P9-CAF-248

Cisco Networking Academy Program: First-Year Companion Guide

Second Edition

Cisco Systems, Inc.

Cisco Networking Academy Program

Cisco Press

Cisco Press
201 West 103rd Street
Indianapolis, IN 46290 USA

Cisco Networking Academy Program: First-Year Companion Guide

Second Edition

Cisco Systems, Inc.

Cisco Networking Academy Program

Copyright © 2002 Cisco Systems, Inc.

Published by:

Cisco Press
201 West 103rd Street
Indianapolis, IN 46290 USA

All rights reserved. No part of this book may be reproduced or transmitted in any form or by any means, electronic or mechanical, including photocopying, recording, or by any information storage and retrieval system, without written permission from the publisher, except for the inclusion of brief quotations in a review.

International Standard Book Number: 1-58713-025-4

Library of Congress Catalog Card Number: 2001087345

04 03 02 01 5 4 3 2

Interpretation of the printing code: The rightmost double-digit number is the year of the book's printing; the rightmost single-digit, the number of the book's printing. For example, the printing code 01-2 shows that the second printing of this book occurred in 2001.

Trademark Acknowledgments

All terms mentioned in this book that are known to be trademarks or service marks have been appropriately capitalized. Cisco Press or Cisco Systems, Inc., cannot attest to the accuracy of this information. Use of a term in this book should not be regarded as affecting the validity of any trademark or service mark.

Warning and Disclaimer

This book is designed to provide information on networking fundamentals. Every effort has been made to make this book as complete and as accurate as possible, but no warranty or fitness is implied.

The information is provided on an as-is basis. Cisco Press and Cisco Systems, Inc., shall have neither liability nor responsibility to any person or entity with respect to any loss or damages arising from the information contained in this book or from the use of the discs or programs that may accompany it.

The opinions expressed in this book belong to the author and are not necessarily those of Cisco Systems, Inc.

Feedback Information

At Cisco Press, our goal is to create in-depth technical books of the highest quality and value. Each book is crafted with care and precision, undergoing rigorous development that involves the unique expertise of members from the professional technical community.

Readers' feedback is a natural continuation of this process. If you have any comments regarding how we could improve the quality of this book, or otherwise alter it to better suit your needs, you can contact us at feedback@ciscopress.com. Please make sure to include the book title and ISBN in your message.

We greatly appreciate your assistance.

Publisher	*John Wait*
Senior Editor	*Carl Lindholm*
Product Manager	*Shannon Gross*
Cisco Systems Management	*Michael Hakkert* *Tom Geitner* *William Warren*
Managing Editor	*Patrick Kanouse*
Senior Project Editor	*Sheri Replin*
Copy Editor	*Krista Hansing*
Technical Reviewers	*Wayne Lewis* *Wayne Jarvimaki* *Cheryl Schmidt* *Richard Reynolds* *Tanna Kincaid* *Truett Clearman* *Charles Schultz* *Lynn Bloomer* *Elaine Horn* *Harry Lawhorn* *Mark McGregor* *Barb Nolley*
Cover Designer	*Louisa Klucznik*
Compositor	*Steve Gifford*
Indexers	*Tim Wright* *Larry Sweazy*

Overview

Table of Contents

Preface

Since 1997, the Cisco Networking Academy Program has instituted an e-learning model that integrates the multimedia delivery of a networking curriculum with testing, performance-based skills assessment, evaluation, and reporting through a Web interface. The Cisco Networking Academy curriculum goes beyond traditional computer-based instruction by helping students develop practical networking knowledge and skills in a hands-on environment. In a lab setting that closely corresponds to a real networking environment, students work with the architecture and infrastructure pieces of networking technology. As a result, students learn the principles and practices of networking technology.

The Cisco Networking Academy Program provides in-depth and meaningful networking content, which is being used by Regional and Local Academies to teach students around the world by utilizing the curriculum to integrate networking instruction into the classroom. The focus of the Networking Academy program is on the integration of a Web-based network curriculum into the learning environment. This element is addressed through intensive staff development for instructors and innovative classroom materials and approaches to instruction, which are provided by Cisco Systems. The participating educators are provided with resources, the means of remote access to online support, and the knowledge base for the effective classroom integration of the Cisco Networking Academy curriculum into the classroom learning environment. As a result, the Networking Academy program provides the means for the dynamic exchange of information by providing a suite of services that redefine the way instructional resources are disseminated, resulting in a many-to-many interactive and collaborative network of teachers and students functioning to meet diverse educational needs.

The Networking Academy curriculum is especially exciting to educators and students because the courseware is interactive. Because of the growing use of interactive technologies, the curriculum is an exciting new way to convey instruction with new interactive technologies that allow instructors and trainers to mix a number of media, including audio, video, text, numerical data, and graphics. Consequently, students can select different media from the computer screen and tweak their instructional content to meet their instructional needs, and educators have the option of either designing their own environment for assessment or selecting from the applicable assessments.

Finally, by developing a curriculum that recognizes the changing classroom and workforce demographics, the globalization of the economy, changing workforce knowledge and skill requirements, and the role of technology in education, the Cisco Networking Academy Program supports national educational goals for K–12 education. As support for the Networking Academy program, Cisco Press has published this book, *Cisco Networking Academy Program: First-Year Companion Guide*, Second Edition, as a companion guide for the curriculum used in the Cisco Networking Academy Program.

Introduction

Cisco Networking Academy Program: First-Year Companion Guide, Second Edition, is designed to act as a supplement to your classroom and laboratory experience with the Cisco Networking Academy Program, whose curriculum is designed to empower you to enter employment or further education and training in the computer networking field.

The book is designed to further train you beyond the online training materials that you have already used in this program, along with the topics pertaining to the Cisco Certified Network Associate (CCNA) exam. The book closely follows the style and format that Cisco has incorporated into the curriculum. In addition, the book follows the two-semester curriculum model that has already been developed for the Cisco Networking Academy Program. Finally, this book is complemented by a CD-ROM, which contains cross-referenced e-lab activities, practice questions, and movies presented in an interactive multimedia format as learning reference materials.

This book introduces and extends your knowledge and practical experience with the design, configuration, and maintenance of local-area networks (LANs). The concepts covered in this book enable you to develop practical experience in skills related to cabling, routing, IP addressing, routing protocols, and network troubleshooting. Finally, this book aims not only to prepare you for your CCNA test and certification, but also to prepare you for the CompTIA Net+ networking certification exam. The OSI model is absolutely essential for all networking students preparing for the CCNA exam. The sections on collisions and segmentation are also very important for the CCNA exam, along with Ethernet, which is important to understand the dominant LAN technology. The IP addressing chapters are perhaps the most conceptually difficult, yet are very important chapters, especially for the CCNA exam. Lastly, the skills in the structured cabling and electricity chapters are crucial if you are seeking network-cabling related employment.

The Goal of This Book

The goal of this book is to educate you about Cisco-supported networking technologies and to help you understand how to design and build networks and to configure Cisco routers. It is designed for use in conjunction with the Cisco Networking Academy Program curriculum or as a stand-alone reference.

This Book's Audience

This book is written for anyone who wants to learn about networking technologies. The main target audience for this book is students in high schools, community colleges, and four-year institutions. Specifically, in an educational environment, this book could be used both in the classroom as a textbook companion and in computer labs as a lab manual.

The secondary target audience is corporate training faculty and staff members. In order for corporations and academic institutions to take advantage of the capabilities of networking, a large number of individuals have to be trained in the design and development of networks.

A third target audience is general users. The book's user-friendly and non-technical approach should be appealing to readers who prefer to stay away from technical manuals.

This Book's Features

Many of this book's features help facilitate a full understanding of the networking and routing covered in this book:

- **Objectives**—At the beginning of each chapter is a list of objectives to be mastered by the end of the chapter. In addition, the list provides a reference to the concepts covered in the chapter, which can be used as an advanced organizer.
- **Figures, examples, and tables**—This book contains figures, examples, and tables that help explain theories, concepts, commands, and setup sequences; they reinforce concepts and help you visualize the content covered in the chapter. In addition, examples and tables provide such things as command summaries with descriptions, examples of screen outputs, and practical and theoretical information.
- **Chapter summaries**—At the end of each chapter is a summary of the concepts covered in the chapter; it provides a synopsis of the chapter and serves as a study aid.
- **Check Your Understanding questions**—The end of each chapter presents review questions that serve as an end-of-chapter assessment. In addition, the questions reinforce the concepts introduced in the chapter and help you test your understanding before you move on to new concepts.

MORE INFORMATION

Throughout the book, a More Information section provides you additional content related to the chapter. The More Information section can be useful if you are seeking to reinforce your understanding of complex subjects.

SKILL BUILDER

Throughout the book, you see references to the lab activities found in the *Cisco Networking Academy Program: Lab Companion*, Volume I, Second Edition. These labs allow you to make a connection between theory and practice.

e-LAB ACTIVITIES

In each chapter, you see references to e-Lab activities, which are located on the accompanying CD-ROM. These activities emphasize not only the conceptual material, but also the important practice that facilitates the learning of networking concepts.

MOVIES

Throughout this book, you see references to movies, which are located on the companion CD-ROM. These movies emphasize the conceptual material and help you to make a connection between theory and practice.

About the CD-ROM

A CD complements this book. The CD contains e-Lab activities, practice questions, and movies presented in an interactive multimedia format. The learning reference materials are cross-referenced and aligned to the content in the textbook. These materials effectively support self-directed learning by allowing you to engage in your learning and skill building. Additionally, these learning reference materials provide the following:

- An easy-to-use graphical user interface
- Accurate and concise feedback
- Frequent interaction with content
- Support for guided and exploratory navigation
- Guidance and external control over navigation
- Learner-direction and support
- Flexibility to learners at different levels of expertise

Finally, these learning reference materials emphasize not only the conceptual material, but also the important practice that facilitates the learning of networking concepts and help you to make a connection between theory and practice.

Conventions Used in This Book

In this book, the following conventions are used:

- Important or new terms are *italicized.*
- All code examples appear in monospace type, and parts of code use the following conventions:
  - — Commands and keywords are in a **bold** type.
  - — Arguments, which are placeholders for values the user inputs, appear in *italics*.

— Square brackets ([ ]) indicate optional keywords or arguments.
— Braces ({ }) indicate required choices.
— Vertical bars (|) are used to separate required choices.

This Book's Organization

This book is divided into 30 chapters, 4 appendixes, and a glossary.

Chapter 1, "Computer Basics," covers the components of a computer and at the role of computers in a networking system. It discusses the "ground up" approach to learning networking, starting with the most basic component of a network—the computer.

Chapter 2, "The OSI Model," discusses the seven-layer Open System Interconnection (OSI) reference model and the communication process between the model's layers.

Chapter 3, "Local-Area Networks," covers basic LAN devices and the evolution of networking devices. It describes how the networking devices operate at each layer of the OSI model and how packets flow through each device as they go through the layers of the OSI model.

Chapter 4, "Layer 1: Electronics and Signals," presents the basic theory of electricity. It also presents how data is transmitted through physical media, such as cables and connectors. Finally, it covers the different factors that affect data transmission, such as alternating current (AC) power-line noise.

Chapter 5, "Layer 1: Media, Connections, and Collisions," presents the network functions that occur at the physical and data link layers of the OSI reference model, and the different types of networking media that are used at the physical layer.

Chapter 6, "Layer 2: Concepts," discusses the fact that access to the networking media occurs at the data link layer of the OSI model, and how data is able to locate its intended destination on a network.

Chapter 7, "Layer 2: Technologies," covers Ethernet, FDDI, and Token Ring, along with the IEEE specifications for each of these technologies and the LAN standards that specify cabling and signaling at the physical and data link layers of the OSI reference model.

Chapter 8, "Design and Documentation," discusses how network physical and logical topologies should be designed and documented and it presents structured cabling and electrical specifications used in LANs and wiring and electrical techniques used in building networks.

Chapter 9, "Structured Cabling Project," presents how to use appropriate and recommended techniques for dressing and securing the cable.

Chapter 10, "Layer 3: Routing and Addressing," describes IP addresses and the three classes of networks in IP addressing schemes. It also discusses subnetworks and subnet masks and describes their IP addressing schemes.

Chapter 11, "Layer 3: Protocols," discusses how devices on LANs use the Address Resolution Protocol (ARP) before forwarding data to a destination and what happens when a device on one network does not know the MAC address of a device on another network.

Chapter 12, "Layer 4: The Transport Layer," explains the primary functions that occur at the transport layer.

Chapter 13, "Layer 5: The Session Layer," explains the primary functions that occur at the session layer.

Chapter 14, "Layer 6: The Presentation Layer," explains the primary functions that occur at the presentation layer.

Chapter 15, "Layer 7: The Application Layer," explains the primary functions that occur at the application layer.

Chapter 16, "WANs and Routers," covers WAN devices, technologies, and standards, along with the function of a router in a WAN.

Chapter 17, "Router CLI," discusses how to operate a router to ensure delivery of data on a network with routers.

Chapter 18, "Router Components," describes the correct procedures and commands to access a router, examine and maintain its components, and test its network connectivity.

Chapter 19, "Router Startup and Setup," explains how to start a router when it is used the first time by using the correct commands and startup sequence to do an initial router configuration.

Chapter 20, "Router Configuration 1,"discuuses how to use router modes and configuration methods to update a router's configuration file by using current and older versions of the Cisco Internetwork Operating System.

Chapter 21, "IOS Images," explains how to use a variety of Cisco IOS software source options, execute commands to load Cisco IOS software onto the router, maintain backup files, and upgrade Cisco IOS software.

Chapter 22, "Router Configuration 2," provides information that helps you practice configuring a router.

Chapter 23, "TCP/IP," describes Transmission Control Protocol/Internet Protocol (TCP/IP) and its operation to ensure communication across any set of interconnected networks.

Chapter 24, "IP Addressing," describes the process of configuring IP addresses.

Chapter 25, "Routing," describes the router's use and operations in performing the key internetworking functions of the OSI reference model network layer.

Chapter 26, "Routing Protocols," describes the initial configuration of a router to enable the IP routing protocols RIP and IGRP.

Chapter 27, "Network Troubleshooting," explores troubleshooting and covers some principles that are common to any troubleshooting methodology.

Chapter 28, "Introduction to Network Security," discusses primary threats to network security and the different types of network attacks.

Chapter 29, "Network Management," discusses the basic fundamentals of managing a network by using techniques such as documenting, auditing, monitoring, and evaluating.

Chapter 30, "Introduction to Residential Networking," presents the emerging Home Network integration industry and explores the evolution of the subsystems in the home as individual networks into an integrated home network.

Appendix A, "Check Your Understanding Answer Key," provides the answers to the Check Your Understanding questions that you find at the end of each chapter.

Appendix B, "Command Summary," describes and defines the commands related to configuring and using Cisco routers that are used throughout this book. It is arranged alphabetically so that you can easily find information on a given command, and each command is also cross-referenced to the chapters where it is used so you can easily find more information.

Appendix C, "e-Lab Activity Index," contains cross-referenced information about each of the e-lab activities contained on the CD-ROM.

Appendix D, "Movie Index," contains cross-referenced information about each of the movies contained on the CD-ROM.

The Glossary defines the terms and abbreviations related to networking utilized in this book.

Objectives

After reading this chapter, you will be able to

- Describe the basic computer hardware components
- Understand computer software basics
- Understand the binary numbering system
- Define networks and networking
- Define digital bandwidth

Chapter 1

Computer Basics

Introduction

In this introductory chapter, you learn about the components of a computer and about the role of computers in a networking system. You use the "ground up" approach to learn networking, starting with the most basic component of a network: the computer. The more you know about computers, the easier it is to understand networks, including how they are designed and built.

To help you understand the role computers play in a networking system, consider the Internet. Think of the Internet as a tree, and computers as leaves on the tree. Computers are the sources of information and the receivers of information, both giving to and taking from the Internet. Computers can function without the Internet but the Internet cannot exist without computers. Computer users are becoming increasingly dependent on the Internet.

Computers, along with being an integral part of a network, play a vital role in the work world. Businesses use their computers for a variety of purposes, including some common ways. They use servers to store important data and to manage employee accounts. They use spreadsheet software to organize financial information; word-processor software to maintain records and correspondence; and Web browsers to access company Web sites. With all this in mind, you can begin looking at the inner workings of a computer. This will give you the foundation you need to begin your study of networking.

Computer Hardware Components

Because computers are important building blocks in a network, it is important to be able to recognize and name the major components of a *personal computer (PC)*.

SKILL BUILDER

Lab Activity: PC Hardware

In this lab, you become familiar with the basic external peripheral components of a PC system and their connections, including network attachment.

Many networking devices are themselves special-purpose computers and have many of the same parts as "normal" PCs. To use your computer as a reliable means of obtaining information, such as accessing Web-based curriculum, your computer must be in good working order. You might occasionally need to troubleshoot simple hardware and software problems. You should be able to recognize, name, and state the purpose of the following PC components.

Electronic Components

The following items are electronic components of a PC:

- **Capacitor**—Stores energy in the form of an electrostatic field (see Figure 1-1).

FIGURE 1-1
A capacitor consists of two conducting metal plates separated by an insulating material.

- **Connector**—The part of a cable that plugs into a port or an interface.
- **Integrated circuit** (IC)—A device made of semiconductor material; it contains many transistors and performs a specific task.
- **Light emitting diode** (LED)—A semiconductor device that emits light when a current passes through it.
- **Resistor**—A device made of a material that opposes the flow of electric current.
- **Transistor**—A device that amplifies a signal or opens and closes a circuit.

Personal Computer Subsystems

The following items are personal computer subsystems:

- **Bus**—A collection of wires through which data is transmitted from one part of a computer to another. It connects all the internal computer components to the CPU. The industry standard architecture (ISA) and the peripheral component interconnect (PCI) are two types of buses.
- **CD-ROM drive**—A compact disk read-only memory drive; a device that can read information from a CD-ROM.
- **Central processing unit** (CPU)—The brains of the computer, where most calculations take place (see Figure 1-2).

FIGURE 1-2
The CPU is a silicon-based microprocessor.

- **Expansion card**—A printed circuit board you can insert into a computer to give it added capabilities (see Figure 1-3).

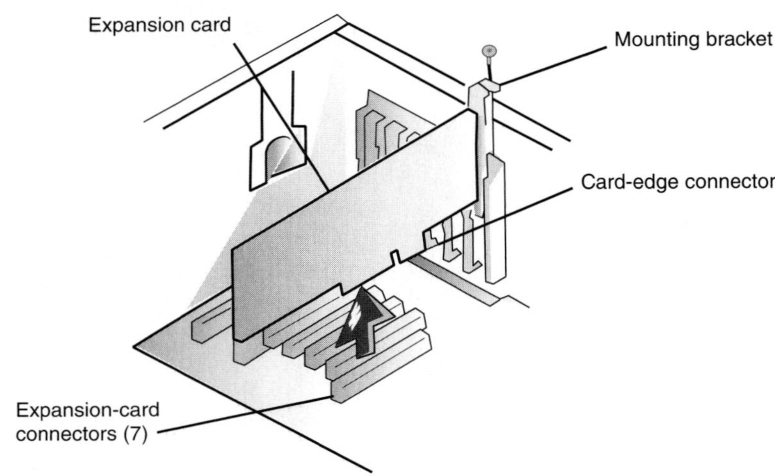

FIGURE 1-3
Examples of expansion cards include video cards, sound cards, and internal modems.

- **Expansion slot**—An opening in a computer where a circuit board can be inserted to add new capabilities to the computer (see Figure 1-4).

FIGURE 1-4
The expansion slot serves as an interface between the system and the devices attached to it.

- **Floppy disk drive**—A disk drive that can read and write to floppy disks (see Figure 1-5).

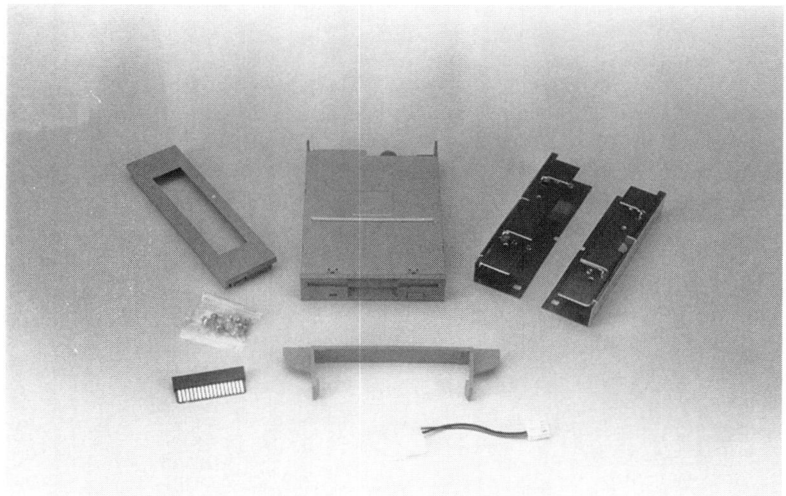

FIGURE 1-5
A floppy disk drive uses removable storage media called floppy disks.

- **Hard disk drive**—The device that reads and writes data on a hard disk.
- **Microprocessor**—A silicon chip that contains a CPU.
- **Motherboard**—The main printed circuit board of a microcomputer (see Figure 1-6).
- **Power supply**—The component that supplies power to a computer (see Figure 1-7).

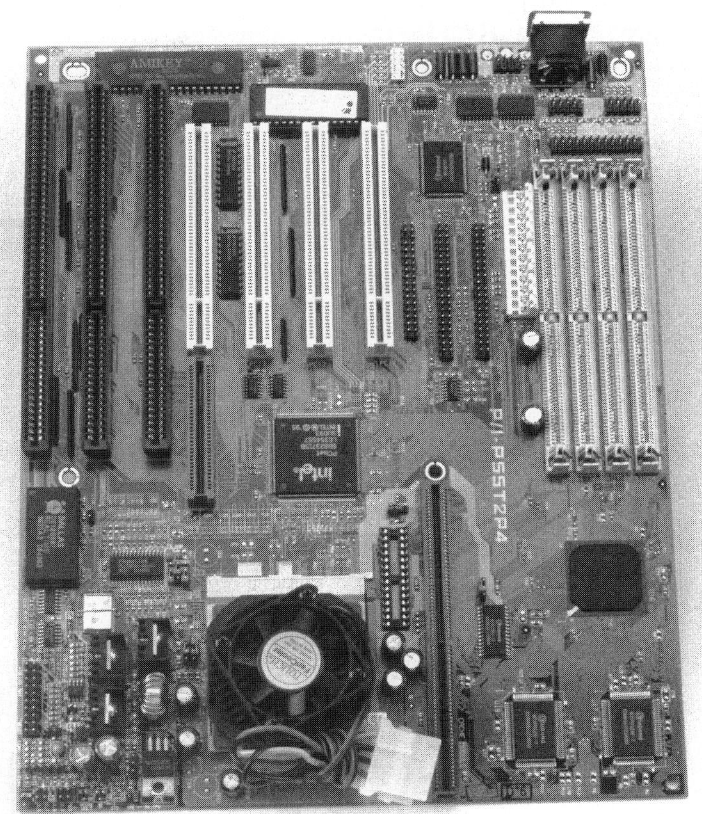

FIGURE 1-6 The motherboard contains the primary components of the computer system.

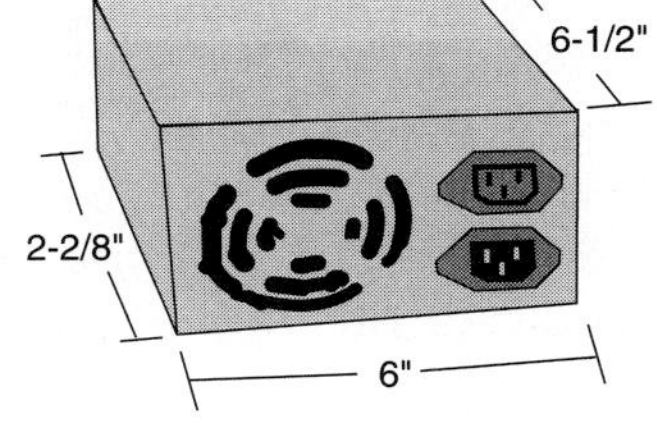

FIGURE 1-7 The power supply converts AC electricity from a power outlet to DC electricity.

- **Printed circuit board (PCB)**—A thin plate on which chips (integrated circuits) and other electronic components are placed.

- **Random-access memory (RAM)**—Also known as read-write memory, RAM can have new data written into it and stored data read from it. A drawback of RAM is that it requires electrical power to maintain data storage (see Figure 1-8).

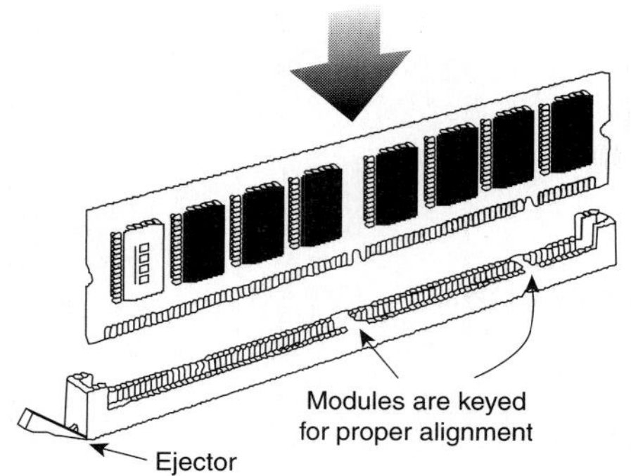

FIGURE 1-8
If the computer is turned off or loses power, all data stored in RAM is lost unless the data was saved to a disk.

- **Read-only memory (ROM)**—Computer memory on which data has been prerecorded (see Figure 1-9).

FIGURE 1-9
After data is written to a ROM chip, it cannot be removed; it only can be read.

- **System unit**—The main part of a PC; the system unit includes the chassis, the microprocessor, the main memory, the bus, and the ports. It does not include the keyboard or the monitor, or any external devices connected to the computer.

MORE INFORMATION

Hard Drive Interfaces

The drive *interface* is the way the drive communicates with the computer. The interface defines a sort of language that allows the drive and the computer to talk to each other. Two main types of drive interfaces are current in today's computers: the Integrated Drive Electronics (IDE) drive and the Small Computer System Interface (SCSI; pronounced *scuzzy*) drive. These drive interfaces place most of the controller circuitry directly on the hard drive, which alleviates a lot of the problems the older hard disks had to deal with.

MORE INFORMATION

Modems

Computers today are used for a variety of purposes, including to connect to remote computers. People dial in to the Internet, telecommute, and regularly exchange data between computers through telephone lines. All this communicating is possible, in part, because of the modem. Although many types of specialized modems exist, this lesson focuses on the asynchronous modem, the modem most commonly used in computer systems, and the processes of modem-based communications.

Modulating and *demodulating* describe how a modem, an electronic computer communication device, sends data signals over the telephone line. The basic purpose of a modem is to enable two computers to send and receive data via a telephone line. The modem must convert digital data from its local computer into analog tones and pulses that can be sent over the telephone line, whereupon the modem at the other end converts these signals back into data to be processed by the receiving computer system. The period of communication between these modems is called a *session*. Modem-equipped computers can communicate via the standard *public switched telephone network (PSTN)*.

The modem comes in two basic form factors: external and internal. External modems sit outside the computer system and are linked to it by a cable, which typically is attached to an RS-232 serial I/O port. An external modem has its own power supply and has a plug-in port for a telephone line, which goes from the I/O port to the wall plug-in and from there to the PSTN. All communications between external modems and the system CPU go through this same I/O port.

The internal modem is plugged into an expansion slot on the ISA bus of the system motherboard or a PCI slot. An internal modem communicates directly with the system CPU by means of this bus without a serial port, relying on the motherboard for its power.

MORE INFORMATION

The Function of the Power Supply

Power lines carry electricity to homes, schools, and offices. To be transported over long distances, electricity carried by power lines is in the form of *alternating current (AC)* electricity. Most modern electronic devices, including computers, do not use AC. Instead, they generally use a form of electricity called *direct current (DC)*. The power supply converts AC to DC.

The *power supply* provides electrical power for all the components inside the computer. The computer system plugs into a wall socket to access electrical power. The power supply converts electrical power from the wall outlet so it can be used by the computer circuitry. The power supply is one of the most important computer components because the type of power supply restricts the type of components that can be used. For example, the type of power supply determines what motherboard and case can be used.

The power supply contains two major components:

- Fan
- AC/DC converter, including regulator, rectifier, resistors, capacitors, and transformer

It is important that you are aware that care must be taken when handling a power supply. A power supply has a caution label translated into multiple languages, cautioning you to beware. Do not open a power supply—capacitors hold a charge that can be fatal.

Backplane Components

The following items are backplane components of a PC:

- **Backplane**—The large circuit board that contains slots for expansion cards.
- **Interface**—A piece of hardware, such as a modem connector, that allows two devices to be connected.
- **Mouse port**—A port designed to connect a mouse to a PC.
- **Network card**—An expansion board inserted into a computer so that the computer can be connected to a network.
- **Parallel port**—An interface capable of transferring more than one bit simultaneously. It is used to connect external devices, such as printers (see Figure 1-10).
- **Port**—An interface on a computer to which you can connect an electronic device.
- **Power cord**—A cord used to connect an electrical device to an electrical outlet in order to provide power to the device.

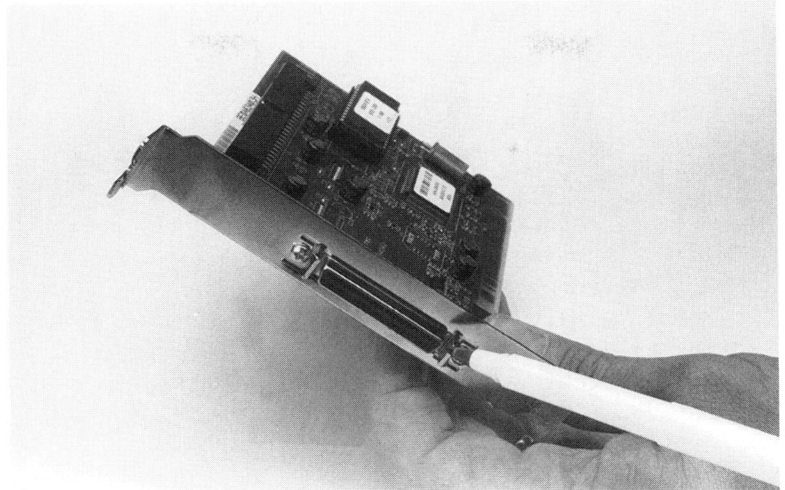

FIGURE 1-10
An expansion card is used to connect peripherals.

- **Serial port**—An interface that can be used for serial communication in which only one bit is transmitted at a time (see Figure 1-11).

FIGURE 1-11
A serial port can be used to connect a modem, a scanner, a mouse, or another device that uses a serial interface.

- **Sound card**—An expansion card that handles all sound functions.
- **Video card**—A board that plugs into a PC to give it display capabilities (see Figure 1-12).

FIGURE 1-12
The video card translates data from the CPU into a format that a monitor can display.

MORE INFORMATION

Processing Data

Working together, the system unit, the output device, and the input device (the hardware components previously discussed) enable the computer to process information called *data*. You input, manipulate, store, and output data to create a work product or to perform complex analyses. Computer data is written in a digital format that uses a binary number system.

When you type on the keyboard or use another method to input information, you generate data that the computer's operating system deciphers. The computer stores the data in its random access memory (RAM) chips. RAM manipulates data at very high speeds. From RAM, data is moved into the central processing unit (CPU). Think of the CPU as the computer's brain. The CPU's job is to analyze and process instructions and to perform any tasks that might have been requested. Information created as a result of CPU data processing output can be displayed on the monitor. For data to be processed, it needs to flow through a computer's components and eventually go through a network interface card (NIC) so that it can be shared through a network. The next section explains the information flow through a computer and the role of the NIC in the communication between the PC and a network.

Information Flow in an Idealized Computer

Figure 1-13 shows the basic components of an idealized computer. You can think of the internal components of a PC as a network of devices, all attached to the system bus. In a way, a PC is a small computer network.

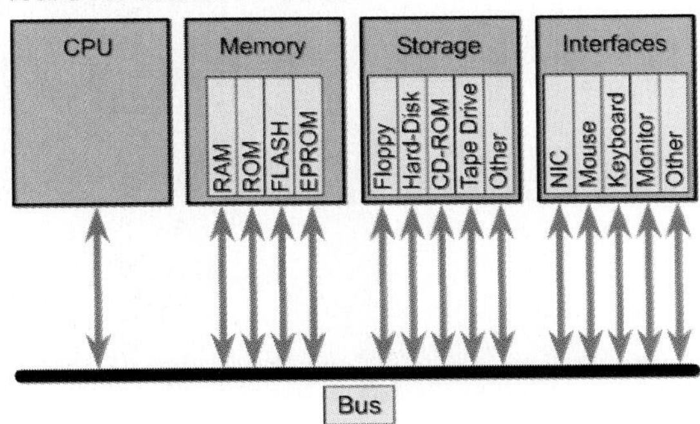

FIGURE 1-13
All computers have a CPU, memory, storage, and interfaces.

Information and electric power are constantly flowing in a PC. It helps to understand networking by thinking of the computer as a miniature network, with the various devices in the system unit attached to, and communicating with, each other. As shown in Figure 1-13, the following are some of the important information flows (almost all of which occur through the bus):

- **Boot instructions**—Stored in ROM until they are sent out.
- **Software applications**—Stored in RAM after they are loaded.
- **RAM and ROM**—Constantly talk to the CPU through the bus.
- **Application information**—Stored in RAM while applications are being used.
- **Saved information**—Flows from RAM to some form of storage device.
- **Exported information**—Flows from RAM and the CPU, through the bus and expansion slots, to the printer, the video card, the sound card, or the network card.

Network Interface Cards

As shown in Figure 1-14, a *network interface card (NIC)* is a printed circuit board that provides network communication capabilities to and from a personal computer. Also called a *LAN adapter*, it plugs into a motherboard and provides a port to connect to the network. This card can be designed as an Ethernet card, a Token Ring card, or a Fiber Distributed Data Interface (FDDI) card, among others.

FIGURE 1-14
A NIC provides a port for the computer's network access.

A NIC communicates with the network through a serial connection, and with the computer through a parallel connection. Each card requires an IRQ, an I/O address, and an upper memory address to work with DOS or Windows 95/98. An *interrupt request line (IRQ)* is a signal informing a CPU that an event that needs its attention has occurred. An IRQ is sent over a hardware line to the microprocessor. For example, when you press a key on the keyboard, the CPU must move the character from the keyboard to RAM. An I/O address is a location in memory used to enter data or to retrieve data from a computer by an auxiliary device. In DOS-based systems, upper memory refers to the memory area between the first 640 kilobytes (K) and 1 megabyte (M) of RAM.

When you select a network card, consider the following three factors:

- Type of network
- Type of media
- Type of system bus

Installing a NIC in a PC

The NIC enables hosts to connect to the network and is, therefore, considered a key network component. From time to time, you might need to install a NIC. Some possible situations that might require you to do so include the following:

- Adding a NIC to a PC that does not already have one
- Replacing a bad or damaged NIC

- Upgrading from a 10 Mbps NIC to a 10/100 Mbps NIC
- Altering settings on a NIC using a jumper (a jumper is a metal bridge that closes an electrical circuit; typically, a jumper consists of a plastic plug that fits over a pair of pins)

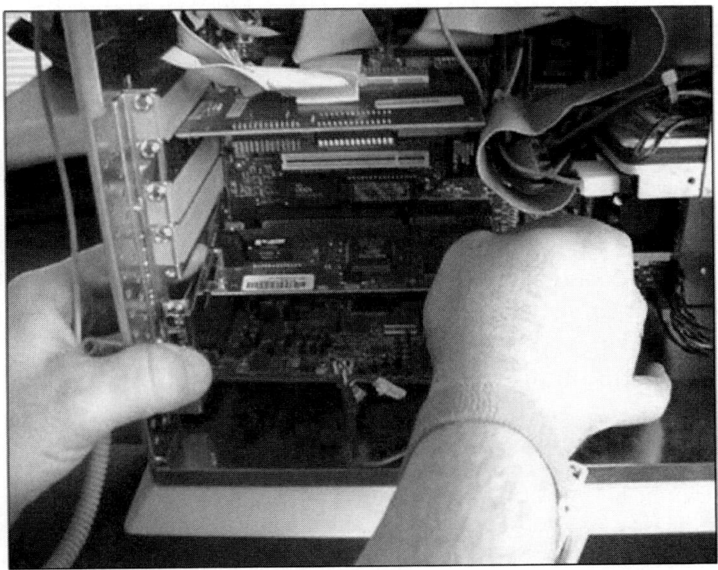

FIGURE 1-15
A NIC plugs into the motherboard and provides ports for network connectivity.

SKILL BUILDER

Lab Activity: NIC Installation

In this lab, you learn how to properly install a NIC in a PC.

To perform the installation, you need to have the following resources:

- Knowledge of how the NIC is configured, including jumpers, plug-and-play software, and erasable programmable read-only memory (EPROM is a type of memory that retains its contents until it is exposed to ultraviolet light)
- Use of network card diagnostics, including the vendor-supplied diagnostics and loopback test (see the documentation for the card)
- Ability to resolve hardware resource conflicts, including IRQ, I/O Base Address, and DMA (direct memory address is used to transfer data from RAM to a device without going through the CPU)

PC Components Versus Laptop Components

Laptop computers and notebook computers are becoming increasingly popular, as are palm top computers, personal digital assistants, and other small computing devices. The information described in the previous sections also pertains to laptops. The main difference is that components in a laptop are smaller—the expansion slots become PCMCIA or PC slots, where NICs, modems, hard drives, and other useful devices, usually the size of a thick credit card, can be inserted into the PCMCIA slots along the perimeter.

Computer Software

Now that you have an idea of what's involved with computer hardware, you need the second ingredient—computer software. The purpose of software is to allow you to interact with the computer or the networking device to get it to do what you want. In this section, you learn about Web browsers (such as Netscape and Internet Explorer), plug-ins, and office applications.

SKILL BUILDER

Lab Activity: TCP/IP Network Settings

In this lab, you configure the network settings required to connect your PC to a LAN and to gain access to the Internet (World Wide Web) and Intranet (internal local Web servers), which enables you to view the curriculum.

Web Browsers

A Web browser acts on behalf of a user by

- Contacting a Web server
- Requesting information
- Receiving information
- Displaying the results on a screen

A *browser* is software that interprets hypertext markup language (HTML), which is the language used to code Web page content. HTML can display graphics and play sounds, movies, and other multimedia files. *Hyperlinks* (computer program commands that point to other places inside a PC or on a network) connect to other Web pages and to files that can be downloaded.

The two most common browsers are Netscape Communicator and Internet Explorer (IE). Table 1-1 illustrates the similarities and differences between these two browsers.

TABLE 1-1 Comparing Browsers

Netscape	Internet Explorer (IE)
First popular browser	Powerfully connected to other Microsoft products
Takes less disk space than IE	Takes more disk space than Netscape
Considered by many to be easy to use	Considered difficult to use
Displays HTML files, does e-mail, transfers files, and performs other functions	Displays HTML files, does e-mail, transfers files, and performs other functions

Plug-Ins

There also are many proprietary (that is, privately owned and controlled) file types that standard Web browsers cannot display. To view these files, you must configure your browser to use plug-in applications. These applications work in conjunction with the browser to launch the program required to view the special files. Some of the more popular proprietary plug-ins include:

- **Flash/Shockwave**—Plays multimedia (integrated text, graphics, video, animation, and/or sound) files; created by Macromedia Authorware, Director, and Flash programs.
- **QuickTime**—Plays movies and sounds that are saved in the Apple QuickTime file format.
- **RealAudio**—Plays audio files that are saved in RealAudio format.
- **RealPlayer G2**—Plays movie files with high resolution that are saved in RealPlayer format.

SKILL BUILDER

Lab Activity: PC Software

In this lab, you verify that the PC is configured properly to run the multimedia-based CNAP Curriculum and practice exams.

SKILL BUILDER

Lab Activity: Web Browser Literacy

In this lab, you learn how to use a Web browser to access Internet sites and to become familiar with the concept of an URL.

MORE INFORMATION

Office Applications

Beyond configuring your computer to view Web-based curriculum, you use your computer to perform many other useful tasks. In business, employees regularly use a set of applications that come in the form of an office suite, such as Microsoft Office. The office applications typically include spreadsheet software, word processing software, database management software, presentation software, and a personal information manager that includes an e-mail program.

Spreadsheet software contains tables consisting of columns and rows and often is used with formulas to process and analyze data. Word-processing software is an application used to create and edit text documents; modern word-processor programs allow the user to create sophisticated documents that include graphics and richly formatted text. Database software is used to store, maintain, organize, sort, and filter records (a *record* is a collection of information identified by a common theme, such as a customer's name).

Presentation software designs and develop presentations to deliver at meetings, classes, or sales presentations. Personal information managers include such things as e-mail, contact lists, a calendar, and a to-do list. Office applications are now as much a part of everyday work as typewriters were before the advent of the PC.

SKILL BUILDER

Lab Activity: Basic Troubleshooting

In this lab, you learn the proper sequence for troubleshooting computer- and network-related problems and you become familiar with some of the more common hardware and software problems.

Binary Number System

Computers are electronic devices made up of electronic switches. At the lowest levels of computation, computers depend on these electronic switches to make decisions. As such, computers react only to electrical impulses. These impulses are understood by the computer as either "on" or "off" states, or as 1s or 0s. Because the computer can't speak your language, you need to learn to speak the computer's language: the language of binary arithmetic.

Computers don't think in the decimal number system, or Base 10, as humans do. Electronic devices are structured in such a way that binary numbering is natural: computers have to translate in order to use decimal numbering. It's like a person who speaks two languages, one is their first language and the other is their second language: it is faster and more accurate to communicate in the first language.

The binary number system, or Base 2, is made up entirely of 0s and 1s. Computers use Base 2 in expressing IP addresses. One of the goals of this chapter is to provide a better understanding of the process of converting between binary numbers (used with IP addresses) and their equivalent decimal values.

In this section, you learn how to think in the binary numbering system so you can make the necessary translations when performing certain networking tasks, such as designing an IP addressing scheme for a network (binary). As you know, it takes time and practice to learn new concepts in math. You probably won't master binary numbers the first time you read about them. So, if you are learning about the binary numbering system for the first time, remember that it is a step-by-step process.

Knowing What Base Someone Refers To

The binary numbering system uses two characters: 0 and 1. Any decimal number you can imagine can be expressed in binary. The characters used in the decimal number system are 0, 1, 2, 3, 4, 5, 6, 7, 8, and 9. Because both number systems use the characters 0 and 1, there's a potential for confusion. For example, what does 10110 mean? It depends on whether you're referring to 10110 in Base 10 or 10110 in Base 2. Because of the potential for confusion, sometimes mathematicians write 10110_{10} to mean 10110 in Base 10 and 10110_2 to mean 10110 in Base 2. However, writing down these subscripts every time you write a number quickly becomes tedious, so what you usually do is make it clear from the context what base is being referred to without explicitly writing down the base.

First, make sure you are clear in your mind when you look at a string of characters, such as 10110, that you know what base the person who wrote 10110 was thinking of when he wrote it. If you are unsure, the person who wrote it did a poor job of making it clear or did not intend to refer to a particular base.

One important *convention* (an agreed-upon rule) should be made clear and almost goes without saying. It is taken for granted after years of working with decimal numbers: The convention is to read, write, and pronounce strings, such as 10110, from left to right. For example, you read 10110 as "one, zero, one, one, zero."

If you come across a string like 10110, it usually is coming from some kind of computer output. There are specific notations that certain programs, such as protocol analyzers, use to differentiate between binary, decimal, and hexadecimal notation. For example, the % sign precedes a binary string; thus, %10110 means 10110 in Base 2.

One practical consideration to keep in mind when using different bases is that the bigger the base, the less characters used to express the number. For example, the decimal (Base 10) number 16 in Base 2 is 10000. In addition, although we focus only on Base 2, there is no numerical limit to the base you can use. Although it is not practical for computer-related work, you could work in Base 23,037 or Base 1,002,395. To illustrate, the decimal number 15 is represented by the letter F in Base 16, the decimal number 20 is represented by the letter K in Base 21, and the decimal number 29 is represented by the letter T in Base 30.

Another important fact to keep in mind is that each base you work in has a fixed set of characters. For example, Base 2 has two characters, and Base 10 has 10 characters. Note that character 2 does not exist in Base 2 (just 0 and 1—you know you aren't working in binary if there's a number with a 2 in it!). No character 3 exists in Base 3 (just 0, 1, and 2). No character 9 exists in Base 9 (just 0, 1, 2, 3, 4, 5, 6, 7, and 8). No character A exists in Base 10 (just 0, 1, 2, 3, 4, 5, 6, 7, 8, and 9). No character G exists in Base 16 (just 0, 1, 2, 3, 4, 5, 6, 7, 8, 9, A, B, C, D, E, and F). You get the idea. Also, note that the number of characters in a base is equal to the decimal value of the base. Here are a couple silly examples: 0 is the only character in Base 1 (so you can't express any number greater than 0 in Base 1!) and there are no characters in Base 0.

Whether you work in Base 2, 10, or whatever, numbers are expressed as strings of characters, such as 101011 in Base 2, 14932 in Base 10. This is actually a convenience. Did you know that writing the decimal number 124 is actually a shortcut? It is short for $1 \times 100 + 2 \times 10 + 4 \times 1$, which would be tedious to write out. Imagine if every time you wrote down a decimal number you had to express it this way! Each number in a string of characters represents a value that depends on its *place* in the string. For example, the character 7 in the Base 10 number 23761 represents 7×100, or 700. You also can use tables with columns to emphasize the importance of place value when converting between bases. Among other things, the tables help illustrate that when you read strings of characters from left to right, the characters represent decreasing place values. For example, in the decimal number 234, 2 represents 2 hundreds, 3 represents 3 tens, and 4 represents 4 ones. In summary, two things are essential to understand with each string of characters: the characters in the string and their place value in the string.

Base Conventions

You use the words *ten*, *eleven*, *twelve*, *thirteen*, *twenty*, *twenty-one*, and so on only when working in decimal. These *are* decimal (Base 10) numbers. When you say *thirty*, it is just a short way of saying *three tens*. When you talk about the string 23 in Base 5, you don't say *twenty-three in Base 5*, you say *two three in Base 5*. Saying *twenty-three* would mean *two tens and three*; you are talking in Base 10 when you say *twenty-three*. You pronounce numbers differently when working in bases *other than ten*. As another example, 101 in Base 2 is spoken *one zero one in Base 2*, or just *one zero one* if it's clear that you're referring to Base 2. You wouldn't say *one hundred one* in Base 2 or *one hundred one*. The reason for this is you don't want to confuse people by verbalizing a string of characters in Base 10 when the string represents a Base 2 number.

One other thing to keep in mind is the role of the character 0. Every base uses the character 0. Whenever the character 0 appears on the left side of a string of characters, you can remove it without changing the value of the string of characters. In Base 10, for example, 02947 equals 2947. In Base 2, 0001001101 equals 1001101. Sometimes, people include 0s on the left side of a number to emphasize places that would otherwise not be represented. For example, it's not unusual to express the binary number 10000 as 00010000.

Working with Exponents

You need to work with powers of numbers, called *exponents*, when dealing with different number systems. Recall from mathematics that powers are used to represent repeated multiplication of the same number. The following example illustrates how exponents work with the number 2 (the rules hold for other numbers as well). First, $2^0=1$, which is spoken *two to the zero equals one* (2 is called the *base* and 0 is called the *exponent*). This fact is not derived from previous knowledge; it is part of the definition of 2^n, where *n* is an *integer*. Second, $2^1 = 2$ is spoken *two to the one equals two*, according to mathematical definition. Third, $2^2 = 2 \times 2 = 4$: *two to the two equals two times two equals four*. Continuing, $2^3 = 2 \times 2 \times 2 = 8$: *two to the three equals two times two times two equals eight*. This provides a pattern that can be used for any power of 2. A common mistake is to confuse taking powers with multiplying, so be careful: $2^4 \neq 2 \times 4 = 8$, $2^4 = 2 \times 2 \times 2 \times 2 = 16$.

Exponents are convenient when you work with binary numbers. For example, the number of objects that *n* bits can represent is calculated by using the formula s^n. If 8 bits are set aside for describing or naming an object, then there are $2^8 = 256$ possible variations for assigning a binary number to that object. This fact is important to understand. If 8 bits are available, that means there are eight *slots* or places for a binary number. Eight bits can express 256 different binary numbers and 8 slots or places can form 256 different strings consisting of 0s and 1s.

Binary Numbers

You have seen many concepts up to this point regarding different bases and how to work with them. You should now have a better understanding of the fundamentals necessary to be able to work in different numbering systems.

In this section, you learn how to use tables to represent numbers in a particular base. Then you learn about the two main concepts of interest: converting binary numbers to decimal numbers, and converting decimal numbers to binary numbers.

In Base 10, you work with powers of ten. For example, 23,605 in Base 10 means $2 \times 10{,}000 + 3 \times 1000 + 6 \times 100 + 0 \times 10 + 5 \times 1$. Note that $10^0 = 1$, $10^1 = 10$, $10^2 = 100$, $10^3 = 1000$, and $10^4 = 10{,}000$. In addition, even though $0 \times 10 = 0$, you don't leave out the 0 in 23,605 because, if you did, you would have $2365 = 2 \times 1000 + 3 \times 100 + 6 \times 10 + 5 \times 1$, which is not what you meant to express by 23,605. The 0 acts as a *placeholder.* On the other hand, if for some reason you want to focus on the one hundred thousand place and the one million place, you express 23,605 as 0,023,605.

As the previous paragraph demonstrates, if you want to literally express the meaning of a decimal number, you can use powers of 10 (10^0, 10^1, 10^2, and so on). You use the expanded form of the powers (1, 10, 100, and so on) when you focus on the actual value of a decimal number. It helps to use tables to keep track of all this. Table1-2 has three rows: the first row lists *powers of 10*; the second row expresses the *expanded* (multiplied out) *powers of 10*; and the third row is where you place numbers to communicate how many (between 0 and 9) of that power of 10 you want.

TABLE 1-2 Base 10 Table

10^7	10^6	10^5	10^4	10^3	10^2	10 1	10 0
10,000,000	1,000,000	100,000	10,000	1000	100	10	1

For example, Table 1-3 shows how to express 23,605 in a Base 10 table.

TABLE 1-3 23,605 in a Base 10 Table

10^4	10^3	10^3	10^1	10^0
10,000	1000	100	10	1
2	3	6	0	5

The pattern for expressing binary numbers is similar to what you just read about decimal numbers. Binary numbers use the principle of place value just as decimal numbers do. The difference is that you use powers of 2 instead of powers of 10, and you use only the characters 0 and 1 (there's no 2, 3, 4, 5, 6, 7, 8, or 9). So, the binary table (comparable to Table1-2) has three rows. The first row lists *powers of* 2; the second row expresses the *expanded* (multiplied out) *powers of* 2; and the third row is where you place numbers to communicate how many (between 0 and 1) of that power of 2 you want (see Table 1-4). Notice that the second row has numbers written in Base 10.

TABLE 1-4 Base 2 Table

2^7	2^6	2^5	2^4	2^3	2^2	2^1	2^0
128	64	32	16	8	4	2	1

As an example, you can *break down* the binary number 1101 by placing the digits in a binary table (see Table 1-5). After making the table, you can use it to convert the binary number to its Base 10 equivalent.

TABLE 1-5 The Binary Number 1101 in a Base 2 Table

2^3	2^2	2^1	2^0
8	4	2	1
1	1	0	1

You can use Table 1-5 to *convert* the binary number 1101 to Base 10:

$$1101 = 1 \times 8 + 1 \times 4 + 0 \times 2 + 1 \times 1 = 8 + 4 + 0 + 1 = 13$$

As another example, you can examine the binary number 10010001 by placing the digits in a binary table (see Table 1-6). After making the table, you can use it to convert the binary number to its Base 10 equivalent.

TABLE 1-6 The Binary Number 10010001 in a Base 2 Table

2^7	2^6	2^5	2^4	2^3	2^2	2^1	2^0
128	64	32	16	8	4	2	1
1	0	0	1	0	0	0	1

You can use Table 1-6 to convert the binary number 10010001 to Base 10

$$10010001 = 1 \times 128 + 0 \times 64 + 0 \times 32 + 1 \times 16 + 0 \times 8 + 0 \times 4 + 0 \times 2 + 1 \times 1 = 128 + 16 + 1 = 145.$$

The binary number 11111111 occurs as often as any other in networking (see Table 1-7).

TABLE 1-7 The Binary Number 11111111 in a Base 2 Table

2^7	2^6	2^5	2^4	2^3	2^2	2^1	2^0
128	64	32	16	8	4	2	1
1	1	1	1	1	1	1	1

You can use Table 1-7 to convert the binary number 11111111 to Base 10:

$$11111111 = 1 \times 128 + 1 \times 64 + 1 \times 32 + 1 \times 16 + 1 \times 8 + 1 \times 4 + 1 \times 2 + 1 \times 1 = 255.$$

Most of the work you do with binary numbers in networking involves working with one byte, or one octet, at a time; that is, working with 8-bit binary numbers.

An IP address is expressed as a dotted-decimal number, W.X.Y.Z, where W, X, Y, and Z are decimal numbers whose binary representations each consist of 8 bits. The smallest decimal value that can be represented by one byte (00000000 in binary) is 0. The largest decimal value that can be represented by one byte (11111111 in binary) is 255, as calculated in Table 1-7. It follows that the range of decimal numbers that can be represented by a byte is 0 to 255, a total of 256 possible values. Therefore, in an IP address, the decimal numbers (W, X, Y, and Z) are between 0 and 255. Some examples of IP addresses are 140.57.255.0, 204.65.103.243, and 5.6.7.8.

Now you know how to convert a binary number to a decimal number. As an exercise, use a table to show that the binary number 11111001 is equal to the decimal number 249. After doing several problems like this, you can develop your own shortcuts that might not include a table at all.

Converting a Decimal Number to a Binary Number

Converting a decimal number to a binary number is one of the most common procedures performed while working with IP addresses. As with most problems in math, there are several ways to solve the problem. This section introduces one method, but feel free to use another method if you find it easier.

To convert a decimal number to binary, you first find the largest power of 2 that fits into the decimal number. Consider the decimal number 35. Referring to Table 1-4, what's the largest power of 2 that is less than or equal to 35? Well, 64 is too large but 32 just fits, so you know that there is a 1 in the 2^5 column. Now, how much is leftover? You find this by subtracting 32 from 35: 35 – 32 = 3. Next, you look at each remaining power of 2, one column at a time. Because the next smaller power of 2 is 2^4, you determine whether 2^4, or 16, is less than or equal to 3. Because it is not, you put a 0 in the 2^4 column. The next power is 2^3, so you decide whether 2^3, or 8, is less than or equal to 3. It is not, so you put a 0 in the 2^3 column as well. Next, is 2^2 (or 4) less than or equal to 3? It is not, so place a 0 in the 2^2 column. Next, is 2^1 (or 2) less than or equal to 3? It is, so place a 1 in the 2^1 column. Now, how much is leftover? Time to subtract: 3–2=1. Finally, you ask whether 2^0 (or 1) is less than or equal to the remainder 1. Because it is, you put a 1 in the 2^0 column. Therefore, the decimal number 35 is equal to the binary number 00100011 or 100011. That's it. Table 1-8 summarizes this process.

TABLE 1-8 The Decimal Number 35 Is Equal to the Binary Number 00100011

2^7	2^6	2^5	2^4	2^3	2^2	2^1	2^0
128	64	32	16	8	4	2	1
0	0	1	0	0	0	1	1

As a second example of converting a decimal number to binary, consider the decimal number 239. Notice that you're taking the byte-oriented approach here; that is, you're working with numbers between 0 and 255, which are the decimal numbers that can be expressed with one byte. If you refer to Table 1-4, what's the largest power of 2 that is less than or equal to 239? You can see that 128 meets the criteria, so you put a 1 in the 2^7 column. Now, how much is leftover? You find this by subtracting 128 from 239: 239 – 128 = 111. Because the next smaller power of 2 is 2^6, you determine whether 2^6 (or 64) is less than or equal to 111. Because it is, you put a 1 in the 2^6 column. How much is leftover? You find this by subtracting 64 from 111: 111 – 64 = 47. The next power is 2^5, so you decide whether 2^5 (or 32) is less than or equal to the remainder 47. It is, so you put a 1 in the 2^5 column as well. How much is leftover? Find this by subtracting 32 from 47: 47 – 32 = 15. Next, is 2^4 (or 16) less than or equal to 15? It is not, so place a 0 in the 2^4 column. Next, is 2^3 (or 8) less than or equal to 15? It is, so place a 1 in the 2^3 column. How much is leftover? Time to subtract: 15 – 8 = 7. Next, is 2^2 (or 4) less than or equal to the remainder 7? It is, so place a 1 in the 2^2 column. How much is leftover? Subtract: 7 – 4 = 3. Next, is 2^1 (or 2) less than or equal to 3? It is, so you put a 1 in the 2^1 column. How much is leftover? Subtract: 3 – 2 = 1. Finally, you ask whether 2^0 (or 1) is less than or equal to the remainder 1? Because it is, you put a 1 in the 2^0 column. Therefore, the decimal number 239 is equal to the binary number 11101111. Table1-9 summarizes the result.

TABLE 1-9 The Decimal Number 239 Is Equal to the Binary Number 11101111

2^7	2^6	2^5	2^4	2^3	2^2	2^1	2^0
128	64	32	16	8	4	2	1
1	1	1	0	1	1	1	1

This procedure works for any decimal number. Consider the decimal number 1,000,000 (one million). What's the largest power of 2 less than or equal to 1,000,000? With a little patience, you can find that 2^{19}=524,288 and 2^{20}=1,048,576, so 2^{19} is the largest power of 2 that fits into 1,000,000. If you continue with the procedure previously described, you determine that the decimal number 1,000,000 is equal to the binary number 11110100001001000000.

You see that binary numbers take up more space than decimal numbers. This is partly why humans don't think in binary. Probably the main reason why humans use Base 10, however, is because we have 10 fingers. If we had 12 fingers, we probably would use Base 12.

Even and Odd

Sometimes, it's useful to recognize how the concepts of *even* and *odd* translate into binary numbers. An even decimal number is one that is a multiple of 2 (such as 0, 2, 4, 6, 8, 10, 12, and so on). Notice in the second row of Table 1-10 that all the numbers are multiples of 2 except the one in the last column: 1.

TABLE 1-10 All the Numbers Are Multiples of 2 Except the One on the Right

2^7	2^6	2^5	2^4	2^3	2^2	2^1	2^0
128	64	32	16	8	4	2	1

This means that a binary number is a multiple of 2 if and only if the rightmost digit is a 0. Therefore, a binary number is even if and only if the rightmost digit is 0. An odd number is one that is not even (such as the decimal numbers 1, 3, 5, 7, 9, 11, and so on). Hence, a binary number is odd if and only if the rightmost digit is 1.

Here are some examples: the binary number 10011 is odd (19 in decimal) and the binary number 1010100010 is even (674 in decimal).

Exercises

The following exercises help you acclimate to thinking in binary:

1. Convert the binary number 1010 to Base 10.
2. Convert the Base 2 number 11110000 to decimal notation.
3. Convert the binary number 10101111 to a decimal number.
4. Convert the decimal number 1111 to binary notation.
5. Convert the decimal number 249 to Base 2.
6. Convert the decimal number 128 to Base 2.
7. Convert the decimal number 65 to a binary number.
8. Convert the Base 10 number 63 to binary notation.
9. Convert the Base 10 number 31 to a binary number.
10. Convert the decimal number 198 to binary notation.
11. Is the binary number 11100011 even or odd?

SKILL BUILDER

Lab Activity: Binary Numbering

In this lab, you learn to work with the binary numbering system. You convert binary numbers (Base 2) to decimal numbers (Base 10) and decimal to binary.

Networks and Networking

A *network* is an intricately connected system of objects or people. Networks are all around us, even inside us. Your own nervous system and cardiovascular system are networks. The cluster diagram in Figure 1-16 shows several types of networks; you might think of others. Notice the following groupings:

- Communications
- Transportation

- Social
- Biological
- Utilities

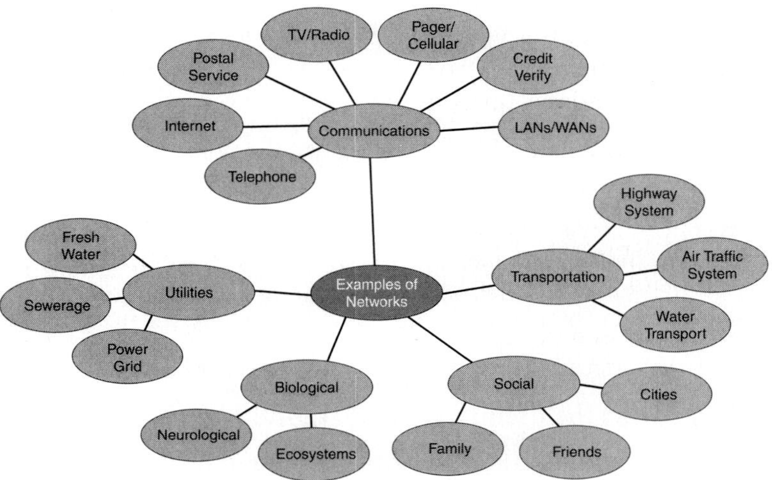

FIGURE 1-16
The term *network* is used in many ways, but the meaning is similar in each case to that of a computer network.

MORE INFORMATION

Circuit Switching Versus Packet Switching Communication Networks

The public telephone system, sometimes referred to as POTS (plain old telephone service), is a switched-circuit communications network. What this means is that when you place a telephone call, the same physical path from one end to the other end is used for the duration of that call. This circuit is maintained for your exclusive use, until you end the connection by hanging up your telephone.

In a circuit-switched network, a physical end-to-end connection is established and bandwidth is reserved. All signals are passed over this circuit for the duration of the session. If you disconnect and reconnect, a different circuit might be used, as represented by the broken line.

In a packet-switched network, there is no physical end-to-end connection established. Communications from different sources can share the same line, rather than having the line dedicated to one end-to-end communication for the duration of a session, as is the case with circuit switching. Because typically there is also no logical end-to-end connection, or virtual circuit, each individual packet of data can take a different path. Packet switching is sometimes referred to as a *connectionless technology* because the network layer does not set up a connection—data is just sent.

Data Networks

Data networks came about as a result of mainframe computer applications that had been written for businesses. However, at the time when these applications were written, businesses owned computers that were stand-alone devices and each one operated on its own, independent from any other computers. Therefore, it became apparent that this was not an efficient or cost effective manner in which to operate businesses. They needed a solution that would successfully address the following two questions:

- How do you avoid duplicating equipment and resources?
- How do you communicate efficiently?

MOVIE 1.1

What Is Internetworking?

A collection of networks.

Businesses recognized how much money they could save and how much productivity they could gain by using networking technology. They started adding networks and expanding existing networks almost as rapidly as new network technologies and products were introduced. As a result, the early 1980s saw a tremendous expansion in networking; however, the early development of networks was chaotic in many ways.

MOVIE 1.2

The Evolution of Networking

The growth of the computer industry.

MORE INFORMATION

The Benefits of a Network

The costs involved in networking computers often pays for itself many times over by reducing expenditures and lost production time. The benefits of networking include the sharing of

- Output devices, such as printers
- Input devices, such as scanners

continues

MORE INFORMATION (CONTINUED)

- Storage devices, such as CD-ROMs, ZIP drives, and JAZ drives
- Modems and Internet connections
- Data and applications

By the mid-1980s, growing pains were felt. Many of the network technologies that had emerged had been created with a variety of different hardware and software implementations. Consequently, many of the new network technologies were incompatible with each other.

MOVIE 1.3

The Evolution of Networking

Stand-alone computers with printers attached.

It became increasingly difficult for networks that used different specifications to communicate with each other. Because they could connect all the workstations, peripherals, terminals, and other devices in a single building, local-area networks (LANs) made it possible for businesses using computer technology to efficiently communicate and share such things as files and printers.

MOVIE 1.4

The Evolution of Networking

Replacing old printers on a LAN with high-speed network printers.

As the use of computers in businesses grew, it soon became obvious that even LANs were not sufficient. In a LAN system, each department or company is a kind of electronic island. What was needed was a way for information to move efficiently and quickly, not only within a company but from one business to another. The solution, then, was the connecting of LANs with metropolitan-area networks (MANs) and wide-area networks (WANs). Because WANs could connect user networks over large geographic areas, they made it possible for businesses to communicate with each other across great distances.

MOVIE 1.5

The Evolution of Internetworking

New offices—each has a LAN, software, hardware, and network administrator.

Data Networking Solutions

For your CCNA studies, most data networks are classified as either LANs or WANs. LANs usually are located in single buildings or campuses, and handle interoffice communications. WANs cover a large geographical area, and connect cities and countries. In addition, LANs and/or WANs also can be linked by internetworking.

Local-Area Networks

LANs consist of computers, network interface cards, networking media, network traffic control devices, and peripheral devices. LANs make it possible for businesses that use computer technology to efficiently share, items such as files and printers, and to make possible communications, such as e-mail. They tie together data, communications, computing, and file servers.

LANs are designed to do the following:

- Operate within a limited geographic area
- Allow many users to access high-bandwidth media
- Provide full-time connectivity to local services
- Connect physically adjacent devices

Wide-Area Networks

As a result of being networked or connected, computers, printers, and other devices on a wide-area network (WAN) could communicate with each other to share information and resources, as well as to access the Internet.

Some common WAN technologies include the following:

- Analog modems
- ISDN (Integrated Services Digital Network)
- DSL (Digital Subscriber Line)
- Frame Relay

- ATM (Asynchronous Transfer Mode)
- The T (US) and E (Europe) Carrier Series: T1, E1, T3, E3, and so on
- SONET (Synchronous Optical Network): STS-1 (OC-1), STS-3 (OC-3), and so on

MORE INFORMATION

Emerging Home Networking Applications

People now design and build their homes to be Internet homes, wiring them for Ethernet connectivity. People integrate their computer(s) with their phone system, security system, home theater system, heating and air conditioning, lighting and other electronic components to be able to control them all with the click of a mouse or even via voice command.

Service providers have built cellular- and satellite-based carrier networks that now offer sophisticated services, such as wireless Internet access. In addition, local exchange carriers (LECs), commonly referred to as local telephone companies, are implementing high speed services for data transfer, such as Digital Subscriber Line (DSL) services at a cost low enough to market to home users.

People also are integrating the PC and the telephone, allowing for automatic answering and message storage and retrieval via computer. In addition, the Internet phone, which uses IP telephony technology and Voice over IP (VoIP), allows people to bypass the telephone lines entirely with an Internet connection through cable, wireless, or some other media, to make long distance calls without paying long distance charges.

Digital Bandwidth

LANs and WANs have always had one thing in common: the use of the term *bandwidth* to describe their capabilities. This term is essential to understand networks but can be confusing at first. Let's take a detailed look at this concept before we get too far into networking.

Bandwidth is the measure of how much information can flow from one place to another in a given amount of time. There are two common uses of the word *bandwidth*: one deals with analog signals, and the other with digital signals. You will work with digital bandwidth, called simply *bandwidth* for the remainder of the text.

You have already learned that the term for the most basic unit of information is the bit. You also know that the basic unit of time is the second. So if you want to describe the *amount* of information flow in a *specific* period of time, you could use the units "bits per second" to describe this flow.

Bits per second is a unit of bandwidth. Of course, if communication happened at this rate, 1 bit per 1 second, it would be very slow. Imagine trying to send the ASCII code for your name and address—it would take minutes! Fortunately, much faster communications are now possible. Table 1-11 summarizes the various units of bandwidth.

TABLE 1-11 Units of Bandwidth

Unit of Bandwidth	Abbreviation	Equivalent
Bits per second	bps	1 bps = fundamental unit of bandwidth
Kilobits per second	Kbps	1 kbps = 1000 = 10^3bps
Megabits per second	Mbps	1 Mbps = 1,000,000 bps + 10^6 bps
Gigabits per second	Gbps	1 Gbps = 1,000,000,000 bps = 10^9 bps

Two Analogies that Describe Digital Bandwidth

Bandwidth is an important element of networking, yet it can be rather abstract and difficult to understand. The following are three analogies that can help you picture what bandwidth is.

- **Bandwidth is like the width of a pipe, as shown in Figure 1-17.** Think of the network of pipes that brings water to your home and carries sewage away from it. Those pipes have different diameters. The city's main water pipe might be 2 meters in diameter, whereas the kitchen faucet might be 2 centimeters. The width of the pipe measures the water-carrying capacity of the pipe. In this analogy, the water is like information and the width of the pipe is like bandwidth. In fact, many networking experts talk in terms of "putting in bigger pipes," meaning more bandwidth (more information-carrying capacity).
- **Bandwidth is like the number of lanes on a highway, as shown in Figure 1-18.** Think about a network of roads that serves your city or town. There might be eight-lane highways, with exits onto two- and three-lane roads, which might then lead to two-lane undivided streets, and eventually to your driveway. In this analogy, the number of lanes is like the bandwidth, and the number of cars is like the amount of information that can be carried.

Keep in mind that the true, actual meaning of bandwidth, in this context, is the maximum number of bits that theoretically can pass through a given area of space in a specified amount of time (under the given conditions). These analogies are only to make it easier to understand the concept of bandwidth.

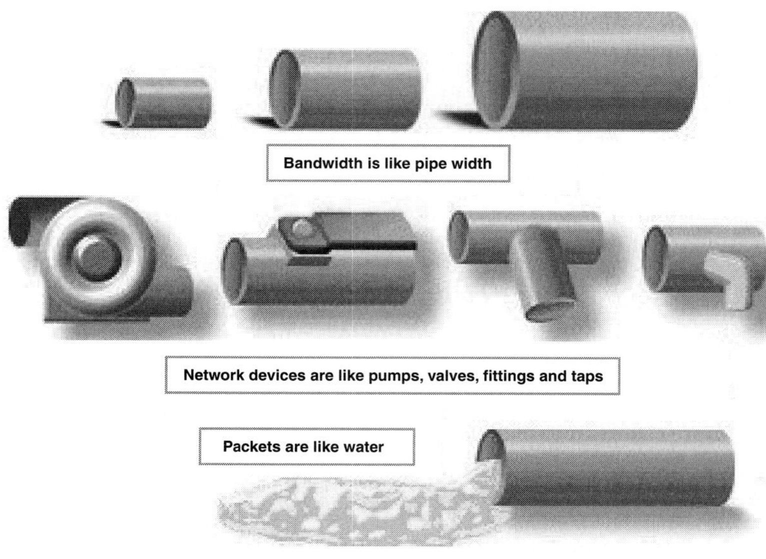

FIGURE 1-17
The wider the pipe, the greater the rate of fluid that can flow through it.

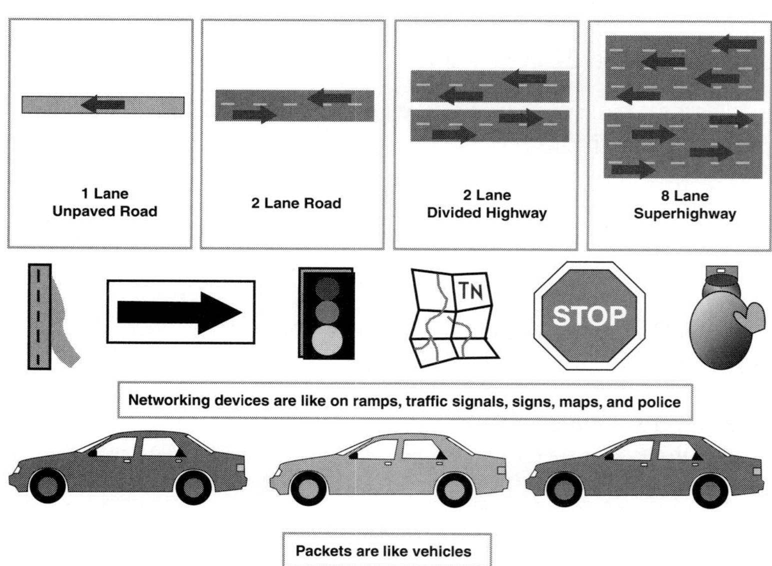

FIGURE 1-18
The more lanes in a highway, the greater the capacity for traffic flow.

Media Bandwidth Differences

Bandwidth is a useful concept. It does, however, have limitations. No matter how you send your messages, no matter which physical medium you use, bandwidth is limited. This is due both to the laws of physics and to the current technological advances.

Table 1-12 lists the maximum digital bandwidth that is possible, including length limitations, for some common networking media. Always remember that limits are both physical and technological.

TABLE 1-12 Maximum Bandwidths and Length Limitations

Typical Media	Maximum Theoretical Bandwidth	Maximum Physical Distance
50-Ohm Coaxial Cable (Ethernet 10Base2, ThinNet)	10–100 Mbps	185 m
75-Ohm Coaxial Cable (Ethernet 10Base5, Thicknet)	10–100 Mbps	500 m
Category 5 Unshielded Twisted Pair (UTP) (Ethernet 10BaseT)	10 Mbps	100 m
Category 5 Unshielded Twisted Pair (UTP) (Ethernet 100BaseTX) (Fast Ethernet)	100 Mbps	100 m
Multimode (62.5/125um) Optical Fiber 100BaseFX	100 Mbps	2000 m
Singlemode (10um core) Optical Fiber 1000BaseLX	1000 Mbps (1.000 Gbps)	3000 m
Wireless	11.0 Mbps	A few 100 meters

Table 1-13 summarizes different WAN services and the bandwidth associated with each service. Which service do you use at home? At school?

TABLE 1-13 WAN Services and Bandwidths

Type of WAN Service	Typical User	Bandwidth
Modem	Individuals	56 Kbps = 0.056 Mbps
ISDN	Telecommuters and small businesses	128 Kbps = 0.128 Mbps

continues

TABLE 1-13 WAN Services and Bandwidths (Continued)

Type of WAN Service	Typical User	Bandwidth
Frame Relay	Small institutions (schools) and reliable WANs	56 Kbps to 1544 Mbps = 0.056 Mbps to 1.544 Mbps
T1	Larger entities	1.544 Mbps
T3	Larger entities	44.736 Mbps
STS-1 (OC-1)	Phone companies; Data-Comm company backbones	51.840 Mbps
STS-3 (OC-3)	Phone companies; Data-Comm company backbones	155.251 Mbps
STS-48 (OC-48)	Phone companies; Data-Comm company backbones	2.488320 Gbps

Data Throughput in Relation to Digital Bandwidth

Imagine that you are lucky enough to have a brand new cable modem, or your local store just installed an ISDN line, or your school just received a 10 Megabit per second Ethernet LAN. Now imagine that the movie you want to view, or the Web page you want to load, or the software you want to download still takes forever to receive. Did you believe you were getting all that bandwidth that was advertised? There is another important concept you should understand: it's called *throughput.*

Throughput refers to the actual, measured bandwidth, at a specific time of day, using specific Internet routes, while downloading a specific file. Unfortunately, for many reasons, the throughput is often far less than the maximum possible digital bandwidth of the medium that is being used.

Some of the factors that determine throughput and bandwidth include the following:

- Internetworking devices
- Type of data being transferred
- Topology
- Number of users
- User's computer

- Server computer
- Power- and weather-induced outages
- Congestion

When you design a network, it's important that you consider the theoretical bandwidth. Your network cannot be faster than your media allows. When you actually work on networks, you must measure throughput and decide whether the throughput is adequate for the user (see Figure 1-19).

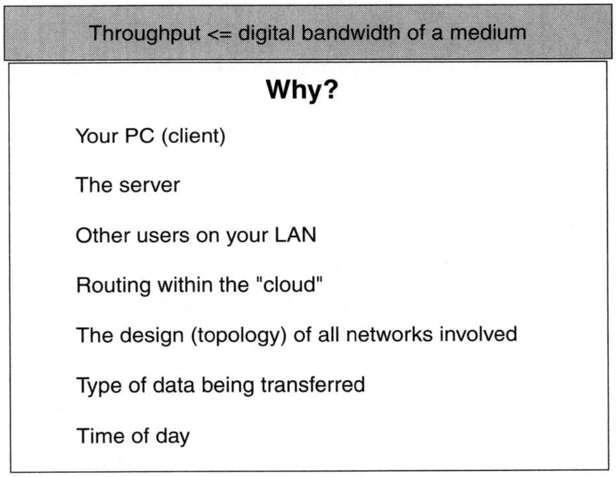

FIGURE 1-19 Throughput is the actual amount of data passing through a given area of space in a specific amount of time.

Throughput <= digital bandwidth of a medium

Why?

Your PC (client)

The server

Other users on your LAN

Routing within the "cloud"

The design (topology) of all networks involved

Type of data being transferred

Time of day

Data Transfer Calculation

An important part of networking involves making decisions about which medium to use. This often leads to questions regarding the bandwidths that the user's applications require. Figure 1-20 summarizes a simple formula that can help you with such decisions. The formula is Estimated Time = Size of File / Bandwidth. The resulting answer represents the fastest that data could be transferred. It does not take into account any of the previously discussed issues that affect throughput, but does give you a rough estimate of the time it takes to send information using that specific medium/application.

FIGURE 1-20 Here's a formula for computing the time it takes to download a file.

BW = Maximum theoretical bandwidth of the "slowest" link between the source host and the destination host.

P = Actual throughput at the moment of transfer.

T = Time for file transfer to occur.

S = File size in bits.

Best download $T = \frac{S}{BW}$

Typical Download $T = \frac{S}{P}$

Now that you are familiar with the units for digital bandwidth, try the following sample problem:

Which would take less time: sending a floppy disk (1.44 MB) full of data over an ISDN line, or sending a 10 GB hard drive full of data over an OC-48 line? Use figures from the bandwidth chart shown earlier to find the answer.

Why Is Bandwidth Important?

Bandwidth is finite. Regardless of the media, bandwidth is limited by the laws of physics. Due to the physical properties of the twisted-pair phone wires that come into many homes limits the throughput of conventional modems to about 56 kbps. The bandwidth of the electromagnetic spectrum is finite in that there are only so many frequencies in the radio wave, microwave, and infrared spectrum. Because this is so, the FCC has a division devoted to controlling bandwidth and who uses it. Optical fiber has virtually limitless bandwidth. However, the rest of the technology to make extremely high bandwidth networks that fully use the potential of optical fiber are just now being developed and implemented.

Knowing how bandwidth works, and that it is finite, can save you lots of money. For example, the cost of various connection options from Internet service providers depends, in part, on how much bandwidth, on average and at peak usage, you require. In a way, you pay for bandwidth.

As a networking professional, you will be expected to know about bandwidth and throughput. They are major factors in analyzing network performance. In addition, as a network designer of new networks, bandwidth will always be one of the major design issues.

There are two major concepts to understand concerning the *information superhighway*. The first is that any form of information can be stored as a long string of bits. The second is that storing information as bits, although useful, is not the truly revolutionary technology. The fact that we can share those bits (trillions of them in one second) means modern civilization is approaching the time when any computer, anywhere in the world or in space, can communicate with any other computer, in a few seconds or less.

It is not uncommon that when a person or an institution starts using a network, they eventually want more and more bandwidth. New multimedia software programs require much more bandwidth than those used in the mid-1990s. Creative programmers are busily designing new applications that are capable of performing more complex communication tasks, thus requiring greater bandwidth.

Summary

In this chapter, you learned about the components of a computer and the role of computers in a networking system. More specifically, you learned the following:

- Computers are vital components of every network. The more you know about computers, the easier it is to understand networks.
- It is important to be familiar with the components of a computer and to be able to install a NIC. Also, troubleshooting PCs is a necessary skill for someone who works on networks.
- Software is the piece of the puzzle that allows the user to interface with the hardware. In networking, Web browsers and e-mail are commonly used software programs. In general, office applications, browsers, and e-mail programs are used to perform business tasks.
- Computers can understand and process data that is in a binary format only. Binary format is represented by 0s and 1s.
- The two main types of networks are LANs and WANs. WANs connect LANs together. LANs and WANs use protocols as languages to allow for computers and networking devices to communicate with each other.
- Bandwidth and throughput are measures of the speed or the capacity of a network.

In the next chapter, you learn about the OSI reference model and how each layer of the OSI model performs certain functions as data travels through the layers.

Check Your Understanding

1. The network card, the monitor connect, and the mouse port are:
   - **A.** Personal computer subsystems
   - **B.** Small, discrete components of a system
   - **C.** Back plane components
   - **D.** Ports of the system
2. Match the following:

a) Boot instructions	1) Stored in ROM until they are sent out
b) Software applications	2) Flows from RAM and the CPU, via the bus and expansion slots, to the interfaces
c) Application information	3) Flows from RAM to some form of storage device
d) Saved information	4) After they are loaded, they are stored in RAM temporarily
e) Exported information	5) Stored in RAM as long as the application is being used

   - **A.** a-1, b-4, c-5, d-3, e-2
   - **B.** a-2, b-5, c-1, d-3, e-4
   - **C.** a-5, b-4, c-3, d-2, e-1
   - **D.** a-1, b-4, c-3, d-5, e-2
3. What is a NIC?
   - **A.** A WAN adapter
   - **B.** A printed circuit board that provides network communication
   - **C.** A card used only for Ethernet networks
   - **D.** A standardized data link layer address
4. A network card communicates with the network through a
   - **A.** Serial connection
   - **B.** Parallel connection
   - **C.** Back plane
   - **D.** None of the above

5. Why do you need to use a static mat and a wrist strap?
   - **A.** To protect yourself from any charge
   - **B.** To ground yourself
   - **C.** To enable easy handling of the equipment
   - **D.** All of the above
6. PCMCIA slots are
   - **A.** Slots used in laptops
   - **B.** Used as expansion slots in all computers
   - **C.** Expansion slots for a NIC card
   - **D.** Slots for certain specialized devices
7. What must computers on a network have in common to communicate directly with each other?
   - **A.** Use the same operating system
   - **B.** Use the same hardware
   - **C.** Use the same protocol
   - **D.** Built by the same company
8. What is a LAN?
   - **A.** A network that connects workstations, terminals, and other devices in a geographically limited area
   - **B.** A network that connects workstations, terminals, and other devices in a large metropolitan area
   - **C.** A network that serves users across a geographically large area and often uses transmission devices provided by a common carrier
   - **D.** A network that covers a larger area than a MAN
9. What do WANs do?
   - **A.** Allow printer and file sharing
   - **B.** Operate over a large geographic area
   - **C.** Operate over a metropolitan area
   - **D.** Provide host-to-host connectivity within a limited area

10. What type of numbering system is characterized by 0s and 1s?
    A. Base 4
    B. Base 10
    C. Binary
    D. Hexadecimal
11. Which numbering system is based on powers of 2?
    A. Octal
    B. Hexadecimal
    C. Binary
    D. ASCII
12. What is the decimal number 151 in binary?
    A. 10100111
    B. 10010111
    C. 10101011
    D. 10010011
13. What is the binary number 11011010 in decimal?
    A. 186
    B. 202
    C. 222
    D. 218
14. What is the binary number 10110 decimal?
    A. 28
    B. 22
    C. 24
    D. 23
15. What is the decimal number 202 in binary?
    A. 11000100
    B. 11000101
    C. 11001010
    D. 11000111

16. What is the binary number 11101100 in decimal form?

A. 234

B. 236

C. 262

D. 242

17. What best describes how much information can flow from one place to another in a given amount of time?

A. Mbps

B. Transfer-rate

C. Reliability

D. Bandwidth

18. Bandwidth is described in

A. Bytes per second

B. Bits per second

C. Megabits per millisecond

D. Centimeters

19. Which of the following statements is false?

A. Throughput usually refers to actual, measured bandwidth, at a specific time of day, using specific Internet routes.

B. Throughput is less than the bandwidth.

C. Throughput is the maximum amount of information that can flow from one point to another.

D. Factors that determine throughput include internetworking devices and the type of data being transferred.

20. What term is used to describe the rated throughput capacity of a given network medium or protocol?

A. TCP/IP

B. Ethernet

C. Bandwidth

D. Routing protocol

Objectives

After reading this chapter, you will be able to

- Describe a general model of communication
- Describe the OSI reference model
- Compare the OSI model and the TCP/IP model

Chapter 2

The OSI Model

Introduction

In the late 1980s and early 1990s, there was a significant increase in the number and overall size of networks. Many of the networks, however, were built using different implementations of hardware and software. As a result, many of the networks were incompatible and it became difficult for networks using different specifications to communicate with each other. To address this problem, the International Organization for Standardization (ISO) researched many network schemes. The ISO recognized the need to create a network model that would help network builders implement networks that could communicate and work together (interoperability) and, therefore, released the OSI reference model in 1984.

This chapter explains how standards ensure greater compatibility and interoperability between various types of network technologies. In this chapter, you learn how the OSI reference model networking scheme supports networking standards. In addition, you see how information or data makes its way from application programs (such as spreadsheets) through a network medium (such as wires) to other application programs located on other computers on a network. As you work through this chapter, you learn about the basic functions that occur at each layer of the OSI model, which will serve as a foundation as you begin to design, build, and troubleshoot networks.

A General Model of Communication

Learning about networking is easier when you start with theory and concepts and then move on to the more concrete aspects of implementation. As network professionals, you need to learn the theory of how networks communicate before designing, building, and maintaining networks.

Learning the concept of layers can help you understand the action that occurs during communication from one computer to another. The following questions involve the movement of physical objects, such as highway traffic, or electronic data:

- What is flowing?
- What different forms flow?

- What rules govern flow?
- Where does the flow occur?

This motion of objects, whether it is physical or logical, is referred to as *flow*. Many layers help describe the details of the flow process. Other examples of systems that flow are the public water system, the highway system, the postal system, and the telephone system.

Now examine the chart shown in Figure 2-1. What network are you examining? What is flowing? What are the different forms of the object that is flowing? What are the rules for flow? Where does the flow occur? The networks listed in this chart give you analogies that help you understand computer networks.

FIGURE 2-1
A comparison of various networks.

Network?	What is Flowing?	Different Forms?	Rules?	Where?
Water	Water	Hot; cold; drinkable; wastewater/ sewer	Access rules (turning taps) flushing; not putting certain things in drains	Pipes
Highway	Vehicles	Trucks, cars, cycles	Traffic laws and rules for politeness	Roads and Highways
Postal	Objects	Letters (written information); packages	Rules for packaging and attaching postage	Postal service boxes, offices, truckes, planes, delivery people
Telephone	Information	Spoken languages	Rules for accessing phone and rules for politeness	Phone system wires, EM waves etc.

The network communication process is complex. The data, in the form of electronic signals, must travel across media to the correct destination computer and then be converted back into its original form in order to be read by the recipient. Several steps are involved in this process and, for this reason, the most efficient way to implement network communications would be as a layered process. In a layered communication process, each layer performs a specific task.

In the next section, you see how the network communication process is broken using a layered model. You also see how data is sent out over the network and how it reaches its intended destination. As you learn about the network communication process, it is important for you to understand the various steps, components, and protocols of the network communication process. This understanding provides you with valuable troubleshooting information when the communications process does not proceed smoothly.

Source, Destination, and Data Packets

As you learned in Chapter 1, the most basic level of computer information consists of binary digits, or bits (0s and 1s). Computers that send one or two bits of information, however, are not useful, so other groupings (such as bytes, kilobytes, megabytes, and gigabytes) are necessary. For computers to send information through a network, all communications on a network originate at a source and travel to a destination. Before data can be sent across a network as electrical impulses, it first must be broken into manageable chunks. The *data* is not the information itself; it is the encoded form of the information, which is the series of electrical impulses into which the information is translated for sending.

As illustrated in Figure 2-2, the information that travels on a network is referred to as data, packet, or data packet. A data packet is a logically grouped unit of information that moves between computer systems. It includes the destination and source information along with other elements that are necessary in order to make communication possible and reliable with the destination device.

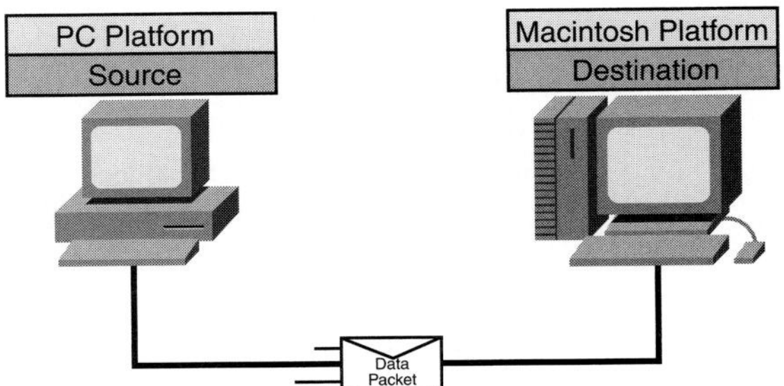

FIGURE 2-2
Packets are the small, easily transmitted units into which data is broken for transmission between a source and a destination.

The small, easily transmitted units into which computer data is broken for transmission across a network are called *packets*. Depending on the networking architecture and the point in the communications process the unit has reached, the term *frames* can be used to talk about packets. In addition, the word *segment* refers to a unit of data transmitted by the Transmission Control Protocol (TCP). We use the term *packet* to refer to these manageable chunks in general. The source IP address in a packet specifies the identity of the original host sending the packet. The destination IP address specifies the identity of the host that should receive the packet.

MORE INFORMATION

Advantages of Dividing Data into Packets

Transmitting data in small packets has several advantages:

- Computers on the network can take turns sending packets, and one computer with a large amount of data to transmit won't monopolize the network's bandwidth.
- If network communication is disrupted and a packet is lost, only that small amount of data, rather than the entire file, must be retransmitted.
- Depending on the network's architecture and link type, each packet can take a different path to reach the destination. Thus, if one pathway becomes congested or slows down, subsequent packets can take a more efficient route.

NOTE

The plural form of *medium* is *media.*

Media

During your study of networking, you might hear references to the word *medium*. In networking, a medium is a material through which data packets travel. It could be any of the following materials:

- Telephone wires (UTP)
- Category 5 UTP (used for 10BASE-T Ethernet)
- Coaxial cables
- Optical fibers (thin glass fibers that carry light)

Another type of media is the atmosphere that carries radio waves, microwaves, and light. Communication without some type of wires or cables is called wireless or free-space communication. This is made possible using electromagnetic (EM) waves. In a vacuum, EM waves travel at the speed of light. EM waves include power waves, radio waves, microwaves, infrared light, visible light, ultraviolet light, x-rays, and gamma rays. EM waves travel through the atmosphere (mostly oxygen, nitrogen, and water), but they also travel through the vacuum of outer space (where virtually no matter, no molecules, and no atoms exist).

Protocol

For data packets to travel from a source to a destination on a network, it is important that all the devices on the network speak the same language, or protocol. A network protocol is a set of rules that makes communication on a network both possible and more efficient. Some common examples of non-networking protocols are as follows:

- In Congress, a form of Roberts Rules of Order makes it possible for hundreds of representatives to take turns and to communicate their ideas in an orderly manner.

- When driving a car, other cars (should!) signal when they want to make a turn; if they do not, the roads become chaotic.
- When flying an airplane, pilots obey specific rules for communication with other airplanes and with air-traffic control.
- When answering the telephone, someone says, "Hello," and the person calling says, "Hello. This is…"; and so it goes back and forth.

The following is one technical definition of a data communications protocol: a set of rules, or an agreement, that determines the format and transmission of data. Layer *n* on one computer communicates with Layer *n* on another computer. The rules and conventions used in this communication are known collectively as the Layer *n* protocol (see Figure 2-3).

FIGURE 2-3
Each layer's protocol exchanges information called protocol data units (PDUs) with peer layers.

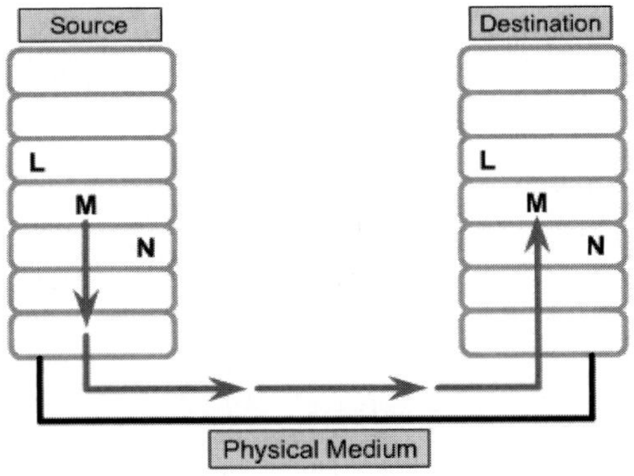
Source
Destination
L
M
N
L
M
N
Physical Medium
• L, M, N - layers in our model of computer communications
• Msource, Mdestination - peer layers
• - peer to peer communications
• M Layer Protocol - the rules by which Msource communicates with Mdestination

MORE INFORMATION

Grouping of Users

Because companies have adopted their internetwork as part of their business strategy, it is typical to subdivide and map corporate internetworks to the corporate business structure. In Figure 2-4, for example, the internetwork is defined based on the grouping of employees (users) in the following ways:

continues

MORE INFORMATION (CONTINUED)

- A main office where everyone is connected via a LAN and where the bulk of the corporate information is located. A main office can have hundreds, or even thousands, of people who depend on network access to do their jobs. It might have several LANs or be a campus that contains several buildings. Because everyone needs access to central resources and information, it is common to see a high-speed backbone LAN and a legacy data center with mainframe computers and applications.

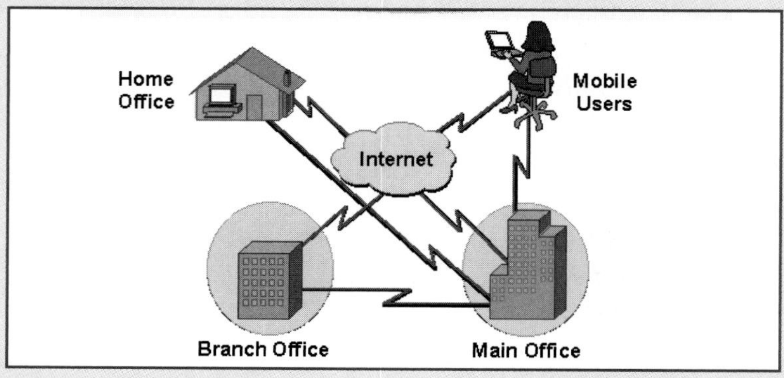

FIGURE 2-4
One of the primary purposes of an internetwork is to increase productivity by linking computers and computer networks so that people have easy access to information.

- A variety of remote-access locations that connect to the main office and/or each other using wide-area network (WAN) services. The following are some examples of possible remote-access locations:
  - **Branch offices**—Small groups of people connect to each other through a LAN. To connect to the main office, these users have to use WAN services. Although some corporate information can be stored at a branch office, it is more likely that it houses user resources, such as printers, but accesses information directly from the main office. The frequency of accessing the main office determines whether the WAN should be based on permanent or dial up connections.
  - **Home offices**—These individuals work from their homes. They most likely require on-demand connections to the main office and/or the branch office to access information or to use network resources, such as file servers.

MORE INFORMATION (CONTINUED)

— **Mobile users**—These individuals connect to the main office LAN when they are at the main office, when they are at the branch office, or when they are on the road. Their network access needs are based on where they are located at a given point in time.

The Evolution of ISO Networking Standards

The early development of LANs, MANs, and WANs was chaotic in many ways. The early 1980s saw tremendous increases in the numbers and sizes of networks. As companies realized they could save money and gain productivity by using networking technology, they added networks and expanded existing networks almost as rapidly as new network technologies and products could be introduced.

By the mid-1980s, these companies began to experience growing pains from all the expansions they made. It became harder for networks that used different specifications and implementations to communicate with each other. They realized that they needed to move away from proprietary networking systems.

MOVIE 2.1

The Evolution of Internetworking

Two Problems: Avoiding duplication of equipment and resources, and the inability to communicate efficiently.

Proprietary systems are privately developed, owned, and controlled. In the computer industry, proprietary is the opposite of open. Proprietary means that one or a small group of companies controls all usage and evolution of the technology. Open means that free usage of the technology is available to the public.

To address the problem of different network systems being incompatible and incapable of communicating with each other, the International Organization for Standardization (ISO) researched network schemes, such as DECnet, SNA, and TCP/IP, to find a set of rules. As a result of this research, the ISO created a network model that could help vendors create networks that would be compatible with, and interoperate with, other networks.

MOVIE 2.2

The OSI Model

The ISO researched networks, including DECnet, SNA, and TCP/IP.

MORE INFORMATION

Other Standards-Setting Bodies

The IETF

The *Internet Engineering Task Force (IETF)* is part of the Internet Architecture Board (IAB), which in turn is a technical advisory group that belongs to the Internet Society (ISOC).

The IETF is divided into working groups, each of which addresses a different issue related to the establishment of Internet standards. The membership is open; any interested party can join.

The primary task of the IETF working groups involves developing and submitting Internet drafts. These Internet drafts evolve into official *Request For Comment (RFC)* documents, which go through an established approval process to become Internet standards.

RFCs and Internet Standards

As a networking professional, you might see references to "RFC [number]" for more information on the characteristics of certain networking services and protocols. These services and protocols include such items as the following:

- Implementation of the Domain Name System (DNS)
- TCP/IP extensions
- Specifications for Network Address Translation (NAT) software

Although many RFCs originate with the IETF, anyone can submit RFC proposals. Not all RFCs describe standards, but if a document is to become a standard, it goes through three stages:

- Proposed Standard
- Draft Standard
- Internet Standard

MORE INFORMATION (CONTINUED)

The IEEE

The IEEE (often called the "Eye-triple E" by members of the industry) promotes the exchange of information and develops standards and specifications primarily for lower level networking technologies (those at the physical and data link layers).

Of particular interest to networking professionals are the specifications that make up the IEEE 802 project. The name is based on the date of the committee meeting. The 80 designates the year (1980) and the 2 designates the month (February).

The OSI reference model, released in 1984, was the descriptive scheme they created. It provided vendors with a set of standards that could enable greater compatibility and interoperability between the various types of network technologies that were produced by the many companies around the world.

The Purpose of the OSI Reference Model

The OSI reference model is the primary model for network communications. A primary objective of the OSI reference model is to accelerate the development of future networking products. Although there are other models in existence, most network vendors today relate their products to the OSI reference model, especially when they want to educate users on the use of their products. They consider it the best tool available to teach people about sending and receiving data on a network.

MOVIE 2.3

The OSI Model

The OSI model enhances interoperability and comprehension.

The OSI reference model allows you to view the network functions that occur at each layer. More importantly, the OSI reference model is a framework you can use to understand how information travels throughout a network. In addition, the OSI reference model can be used to visualize how information, or data packets, travels from application programs (for example, spreadsheets, documents, and so on), through a network medium (for example, wires), to other application programs that are located in another computer on a network, even if the sender and the receiver have different types of network media.

MOVIE 2.4

The OSI Model Conceptual Framework

Protocols allow communication to occur.

In the OSI reference model, there are seven numbered layers. Each layer illustrates a particular network function. This separation of networking functions is called *layering*. Dividing the network into these seven layers provides the following advantages:

- It breaks network communication into smaller, simpler parts that are easier to develop.
- It facilitates standardization of network components to allow multiple-vendor development and support.
- It allows different types of network hardware and software to communicate with each other.
- It prevents changes in one layer from affecting the other layers, so that they can develop more quickly.
- It breaks network communication into smaller parts to make learning it easier to understand.

The Seven Layers of the OSI Reference Model

The process of moving information between computers is divided into seven smaller and more manageable steps in the OSI reference model. Each of the seven smaller problems is represented by its own layer in the model. The seven layers of the OSI reference model are

- Layer 7: The application layer

- Layer 6: The presentation layer
- Layer 5: The session layer
- Layer 4: The transport layer
- Layer 3: The network layer
- Layer 2: The data link layer
- Layer 1: The physical layer

During the course of this semester, you start your studies with Layer 1 and work your way through the OSI model, layer by layer. By working through the layers of the OSI reference model, you can understand how data travels through a network and what devices operate at each layer as data travels through them. As a result, you can understand how to troubleshoot network problems as they occur during data packet flow. Each OSI layer has a set of functions that it must perform for data to travel from a source to a destination on a network. The following sections provide a brief description of each layer in the OSI reference model, as shown in Figure 2-5.

MOVIE 2.5

The Internet

Technology and networking.

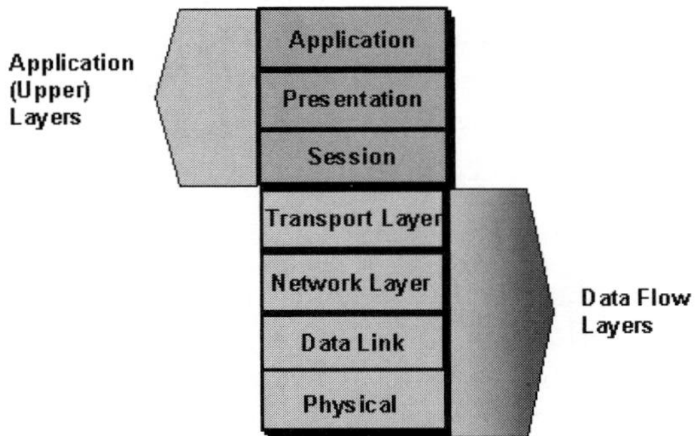

FIGURE 2-5
The seven layers of the OSI model.

The Upper Layers

The three upper layers of the OSI reference model are referred to as the *application layers*. Figure 2-6 shows the upper layers and provides information on their functionality with some examples.

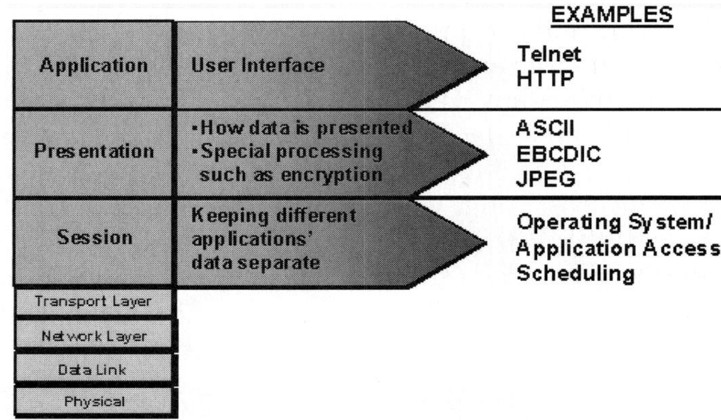

FIGURE 2-6 The upper layers of the OSI model deal with the user interface, data formatting, and the application access.

Layer 7: The Application Layer

The application layer is the OSI layer that is closest to the user. It provides network services, such as file access and printing, to the user's applications. It differs from the other layers in that it does not provide services to any other OSI layer, but rather, only to applications outside the OSI model. Examples of such applications are spreadsheet programs, word-processing programs, and bank terminal programs. The application layer establishes the availability of intended communication partners. It also synchronizes and establishes an agreement on procedures for error recovery and control of data integrity. If you want to remember Layer 7 in as few words as possible, think of browsers.

Layer 6: The Presentation Layer

The presentation layer ensures that the information that the application layer of one system sends out is readable by the application layer of another system. If necessary, the presentation layer translates between multiple data formats by using a common format. This layer also is responsible for compression and encryption. If you want to think of Layer 6 in as few words as possible, think of a common data format.

Layer 5: The Session Layer

As its name implies, the session layer establishes, manages, and terminates sessions between two communicating hosts. The session layer provides its services to the presentation layer. It also synchronizes dialogue between the two hosts' presentation layers and manages their data exchange. In addition to session regulation, the session layer offers provisions for efficient data transfer, class of service, and exception reporting of session layer, presentation layer, and application layer problems. If you want to remember Layer 5 in as few words as possible, think of dialogues and conversations.

The Lower Layers

The four lower layers of the OSI model define how data is transferred across a physical wire through internetworking devices, to the desired end station, and finally to the application. Figure 2-7 summarizes the basic function of these four layers. Later in this book, each layer is discussed in greater detail.

FIGURE 2-7
The lower layers control the physical delivery of data.

Layer	Function	EXAMPLES
Application		
Presentation		
Session		
Transport	• Reliable or unreliable delivery • Error correction before retransmit	TCP UDP SPX
Network	Provide logical addressing which routers use for path determination	IP IPX
Data Link	• Combines bits into bytes and bytes into frames • Access to media using MAC address • Error detection not correction	802.3 / 802.2 HDLC
Physical	• Move bits between devices • Specifies voltage, wire speed and pin-out cables	EIA/TIA-232 V.35

Layer 4: The Transport Layer

The transport layer segments data from the sending host's system and reassembles the data into a data stream on the receiving host's system. The boundary between the transport layer and the session layer can be thought of as the boundary between application protocols and data-flow protocols. Whereas the application, presentation, and session layers are concerned with application issues, the lower four layers are concerned with data transport issues.

The transport layer attempts to provide a data transport service that shields the upper layers from transport implementation details. Specifically, such issues as how reliable transport between two hosts is accomplished is the concern of the transport layer. In providing communication service, the transport layer establishes, maintains, and properly terminates connection-oriented circuits. In providing reliable service, transport error detection-and-recovery and information flow control are used. If you want to remember Layer 4 in as few words as possible, think of flow control and reliability.

Layer 3: The Network Layer

The network layer is a complex layer that provides connectivity and path selection between two host systems that might be located on geographically separated networks. If you want to remember Layer 3 in as few words as possible, think of path selection, routing, and logical addressing.

Layer 2: The Data Link Layer

The data link layer provides the transit of data across a physical link. In so doing, the data link layer is concerned with physical (as opposed to logical) addressing, network (sometimes called logical) topology, network media access, and error detection. If you want to remember Layer 2 in as few words as possible, think of frames and media access control.

Layer 1: The Physical Layer

The physical layer defines the electrical, mechanical, procedural, and functional specifications for activating, maintaining, and deactivating the physical link between end systems. Such characteristics as voltage levels, timing of voltage changes, physical data rates, maximum transmission distances, physical connectors, and other, similar, attributes are defined by physical layer specifications. If you want to remember Layer 1 in as few words as possible, think of signals and media.

Encapsulation

All communications on a network originate at a source, are sent to a destination. The information that is sent on a network is referred to as data or data packets. If one computer (Host A) wants to send data to another computer (Host B), the data first must be packaged by a process called *encapsulation*. Encapsulation wraps data with the necessary protocol information before network transit.

> **NOTE**
>
> The word *header* means that information was added to the front of the packet, just as trailers are added at the end. In addition, an address is an important piece of information that gets added.

Therefore, as the data packet moves down through the layers of the OSI model, it receives headers, trailers, and other information.

To see how encapsulation occurs, let's examine the manner in which data travels through the layers, as illustrated in Figure 2-8. When the data is sent from the source, as shown in Figure 2-8, it travels through the application layer down through the other layers. As you can see, the packaging and the flow of the data that is exchanged goes through changes as the layers perform their services for end users.

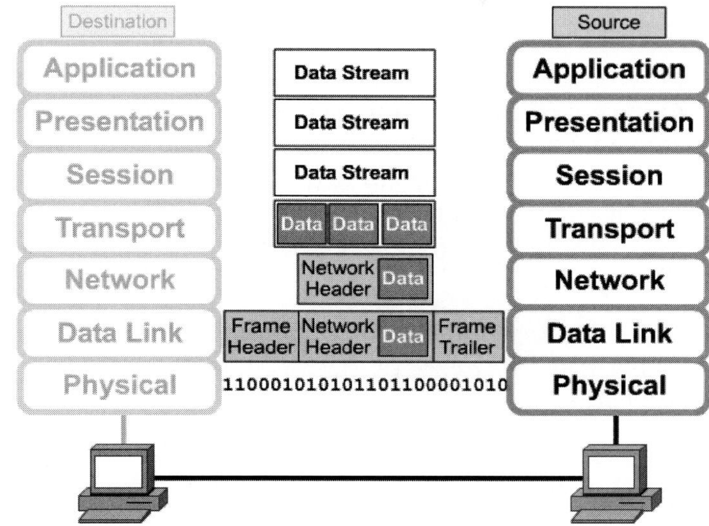

FIGURE 2-8
The lower layer uses encapsulation to put the PDU from the upper layer into its data field and to add headers and trailers the layer can use to perform its function.

The data, in the form of electronic signals, must travel across a cable to the correct destination computer, and then be converted to its original form to be read by the recipient. As you can imagine, several steps are involved in this process. For this reason, developers of hardware, software, and protocols recognized that the most efficient way to implement network communications would be as a layered process.

As illustrated in Figure 2-9, networks must perform the following five conversion steps in order to encapsulate data:

1. **Build the data.** As a user sends an e-mail message, its alphanumeric characters are converted to data that can travel across the internetwork.

2. **Package the data for end-to-end transport.** The data is packaged for internetwork transport. By using segments, the transport function ensures that the message hosts at both ends of the e-mail system can reliably communicate.

3. **Add the network address to the header.** The data is put into a packet or a datagram that contains a network header with source and destination

logical IP addresses. These addresses help network devices send the packets across the network along a dynamically chosen path.

4. **Add the local (MAC) address to the data link header.** Each network device must put the packet into a frame. The frame includes a header with the physical address of the next directly connected device in the path.

5. **Convert to bits for transmission.** The frame must be converted into a pattern of 1s and 0s (bits) for transmission on the medium (usually a wire). A clocking function enables the devices to distinguish these bits as they travel across the medium. The medium on the physical internetwork can vary along the path used. For example, the e-mail message can originate on a LAN, across a campus backbone, and go out a WAN link until it reaches its destination on another remote LAN.

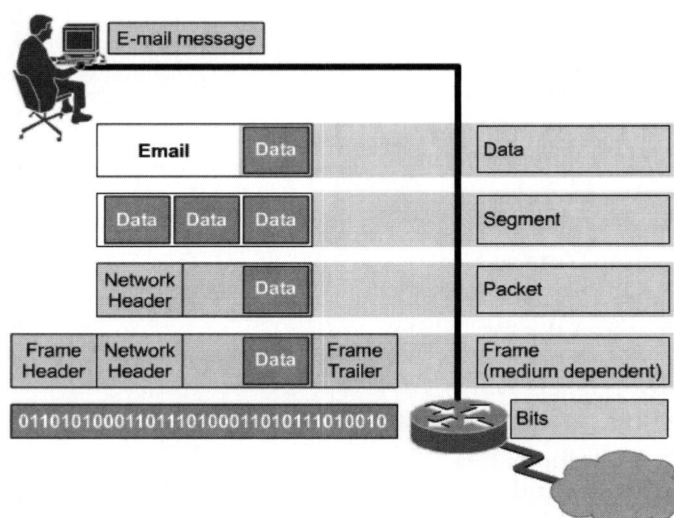

FIGURE 2-9
Headers and trailers are added as data moves down through the layers of the OSI model.

De-Encapsulation

When the remote device receives a sequence of bits, it passes them to the data link layer for frame manipulation. When the data link layer receives the frame, it does the following:

- It reads the physical address and other control information provided by the directly connected peer data link layer.
- It strips the control information from the frame, thereby creating a datagram.

- It passes the datagram up to the next layer, following the instructions that appeared in the control portion of the frame.

This process is referred to as *de-encapsulation*. Each subsequent layer performs a similar de-encapsulation process.

MORE INFORMATION

Cyclical Redundancy Check

Each data packet has information added to the raw data itself, in the form of *packet headers*. The headers contain addressing information so the packets reach the correct destination. They also contain sequencing information so the data can be reassembled accurately when all packets reach the receiving computer.

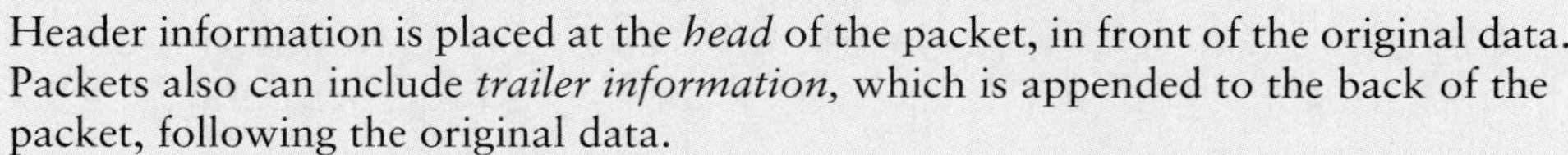

Header information is placed at the *head* of the packet, in front of the original data. Packets also can include *trailer information,* which is appended to the back of the packet, following the original data.

The error-checking component in the trailer is called a *cyclical redundancy check (CRC)*. The CRC performs calculations on the packet before it leaves the source computer and again when it reaches the destination. If the results of these calculations are different, the data has changed. This can occur because of a disruption of the electrical signals that represent the 0s and 1s making up the data. If a discrepancy is found, that packet can be resent.

Names for Data at Each Layer of the OSI Model

For data to travel from the source to the destination, as shown in Figure 2-10, each layer of the OSI model at the source must communicate with its peer layer at the destination. This form of communication is referred to as *Peer-to-Peer Communication*. During this process, each layer's protocol exchanges information, called *protocol data units (PDUs)*, between peer layers. Each layer of communication, on the source computer, communicates with a layer-specific PDU, and with its peer layer on the destination computer as illustrated in Figure 2-11.

Data packets on a network originate at a source, and then travel to a destination. Each layer depends on the service function of the OSI layer below it. To provide this service, the lower layer uses encapsulation to put the PDU from the upper layer into its data field; then it adds whatever headers and trailers the layer needs to perform its function. Next, as the data moves down through the layers of the OSI model, additional headers and trailers are added. After Layers 7, 6, and 5 have added their information, Layer 4 adds more information. This grouping of data, the Layer 4 PDU, is called a *segment*.

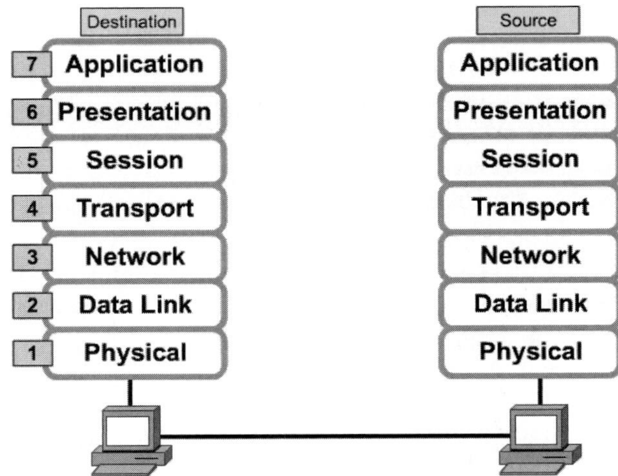

FIGURE 2-10 Data packets on a network originate at a source and are sent to a destination.

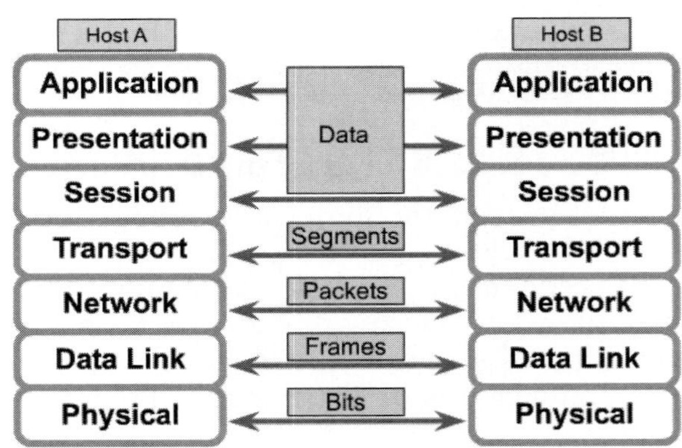

FIGURE 2-11 To communicate with its peer layer in the other system, each layer uses its own layer protocol data units.

The network layer, for example, provides a service to the transport layer, and the transport layer presents data to the network layer, which has the task of moving the data through the internetwork. It accomplishes this task by encapsulating the data and attaching a header creating a packet or a datagram (the Layer 3 PDU). The header contains information required to complete the transfer, such as source and destination logical addresses.

The data link layer provides a service to the network layer. It encapsulates the network layer information in a frame (the Layer 2 PDU); the frame header contains information (for example, physical addresses) required to complete the data link functions. Also, the data link header information is local and is meaningful only to the directly connected devices.

The physical layer also provides a service to the data link layer. The physical layer encodes the data link frame into a pattern of 1s and 0s (bits) for transmission on the medium (usually a wire) at Layer 1. The bits then are transmitted to the next directly connected device in the end-to-end path.

MORE INFORMATION

Mapping Business Needs to a Hierarchical Model

When you understand how an internetwork is used from a business's and a user's standpoint and can map those needs to a model, you are ready to understand how to build the internetwork. To simplify network design, implementation and management, Cisco uses a hierarchical model to describe a network. Although using a model typically is associated with designers, it is important as an implementer that you understand the model. Understanding the model allows you to know what type of equipment and features are required for each device in your internetwork.

User demands and complex applications have forced network designers and implementers to use the traffic patterns in the network as the criteria for building an internetwork. Networks cannot be divided into subnetworks based only on the number of users. The emergence of servers that run global applications also has a direct effect on the load across the internetwork. A higher traffic load across the entire internetwork results in the need for more efficient routing and switching techniques.

In the new campus model, traffic patterns dictate the grouping and resulting placement of the services required by the end user. To properly build a network that can view and address traffic pattern (user) requirements, the three-layer hierarchical model is organized as follows:

- Access layer
- Distribution layer
- Core layer

The access layer of the network is the point at which end users are connected to the network. This is why it is sometimes referred to as the desktop layer. Users and the resources they need to access most are locally available. Traffic to and from local resources is confined between the resources, the switches, and the end users. Multiple groups of users and their resources exist at the access layer. In many networks, it is not possible to provide users with local access to all services, such as printers, or centralized file storage devices, or dial-out access to the Web. In these cases, user traffic for these services is directed to a layer in the network called the distribution layer.

continues

MORE INFORMATION (CONTINUED)

Distribution Layer

The distribution layer of the network, also referred to as the *workgroup layer*, marks the point between the access layer and the main "motorway" of the internetwork, called the *core*. The primary function of this layer is to perform potentially "expensive" packet manipulations, such as routing, filtering, and WAN access. The distribution layer determines the fastest way for a user request, such as file server access, to be forwarded to the server. After the distribution layer decides the path, it forwards the request to the core layer. The core layer then quickly transports the request, using the instructions from the distribution layer.

Core Layer

The sole purpose of the core layer of the network is to switch traffic as fast as possible. Typically, the traffic being transported is to and from services that are common to a majority of users. These services are referred to as enterprise services. Examples of enterprise services would be e-mail, Internet access, or video conferencing. When a user must have access to enterprise services, the user's request is processed at the distribution layer. The distribution layer devices then forward the user requests to the core, or the backbone. The backbone simply provides quick transport to the desired enterprise service. If and how a packet can get transported through the core is the role of the distribution layer.

The TCP/IP Reference Model

Although the OSI reference model is recognized universally, the historical and technical open standard of the Internet is Transmission Control Protocol/Internet Protocol (TCP/IP). The TCP/IP reference model and the TCP/IP protocol stack make data communication possible between any two computers, anywhere in the world. The TCP/IP model has historical importance, just like the standards that allowed the telephone, electrical power, railroad, television, and videotape industries to flourish.

The Layers of the TCP/IP Reference Model

The U.S. Department of Defense (DoD) created the TCP/IP reference model because it wanted a network that could survive any condition, even a nuclear war. To illustrate further, imagine a world at war, criss-crossed by different kinds of connections: wires, microwaves, optical fibers, and satellite links. Then imagine that you need information/data (in the form of packets) to flow, regardless of the condition of any particular node or network on the internetwork (which, in this case, might have been destroyed by the war). The DoD wants its packets to get through every time, under any condition, from any one point to any other point. It was this very difficult design problem that brought about the creation of the TCP/IP reference model, which is the standard on which the internet has grown.

As you read about the TCP/IP model layers, keep in mind the original intent of the Internet; it can help explain why certain things are as they are. The TCP/IP model has four layers: the application layer, the transport layer, the internet layer, and the network access layer.

CAUTION

Some of the layers in the TCP/IP model have the same name as layers in the OSI model. Do not confuse the layers of the two models—the application layer has different functions in each model.

Application Layer

The designers of TCP/IP felt that the higher level protocols should include the session and presentation layer details. They simply created an application layer that handles high-level protocols, issues of representation, encoding, and dialog control. The TCP/IP combines all application-related issues into one layer, and ensures this data is properly packaged for the next layer. This is also referred to as the process layer.

Transport Layer

The transport layer typically deals with the issues of reliability, flow control, and retransmission. One of its protocols, the transmission control protocol (TCP), provides excellent and flexible ways to create reliable, well-flowing, network communications. TCP is a connection-oriented protocol. It supports dialogues between source and destination while packaging application layer information into units called *segments*. Connection-oriented does not mean that a physical circuit exists between the communicating computers (that would be circuit switching). It does mean that Layer 4 segments must travel back and forth between two hosts to set up a logical connection before data can be sent. This layer is also sometimes called the *host-to-host layer.*

Internet Layer

The purpose of the internet layer is to send source packets from any network on the internetwork and have them arrive at the destination independent of the path and networks they took to get there. The specific protocol that governs this layer is called the Internet Protocol (IP). Best path determination and packet switching occur at this layer. Think of it in terms of the postal system. When you mail a letter, you do not know how it gets there (there are various possible routes), but you do care that it arrives.

Network Access Layer

The name of this layer is broad and somewhat confusing. It also is called the host-to-network layer. Sometimes, it's shown as two layers, as in the OSI model. The network access layer is concerned with all the issues that an IP packet requires to actually cross a physical link from one device to a directly connected one. It includes the LAN and WAN technology details, and all the details in the OSI physical and data link layers.

TCP/IP Protocol Graph

The diagram shown in Figure 2-12 is called a *protocol graph*. At the application layer, you see different network tasks you might not recognize but, as a user of the Internet, probably use every day. You will examine all of these during the course of the curriculum. These applications include the following:

- **FTP**—File Transfer Protocol
- **HTTP**—Hypertext Transfer Protocol
- **SMTP**—Simple Mail Transfer protocol
- **DNS**—Domain Name System
- **TFTP**—Trivial File Transfer Protocol

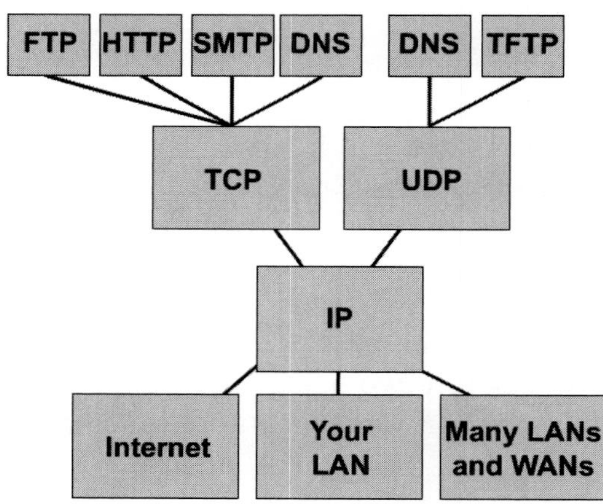

FIGURE 2-12
These common protocols are specified by the TCP/IP reference model.

The TCP/IP model emphasizes maximum flexibility, at the application layer, for developers of software. The transport layer supports two protocols: Transmission Control Protocol (TCP) and user datagram protocol (UDP). You examine these in detail later in the CCNA curriculum. The lowest layer, the network access layer, refers to the particular LAN or WAN technology that is being used.

In the TCP/IP model, regardless of which application requests network services, and regardless of which transport protocol is used, there is only one network protocol: Internet Protocol (IP). This is a deliberate design decision. IP serves as a universal protocol that allows any computer, anywhere, to communicate at any time.

The OSI Model and the TCP/IP Model

If you compare the OSI model and the TCP/IP model, you can notice that they have similarities and differences (see Figure 2-13). Examples include the following:

Similarities

- Both have layers.
- Both have application layers, although they include very different services.
- Both have comparable transport and network layers.
- Packet-switched (not circuit-switched) technology is assumed.
- Networking professionals need to know both models.

Differences

- TCP/IP combines presentation and session layer functions into its application layer.
- TCP/IP combines the OSI data link and physical layers into one layer.
- TCP/IP appears simpler because it has fewer layers; however, this is a misconception. The OSI reference model, with its less complex and multiple layers, is simpler to develop and troubleshoot.
- TCP/IP protocols are the standards around which the Internet was developed, so the TCP/IP model gains credibility just because of its protocols. In contrast, networks typically aren't built with the OSI protocols, although the OSI model is used as a guide.

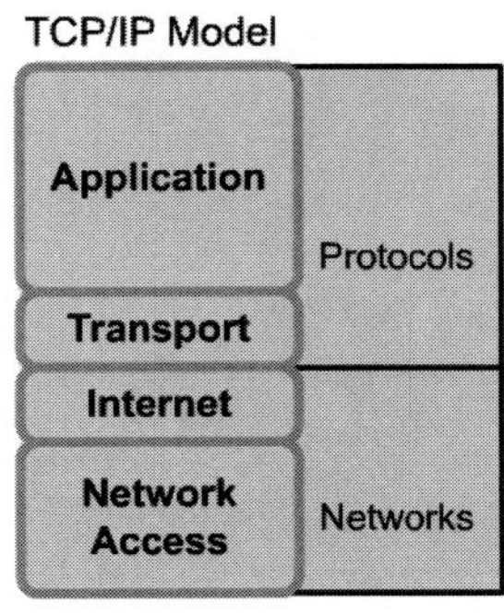

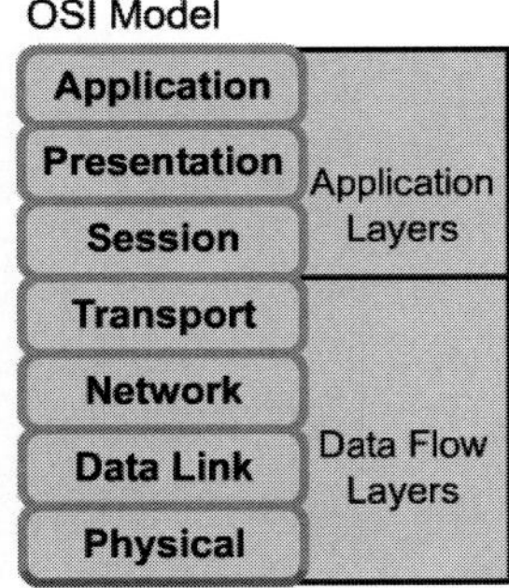

FIGURE 2-13 Comparison of the OSI model and the TCP/IP model.

SKILL BUILDER

Lab Activity: OSI Model and TCP/IP

In this lab, you learn how to relate the seven layers of the OSI model to the four layers of the TCP/IP model. You also learn to name the primary TCP/IP protocols and utilities that operate at each layer.

Use of the OSI and the TCP/IP Models in the CCNA Curriculum

Although TCP/IP protocols are the standards upon which the Internet has grown, this curriculum uses the OSI model for the following reasons:

- It is a worldwide, generic, protocol-independent standard.
- It has more details, which makes it more helpful for learning and troubleshooting.

Many networking professionals have different opinions on which model to use. You should become familiar with both. You can use the OSI model as the microscope through which to analyze networks, but you also can use the TCP/IP protocols throughout the curriculum. Remember that there is a difference between a model (that is, layers, interfaces, and protocol specifications) and an actual protocol that is used in networking.

You will focus on TCP as an OSI Layer 4 protocol, IP as an OSI Layer 3 protocol, and Ethernet as a Layer 2 and Layer 1 technology. The diagram in Figure 2-14 shows that, later in the course, you will examine one particular data link and physical layer technology, Ethernet, out of the many choices available. You learn more about Ethernet in Chapters 5 and 6.

FIGURE 2-14
The focus of the CCNA curriculum.

The OSI Model

7	Application	FTP, TFTP, HTTP, SMTP, DNS, TELNET, SNMP
6	Presentation	Very little focus
5	Session	
4	Transport	TCP (the Internet)
3	Network	IP (the Internet)
2	Data Link	Ethernet (common LAN technology)
1	Physical	

SKILL BUILDER

Lab Activity: OSI Model Layers

In this lab, you identify the characteristics of each layer as well as the terminology and physical devices that operate at each layer.

Summary

This chapter described how layers are used for general forms of communication. You learned that data travels from a source to a destination over media and that a protocol is a formal description of a set of rules and conventions that govern how devices on networks exchange information.

Following the discussion on layered communication, you learned that the OSI reference model is a descriptive network architecture whose standards help achieve greater compatibility and interoperability between various types of network technologies. You also learned that the OSI reference model organizes network functions into seven numbered layers:

- **Layer 7**—The application layer
- **Layer 6**—The presentation layer
- **Layer 5**—The session layer
- **Layer 4**—The transport layer
- **Layer 3**—The network layer
- **Layer 2**—The data link layer
- **Layer 1**—The physical layer

Encapsulation is the process in which data is wrapped in a particular protocol header and, possibly, trailer before it is sent across the network. During Peer-to-Peer Communications, each layer's protocol exchanges information, called protocol data units (PDUs), with peer layers.

In the last section of the chapter, you learned about the TCP/IP model and how it compares to the OSI model. Now you have a basic understanding of the OSI model and can start looking at each layer in more depth in the following chapters.

Check Your Understanding

1. At its most basic level, computer data consist of
   A. Bits
   B. Bytes
   C. Packets
   D. None of the above
2. Which of the following is not a form of cable media?
   A. Coaxial cables
   B. Optical fibers
   C. Category 5 UTP
   D. None of the above
3. A protocol is not
   A. A set of rules
   B. An agreement
   C. A connection layer
   D. A definitive outline
4. Which of the following is a feature of layering in the network model?
   A. Combines the complexity of internetworking into one single non-modular entity
   B. Defines standard interfaces for plug-and-play compatibility and multi-vendor integration
   C. Layering ensures proper interaction among the layer protocols
   D. None of the above
5. Which of the following is not a reason why the OSI model is a layered network model?
   A. A layered model increases complexity.
   B. A layered model standardizes interfaces.
   C. A layered model enables specialized development effort.
   D. A layered model uses peer-to-peer communication.

6. Which of the following is the correct order for the network layers?

A.

1: Physical

2: Data Link

3: Transport

4: Network

5: Presentation

6: Session

7: Application

B.

1: Physical

2: Data Link

3: Network

4: Transport

5: Session

6: Presentation

7: Application

C.

1: Physical

2: Data Link

3: Network

4: Session

5: Transport

6: Application

7: Presentation

D.

1: Physical

2: Network

3: Session

4: Data Link

5: Transport

6: Application

7: Presentation

7. Which layer of the OSI model handles error detection, network topology, and medium access?

A. The physical layer

B. The data link layer

C. The transport layer

D. The network layer

8. Which layer of the OSI model establishes, maintains, and manages sessions between applications?

A. The transport layer

B. The session layer

C. The presentation layer

D. The application layer

9. Which best describes the function of the presentation layer?

A. It provides data representation and code formatting.

B. It handles error notification, network topology, and flow control.

C. It provides network services to user applications.

D. It provides electrical, mechanical, procedural, and functional means for activating and maintaining the link between systems.

10. Which layer of the OSI model provides network services to user applications?

A. The transport layer

B. The session layer

C. The presentation layer

D. The application layer

11. Which layer offers provisions for data expedition, class of service, and exception reporting?

A. Session

B. Presentation

C. Network

D. Data link

12. Which of the following statements regarding encapsulation is untrue?

A. Encapsulation allows computers to communicate data.

B. If one computer wants to send data to another computer, the data first must be packaged by a process called encapsulation.

C. Encapsulation occurs at one layer.

D. Encapsulation wraps data with the necessary protocol information before network transit.

13. Which of the following correctly describes the five conversion steps of data encapsulation when one computer sends an e-mail message to another computer?

A. Data, segments, packets, frames, bits

B. Bits, frames, packets, segments, data

C. Packets, segments, data, bits, frames

D. Segments, packets, frames, bits, data

14. An e-mail message is sent from Host A to Host B on a LAN. To send this message, the data must be encapsulated. Which of the following best describes the first step of data encapsulation?

A. Alphanumeric characters are converted into data.

B. The message is segmented into easily transportable chunks.

C. A network header is added to the message (source and destination addresses).

D. The message is converted into binary format.

15. An e-mail message is sent from Host A to Host B on a LAN. Before you can send this message, the data must be encapsulated. Which of the following best describes what happens after a packet is constructed?

    A. The packet is transmitted along the medium.

    B. The packet is put into a frame.

    C. The packet is segmented into frames.

    D. The packet is converted to binary format.

16. An e-mail message is sent from Host A to Host B on a LAN. Before you can send this message, the data must be encapsulated. Which of the following best describes what happens after the e-mail message's alphanumeric characters are converted into data?

    A. The data is converted into binary format.

    B. A network header is added to the data.

    C. The data is segmented into smaller chunks.

    D. The data is put into a frame.

17. Which best describes a datagram?

    A. A message sent to the source to confirm the receipt of uncorrupted data

    B. A binary representation of routing information

    C. A data packet less than 100 bytes in size

    D. A network layer packet

18. Which of the following is the PDU for the transport layer?

    A. Frame

    B. Degment

    C. Packet

    D. Frame

19. Which of the following layers of the OSI model is *not* present in the TCP/IP protocol stack?

    A. Transport

    B. Network

    C. Internet

    D. Data link

20. Which of the following protocols has TCP/IP as its underlying protocols?

A. SMTP

B. FTP

C. DNS

D. TFTP

Objectives

After reading this chapter, you will be able to

- Describe network topologies
- Describe basic LAN devices
- Describe the evolution of network devices
- Describe the basics of data flow through LANs
- Describe how to build a LAN

Chapter 3

Local-Area Networks

Introduction

You should have a basic understanding of the OSI model and what happens to data packets as they travel through the layers, so it is time for you to look at basic networking devices. By working through the layers of the OSI reference model, you can learn what devices operate at each layer as data packets travel through them from the source to the destination. The focus of this chapter is *local-area networks (LANs)*. As you know, LANs are high-speed, low-error data networks that cover a relatively small geographic area (up to a few thousand meters). LANs connect workstations, peripherals, terminals, and other devices in a single building or other geographically limited area.

Although sending out data to every device on a network might work for a relatively small network, it is easy to see that the larger a network is, the more traffic there is. This can present a serious problem because only one data packet can be on a cable at any one time. If only one cable interconnects each device on a network, the flow of data over the network is slowed down considerably. Network devices are products used to connect networks. As computer networks grow in size and complexity, so do the network devices used to connect them. Network devices can control the amount of traffic on a network and can speed up the flow of data over a network.

In this chapter, you learn about network topologies, basic LAN devices, and the evolution of network devices. You also learn about the network devices that operate at each layer of the OSI model and how packets flow through each device as they go through the layers of the OSI model. Finally, you learn about the basic steps in building LANs.

Topology

Topology defines the structure of the network. The topology definition contains two parts: the physical topology, which is the actual layout of the wire (media), and the logical topology, which defines how the media is accessed by the hosts. The physical topologies that are used commonly are bus, ring, star, extended star, hierarchical, and mesh (see Figure 3-1).

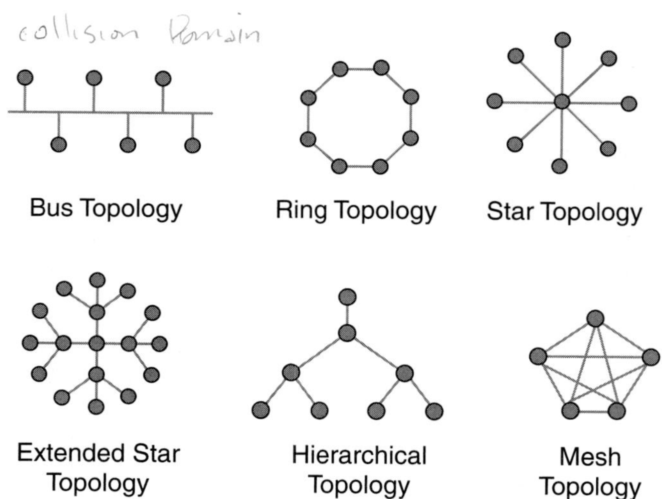

FIGURE 3-1 The physical layout, which describes how a LAN is constructed, is called the topology.

The commonly used physical topologies are:

- **Bus topology**—Uses a single backbone segment (length of cable) to which all the hosts directly connect.
- **Ring topology**—Connects one host to the next and the last host to the first. This creates a physical ring of cable.
- **Star topology**—Connects all cables to a central point of concentration. This point is usually a hub or a switch (hubs are described later in this chapter).
- **Extended star topology**—Uses the star topology. It links individual stars together by linking the hubs/switches. This, as you learn later in the chapter, extends the length and the size of the network.
- **Hierarchical topology**—Similar to an extended star topology, but instead of linking the hubs/switches together, each secondary (subordinate) system is linked to a primary computer that controls the traffic on the topology.
- **Mesh topology**—Used when there can be absolutely no break in communication—for example, the control systems of a nuclear-power plant. As you can see in Figure 3-1, with a full mesh topology, each host has its own connections to all other hosts. A partial mesh reflects the design of the Internet, which has multiple paths to any one location, although not a connection from every host to every other host.

Figure 3-2 shows many topologies. It shows a LAN of moderate complexity that is typical of a school or a small business. It has many symbols, and it depicts many networking concepts that you will learn throughout this book.

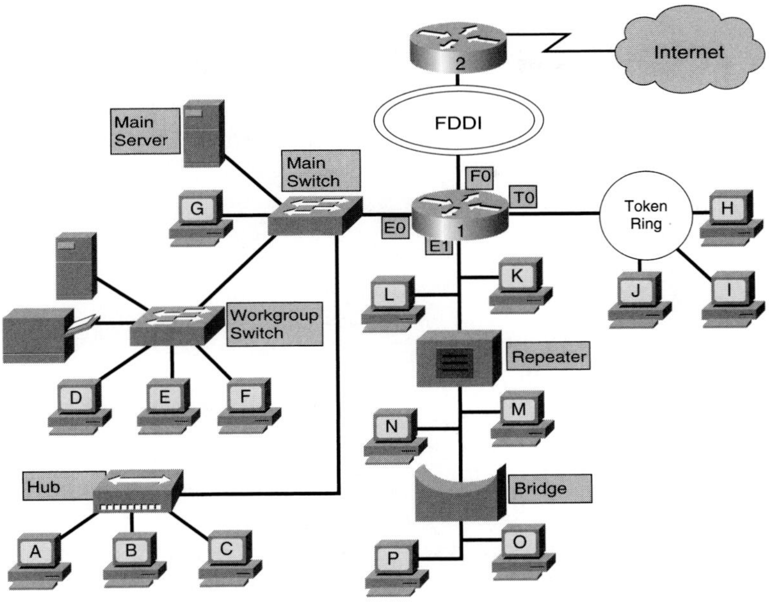

FIGURE 3-2 This LAN is typical of a small campus, and represents most of the devices that you will study for your CCNA.

LAN Devices in a Topology

Devices that connect directly to a network segment often are referred to as *hosts*. These hosts include computers (both clients and servers), printers, scanners, and many other user devices. The host devices can exist without a network, but its capabilities are greatly limited.

Host devices are not part of any layer. They have a physical connection to the network media by having a network interface card (NIC) and the functions of the other OSI layers are performed in software inside the host. This means that they operate at all seven layers of the OSI model. Host devices perform the entire process of encapsulation and de-encapsulation to do their job of sending e-mails, printing reports, scanning pictures, or accessing databases. For those who are familiar with the inner workings of PCs, think of the PC itself as a tiny network that connects the bus and the expansion slots to the CPU, the RAM, and the ROM.

There are no standardized symbols within the networking industry for hosts, but they usually are fairly easy to figure out. As shown in Figure 3-3, they look like the real device so you are constantly reminded of that device.

FIGURE 3-3
These devices provide the users with a connection to the network, with which the users share, create, and obtain information.

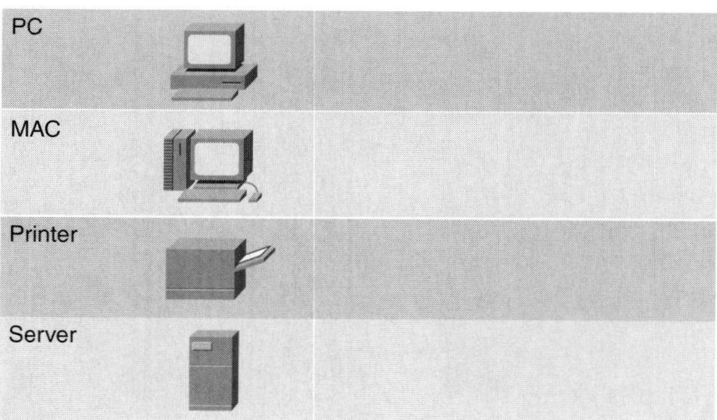

The basic function of computers on the LAN is to provide the user with an almost limitless set of opportunities. Modern software, microelectronics, and a relatively small amount of money enable you to run word-processing, presentation, spreadsheet, and database programs. They also enable you to run a Web browser, which gives you almost instant access to information via the World Wide Web. You can send e-mail, edit graphics, save information in databases, play games, and communicate with other computers around the world. The list of applications grows each day.

NICs

So far in this chapter, you dealt with Layer 1 devices and concepts. Starting with the *network interface card (NIC)*, the discussion moves to layer two, the data link layer, of the OSI model. NICs are considered Layer 2 devices because each individual NIC throughout the world carries a unique code, called a *Media Access Control (MAC)* address. This address is used to control data communication for the host on the network. You can learn more about the MAC address in Chapter 6. As the name implies, the NIC controls the host's access to the medium.

In terms of physical appearance, a NIC is a printed circuit board, as shown in Figure 3-4, that fits into the expansion slot of a bus on a computer's motherboard or peripheral device. It is also called a network adapter. On laptop/notebook computers, NICs are usually the size of a PCMCIA card. Its function is to adapt the host device to the network medium.

The NIC is the basic hardware component of network communications. It translates the parallel signal produced by the computer into the serial format that is sent over the network cable. The 1s and 0s of binary communication are turned into electrical impulses, pulses of light, radio waves, or whatever signaling scheme the network media uses.

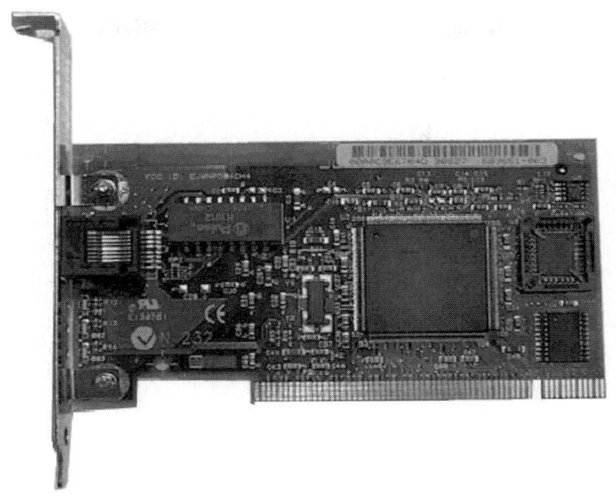

FIGURE 3-4 Along with preparing the data to go onto the network media, the NIC is responsible for controlling the flow of data between computers and media and for receiving incoming data.

MOVIE 3.1

Network Interface Cards

The MAC address is hard coded onto the NIC.

An important part of the network interface is the transceiver. Some NICs, such as those made for 10Base2 and 10BaseT networks, have the transceiver built onto the card itself. Others, such as those made for 10Base5 networks, have an attachment unit interface (AUI) connector by which a cable is attached to an external transceiver. The transceiver, as its name indicates, sends and receives signals.

In some cases, the type of connector on the NIC does not match the type of media to which you need to connect. A good example is your Cisco 2500 router. On the router, you can see AUI (Attachment Unit Interface) connectors. You need to connect the router to a UTP Category 5 Ethernet cable. To do this, a transceiver (transmitter/receiver) is used. A transceiver converts one type of signal and/or connector to another (for example, to connect a 15-pin AUI interface to an RJ-45 jack, or to convert electrical signals to optical signals). It is considered a Layer 1 device because it looks only at bits and not at any address information or higher-level protocols.

NICs have no standardized symbol. It is implied that, whenever you see networking devices attached to network media, there is some sort of NIC or NIC-like device present (although it is generally not shown). Wherever you see a dot on a topology, there is either a NIC or an interface (port) that acts like at least part of a NIC.

MORE INFORMATION

Selecting a NIC

When selecting a NIC for a computer, you should consider the following:

- Network architecture
- Operating system
- Media type
- Data transfer speed
- Available bus types

Several different bus architectures exist for which NICs are made:

- ISA (Industry Standard Architecture)
- EISA (Extended ISA)
- PCI (Peripheral Component Interconnect)
- MCA (Micro Channel Architecture)
- PCMCIA (Personal Computer Memory Card International Association)

Also, some NICs connect through the SCSI bus. A few universal serial bus (USB) network cards are available, but these are not common. Some computers come with a NIC that is integrated into the motherboard.

Media

The symbols for media vary, as shown in Figure 3-5. For example, the Ethernet symbol is typically a straight line with perpendicular lines projecting from it; the Token Ring network symbol is a circle with hosts attached to it; and for FDDI, the symbol is two concentric circles with attached devices.

The basic functions of media are to carry a flow of information, in the form of bits, through a LAN. Other than wireless LANs (that use the atmosphere, or space, as the medium) and the new PANs (personal-area networks, which use the human body as a networking medium!), networking media confine network signals to wire, cable, or fiber. Networking media are considered Layer 1 components of LANs.

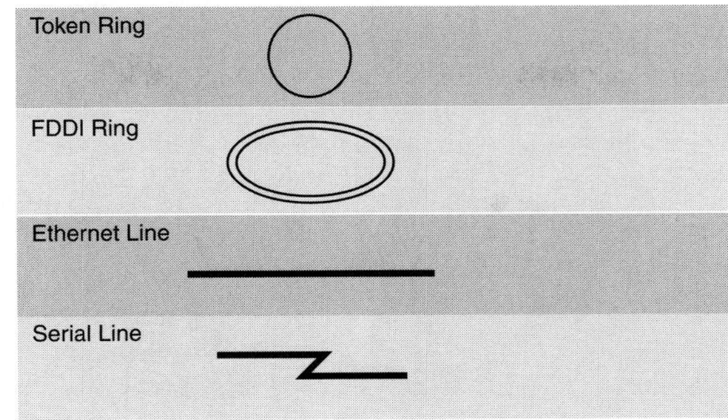

FIGURE 3-5
The network media is the means by which the signals travel from one networked device to another.

You can build computer networks with many different media types. Each media has advantages and disadvantages. What is an advantage for one media (Category 5 cost) might be a disadvantage for another (fiber optic cost). Some of the possible advantages or disadvantages include the following:

- Cost
- Ease of installation
- Maximum cable length

Coaxial cable, optical fiber, and even free space can carry network signals. However, the principal medium you will study is called Category 5 unshielded twisted-pair (CAT 5 UTP) cable because it is the most-used medium in network installations.

MORE INFORMATION

Bus Topology Operation

In a LAN, workstations must be connected. If a file server is included in the LAN, it too is connected to the workstations. Networking media make this connection (see Figure 3-6).

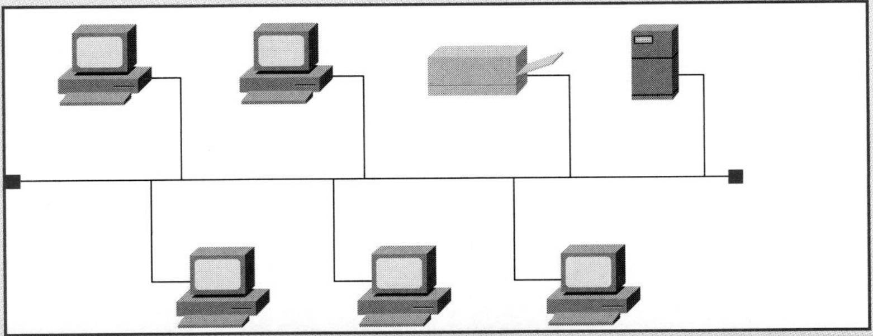

FIGURE 3-6
A bus topology is typical of Ethernet LANs, including 10Base2 and 10Base5.

continues

MORE INFORMATION (CONTINUED)

A bus topology is one in which all devices on the LAN are attached to a linear networking medium. This linear networking medium often is referred to as the trunk line, bus, or highway. As shown in Figure 3-7, every device, such as a workstation or a server, is attached independently to the common bus wire through some kind of connection. The bus wire must end in a terminating resistance, or terminator, which absorbs electrical signals so they don't bounce, or reflect, back and forth on the bus.

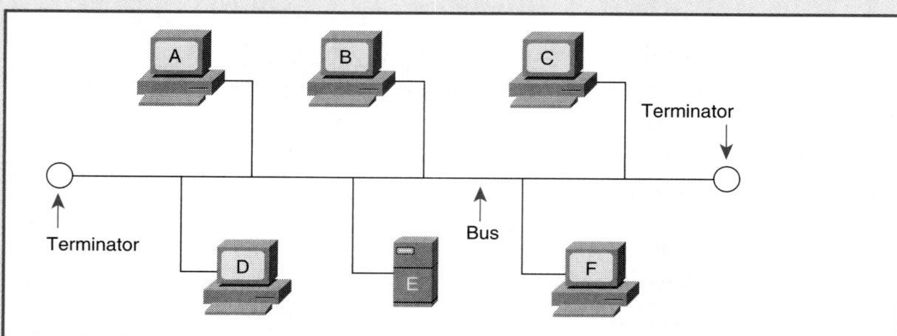

FIGURE 3-7 Electrical signals are absorbed in a bus wire by a terminator.

Signal Transmission over a Bus Topology

As shown in Figure 3-8, the signal travels in both directions from the source when data is transmitted over the networking media in a bus topology. These signals are made available to all devices on the LAN. As you learned in previous lessons, each device checks the data as it passes. If the destination MAC address carried by the data does not match that of a device, the device ignores the data. However, if the destination MAC address carried by the data does match that of a device, the device copies the data and passes it up to the data link and network layers of the OSI reference model.

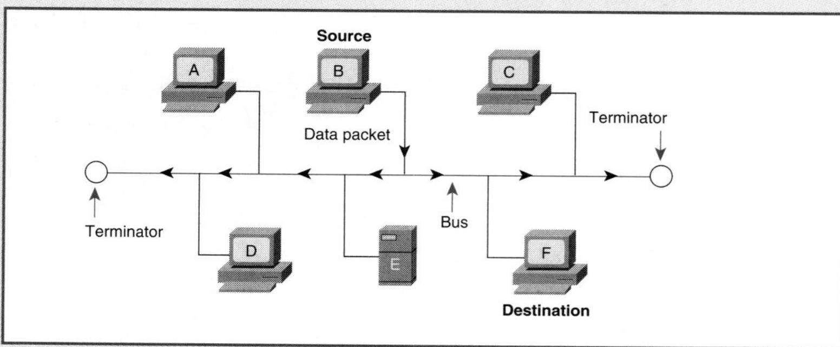

FIGURE 3-8 Data transmitted over a bus topology travels in both directions.

As you can see in Figure 3-8, each end of the cable has a terminator. When a signal reaches the end of the bus, it is absorbed by the terminator. This prevents signals from bouncing back and being received again by workstations attached to the bus.

MORE INFORMATION (CONTINUED)

To ensure that only one workstation transmits at a time, a bus topology uses collision detection because, if more than one node attempts to transmit at the same time, a collision occurs. Because it is based on an algorithm, the length of this enforced retransmission delay is different for every device on the network, thus minimizing the likelihood of another collision.

Advantages and Disadvantages of a Bus Topology

A typical bus topology has a simple wiring layout that uses short lengths of networking media. Therefore, the cost of implementing this type of topology is usually low compared with that of other topologies. However, the low-cost implementation of this topology is offset by its high management costs. In fact, the biggest disadvantage of a bus topology is that fault diagnosis and isolation of networking problems can be difficult.

Because the networking medium does not pass through the nodes attached to it, if one device goes down on the network, it doesn't affect other devices on the network. Although this can be considered an advantage of bus topology, it is also offset by the fact that the single cable used in this type of topology can act as a single point of failure. In other words, if the networking medium used for the bus breaks, none of the devices located along it will be capable of transmitting signals.

MOVIE 3.2

Internetworking Devices Connect Networks

Repeaters, bridges, LAN extenders, routers, and WANs are introduced.

Repeaters

As mentioned in the "Media" section, many types of media exist and each type has advantages and disadvantages. One of the disadvantages of the type of cable that we primarily use, CAT5 UTP, is cable length. The maximum length for UTP cable in a network is 100 meters (approximately 333 feet). If you need to extend beyond the network limit, as shown in Figure 3-9, you must add a device to your network. This device is called a repeater.

The term *repeater* comes from the early days of visual communication, when a man situated on a hill received a signal from a person on the hill to his left, and then repeated the signal to the person on the hill to his right. It also comes from telegraph, telephone, microwave, and optical communications, all of which use repeaters to strengthen their signals over long distances to prevent the signals from fading or dying out.

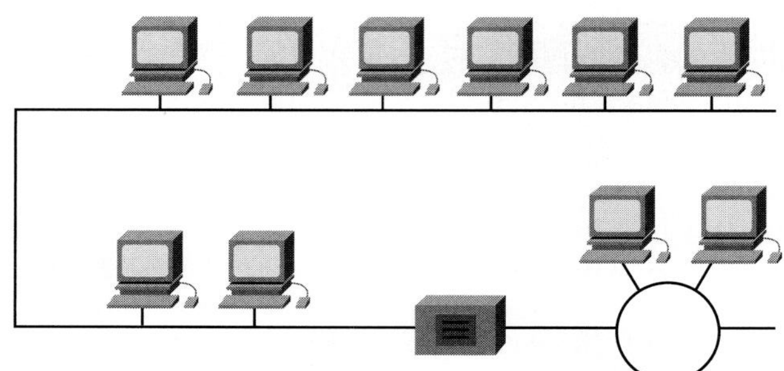

FIGURE 3-9
Common networking problems are too many nodes and not enough cables. A repeater solves both of these problems.

Like networking media, repeaters are networking devices that exist at Layer 1, the physical layer, of the OSI reference model. To begin understanding how a repeater works, it is important to understand first that as data leaves a source and goes out over the network, it is transformed into either electrical or light pulses that pass along the networking media. These pulses are referred to as *signals*. When signals first leave a transmitting station, they are clean and easily recognizable. However, the longer the cable length, the weaker and more deteriorated the signals become as they pass along the networking media. For example, specifications for Category 5 twisted-pair Ethernet cable establish the maximum distance that signals can travel along a network as 100 meters. If a signal travels beyond that distance, there is no guarantee that a NIC can read the signal. A repeater can provide a simple solution if this problem exists.

MOVIE 3.3

Repeaters Amplify Signals

A repeater cleans, amplifies, and resends a signal that is weakened by long cable length.

The purpose of a repeater is to regenerate and retime network signals at the bit level to allow them to travel a longer distance on the media. Watch out for the Four Repeater Rule for 10Mbps Ethernet, also known as the 5-4-3 Rule, when extending LAN segments. This rule states that you can connect five network segments end-to-end using four repeaters, but only three segments can have hosts (computers) on them.

The term repeater originally meant a single port "in" and a single port "out" device. But today, multiple-port repeaters also exist. Repeaters are classified as Layer 1 devices in the OSI model, because they act only on the bit level and look at no other information. (The symbol for repeaters is not standardized—the symbol shown in Figure 3-9 represents a repeater throughout this book.)

MOVIE 3.4

Repeater Disadvantages

Repeaters can't filter traffic.

MORE INFORMATION

The Use of Repeaters in an Extended Star Topology

If a simple star topology cannot provide enough coverage for the area to be networked, you can extend it by using internetworking devices that do not result in attenuation of the signal; the resulting topology is referred to as an *extended star topology*.

Imagine that you have a building that is 250 meters by 250 meters. For a star topology to be used effectively in this building, it must be extended. You don't do this by extending the horizontal cabling beyond the recommended maximum length. Instead, you use networking devices that strengthen the signal.

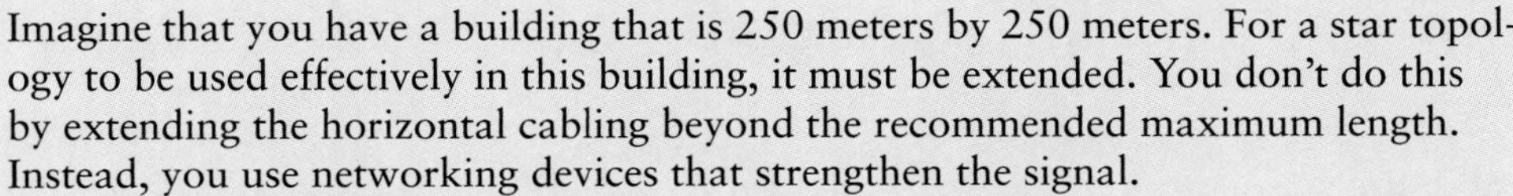

Signals do not become unrecognizable to devices receiving them on the network if repeaters take in weakened signals, clean them up, regenerate them, and send them on their way along the network. By using repeaters, you can extend the distance over which a network can reach. Repeaters work in tandem with the networking media and, therefore, exist at the physical layer of the OSI reference model.

Hubs

Generally speaking, the term *hub* is used instead of repeater when referring to the device that serves as the center of a network, as shown in Figure 3-10. Although a hub operates in physical star topology, it creates the same contention environment as a bus. This is because when one device transmits, all other devices hear it and the contention creates a logical bus.

The purpose of a hub is to regenerate and retime network signals. This is done at the bit level for a large number of hosts (for example, 4, 8, or even 24). This is known as concentration. The following are the most important properties of hubs:

- They regenerate and repeat signals.
- They propagate signals through the network.
- They cannot filter network traffic.
- They cannot determine the best path.
- They are used as network concentration points.

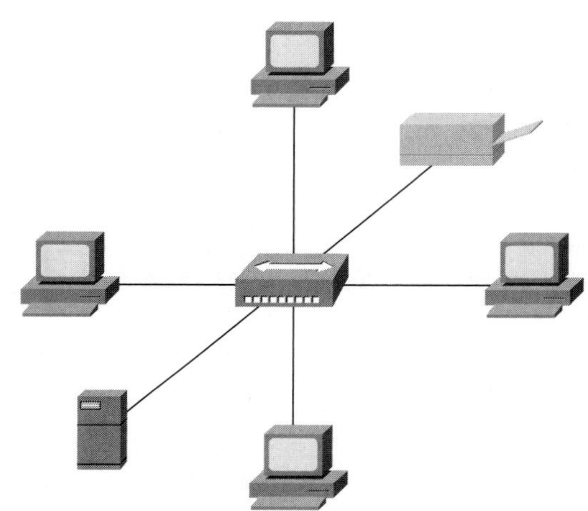

FIGURE 3-10
A star topology is typically used in Ethernet and Token Ring networks, where the center of the network is a hub, repeater, or concentrator.

You will notice the characteristics of a hub are similar to the repeater's, which is why a hub is also known as a *multi-port repeater.* The difference is the number of cables that connect to the device. Where a repeater typically has only two ports, a hub generally has from four to twenty or more ports, as shown in Figure 3-11. Whereas a repeater receives on one port and repeats on the other, a hub receives on one port and transmits on all other ports.

Hubs are used most commonly in Ethernet 10BaseT or 100BaseT networks. The hub's role in a Token Ring network is played by a *Media Access Unit (MAU)*. Physically, it resembles a hub, but Token Ring technology is very different, as you learn in Chapter 7. In FDDI, the connecting device is called a *concentrator.* MAUs and concentrators are also Layer 1 devices.

Two reasons to use hubs are to create a central connection point for the wiring media, and to increase the reliability of the network. The reliability of the network is increased by allowing any single cable to fail without disrupting the entire network. This differs from the bus topology where having one cable fail disrupts the entire network. Hubs are considered Layer 1 devices because they only regenerate the signal and repeat it out all of their ports (network connections).

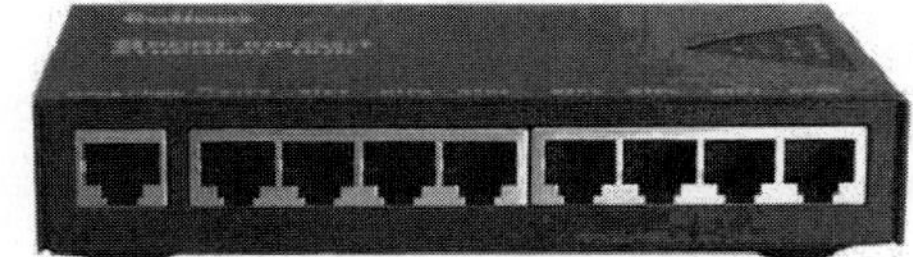

FIGURE 3-11
Hubs also are called concentrators because they serve as central connection points.

There are different classifications of hubs in networking. (You will see the hub symbol shown in Figure 3-12 throughout this book.) The first classification is passive or active hubs. Most modern hubs are active; they take energy from a power supply to regenerate network signals. Some hubs are called passive devices because they merely split the signal for multiple users, like using a "Y" cord on a CD player to use more than one set of headphones. Passive hubs do not regenerate bits, so they do not extend a cable's length, they allow only two or more hosts to connect to the same cable segment. As a result, passive hubs weaken the signal.

Active hubs also are called multiport repeaters because they have multiple ports (like a passive hub) and they regenerate the signal coming into one port before sending it back out the other port (like a repeater). Active hubs require electrical power. The intelligent hub is a special type of active hub. It not only regenerates the signal, it also has an onboard processor that enables you to perform diagnostics and to detect whether there is a problem with a particular port.

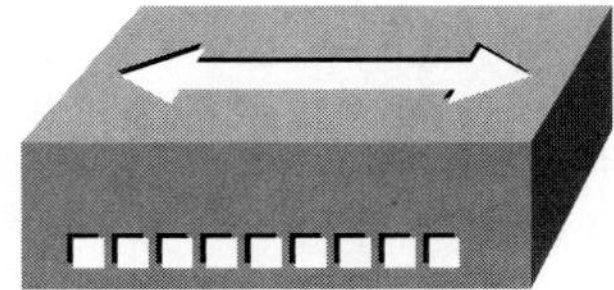

FIGURE 3-12
The symbol for a hub is not standardized.

MORE INFORMATION

Using Hubs in a Star Topology

In LANs where the star topology is used, the networking media run from a central hub out to each device attached to the network. As shown in Figure 3-13, the physical layout of the star topology resembles spokes radiating from the hub of a wheel. A star topology uses a central point.

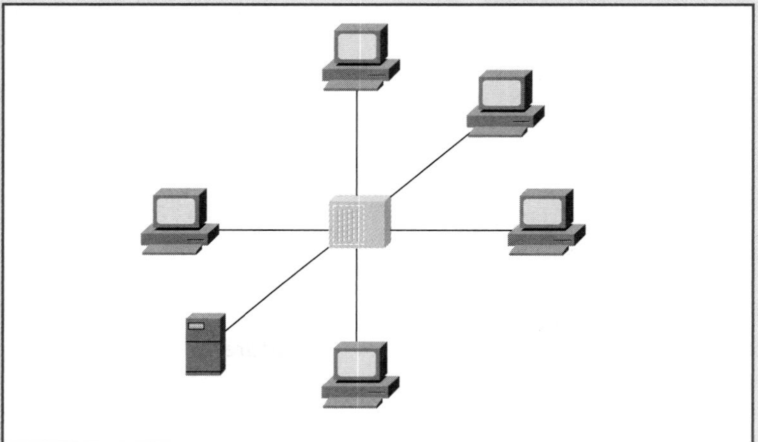

FIGURE 3-13 A star topology resembles a hub-and-spokes configuration.

When a star topology is used, communication between devices attached to the LAN is through point-to-point wiring to the hub. All network traffic in a star topology passes through the hub.

In a star topology, the hub can be either active or passive. If it is active, the hub not only connects the networking media, it also regenerates the signal and acts as a multiport repeater, sometimes referred to as a concentrator. By regenerating the signal, such active hubs enable data to travel over greater distances. By contrast, a passive hub simply connects networking media.

Advantages and Disadvantages of a Star Topology

Most LAN designers consider a star topology to be the easiest to design and install because the networking media run directly out from a central hub to each workstation area. Another advantage of a star topology is ease of maintenance. In a star topology, the layout used for the networking media is easy to modify, and problem diagnosis is relatively easy to perform. Moreover, workstations can be added easily to a network employing a star topology by plugging into the hub the cable connected to the new workstation. If one run of networking media is broken or shorted, only the device attached at that point is out of commission. However, the rest of the LAN remains functional. In short, a star topology means greater reliability.

MORE INFORMATION (CONTINUED)

In some ways, a star topology's advantages also can be considered disadvantages. For example, although limiting one device per run of networking media can make diagnosis of problems easier, it also increases the amount of networking media required. This results in increased costs in setting up a star topology LAN. Moreover, the hub can make maintenance easier because all data has to pass through this central point; if the hub fails, however, the entire network fails also.

The Area Covered by a Star Topology

The maximum distance for a run of networking media, which is referred to as *horizontal cabling*, in the area extending from the wiring closet to a workstation, or the area that extends from the hub to any workstation, is 100 meters.

In a star topology, each of the horizontal cabling runs can radiate from the hub, much like the spokes of a wheel; therefore, a LAN using this type of topology could cover a 200-meter by 200-meter area. As you can imagine, times arise when the area to be covered by a network exceeds what a simple star topology can accommodate. This is when an extended star topology is deployed.

The disadvantage of using a hub is that it can't filter network traffic. *Filtering* generally refers to a process or a device that screens network traffic for certain characteristics, such as source address, destination address, or protocol, and determines whether to forward or discard that traffic based on the established criteria. On a hub, data arriving at one port gets sent out on all other ports. Consequently, a hub passes data to all other sections or segments of a network, regardless of whether the data needs to go there.

If only one cable interconnects all the devices on a network or if segments of a network are connected by only nonfiltering devices, such as hubs, more than one user can try to send data on the network at the same time. If more than one node attempts to transmit at the same time, a collision occurs. When a collision occurs, the data from each device hits each other and is damaged. The network area within which data packets originate and collide is called a *collision domain*. One way to solve the problems of too much traffic on a network and too many collisions is to use a bridge.

FOR MORE INFORMATION

Cisco Hub Products

As shown in Figure 3-14, Cisco offers a wide range of hub products. The series of hubs displayed in this figure reflects a snapshot of some Cisco offerings. Cisco's product line continuously evolves in response to customer needs and other technology migration issues.

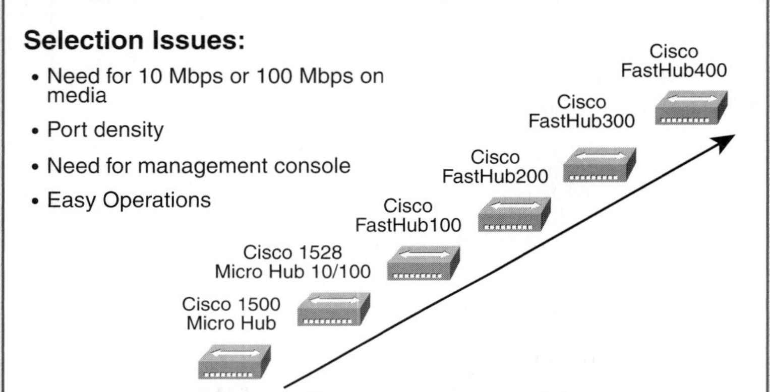

FIGURE 3-14 Cisco offers many hub products.

Criteria used in selecting hubs includes the media speed needed, the number of ports needed, the ease of installation, and the need for remote management. Before implementing hubs, assess which workstations need 10 Mbps and which higher end workstations need an upgrade to 100 Mbps. Lower-end hubs offer only 10 Mbps whereas mid-range hubs autosense the data rates of Ethernet frames and provide for either 10 Mbps or 100 Mbps. This middle range can handle both current and future bandwidth needs.

The scope of consolidated connections refers to the issue of how many hub ports your users require. Hubs allow for a variety of port densities and you can stack hubs to get multiples of the hubs densities. Most hubs are simple to plug in and operate. For most hubs, there is no console port. If you want a managed hub that has an integral console, select from the higher end hub series.

Bridges

A *bridge* is a Layer 2 device designed to create two or more LAN segments, each of which is a separate collision domain. That is, they were designed to create more useable bandwidth. The purpose of a bridge is to filter traffic on a LAN—to keep local traffic local—yet allow connectivity to other parts (segments) of the LAN for traffic that is directed there. You might wonder, then, how the bridge knows which traffic is local and which is not. The answer is the same one the postal service uses when asked how it knows which mail is local. It looks at the local address. Every networking device has a unique MAC address on the NIC. The bridge keeps track of which MAC addresses are on each side of the bridge and makes its decisions based on this MAC address list.

Bridges filter network traffic by looking only at the MAC address. Therefore, they can rapidly forward traffic representing any network layer protocol. Because bridges look only at MAC addresses, they are not concerned with network layer protocols. Consequently, bridges are concerned only with passing or not passing frames, based on their destination MAC addresses. The following are the important properties of bridges:

- They are more intelligent than hubs—that is, they can analyze incoming frames and forward (or drop) them based on addressing information.
- They collect and pass packets between two or more LAN segments.
- They create more collision domains, allowing more than one device to transmit simultaneously without causing a collision.
- They maintain address tables.

MOVIE 3.5

Bridges

Bridges divide a network into segments and filter traffic.

MOVIE 3.6

Bridge Problems

Bridges always propagate frames.

Figure 3-15 shows an example of how a bridge is used. The appearance of bridges varies greatly depending on the type. Although routers and switches have taken over much of the bridge's functions, bridges as separate devices nonetheless remain important in many networks. To understand switching and routing, you first must understand bridging. Figure 3-15 shows the bridge symbol, which resembles a suspension bridge. Traditionally, the term bridge refers to a device that has just two ports. However, you also see references to bridges with three or more ports.

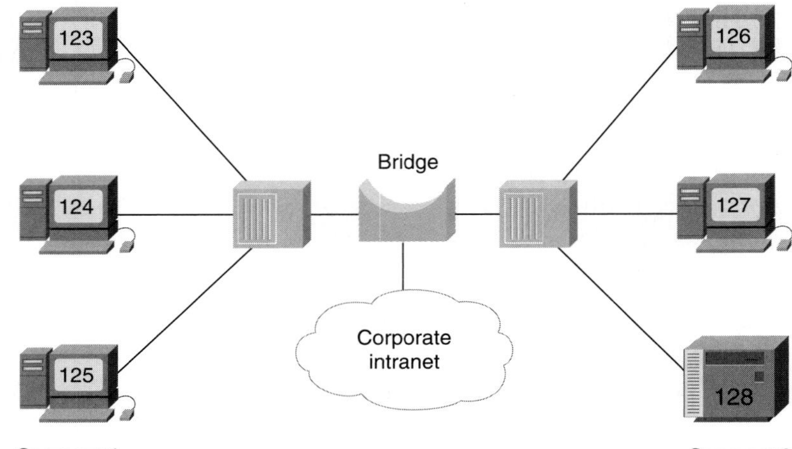

FIGURE 3-15
Bridges operate at Layer 2, the data link layer, of the OSI reference model and are not required to examine upper-layer information.

What really defines a bridge is its Layer 2 filtering of frames and how this is actually accomplished. Just as was the case of the repeater/hub combination, another device, called a *switch* (which you learn about in the next section), is used for multiple bridge connections.

MORE INFORMATION

Bridge Operation

To filter or selectively deliver network traffic, bridges build tables of all MAC addresses located on a network. If data comes along the networking media, a bridge compares the destination MAC address carried by the data to the MAC addresses contained in its tables. If the bridge determines that the destination MAC address of the data is from the same network segment as the source, as shown in Figure 3-16, it does not forward the data to other segments of the network.

MORE INFORMATION (CONTINUED)

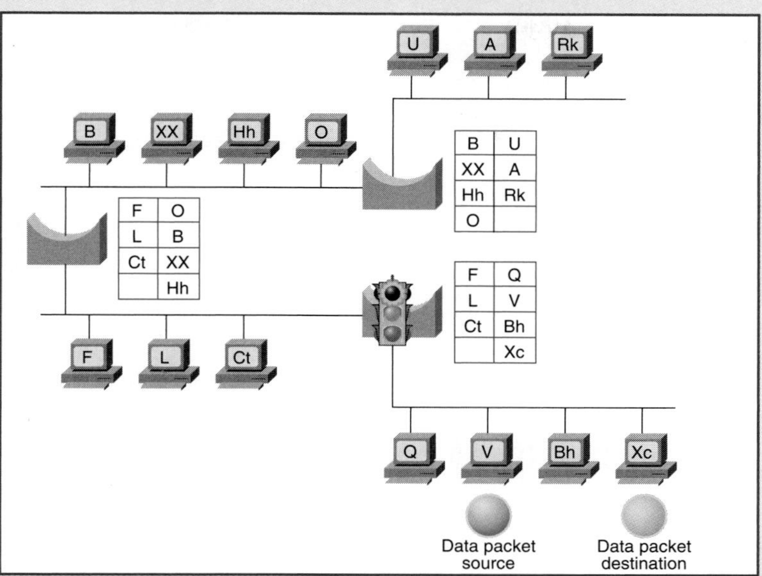

FIGURE 3-16 Bridges do not forward data to other segments of a network if the destination MAC address is on the same network segment. In this example, a data packet originates from Computer V and its destination is Computer Xc.

If the bridge determines that the destination MAC address of the data is not from the same network segment as the source, as shown in Figure 3-17, it forwards the data to all other segments of the network. Therefore, bridges can significantly reduce the amount of traffic between network segments by eliminating unnecessary traffic.

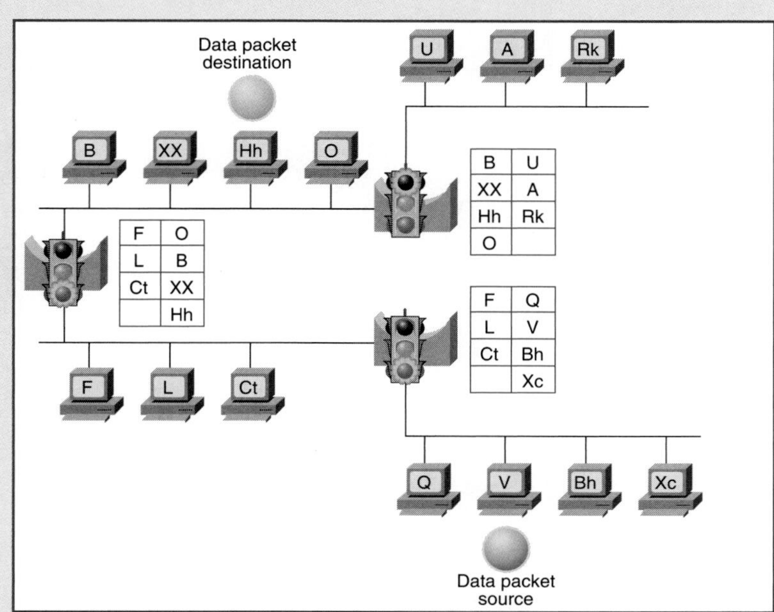

FIGURE 3-17 Bridges forward data to other segments of a network if the destination MAC address is not on the same network segment. In this example, a data packet originates from Computer V and its destination is Computer Hh.

Switches

A *switch* is a Layer 2 device just as a bridge is. In fact, a switch is sometimes called a multi-port bridge, just like a hub is called a multi-port repeater. The difference between the hub and the switch is the same as the difference between a repeater and a bridge: switches make decisions based on MAC addresses and hubs don't make decisions at all.

Because of the decisions that switches make, they make a LAN much more efficient. They do this by "switching" data only out the port to which the proper host is connected. In contrast, a hub sends the data out all its ports so that all the hosts have to see and process (accept or reject) all the data.

Switches, at first glance, often look like hubs. Both hubs and switches have many connection ports because part of their function is connectivity concentration (allowing many devices to be connected to one point in the network). The difference between a hub and a switch is what happens inside the device. Figure 3-18 shows the symbol for a switch. The arrows on top represent the separate paths data can take in a switch, unlike the hub, where all data flows on all paths.

FIGURE 3-18
Layer 2 switches are devices that function at the data link layer of the OSI model.

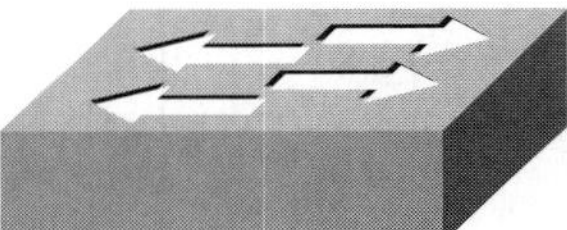

The purpose of a switch is to concentrate connectivity while making data transmission more efficient. For now, think of the switch as something that combines the connectivity of a hub with the traffic regulation of a bridge on each port. It switches frames from incoming ports (interfaces) to outgoing ports while providing each port with full bandwidth (the transmission speed of data on the network backbone). You learn more about this in Chapter 7.

MORE INFORMATION

Catalyst Switch Products

The series of switches in Figure 3-19 reflects some Cisco switch products.

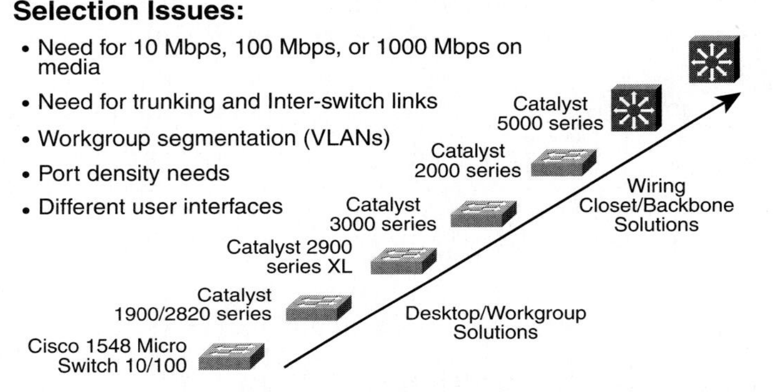

FIGURE 3-19 Cisco's product line continuously evolves in response to customer needs and other technology migration issues.

As you move up to higher-end Catalyst switches, port density (the number of available ports on the switch) gets very high (well over 100 Fast Ethernet ports per switch). The upper-end switches also can integrate modules to switch packets with ATM.

Routers

The router is the first device you work with that is at the OSI network layer, otherwise known as Layer 3. Working at Layer 3 allows the router to make decisions based on network addresses as opposed to individual Layer 2 MAC addresses. Routers also can connect different Layer 2 technologies, such as Ethernet, Token Ring, and FDDI. However, because of their capability to route packets based on Layer 3 information, routers have become the backbone of the Internet, running the IP protocol.

MOVIE 3.7

Routers

A router can solve the problem of excessive broadcast traffic.

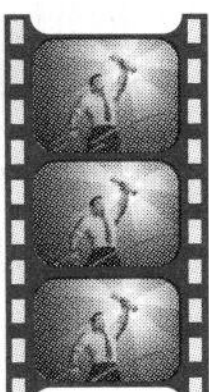

The purpose of a router is to examine incoming packets (Layer 3 data), choose the best path for them through the network, and then switch them to the proper outgoing port. Routers are the most important traffic-regulating devices on large networks. They enable virtually any type of computer to communicate with any other computer anywhere in the world! While performing these basic functions, routers also can execute many other tasks, which are covered in later chapters.

Routers differ from bridges in several respects. First, bridging occurs at Layer 2, the data link layer, whereas routing occurs at Layer 3, the network layer of the OSI reference model. Second, bridges use physical or MAC addresses to make data forwarding decisions. Routers use a different addressing scheme that occurs at Layer 3 to make forwarding decisions. They use network-layer addresses, which are referred to as Internet Protocol (IP), or logical, addresses, rather than MAC addresses. Routers match information in the routing table with the data's destination IP address and send incoming data toward the correct subnetwork and host. Because IP addresses are implemented in software and refer to the network on which a device is located, sometimes these Layer 3 addresses are referred to as protocol addresses or network addresses. Physical, or MAC, addresses usually are assigned by the NIC manufacturer and are hard-coded into the NIC. Network-layer addresses, or IP addresses, on the other hand, usually are assigned by the network administrator.

MOVIE 3.8

Router/Bridge Difference

Bridging occurs at Layer 2 and routing occurs at Layer 3.

The symbol for a router, shown in Figure 3-20, is suggestive of its two primary purposes: path selection, and switching of packets to the best route. A router can have many different types of interface ports.

FIGURE 3-20
The router symbol (note the inward- and outward-pointing arrows).

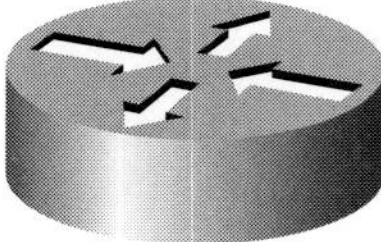

Figure 3-21 shows a fixed interface for a 2500 series router with an Ethernet port for a LAN connection.

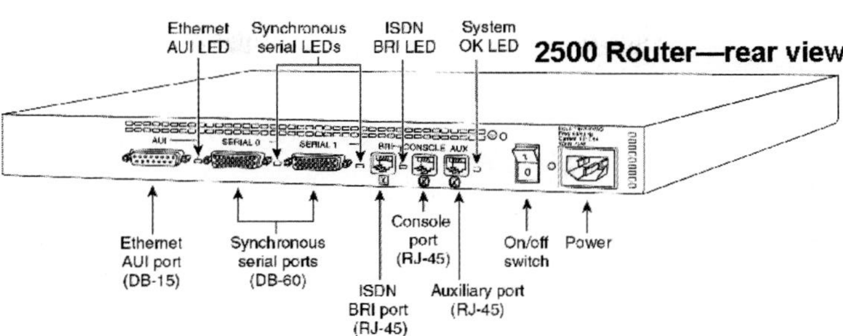

FIGURE 3-21
The console port connection allows direct connection to the router to be able to configure it.

Figure 3-22 shows interfaces for the 1603 and 3640 series routers.

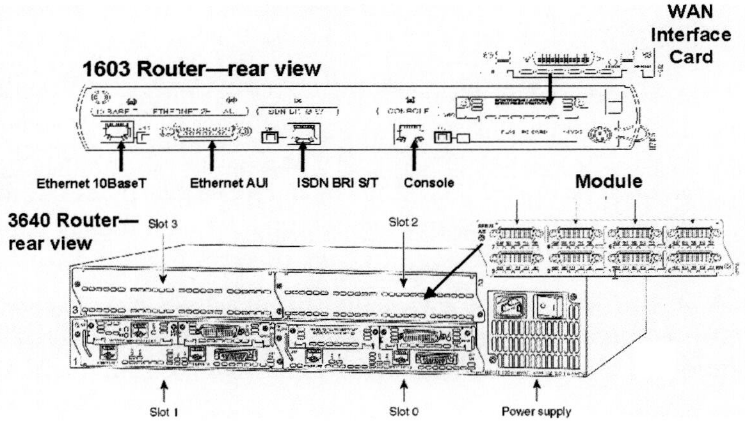

FIGURE 3-22
These particular routers have both a 10BaseT and an AUI connector for the Ethernet connection.

MORE INFORMATION

Router Products

The series of routers in Figure 3-23 reflects a snapshot of some Cisco offerings.

continues

MORE INFORMATION (CONTINUED)

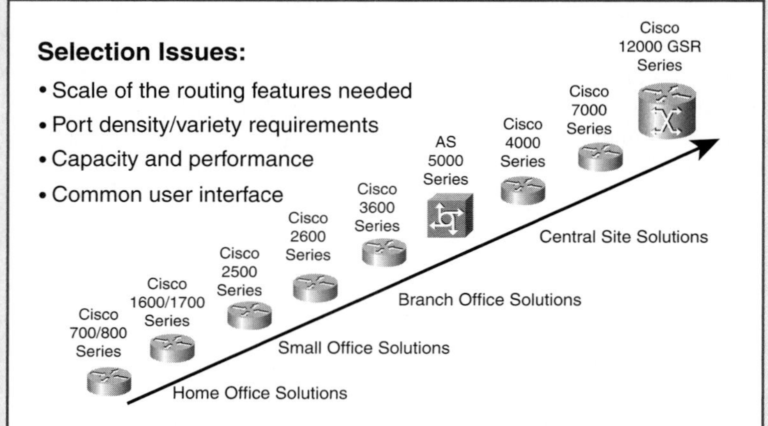

FIGURE 3-23 Cisco's product line continuously evolves in response to customer needs and other technology migration issues.

A key criterion in router selection is knowing what router service features are needed. Different routers in the Cisco product line incorporate different feature sets. You learn about many advanced router features throughout this book.

Port densities and interface speeds generally increase as you move to the upper end of the various Cisco router families. For example, the 12000 series is the first in a product class of gigabit switch routers (GSRs). The Cisco 12000 GSR initially supports IP backbone links at OC-12 (622 Mbps), and can scale to handle links at OC-48 (2.4 Gbps).

If your network requires WAN links, the router selection issue involves which router provides the necessary links in a cost-effective manner. Generally, a production network has several LAN switches interconnected to the WAN by routers.

Clouds

The cloud symbol in Figure 3-24 suggests another network, or perhaps the entire Internet. It reminds you that there is a way to connect to that other network (for example, the Internet), but does not supply all the details of either the connection or the network.

The physical features of the cloud are many. To help you understand, you might think of all the devices that connect your computer to some very distant computer, perhaps on another continent. There is no single picture that could display all the processes and equipment that would be involved in making that connection.

FIGURE 3-24
The cloud represents a large group of details that are not pertinent to a situation or description at a given time.

It is important to remember that, at this point in the book, you are interested only in how LANs connect to larger WANs and to the Internet (the ultimate WAN), so that any computer can talk to any other computer, any place and any time. Because the cloud is not really a single device, but represents a collection of devices that operate at all levels of the OSI model, it could be classified as a Layer 1 through 7 device.

Network Segments

The term *segment* has many meanings in networking. The correct definition depends on the situation in which it is used. Historically, a segment identifies the Layer 1 media that is the common path for data transmission in a LAN. As previously mentioned in the "Media" section, there is a maximum length for data transmission on each type of media. Each time an electronic device is used to extend the length or to manage data on the media, a new physical segment is created (see Figure 3-25). The rest of this chapter covers the devices used to create new segments. Some people refer to segments by the term *wires*, although the "wire" might be optical fiber, wireless medium, or copper wire.

Other definitions of the term segment are used commonly in networking, and are used in later networking topics. Because these topics are covered later, you might not understand what they mean right now. The only reason that this is discussed here is to eliminate confusion later when the term *segment* has a different network meaning.

A second definition, more commonly used by Cisco today, defines a segment as a *collision domain*. The difference between the first and second definitions is very small and is defined in Chapter 7, when collision domains are defined. Finally, a third definition for segment that you might hear describes a Layer 4 Protocol Data Unit (PDU).

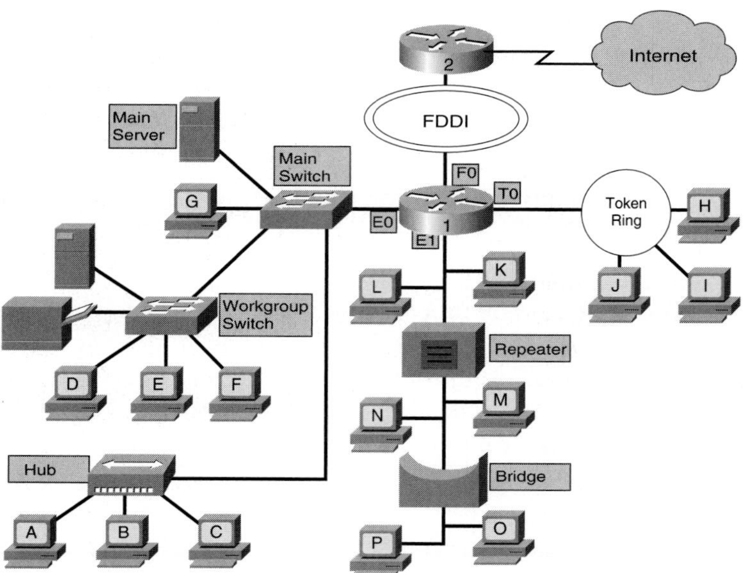

FIGURE 3-25
A network can be made up of multiple segments that are connected by networking devices.

Evolution of Network Devices

The history of computer networking is complex, involving many people from all over the world over the past thirty years or so. What is presented here is a simplified view of how the devices you have been studying evolved from each other. The processes of invention and commercialization are far more complicated, but it is helpful to look at the problems that each network device solved and the problems that still remain.

In the 1940s, computers were huge electromechanical devices that were prone to failure. In 1947, the invention of a semiconductor transistor opened up many possibilities for making smaller, more reliable computers. In the 1950s, mainframe computers, run by punched-card programs, began to be used commonly by large institutions. In the late 1950s, the integrated circuit was invented. It combined several, many, and later millions of transistors on one small piece of semiconductor. Through the 1960s, mainframes with terminals were commonplace, and integrated circuits became more widely used.

In the late 1960s and 1970s, smaller computers, called minicomputers (although still huge by today's standards), came into existence. In 1978, the Apple Computer company introduced the personal computer. In 1981, IBM introduced the open-architecture personal computer. The user-friendly Mac, the open architecture IBM PC, and the further micro-miniaturization of integrated circuits lead to widespread use of personal computers in homes and businesses. As the late 1980s began, computer users—with their stand-alone computers—started to share data (files) and resources (printers). People asked, "Why not connect them?"

Starting in the 1960s and continuing through to the 1990s, the Department of Defense (DoD) developed large, reliable, *wide-area networks (WANS)*. Some of their technology was used in the development of LANs, but more importantly, the DoDs WAN eventually became the Internet.

> **NOTE**
>
> While all this was happening, telephone systems continued to improve. Especially in the areas of switching technology and long-distance service (because of such new technologies as microwaves and optical fibers), a worldwide, reliable telephone system evolved.

To help you understand the next technological advancement, the development of local-area networks (LANs), consider the following problem. Somewhere in the world, multiple computers wanted to communicate with each other. To do so, they needed some kind of device that could talk to the computers and to the media (the NIC), and some way for the messages to travel (the medium). Suppose also, that the computers wanted to communicate with other computers that were a greater distance away. The answer to this problem came in the form of repeaters and hubs. The repeater was introduced to enable computer data signals to travel farther. The multi-port repeater, or hub, was introduced to enable a group of users to share files, servers, and peripherals. You might call this a workgroup network.

Soon, workgroups wanted to communicate with other workgroups. Because of the functions of hubs (they broadcast all messages to all ports, regardless of destination), as the number of hosts and the number of workgroups grew, there were larger and larger traffic jams. The bridge was invented to segment the network into multiple collision domains to introduce some traffic control.

The best feature of the hub—concentration/connectivity—and the best feature of the bridge—segmentation—were combined to produce a switch. It has many ports, but allows each port to pretend it has a connection to the other side of the bridge, thus allowing more users and lots of communications.

In the mid-1980s, special-purpose computers, originally called *gateways* (and then routers), were developed. These devices allowed the interconnection of separate LANs. Internetworks were created. The DoD already had an extensive internetwork, but the commercial availability of routers, which carried out best path selections and switching for data from many protocols, allowed the explosive growth of networks that we are experiencing today. The cloud represents that growth.

With the arrival of the new century, the next step is the convergence of computer and communications technology (specifically, the convergence of voice, video, and data, which traditionally have traveled via different systems) into one information stream. Now that you have an understanding of the evolution of networking devices, the next section explains how networking devices operate within the OSI model.

Evolution of Networking Devices and the OSI Layers

Hosts and servers operate at Layers 1 through 7; they perform the encapsulation process. Figure 3-26 shows the symbols for each of the networking devices related to each of the OSI model layers. Transceivers, repeaters, and hubs are all considered active Layer 1 devices because they act only on bits and require energy. Patch cables, patch panels, and other interconnection components are considered passive Layer 1 components because they simply provide some sort of conducting path.

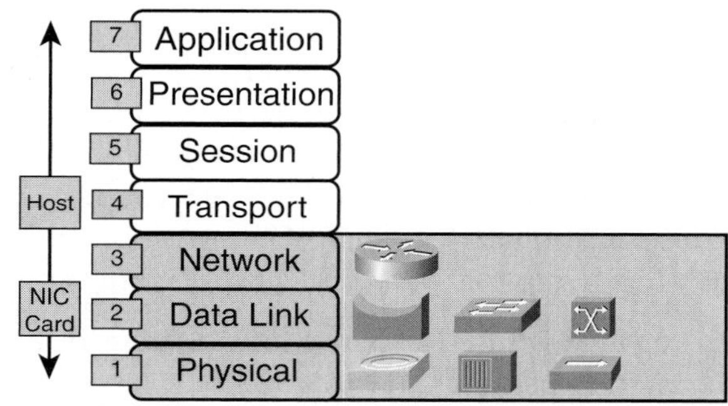

FIGURE 3-26
Each device has specific functions that operate at each of the OSI model layers.

NICs are considered Layer 2 devices because they are the location of the MAC address; but because they often handle signaling and encoding, they are also Layer 1 devices. Bridges and switches are considered Layer 2 devices because they use Layer 2 (MAC address) information to make decisions about whether to forward packets. They also operate on Layer 1 to allow bits to interact with the media.

Routers are considered Layer 3 devices because they use Layer 3 (network) addresses to choose best paths and to switch packets to the proper route. Router interfaces operate at Layers 2 and 1, as well as Layer 3. Clouds, which might include routers, switches, servers, and many devices not yet introduced, involve Layers 1 through 7.

Basics of Data Flow Through LANs

For reliable communications to take place over a network, data to be sent must be put in manageable traceable packages. This is done through the process of encapsulation (as covered in Chapter 2). A brief review of the process states that the top three layers—application, presentation, session—prepare the data for transmission by creating a common format for transmission.

The transport layer breaks up the data into manageable size units called segments. It also assigns sequence numbers to the segments to make sure the receiving host puts the data back together in the proper order. The network layer then encapsulates the segment creating a packet. It adds a destination and a source network address, usually IP, to the packet.

The data link layer further encapsulates the packet and creates a frame. It adds the source and destination local (MAC) addresses to the frame. The data link layer then transmits the binary bits of the frame over the physical layer media.

When the data is transmitted on just a LAN, we talk about the data units as frames because the MAC address is all that is necessary to get from source to destination host. But if we need to send the data to another host over an intranet or the Internet, packets or datagrams become the data unit that is referred to. This is because the network address in the packet contains the final destination address of the host to which the data (packet) is being sent, whereas the data link layer information is local. That is, it changes as it passes through each network. The bottom three layers (network, data link, physical) of the OSI model are the primary movers of data across an intranet or Internet.

Packet Flow Through Layer 1 Devices

The packet flow through Layer 1 devices is simple. Physical media are considered Layer 1 components. All they attend to are bits (for example, voltage or light pulses). If the Layer 1 devices are passive (for example, plugs, connectors, jacks, patch panels, physical media), then the bits simply travel through the passive devices, hopefully with a minimum of distortion. If the Layer 1 devices are active (such as repeaters or hubs), the bits actually are regenerated and retimed. Transceivers, also active devices, can act as connector adapters (AUI port to RJ-45) or as media converters (RJ-45 electrical to ST Optical), in addition to transmitting and receiving on the media. In all cases, the transceivers act as a Layer 1 devices. No Layer 1 device examines any of the headers or data of an encapsulated packet. They work only with bits.

Packet Flow Through Layer 2 Devices

It is important to remember that packets are contained inside frames, so to understand how packets travel on Layer 2 devices, you work with the packets encapsulated form: the frame. Just remember that anything that happens to the frame also happens to the packet.

NICs, bridges, and switches involve the use of data link (MAC) address information to direct frames, which means they are referred to as Layer 2 devices. The unique MAC address resides in a NIC. The MAC address creates the frame.

Bridges work by examining the MAC address of incoming frames. If the frame is local (with a MAC address on the same network segment as the incoming port of the bridge), the frame is not forwarded across the bridge. If the frame is non-local (with a MAC address not on the incoming port of the bridge), it is forwarded to the next network segment. Consider a switch to be a hub with individual ports that act like bridges. The switch takes a data frame, reads the frame, examines the Layer 2 MAC address, and forwards the frames (switches them) to the appropriate ports.

Packet Flow Through Layer 3 Devices

The main device that is discussed at the network layer is the router. Routers actually operate at Layer 1 (bits on the medium at router interfaces), Layer 2 (frames switched from one interface to another), based on packet information and Layer 3 (routing decisions).

Packet flow through routers (that is, selection of best path and actual switching to the proper output port) involves the use of Layer 3 network addresses. After the proper port is selected, the router encapsulates the packet in a frame again to send the packet to its next destination. This process happens for every router in the path from the source host to the destination host.

Packet Flow Through Layer 1–7 Devices

Some devices (such as your PC) are Layer 1-7 devices. In other words, they perform processes that can be associated with every layer of the OSI model. Encapsulation and de-encapsulation are two examples of this. A device called a gateway (essentially a computer which converts information from one protocol to another) can operate on a single layer or multiple layers. An example of a gateway would be a computer on a LAN that allows the network to connect to an IBM mainframe computer or to a network-wide facsimile (fax) system. In both of these examples, the data would have to go all the way up the OSI model stack to be converted into a data format the receiving device, either the mainframe or the fax unit, could use.

Packet Flow Through Clouds

Finally, clouds might contain several kinds of media: NICs, switches, bridges, routers, gateways, and other networking devices. Because the cloud is not really a single device but a collection of devices that operate at all levels of the OSI model, it can be classified as a Layer 1 through 7 device.

You can follow the path of the data generated by the **ping** command. The **ping** command sends some IP data to the device you specify in the command. If the device is configured correctly, it answers back. If you receive an answer, then you know the device exists and is active. If you don't receive a response, then you can assume there's a problem somewhere between your host and the destination.

SKILL BUILDER

Lab Activity: Building a Simple Network

Before you can build a complex LAN, you must start with a simpler LAN. In this lab, you build a very simple network. It presents many of the same issues you would encounter if you were to build a larger network, or even a whole Internet. Here are some questions you should ask yourself before you begin:

- Do I know a simple test for finding the Media Access Control (MAC, physical, Ethernet) address and the Internet Protocol (IP) address setting on my workstation for every installed adapter? (Write down the output.)
- Do I know where I might go to change these settings? (Describe how you get there and what things you can change.)
- Can I recognize and draw, from memory, the basic networking devices: repeaters, hubs, bridges, switches, PCs, servers, and a cloud? (Draw the symbols.)
- Can I draw, using 10 dots, six different topologies? (Draw them; refer to a graphic you have seen. Comment on the pros and cons of each topology for connecting 10 dots.)
- Can I draw a diagram of the following networks: PC to PC; four PCs connected to a hub; four PCs connected to a switch; two groups of four PCs, each connected to a router?
- Can I recognize a hub and explain all the lights and ports? (Sketch and label.)
- Can I recognize a Category 5 UTP straight-through cable? (Sketch and label, including the color codes in the plugs on both ends of the cable.)
- Can I recognize a Category 5 UTP cross-connect cable? (Sketch and label, including the color codes in the plugs on both ends of the cable.)
- Can I recognize an installed NIC and explain all the lights and ports?

The purpose of this lab is to build a simple workgroup. You first connect two PCs, as shown in Figure 3-27.

continues

SKILL BUILDER (CONTINUED)

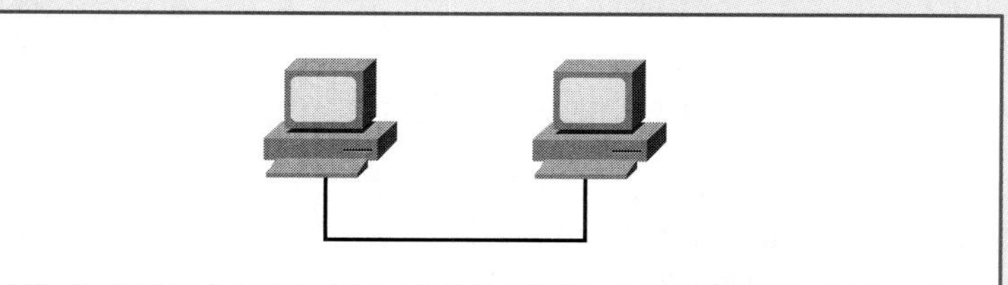

FIGURE 3-27 A simple network made up of two nodes.

Then, as shown in Figure 3-28, you connect four hosts to a hub, which provides connectivity between four hosts.

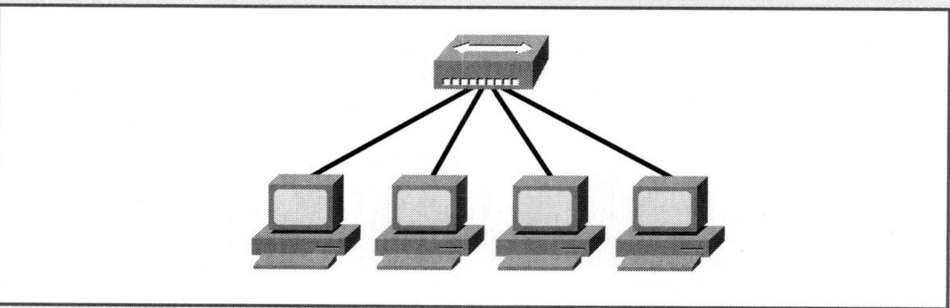

FIGURE 3-28 Four nodes with file sharing capabilities.

Last, you configure the hosts with approved IP addresses, and a Layer 1 connection to the school's network cloud (which is connected to the district's ISP). You have completed the lab when you connect the hosts to the Internet, as shown in Figure 3-29.

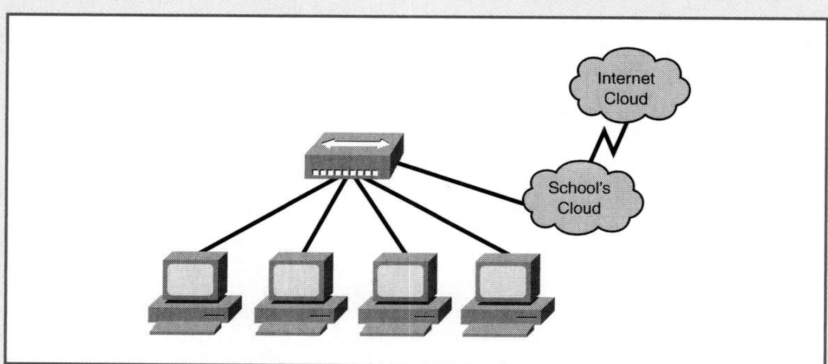

FIGURE 3-29 Four nodes with Internet access via LAN and ISP.

Summary

The purpose of this chapter was to introduce you to basic LAN devices and data flow, so you can begin thinking about building LANs. Now that you have completed this chapter, you should have a firm understanding of the following:

- LAN devices, such as routers, switches, and hubs
- Evolution of networking devices
- Basics of data flow
- Basics related to building LANs

In the next chapter, you learn about electronics and signals as they relate to Layer 1 of the OSI model. By understanding how signals operate at Layer 1, you begin to understand how data is transmitted through a network. In addition, this prepares you in your effort to design, build, and troubleshoot networks.

Check Your Understanding

1. Which of the following best describes topology?
   - **A.** A connection of computers, printers, and other devices for the purpose of communications
   - **B.** The physical arrangement of network nodes and media within an enterprise networking structure
   - **C.** A network type that prevents collisions of data packets
   - **D.** A method for filtering network traffic to reduce the chance of bottlenecks and slowdowns
2. Which of the following best describes a star topology?
   - **A.** A LAN topology in which a central hub is connected by vertical cabling to other hubs that are dependent on it
   - **B.** A LAN topology in which transmissions from network stations propagate the length of the medium and are received by all other stations
   - **C.** A LAN topology in which endpoints on a network are connected to a common central point
   - **D.** A LAN topology in which central points on a network are connected to a common central switch by linear links
3. Why are networking devices used?
   - **A.** They allow a greater number of nodes, extend the network distance, and connect separate networks.
   - **B.** They allow the connection of devices within an entire building.
   - **C.** They provide redundant pathways and thus prevent signal loss and corruption.
   - **D.** Both A and B.
4. Which of the following best describes a node?
   - **A.** An endpoint of a network connection or a junction common to two or more lines in a network that serve as control points
   - **B.** An application that establishes, manages, and terminates sessions between devices and manages data exchange between presentation layer entities

C. An application that synchronizes cooperating devices and establishes agreement on procedures for error recovery and control of data integrity

D. All of the above

5. Which of the following best defines digital signals?

A. Electrical pulses representing data

B. Amplification of data

C. Conversion of data

D. Officially specified rules or procedures

6. A NIC is considered an OSI Layer _____ device.

A. 1

B. 2

C. 3

D. 4

7. Repeaters are

A. Bridges

B. Switches

C. Signal regenerators

D. None of the above

8. For which of the following problems can repeaters provide a simple solution?

A. Too many types of incompatible equipment on the network

B. Too much traffic on a network

C. Too slow data transmission rates

D. Too many nodes and/or not enough cable

9. A hub is an OSI Layer _____ device.

A. 1

B. 2

C. 3

D. 4

10. What is one disadvantage of using a hub?

A. A hub cannot extend the network operating distance.

B. A hub cannot filter network traffic.

C. A hub cannot send weakened signals over a network.

D. A hub cannot amplify weakened signals.

11. A bridge is an OSI Layer _____ device.

A. 1

B. 2

C. 3

D. 4

12. Which of the following is true concerning a bridge and its forwarding decisions?

A. They operate at OSI Layer 2 and use IP addresses to make decisions.

B. They operate at OSI Layer 3 and use IP addresses to make decisions.

C. They operate at OSI Layer 2 and use MAC addresses to make decisions.

D. They operate at OSI Layer 3 and use MAC addresses to make decisions.

13. A switch is an OSI Layer _____ device.

A. 1

B. 2

C. 3

D. 4

14. Which of the following is true concerning the function of a switch?

A. Increases the sizes of collision domains

B. Combines the connectivity of a hub with the traffic regulation of a bridge

C. Combines the connectivity of a hub with the traffic directing of a router

D. Performs Layer 4 path selection

15. A router is an OSI Layer _____ device.

    A. 1

    B. 5

    C. 3

    D. 4

16. What do routers connect?

    A. Bridges and repeaters

    B. Bridges and hubs

    C. Two or more networks

    D. Hubs and nodes

17. What does a router route?

    A. Layer 1 bits

    B. Layer 2 frames

    C. Layer 3 packets

    D. Layer 4 segments

18. What does a router do?

    A. It matches information in the routing table with the data's destination IP address and sends incoming data to the correct subnetwork and host.

    B. It matches information in the routing table with the data's destination IP address and sends incoming data to the correct subnetwork.

    C. It matches information in the routing table with the data's destination IP address and sends incoming data to the correct network.

    D. It matches information in the routing table with the data's destination IP address and sends incoming data to the correct subnet.

19. To construct a simple LAN of four computers, you connect them with a ______?

    A. Cross-connect cable

    B. Serial line

    C. Hub

    D. Router

20. If four hosts are connected to a hub and then to the Internet, how many IP addresses are required for these five devices?

A. One

B. Two

C. Four

D. Five

Objectives

After reading this chapter, you will be able to

- Understand the basics of electricity
- Understand the basics of digital multimeters
- Understand the basics of signals and noise in communications systems
- Understand the basics of encoding networking signals

Layer 1: Electronics and Signals

Introduction

The function of the physical layer is to transmit data by defining the electrical specifications between the source and destination. After it reaches a building, electricity is carried to workstations, servers, and network devices via wires concealed in walls, floors, and ceilings. Data, which can consist of such things as text, pictures, audio, or video, travels through the wires and is represented by the presence of either electrical pulses on copper conducting wires or light pulses in optical fibers.

In this chapter, you learn about the basic theory of electricity, which provides a foundation for understanding networking at the physical layer of the OSI model. You also learn how data is transmitted through physical media, such as cables and connectors. Last, you learn about the different factors that affect data transmission, such as alternating current (AC) power line noise.

Electricity Basics

The basic unit of all matter is an atom. The atom is made of three tiny parts: protons, neutrons, and electrons. The protons and neutrons are lumped together in a small grouping called a *nucleus* (the electron flows freely around this nucleus). When these three parts come together, they form an atom. All matter is composed of atoms. The Periodic Table of Elements, shown in Figure 4-1, lists all the known types of atoms and their properties.

The names of the parts of the atom are

- **Nucleus**—The center part of the atom, formed by protons and neutrons
- **Protons**—Particles have a positive charge, and along with neutrons, form the nucleus
- **Neutrons**—Particles have no charge (neutral), and along with protons, form the nucleus
- **Electrons**—Particles have a negative charge and orbit the nucleus

To help you understand the electrical properties of elements/materials, locate helium on the periodic table. It has an atomic number of 2, which means that it has 2 protons and 2 electrons. It has an atomic weight of 4. By subtracting the atomic number (2) from the atomic weight (4), you learn that helium also has 2 neutrons.

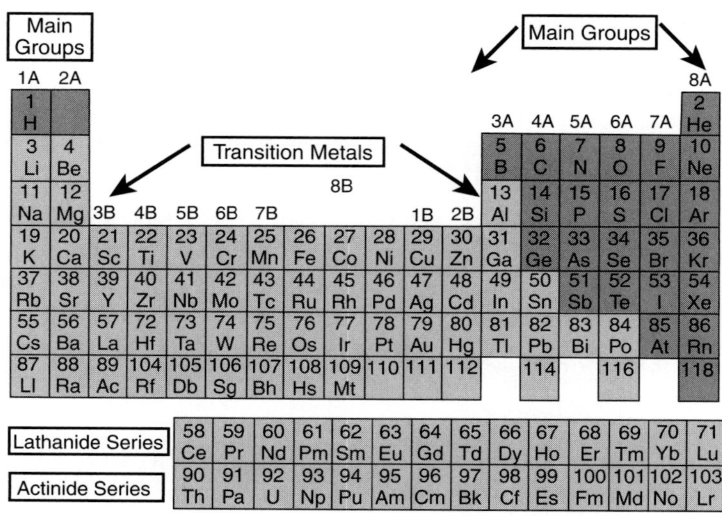

FIGURE 4-1
The Periodic Table of Elements.

The Danish physicist, Niels Bohr, developed a simplified model to illustrate atoms. Figure 4-2 shows the model for a helium atom. Notice the scale of the parts. If the protons and the neutrons of this atom were the size of a soccer ball, in the middle of a soccer field, the only thing smaller than the ball would be the electrons. They would be the size of cherries, and would be orbiting near the outermost seats of the stadium. The only thing larger than the soccer ball would be the space inside the atom, which would be the size of the soccer field.

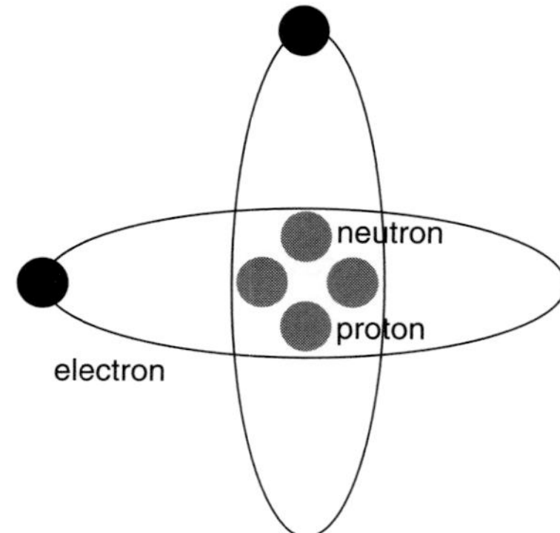

FIGURE 4-2
The helium atom has two protons, two electrons, and two neutrons.

Creating Stable Atoms

One of the laws of nature, called Coulomb's Electric Force Law, states that opposite charges react to each other with a force that causes them to be attracted to each other. Like charges react to each other with a force that causes them to repel each other. A force is a pushing or pulling motion. In the case of opposite and like charges, the force increases as the charges move closer to each other.

Examine Bohr's model of the helium atom. If Coulomb's Law is true, and if Bohr's model describes helium atoms as stable, other laws of nature must be at work. How can they both be true?

> **Coulomb's Law**—Opposite charges attract.
>
> **Bohr's model**—Protons are positive charges, and electrons are negative charges.

Question 1: Why don't the electrons fly in toward the protons?

1. **Coulomb's Law**—Like charges repel.
2. **Bohr's model**—Protons are positive charges. There is more than one proton in the nucleus.

Question 2: Why don't the protons fly away from each other?

The answer to these questions is that other laws of nature must be considered. Following are the answers to each of the above questions.

Answer 1: The electrons stay in orbit, even though they are attracted by the protons. They have just enough velocity to keep orbiting, just like the moon around the Earth, and to not let themselves be pulled into the nucleus.

Answer 2: The protons do not fly apart from each other because of a nuclear force that is associated with neutrons. The nuclear force is an incredibly strong force that acts as a kind of glue to hold the protons together.

The protons and neutrons are bound together by a powerful force; however, the force that binds electrons to their orbit around the nucleus is weaker. Figure 4-3 illustrates these forces. Electrons in certain atoms can be pulled free from the atom and made to flow. This is electricity—a free flow of electrons.

Static Electricity

Loosened electrons that stay in one place, without moving and with a negative charge, are called *static electricity* (see Figure 4-4). If these static electrons have an opportunity to jump to a conductor, this can lead to electrostatic discharge (ESD). Electrostatic discharge, although usually harmless to people, can create serious problems for sensitive electronic equipment unless dealt with properly.

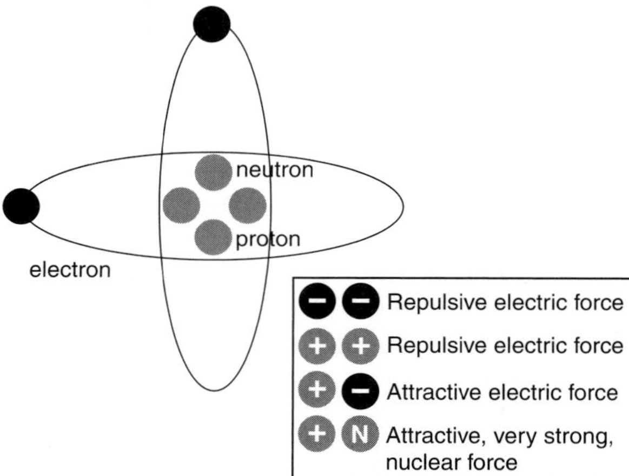

FIGURE 4-3
Forces within an atom.

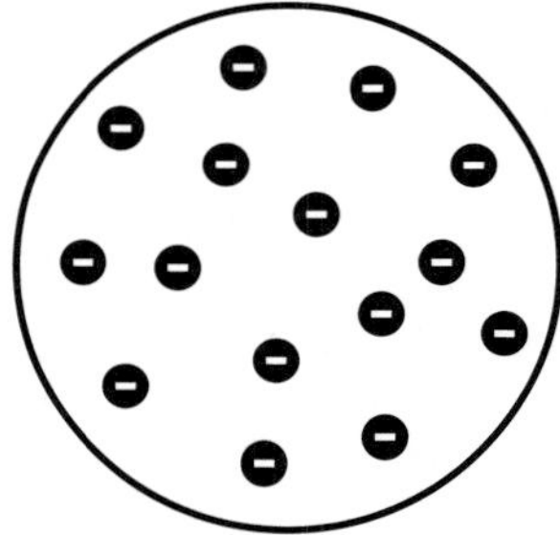

FIGURE 4-4
Because electrons do not feel net electric force, they do not move.

If you walk across a carpet in a cool and dry room, a spark could jump from your fingertips to the next object you touch. You would feel a small electric shock. You know from experience that an electrostatic discharge can be uncomfortable, although it is quite harmless. However, when a computer experiences an ESD, the result can be disastrous. A static discharge can randomly damage computer chips and/or data.

Types of Electrical Materials

Atoms, or groups of atoms called molecules, can be referred to as materials. Materials are classified as belonging to one of three groups, depending on how easily electricity, or free electrons, flows through them. The three types of electrical materials discussed in this section are electrical insulators, electrical conductors, and electrical semiconductors. See Table 4-1 for a summary.

Electrical Insulators

Electrical insulators are materials that allow electrons to flow through them with great difficulty or not at all. Examples of electrical insulators include plastic, glass, air, dry wood, paper, rubber, and helium gas. These materials have stable chemical structures, with orbiting electrons tightly bound within the atoms.

Electrical Conductors

Electrical conductors are materials that allow electrons to flow through them with great ease. They flow easily because the outermost electrons are bound very loosely to the nucleus and are freed easily. At room temperature, these materials have a large number of free electrons that can provide conduction. The introduction of voltage causes the free electrons to move, causing a current to flow.

The periodic table categorizes groups of atoms by listing them in the form of columns. The atoms in each column belong to particular chemical families. Although they might have different numbers of protons, neutrons, and electrons, their outermost electrons have similar orbits and behave similarly when interacting with other atoms and molecules. The best conductors are metals, such as copper (Cu), silver (Ag), and gold (Au). All these metals are located in one column of the periodic table and have electrons that are freed easily, making them excellent materials for carrying a current.

Other conductors include solder, which is a mixture of lead (Pb) and tin (Sn), and water with ions. An ion is an atom that has more or less electrons than a neutral atom. The human body is made of approximately 70 percent water with ions, which means that it, too, is a conductor.

Electrical Semiconductors

Semiconductors are materials where the amount of electricity they conduct can be controlled precisely. These materials are listed together in one column of the periodic chart. Examples include carbon (C), germanium (Ge), and the alloy gallium arsenide (GaAs). The most important semiconductor, the one that makes the best microscopic-sized electronic circuits, is silicon (Si).

Silicon is common and can be found in sand, glass, and many types of rocks. The region around San Jose, California, is known as Silicon Valley because the computer industry, which depends on silicon microchips, started in that area. The switches, or gates, inside a microprocessor are made up of semiconductors.

TABLE 4-1 A Summary of the Three Main Types of Electrical Materials

Material	Flow	Examples
Insulators	Electrons flow poorly.	Plastic, paper, rubber, dry wood, air, and glass
Conductors	Electrons flow well.	Copper (Cu), silver (Ag), gold (Au), solder, water with ions, and humans
Semicon-ductors	Electron flow can be controlled precisely.	Carbon (C), germontum (Ge), gallium arsenide (GaAs), and silicon (Si)

Whether materials are classified as insulators, conductors, or semiconductors, it is the knowledge of how each one controls the flow of electrons, and of how they work together in various combinations, that is the basis for all electronic devices.

Measuring Electricity

As with any other physical process or concept, you need to be able to measure electricity in order to make use of it. There are numerous ways to measure electricity, but in this section, you focus on voltage, current, resistance, and impedance. These networking media terms are used to discuss measuring electricity, which is done with tools like multimeters (also covered in this section).

Voltage

Voltage, sometimes referred to as electromotive force (EMF), is an electrical force, or pressure, that occurs when electrons and protons are separated. The force that is created pulls toward the opposite charge and pushes away from the like charge. This process occurs in a battery, where chemical action causes electrons to be freed from the battery's negative terminal, and to travel to the opposite, or positive, terminal through an external circuit—not through the battery itself. The separation of charges results in voltage. Voltage also can be created by friction (static electricity), magnetism (electric generator), or light (solar cell).

Voltage is represented by the letter *V*, and sometimes by the letter *E* for electromotive force. The unit of measurement for voltage is volt (V), and is defined as the amount of work, per unit charge, needed to separate the charges.

Current

Electrical current, or current, is the flow of charges that is created when electrons move. In electrical circuits, current is caused by a flow of free electrons. When voltage (electrical pressure) is applied, and there is a path for the current, electrons move from the negative terminal (which repels them), along the path, to the positive terminal (which attracts them).

Current is represented by the letter *I*. The unit of measurement for current is Ampere (Amp), and is defined as the number of charges per second that pass by a point along a path.

Resistance

Materials through which current flows offer varying amounts of opposition, or resistance, to the movement of the electrons. Materials that offer very little, or no, resistance, are called *conductors*. Those that do not allow the current to flow, or severely restrict its flow, are called *insulators*. The amount of resistance depends on the chemical composition of the materials. Resistance is represented by the letter *R*. The unit of measurement for resistance is the ohm (Ω). The symbol comes from the Greek capital letter Ω, omega.

Alternating Current

Alternating current (AC) is one of the two ways in which current flows. AC and voltages vary with time by changing their polarity, or direction. AC flows in one direction, and then reverses its direction and repeats the process. AC voltage is positive at one terminal and negative at the other; then, it reverses its polarity so the positive terminal becomes negative and the negative terminal becomes positive. This process repeats itself continuously.

Direct Current

Direct current (DC) is the other way in which current flows. DC always flows in the same direction, and DC voltages always have the same polarity. One terminal is always positive, and the other is always negative. They do not change or reverse.

Impedance

Impedance is the total opposition to current flow (due to AC and DC voltages). The term *resistance* generally is used when referring to DC voltages. Impedance is the general term, and is the measure of how the flow of electrons is resisted, or impeded. Impedance is represented by the letter *Z*. Its unit of measurement, like that for resistance, is the ohm (Ω).

Voltage, Current, Resistance Relationship

Currents only flow in closed loops called *circuits*. These circuits must be composed of conducting materials, and must have sources of voltage. Voltage causes current to flow, while resistance and impedance oppose it. Knowing these facts allows people to control a flow of current.

Ground

The term ground can be a difficult concept to understand completely because people use the term for many different purposes.

Ground can refer to the place on the earth that touches your house (probably via the buried water pipes), eventually making an indirect connection to your electric outlets. When you use an electric appliance that has a plug with three prongs, the third prong is the ground. It gives the electrons an extra conducting path to flow to the earth rather than through your body.

NOTE

A *multimeter* is test equipment used to measure voltage, current, resistance, and possibly other electrical quantities, and displayed the value in numeric form.

Ground also can mean the reference point, or the 0 volts level, when making electrical measurements. Voltage is created by the separation of charges, which means that voltage measurements must be made between two points. A multimeter (which measures voltage, current, and resistance) has two wires for that reason. The black wire is referred to as the ground, or reference ground. A negative terminal on a battery also is referred to as 0 volts, or reference ground.

Analogy for Voltage, Resistance, and Current

Water flow, as illustrated in Figure 4-5, can help you understand the concepts of voltage, current, and resistance. The higher the water and the greater the pressure, the more the water flows. The water current depends on how much the tap (valve) is opened. Similarly, the higher the voltage and the greater the electrical pressure, the more current is produced. The electric current then encounters resistance, which reduces flow (like the water tap). If it is on an AC circuit, the amount of current depends on how much impedance (resistance) is present. The pump is like a battery. It provides pressure to keep the flow moving.

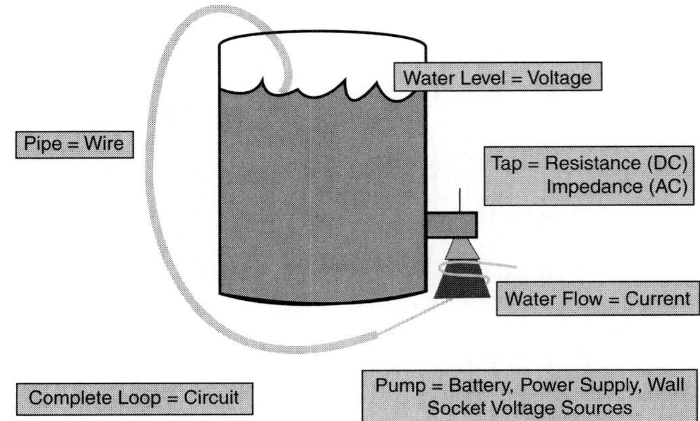

FIGURE 4-5 Useful parallels can be made between water flow and electricity.

Graphing AC and DC Voltage

An *oscilloscope* is an important and sophisticated electronic device used to study electrical signals. Because it is possible to control electricity precisely, deliberate electrical patterns called *waves* can be created. An oscilloscope graphs the electrical waves, pulses, and patterns. It has an x-axis that represents time, and a y-axis that represents voltage. There are usually two y-axis voltage inputs so that two waves can be observed and measured at the same time.

Power lines carry electricity to your home, school, and office. The power lines carry electricity in the form of alternating current (AC) (see Figure 4-6). Another type of current, called direct current (DC), can be found in flashlight batteries, car batteries, and as power for the microchips on the motherboard of a computer (see Figure 4-7). It is important to understand the difference between these two types of current.

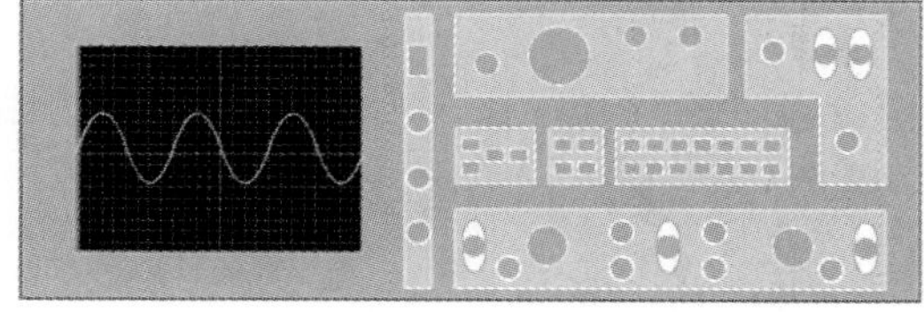

FIGURE 4-6
AC is a form of electricity where the current changes direction regularly.

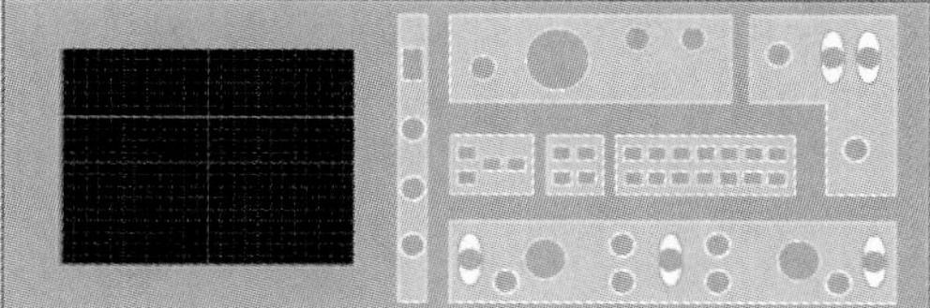

FIGURE 4-7
DC moves in a single direction in a steady flow around a circuit.

Constructing a Simple Series Electrical Current

Electrons flow only in circuits that are closed, or complete, loops. Figure 4-8 shows a simple circuit, typical of a lantern-style flashlight. The chemical processes in the battery cause charges to be separated, which provides a voltage, or electrical pressure, which enables electrons to flow through various devices. The lines represent a conductor (usually copper wire).

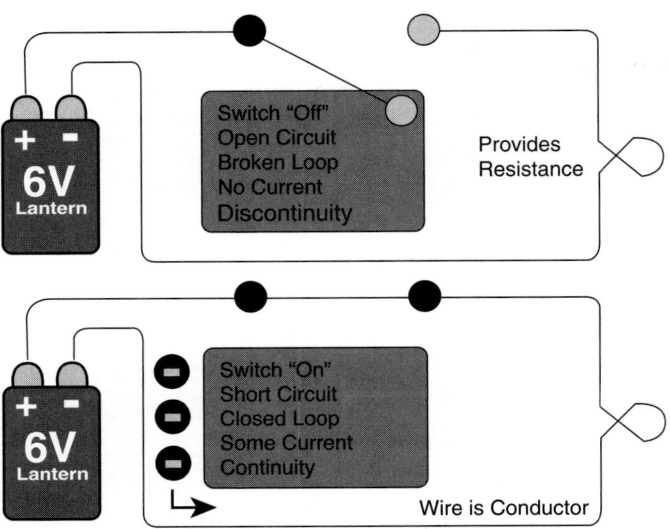

FIGURE 4-8
A 6-volt flashlight uses a simple circuit.

You can think of a switch as two ends of a single wire that can be opened (or broken) and closed (also known as fixed or shorted) to prevent or to allow, respectively, electrons to flow. Finally, the bulb provides resistance to the flow of electrons, causing the electrons to release energy in the form of light. The circuits involved in networking use the same concepts as this simple circuit, but are much more complex.

The following list summarizes the electrical concepts that you learned so far. These concepts are the basis upon which signaling and data transmissions are described later in this chapter. Understanding these electrical concepts makes it relatively easy to understand the processes occurring at the physical layer of the OSI model.

- Electrons flow in closed loops called circuits.
- Definitions:
  - **Voltage** (V)—Electrical pressure due to the separation of electrical charge (+ and –)
  - **Current** (I)—Flow of charged particles, usually electrons
  - **Resistance**—Property of a material that opposes and can control electrical flow
  - **Impedance**—Equivalent to resistance but for AC and pulsed circuits
  - **Short circuit**—Conducting path
  - **Open circuit**—Discontinuity in conducting path
- Voltage causes currents; resistance and impedance limit currents.

Electrical Grounds

For AC and DC electrical systems, the flow of electrons is always from a negatively charged source to a positively charged source. However, for the controlled flow of electrons to occur, a complete circuit is required. Generally speaking, electrical current follows the path of least resistance.

Because metals, such as copper, provide little resistance, they frequently are used as conductors for electrical current. Conversely, materials such as glass, rubber, and plastic provide more resistance. Therefore, they do not make good electrical conductors. Instead, these materials frequently are used as insulators. They are used on conductors to prevent shock, fires, and short circuits.

Electrical power usually is delivered to a pole-mounted transformer. The transformer reduces the high voltages, used in the transmission, to the 120 or 240 volts used by typical consumer electrical appliances.

Figure 4-9 shows an electrical outlet. Electricity is supplied through wall outlets in the US (other nations have different wall outlet configurations). The top two connectors supply power. The round connector on the bottom protects people and equipment from shocks and short circuits. This connector is called the *safety ground connection*. In electrical equipment where this is used, the safety ground wire is connected to any exposed metal part of the equipment. The motherboards and the computing circuits in computing equipment are connected electrically to the chassis. This also connects them to the safety grounding wire, which dissipates static electricity.

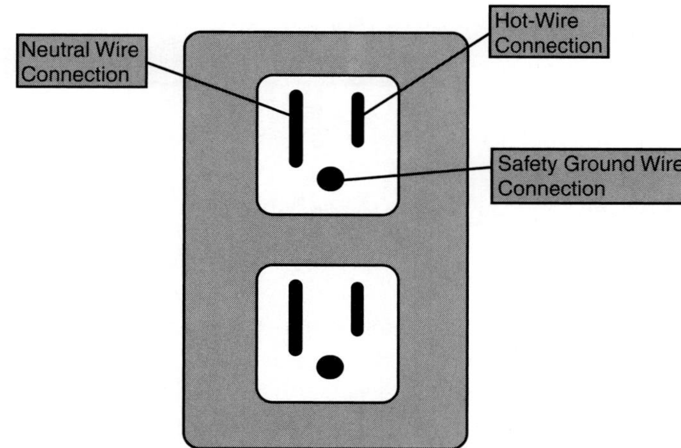

FIGURE 4-9
The familiar neutral, hot, and safety ground wires in a wall outlet.

The purpose of connecting the safety ground to exposed metal parts of the computing equipment is to prevent such metal parts from becoming energized with a hazardous voltage resulting from a wiring fault inside the device.

An accidental connection between the hot wire and the chassis is an example of a wiring fault that could occur in a network device. If such a fault were to occur, the safety ground wire connected to the device would serve as a low resistance path to the earth ground. The safety ground connection provides a lower resistance path than your body.

When properly installed, the low resistance path, which is provided by the safety ground wire, offers sufficiently low resistance and current carrying capacity to prevent the build up of hazardously high voltages. The circuit links directly to the hot connection to the earth, as shown in Figure 4-10.

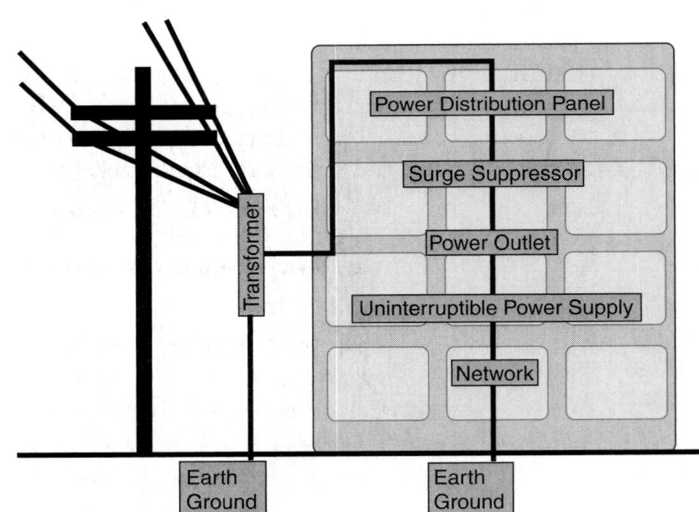

FIGURE 4-10 Surge suppressors, uninterruptible power supplies, and wall outlets all connect to a transformer and to the earth ground.

Safe Handling and Use of the Multimeter

The multimeter can perform voltage, resistance, and continuity measurements, which are important in networking. You can learn about the multimeter from two different sources: the hard copy (paper) manual, and the online (manufacturer's Web site) version of the manual.

SKILL BUILDER

Lab Activity: Safe Handling and Use of Multimeter

In this lab, you learn how to use or handle a multimeter correctly.

Using a Multimeter to Make Resistance Measurements

If you intentionally make a path into a low-resistance path, for use by two connected electrical devices, then the path has *continuity*. If a path is made unintentionally into a low-resistance path, then it is called a *short circuit*. The unit of measurement for both is the ohm (Ω). Continuity refers to the level of resistance of a path.

With either measurement, the multimeter emits a high-pitched sound when it detects a low-resistance path. You perform measurements on the following:

- CAT 5 cable
- Terminated CAT 5 cable
- Terminated coaxial cable
- Telephone wire
- CAT 5 jacks
- Switches
- Wall outlets

SKILL BUILDER

Lab Activity: Resistance Measurements

In this lab, you demonstrate your ability to measure resistance and continuity with the multimeter.

Using a Multimeter to Make Voltage Measurements

Two types of voltage measurements exist: DC and AC. For your personal safety, and to protect the meter, it is important that you understand the differences between the two.

DC Voltage

The meter must be set to DC when measuring DC voltages. This includes the following:

- Batteries
- Outputs of computer power supplies

CAUTION

Line voltage can kill you! You must remember to use the correct setting on the multimeter.

- Solar cells
- DC generators

AC Voltage

The meter must be set to AC when you measure AC voltages. If you measure a wall socket, for example, you must assume that line voltage is present. Line voltage is 120 V AC in the US, and 220 V AC in most other places around the world.

SKILL BUILDER

Lab Activity: Voltage Measurements

In this lab, you demonstrate your ability to measure voltage safely with the multimeter.

SKILL BUILDER

Lab Activity: Series Circuits

In this lab, you build series circuits and explore their basic properties.

SKILL BUILDER

Constructing a Simple Electrical Communication System

Figure 4-11 shows part of the circuits that allow Ethernet NICs to communicate with each other. This should give you a hint on how to approach your challenge in this lab, which is to design, build, and demonstrate a simple electrical communication system.

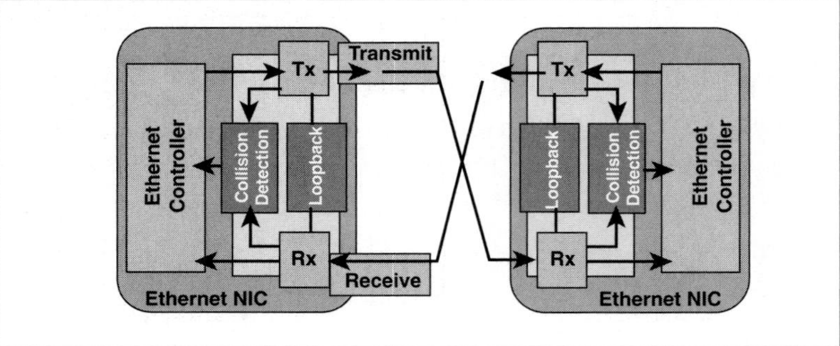

FIGURE 4-11 Ethernet physical connector provides several circuits.

SKILL BUILDER (CONTINUED)

Lab Activity: Communication Circuit

In this lab, you design, build, and test a simple, complete, fast, and reliable communication system using common materials.

Signals and Noise in Communication Systems

The term *signal* refers to a desired electrical voltage, light pattern, or modulated electromagnetic wave. There are many ways in which a signal can be created physically: as electrical pulses that travel over copper wire, as pulses of light that travel through strands of glass or plastic, as radio transmissions that travel over the airwaves, as laser or satellite transmissions, and as infrared pulses. Each of these entities can carry networking data. When the 1s and 0s that represent computer data turn into pulses of energy, they are encoded, or modulated. The two main types of signaling are *analog* and *digital*. In this section, you study the specific attributes of each of these types of signals.

Comparing Analog and Digital Signals

Analog signals can be illustrated graphically as waveforms because they change gradually and continuously. An analog signal is an electromagnetic wave that constantly changes. Figure 4-12 is a pictorial representation of an analog signal. An analog signal has the following characteristics:

- Waviness
- A continuously varying voltage-versus-time graph
- Typical of things in nature
- Used widely in telecommunications for more than 100 years

Figure 4-12 shows a pure sine wave. The two important characteristics of a sine wave are its amplitude (A), its height and depth, and its period (T), which is the length of time to complete one cycle. You can calculate the frequency (f), wiggleyness, of the wave with the formula f = 1/T.

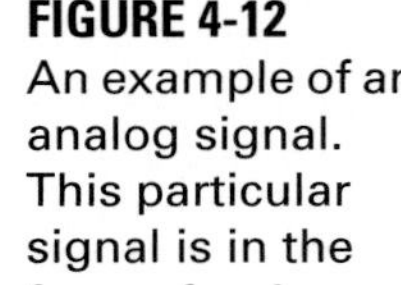

FIGURE 4-12
An example of an analog signal. This particular signal is in the form of a sine wave.

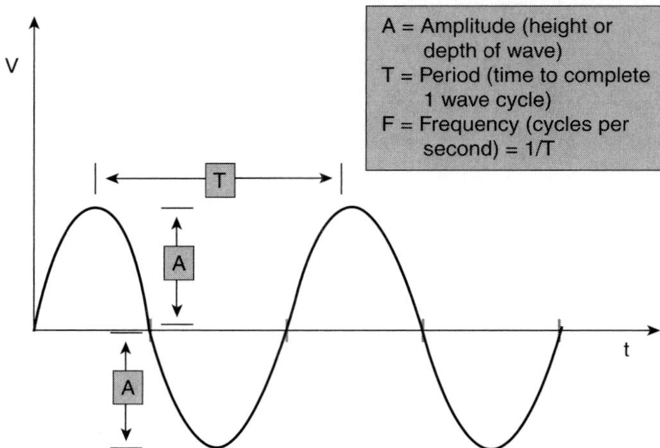

Digital signals change from one state to another almost instantaneously, without stopping at an in-between state. Figure 4-13 illustrates digital signaling. A digital signal has the following characteristics:

- Discrete, or jumpy, voltage-versus-time graphs
- Typical of technology instead of nature

FIGURE 4-13
An example of a digital signal.

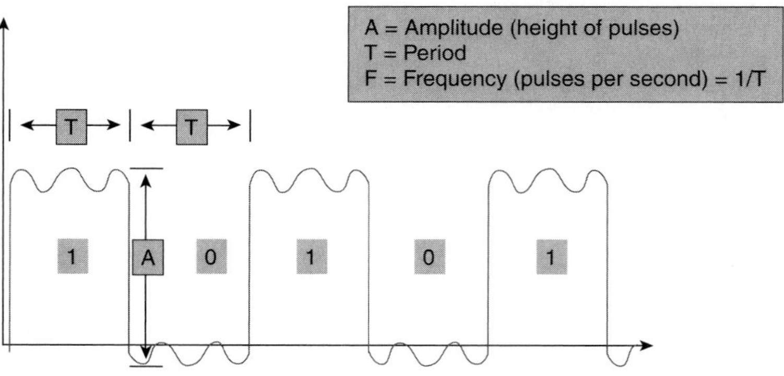

MORE INFORMATION

Measuring Analog Signals

Analog signals are measured in cycles, with one cycle representing the change from high to low and back again (or vice versa). The following three characteristics are measured:

- **Amplitude**—The strength of the signal, represented by the height of the wave.
- **Frequency**—Frequency is represented as hertz (cycles per second).
- **Phase**—The relative state of one wave to another, measured in degrees.

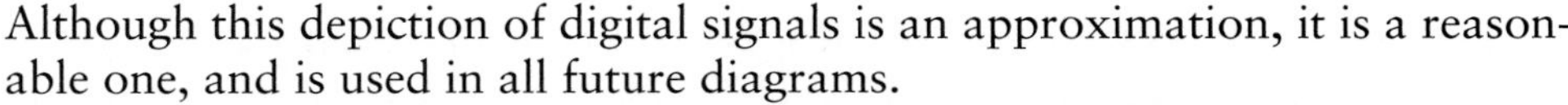

Although this depiction of digital signals is an approximation, it is a reasonable one, and is used in all future diagrams.

MORE INFORMATION

Digital and Analog Signaling

Digital signaling often is the most appropriate format for transmitting computer data, and most networks use digital signaling methods for that reason. Because it is a simpler technology, digital signaling has some advantages over analog:

- It is generally less expensive to make digital equipment.
- Digital signals are generally less vulnerable to errors caused by interference. The discrete state of on or off is not as easily affected by a small distortion as is a continuous waveform.

Analog signals also have advantages:

- Analog signals can be easily multiplexed; that is, signals can be combined to increase bandwidth.
- Analog signals are less vulnerable to the problem of attenuation (that is, signal loss) because of distance, so they can travel farther without becoming too weak for reliable transmission. On the other hand, when an analog signal is amplified, the noise is amplified along with the signal.

Digital connectivity solutions generally offer better security, faster performance, and higher reliability. In addition, digital lines are far less error-prone than are analog lines. LANs generally rely on cabling over which digital signals are transmitted.

continues

MORE INFORMATION (CONTINUED)

Multiplexing

Multiplexing is a method of sending different streams of information on a link at the same time, in the form of a single, complex signal. The separate streams then are recovered at the receiving end. Both analog and digital signals can be multiplexed.

Frequency-Division Multiplexing

Analog signals typically are multiplexed using *frequency-division multiplexing (FDM)*. Multiple channels are combined on a single line for transmission, and each channel is assigned a different frequency. A two-way communications circuit requires a multiplexer/demultiplexer at each end. FDM assigns each channel a separate frequency and combines all frequencies for simultaneous transmission on a single line. The cable TV system is an excellent example of an FDM system.

Time-Division Multiplexing

Digital signals usually use *time-division multiplexing (TDM)*. This method combines signals for transmission on a single communications line and breaks each signal into segments with short durations. The signals then are carried over the line in alternating time slots, one after another. At the other end, they are separated by a demultiplexer. TDM breaks each signal into segments of short duration and transmits all segments over a single line one after the other

Dense Wavelength Division Multiplexing

Networks that run over fiber-optic cable can use yet another type of multiplexing: *dense wavelength division multiplexing (DWDM)*. With DWDM, each signal is carried on a separate wavelength of light. Different data formats (for instance, SONET and ATM) can travel simultaneously over the same optical fiber. DWDM carries each signal on a separate wavelength of light, within a single fiber. This is analogous to FDM, with wavelengths instead of frequencies.

Using Analog Signals to Build Digital Signals

Jean Baptiste Fourier is responsible for one of the greatest mathematical discoveries. He proved that a special sum of sine waves, of harmonically related frequencies, which are multiples of some basic frequency, could be added together to create any wave pattern. This is how voice recognition devices and heart pacemakers work. Complex waves can be built out of simple waves. A square wave, or a square pulse, can be built by using the right combination of sine waves. Figure 4-14 shows how the square wave (digital signal) can be built with sine waves (analog signals). This is important to remember as you examine what happens to a digital pulse as it travels along networking media.

FIGURE 4-14
A square wave that is being approximated by a series of sine waves.

MORE INFORMATION

Simplex, Half-Duplex, and Full-Duplex Transmission

The data channels over which a signal is sent can operate in one of three ways: *simplex*, *half-duplex*, or *full-duplex*. The distinction between these three is in the way the signal can travel.

Simplex Transmission

Simplex transmission, as its name implies, is simple. It is also called unidirectional because the signal travels in only one direction, just like traffic flows on a one-way street. Television transmission is an example of simplex communication. The data (that is, the television programs) are sent to your TV. No signals are transmitted back from the television to the broadcaster or cable company. This is why a TV has a receiver, but no transmitter.

Half-Duplex Transmission

Half-duplex transmission is an improvement over simplex transmission; the traffic can travel in both directions. Unfortunately, the road isn't wide enough to accommodate bidirectional signals simultaneously. This means that only one side can transmit at a time. Half-duplex transmission enables signals to travel in either direction, but not in both directions simultaneously.

continues

MORE INFORMATION (CONTINUED)

Full-Duplex Transmission

Full-duplex transmission operates like a two-way, two-lane street. Traffic can travel in both directions at the same time. Full-duplex networking technology increases performance because data can be sent and received at the same time.

Representing One Bit on a Physical Medium

Data networks have become increasingly dependent on binary (two-state) systems. The basic building block of information is 1 binary digit, known as the bit or pulse. One bit, on an electrical medium, is the electrical signal corresponding to binary 0 or binary 1. This can be as simple as 0 volts for binary 0, and +5 volts for binary 1, or a more complex encoding. Signal reference ground is an important concept relating to all networking media that use voltages to carry messages.

To function correctly, a signal reference ground must be close to a computer's digital circuits. Engineers have accomplished this by designing ground planes into circuit boards. The computer cabinets are used as the common point of connection for the circuit board ground planes to establish the signal reference ground. Signal reference ground establishes the 0 volts line in the signal graphics.

With optical signals, binary 0 would be encoded as a low-light, or no-light, intensity (darkness). Binary 1 would be encoded as a higher-light intensity (brightness), or other more complex patterns.

With wireless signals, binary 0 might be a short burst of waves; binary 1 might be a longer burst of waves, or another more complex pattern. The 0 bit commonly is represented by a horizontal line appearing on the t-axis (it's black in Figure 4-15). It's also common to use +5 volts to indicate the 1 bit (the upper horizontal black line in the voltage versus time graph on the left).

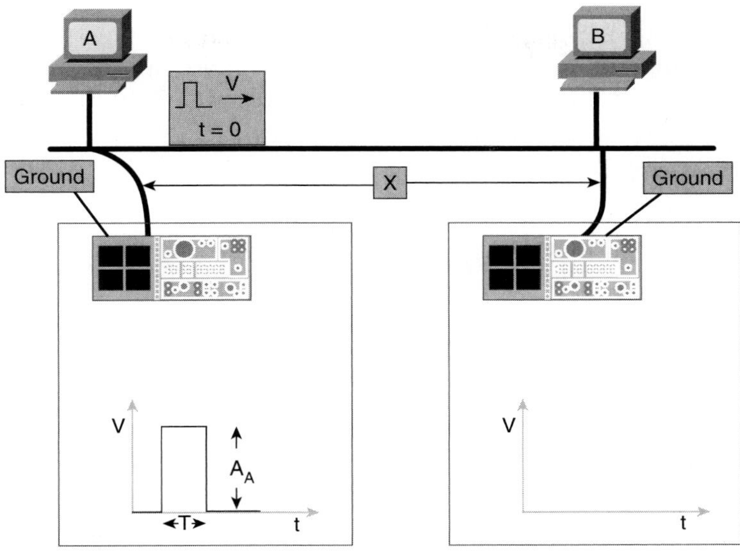

FIGURE 4-15
The signal reference ground sets a baseline.

MORE INFORMATION

Baseband and Broadband

The entire capacity of an Ethernet cable is used for transmitting the data in one channel. This makes Ethernet a *baseband* technology. A *channel* is an allocated portion of the media's available bandwidth that can be used for transmission. Baseband transmission is simple. The signal has the benefits of having the entire bandwidth to itself. Baseband usually is associated with digital signaling (although it can be used with analog). Most computer communications are baseband; for example, the signals from computers to monitors, printers, and other peripherals are baseband because they are analog modem communications. Baseband signaling is bidirectional; the signal can flow both ways so you can transmit and receive over the same cable.

Broadband technologies allow for dividing the capacity of a link into two or more channels, each of which can carry a different signal. All channels can send simultaneously. ISDN is an example of a broadband technology because multiple signals can be carried over separate channels on a single wire. In addition to satellite and other wireless technologies, Digital Subscriber Line (DSL) is another example of a broadband technology because data and voice can travel simultaneously over the same line.

Signaling and Communications Problems

The signals that make computer communications possible are subject to various problems and limitations. Some cable types and signaling methods are more susceptible to certain problems than others. In this section, you examine six things that can happen to 1 bit:

- Propagation
- Attenuation
- Reflection
- Noise
- Timing problem
- Collisions

Network Signal Propagation

Propagation means travel. When a NIC puts a voltage or light pulse onto a physical medium, that square pulse made up of waves travels along the medium (propagates). Propagation means that a lump of energy, representing 1 bit, travels from one place to another. The speed at which it propagates depends on the actual material used in the medium, the geometry (structure) of the medium, and the frequency of the pulses. The time it takes the bit to travel from one end of the medium and back is referred to as the round trip time (RTT). Assuming no other delays, the time it takes the bit to travel down the medium to the far end is RTT/2 (see Figure 4-16).

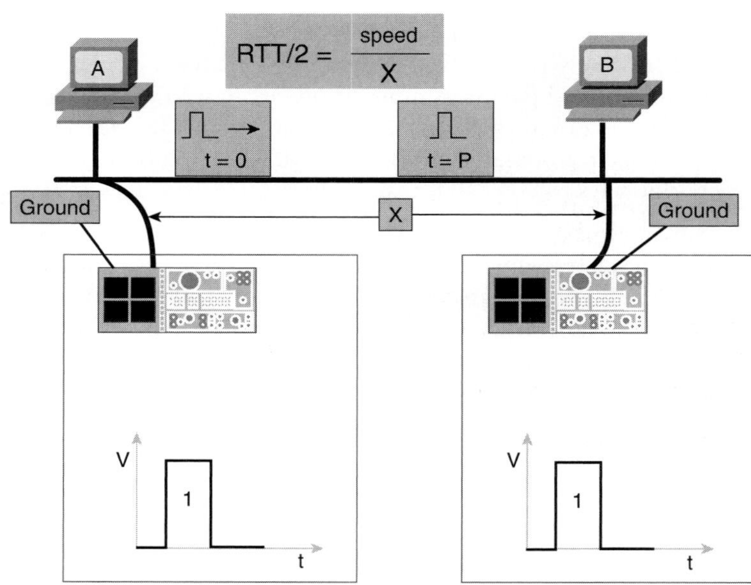

FIGURE 4-16 The formula Distance = Rate × Time comes in handy in networking. Here's one application of the D=RT formula: computing the propagation delay (half the round-trip time) for a bit traveling from Host A to Host B.

The fact that the bit takes a small amount of time to travel along the medium does not normally cause network problems. However, with the ever-increasing data transmission rates of today's networks, sometimes you must account for the amount of time it takes the signal to travel.

Network Attenuation

Attenuation is the loss of signal strength over distance. This means that a 1-bit voltage signal loses amplitude as energy passes from the signal to the cable (see Figure 4-17). Choosing materials carefully (for example, using copper instead of carbon) and using geometry wisely (the shape and positioning of the wires) can reduce electrical attenuation.

FIGURE 4-17 Attenuation is the loss of signal energy as the distance traveled by a bit on the cable increases. This is indicated by the reduced height and protracted base of the square wave pictured on the right relative to its original condition on the left.

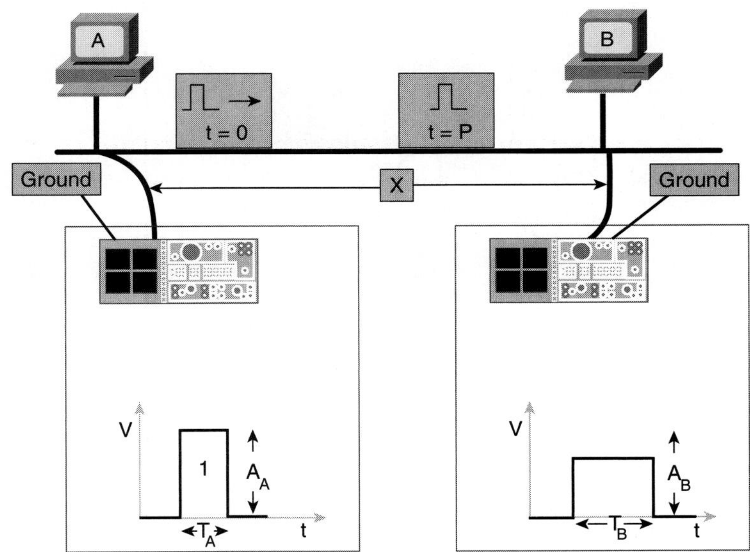

Some loss is always unavoidable when electrical resistance is present. Attenuation also happens to optical signals; the optical fiber absorbs and scatters some of the light energy as the light pulse, 1 bit, travels down the fiber. The wavelength, or color, of the light you choose can minimize attenuation. Attenuation also can be minimized by whether or not you use single mode or multi-mode fiber, and by the actual glass that is used for the fiber. Even with these choices, some signal loss is unavoidable.

Attenuation also happens to radio waves and microwaves as they are absorbed and scattered by specific molecules in the atmosphere. Attenuation can affect a network because it limits the length of network cabling over which you can send a message. If the cable is too long or too attenuating, a 1 bit sent from the source can look like a 0 bit by the time it reaches the destination.

Network Reflection

Reflection occurs in electrical signals. When voltage pulses, or bits, hit a discontinuity, some energy can be reflected (see Figure 4-18). If not controlled carefully, this energy can interfere with later bits. Remember, while you are focused on only 1 bit at a time right now, in real networks, you will want to send millions and billions of bits every second, thus requiring you to keep track of this reflected pulse energy. Depending on the cabling and the connections the network uses, reflections might or might not be a problem.

FIGURE 4-18
Reflection is caused by discontinuities in the medium. This could be a result of kinks in a cable or poorly terminated cables.

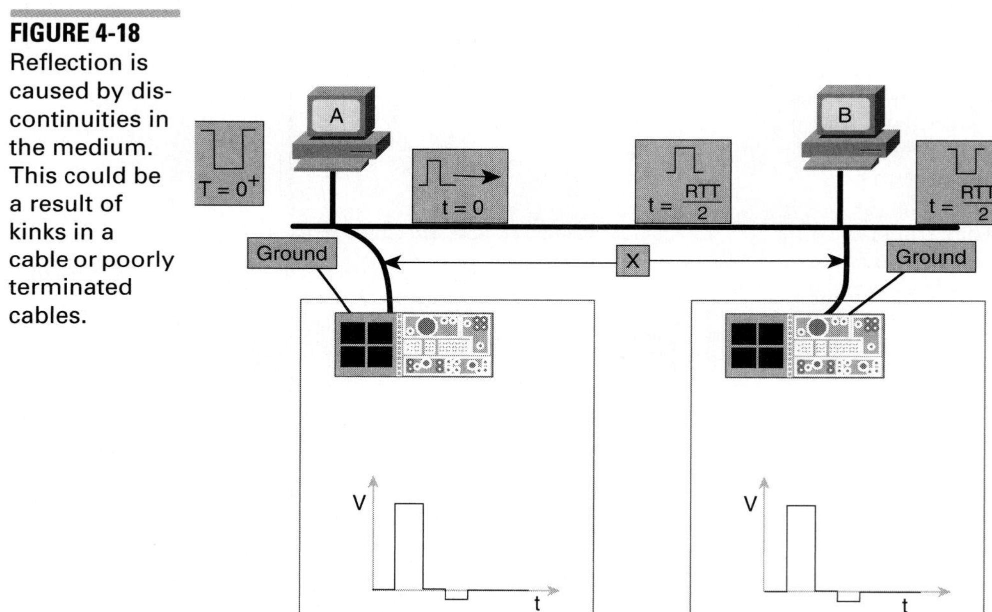

Reflection also occurs with optical signals. Optical signals reflect whenever they hit a discontinuity in the glass fiber, such as when a connector is plugged into a device. You can see this effect at night if you look out a window. You can see your reflection in the window even though the window is not a mirror. Some of the light that is reflected off your body reflects in the window. This also happens with radio waves and microwaves as they encounter different layers in the atmosphere.

This can cause problems on your network. For optimal network performance, it is important that the network media have a specific impedance to match the electrical components in the NICs. Unless the network media has the correct impedance, the signal suffers some reflection and interference is created. Then multiple reflecting pulses can occur. Whether the system is electrical, optical, or wireless, impedance mismatches cause reflections. If enough energy is reflected, the binary, two-state system can become confused by all the extra energy bouncing around. You can resolve this by ensuring that all networking components are carefully impedance matched. This is why you must have a terminator (resister) at the endpoints of Ethernet coaxial LANs.

Noise

Noise is unwanted additions to optical or electromagnetic signals. No electrical signal is without noise; however, it is important to keep the signal-to-noise (S/N) ratio as high as possible. The S/N ratio is an engineering calculation and measurement that involves dividing the signal strength by the noise strength; it gives a measure of how easy it is to decipher the desired, intended signal from the unwanted, but unavoidable, noise. In other words, each bit receives additional unwanted signals from various sources. Too much noise can corrupt a bit, turning a binary 1 into a binary 0, or a 0 into a 1, which destroys the message. Figure 4-19 shows five sources of noise that can affect a bit on a wire.

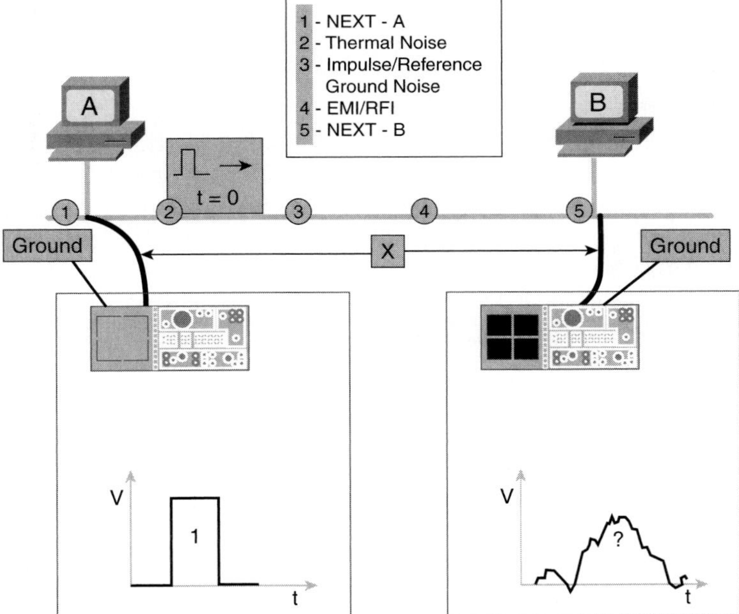

FIGURE 4-19
Five sources of noise on a cable.

NEXT-A and NEXT-B

When electrical noise on the cable originates from signals on other wires in the cable, this is known as crosstalk. NEXT stands for *near-end crosstalk*. When two wires are near each other and untwisted, energy from one wire can wind up in an adjacent wire and vice versa. This can cause noise at both ends of a terminated cable. There are actually many forms of crosstalk that must be considered when building networks.

NEXT can be addressed by strict adherence to standard termination procedures, proper installation methods, and use of quality twisted pair cables. NEXT-A stands for Near End Crosstalk at computer A and NEXT-B stands for Near End Crosstalk at computer B.

Thermal Noise

Thermal noise, due to the random motion of electrons, is unavoidable but usually relatively small compared to our signals.

AC Power/Reference Ground Noise

AC power and reference ground noises are crucial problems in networking. AC line noise creates problems in our homes, schools, and offices. Electricity is carried to appliances and machines by wires concealed in walls, floors, and ceilings. Consequently, inside these buildings, AC power line noise is all around us. If not properly prevented, power line noise can cause problems for a network.

Ideally, the signal reference ground should be completely isolated from the electrical ground. Isolation could keep AC power leakage and voltage spikes off the signal reference ground.

But the chassis of a computing device serves as the signal reference ground, and as the AC power line ground. Because there is a link between the signal reference ground and the power ground, problems with the power ground can lead to interference with the data system. Such interference can be difficult to detect and trace. Usually, it stems from the fact that electrical contractors and installers don't care about the length of the neutral and ground wires that lead to each electrical outlet. Unfortunately, when these wires are long, they can act as an antenna for electrical noise. It is this noise that interferes with the digital signals (bits) a computer must be able to recognize and process.

You will discover that AC line noise coming from a nearby video monitor or hard disk drive can be enough to create errors in a computer system. It does this by interfering (changing the shape and the voltage level) with the desired signals and preventing a computer's logic gates from detecting the leading and trailing edges of the square waves. This problem can be further compounded when a computer has a poor ground connection.

EMI and RFI

External sources of electrical impulses that can attack the quality of electrical signals on the cable include lighting, electrical motors, and radio systems. These types of interference are referred to as *electromagnetic interference (EMI)* and *radio frequency interference (RFI)*. Each wire in a cable can act like an antenna. When this happens, the wire actually absorbs electrical signals from other wires in the cable and from electrical sources outside the cable. If the resulting electrical noise reaches a high enough level, it can become difficult for NICs to discriminate the noise from the data signal. This is particularly a problem because most LANs use frequencies in the 1-100 megahertz (MHz) frequency region, which happens to be where FM radio signals, TV signals, and lots of appliances have their operating frequencies as well.

Look at how electrical noise, regardless of the source, impacts digital signals. Imagine that you want to send data, represented by the binary number 1011001001101, over the network. Your computer converts the binary number to a digital signal. Figure 4-20 shows what the digital signal for 1011001001101 looks like. The digital signal travels through the networking media to the destination. The destination happens to be near an electrical outlet that is fed by both long neutral and long ground wires. These wires act as possible antennas for electrical noise. Figure 4-20 shows what electrical noise looks like.

Because the destination computer's chassis is used for both the earth ground and the signal reference ground, the noise generated interferes with the digital signal that the computer receives. Figure 4-20 shows what happens to the signal when it is combined with this electrical noise. Instead of reading the signal as 1011001001101, the computer reads the signal as 1011000101101, making the data unreliable (corrupted).

Unlike copper wire, optical and wireless systems experience some of these forms of noise but are immune to others. For example, optical fiber is immune to NEXT and AC power/reference ground noise, and wireless systems are particularly prone to EMI/RFI. The focus here has been on noise in copper-based wiring systems. The problem of NEXT can be addressed by strict adherence to standard termination procedures and the use of quality twisted pair cables.

Nothing can be done about thermal noise, other than to give the signals a large enough amplitude so it doesn't matter. To avoid the problem of AC/reference ground as described previously, it is important to work closely with your electrical contractor and power company. This can enable you to get the best and shortest electrical ground. One way to do this is to investigate the cost of installing a single power transformer, dedicated to your LAN installation area. If you can afford this option, you can control the attachment of other devices to your power circuit. Restricting how and where devices, such as motors or high-current electrical heaters, are attached can eliminate much of the electrical noise generated by them.

When working with your electrical contractor, you should ask that separate power distribution panels, known as breaker boxes, be installed for each office area. Because the neutral wires and the ground wires from each outlet come together in the breaker box, taking this step can increase your chances of shortening the length of the signal ground. While installing individual power distribution panels for every cluster of computers can increase the up-front cost of the power wiring, it reduces the length of the ground wires, and limits several kinds of signal-burying electrical noise.

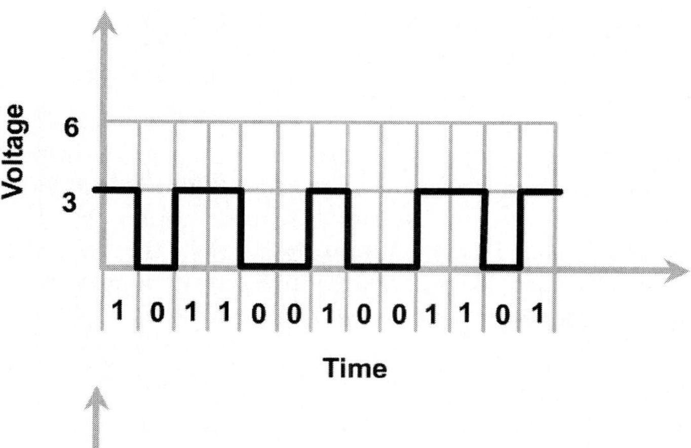

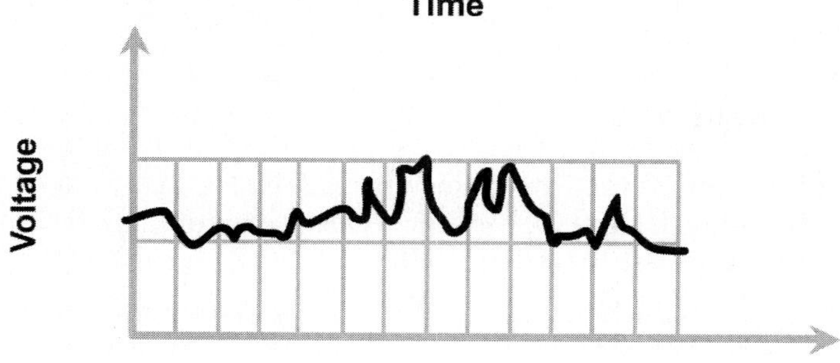

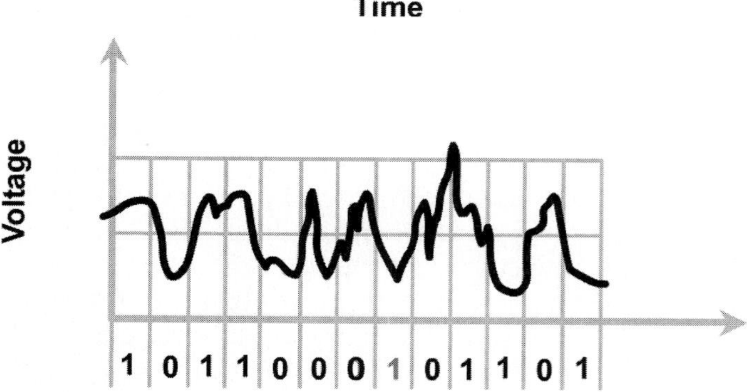

FIGURE 4-20
The first graph is a digital signal, the second graph represents electrical noise, and the third graph shows the combined result.

You can limit EMI and RFI in a number of ways. One way is to increase the size of the conductor wires. Another way is to improve the type of insulating material used. However, such changes increase the size and cost of the cable faster than they improve its quality. Therefore, it is more typical for network designers to specify a cable of good quality, and to provide specifications for the maximum recommended cable length between nodes. Two techniques that cable designers have used successfully in dealing with EMI and RFI are *shielding* and *cancellation*.

Shielding

In cable that employs shielding, a metal braid or foil surrounds each wire pair or group of wire pairs. This shielding acts as a barrier to any interfering signals. However, as with increasing the size of the conductors, using braid or foil covering increases the diameter of the cable and the cost as well. Therefore, cancellation is the more commonly used technique to protect the wire from undesirable interference.

Cancellation

When electrical current flows through a wire, it creates a small, circular magnetic field around the wire (see Figure 4-21). The direction of these magnetic lines of force is determined by the direction in which the current flows along the wire. If two wires are part of the same electrical circuit, electrons flow from the negative voltage source to the destination along one wire. Then, the electrons flow from the destination to the positive voltage source along the other wire.

When two wires in an electrical circuit are placed close together, their magnetic fields are the exact opposite of each other. Thus, the two magnetic fields cancel each other out. They also cancel out any outside magnetic fields as well. Twisting the wires can enhance this cancellation effect. By using cancellation in combination with twisting of wires, cable designers can provide an effective method of providing self-shielding for wire pairs within the network media.

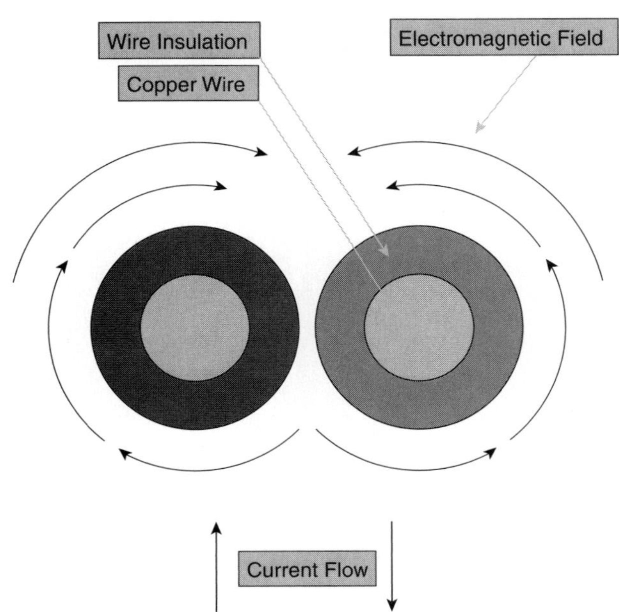

FIGURE 4-21 Electrical current in a wire induces a magnetic field around the wire.

Dispersion, Jitter, and Latency

Dispersion, jitter, and latency are actually three different things that can happen to a bit. They are grouped together because each affects the same thing: the timing of a bit. Because you are trying to understand what problems might occur as millions and billions of bits travel on a medium in one second, timing matters a great deal.

Dispersion is when the signal broadens in time (see Figure 4-22). It is caused by the type of media involved. If serious enough, 1 bit can start to interfere with the next bit and confuse it with the bits before and after it. Because you want to send billions of bits per second, you must be careful not to allow the signals to spread out. Dispersion can be fixed by proper cable design, limiting cable lengths, and finding the proper impedance. In optical fibers, dispersion can be controlled by using laser light of a very specific wavelength. For wireless communications, dispersion can be minimized by the frequencies used to transmit.

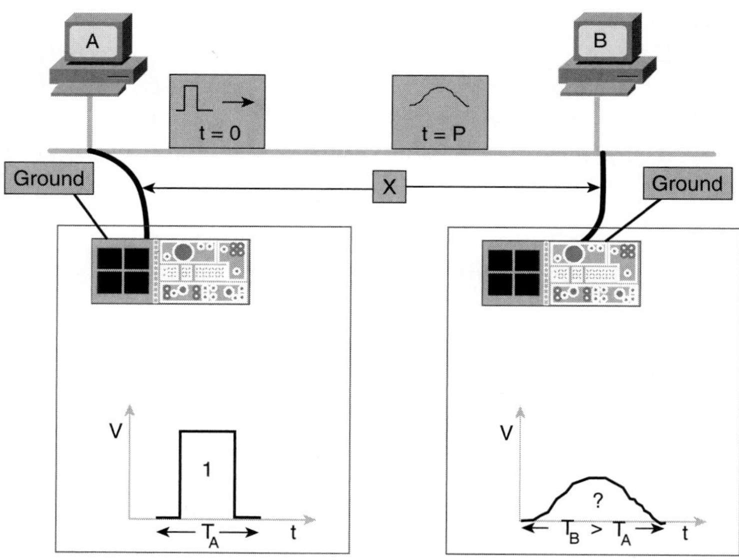

FIGURE 4-22 Dispersion sometimes elongates digital signals to the point where networking devices cannot distinguish where one bit ends and another begins.

All digital systems are clocked, meaning clock pulses cause everything to happen. Clock pulses cause a CPU to calculate, data to store in memory, and the NIC to send bits. If the clock on the source host is not synchronized with the destination, which is quite likely, you get timing jitter. This means that bits arrive a little earlier and later than expected. Jitter can be fixed by a series of complicated clock synchronizations, including hardware and software, or protocol synchronizations.

Latency, also known as delay, has two main causes. First, Einstein's theory of relativity states that "nothing can travel faster than the speed of light in a vacuum (3.0 × 108 meters/second)." Wireless networking signals travel at slightly less than the speed of light in a vacuum. Networking signals on copper media travel in the range of 1.9 × 108 m/s to 2.4 × 108 m/s. Networking signals on optical fiber travel at approximately 2.0 × 108 m/s. To travel a distance, a bit takes at least a small amount of time to get to where it's going. Second, if the bit goes through any devices, the transistors and the electronics introduce more latency. The solution to the problem of latency is the careful use of internetworking devices, different encoding strategies, and various layer protocols.

Collision

A collision occurs when two bits from two different communicating computers are on a shared medium at the same time. In the case of copper media, the voltages of the two binary signals are added and cause a third voltage level. This voltage variation is not allowed in a binary system, which understands only two voltage levels. The bits are corrupted (or destroyed). Figure 4-23 illustrates a collision.

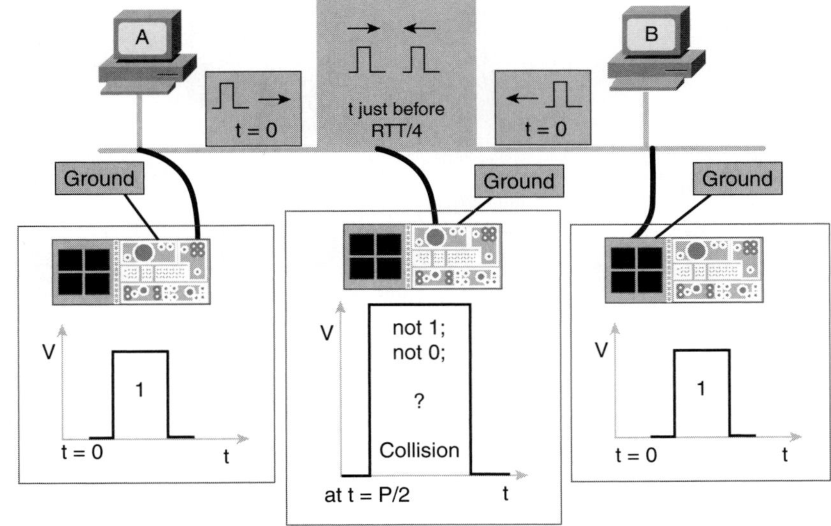

FIGURE 4-23 Collisions are a common phenomenon on Ethernet networks.

In some technologies, such as Ethernet, collisions are a natural part of the functioning of a network. However, excessive collisions can slow the network down or bring it to a halt. Therefore, a lot of network design goes into minimizing and localizing collisions.

You can deal with collisions in many ways. One way is to detect them and simply have a set of rules for dealing with them when they occur, as in Ethernet. LocalTalk and 802.11 attempt to avoid the collisions: The transmitter exchanges a very short message with the intended receiver before sending the actual data. Deterministic protocols, such as Token Ring, FDDI, and polling, do not have collisions at all.

Messages in Terms of Bits

After a bit reaches a medium, it propagates and might experience attenuation, reflection, noise, dispersion, or collision. You want to transmit far more than 1 bit. In fact, you want to transmit millions of bits in one second. All the effects, so far described, that can occur to 1 bit, apply to the various protocol data units (PDUs) of the OSI model. Eight bits equal 1 byte. Multiple bytes equal 1 frame (see Figure 4-24). Frames contain datagrams, or packets. Packets carry the message you want to communicate. Networking professionals often talk about attenuated, reflected, noisy, dispersed, and collided frames and packets.

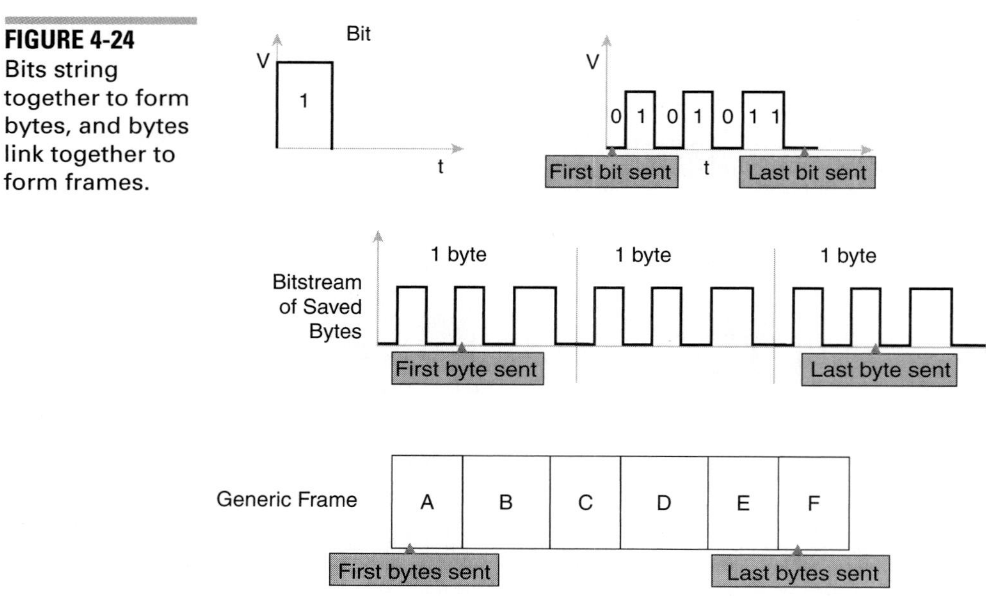

FIGURE 4-24 Bits string together to form bytes, and bytes link together to form frames.

Encoding Networking Signals

When you want to send a message over a long distance, you must solve two problems: first, how to express the message (encoding or modulation), and second, which method to use to transport the message (carrier). Throughout history, there have been a variety of ways in which the problem of carrying a long-distance communication has been solved: runners, riders, horses, optical telescopes, carrier pigeons, smoke signals, and so on. Each method of delivery requires a form of encoding. For example, smoke signals announcing that good hunting has just been found might be three short puffs of smoke. A carrier pigeon message that someone has reached a destination safely might be a picture of a smiling face. In more modern times, the creation of Morse code revolutionized communications. Two symbols, the dot and the dash, are used to encode the alphabet. For example, ×××- - - ××× means SOS, the universal distress signal (see Figure 4-25). Modern telephones, FAX, AM radio, FM radio, short wave radio, and TV all encode their signals electronically. Typically, they use the modulation of waves from different parts of the electromagnetic spectrum.

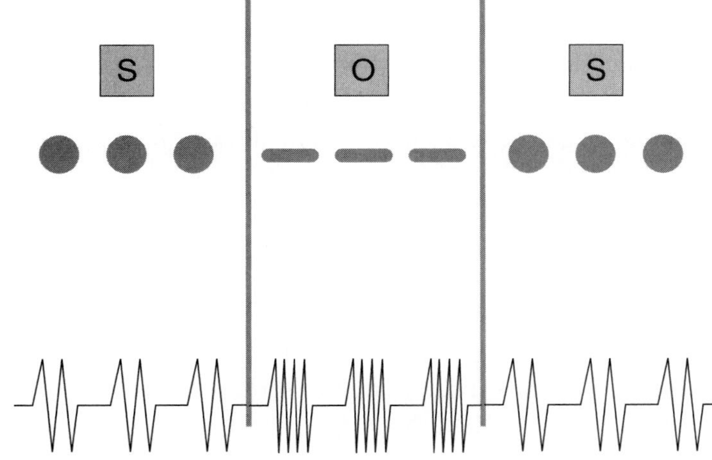

FIGURE 4-25
Historical versions of transmitting signals with encoding.

Encoding means to convert binary data into a form that can travel on a physical communications link. Modulation means using the binary data to manipulate an analog wave. Computers use three particular technologies, all of which have their counterparts in history. These technologies are as follows: encoding messages as voltages on various forms of copper wire; encoding messages as pulses of guided light on optical fibers; and modulating messages as radiated electromagnetic waves.

Encoding

Encoding means converting 1s and 0s into something real and physical, such as the following:

- An electrical pulse on a wire
- A light pulse on an optical fiber
- Electromagnetic waves into space

Two methods of accomplishing this are *transistor-transistor logic (TTL)* encoding and *Manchester encoding*. Figure 4-26 illustrates these and other methods.

TTL Encoding

TTL encoding is the simplest. It is characterized by a high signal and a low signal (often +5 or +3.3 V for binary 1 and 0 V for binary 0). In optical fibers, binary 1 might be a bright LED or laser light, and binary 0 dark or no light. In wireless networks, binary 1 might mean a carrier wave is present, and binary 0 no carrier at all.

Manchester Encoding

Manchester encoding is more complex, but is more immune to noise and is better at remaining synchronized. In Manchester encoding, the voltage on copper wire or the brightness of LED or laser light in optical fiber has the bits encoded as transitions. Observe that the Manchester encoding results in 1 being encoded as a low-to-high transition and 0 being encoded as a high-to-low transition.

A mid-bit transtion is guaranteed to be there that allows the timing to be recovered from the received signal.The receiver knows that there will be a transition and, hence, can use that knowledge to remain synchronized with the transmitter. The information, then, is contained in the direction of the guaranteed state change. In fact, this method of bit synchronization is often called "guaranteed state change."

Modulation

Closely related to encoding is modulation, which specifically means taking a wave and changing (or modulating) it so that it carries information. To give you an idea of what modulation is, examine three forms of modifying (or modulating) a carrier wave to encode bits:

- **AM (amplitude modulation)**—The modulation, or height, of a carrier sine wave is varied to carry the message.
- **FM (frequency modulation)**—The frequency, or wigglyness, of the carrier wave is varied to carry the message.
- **PM (phase modulation)**—The phase, or beginning and ending points of a given cycle, of the wave is varied to carry the message.

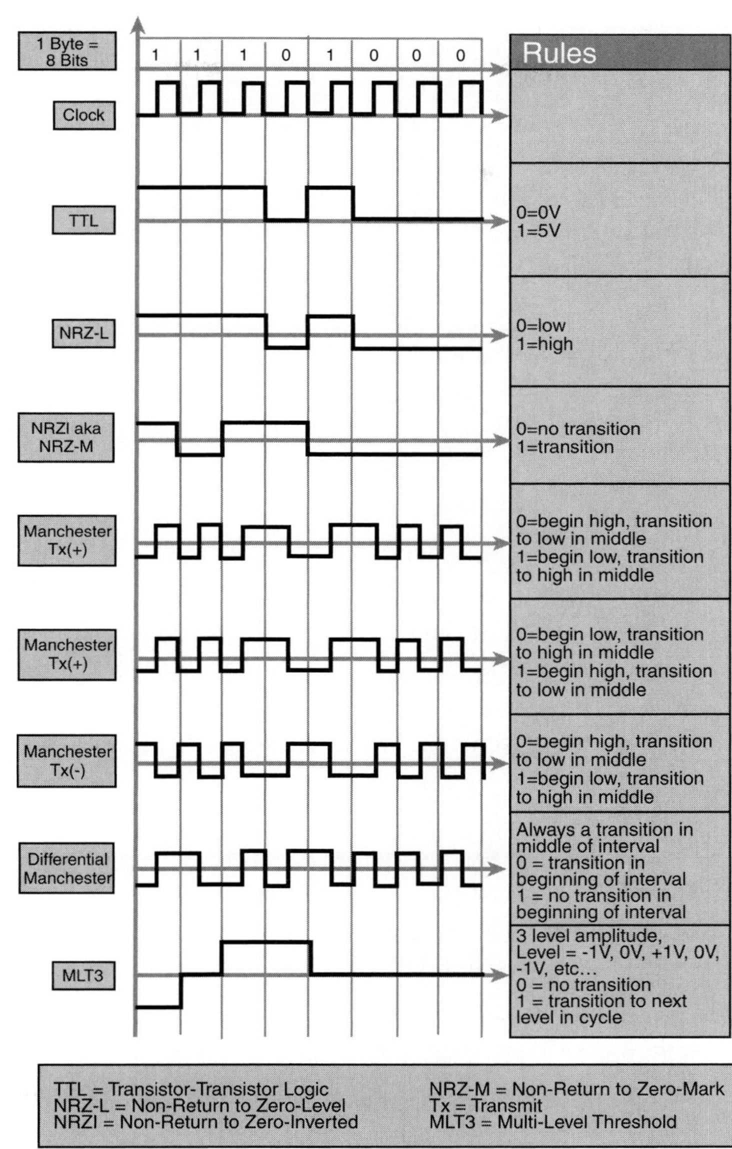

FIGURE 4-26
The primary methods of encoding.

Other more complex forms of modulation also exist. Figure 4-27 shows three ways binary data can be encoded onto a carrier wave by the process of modulation. Binary 11 (read as one one, not eleven!) can be communicated on a wave by either AM (wave on/wave off), FM (wave wiggles a lot for 1s, a little for 0s), or PM (one type of phase change for 0s, another for 1s).

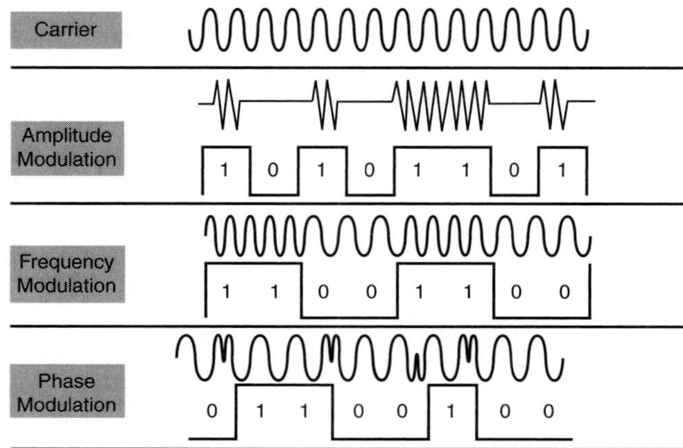

FIGURE 4-27 Three ways for encoding binary data into a carrier wave.

Messages can be encoded in a variety of ways:

- As a voltage level, as with TTL and NRZ-L
- As transition or lack of, as with NRZI and differential manchester
- By the direction of the transition, as with Machester

Manchester and NRZI encoding are popular on copper-based networks. Manchester and 4B/5B encoding are popular on fiber-based networks. Last, a variety of encoding schemes (variations on AM, FM, and PM) are used on wireless networks.

Summary

This chapter provided you with the basic theory of electricity and the factors that affect data transmission. More specifically, you learned the following:

- Electricity is based on the ability of electrons of certain types of atoms to separate, or flow, from the confines of these atoms.
- Opposite charges attract and like charges repel. Electricity flows from negative to positive within electrical circuits.
- Materials can be classified as either insulators, conductors, or semiconductors, depending on their ability to allow electrons to flow.
- The concepts of voltage, current, resistance, and impedance provide a means of measuring electricity, which is required to be able to design and manufacture electronic devices.

- Alternating current and direct current are the two types of current. AC provides power to our homes, schools, and work places. DC is used with electrical devices that depend on a battery to function.
- Electrical grounds provide a baseline from which to measure voltage. They also are used as a safety mechanism to prevent hazardous shocks.
- All electronic equipment is composed of electrical circuits that regulate the flow of electricity via switches.
- The computer converts the binary number to a digital signal.
- When a computer attached to a network receives data in the form of digital signals, it recognizes the data by measuring and comparing the voltage signals it receives to a reference point called the signal reference ground.
- Ideally, the signal reference ground should be completely isolated from the electrical ground. Isolation keeps AC power leakage and voltage spikes off the signal reference ground.
- If not properly addressed, power line noise can present serious problems for a network.
- The five types of noise are NEXT, thermal noise, AC power/reference, ground noise, and EMI/RFI.
- Timing problems include dispersion, jitter, and latency.
- Collisions occur when two bits from two different communicating computers simultaneously propagate on a shared medium.

The next chapter discusses the different types of networking media that are used at the physical layer. In addition, it describes how network devices, cable specifications, network topologies, collisions, and collision domains can help determine such things as how much data can travel across the network and how fast.

Check Your Understanding

1. Match the columns:

1) Nucleus	a) Particles that have a negative charge, and orbit the nucleus
2) Protons	b) Particles that have no charge (neutral), and along with protons, form the nucleus
3) Neutrons	c) The center part of the atom, formed by protons and neutrons
4)Electrons	d) Particles that have a positive charge and, along with neutrons, form the nucleus

A. 1-c, 2-d, 3-b, 4-a

B. 1-d, 2-c, 3-a, 4-b

C. 1-c, 2-b, 3-d, 4-a

D. 1-a, 2-c, 3-b, 4-d

2. Which of the following statements regarding static electricity is untrue?

A. Opposite charges react to each other with a force that causes them to be attracted to each other.

B. Like charges react to each other with a force that causes them to repel each other.

C. In the case of opposite and like charges, the force increases as the charges move closer to each other.

D. None of the above.

3. Which of the following statements regarding static electricity is untrue?

A. Static electricity is also called electrostatic discharge.

B. Static electricity is harmless to humans and equipment.

C. ESD causes a small electric shock.

D. None of the above.

4. Match the following to their respective units of measurement:

1) Voltage	a) Ohm
2) Current	b) Ampere
3) Resistance	c) Volt

A. 1-c, 2-b, 3-a

B. 1-b, 2-c, 3-a

C. 1-a, 2-c, 3-b

D. 1-c, 2-b, 3-a

5. What kind of power is supplied to the microchips on the motherboard of a computer?

A. AC

B. DC

C. RC

D. MC

6. An oscilloscope cannot be used to measure which of the following:

A. Voltage

B. Resistance

C. Current

D. None of the above

7. Where is the safety ground connected for a computer?

A. Exposed metal parts

B. The monitor

C. The mouse

D. The network connection

8. Electrons flow in ______ loops called ______.

A. Open; voltage

B. Closed; voltage

C. Open; circuits

D. Closed; circuits

9. A half-duplex circuit means
   A. Only one side can talk at a time
   B. The signal strength is cut in half
   C. The signal strength is doubled
   D. Two hosts can talk simultaneously
10. Attenuation means
   A. Travel
   B. Delay
   C. A signal losing strength over distance
   D. Loss of signal due to EMI
11. What is ideal about the signal reference ground?
   A. Signal reference ground is the ground voltage of 0 volts.
   B. Signal reference should be completely isolated from the electrical ground.
   C. Signal reference ground is a voltage of +5 volts.
   D. None of the above.
12. Which of the following is an external source of electrical impulses that can attack the quality of electrical signals on a cable?
   A. EMI caused by electrical motors
   B. RFI caused by electrical motors
   C. Impedance caused by radio systems
   D. EMI caused by lightning
13. What is the primary cause of crosstalk?
   A. Cable wires that are too large in diameter
   B. Too much noise in a cable's data signal
   C. Electrical motors and lighting
   D. Electrical signals from other wires in a cable

14. Which of the following describes cancellation?

A. Wires in the same circuit cancel each other's electrical current flow.

B. Cancellation is a commonly used technique to protect the wire from undesirable interference.

C. The magnetic fields from one cable run cancel magnetic fields of another cable run.

D. External magnetic fields cancel the fields inside network cabling.

15. What is it called when two bits from two different communicating computers are on a shared medium at the same time?

A. Latency

B. Dispersion

C. Collision

D. Obstruction

16. Reflection does not occur with what kind of signals?

A. Electrical

B. Radio waves

C. Microwaves

D. None of the above

17. _______ means to convert binary data into a form that can travel on a physical communications link.

A. Encoding

B. Decoding

C. Encrypting

D. Decrypting

18. On copper-based networks, commonly, encoding is done using

A. Manchester and NRZI

B. 4B/5B

C. AM, FM, and PM

D. All of the above

19. On fiber-based networks, commonly, encoding is done using
    - **A.** Manchester and NRZI
    - **B.** Manchester and 4B/5B
    - **C.** AM, FM, and PM
    - **D.** All of the above
20. On wireless networks, commonly, encoding is done using
    - **A.** Manchester and NRZI
    - **B.** 4B/5B
    - **C.** AM, FM, and PM
    - **D.** All of the above

Objectives

After reading this chapter, you will be able to

- Describe LAN media
- Understand cable specifications and cable termination
- Describe how to make and test cable
- Describe LAN technologies
- Describe Layer 1 components and devices
- Understand collisions and collision domains
- Describe the basic topologies used in networking

Chapter 5

Layer 1: Media, Connections, and Collisions

Introduction

Like a well-constructed house, a network must be built on a solid foundation. In the OSI reference model, this foundation is called *Layer 1* or the *physical layer*. This chapter describes how network functions are linked to Layer 1 of the OSI reference model. The physical layer is the layer that defines electrical, mechanical, procedural, and functional specifications for activating, maintaining, and deactivating the physical link between end systems.

In this chapter, you learn about the network functions that occur at the physical layer of the OSI model. You learn about different types of networking media that are used at the physical layer, including shielded twisted-pair cable, unshielded twisted-pair cable, coaxial cable, and fiber-optic cable. In addition, you learn how network devices, cable specifications, network topologies, collisions, and collision domains can help determine how fast data can travel across the network.

LAN Media

The function of the physical layer is to transmit data. Data, which can be such information as text, pictures, and sounds, is represented by the presence of either electrical pulses, referred to as voltage, on copper conducting wires or light pulses within optical fibers. This transmission process, referred to as *encoding* or *modulation*, is accomplished by using cables and connectors. These Layer 1 devices help to comprise LAN media.

LAN media refers to the various physical environments through which transmission signals pass. For computers to communicate encoded information with each other, networking media must connect them physically together. The LAN media used to connect computers varies greatly. The following cable types can be used to connect computers:

- Shielded twisted-pair cable
- Unshielded twisted-pair cable
- Coaxial cable
- Fiber-optic cable

Shielded Twisted-Pair Cable

Shielded twisted-pair (STP) cable combines the techniques of shielding and cancellation via the twisting of wires. Each pair of wires is wrapped in metallic foil, as shown in Figure 5-1. The four pairs of wires are wrapped in an overall metallic braid or foil. (It is normally 150Ohm cable.) STP reduces electrical noise originating inside the cable (crosstalk) and outside the cable (electromagnetic interference [EMI] and radio frequency interference [RFI]). Shielded twisted-pair cable shares many of the advantages and disadvantages of unshielded twisted-pair (UTP) cable. STP affords greater protection from all types of external interference, but it is more expensive and difficult to install than UTP.

FIGURE 5-1
STP often is used for LocalTalk and Token Ring networks.

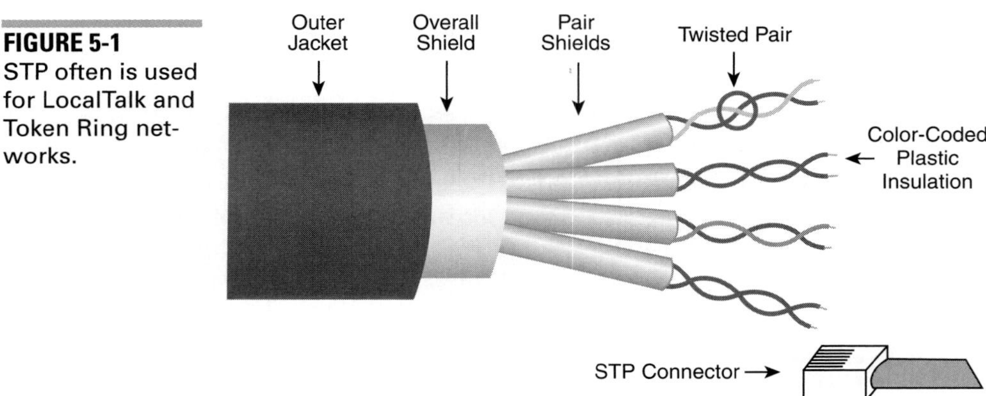

A new hybrid of UTP with traditional STP is screened UTP (ScTP), also known as foil twisted-pair (FTP). ScTP is essentially UTP wrapped in a metallic foil shield, or "screen," as shown in Figure 5-2. (It is usually 100- or 120-Ohm cable.)

The metallic shielding materials in STP and ScTP need to be grounded at both ends. However, 10 Mbps Ethernet, which is still common, needs only one end to be grounded for proper operation. If improperly grounded or if any discontinuities exist in the entire length of the shielding material (likely due to poor termination or installation), STP and ScTP become susceptible to experiencing major noise problems because the shield acts like an antenna, picking up unwanted signals. However, the effect of shielding works both ways. Not only does the foil (shield or screen) prevent incoming electromagnetic waves from causing noise on data wires, it minimizes the outgoing radiated electromagnetic waves, which can cause noise in other devices. Like UTP, you cannot run STP and ScTP cable as far as some other types of networking media, such as

FIGURE 5-2
The maximum cable length for STP and ScTP is 100 m.

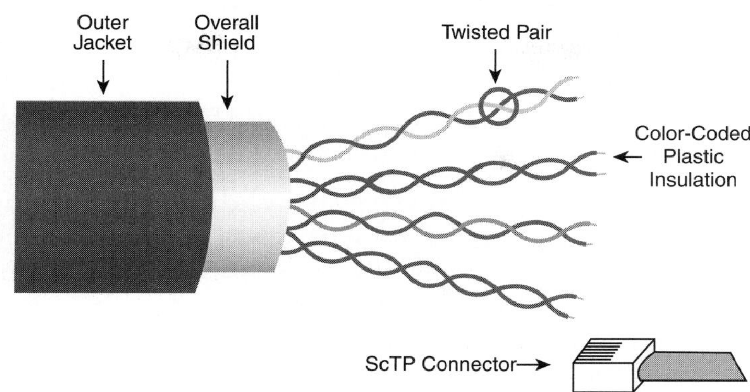

coaxial cable and optical fiber, without the signal being repeated. Also, the insulation and shielding add considerably to the size, weight, and cost of the cable. And the shielding materials make terminations more difficult and susceptible to poor workmanship. However, STP and ScTP still have a role—for example, a wide base of these types of installations exist in Europe.

Unshielded Twisted-Pair Cable

As shown in Figure 5-3, unshielded twisted-pair (UTP) cable is a four-pair wire medium used in a variety of networks. Insulating material covers each of the eight individual copper wires in the UTP cable. In addition, each pair of wires is twisted around each other. This type of cable relies solely on the cancellation effect, produced by the twisted wire pairs, to limit signal degradation caused by EMI and RFI. To further reduce crosstalk between the pairs in UTP cable, the number of twists in the wire pairs varies. Like STP cable, UTP cable must follow precise specifications as to how many twists or braids are permitted per foot of cable.

FIGURE 5-3
A variety of networks use UTP, which is a type of four-pair wire medium.

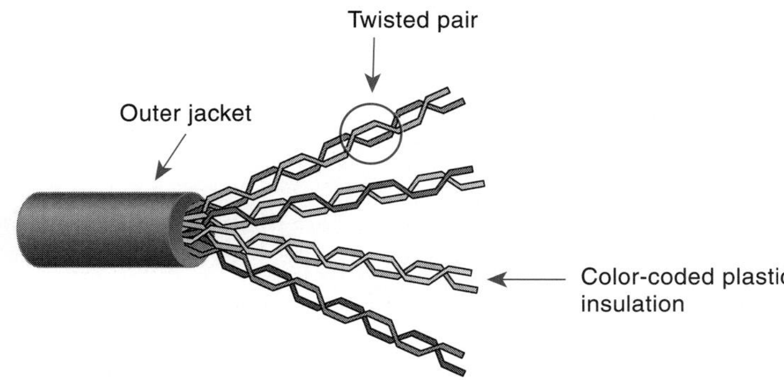

When used as a networking medium, UTP cable has four pairs of either 22- or 24-gauge copper wire. UTP has an impedance of 100 ohms. This differentiates it from other types of twisted-pair wiring, such as telephone wiring.

Because UTP has an external diameter of approximately .43 cm, its small size is an advantage for installations. Because UTP can be used with most of the major networking architectures, it continues to dominate as a LAN media.

Unshielded twisted-pair cable has many advantages. It is easy to install and is less expensive than other types of networking media. In fact, UTP typically costs less per meter than any other type of LAN cabling. However, the real advantages of UTP include the size versus thicknet, the fact that the wiring methods are well understood because the technology has been used by the PSTN for so long, and the physical topology used with UTP, which is considered better for troubleshooting.

Because it has such a small external diameter, UTP does not fill up wiring ducts as rapidly as other types of cable. This is an extremely important factor to consider, particularly when installing a network in an older building. Moreover, UTP cable often is installed using a registered jack (RJ) connector (shown in Figure 5-4). RJ connectors are standard connectors originally used to connect telephone lines and are now used in connecting networks.

FIGURE 5-4
UTP uses RJ connectors.

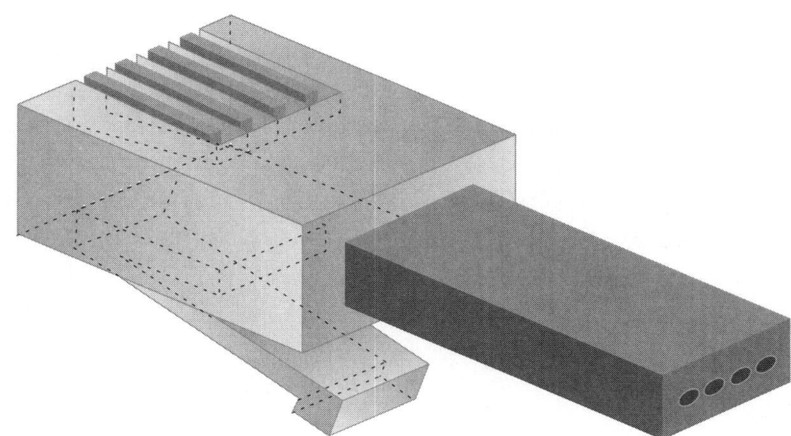

Using twisted-pair cabling does have its disadvantages. UTP cable is more prone to electrical noise and interference than other types of networking media, and the distance between signal boosts is shorter for UTP than it is for coaxial and fiber-optic cables. UTP once was considered to be relatively slow at transmitting data compared to other types of copper cable. However, this is no longer true. In fact, today, UTP is considered to be the fastest copper-based media.

Coaxial Cable

Coaxial cable, illustrated in Figure 5-5, consists of a hollow outer cylindrical conductor that surrounds a single inner wire conductor—the two conductors are separated by insulation. In the center of the cable is a single copper wire. A layer of flexible insulation surrounds it. Over this insulating material, a woven copper braid or metallic foil acts as the second of two wires in the circuit. It also acts as a shield for the inner conductor. This second layer, or shield, helps reduce the amount of outside interference. The cable jacket covers this shield.

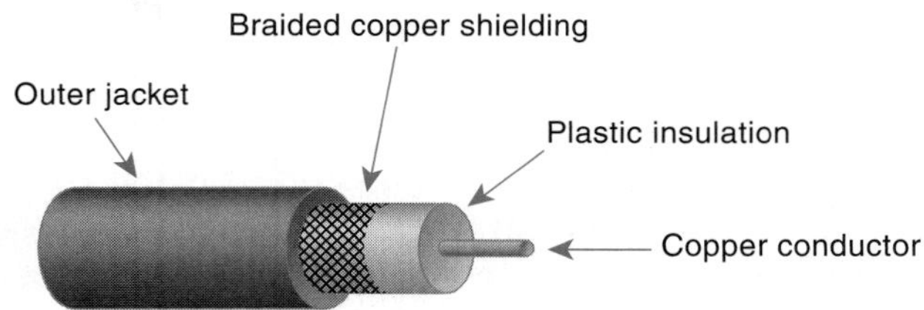

FIGURE 5-5
Coaxial cable is made up of a single inner wire conductor that is surrounded by a hollow cylindrical conductor.

For LANs, coaxial cable offers several advantages. It can be run (without boosts from repeaters) for longer distances between network nodes than either STP or UTP cable. Repeaters regenerate the signals in a network so they can cover greater distances.

Coaxial cable is less expensive than fiber-optic cable, and the technology is well known. It has been used for many years for various types of data communication. Can you think of another type of communication that utilizes coaxial cable?

When working with cable, it is important to consider its size. As the thickness (or diameter) increases, so does the difficulty in physically handling the cable. Keep in mind that cable must be pulled through conduits and troughs that are limited in size. Coaxial cable comes in a variety of sizes. This type of coaxial cable frequently is referred to as *thicknet*. As its nickname suggests, this type of cable, because of its thickness, can be too rigid to allow for an easy installation install. The rule of thumb: The more difficult the network media is to install, the more expensive it is to install. Coaxial cable is more expensive to install than twisted-pair cable. Thicknet cable is practically never used anymore, except for special purpose installations.

Coaxial cable with an outside diameter of only .35 cm (sometimes referred to as *thinnet*) was used in Ethernet networks. It was useful especially for cable installations that required the cable to make many twists and turns. Because it was easier to install than Thicknet, it also was cheaper to install. This led some people to refer to it as *cheapernet*. However, because the outer copper or metallic braid in coaxial cable comprises half the electrical circuit, special care must be taken to ensure that it is grounded properly. This is done by ensuring that a solid electrical connection exists at both ends of the cable. Frequently, installers fail to do this.

As a result, poor shield connection is one of the most common connection problems involved with the installation of coaxial cable. Connection problems result in electrical noise that interferes with signal transmission on the networking media. For this reason, despite its small diameter, thinnet is no longer used much in Ethernet networks.

Fiber-Optic Cable

Fiber-optic cable, illustrated in Figure 5-6, is a networking medium capable of conducting modulated light transmission. It is more expensive than other networking media; however, it is not susceptible to electromagnetic or radio frequency interference and is capable of higher data rates than the other types of networking media. Fiber-optic cable does not carry electrical pulses as do other forms of networking media that employ copper wire. Instead, signals that represent bits are converted into pulses of light. Although light is an electromagnetic wave, light within a fiber is not considered wireless communication because the electromagnetic waves are guided through the optical fiber. The term *wireless* is reserved for radiated, or unguided, electromagnetic waves.

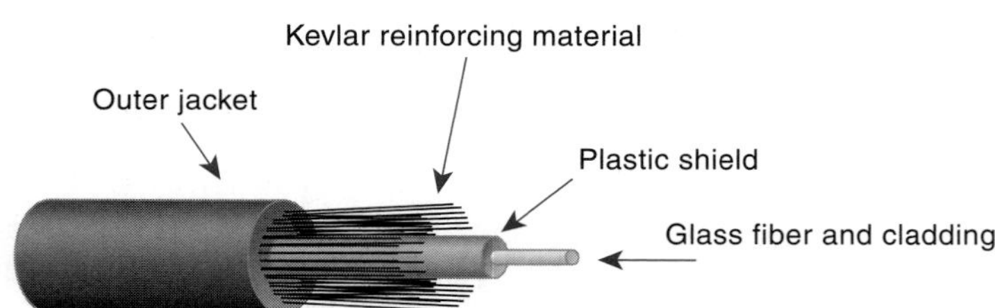

FIGURE 5-6
Fiber-optic cable is a networking medium capable of carrying modulated light transmissions.

Fiber-optic communication is rooted in a number of inventions made in the last century. It was not until the 1960s, when solid-state laser light sources and high-quality impurity-free glasses were introduced, that fiber-optic communication became practical. Its use on a widespread basis was pioneered by telephone companies that realized its benefits for long-distance communication.

Fiber-optic cable used for networking consists of two fibers encased in separate sheaths. If you view it in a cross section, you can see that layers of protective buffer material, usually a plastic (such as Kevlar), and an outer jacket surround each optical fiber. The outer jacket provides protection for the entire cable. Usually made of plastic, it conforms to appropriate fire and building codes. The purpose of the Kevlar is to furnish additional cushioning and protection for the fragile hair-thin glass fibers. Where buried fiber-optic cables are required, a stainless steel wire is sometimes included for added strength.

The light-guiding parts of an optical fiber are called the *core* and the *cladding*. The core is usually pure glass with a high index of refraction. When a cladding layer of glass or plastic with a low index of refraction surrounds the core glass, light can be trapped in the fiber core. This process is called total internal reflection, and it allows the optical fiber to act like a light pipe, guiding light for tremendous distances, even around bends.

MORE INFORMATION

Fiber-Optic Mode Types and Light Sources

Fiber-optic mode types include the following:

- **Single mode**—Single mode also is called axial because the light travels down the axis of the cable.
- **Multimode**—In multimode fiber, light waves enter the glass pipe at different angles and travel nonaxially, which means they bounce back and forth off the walls of the glass tube.

Single-mode fiber is faster than multimode (up to 10 Gbps) because of the *dispersion* (scattering or separation of light waves) in multimode caused by the light pulses arriving at the end of the cable at different times. Single mode typically is used for WANs (for example, telephone company switch-to-switch connections). Multimode often is used in LANs.

The reason why single-mode fiber is faster is that it is so much smaller in diameter than multimode fiber. Single-mode fiber allows only a single mode or color of light; it is so narrow that the bouncing around and, thus, the dispersion that limits the frequencies cannot occur. Multimode fiber is much larger and multiple modes of light can pass. The light waves have room to bounce around, losing energy and spreading out the pulse.

Fiber-optic transmission can be categorized by the type of light source used:

- **LED (light emitting diode)**—LED commonly is used with multimode fiber.
- **ILD (injection laser diode)**—ILD emits a strong, intense, narrowly focused light beam. It commonly is used with single-mode fiber but also is used with multimode.

Both lasers and single-mode fiber add to the cost; however, you can achieve higher data rates.

Wireless Communication

Wireless signals are electromagnetic waves that can travel through the vacuum of outer space and through media, such as the air in our atmosphere. Therefore, no cable medium is necessary for wireless signals. This makes wireless communication a versatile means of building a network. Figure 5-7 represents an electromagnetic wave.

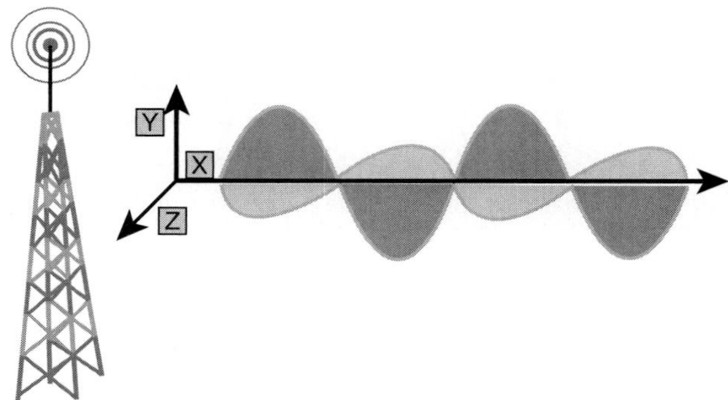

FIGURE 5-7
Encoding signals as electromagnetic waves.

Power waves, radio waves, microwaves, infrared light waves, visible light waves, ultraviolet light waves, x-rays, and gamma rays are distinct components of the electromagnetic spectrum; however, they share some important characteristics:

- These waves have an energy pattern similar to that represented in Figure 5-7.
- These waves travel at the speed of light (c = 299, 792, 458 meters per second) in a vacuum. This speed might more accurately be called the speed of electromagnetic waves.
- These waves obey the equation (frequency) × (wavelength) = c.
- These waves can travel through a vacuum; however, they interact differently with various materials.

The primary way of distinguishing between the different electromagnetic waves is by their frequency. Low frequency electromagnetic waves have a long wavelength (the distance from one peak to the next on the corresponding sine wave), whereas high frequency electromagnetic waves have a short wavelength.

MORE INFORMATION

Wireless Transmission Methods

Laser

Laser is an acronym for "light amplification by stimulated emission of radiation." A laser outputs a coherent (focused) electromagnetic energy field in which all waves are at the same frequency and are aligned in phase.

Infrared

Infrared, like laser, is normally a line-of-sight technology. However, in some implementations, the signal can be bounced or redirected. Even in these implementations, however, infrared cannot go through opaque objects, such as walls.

Radio

Radio waves can carry data signals and can pass through walls. There are both terrestrial and satellite radio technologies.

A common application of wireless data communication is mobile use. Some examples of mobile use include the following:

- Cars or airplanes
- Satellites
- Remote space probes
- Space shuttles and space stations
- Anyone/anything/anywhere/anytime that requires network data

Another common application of wireless data communication is wireless LANs (WLANs), which are built in accordance with the IEEE 802.11 standards. WLANs typically use radio waves (for example, 902 MHz), microwaves (for example, 2.4 GHz), and infrared waves (for example, 820 nanometers) for communication. Wireless technologies are a crucial part of the future of networking.

MORE INFORMATION

Selecting the Right Networking Media

Various criteria, such as rate of data transfer and cost, help determine which networking medium should be used. The type of connecting material used in a network determines such things as how much data can travel across the network and how quickly. Other factors, such as expense and where the cable is used, are important as well.

MORE INFORMATION (CONTINUED)

To ensure optimal performance, it is important for the networking media to carry the signal from one device to another with as little degradation as possible. In networking, several factors can cause the signal to degrade. All networking media use shielding and/or cancellation techniques to prevent signal degradation. However, the differences in the types of shielding and cancellation used in various networking media cause cables to differ in size, cost, and difficulty of installation.

In addition, networking media can employ different types of cable jackets. The jacket is the outside covering of the cable, which usually is made of some form of plastic, nonstick coating, or composite material. When designing a LAN, it is important to remember that networking media installed between walls, in an elevator shaft, or passing through an air-handling unit could become a torch capable of carrying fire from one part of a building to another. Moreover, plastic cable jackets can create toxic smoke when they burn. To guard against such occurrences, fire codes, building codes, and safety standards have been implemented that govern the type of cable jackets that can be used. Therefore, adherence to such codes must be taken into consideration (along with such factors as cable size, speed, cost, and difficulty of installation) when determining what type of networking media to use in a LAN.

To understand this concept of selecting networking media more fully, think of two cities located several miles apart. Although they are several miles apart, the cities are connected to each other by means of roads. Some of the roads might be basic in terms of size and the types of materials used to construct them; an example of this is an unimproved one-lane gravel road. Other roads might be larger in size and constructed of more sophisticated materials; an example of this is a reinforced, concrete, four-lane superhighway.

If you are interested in taking a leisurely Sunday afternoon sightseeing drive from City A to City B, you might choose the unimproved one-lane gravel road for your trip. On the other hand, if you drive an ambulance in City A and need to deliver a critically ill patient to a hospital in City B, it is foolhardy to follow the same route. Because it is faster, smoother, and wider, the four-lane superhighway could accommodate your needs as an ambulance driver, whereas the one-lane country road would not. The cities are like two computers trying to communicate, and the roads are like networking media operating at the physical layer. As in the cities and roads example, the type of connecting material used by a network determines the amount of data that can travel across the network and its speed.

Cable Specification and Termination

Until recently, there was a somewhat confusing mix of standards governing networking media. Standards ranged from fire and building codes to detailed electrical specifications. Others focused on tests to ensure safety and performance.

As you design and build networks, make sure you comply with all applicable fire codes, building codes, and safety standards. You also should follow any established performance standards to ensure optimal network operation and, because of the variety of options available today in networking media, to ensure compatibility and interoperability. Your work in this curriculum focuses on the standards for networking media that were developed and issued by the following groups:

- **IEEE**—Institute of Electrical and Electronics Engineers
- **UL**—Underwriters Laboratories
- **EIA**—Electronic Industries Alliance
- **TIA**—Telecommunications Industry Association
- **ANSI**—American National Standards Institute

The latter two organizations jointly issued a list of standards that you often see listed as the TIA/EIA standards. In addition to these groups and organizations, local, state, county, and national government agencies issue specifications and requirements that can impact the type of cabling that can be used in a LAN.

The IEEE has outlined cabling requirements in its 802.3 and 802.5 specifications for Ethernet and Token Ring systems, and other standards for FDDI. Underwriters Laboratories issues cabling specifications that are concerned primarily with safety standards; however, they also rate twisted-pair networking media for performance. The Underwriters Laboratories established an identification program that lists markings for shielded and unshielded twisted-pair networking media to simplify the job of ensuring that materials used in LAN installations meet specifications.

TIA/EIA Standards

Of all the organizations mentioned here, the TIA/EIA has the greatest impact on networking media standards. Specifically, TIA/EIA-568-A and TIA/EIA-569-A have been and continue to be the most widely used standards for technical performance of networking media.

The TIA/EIA standards specify the minimum requirements for multi-product and multi-vendor environments. They allow for the planning and the installation of LAN systems without dictating the use of specific equipment, thus giving LAN designers the freedom to create options for improvement and expansion.

TIA/EIA-568-A

The TIA/EIA standards address six elements of the LAN cabling process. These are:

- Horizontal cabling
- Telecommunications closets
- Backbone cabling
- Equipment rooms
- Work areas
- Entrance facilities

This book focuses on TIA/EIA-568-A standards for horizontal cabling, which defines horizontal cabling as cabling that runs from a telecommunications outlet to a horizontal cross-connect. It includes the networking medium that runs along a horizontal pathway, the telecommunications outlet or connector, the mechanical terminations in the wiring closet, and the patch cords or jumpers in the wiring closet. In short, horizontal cabling includes the networking media that is used in the area that extends from the wiring closet to a workstation. Figure 5-8 shows horizontal cabling, which typically runs from the wiring closet to a single workstation.

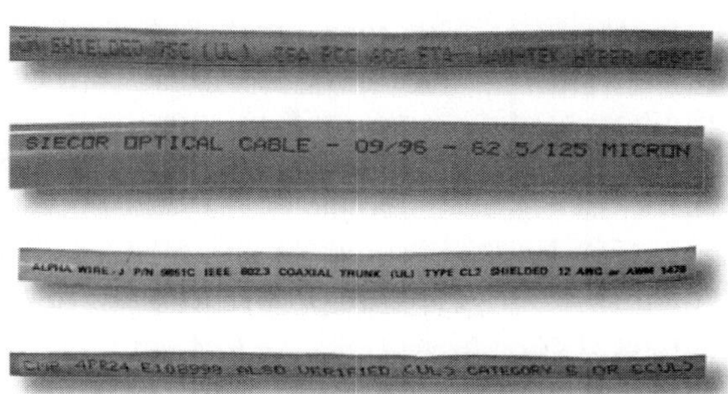

FIGURE 5-8 Horizontal cabling with marking specified for shielded twisted-pair (STP) and unshielded twisted-pair (UTP) cables.

TIA/EIA-568-A contains specifications governing cable performance. It calls for running two cables, one for voice and one for data, to each outlet. Of the two cables, the one for voice must be four-pair UTP. The TIA/EIA-568-A standard specifies five categories in the specifications. These are category 1 (CAT 1), category 2 (CAT 2), category 3 (CAT 3), category 4 (CAT 4), and category 5 (CAT 5) cabling. Of these, only CAT 3, CAT 4, and CAT 5 qualify for use in

LANs. Of these three categories, CAT 5 is by far the most frequently recommended and implemented in installations today. The networking media that are recognized by TIA/EIA, as shown in Figure 5-9, are:

- Shielded twisted-pair cable
- Unshielded twisted-pair cable
- Screened twisted-pair cable
- Fiber-optic cable
- Coaxial cable

FIGURE 5-9
Common networking media include coaxial, twisted-pair, and fiber-optic cable.

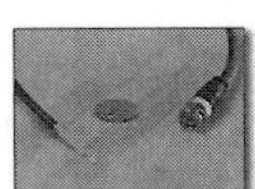

Coaxial

Unshielded twisted-pair

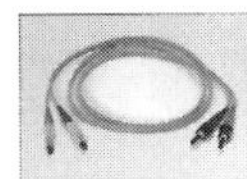

Fiber-optic

For shielded twisted-pair cable, the TIA/EIA-568-A standard calls for two pairs of 150-ohm cable. For unshielded twisted-pair cable, the standard calls for four pairs of 100-ohm cable, which is shown in Figure 5-10.

FIGURE 5-10
100-ohm UTP cable containing four pairs.

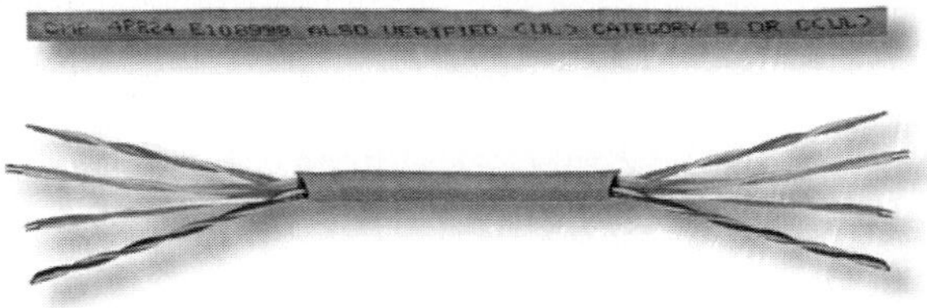

For fiber-optic, the standard calls for two fibers of 62.5/125 multimode cable, which is shown in Figure 5-11.

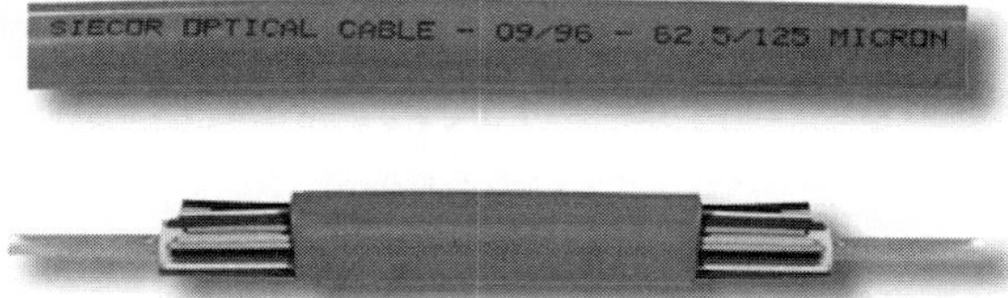

FIGURE 5-11 62.5/125 multimode fiber-optic cable.

Although 50-ohm coaxial cable, which is shown in Figure 5-12, is a recognized type of networking media in TIA/EIA-568-A, it is not recommended for new installations. Moreover, this type of coaxial cable is expected to be removed from the list of recognized networking media in the next revision of this standard.

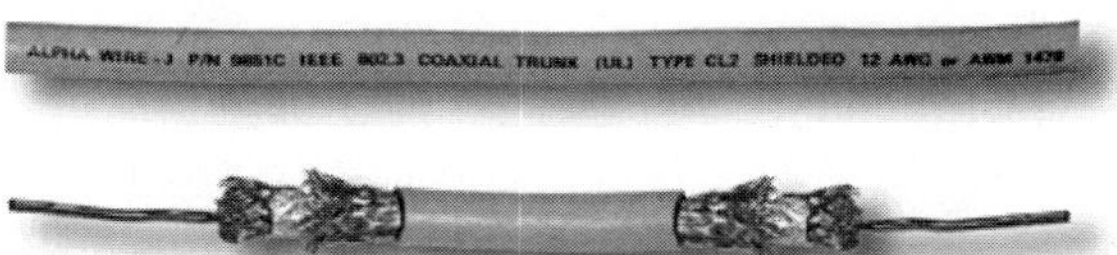

FIGURE 5-12 50-ohm coaxial cable is not recommended for new installations.

For the horizontal cabling component, TIA/EIA-568-A requires a minimum of two telecommunications outlets or connectors at each work area. Two cables support this telecommunications outlet/connector. The first is a four-pair, 100-ohm CAT 3 or higher UTP cable along with its appropriate connector (see Figure 5-13). The second can be any one of the following:

- Four-pair, 100-ohm unshielded twisted-pair cable and its appropriate connector
- 150-ohm shielded twisted-pair cable and its appropriate connector
- Coaxial cable and its appropriate connector
- Two-fiber, 62.5/125 µ optical fiber cable and its appropriate connector

According to TIA/EIA-568-A, the maximum distance for UTP cable runs in horizontal cabling is 90 meters (m). This is true for all types of CAT 5 UTP networking media. The standard also specifies that patch cords or cross-connect jumpers located at the horizontal cross-connect cannot exceed 6 m in length. TIA/EIA-568-A also allows 3 m for patch cords that connect equipment at the work area. The total length of the patch cords and cross-connect jumpers used in the horizontal cabling cannot exceed 10 m.

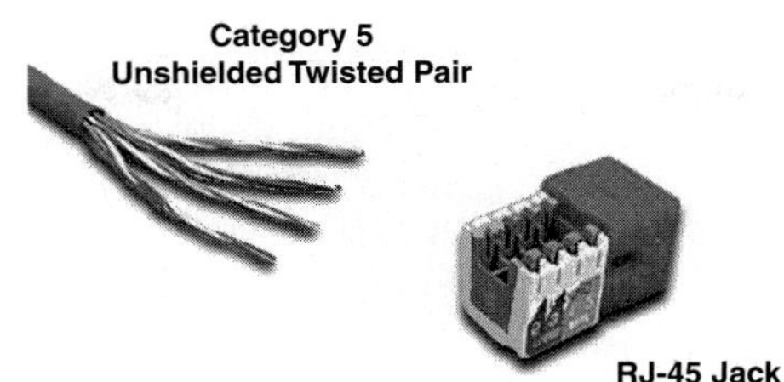

FIGURE 5-13
Category 5 UTP and an RJ45 jack.

A final specification for horizontal cabling contained in TIA/EIA-568-A requires that all grounding and bonding must conform to TIA/EIA-607 as well as to any other applicable codes. The latest industry standards being developed are for CAT 5e, CAT 6, and CAT 7 cabling, all offering improvements over CAT 5.

Differentiating Between Connections

Figure 5-14 illustrates the different connection types used by each physical layer implementation of 802.3. Of the three examples shown, the RJ-45 connector and the jack are the most prevalent. UTP implementation and the RJ-45 connector is discussed in the following section.

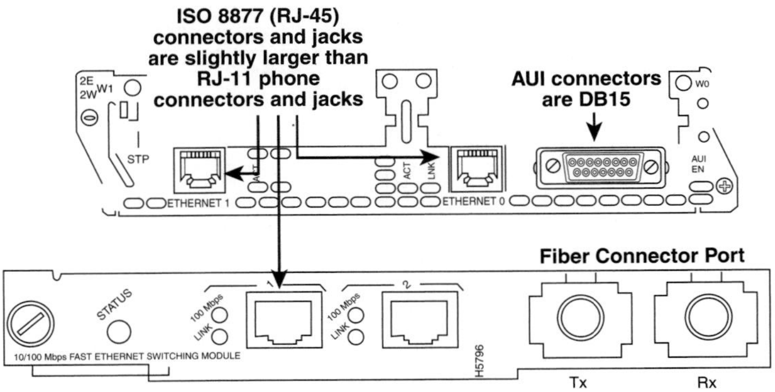

FIGURE 5-14
Connector types for Ethernet cabling.

UTP Implementation

If you look at an RJ-45 connector terminating a UTP connection, you see eight colored wires. These wires are twisted into four pairs within the outer jacket. Four of the wires are tip conductors (T1 through T4) and the other four are ring conductors (R1 through R4). *Tip* and *ring* are terms coined in the early days of the telephone. Today, these terms refer to the *positive* and *negative* wires, respectively, in a pair. The wires in the first pair in a cable or connector are designated as T1 and R1, the second pair is T2 and R2, and so on.

The RJ-45 connector is a male interface on the end of a cable. As you look at the male connector from the front, the pin locations are numbered 8 on the left down to 1 on the right.

The jack is the female component in a network device, wall or cubicle partition outlet, or patch panel. As you look at the device port, the corresponding female plug locations are 1 on the left up to 8 on the right.

For electricity to run between the connector and the jack, the order of the wires must follow the EIA/TIA-568-A and 568-B standards, as shown in Figure 5-15. In addition to identifying the correct EIA/TIA category of cable to use for connecting a device, depending on what standard is being used by the jack on the network device, you need to determine whether to use either of the following:

- A straight-through cable
- A crossover cable

FIGURE 5-15
The RJ-45 connector.

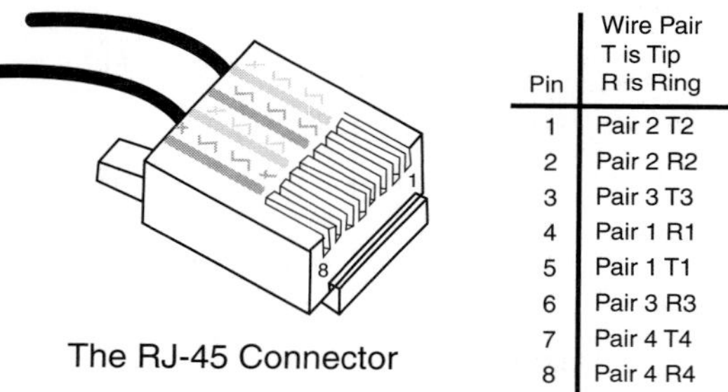

Pin	Wire Pair T is Tip R is Ring
1	Pair 2 T2
2	Pair 2 R2
3	Pair 3 T3
4	Pair 1 R1
5	Pair 1 T1
6	Pair 3 R3
7	Pair 4 T4
8	Pair 4 R4

Making and Testing Cable

As you learned earlier, the foundation of the OSI reference model is the networking media; every other layer of that model depends on and is supported by the networking media. You read that a network is only as reliable as its cabling—according to many experts, the network's cabling is the most important component of the network.

Therefore, after the networking media is installed, it is important to determine how reliable your network's cables are. Even with a great investment in the best-quality cable, connectors, patch panels, and other equipment, poor installation practices can prevent your network from operating at an optimal level. Therefore, you should test the entire installation after it is in place.

When you test your network, follow these steps:

1. Break the system into logically conceived functional elements.
2. Note any symptoms.
3. Based on the symptoms you observe, determine what is the most likely dysfunctional element.
4. Use substitution or additional testing to discover whether the likely element is, in fact, dysfunctional.
5. If the element suspected of being dysfunctional proves not to be the problem, proceed to the next most likely element you suspect.
6. When you find the dysfunctional element, repair it if possible.
7. If it is not possible to repair the dysfunctional element, replace it.

The IEEE and TIA/EIA have established standards that allow you to evaluate whether your network is operating at an acceptable level after installation is completed. Provided that your network passes this test and has been certified as meeting the standards, you can use the network's initial operating level as an established baseline.

Knowing this baseline measurement is important because the need to test does not end just because your network installation is certified as meeting the standards. Continue testing your network periodically to ensure optimal network performance. You can do this by comparing recorded measurements taken when the system was known to be operating properly against current measurements. A significant drop from the baseline measurement is an indication that something is wrong with the network.

Repeated testing of your network and comparison against its baseline can help you spot specific problems and can allow you to track degradation caused by aging, poor maintenance practices, weather, or other factors. You might think testing cable is a simple matter of substituting one cable for another. However, this does not provide certain proof of anything because a common problem can affect all cables on a LAN. For this reason, it is recommended that you use a cable tester to measure network performance. Cable testers are handheld devices you can use to certify that the cable meets the required IEEE and TIA/EIA standards. Cable testers vary in the types of testing functions they provide. Some provide printouts; others can be attached to a PC to create a data file.

Cable Testers

Cable testers have a wide range of features and capabilities. Therefore, the list of things cable testers can measure is intended to give you a general overview of the available features. You need to determine what features best meet your needs and make your selection accordingly.

Generally, cable testers can perform tests that measure the overall capability of a cable run. This includes determining cable distance, locating bad connections, providing wire maps for detecting crossed pairs, measuring signal attenuation, detecting near-end crosstalk, detecting split pairs, performing noise level tests, and tracing cable behind walls.

It is important to measure the distance of the cable because the overall length of the cable runs can affect the capability of devices on the network to share the networking media. As you have learned already, cable that exceeds the maximum length specified by EIA/TIA-568A causes signal degradation.

Cable testers, referred to as *time domain reflectometers (TDRs)*, measure the distance to open-ended or shorted cable. The TDR does this by sending an electrical pulse down the cable. The device then times the signal's reflection back from the end of the cable. Distance readings provided using this technique are expected to be accurate to within 2 feet.

When you use UTP cable for a LAN installation, use distance measurements to determine whether the connections at the patch panel and at the telecommunications outlets are good. To understand how this works, you must understand more about how the TDR works.

When TDR measures distance on a cable, it sends an electrical signal that is reflected when it encounters the open connection. Imagine that you will use this device to determine which connections in a cable run are faulty. Begin by attaching the device to the patch cord at the patch panel. If the TDR reports the distance to the patch panel instead of the distance to a further point, then you know you have a connection problem. The same procedure can be used at the opposite end of the cable to measure through the RJ-45 jack located at the telecommunications outlet.

Wire Maps

Cable testers use a *wire map* to indicate which wire pairs connect to what pins on lugs or sockets. This test shows whether an installer connected wires to a plug or a jack properly or in reverse order. Wires connected in reverse order are referred to as *crossed pairs*. This is a common problem unique to UTP cable installations. When crossed pairs are detected in UTP LAN cabling systems, the connection is not good. When crossed pairs are detected, the wiring must be redone.

SKILL BUILDER

Lab Activity: Basic Cable Tester

In this lab, the instructor provides functional, intermittent, and bad cables (Ethernet 10BaseT RJ-45 568-B) to test for continuity using the Fluke 620 cable tester (or its equivalent).

Straight-Through Cable

A straight-through cable maintains the pin connection all the way through the cable, thus the wire connected to pin 1 is the same on both ends of the cable. Figure 5-16 illustrates that the RJ-45 connectors on both ends have all their wires in the same order. If you hold the two RJ-45 ends of a cable side by side in the same orientation, you can see the colored wires (or strips or pins) at each connector end. If the order of the colored wires is the same at each end, the cable is straight-through.

FIGURE 5-16
The wire on the cable ends are in the same order.

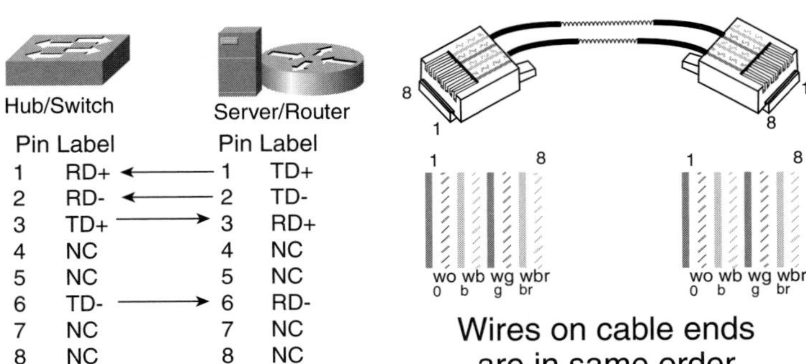

Use a straight-through cable to connect such devices as PCs or routers to other devices, such as hubs or switches. Figure 5-17 shows the connection guidelines when using straight-through cable.

SKILL BUILDER

Lab Activity: Straight-Through Cable

As specified in the 568 standards, your cable can have a maximum length of 3 m. In this lab, you use the following steps to make and test a straight-through patch cable:

1. Cut a length of cable.
2. Strip off the jacket.

continues

SKILL BUILDER (CONTINUED)

3 Separate the four pairs of wires.

4 Untwist the wires.

5 Organize the wires according to the proper color code and flatten the wires.

6 Maintain the color order and flatness of the wires, and then clip their length so that a maximum of 1.2 cm of untwisted wire is present.

7 Insert the ordered wires into a RJ-45 plug; make sure the jackets are inserted into the plug.

8 Push the wires in firmly enough to make sure the conductors are all visible when you look at the plug from the end.

9 Inspect the color code and the jacket location to be sure they are correct.

10 Insert the plug firmly into the crimp tool and crimp down completely.

11 Inspect both ends visually and mechanically.

12 Use a cable tester to verify the quality of the cable.

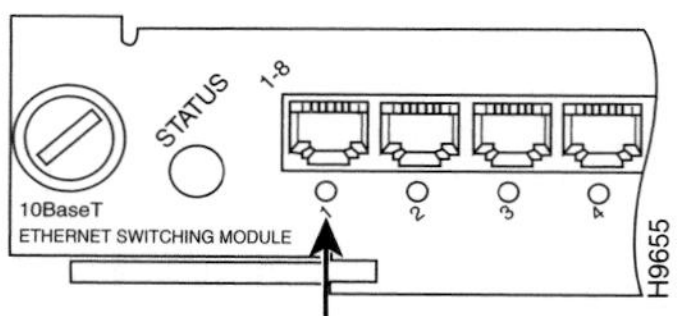

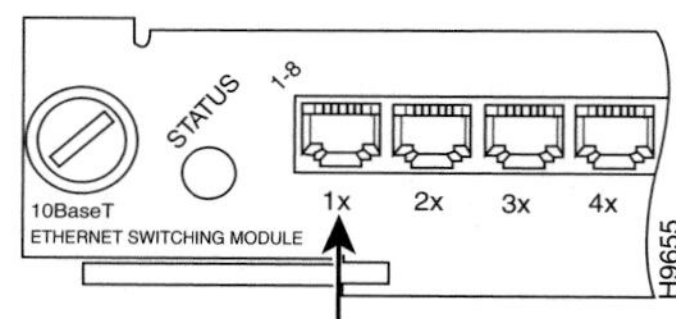

FIGURE 5-17 Use a straight-through cable when only one port is designated with an X.

SKILL BUILDER

Lab Activity: Rollover Cable

In this lab, you make and test a rollover or console cable. This cable is used to connect a workstation to the console port on a router or switch for purposes of accessing the router or switch.

Crossover Cable

A crossover cable crosses the critical pair to properly align, transmit, and receive signals on devices with like connections. The RJ-45 connectors on both ends show that some of the wires on one side of the cable are crossed to a different pin on the other side of the cable. Specifically for Ethernet, pin 1 at one RJ-45 end should be connected to pin 3 at the other end; pin 2 at one end should be connected to pin 6 at the other end (see Figure 5-18).

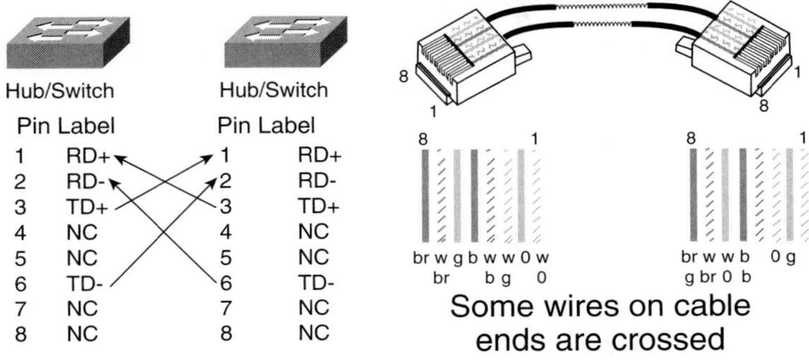

FIGURE 5-18 Some wires on cable ends are crossed.

You can use a crossover cable to connect similar devices: switch to switch, switch to hub, hub to hub, router to router, or PC to PC. Figure 5-19 shows some guidelines for using crossover cables.

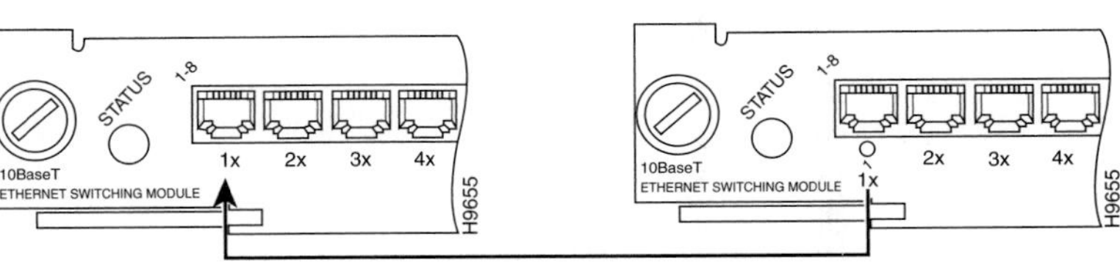

FIGURE 5-19 Use a crossover cable when both ports are designated with an X or when neither port is designated with an X.

SKILL BUILDERS

Lab Activity: Crossover Cable

In this lab, you make and test a crossover cable. Crossover cables connect one device to another like device.

Lab Activity: Cable Tester—Wire Map

In this lab, you learn the advanced features of the Fluke 620 LAN CableMeter (or its equivalent).

continues

SKILL BUILDERS (CONTINUED)

Lab Activity: Straight-Through Cable Tester

In this lab, you perform cable identification experiments using the Fluke 620 LAN CableMeter (or its equivalent).

Lab Activity: Cable Tester Length

In this lab, you perform length measurements using the Fluke 620 LAN CableMeter (or its equivalent).

LAN Technologies

This book introduces you to three LAN technologies: Ethernet, Token Ring, and FDDI. All three have a variety of Layer 1 components and devices. Ethernet, Fiber Distributed Data Interface (FDDI), and Token Ring are widely used LAN technologies that account for virtually all deployed LANs (see Figure 5-20). LAN standards specify cabling and signaling at the physical and data link layers of the OSI reference model. Because they are widely adhered to, this book covers the Ethernet and IEEE 802.3 LAN standards.

NOTE

Ethernet was developed by Xerox Corporation's Palo Alto Research Center (PARC) in the 1970s.

Ethernet and IEEE 802.3 LAN Standards

Ethernet is the most popular LAN standard today. Ethernet LANs have millions of devices or nodes. The early LANs required little bandwidth to perform the simple network tasks required at that time: sending and receiving e-mail, transferring data files, and handling print jobs.

In 1980, the Institute of Electrical and Electronic Engineers (IEEE) released the IEEE 802.3 specification. Ethernet was the technological basis for this specification. Shortly thereafter, Digital Equipment Corporation, Intel Corporation, and Xerox Corporation jointly developed and released an Ethernet specification (Version 2.0) that is substantially compatible with IEEE 802.3. Together, Ethernet and IEEE 802.3 currently maintain the greatest market share of any LAN standard.

An Ethernet LAN transports data between network devices, such as computers, printers, and file servers. Ethernet is known as a sharedmedia technology; that is, all the devices are connected to the same delivery media or cable. For example, a handwritten letter can be sent (transmitted) using one of many delivery methods, such as the U.S. postal service, Federal Express, or a fax. Electronic data can be transmitted via copper cable, thick coaxial cable, thinnet, wireless data transfer, and so on.

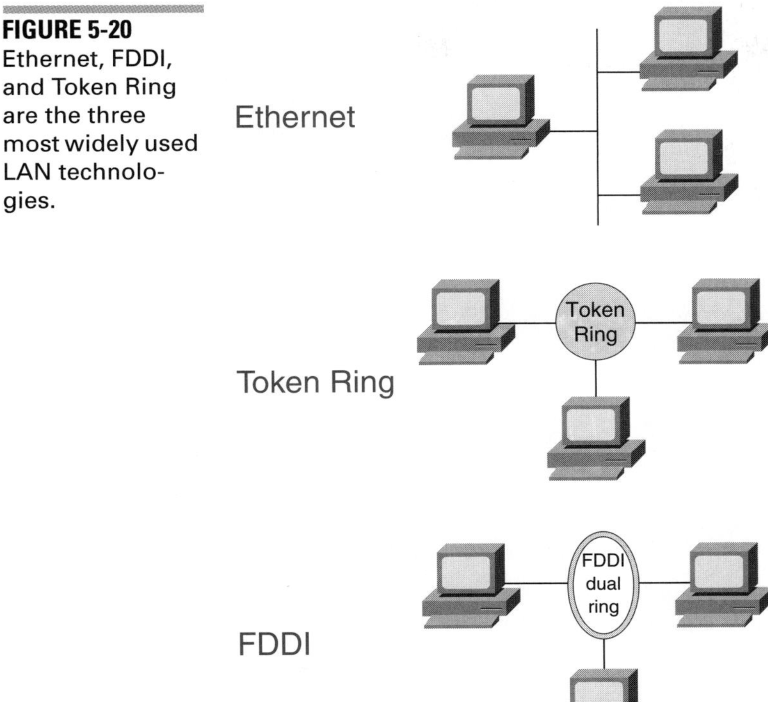

FIGURE 5-20 Ethernet, FDDI, and Token Ring are the three most widely used LAN technologies.

LANs and the Physical Layer

When Ethernet was developed, it was designed to fill the middle ground between long distance, low-speed networks and specialized, computer-room networks that carried data at high speeds for limited distances. Ethernet is well suited to applications in which a local communication medium must carry sporadic, occasionally heavy, traffic at high-peak data rates.

The Ethernet and IEEE 802.3 standards define a bus-topology LAN that operates at a baseband signaling rate of 10 Mbps, which is referred to as 10Base. The focus of this chapter is Ethernet 10BaseT technology, which has a star topology. Figure 5-21 illustrates three defined wiring standards:

- **10Base2**—Known as thin Ethernet; allows network segments up to 185 m on coaxial cable.
- **10Base5**—Known as thick Ethernet; allows network segments up to 500 m on coaxial cable.
- **10BaseT**—Carries Ethernet on inexpensive twisted-pair wiring.

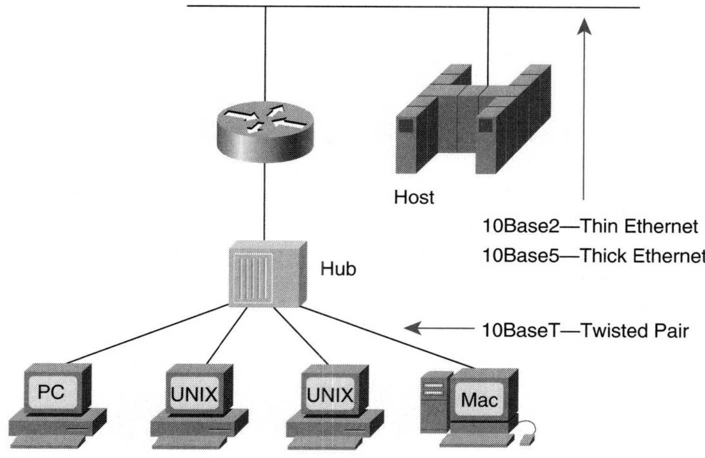

FIGURE 5-21
A network can use a combination of different Ethernet/802.3 access types.

MORE INFORMATION

Gigabit Ethernet

Gigabit Ethernet is an extension of the IEEE 802.3 Ethernet standard. Gigabit Ethernet offers 1000 Mbps of raw data bandwidth. Some of the features of Gigabit Ethernet include

- Full-duplex operating modes for switch-to-switch and switch-to-end-station connections
- Half-duplex operating modes for shared connections using repeaters and CSMA/CD
- Uses the same frame format, frame size, and management objects used in existing IEEE 802.3 networks

The 10Base5 and 10Base2 standards provide access for multiple stations on the same segment. 10Base5 (thicknet) stations are attached to the segment by a drop cable that runs from an attachment unit interface (AUI) in the station to a transceiver that is attached directly to the Ethernet coaxial cable. For thinnet and 10BaseT, the AUI and the transceiver are co-located in the station itself (on the NIC), and no drop cable is required. Because the 10BaseT standard provides access for a single station only, stations attached to an Ethernet LAN by 10BaseT are connected to a switch or a hub. In a hub arrangement, the hub is analogous to an Ethernet segment.

TABLE 5-1 Ethernet Specifications Summary

	10Base2	10Base5	10BaseT	100BaseTX	100BaseFX
Media	Thin coax RG-58 A/U	Thick coax RG-8 or RG-11	TIA/EIA UTP Cat 3, 4, 5, and 5e, 2pair	TIA/EIA UTP Cat 5 and 5e, 2-pair	62.2/125 micron multimode fiber
Connector Type	BNC connector	AUI/ DIX (to transceiver)	RJ-45 modular	RJ-45 modular	Duplex media interface connector (MIC) ST
Maximum Segment Length	185 m	500 m	100 m	100 m	412 m
Topology	Bus	Bus	Star	Star	Point-to-Point
Transfer Rate	10 Mbps	10 Mbps	10 Mbps	100 Mbps	100 Mbps

The Ethernet 10BaseT technologies carry Ethernet frames on inexpensive twisted-pair wiring. You study four components and three devices that are related to these technologies. The first four components are passive, meaning they require no energy to operate. They are:

- Cabling
- Jacks
- Plugs
- Patch panels

The last three components are active. They are:

- Transceivers
- Repeaters
- Miniport repeaters (hubs)

Cabling, Jacks, and Plugs

The standard 10BaseT cable is CAT 5 twisted-pair cable, which is composed of four twisted pairs that reduce noise problems. CAT 5 is thin, inexpensive, and easy to install. The function of CAT 5 cable is to transmit bits in the form of signals; therefore, it is a Layer 1 component.

The standard 10BaseT termination is the registered jack-45 (RJ-45) connector. It reduces noise, reflection, and mechanical stability problems, and resembles a phone plug, except that it has eight conductors instead of four. It is considered a passive networking component because it serves only as a conducting path between the four pairs of Category 5 twisted cable and the prongs of the RJ-45 jack. It is considered a Layer 1 component, rather than a device, because it serves only as a conducting path for signals.

RJ-45 plugs fit into RJ-45 jacks or receptacles. The RJ-45 jack has eight conductors, which snap together with the RJ-45 plug. On the other side of the RJ-45 jack is a punch down block where wires are separated out and forced into slots with a fork-like tool, called a *punch-down tool*. This provides a copper-conducting path for the signals. The RJ-45 jack is a Layer 1 component.

Patch Panels

Patch panels are convenient groupings of RJ-45 jacks. They come in 12, 24, and 48 ports, and typically are rack-mounted (see Figure 5-22). The front sides are RJ-45 jacks; the back sides are punch-down blocks that provide connectivity or conducting paths. They are classified as Layer 1 components.

FIGURE 5-22
RJ-45 ports are located on the front of the patch panel.

Transceivers

A *transceiver* is a combination of transmitter and receiver (see Figure 5-23). In networking applications, this means they convert one form of signal to another form. For example, many networking devices come with an auxiliary unit interface and a transceiver that allows a 10Base2, 10Base5, 10BaseT, or 10/100 BaseFX to be connected to the port. A common application is the conversion of AUI ports to RJ-45 ports. They are Layer 1 devices. They transmit from one pin configuration and/or media to another. Transceivers often are built into NICs. Transceivers on NICs are called *signaling components*, which means they encode signals onto the physical medium.

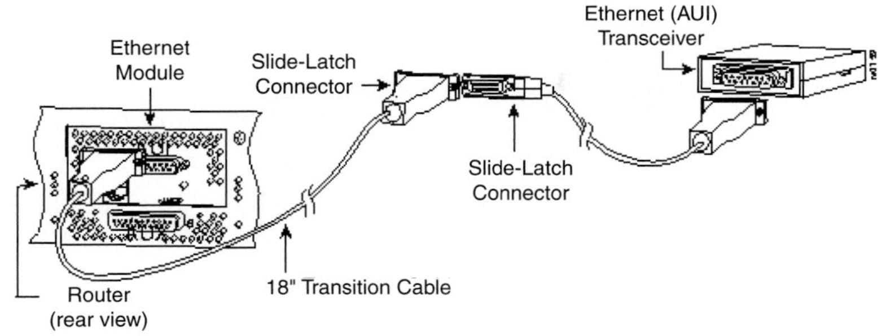

FIGURE 5-23 The transceiver performs many of the physical layer functions, including collision detection.

Repeaters

Repeaters regenerate and retime signals, thereby increasing the distance that signals can travel and still be clearly interpreted at the destination. Repeaters deal only with packets at the bit level; therefore, they are Layer 1 devices. Repeaters are internetworking devices that exist at the physical layer (Layer 1) of the OSI model. They can increase the number of nodes that can be connected to a network and, thus, the distance over which the network can extend. Repeaters re-shape, regenerate, and retime signals before sending them on along the network.

The disadvantage of using repeaters is that they cannot filter network traffic. Signals that arrive on one port of a repeater are sent out on all other ports. The data gets passed along to all other LAN segments of a network regardless of whether it needs to go there.

Multiport Repeaters (Hubs)

As you have learned already, multiport repeaters combine connectivity with the amplifying and re-timing properties of repeaters. It is typical to see 4, 8, 12, and up to 24, ports on multiport repeaters. This allows many devices to be cheaply and easily interconnected. Multiport repeaters often are called hubs, instead of repeaters, when referring to the devices that serve as the center of a star topology network. Hubs are very common internetworking devices. Because the typical unmanaged hub requires only power and plugged-in RJ-45 jacks, they are great for setting up a network quickly. Like repeaters, hubs deal only with signals and are Layer 1 devices.

All these devices—passive and active—create or act on the signals. They recognize no information patterns in the signals, no addresses, and no data. Their function is simply to facilitate the transmission of signals. Layer 1 is fundamental to troubleshooting networks, and should never be underestimated. Many network problems are traceable to bad RJ-45 terminations, jacks, punch-downs, repeaters, hubs, or transceivers.

MORE INFORMATION

Positioning Ethernet in the Campus Network

Given the variety of Ethernet speeds that can be deployed in the campus network, you need to determine when, if, and where you want to upgrade to one or more of the Fast Ethernet implementations. Note that today you can run 10 Mb or 100 Mb Ethernet anywhere in the network, provided you have the correct hardware.

In today's installations, although businesses are considering putting 100 Mbps Ethernet from the core to the access layer, costs for cabling and adapters can make this prohibitive. However, before making this decision, you must determine your network requirements. For example, if you are using a new generation of multimedia, imaging, and database products, these can easily overwhelm a network running at traditional Ethernet speeds of 10 Mbps.

In general, Fast Ethernet technology can be used in a campus network in several different ways:

- Fast Ethernet is used as the link between the access and distribution layer devices, supporting the aggregate traffic from each Ethernet segment on the access link.
- Many client/server networks suffer from too many clients trying to access the same server, creating a bottleneck where the server attaches to the LAN. To enhance client/server performance across the campus network, enterprise servers are connected by Fast Ethernet links to ensure the avoidance of bottlenecks at the server. Fast Ethernet, in combination with switched Ethernet, creates an effective solution in this case.
- Fast Ethernet links also can be used to provide the connection between the distribution layer and the core. Because the campus network model supports dual links between each distribution layer router and core switch, the aggregated traffic from multiple access switches can be load balanced across these links.

Collisions and Collision Domains in Shared Medium Environments

As illustrated in Figure 5-24, some of the various types of directly connected networks include the following:

- **Shared media environment**—Occurs when multiple hosts have access to the same medium. For example, if several PCs are attached to the same physical wire or optical fiber, or share the same airspace, they all share the same media environment. Occasionally, you might hear someone say "all the computers are on the same wire." It means they all share the same media even though the "wire" might be CAT 5 UTP, which has four pairs of wire.
- **Extended shared media environment**—This is a special type of shared media environment in which networking devices (that is, repeaters) can extend the environment so it can accommodate even more users than the shared media environment. There are, however, negative aspects to this as well as positive aspects.
- **Point-to-point network environment**—This is widely used in dial-up network connections, and is the one with which you most likely are familiar. It is a shared networking environment in which one device is connected to only one other device via a link, such as connecting to an Internet service provider by a phone line.

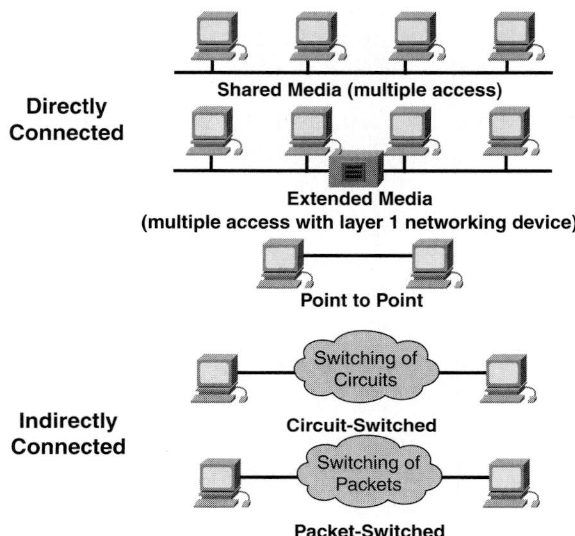

FIGURE 5-24
Various types of networks.

Some networks are indirectly connected, meaning that some higher layer networking devices and/or significant geographical distance exist between the two communicating hosts. The two types of indirectly connected networks are described as follows:

- **Circuit-switching**—An indirectly connected network in which actual electrical circuits are maintained for the duration of the communication. Circuit switching sets up a physical, end-to-end connection between the endpoints. The bandwidth is dedicated to this point-to-point connection. The current telephone system is still, in part, circuit-switched, although the telephone systems in many countries are now concentrating less on circuit-switched technologies.
- **Packet-switching**—Rather than dedicating a link as an exclusive circuit connection between two communicating hosts, the source sends messages in packets. Each packet contains enough information for it to be routed to the proper destination host. The advantage: Many hosts can share the same link; the disadvantage: Conflicting demands on the network can occur because nodes must share the media and each node does not have dedicated bandwidth.

Collisions and Collision Domains

A *collision* is a situation that can occur when two bits propagate at the same time on the same network. A small, slow network could work out a system that allowed only two computers, each agreeing to take turns, to send messages. The problem is that many computers are connected to large networks, each one wanting to communicate millions of bits every second. It's also important to remember that the "bits" are sent in contiguous groups (packets).

Serious problems can occur as a result of too much traffic on a network. If, for example, only one cable interconnects all the devices on a network, the possibility of conflicts with more than one user sending data at the same time is high. The same is true if segments of a network are connected only by non-filtering devices, such as repeaters. Ethernet allows only one data packet to access the cable at any one time. If more than one node attempts to transmit at the same time, a collision occurs, and the data from each device suffers damage.

The area within the network from where the data packets originated and collided is called a *collision domain*. All shared media environments are collision domains. One wire might be connected to another wire through patch cables, transceivers, patch panels, repeaters, and hubs. All these Layer 1 interconnections are part of a collision domain.

Signals in a Collision

When a collision occurs, the data packets that are involved are destroyed, bit by bit. To avoid this problem, the network should have in place a system that can manage the competition for the medium (contention). For example, a binary system can recognize only two voltage, light, or electromagnetic wave states. Therefore, in a collision, the signals interfere, or collide, with each other and create a third and invalid state. Just as two cars cannot occupy the same space, as shown in Figure 5-25, on the same road at the same time, neither can two signals occupy the same medium at the same time.

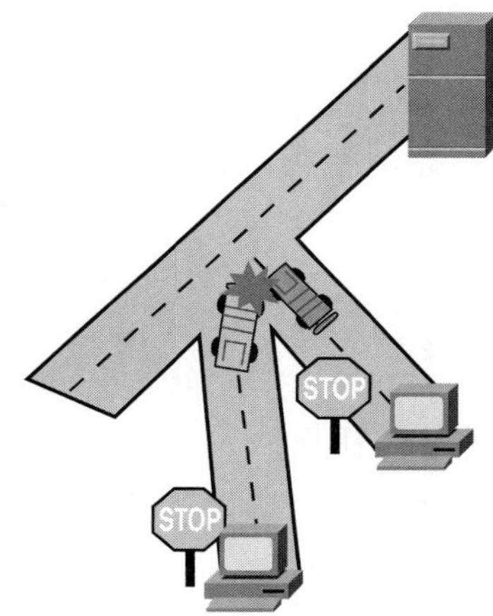

FIGURE 5-25
A problem can occur when too many end stations try to access the same segment.

You might think that collisions are detrimental because they decrease network performance. However, a certain amount of collisions are a natural function of a shared media environment (that is, collision domain). This is because large numbers of computers are trying to communicate with each other at the same time by using the same wire.

The history of how Ethernet handles collisions dates back to research at the University of Hawaii. In its attempts to develop a wireless communication system between the Islands of Hawaii, university researchers developed a protocol called *Aloha*. This protocol was instrumental in the development of Ethernet.

As a networking professional, one important skill is the ability to recognize collision domains. If you connect several computers to a single medium that has no other networking devices attached, you have a shared-access situation and you have a single collision domain (see Figure 5-26). Depending on the particular technology used, this situation limits the number of computers that can use that portion of the medium, also called a *segment*.

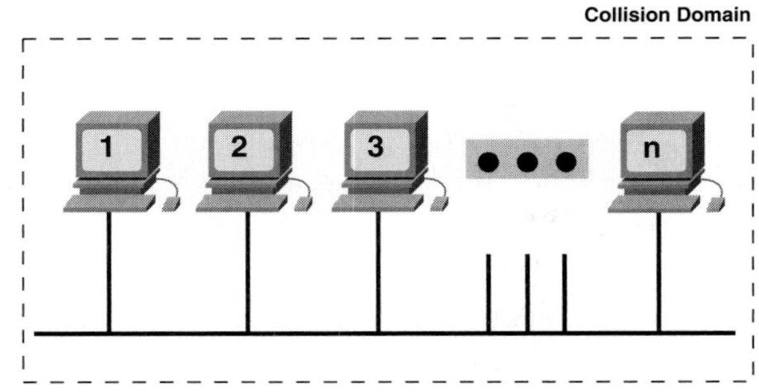

FIGURE 5-26
Collision domain: basic shared access.

Repeaters, Hubs, and Collision Domains

Repeaters regenerate and retime bits, but they cannot filter the flow of traffic that passes through them. Signals that arrive at one port of a repeater are sent out on all other ports.

Using a repeater extends the collision domain; therefore, the network on both sides of the repeater is one large collision domain.

You have learned already that another name for a hub is a *multiport repeater.* Any signal that comes in one port of the hub is regenerated, retimed, and sent out every other port.

Therefore, hubs, which are useful for connecting large numbers of computers, extend collision domains. The extended collision domain introduced by a hub results in diminished network performance. The degradation in performance depends on the degree of usage of the network by the computers on that network.

Both repeaters and hubs are Layer 1 devices; therefore, they perform no filtering of network traffic. Extending a run of cable with a repeater, and ending that run with a hub, results in a larger collision domain, as shown in Figure 5-27.

The Four Repeater Rule

The four repeater rule in Ethernet states that no more than four repeaters or repeating hubs can be installed between any two computers on the network. If followed, the rules guarantee that if a collison occurs, every node in the collision domain knows it has occurred. This is crucial to the successful operation of the network protocol.

When this delay limit is exceeded, the number of late collisions dramatically increases. A late collision is when a collision happens after transmitting the first 64 bytes of the frame.

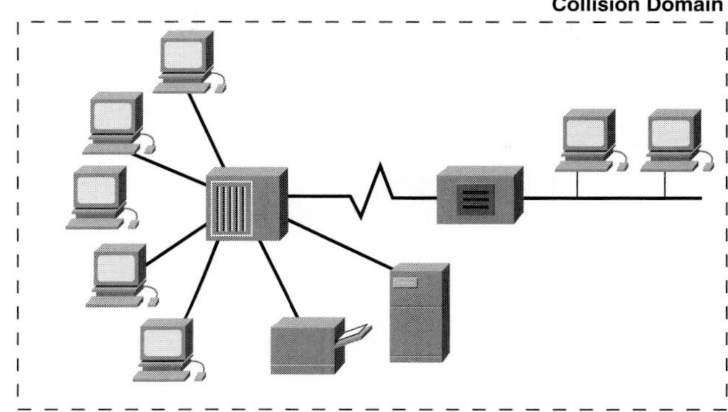

FIGURE 5-27
Collision domain: extended by a hub and repeater.

These late collision frames add delay referred to as *consumption delay.* As consumption delay and latency increase, network performance decreases. This Ethernet rule of thumb also is known as the 5-4-3-2-1 rule. Five sections of the network, four repeaters or hubs, three sections of the network are "mixing" sections (with hosts), two sections are link sections (for link purposes), and one large collision domain (as shown in Figure 5-28).

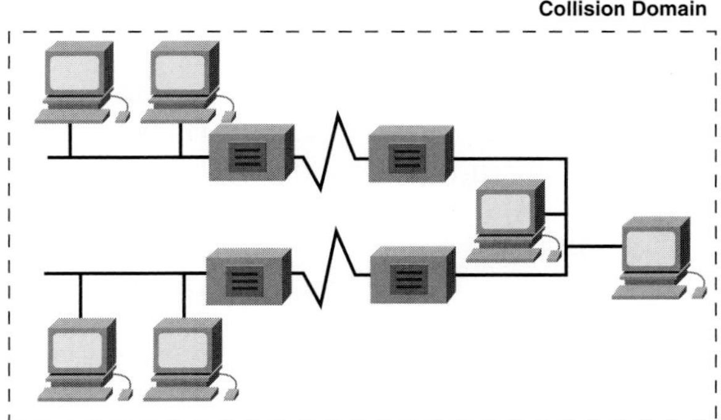

FIGURE 5-28
Collision domain: four repeater rule.

Segmenting Collision Domains

Although repeaters and hubs are useful, inexpensive networking devices, they extend collision domains. If the collision domain becomes too large, this can cause too many collisions and result in poor network performance. You can reduce the size of collision domains by using intelligent networking devices that break up the domains. Examples of this type of networking device are bridges, switches, and routers. As shown in Figure 5-29, this process is called *segmentation.*

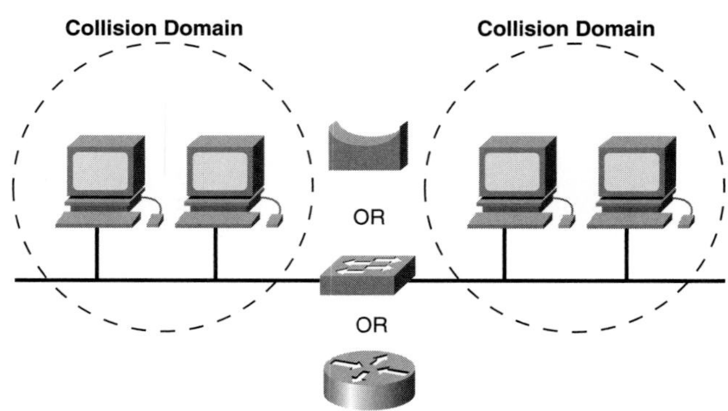

FIGURE 5-29
Limiting the collision domain.

A bridge can eliminate unnecessary traffic on a busy network by dividing a network into segments and filtering traffic based on the station address. Traffic between devices on the same segment does not cross the bridge, and does not affect other segments. This works well as long as the traffic between segments is not too heavy. Otherwise, the bridge can become a bottleneck and actually slow down communication.

Network Topologies

In this section, you review the various topologies used in networking. You learn how a physical topology describes the plan for wiring the physical devices. Finally, you study a logical topology to learn how information flows through a network to determine where collisions might occur. A network might have one type of physical topology and a completely different type of logical topology. For example, Ethernet 10BaseT uses an extended-star physical topology, but acts as though it uses a logical bus topology. Token Ring uses a physical star and a logical ring. FDDI uses a physical ring and a logical ring.

Linear Bus Network Topology

The bus topology has all its nodes connected directly to one link, and has no other connections between nodes, as shown in Figure 5-30. Each host is wired to a common wire. One advantage of this topology is that all hosts are connected to each other, and thus can communicate directly. One disadvantage of this topology is that a break in the cable disconnects hosts from each other. A bus topology enables every networking device to see all signals from all other devices. This can be an advantage if you want all information to go to every device at once.

FIGURE 5-30
A bus topology is a linear LAN architecture in which transmissions from network stations propagate the length of the medium in both directions and are received by all other stations.

Ring Network Topology

A ring topology is a single closed ring consisting of nodes and links, with each node connected to only two adjacent nodes, as shown in Figure 5-31. The topology shows all devices wired directly to each other in what is called a *daisy-chain*. This is similar to the manner in which a mouse on an Apple PC plugs into the keyboard, which in turn connects to the PC. For information to flow, each station must pass the information to an adjacent station. Every frame is still seen by every node, but sequentially, one at a time.

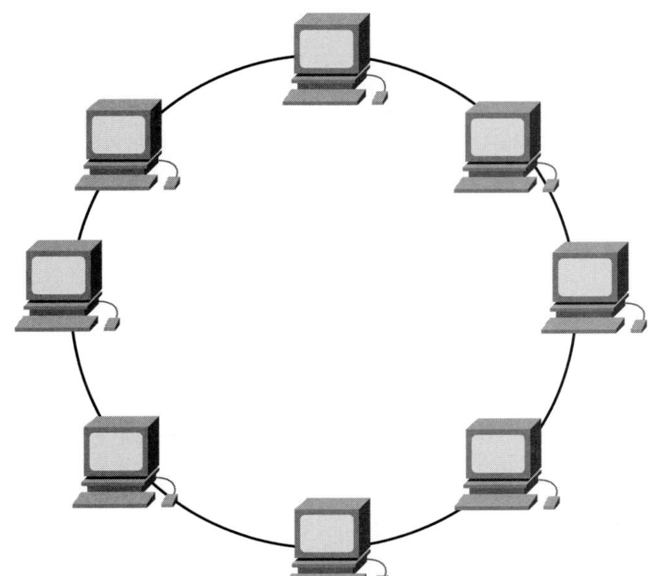

FIGURE 5-31
A ring topology is a LAN architecture that consists of a series of devices connected to one another by unidirectional transmission links to form a single closed loop.

Dual Ring Network Topology

A dual ring topology consists of two concentric rings. As shown in Figure 5-32, the two rings are not connected. A dual ring topology is the same as a ring topology, except that a second, redundant ring connects the same devices. In other words, to provide reliability and flexibility in the network, each networking device is part of two independent ring topologies. Because of the fault tolerant and autorecovery features of this topology, the rings can reconfigure to form one larger ring and the network continues to function when a media failure occurs.

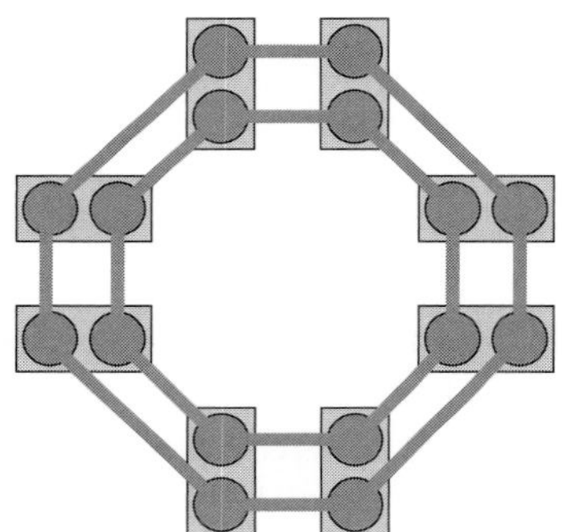

FIGURE 5-32
A dual ring topology acts like two independent rings where only one ring is used at a time.

Star Network Topology

A star topology is a LAN architecture in which the end points on a network are connected to a common central hub or a switch by dedicated links. A star topology has a central node with all links to other nodes radiating from it and allows no other links. Its primary advantage is that it allows all other nodes to communicate with each other conveniently. Figure 5-33 shows an example of a logical bus topology that is implemented physically in a star. Its primary disadvantage is that if the central node fails, the whole network becomes disconnected. Depending on the type of networking device used at the center of the star network, collisions can be a problem. The flow of all information would go through one device. This might be desirable for security or restricted access reasons, but, again, it would be very susceptible to any problems in the star's central node.

Extended Star Network Topology

An extended star topology has a core star topology, with each of the end nodes of the core topology acting as the center of its own star topology, as shown in Figure 5-34. The advantage of this is that it keeps wiring runs shorter and limits the number of devices that need to interconnect to any one central node. An extended star topology is very hierarchical, and can be configured (with the appropriate equipment) to "encourage" traffic to stay local. This is how the phone system is currently structured.

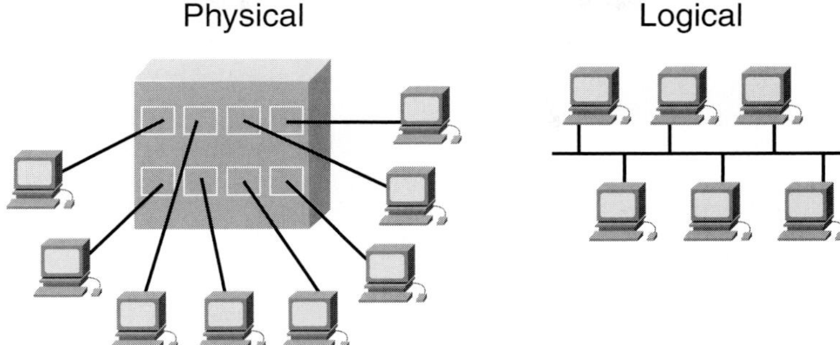

FIGURE 5-33 Logical bus topology often is implemented physically in a star topology.

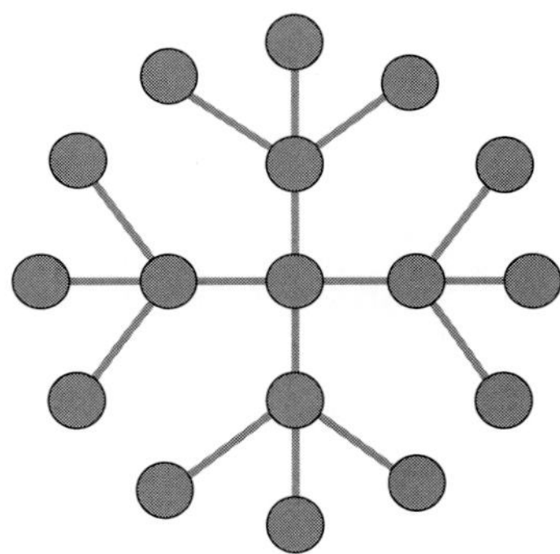

FIGURE 5-34 The phone system is currently structured in an extended star topology.

Tree Network Topology

The tree topology is similar to the extended star topology. The primary difference is that it does not use one central node. Instead, it uses a trunk node from which it branches to other nodes, as shown in Figure 5-35. Two types of tree topologies exist: the binary tree (each node splits into two links) and the backbone tree (a backbone trunk has branch nodes with links hanging from it). The trunk is a wire that has several layers of branches. The flow of information is hierarchical.

Irregular Network Topology

In the irregular network topology, there is no obvious pattern to the links and nodes. The wiring is inconsistent; the nodes have varying numbers of wires leading from them. This is how networks in the early stages of construction, or poorly planned networks, are often wired.

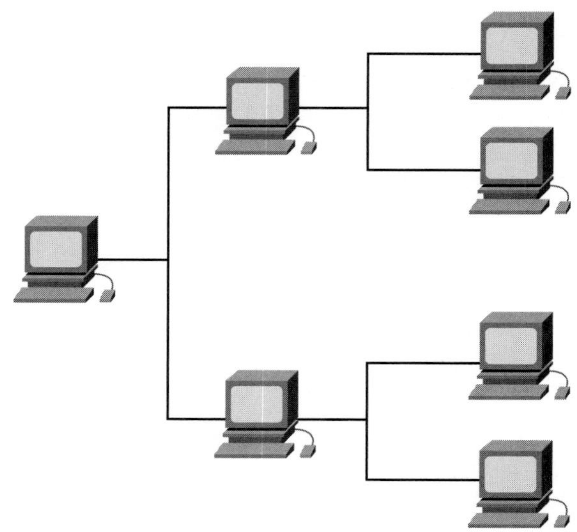

FIGURE 5-35
A tree topology is a LAN architecture that is identical to the bus topology, except that branches with multiple nodes are possible.

Complete (Mesh) Network Topology

In a complete, or mesh topology, every node is linked directly to every other node, as shown in Figure 5-36. This wiring has very distinct advantages and disadvantages. One advantage is every node is connected physically to every other node (creating a redundant connection). Should any link fail, information can flow through many other links to reach its destination. Another advantage of this topology is that it allows information to flow along many paths on its way back through the network. The primary physical disadvantage is that for anything more than a small number of nodes, the amount of media for the links, and the amount of connections on the links becomes overwhelming. For a WAN, a full mesh topology is cost prohibitive because the cost is proportional to the number of links.

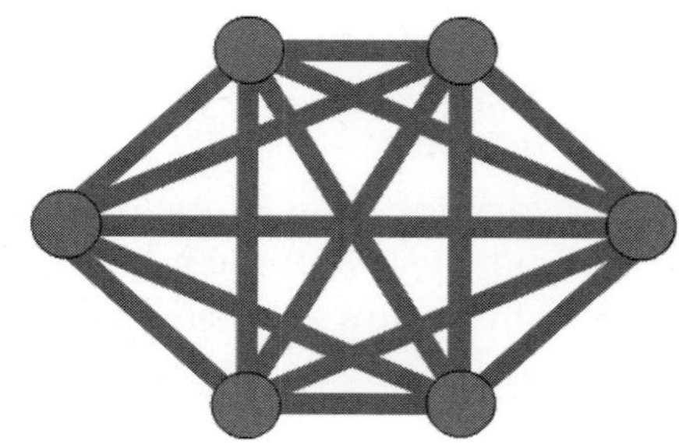

FIGURE 5-36
The behavior of a complete, or mesh, topology depends greatly on the devices used.

Cellular Network Topology

The cellular topology consists of circular or hexagonal areas, each of which has an individual node at its center, as shown in Figure 5-37. The cellular topology is a geographical area divided into regions (cells) for the purposes of wireless technology—a technology that becomes increasingly more important each day. No physical links exist in a cellular topology, only electromagnetic waves. Sometimes, the receiving nodes move (for example, a car cell phone), and sometimes the sending nodes move (for example, satellite communication links).

The obvious advantage of a cellular (wireless) topology is that there is no tangible media other than the earth's atmosphere or the vacuum of space. The disadvantages are that signals are present everywhere in a cell and, thus, are susceptible to disruptions (man-made and environmental) and to security violations (that is, electronic monitoring and theft of service). Cellular technologies communicate directly with each other, but distance limitations and interference sometimes make reception extremely difficult.

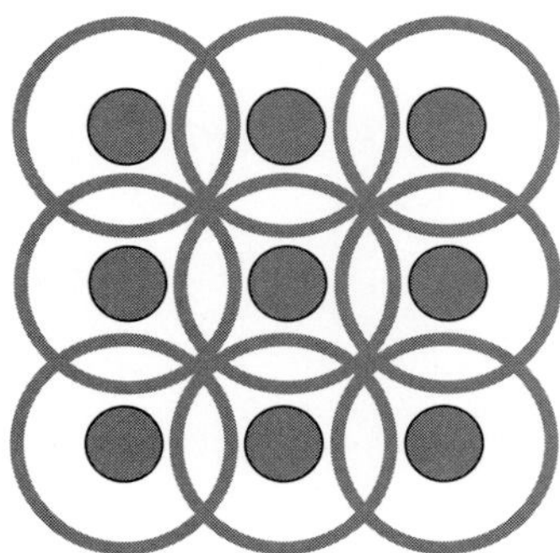

FIGURE 5-37
As a rule, cellular-based topologies are integrated with other topologies, whether they use the atmosphere or satellites.

Summary

In this chapter, you learned that the function of the physical layer is to transmit data. In addition, you learned that the following types of networking media can be used to connect computers:

- Coaxial cable, which consists of a hollow outer cylindrical conductor that surrounds a single inner wire conductor.
- UTP cable, which is a four-pair wire medium used in a variety of networks.
- STP cable, which combines the techniques of shielding, cancellation, and twisting of wires.

- Fiber-optic cable, which is a networking medium capable of conducting modulated light transmissions.

This chapter discussed various criteria, such as rate of data transfer and expense, which help determine what types of networking media should be used. You learned that TIA/EIA-568-A and TIA/EIA-569 are the most widely used standards for technical performance of networking media.

Additionally, this chapter described how signals propagating at the same time on the same network result in a collision. Last, you learned that a network can have one type of physical topology and a completely different type of logical topology. In the next chapter, you learn about the IEEE model and how the data link layer provides transit of data across a physical link by using Media Access Control (MAC) and Layer 2 addressing.

Check Your Understanding

1. What is the maximum cable length for STP (without a repeater, and so on)?
   - **A.** 100 ft
   - **B.** 100 m
   - **C.** 150 ft
   - **D.** 1000 m
2. 150 ohm STP is used primarily for what installation?
   - **A.** Ethernet
   - **B.** Fast Ethernet
   - **C.** Token Ring
   - **D.** None of the above
3. How many pairs of wires make up a UTP cable?
   - **A.** 2
   - **B.** 4
   - **C.** 6
   - **D.** 8
4. Which connector does UTP use?
   - **A.** STP
   - **B.** BNC
   - **C.** RJ-45
   - **D.** RJ-69
5. What is an advantage that coaxial cable has over STP or UTP?
   - **A.** It is capable of achieving 10-100 Mbps.
   - **B.** It is inexpensive.
   - **C.** It can run longer distances unboosted.
   - **D.** None of the above.

6. A more compact version of coaxial cable is known as
   A. Thinnet
   B. BNC
   C. STP
   D. UTP
7. A _______ fiber optic cable allows multiple streams of LED-generated light.
   A. Multimode
   B. Multichannel
   C. Muliphase
   D. None of the above
8. What is the importance of the EIA/TIA standards?
   A. They provide a framework for the implementation of the OSI reference model.
   B. They provide guidelines for NIC manufacturers to follow to ensure compatibility.
   C. They provide the minimum media requirements for multi-product and multi-vendor environments.
   D. None of the above.
9. For the horizontal cabling component, TIA/EIA-568A requires a minimum of how many connectors at each work area?
   A. 1
   B. 2
   C. 4
   D. 6
10. What does the twisting of the wires do in a CAT-5 cable?
   A. It makes it thinner.
   B. It makes it less expensive.
   C. It reduces noise problems.
   D. It allows six pairs to fit in the space of four pairs.

11. The standard 10BaseT cable is Category __.

A. 3

B. 4

C. 5

D. 6

12. The network area within which data packets originate and collide is called a __________?

A. Collision domain

B. Network domain

C. Collision segment

D. Network segment

13. Using repeaters _______ the collision domain.

A. Reduces

B. Has no effect on

C. Extends

D. None of the above

14. The process of installing complex networking devices that break up the domains by using bridges, switches, and routers is known as:

A. Sectioning

B. Segmentation

C. Collision Domain Reduction

D. None of the above

15. What physical topology has all its nodes connected directly to one link, and has no other connections between nodes?

A. Linear bus

B. Star

C. Ring

D. None of the above

16. What physical topology has all the devices daisy-chained together?

A. Linear bus

B. Star

C. Ring

D. None of the above

17. What is the purpose of the second ring in a dual ring network?

A. Duplex

B. Signaling

C. Redundancy

D. None of the above

18. What is the primary disadvantage of the star network topology?

A. It doesn't allow all other nodes to communicate with each other conveniently.

B. If the central node fails, the whole network becomes disconnected.

C. It is much slower than the other topologies.

D. None of the above.

19. In a complete, or full-mesh, topology, every node

A. Is linked directly to every other node

B. Is connected to two central nodes

C. Is linked wirelessly to a central node

D. None of the above

20. The cellular topology uses _______ as its medium.

A. Electromagnetic waves

B. The cellular network

C. Infrared signals

D. The atmosphere or the vacuum of space

After reading this chapter, you will be able to

- Understand how LANs operate at the data link layer
- Understand hexadecimal numbers
- Understand MAC addressing
- Describe framing
- Describe Media Access Control (MAC)

Layer 2: Concepts

Introduction

All data sent out on a network comes from a source and goes to a destination. The data link layer of the OSI model provides access to the networking media, which enables the data to reach its intended destination on a network. In addition, the data link layer functions include error notification, network topology, and flow control; these functions depend on the network topology.

In this chapter, you learn about LAN media and the IEEE model, and you learn how the data link layer provides reliable transit of data across a physical link by using the Media Access Control (MAC) addresses. In so doing, the data link layer is concerned with physical (as opposed to network, or logical) addressing, network topology, line discipline (how end systems use the network link), error notification, ordered delivery of frames, and flow control. In addition, you learn how the data link layer uses MAC addresses to distinguish between multiple stations sharing the same medium. Before a data packet is exchanged with a directly connected device on the same LAN, the sending device needs to have a MAC address it can use as a destination address.

LANs and the Data Link Layer

The physical layer specifies the electrical, mechanical, procedural, and functional requirements for activating, maintaining, and deactivating the physical link between end systems. The physical layer specifies such characteristics as voltage levels, data rates, maximum transmission distances, and physical connectors. The data link layer

- Communicates with the upper layers through Logical Link Control (LLC)
- Uses a flat addressing convention (naming refers to the assignment of unique identifiers/addresses)
- Uses framing to organize or group the bits of the data
- Uses Media Access Control (MAC) to choose which computer transmits binary data from a group in which multiple computers are trying to transmit at the same time

Before a data packet is exchanged with a directly connected device on the same LAN, the sending device needs to have a MAC address it can use as a destination address.

The data link layer provides data transport across the physical link joining two devices. For example, as Figure 6-1 shows, the three devices can be attached directly to each other over the Ethernet LAN. The Macintosh on the left and the Intel-based PC in the middle show MAC addresses used by the data link layer. The router on the right also uses a MAC address for each of its LAN interfaces. To indicate the 802.3 interface on the router, you use the Cisco Internetwork Operating System (IOS) interface type abbreviation E followed by an interface number. For example, E0, as shown in Figure 6-1, is the name of Ethernet/802.3 interface number 0. You can see how MAC addresses operate and are assigned later in this chapter.

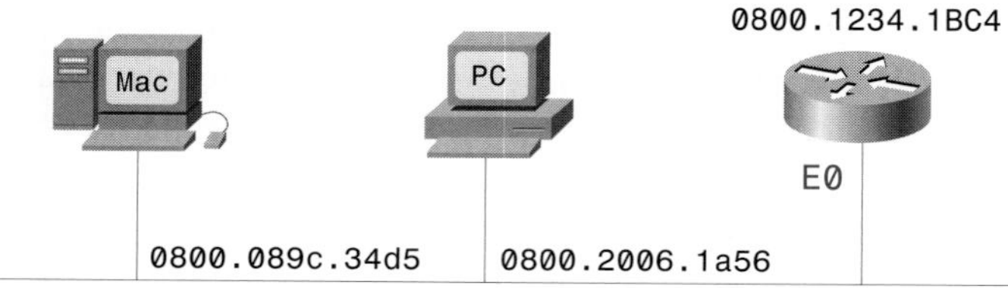

FIGURE 6-1
A Cisco router's data link to Ethernet/802.3 uses an interface named E plus a number.

MORE INFORMATION

LAN Transmission Methods

LAN data transmissions fall into three classifications: unicast, multicast, and broadcast. In each type of transmission, a single packet is sent to one or more nodes.

In a unicast transmission, a single packet is sent from the source to a destination on a network. First, the source node addresses the packet by using the physical address of the destination node. The package then is sent onto the network, and finally, the network passes the packet to its destination.

A multicast transmission consists of a single data packet that is sent to a specific subset of nodes on the network. First, the source node addresses the packet by using a multicast address. Then the packet is transmitted on the network.

A broadcast transmission consists of a single data packet that is transmitted to all nodes on the network. In these types of transmissions, the source node addresses the packet by using the broadcast address. The packet then is transmitted on the network.

LAN Standards

Standards define the physical media and the connectors used to connect devices to media. Standards also define the way devices communicate at the data link layer. The data link layer defines how data is transported over a physical media. In addition, it defines how to encapsulate protocol-specific traffic in such a way that traffic going to different upper-layer protocols can use the same *channel* as it goes up the stack. To provide these functions, the Institute of Electrical and Electronic Engineers (IEEE) Ethernet data link layer has two sublayers:

- **Media Access Control** (MAC) (802.3)—As the name implies, the MAC sublayer defines how to transmit frames on the physical wire. It handles physical addressing associated with each device, network topology definition, and line discipline.
- **Logical Link Control** (LLC) (802.2)—As the name implies, the LLC is responsible for logically identifying different protocol types and then encapsulating them. A type code or a service access point (SAP) identifier performs the logical identification. The type of LLC frame used by an end station depends on what identifier the upper layer protocol expects.

Figure 6-2 illustrates how several popular LAN protocols map to the OSI reference model.

FIGURE 6-2
Popular LAN protocols mapped to the OSI reference model.

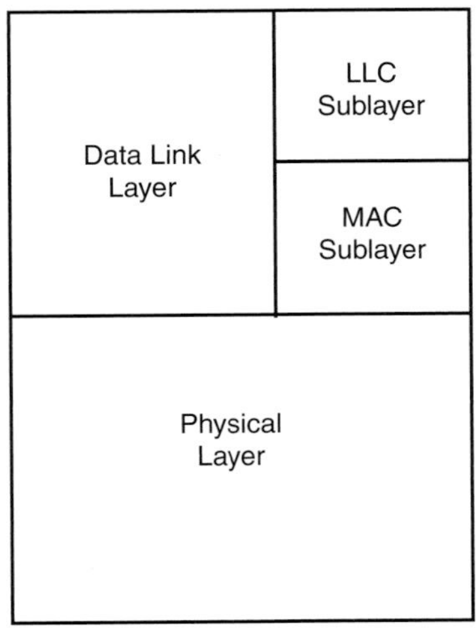

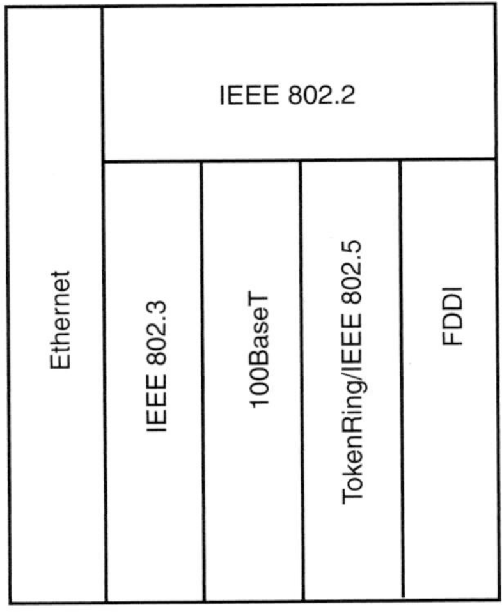

Media Access Control Sublayer

The Media Access Control (MAC) sublayer deals with the protocols that a host follows to access the physical media. Figure 6-3 illustrates the frame structure for MAC sublayer 802.3 frames. This standard frame structure provides an example of how control information is used to transmit information at this layer. The definitions of the MAC sublayer fields are as follows:

> **NOTE**
>
> The 802.3 committee kept the same 8-byte bit pattern for the preamble but broke it into two fields: a seven-byte preamble and a one-byte start of frame delimiter. The Ethernet 2.0 preamble (7 bytes of 1010 and 1 byte of 10101011, which says that the next bit goes into the buffer and is the first bit of the actual frame.

- The IEEE 802.3 frames begin with an alternating pattern of 1s and 0s, called a *preamble*. The preamble tells receiving stations that a frame is coming.
- Immediately following the preamble are the destination and source physical address fields. These addresses are referred to as *MAC layer addresses*. They must be unique for each device on the network. On most LAN-interface cards, the MAC address is burned into ROM; hence the term *burned-in address (BIA)*. When the network interface card initializes, this address is copied into RAM.

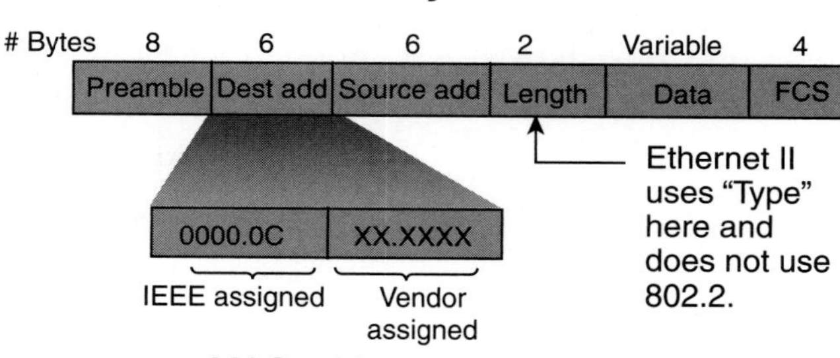

FIGURE 6-3 MAC sublayer frame.

The source address is always a unicast (single node) address, whereas the destination address can be unicast, multicast (group), or broadcast (all nodes).

- In IEEE 802.3 frames, the two-byte field following the source address is a length field, which indicates the number of bytes of data that follow this field and precede the frame check sequence (FCS) field.
- Following the length field there is a data field. This field includes the LLC control information, other upper layer control information, and the user data.
- Following the data field is a four-byte FCS field, which contains a cyclic redundancy check (CRC) value. The sending device creates the CRC; the receiving device recalculates the CRC to check for damage that might have occurred to the frame in transit.

Logical Link Control Sublayer

The Logical Link Control (LLC) sublayer of the data link layer manages communications between devices over a single link on a network. LLC is defined in the IEEE 802.2 specification and supports both connectionless and connection-oriented services. IEEE 802.2 defines fields in the data link layer frames that enable multiple higher-layer protocols to share a single physical data link.

The IEEE created the logical link sublayer to allow part of the data link layer to function independently from existing technologies. This layer provides versatility in services to network layer protocols running above it, while communicating effectively with the variety of technologies running below it. The LLC, as a sublayer, participates in the encapsulation process. Sometimes, the LLC PDU also is called an *LLC packet*, but this is not a widely used term.

LLC takes the network protocol data, the datagram or packet, and adds more control information to help deliver the packet to its destination. It adds two addressing components of the 802.2 specification: the Destination Service Access Point (DSAP) and the Source Service Access Point (SSAP), which identify the upper layer protocol at each end. This repackaged packet then travels to the MAC sublayer for handling by the required specific technology for further encapsulation and data. An example of this specific technology might be one of the varieties of Ethernet, Token Ring, or FDDI.

Hexadecimal Numbers as MAC Addresses

You already studied the decimal and binary numbering systems. Decimal numbers are used in Base 10, and binary numbers are used in Base 2. Another number system you need to be familiar with is the hexadecimal (hex) or Base 16 number system. Think of hex as a shorthand method for representing the 8-bit bytes stored in a computer system. It was chosen to represent the MAC address because it can easily represent the 8-bit byte by using only two hexadecimal symbols.

MAC addresses are 48 bits in length and always are expressed as 12 hexadecimal digits. The first six hexadecimal digits (reading left to right), which the IEEE administers, identify the manufacturer or the vendor and thus comprise the Organizational Unique Identifier (OUI). The remaining six hexadecimal digits comprise the interface serial number, or another value administered by the specific vendor. MAC addresses sometimes are referred to as *burned-in addresses (BIAs)* because they are burned into read-only memory (ROM) and are copied into random-access memory (RAM) when the NIC initializes.

Basic Hexadecimal Numbering

Hexadecimal (hex) is the number system that is used to represent MAC addresses. It is referred to as *Base 16* because it uses 16 symbols; combinations of these symbols can then represent all possible numbers. Because only 10 numeric symbols represent decimal digits (0, 1, 2, 3, 4, 5, 6, 7, 8, 9), and Base 16 requires six more symbols, the extra symbols used are the letters A, B, C, D, E, and F.

The position of each symbol, or digit, in a hex number represents the base number 16 raised to a power, or exponent, associated with this position—just as for decimal and binary. Moving from right to left, the first position represents 16^0, or 1; the second position represents 16^1, or 16; the third position, 16^2, or 256; and so on.

Example:

$4F6A = (4 \times 16^3) + (F[15] \times 16^2) + (6 \times 16^1) + (A[10] \times 16^0) = 20330$ (decimal)

MORE INFORMATION

Hexadecimal Numbers

In Base 16, or *hexadecimal*, you work with powers of sixteen. You use hexadecimal notation with data link layer addressing (such as MAC addresses) and when referring to memory addresses in electronic devices. The 16 hexadecimal characters are 0, 1, 2, 3, 4, 5, 6, 7, 8, 9, A, B, C, D, E, and F. The A corresponds to the decimal number 10; B to 11; C to 12; D to 13; E to 14; and F to 15. Some examples of hexadecimal numbers are 2A384C5D9E7F, A001, and 237. You have to be careful that it is clear from the context what base you're referring to; otherwise, the example given of 237 might be mistaken for a decimal number.

Two special notations are used with hexadecimal numbers. Sometimes, you see notation like 0x1A3B or 1A3Bh. These mean the same thing: 1A3B in hexadecimal. To reiterate, if you see a string preceded by 0x or followed by h, you know to interpret the string as a hexadecimal number. In particular, you see these notations when you work with memory registers.

Another fact that is important to understand: One hexadecimal character can represent any decimal number between 0 and 15. In binary, F (15 decimal) is 1111 and A (10 decimal) is 1010. *It follows that 4 bits are required to represent a single hexadecimal character in binary.* A MAC address is 48 bits long (6 bytes), which translates to $48 \div 4 = 12$ hexadecimal characters required to express a MAC address. You can check this by typing **winipcfg** in Windows 95/98 or **ipconfig /all** in Windows NT4/2000 at the command prompt.

MORE INFORMATION (CONTINUED)

Table 6-1 is a hexadecimal table that has three rows. The first row lists *powers of 16*; the second row expresses the *expanded* (multiplied out) *powers of 16*; and the third row is where you indicate how many (between 0 and F) of that power of 16 you want. *Notice that the second row has numbers written in Base 10!* This table uses only four columns because the powers of 16 become very large as the exponent increases; also, it is common to express hexadecimal characters in groups of two or four.

TABLE 6-1 Hexadecimal Table

16^3	16^2	16^1	16^0
4096	256	16	1

Consider the hexadecimal number 3A. You can determine the value of 3A in decimal by using a hexadecimal table (see Table 6-2).

TABLE 6-2 Hexadecimal Table for 3A

16^1	16^0
16	1
3	A

You can use Table 6-2 to convert the hexadecimal number 3A to Base 10:

$$3A = 3 \times 16 + A \times 1 = 3 \times 16 + 10 \times 1 = 48 + 10 = 58$$

Now, consider the hexadecimal number 23CF. Table 6-3 helps put it in perspective.

TABLE 6-3 Hexadecimal Table for 23CF

16^3	16^2	16^1	16^0
4096	256	16	1
2	3	C	F

You can use Table 6-3 to convert the hexadecimal number 23CF to Base 10:

$$23CF = 2 \times 4096 + 3 \times 256 + C \times 16 + F \times 1 = 2 \times 4096 + 3 \times 256 + 12 \times 16 + 15 \times 1 = 8192 + 768 + 192 + 15 = 9167$$

The smallest decimal value that can be represented by four hexadecimal characters, 0000, is 0. The largest decimal value that can be represented by four hexadecimal characters, FFFF, is 65,535. It follows that the range of decimal numbers that can be represented by four hexadecimal characters (16 bits) is 0 to 65,535, a total of 65,536 or 2^{16} possible values.

Now you know how to convert a hexadecimal number to a decimal number. As an exercise, use a table to show that the hexadecimal number 8D2B3 converts to the decimal number 578,227. As with binary to decimal conversion, after repeating this procedure several times, you'll probably develop your own shortcuts that might include not using a table at all.

Converting Decimal Numbers to Hexadecimal Numbers

There's more than one way to proceed, so stick with your favorite method. The following process demonstrates one way to go about this conversion. If you are already comfortable with a particular method, you might want to skip the next two paragraphs.

To convert a decimal number to a hexadecimal number, the idea is to first find the largest power of 16 that is less than or equal to the decimal number, and then to determine how many times it fits into the decimal number. Because you've been through a similar process with decimal to binary conversion, you can just get right to it. One difference to note is that the highest power of 16 to fit into a decimal number sometimes fits multiple times.

Consider the decimal number 15,211. Looking at Table 6-4, what's the largest power of 16 that is less than or equal to 15,211? Well, 4096 meets this criterion. How many times does it fit in 15,211? Checking, you see that 4096 fits three times and no more (4096 × 3 = 12,288), so you know there will be a 3 in the 4096 (or 16^3) column. Now, how much is left over? You find this by subtraction: 15,211 – 12,288 = 2923. Next, you see that 256 fits 11 times (and no more) into 2923 (256 × 11 = 2816), so you know there is a B (not 11!) in the 256 (or 16^2) place. Subtracting, you get 2923 – 2816 = 107. Because 16 fits six times (and no more) into 107 (16 × 6 = 96), you know there is a 6 in the 16 (or 16^1) column. Subtracting, you get 107 – 96 = 11, so the last digit is a B. The hexadecimal value for the decimal number 15,211 is 3B6B. Table 6-4 summarizes this process.

TABLE 6-4 Hexadecimal Table for 3B6B

16^3	16^2	16^1	16^0
4096	256	16	1
3	B	6	B

As with binary numbers, one method for converting them from decimal to hex can be done with the *remainder method*. In this method, you repeatedly divide the decimal number by the base number (in this case 16). You then convert the remainder each time into a hex number.

Example:

Convert the decimal number 24032 to hex:

1. 24032 / 16 = 1502, with a remainder of 0
2. 1502 / 16 = 93, with a remainder of 14 or E
3. 93 / 16 = 5, with a remainder of 13 or D
4. 5 / 16 = 0, with a remainder of 5

By collecting all the remainders backward, you have the hex number 5DE0.

Converting Hexadecimal Numbers to Decimal Numbers

As you saw earlier, you convert hexadecimal numbers to decimal numbers by multiplying the hex digits by the base number of the system 16, raised to the exponent of the position.

Example:

Convert the hex number 3F4B to a decimal number. (Work from left to right.)

$$\begin{aligned} 3 \times 16^3 &= 12288 \\ F(15) \times 16^2 &= 3840 \\ 4 \times 16^1 &= 64 \\ B(11) \times 16^0 &= 11 \\ \text{decimal equivalent} &= 16203 \end{aligned}$$

Methods for Working with Hexadecimal and Binary Numbers

Converting binary to hexadecimal and hexadecimal to binary is an easy conversion. The reason is that 16 is a power of 2. Every four binary digits (bits) correspond to one hexadecimal digit. The conversion looks like this:

Binary Hex	Binary Hex
0000 = 0	1000 = 8
0001 = 1	1001 = 9
0010 = 2	1010 = A
0011 = 3	1011 = B

0100 = 4 1100 = C

0101 = 5 1101 = D

0110 = 6 1110 = E

0111 = 7 1111 = F

So if you have a binary number that looks like 01011011, you break it into two groups of four bits. These look like this: 0101 and 1011. When you convert these two groups to hex, they look like 5 and B. So converting 01011011 to hex is 5B. To convert hex to binary, do the opposite. Convert hex AC to binary. First convert hex A to 1010 binary, and then convert hex C to 1100 binary. So the conversion for hex AC is 10101100 binary.

No matter how large the binary number, you always apply the same conversion. Start from the right of the binary number and break the number into groups of four. If at the left end of the number it doesn't evenly fit into a group of four, add zeros to the left end until it is equal to four digits (bits), this is called padding with zeros. Then convert each group of four to its hex equivalent. Here is an example:

100100100010111110111110111001001:

0001 0010 0100 0101 1111 0111 1101 1100 1001

Converts to:

1 2 4 5 F 7 D C 9

So:

100100100010111110111110111001001 binary = 1245F7DC9 hex

Converting from hex to binary works in exactly the opposite way. For every one hex digit, you convert it to four binary digits (bits). For example,

AD46BF

A D 4 6 B F

Converts to:

1010 1101 0100 0110 1011 1111

So:

AD46BF hex converts to 101011010100011010111111 binary

Be especially careful to include four binary digits for each hexadecimal character, padding with zeros when necessary, for this method to work. This concludes the description of the method used to convert binary to hexadecimal and hexadecimal to binary.

Exercise:

1. Convert 0xAB to Base 10.
2. Convert ABCDh to Base 10.
3. Convert 0xFF to decimal notation.
4. Convert the decimal number 249 to Base 16.
5. Convert the decimal number 65,000 to hexadecimal notation.
6. Convert 0x2B to Base 2.
7. Convert 0x10F8 to Base 2.
8. Change the MAC address 00-A0-CC-3C-4A-39 to binary notation.
9. Change both the IP address 166.122.23.130 and the subnet mask 255.255.255.128 to dotted-hexadecimal form.

MAC Addressing

Without MAC addresses, you have a group of nameless computers on your LAN. Therefore, at the data link layer, a header and a trailer is added to the upper layer data. The header contains control information intended for the data link layer entity in the destination system. The trailer contains a frame check sequence. Data from upper layer entities is encapsulated in the data link layer header and trailer.

In an Ethernet network, one node's transmission traverses the entire segment and is received and examined by every node. In a linear bus topology, when the signal reaches the end of a segment, terminators absorb it to prevent it from going back onto the segment. Only one transmission is allowed on the LAN at any given time. For example, Figure 6-4 shows a linear bus network with Node A transmitting a packet addressed to Station D. This packet is received by all nodes. Node D recognizes its MAC address and processes the frame. However, nodes B and C do not recognize their address and discard the frame.

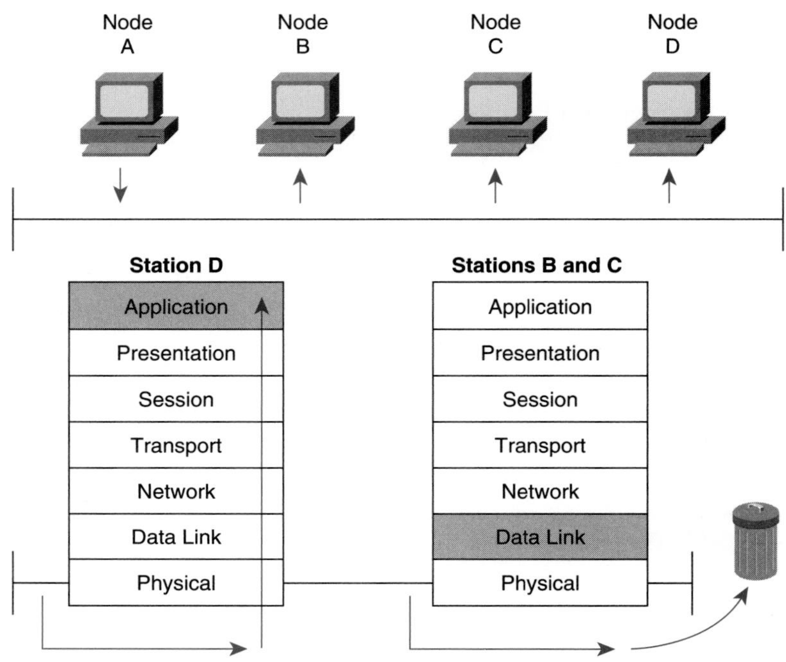

FIGURE 6-4 Node D recognizes its MAC address and processes the frame; Nodes B and C do not recognize their addresses and discard the frame.

MORE INFORMATION

Ethernet/802.3 Broadcast

Broadcasting is a powerful tool that sends a single frame to many stations at the same time. Broadcasting uses a data-link destination address of all 1s (FFFF.FFFF.FFFF or FF-FF-FF-FF-FF-FF in hexadecimal). As Figure 6-5 shows, if Station A transmits a frame with a destination address of all 1s, Stations B, C, and D receive the frame and pass it on to upper layers for further processing.

Broadcasting can seriously affect the performance of stations by interrupting them unnecessarily. For this reason, broadcasts should be used only when the MAC address of the destination is unknown or when the destination is all stations.

MORE INFORMATION (CONTINUED)

FIGURE 6-5 Broadcasting sends a single frame to many stations at the same time by using the data-link broadcast destination address.

Station A	Station B	Station C	Station D
Application	Application	Application	Application
Presentation	Presentation	Presentation	Presentation
Session	Session	Session	Session
Transport	Transport	Transport	Transport
Network	Network	Network	Network
Data link	Data Link	Data Link	Data Link
Physical	Physical	Physical	Physical

MAC Address and NICs

Each network node has a uniquely assigned Media Access Control (MAC) address, which is located on the installed network card (NIC) (see Figure 6-6). Also referred to as the physical address, no two MACs should ever be identical.

FIGURE 6-6 The physical address of a computer is on a NIC.

As stated in the introduction to hexadecimal numbers as MAC addresses, a MAC address is a 48-bit address expressed as 12 hexadecimal digits. The first six hexadecimal digits of a MAC address contain a manufacturer identification (vendor code), also known as the Organizationally Unique Identifier (OUI). The last six hexadecimal digits are administered by each vendor and often represent the interface serial number (see Figure 6-7).

FIGURE 6-7
The MAC address format.

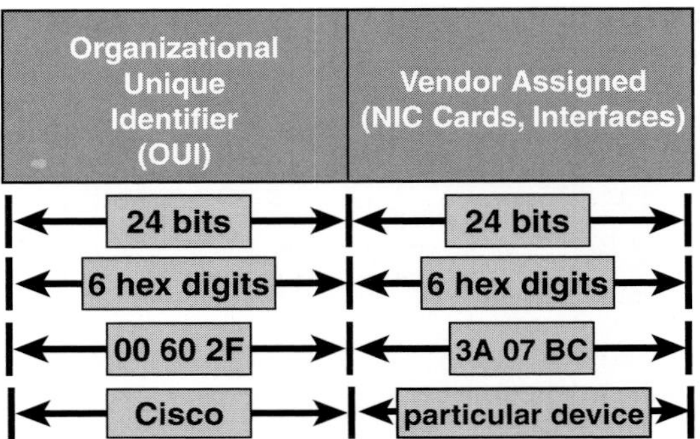

Before it leaves the factory, the hardware manufacturer assigns a physical address to each NIC. MAC addresses do have one major disadvantage. They have no structure, and are considered flat address spaces. As soon as your network grows to more than just a few computers, this disadvantage of a flat address space becomes a real problem. A MAC address is programmed into a chip on the NIC. Because the MAC address is located on the NIC, if the NIC is replaced in a computer, the physical address of the station changes to that of the new MAC address. Again, MAC addresses are written using hexadecimal (Base 16) numbers. There are two formats for MAC addresses: 0000.0c12.3456 or 00-00-0c-12-34-56.

Ethernet and 802.3 LANs are broadcast networks. All stations see all frames. Each station must examine every frame to determine whether that station is the desired destination. On an Ethernet network, when one device wants to send data to another device, it can open a communication pathway to the other device by using its MAC address. When a source device sends data out on a network, the data carries the MAC address of its intended destination. As this data propagates along the network media, the NIC in each device on the network checks to see whether its MAC address matches the physical destination address carried by the data frame. If there is no match, the NIC discards the data frame.

An important part of both encapsulation and de-encapsulation is the addition or removal of source and destination MAC addresses. Information cannot be delivered properly on a network without these addresses. MAC addresses are vital to the functioning of a computer network. They provide a way for computers to identify themselves and each other. They give hosts a permanent, unique name. The number of possible addresses is not going to run out anytime soon, because there are 16^{12} (or 2 trillion!) possible MAC addresses.

Framing

Encoded bit streams on physical media represent a tremendous technological accomplishment, but they alone, are not enough to make communication happen. Framing helps organize essential information that could not, otherwise, be interpreted by an end system (based simply on coded bit streams alone). Examples of such information are

- Which computers are communicating with one another
- When communication between individual computers begins and when it ends
- A record of errors that occurred during the communication
- Whose turn it is to "talk" in a computer "conversation"
- Where the data is located within the frame

When you have a way to identify computers, you can move on to framing. Framing is the Layer 2 encapsulation process; a frame is the Layer 2 protocol data unit. When you work with bits, the most accurate diagram you can use to visualize them is a voltage versus time graph. However, because you usually deal with larger units of data and addressing and control information, a voltage versus time graph could become ridiculously large and confusing. Another type of diagram you could use is the frame format diagram, which is based on voltage versus time graphs. You read them from left to right, just like an oscilloscope graph. The frame format diagram shows different groupings of bits (fields); certain functions are associated with the different fields.

TWO ANALOGIES FOR FRAMES

The following two analogies can help explain frames:

Picture Frame Analogy

A picture frame marks the outside of a painting or a photograph. It makes the painting or the photograph easier to transport and protects the painting or the photograph from physical damage. In computer communication, the picture frame is like the data frame, and the painting or the photograph is like the data. The frame marks the beginning and the end of a piece of data, and makes the data easier to transport. The frame helps protect the data from errors.

continues

TWO ANALOGIES FOR FRAMES (CONTINUED)

Packaging/Shipping Analogy

When you ship a large, heavy package, you usually include various layers of packing material. The last step, before you put it on a truck to be shipped, is to place it on a pallet and wrap it. You can relate this to computer communications by thinking of the securely packed object as the data, and the whole, wrapped package on the pallet as the frame.

Frame Format

Various standards describe many different types of frames. A frame has sections, called *fields*, and each field is composed of bytes (see Figure 6-8). The names of the fields commonly found in a data link layer frame are as follows:

- Frame start field
- Address field
- Length / type / control field
- Data field
- Frame check sequence field
- Frame stop field

FIGURE 6-8
A generic frame format.

Field Names					
A	B	C	D	E	F
Start Frame Field	Address Field	Type/ Length Field	Data Field	FCS Field	Stop Frame Field

Frame Start Field

When computers are connected to a physical medium, there must be a way they can grab the attention of other computers to send the message, "Here comes a frame!" Various technologies have different ways of doing this process, but all frames, regardless of technology, begin with a sequence of signaling bytes.

Address Field

All frames contain identifying information, such as the MAC address of the source computer and the MAC address of the destination computer.

Control Field

Most frames have some specialized fields. In some technologies, a length field specifies the exact length of a frame. Some have a field that specifies the Layer 3 protocol encapsulated by the Layer 2 frame. There is also a set of technologies where no such fields are used.

Data Field

The reason for sending frames is to get higher-layer data, ultimately the user application data, from the source computer to the destination computer. The data package you want to deliver includes the message you want to send (the data). The padding bytes are added sometimes so the frames have a minimum length—this is done for timing purposes. LLC bytes also are included with the data field in the IEEE standard frames. Remember that the Logical Link Control (LLC) sublayer takes the network protocol data, a Layer 3 packet, and adds control information to help deliver that packet to its destination. Layer 2 communicates with upper layers through Logical Link Control (LLC).

Frame Check Sequence Field

All frames (and the bits, the bytes, and the fields contained within them) are susceptible to errors from a variety of sources. You need to know how to detect them. An effective but inefficient way to do this might be to send every frame twice, or to have the destination computer send a copy of the original frame back to the source computer before it can send another frame.

Fortunately, there is a more efficient and effective way, one in which only the bad frames are discarded and retransmitted. The Frame Check Sequence (FCS) field contains a number that is calculated by the source computer and is based on the data in the frame. When the destination computer receives the frame, it recalculates the FCS number and compares it with the FCS number included in the frame. If the two numbers are different, an error is assumed and the frame is discarded.

Three primary ways exist to calculate the Frame Check Sequence number:

- **Cyclic redundancy check** (CRC)—Performs polynomial calculations on the data.
- **Two-dimensional parity**—Adds an 8th bit that makes an 8-bit sequence have an odd or even number of binary 1s.
- **Internet checksum**—Adds the values of all the data bits to arrive at a sum.

Frame Stop Field

To start a frame, the computer that transmits data must get the attention of other devices, and then claim it again, to end the frame. The length field (if applicable) indicates where the end of the frame should occur. The frame ends after the FCS. Sometimes there is a formal byte sequence referred to as an *end-frame delimiter.*

Access Methods for Media Access Control

Media Access Control (MAC) refers to protocols that determine which computer on a shared-medium environment (media access domain) is allowed to transmit the data. MAC, with LLC, comprises the IEEE version of Layer 2. MAC and LLC are both sublayers of Layer 2.

There are two broad categories of Media Access Control: deterministic (taking turns) and non-deterministic (first come, first served). Token Ring and FDDI are deterministic and Ethernet/802.3 is non-deterministic (also called *probabilistic*).

THREE ANALOGIES FOR MAC

Tollbooth Analogy

Consider how a tollbooth controls multiple lanes of vehicles crossing a bridge. Vehicles gain access to the bridge by paying a toll. In this analogy, the vehicle is the frame, the bridge is the shared medium, and paying the fee at the tollbooth is the protocol that allows access to the bridge.

Ticket Line Analogy

Picture yourself waiting in line to ride a roller coaster at an amusement park. The line is necessary to ensure order; there are a specified maximum number of people who can fit on the roller coaster at one time. Eventually, as the line moves, you pay for your ticket and you sit in a car. In this analogy, the people are the data, the cars are the frames, the roller coaster tracks are the shared medium, and the protocol is the waiting in line and the presentation of the ticket.

Meeting Analogy

Imagine yourself at a meeting table with other members of a large talkative group. There is one shared medium—the air around the meeting table—through which signals (spoken words) are communicated. The protocol for determining access to the medium is that the first person who speaks, when everyone quiets down, can talk as long as he/she wants, until finished. In this analogy, the words of the individual members are the packets, the air above the meeting table is the medium, and the first person to speak in the meeting is the protocol.

Deterministic MAC Protocols

Deterministic MAC protocols use a form of taking turns. Some Native American tribes used the custom of passing a talking stick during gatherings. Whoever held the talking stick was allowed to speak. When that person finished, he/she passed it to another person.

In this analogy, the shared media is the air, the data are the words of the speaker, and the protocol is possession of the talking stick. The stick might even be called a token. This situation is similar to a deterministic data link protocol called Token Ring. In a Token Ring network, individual hosts are arranged in a ring, as shown in Figure 6-9. A special data token circulates around the ring. When a host receives the token, it can transmit data, if it has some, instead of the token. This is called *seizing the token*. When the transmitted frame comes back around to the transmitter, the station transmits a new token. The frame thus is removed, or *stripped*, from the ring.

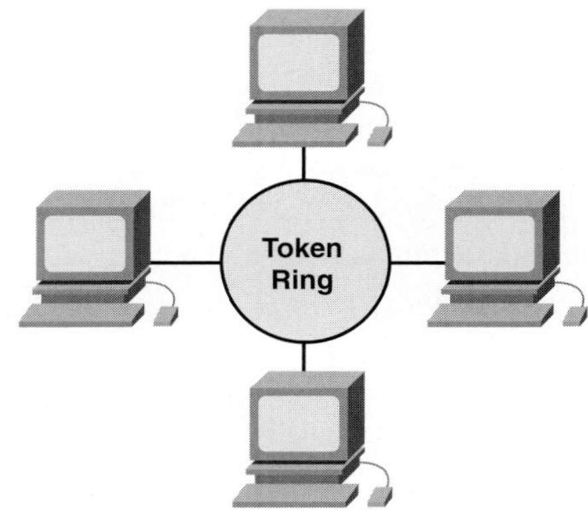

FIGURE 6-9
A Token Ring network with four hosts.

Non-Deterministic MAC Protocols

Non-deterministic MAC protocols use a first-come, first-served (FCFS) approach. In the late 1970s, the University of Hawaii developed and used a radio communication system (ALOHA) that connected the various Hawaiian Islands. The protocol they used allowed anyone to transmit at will. This led to radio wave collisions that could be detected by listeners during transmissions. ALOHA eventually became a modern MAC protocol called *Carrier Sense Multiple Access with Collision Detection (CSMA/CD)*.

To use this shared-medium technology, Ethernet allows the networking devices to arbitrate for the right to transmit. Stations on a CSMA/CD network listen for quiet, at which time it's okay to transmit. However, if two stations transmit at the same time, a collision occurs, and neither station's transmission succeeds. All other stations on the network also hear the collision and wait for silence. The transmitting stations in turn each wait a random period of time (a backoff period) before retransmitting, thus minimizing the probability of a second collision.

Three Specific Topological Implementations and Their MACs

Three common Layer 2 technologies are Token Ring, FDDI, and Ethernet. All three specify Layer 2 functionality (for example, LLC, naming, framing, and

MAC), as well as Layer 1 signaling components and media access. They each have their own topological implementations as well. The specific topologies associated with three LAN technologies are as follows:

- **Ethernet**—Logical bus topology (information flow is on a linear bus) and physical star or extended star (wired as a star).
- **Token Ring**—Logical ring topology (in other words, information flow is controlled in a ring) and a physical star topology (in other words, it is wired as a star).
- **FDDI**—Logical ring topology (information flow is controlled in a ring) and physical dual-ring topology (wired as a dual-ring).

MORE INFORMATION

The Media Access Domain

A media access domain consists of all the devices connected to a LAN that must share the LAN's bandwidth. The name and the nature of this domain depend on the media access methodology employed in the LAN. The two primary methodologies for regulating media access are *collision detection* and *token passing*.

Other media access arbitration techniques exist but these two account for the majority of existing LAN implementations. More importantly, they adequately demonstrate the differences between a media access domain as well as a MAC broadcast domain.

The Collision Domain

In a LAN that uses contention to arbitrate permission to transmit, such as the various Ethernets, this domain is known as a collision domain. This name reflects the fact that this is a competition-based, chaotic, and less-than-perfectly reliable access arbitration technique.

In essence, any device in the contention domain can begin transmitting if it detects no other traffic on the transmission media. The lack of traffic is presumed to mean an idle LAN. In fact, because transmissions are not instantaneous, silence on the LAN might just mean that a device is transmitting but that transmission hasn't reached all the devices yet. Therefore, a device can begin transmitting only to have its transmissions collide with another. In such cases, both transmission streams are compromised and must be retransmitted.

In an Ethernet network, regardless of the media type or transmission speed, a contention domain consists of all the devices that must compete for the right to transmit. IEEE-compliant Ethernet LANs can support up to a maximum of 1,024 station devices in a single contention domain. This means that there can be up to 1,024 total devices competing for the right to transmit in an Ethernet contention domain. In reality, this number is far more than typically is used in a live network—a more realistic figure would be less than 200 devices.

MORE INFORMATION (CONTINUED)

The Token-Passing Domain

In LANs that pass tokens to regulate media access, such as Fiber Distributed Data Interface (FDDI) or Token Ring, the media access domain is called the *token-passing domain*. Media access is arbitrated by passing a token in an orderly, circular fashion between the LAN's peripheral devices. A token is a special pattern of bits that is circulated around the media access domain.

A LAN-attached device can modify the token to form the header of a data frame. This is another way of saying that a node can seize the token. Recipient peripheral devices copy the data in the frame from the LAN. This device also inverts some of the bits in the frame's header to acknowledge its receipt. The frame then is allowed to continue traversing the ring. When it returns to its originator, that device takes the frame off the network and transmits a token, which travels to the next device downstream. Although this might seem complicated, token passing is a highly organized and efficient means of arbitrating media access.

In a token-passing LAN, regardless of the media type or the transmission speed, a token-passing domain consists of all the devices that pass tokens on a *ring*. Here is where a discontinuity in definitions occurs between Token Ring and FDDI, the two most common token-passing LAN architectures. They enjoy similar media access domain characteristics, but they define devices differently.

In a Token Ring network, only the LAN's devices count as devices. The hubs are nothing more than repeaters; they are incapable of modifying token bits. Therefore, they cannot be considered devices or nodes in the parlance of this LAN architecture. FDDI, on the other hand, does count hub ports as devices. This has some significant ramifications on the sizes of the media access domains in these two LAN architectures. Token Ring LANs can support up to a maximum of 260 devices in a single token-passing domain. FDDI can support up to 500 total devices (in its token-passing domain). It implies that you can connect more devices to a Token Ring LAN than you can to a FDDI LAN.

Additionally, FDDI enables devices to be either single-attached (SA) or dual-attached (DA) to the LAN. These describe the number of connections made to the LAN for each device. While providing redundancy, DA FDDI effectively doubles the device count in the token-passing domain. Each attached port must be counted as a separate device.

Expanding Media Access Domains

Many of today's LANs are constructed using repeating hubs. The result is a star-shaped physical topology; devices are interconnected via a central hub. In other words, their connections to the LAN radiate out from a single point much like the rays of a star. Consequently, the physical topologies of Ethernet and Token Ring LANs can be identical regardless of their media access methodology. Figure 6-10 illustrates a media access domain in a star-shaped LAN.

continues

MORE INFORMATION (CONTINUED)

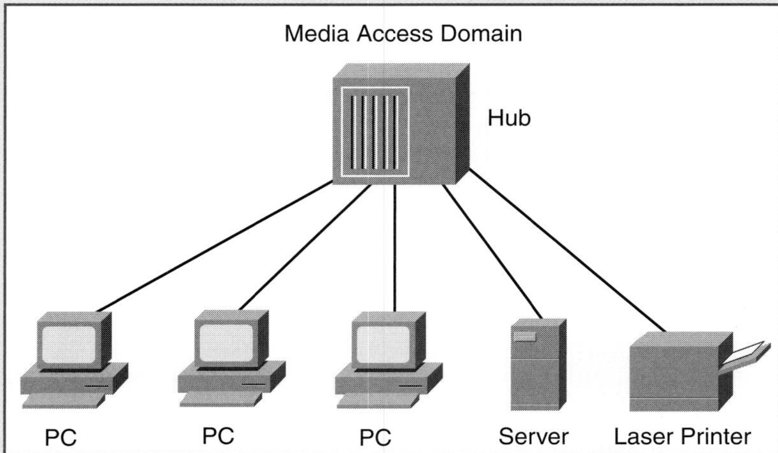

FIGURE 6-10 A media access domain in a star-shaped LAN.

If a given work environment were to install a second Ethernet hub for a second workgroup, it would have two separate Ethernet LANs. That is, each LAN would be completely autonomous and define its own media access and MAC broadcast domains. Figure 6-11 illustrates this.

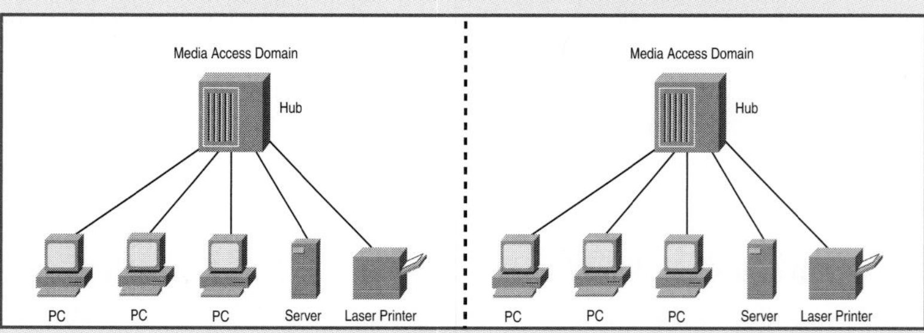

FIGURE 6-11 Two separate LANs, each with its own media access domain.

If the two LANs in Figure 6-11 were to be interconnected directly, the result would be a single LAN. This LAN's media access domain would consist of all the devices that populated the original two LANs. The media access domain also would include the two ports used to interconnect the LANs. Therefore, this LAN would consolidate all LAN-attached devices into a single media access domain. See Figure 6-12.

MORE INFORMATION (CONTINUED)

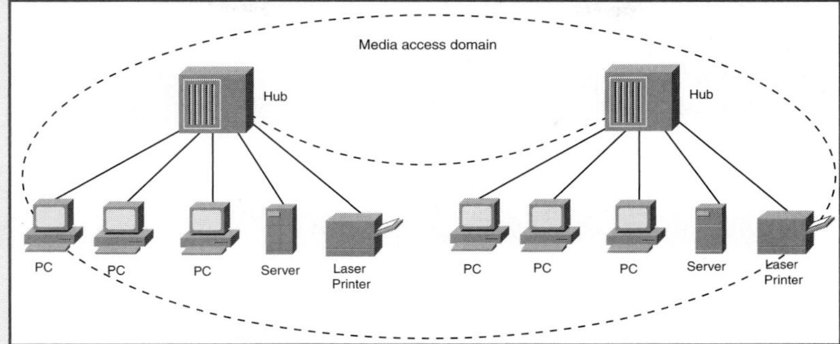

FIGURE 6-12 Making one LAN from the original two.

Interconnecting the hubs of the two LANs, either contention based or token passing, results in a functional consolidation of their media access domains. Depending on the LAN architecture, the expanded media access domain also might have to include the hub ports that are interconnected. This is the only way to expand a media access domain.

Other access domain independent forms of LAN expansion and LAN-to-LAN interconnection are possible but require additional hardware. This hardware can include LAN switches, bridges, and routers. These devices, however, do not increase either the size of the media access domain or the MAC broadcast domain. Therefore, they enable the overall size of a LAN to increase without a commensurate increase in the size of its media access domains.

The MAC Broadcast Domain

A MAC broadcast domain consists of all the devices, which are connected to a LAN, that receive framed data broadcast by a machine to all other machines on the LAN. The concept of a MAC broadcast is virtually universal throughout all IEEE-compliant LANs, regardless of their media access methodology.

Note that FDDI is considered an IEEE-compliant LAN even though IEEE did not create it. This is because the IEEE standards are passed to the American National Standards Institute (ANSI) for integration with its national standards. FDDI is an ANSI specification that complies with the ANSI equivalents of the IEEE 802.1 and 802.2 standards. Therefore, FDDI is IEEE compliant.

In essence, a MAC broadcast domain is the set of devices that can communicate directly without requiring higher-layer protocols or addressing. To better illustrate the difference between MAC broadcast and media access domains, compare Figure 6-13 to Figure 6-10.

continues

MORE INFORMATION (CONTINUED)

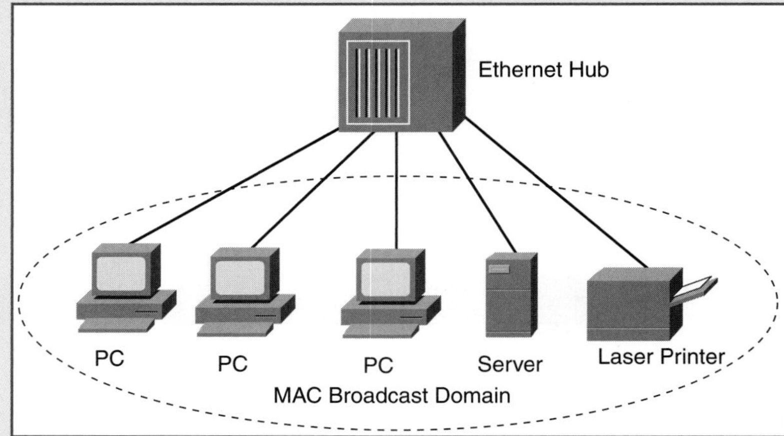

FIGURE 6-13
An Ethernet MAC broadcast domain with five devices.

Figure 6-13 uses the same LAN configuration depicted in Figure 6-10 but identifies its MAC broadcast domain rather than the media access domain. The key distinction between MAC broadcast and media access domains becomes obvious when you examine the various LAN segmentation mechanisms.

As with the media access domain, adding a second isolated LAN creates a second, fully separate broadcast domain. Figure 6-14 identifies the MAC broadcast domains of the LAN configuration presented in Figure 6-11.

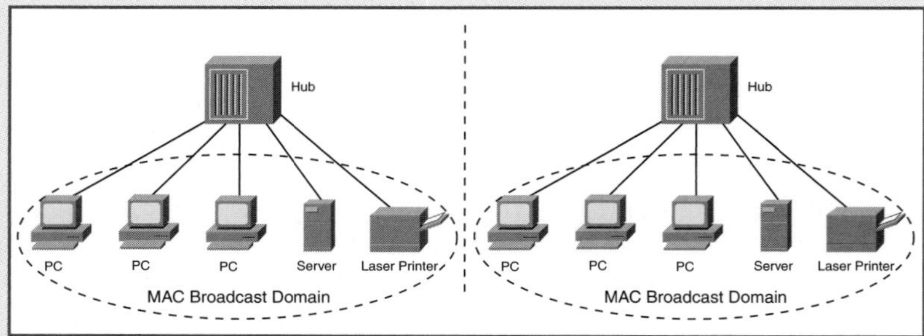

FIGURE 6-14
Two separate Ethernet MAC broadcast domains.

Interconnecting these LANs in the manner demonstrated in Figure 6-12 results in a single, but larger, MAC broadcast domain. Figure 6-15 illustrates this new broadcast domain.

MORE INFORMATION (CONTINUED)

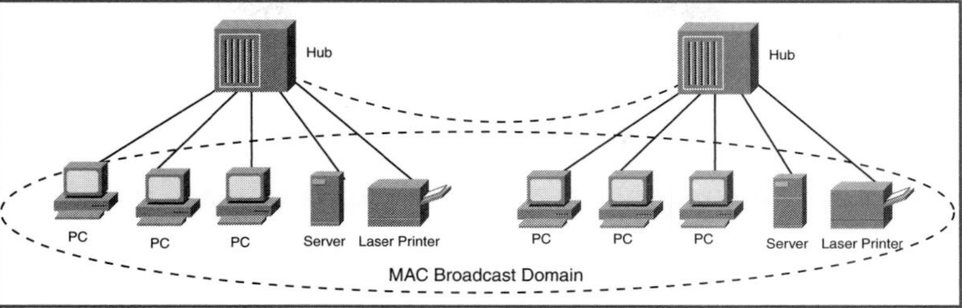

FIGURE 6-15 Making one Ethernet LAN and MAC broadcast domain from the original two.

This LAN's MAC broadcast domain consists of all the devices that populated the original two LANs' broadcast domains. In this scenario, any given broadcast message is now propagated across the network to twice as many devices as before. Therein lies the proverbial double-edged sword of LANs with large MAC broadcast domains: They can become quite large due to the amalgamation of their media access domains, but suffer from the flatness, or lack of hierarchy, inherent in a MAC broadcast domain.

The Trouble with Flat LANs

LANs built with a single MAC broadcast domain are known as *flat LANs*. They are flat because there is no structure or hierarchy to their broadcast domains. The benefit of having a large broadcast domain is that it is extremely easy to reach all the devices that are interconnected on the LAN. The potential danger, also, is that it is extremely easy to reach all the devices on the LAN. The more devices you connect to a flat LAN, the more resources each one consumes.

MAC broadcast message. Using the wrong communications protocol (that is, one that makes extensive use of MAC broadcasting) could easily compromise the performance of the network, as well as all the devices that populate it.

Note that MAC broadcasts are performed by setting the destination MAC address of a frame of data to its highest possible value: FF:FF:FF:FF:FF:FF. This reserved address value, when placed in a frame's destination address field, is interpreted by all IEEE-compliant LANs as being addressed to all local machines. Therefore, all machines process the reserved address value regardless of their individual MAC addresses. In the next chapter, you will learn how to expand the overall size of a LAN and to control the size of the media access and/or MAC broadcast domains.

Summary

In this chapter, you learned that the Institute of Electrical and Electronic Engineers (IEEE) is a professional organization that defines network standards. You should know that IEEE LAN standards (including IEEE 802.3 and IEEE

802.5) are the best-known IEEE communication standards and are the predominant LAN standards in the world today. The IEEE divides the OSI link layer into two separate sublayers:

- Media Access Control (MAC)
- Logical Link Control (LLC)

This chapter explained how Layer 2 of the OSI model provides access to the networking media, which enables the data to reach its intended destination on a network. With this in mind, you should understand the following:

- Layer 2 provides transit of data across a physical link
- Layer 2 uses a system called Media Access Control (MAC)
- Layer 2 uses the MAC address, which is the physical address located on a NIC
- Layer 2 uses framing to organize or group the bits

Now that you have a firm understanding of Layer 2 concepts, you are ready to learn about the Layer 2 technologies, which are discussed in the next chapter.

Check Your Understanding

1. Layer 2 uses _________ to organize or group bits of data.

   A. Framing

   B. Packeting

   C. Encapsulation

   D. De-encapsulation

2. The recognized IEEE sublayers are concerned with what layers of the OSI reference model?

   A. 2 and 3

   B. 1 and 2

   C. 3 and 4

   D. 1 and 3

3. In many technologies, the NIC includes a Layer 1 device called a ________?

   A. Data control module

   B. Transmitter

   C. Transceiver

   D. Repeater

4. The LLC, as a sublayer, participates in the ________ process.

   A. Encryption

   B. Encapsulation

   C. Framing

   D. None of the above

5. The first six hexadecimal numbers in a MAC address represent an ________.

   A. Interface serial number

   B. Organizational unique identifier

   C. Interface unique identifier

   D. None of the above

6. The hexadecimal number system is also know as
   - **A.** Hex 16
   - **B.** Base 2
   - **C.** Base 16
   - **D.** Base 10
7. What is the Base 16 equivalent to the decimal number 24032?
   - **A.** 5DE0
   - **B.** 0ED3
   - **C.** E03D
   - **D.** 3ED0
8. What is the decimal equivalent to the hexadecimal number E6D3?
   - **A.** 59019
   - **B.** 59091
   - **C.** 59136
   - **D.** 59093
9. Convert the decimal number 2989 to hex.
   - **A.** FDD1
   - **B.** BAD
   - **C.** TED
   - **D.** CAD
10. MAC address are ___ bits in length.
    - **A.** 12
    - **B.** 24
    - **C.** 48
    - **D.** 64
11. Where does the MAC address reside?
    - **A.** Transceiver
    - **B.** Computer BIOS
    - **C.** NIC
    - **D.** CMOS

12. Which of the following statements best describes communication between two devices on a LAN?

A. The source device encapsulates data in a frame with the MAC address of the destination device, and then transmits it. Everyone on the LAN sees it, but the devices with non-matching addresses otherwise ignore the frame.

B. The source encapsulates the data and places a destination MAC address in the frame. It puts the frame on the LAN, where only the device with the matching address can check the address field.

C. The destination device encapsulates data in a frame with the MAC address of the source device, puts it on the LAN, and the device with the matching address removes the frame.

D. Each device on the LAN receives the frame and passes it up to the computer, where software decides whether to keep or to discard the frame.

13. Which are the functions associated with framing?

A. Identifies which computers are communicating with one another

B. Signals when communication between individual computers begins and when it ends

C. Flags corrupted frames

D. All of the above

14. How does a computer on a LAN detect an error in a frame?

A. It sends a copy of the frame back to the sender for verification.

B. It checks the destination address to verify that the frame was really intended for them.

C. It compares an FCS in the frame to one that the computer calculates from the contents of the frame.

D. It calculates a checksum from the data in the frame, and then sends it back to the source for verification.

15. Media Access Control refers to what?

A. The state in which a NIC has captured the networking media and is ready to transmit

B. Rules that govern media capturing and releasing

C. Protocols that determine which computer on a shared-medium environment is allowed to transmit the data

D. A formal byte sequence has been transmitted

16. Which best describes a CSMA/CD network?

A. One node's transmission traverses the entire network and is received and examined by every node.

B. Signals are sent directly to the destination if the source knows both the MAC and IP addresses.

C. One node's transmission goes to the nearest router, which sends it directly to the destination.

D. Signals are always sent in broadcast mode.

17. Which best describes broadcasting?

A. Sending a single frame to many stations at the same time

B. Sending a single frame to all routers to simultaneously update their routing tables

C. Sending a single frame to all routers at the same time

D. Sending a single frame to all hubs and bridges at the same time

18. Which protocol listed below is a non-deterministic protocol?

A. Token Ring

B. CSMA/CD

C. IPX

D. RIP

19. FDDI is characterized as

A. Physical ring and logical dual-ring topology

B. Logical ring and physical bus topology

C. Logical ring and physical dual-ring topology

D. Logical ring and linear bus topology

20. Which is true of a deterministic MAC protocol?

A. It defines collisions and specifies what to do about them.

B. It allows the hub to determine the number of users active at any one time.

C. It allows hosts to “take turns” sending data.

D. It allows the use of a “talking stick” by network administers to control the media access of any users considered “troublemakers.”

Objectives

After reading this chapter, you will be able to

- Understand Token Ring basics
- Understand Fiber Distributed Data Interface (FDDI) basics
- Understand Ethernet and IEEE 802.3
- Describe Layer 2 devices
- Describe Ethernet LAN segmentation
- Understand basic Ethernet 10BaseT troubleshooting

Chapter 7

Layer 2: Technologies

Introduction

The previous chapter discussed LAN media access control and the IEEE model, and showed how the data link layer provides transit of data across a physical link by using the Media Access Control (MAC) addresses. This chapter tells you more about Layer 2 LAN technologies. Ethernet, Fiber Distributed Data Interface (FDDI), and Token Ring are widely used LAN technologies that account for virtually all deployed LANs.

In this chapter, you learn more about Ethernet, FDDI, and Token Ring, along with the IEEE specifications for each of these technologies. You learn about the LAN standards that specify cabling and signaling at the physical and data link layers of the OSI reference model. In addition, you look more closely at Layer 2 devices and see some basic Ethernet 10BaseT troubleshooting.

Token Ring/802.5 Basics

IBM developed the first Token Ring network in the 1970s. It is still IBM's primary LAN technology and is second only to Ethernet (IEEE 802.3) in terms of LAN implementations. The IEEE 802.5 specification is almost identical to—and completely compatible with—IBM's Token Ring network. The IEEE 802.5 specification was modeled after IBM's Token Ring and continues to shadow its ongoing development. The term *Token Ring* refers both to IBM's Token Ring and to IEEE's 802.5 specification.

Token Ring Frame Format

Tokens are 3 bytes in length and consist of a start delimiter, an access control byte, and an end delimiter (see Figure 7-1). The start delimiter alerts each station to the arrival of a token, or data/command frame. This field also includes bit patterns that distinguish the byte from the rest of the frame by violating the encoding scheme used elsewhere in the frame.

Access Control Byte

The access control byte contains the priority and reservation fields, a token, and a monitor bit. The token bit distinguishes a token from a data/command frame, and a monitor bit determines whether a frame is continuously circling the ring.

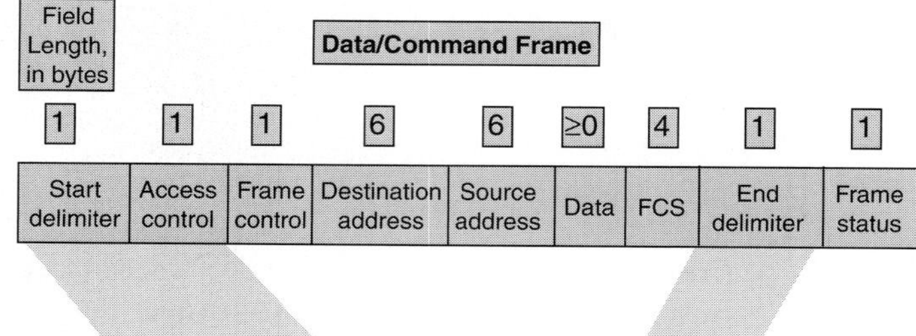

FIGURE 7-1
Data frames carry information for upper-layer protocols, and command frames contain control information and have no data for upper-layer protocols.

The end delimiter signals the end of the token or data/command frame. It contains bits that indicate a damaged frame, as well as bits that indicate whether a frame is the last of a logical sequence.

Data/Command Frames

Data/command frames vary in size depending on the size of the information field. Data frames carry information for upper-layer protocols; command frames contain control information and have no data for upper-layer protocols.

In data/command frames, a frame control byte follows the access control byte. The frame control byte indicates whether the frame contains data or control information. In control frames, this byte specifies the type of control information.

Following the frame control byte are two address fields that identify destination and source stations. As with IEEE 802.5, their addresses are 6 bytes in length. The data field follows the address fields. The length of this field is limited by the ring token that holds the time, thus defining the maximum time a station might hold the token.

Following the data field is the frame check sequence (FCS) field. The source station fills this field with a calculated value dependent on the frame contents. The destination station recalculates the value to determine whether the frame has been damaged in transit. The frame is discarded if it has been damaged. As with the token, the end delimiter completes the data/command frame.

Token Passing

Token Ring and IEEE 802.5 are the primary examples of token-passing networks. Token-passing networks move a small frame, called a token, around the network (see Figure 7-2). Possession of the token grants the right to transmit data. If a node that receives a token has no information to send, it passes the token to the next end station. Each station can hold the token for a maximum period of time, depending on the specific technology that has been implemented.

FIGURE 7-2
In Token Ring, collisions are inherently avoided because there is only one token permitted on the network at time.

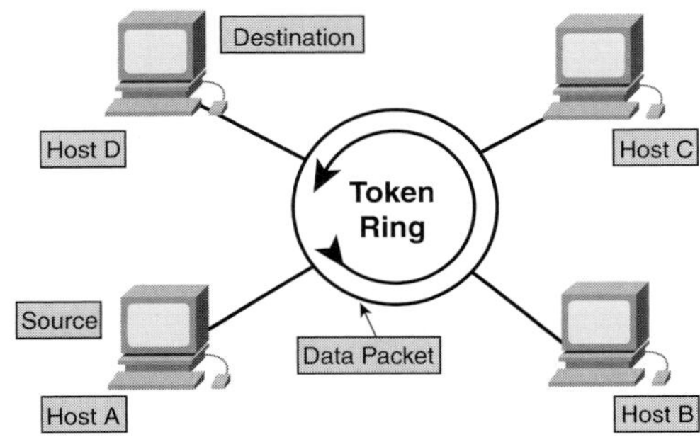

When a token is passed to a host that has information to transmit, the host seizes the token and alters 1 bit of it. The token becomes a data frame. Next, the station appends the information to transmit to the token and sends this data to the next station on the ring. There is no token on the network while the information frame is circling the ring, unless the ring supports early token release. Other stations on the ring cannot transmit at this time; they must wait for the token to become available. Token Ring networks have no collisions. If early token release is supported, a new token can be released by the transmitter when the frame transmission has been completed.

The information frame circulates the ring until it reaches the intended destination station, which copies the information for processing. The information frame continues around the ring until it reaches the sending station, where it is removed. The sending station can verify whether the frame was received and copied by the destination. The destination station also sets bits in the frame status byte: bits to indicate that the destination is active on the ring and bits to indicate the frame was copied without error. The sending station checks the bits in the frame status byte.

Unlike CSMA/CD networks, such as Ethernet, token-passing networks are deterministic. This means that you can calculate the maximum time that will pass before any end station will be capable of transmitting. This feature and several reliability features make Token Ring networks ideal for applications in which any delay must be predictable and robust network operation is important.

Priority System

Token Ring networks use a sophisticated priority system that permits certain user-designated, high-priority stations to use the network more frequently. Token Ring frames have two fields that control priority: the priority field and the reservation field.

Only stations with a priority equal to or higher than the priority value contained in a token can seize that token. After the token is seized and changed to an information frame, only stations with a priority value higher than that of the transmitting station can reserve the token for the next network pass. The next token generated includes the higher priority of the reserving station. Stations that raise a token's priority level must reinstate the previous priority when their transmission has been completed.

Management Mechanisms

Token Ring networks use several mechanisms for detecting and compensating for network faults. One mechanism is to select one station in the Token Ring network to be the active monitor. This station acts as a centralized source of timing information for other ring stations and performs a variety of ring-maintenance functions. The active monitor station can potentially be any station on the network. One of this station's functions is to remove continuously circulating frames from the ring. When a sending device fails, its frame can continue to circle the ring and prevent other stations from transmitting their frames, which can lock up the network. The active monitor can detect these frames, remove them from the ring, and generate a new token.

The IBM Token Ring network's physical star topology also contributes to the overall network reliability. Active multistation access units (MSAUs or MAUs) can see all information in a Token Ring network, thus enabling them to check for problems and to selectively remove stations from the ring whenever necessary. Beaconing, a Token Ring protocol, detects and tries to repair network faults. When a station detects a serious problem with the network, such as a cable break, it sends a beacon frame. This process of each device on the ring sending the beacon frame defines a failure domain. A failure domain includes the station that is reporting the failure, its nearest active upstream neighbor (NAUN), and everything in between. Beaconing initiates another process called autoreconfiguration, in which nodes within the failure domain automatically perform diagnostics. This is an attempt to reconfigure the network around the failed areas. Physically, MSAUs can accomplish this through electrical reconfiguration.

Token Ring Signaling

Manchester encoding results in 0 being encoded as a high-to-low transition and 1 being encoded as a low-to-high transition. The 4/16-Mbps Token Ring networks use differential Manchester encoding (a variation on Manchester encoding). Token Ring uses the differential Manchester encoding method to encode clock and data bit information into bit symbols. A 1 bit is represented by no polarity change at the start of the bit time; a 0 bit is represented by a polarity change at the start of the bit time.

Token Ring Media and Physical Topologies

IBM Token Ring network stations (often using STP and UTP as the media) are directly connected to MSAUs and can be wired together to form one large ring. Patch cables connect MSAUs to other MSAUs that are adjacent. Lobe cables connect MSAUs to stations. MSAUs include bypass relays for removing stations from the ring (see Figure 7-3).

FIGURE 7-3 IBM Token Ring network physical connections.

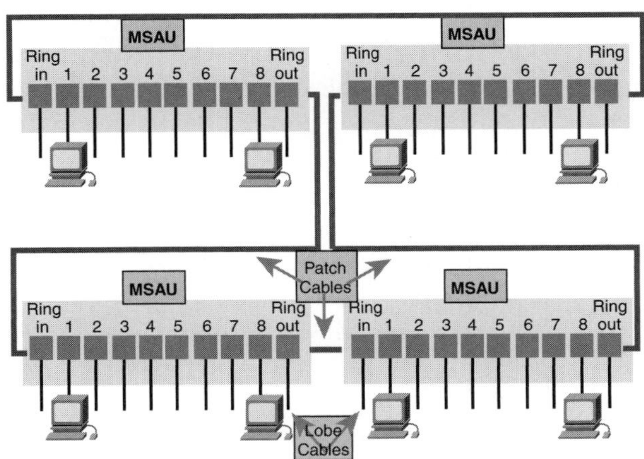

Fiber Distributed Data Interface Basics

In the mid-1980s, high-speed engineering workstations had pushed the capabilities of existing Ethernet and Token Ring LANs to their limits. Engineers needed a LAN that could support their workstations and their new applications. At the same time, system managers became concerned with network reliability issues as mission-critical applications were implemented on the high-speed networks.

To resolve these issues, the ANSI X3T9.5 standards committee produced the *Fiber Distributed Data Interface (FDDI)* standard. After completing the specifications, ANSI submitted FDDI to the International Organization for Standardization (ISO), which then created an international version of the FDDI that is completely compatible with the ANSI standard version.

Although FDDI implementations are not as common today as Ethernet or Token Ring, FDDI has a substantial following and continues to grow as its costs decrease. FDDI is frequently used as a backbone technology and to connect high-speed computers in a LAN.

FDDI has four specifications:

1. **Media Access Control** (MAC)—Defines how the medium is accessed, including these aspects:
   - Frame format
   - Token handling
   - Addressing
   - Algorithm for calculating a cyclic redundancy check and error-recovery mechanisms
2. **Physical Layer Protocol** (PHY)—Defines data encoding/decoding procedures, including these:
   - Clocking requirements
   - Framing
3. **Physical Layer Medium** (PMD)—Defines the characteristics of the transmission medium, including the following:
   - Fiber optic link
   - Power levels
   - Bit error rates
   - Optical components
   - Connectors
4. **Station Management** (SMT)—Defines the FDDI station configuration, including these aspects:
   - Ring configuration
   - Ring control features
   - Station insertion and removal
   - Initialization
   - Fault isolation and recovery

- Scheduling
- Collection of statistics

Figure 7-4 shows the four FDDI specifications and their relationship to one another and to the IEEE-defined Logical Link Control (LLC) sublayer.

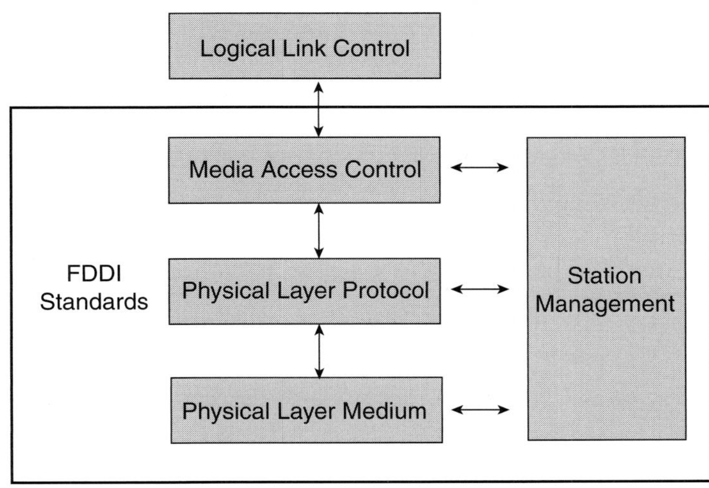

FIGURE 7-4
FDDI is defined by four separate specifications.

FDDI MAC

Fiber Distributed Data Interface (FDDI) specifies a 100-Mbps token-passing, dual-ring LAN using fiber-optic cable. Figure 7-5 shows the counter-rotating primary and secondary FDDI rings. The dual rings consist of a primary and a secondary ring. During normal operation, the primary ring is used for data transmission and the secondary ring remains idle.

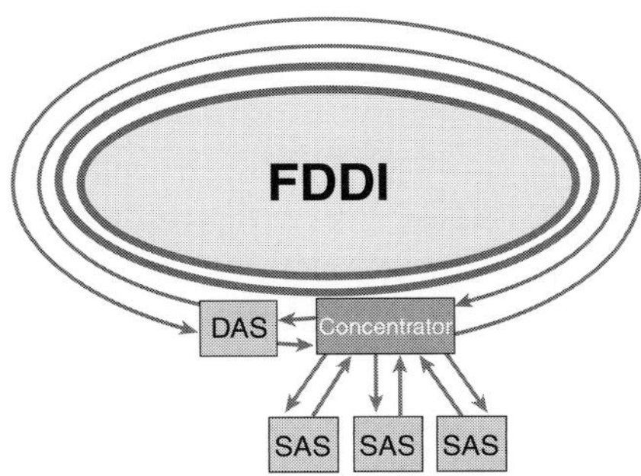

FIGURE 7-5
FDDI uses a dual-ring architecture with traffic on each ring flowing in opposite directions (called counter-rotating).

FDDI uses a token-passing strategy similar to that of Token Ring. FDDI's dual ring ensures not only that stations are guaranteed their turn to transmit, but also that if one part of one ring is damaged or disabled for any reason, the second ring can be used. This makes FDDI fault-tolerant.

FDDI supports real-time allocation of network bandwidth, making it ideal for a variety of different application types. FDDI provides this support by defining two types of traffic: synchronous and asynchronous.

Synchronous

Synchronous traffic can consume a portion of the 100 Mbps total bandwidth of an FDDI network, while asynchronous traffic can consume the rest.

Synchronous bandwidth is allocated to stations requiring continuous transmission capability. This is useful for transmitting voice and video information. The remaining bandwidth is used for asynchronous transmissions.

The FDDI SMT specification defines a distributed bidding scheme to allocate synchronous FDDI bandwidth.

Asynchronous

Asynchronous bandwidth is allocated using an eight-level priority scheme similar to that of Token Ring. Each station is assigned an asynchronous priority level.

FDDI also permits extended dialogues, in which stations can temporarily use all asynchronous bandwidth.

The FDDI priority mechanism can lock out stations that cannot use synchronous bandwidth and those that have too low of an asynchronous priority.

FDDI Signaling

FDDI uses an encoding scheme called 4B/5B. Every 4 bits of data are sent as a 5-bit code. These 5-bit codes—or symbols, as they are called—are chosen so that sufficient transitions occur to maintain bit synchronization. The signal sources in FDDI transceivers are LEDs or lasers.

FDDI Media

FDDI specifies a 100-Mbps token-passing, dual-ring LAN that uses a fiber-optic transmission medium. It defines the physical layer and media access portion of the link layer, which is similar to IEEE 802.3 and IEEE 802.5 in its relationship to the OSI model. Although it operates at faster speeds, FDDI is similar to Token Ring. The two networks share a few features, such as logical topology (ring) and media access technique (token-passing). A characteristic of FDDI is its use of optical fiber as a transmission medium. Optical fiber offers several advantages over traditional copper wiring, including the following:

- **Security**—Optical fiber does not emit electrical signals that can be tapped, and it is detectable if the fiber *is* tapped.
- **Reliability**—Optical fiber is immune to electrical interference.
- **Speed**—Optical fiber has much higher throughput potential than copper cable.

FDDI defines the two specified types of fiber: single-mode (also called monomode) and multimode. Figure 7-6 shows single-mode fiber using a laser light source and multimode fiber using an LED light source: Modes can be thought of as bundles of light rays of the same wavelength entering the fiber at a particular angle. Single-mode fiber allows only one mode of light to propagate through the fiber, while multimode fiber allows multiple modes of light to propagate through the fiber.

Multiple modes of light propagating through fiber might travel different distances, depending on their entry angles. This causes them to arrive at the destination at different times, a phenomenon called modal dispersion. Single-mode fiber is capable of higher bandwidth and greater cable run distances than multimode fiber. Because of these characteristics, single-mode fiber is often used for interbuilding connectivity, while multimode fiber is often used for intrabuilding connectivity. Multimode fiber uses LEDs as the light-generating devices, while single-mode fiber generally uses lasers.

FIGURE 7-6
A mode is a ray of light entering the fiber at a particular angle.

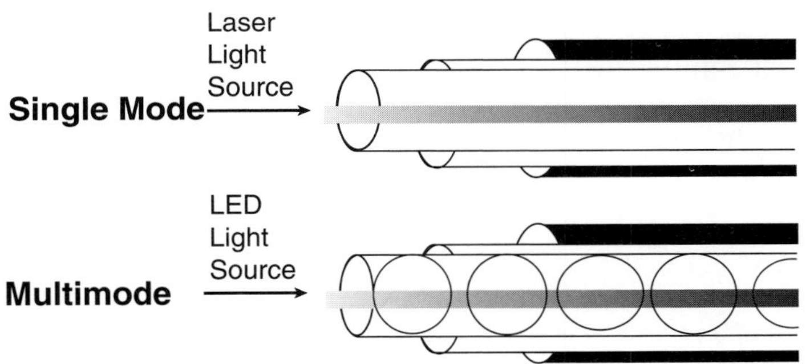

FDDI specifies the use of dual rings for physical connections. Traffic on each ring travels in opposite directions. Physically, the rings consist of two or more point-to-point connections between adjacent stations. One of the two FDDI rings is called the primary ring; the other is called the secondary ring. The primary ring is used for data transmission; the secondary ring is generally used as a backup.

Class B stations, or single-attachment stations (SAS), attach to one ring; Class A stations, or dual-attachment stations (DAS), attach to both rings. SASs are attached to the primary ring through a hub, called a concentrator, which provides connections for multiple SASs. The concentrator ensures that a failure or powerdown of any given SAS does not interrupt the ring. This is particularly useful when PCs or similar devices that frequently power on and off connect to the ring. A typical FDDI configuration with both DASs and SASs is shown in Figure 7-7. Each FDDI DAS has two ports, designated A and B. These ports connect the station to the dual FDDI ring; therefore, each port provides a connection for both the primary ring and the secondary ring. Figure 7-8 shows the ring attachments of an FDDI SAS, DAS, and concentrator.

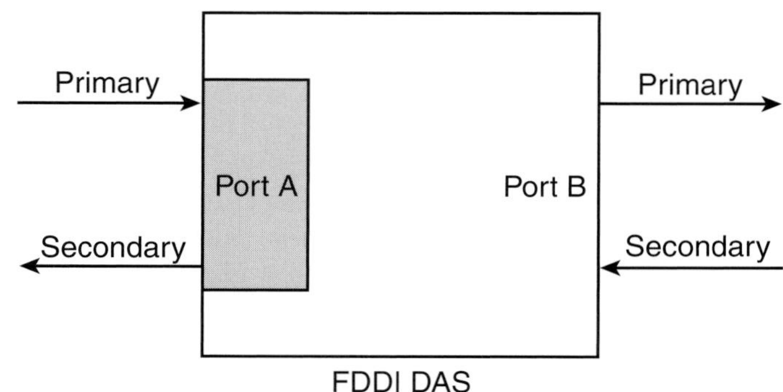

FIGURE 7-7
FDDI DAS A and B ports with attachments to the primary and secondary rings.

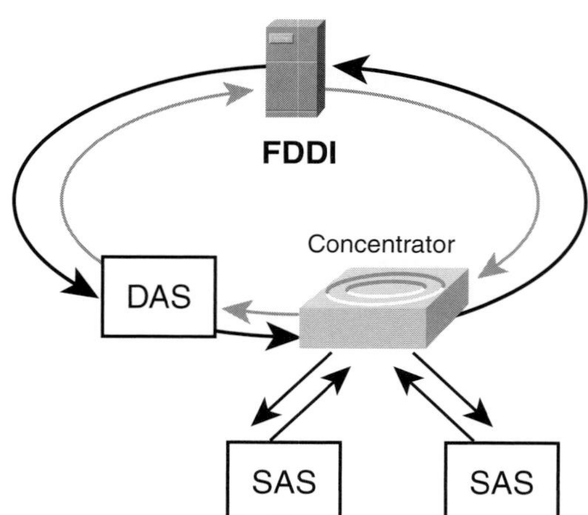

FIGURE 7-8
A FDDI concentrator attaches directly to both the primary and secondary rings, and ensures that failure or power down of any SAS does not bring down the ring.

Ethernet and IEEE 802.3

Ethernet is the most widely used local-area network (LAN) technology. Ethernet was designed to fill the middle ground between long-distance, low-speed networks and specialized, computer-room networks carrying data at high speeds for very limited distances.

Ethernet is well suited to applications in which a local communication medium must carry sporadic, occasionally heavy traffic at high-peak data rates. Ethernet was considered high-speed when it was first available. It was designed to enable sharing resources on a local workgroup level. Design goals included simplicity, low cost, compatibility, fairness, low delay, and high speed.

Xerox Corporation's Palo Alto Research Center (PARC) developed the first experimental Ethernet system in the early 1970s. This was used as the basis for the Institute of Electrical and Electronic Engineers (IEEE) 802.3 specification released in 1980.

Shortly after the 1980 IEEE 802.3 specification was released, Digital Equipment Corporation, Intel Corporation, and Xerox Corporation jointly developed and released an Ethernet specification, Version 2.0, that was substantially compatible with IEEE 802.3. Together, Ethernet and IEEE 802.3 currently maintain the greatest market share of any LAN protocol. Today, the term *Ethernet* is often used to refer to all carrier sense multiple access collision detect (CSMA/CD) LANs that generally conform to Ethernet specifications, including IEEE 802.3.

CSMA/CD is an access method that allows only one station to transmit at a time on a shared medium. The goal of standard Ethernet is to provide a best-effort delivery service. However, standard Ethernet using CSMA/CD takes into consideration all the transmission requests and determines what devices can transmit and when they can transmit for all the devices to receive adequate service.

Ethernet and IEEE 802.3 specify similar technologies; both are CSMA/CD LANs. Stations on a CSMA/CD LAN can access the network at any time. Before sending data, CSMA/CD stations listen to the network to determine whether it is already in use. If it is, then they wait. If the network is not in use, the stations transmit. A collision occurs when two stations listen for network traffic, hear none, and transmit simultaneously. In this case, both transmissions are damaged, and the stations must retransmit at some later time. Backoff algorithms determine when the colliding stations can retransmit. CSMA/CD stations can detect collisions, so they know when they must retransmit.

Both Ethernet and IEEE 802.3 LANs are broadcast networks. This means that every station will see all the frames at the same time, regardless of whether they are the intended destination of that data. Each station must examine the received frames to determine if they are the destination. If so, the frame is passed to a higher-layer protocol within the station for appropriate processing.

Differences between Ethernet and IEEE 802.3 LANs are subtle. Ethernet provides services corresponding to Layer 1 and Layer 2 of the OSI reference model. IEEE 802.3 specifies the physical layer, Layer 1, and the channel-access portion of the data link layer, Layer 2, but does not define the Logical Link Control functionality. Both Ethernet and IEEE 802.3 are implemented through hardware. Typically, the physical part of these protocols is either an interface card in a host computer or circuitry on a primary circuit board within a host computer.

At least 18 varieties of Ethernet have been specified or are in the specification process. Table 7-1 highlights some of the most common and important Ethernet technologies.

TABLE 7-1 Ethernet Technologies

Type	10Base5	10BaseT	10BaseFL	100BaseTX	100BaseFX	1000BaseT
Media	Thick coax RG-8 or RG-11	TIA/EIA UTP Cat 3, 4, 5, and 5e, 2 pair	62.2/125 micron multi-mode fiber	TIA/EIA UTP Cat 5 and 5e, 2 pair	62.2/125 micron multi-mode fiber or single mode fiber	TIA/EIA UTP 5, and 5e, 2 pair
Maximum Segment Length	500 meters	100 meters	2000 meters	100 meters	400/2000 meters (full/half duplex) 10,000 meters	100 meters

TABLE 7-1 Ethernet Technologies (Continued)

Type	10Base-5	10Base-T	10Base-FL	100Base-TX	100Base-FX	1000Base-T
Physical Topology	Bus	Star, Extended Star	Star	Star	Star	Star
Logical Topology	Bus	Bus	Bus	Bus	Bus	Bus
Transfer Rate	10 Mbps	10 Mbps	10 Mbps	100 Mbps	100 Mbps	1000 Mbps

Ethernet Frame Format

Figure 7-9 illustrates the frame fields associated with both Ethernet and IEEE 802.3 frames.

FIGURE 7-9 Ethernet and IEEE 802.3 Frame Formats

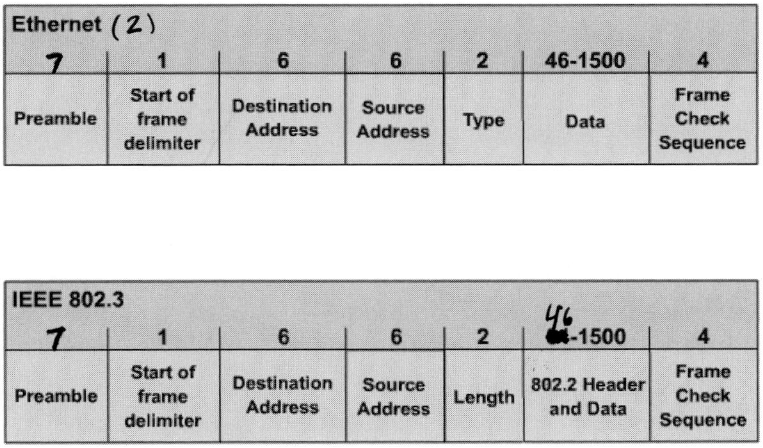

Ethernet

	1	6	6	2	46-1500	4
Preamble	Start of frame delimiter	Destination Address	Source Address	Type	Data	Frame Check Sequence

IEEE 802.3

	1	6	6	2	46-1500	4
Preamble	Start of frame delimiter	Destination Address	Source Address	Length	802.2 Header and Data	Frame Check Sequence

For the 802.3 frame format, there is a question mark for the Preamble field, which should be 7 bytes. Both Ethernet and 802.3 use the same 8-byte pattern: 7 bytes of "10" and an eighth byte of "10101011." 802.3 breaks this into two fields.

The Ethernet and IEEE 802.3 frame fields are described in the following summaries:

- **Preamble**—The purpose of the preamble is synchronization. The Ethernet frame includes an additional byte that is the equivalent of the Start of Frame (SOF) field specified in the IEEE 802.3 frame.
- **Start of Frame (SOF)**—The IEEE 802.3 delimiter byte ends with two consecutive 1 bits, which serve to synchronize the frame-reception portions of all stations on the LAN. SOF is explicitly specified in Ethernet.
- **Destination and source addresses**—The first 3 bytes of the addresses are specified by the IEEE on a vendor-dependent basis. The last 3 bytes are specified by the Ethernet or IEEE 802.3 vendor. The source address is always a unicast (single-node) address. The destination address can be unicast, multicast (group), or broadcast (all nodes).
- **Type (Ethernet)**—The Type field specifies the upper-layer protocol to receive the data after Ethernet processing is completed.
- **Length (IEEE 802.3)**—The Length field indicates the number of bytes of data that follows this field.
- **Data (Ethernet)**—After physical layer and link layer processing is complete, the data contained in the frame is sent to an upper-layer protocol, which is identified in the type field. Although Ethernet version 2 does not specify any specific padding, in contrast to IEEE 802.3, Ethernet expects at least 46 bytes of data, like 802.3.
- **Data (IEEE 802.3)**—After physical layer and link layer processing is complete, the data is sent to an upper-layer protocol, which must be defined within the data portion of the frame. If data in the frame is insufficient to fill the frame to its minimum 64-byte size, padding bytes are inserted to ensure at least a 64-byte frame.
- **Frame check sequence (FCS)**—This sequence contains a 4-byte CRC value that is created by the sending device and is recalculated by the receiving device to check for damaged frames.

NOTE

For Ethernet, physical layer and data link layer processing will identify the upper layer protocol (ULP), which is found in the Type field of the data link header. For 802.3, it is physical layer, MAC sublayer, and logical link control sublayer processing which must take place to identify the ULP. The ULP is found in the LLC header, which is found in the data portion of the frame.

Ethernet MAC

Ethernet is a shared-media broadcast technology. The access method CSMA/CD used in Ethernet performs three functions:

1. Transmitting and receiving frames
2. Decoding frames and checking them for valid addresses before passing them to the upper layers of the OSI model
3. Detecting errors within frames or on the network

MOVIE 7.1

Ethernet and 802.3 LANs

Ethernet and 802.3 LANs are broadcast networks.

In the CSMA/CD access method, networking devices with data to transmit over the networking media work in a listen-before-transmit mode. This means that when a device wants to send data, it must first check to see whether the networking media is busy. The device must check to see if there are any signals on the networking media. After the device determines that the networking media is not busy, the device can begin to transmit its data. While transmitting its data in the form of signals, the device also listens, to ensure that no other stations are transmitting data to the networking media at the same time. If two stations send at the same time, a collision occurs, as illustrated in the upper half of Figure 7-10. After it completes transmitting its data, the device returns to listening mode.

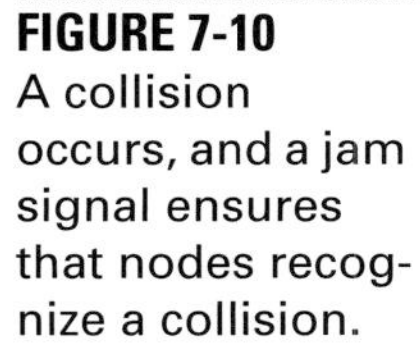

FIGURE 7-10
A collision occurs, and a jam signal ensures that nodes recognize a collision.

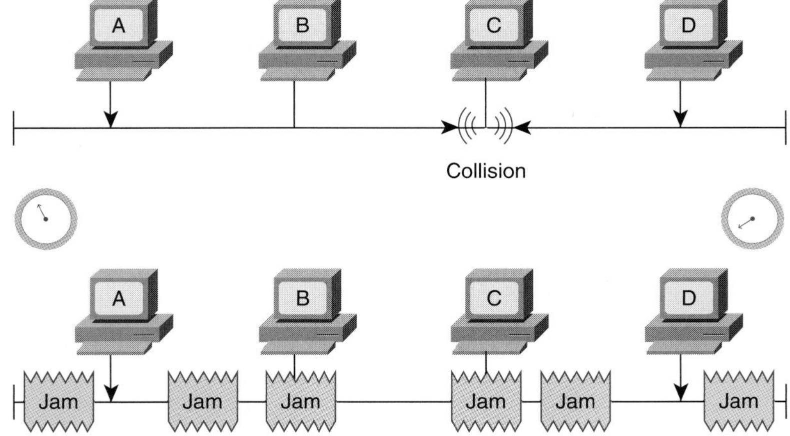

Networking devices are capable of detecting when a collision has occurred because the amplitude of the signal on the networking media increases. When a collision occurs, each device that is transmitting continues to transmit data for a short time, to ensure that all devices see the collision. When all devices on the network have seen that a collision has occurred, each transmitting device invokes what is called the back-off algorithm. After all transmitting devices on the network have backed off for a certain period of time (random and, therefore, different for each device), any device can attempt to gain access to the networking media again. When data transmission resumes on the network, the devices that were involved in the collision do not have priority to transmit data.

MOVIE 7.2

CSMA/CD LANs

CSMA/CD LANs use Ethernet and 802.3

Ethernet is a broadcast transmission medium. This means that all devices on a network can see all data that passes along the networking media. However, not all the devices on the network will process the data. Only the device whose MAC address matches the destination MAC address carried by the data will copy the data.

When a device has verified the destination MAC address carried by the data, it then checks the data packet for transmission errors. If the device detects errors, the data packet is discarded.

> **NOTE**
>
> Manchester encoding results in 0 being encoded as a high-to-low transition and 1 being encoded as a low-to-high transition. Because both 0s and 1s result in a transition to the signal, the clock can be effectively recovered at the receiver from this guaranteed mid-bit transition.

The destination device will not notify the source device, regardless of whether the packet arrived successfully. Ethernet is a connectionless network architecture and is referred to as a best-effort delivery system.

Ethernet Signaling

The rules of Manchester encoding define a 0 as a signal that is high for the first half of the period and low for the second half. The rules define a 1 as a signal that is low for the first half of the period and high for the second half. 10BaseT transceivers are designed to send and receive signals over a segment that consists of four wires—one pair of wires for transmitting data and one pair of wires for receiving data.

Ethernet 10BaseT Media and Topologies

In a LAN with a star topology, the networking media is run from a central hub out to each device attached to the network. The physical layout of the star topology resembles spokes radiating from the hub of a wheel. As Figure 7-11 shows, a central point of connection is used in a star topology. When a star topology is used, communication between devices attached to the LAN is via point-to-point wiring to the central link or hub. All network traffic in a star topology passes through the hub.

FIGURE 7-11
A star topology resembles a hub-and-spokes configuration.

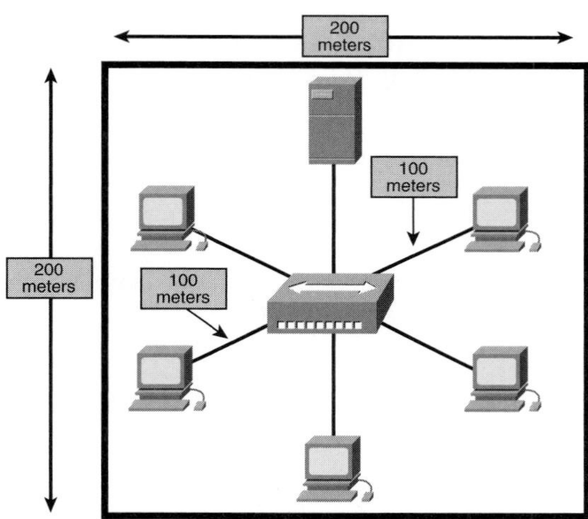

The hub receives frames on a port and then copies and transmits (repeats) the frame to all the other ports. The hub can be either active or passive. An active hub connects the networking media and regenerates the signal. In an Ethernet in which hubs act as multiport repeaters, the hubs are sometimes referred to as concentrators. By regenerating the signal, active hubs enable data to travel over greater distances, but they weaken the signal. A passive hub is a device used simply to connect networking media and does not regenerate a signal.

An advantage of the star topology is that it is considered the easiest to design and install. This is because the networking media is run directly out from a central hub to each workstation area. Another advantage is its ease of maintenance—the only area of concentration is located at the hub. In a star topology, the layout used for the networking media is easy to modify and troubleshoot. Workstations can be easily added to a network employing a star topology. If one run of networking media is broken or shorted, only the device attached at that point is out of commission; the rest of the LAN remains functional. In short, a star topology means greater reliability.

In some ways, a star topology's advantages can also be considered disadvantages. For example, although limiting one device per run of networking media can make diagnosis of problems easier, it also increases the amount of networking media required, which adds to the setup costs. And, although the hub can make maintenance easier, it represents a single point of failure—if the hub breaks, everyone's network connection is lost.

TIA/EIA-568-A specifies that the physical layout, or topology, to be used for horizontal cabling must be a star topology. Every outlet is independently and directly wired to the patch panel. The TIA/EIA-568-A specification for the maximum length of horizontal cabling for unshielded twisted-pair cable is 90 m. The maximum length for patch cords at the telecommunications outlet/connector is 3 m, and the maximum length for patch cords/jumpers at the horizontal cross-connect is 6 m (see Figure 7-12).

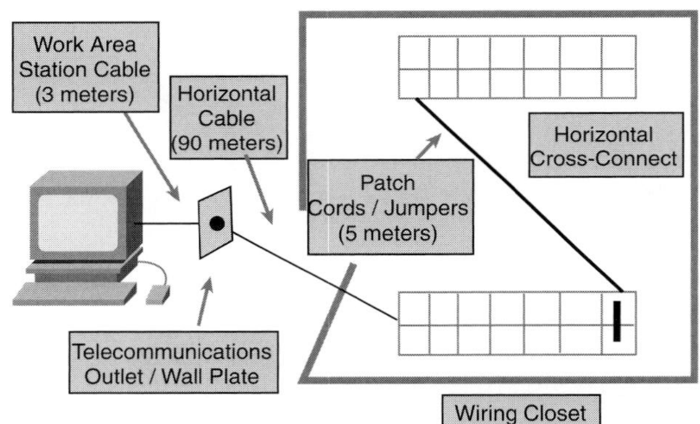

FIGURE 7-12
The termination for each telecommunications outlet/connector is located at the patch panel in the wiring closet.

The maximum distance for a run of horizontal cabling that extends from the hub to any workstation is 100 m (actually 99 m, but it is commonly rounded up to 100 m). Figure 7-13 includes the 90 m for the horizontal cabling, the 3 m for the patch cords, and the 6 m for the jumpers at the horizontal cross-connect. Horizontal cabling runs in a star topology radiate out from the hub, much like the spokes of a wheel.

Sometimes, the area to be covered by a network exceeds the TIA/EIA-568-A specified maximum length that a simple star topology can accommodate. For example, envision a building with the dimensions 200 m × 200 m. A simple star topology that adheres to the horizontal-cabling standard specified by TIA/EIA-568-A cannot provide complete coverage for that building.

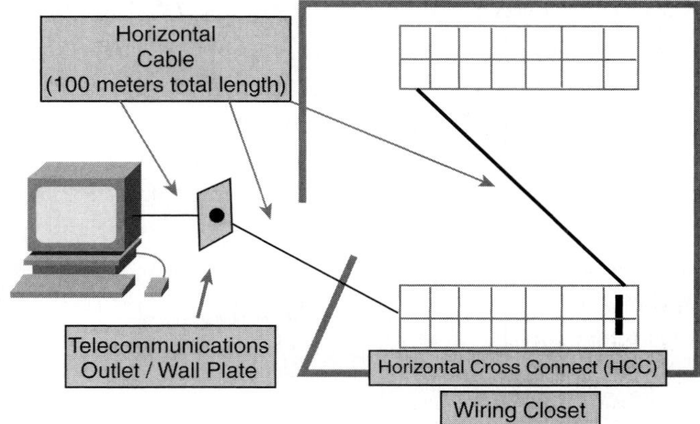

FIGURE 7-13
A LAN that uses a star topology could cover the area of a circle with a radius of 100 m.

As indicated in Figure 7-14, workstations E, F, and C are located outside the area that can be covered by a star topology that adheres to TIA/EIA-568-A specifications. As shown, they are not part of the LAN, so users at these workstations who want to send, share, and receive files would not be able to.

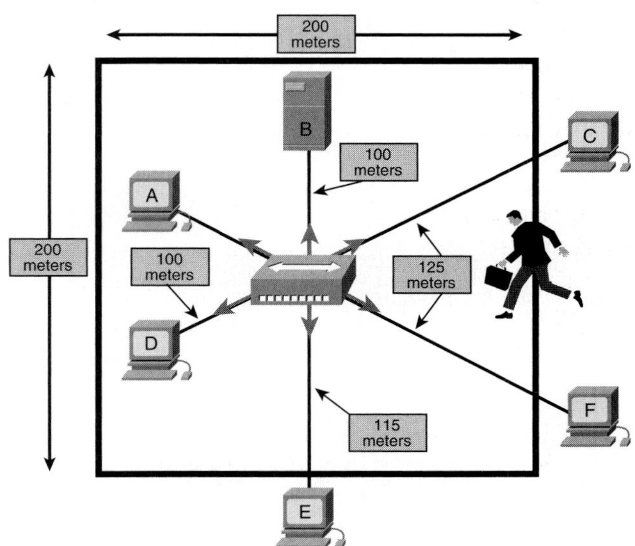

FIGURE 7-14
Some cable installers are tempted to solve the problem of a star topology's inadequate coverage by extending the length of the networking media beyond the TIA/EIA-568-A specified maximum length.

When signals first leave a transmitting station, they are clean and easily recognizable. However, the longer the cable length is, the weaker and more deteriorated the signals become as they pass along the networking media. If a signal travels beyond the specified maximum distance, there is no guarantee that when it reaches a NIC, the NIC will be capable of reading it.

If a star topology cannot provide enough coverage for an area to be networked, the network can be extended through the use of internetworking devices that do not result in attenuation of the signal. This resulting topology is designated as an extended star topology. As indicated in Figure 7-15, the distance over which a network can operate is extended by using repeaters.

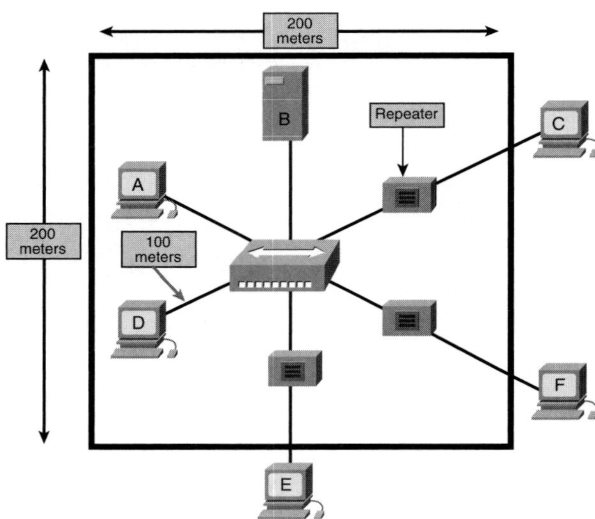

FIGURE 7-15
Repeaters take in weakened signals, regenerate and retime them, and send them back out onto the network.

MORE INFORMATION

Migrating to Gigabit Ethernet

Migration to Gigabit Ethernet will occur gradually. Initial implementation will be in the backbone of existing Ethernet LANs. Next, server connections will be upgraded, and eventually upgrades will reach the desktop as well. Some of the likely points of implementation include:

- **Upgrade switch-to-switch links**—100-Mbps links between Fast Ethernet switches or repeaters can be replaced with 1000-Mbps links, speeding communication between backbone switches and allowing the switches to support a greater number of switched and shared Fast Ethernet segments.
- **Upgrade switch-to-server links**—1000-Mbps connections can be implemented between switches and high-performance servers. This upgrade would require the servers to be outfitted with Gigabit Ethernet NICs.

MORE INFORMATION (CONTINUED)

- **Upgrade a Fast Ethernet backbone**—A Fast Ethernet backbone switch with attached 10/100 switches can be upgraded to a Gigabit Ethernet switch supporting multiple 100/1000 switches, as well as routers and hubs with Gigabit Ethernet interfaces, and Gigabit repeaters.
- **Upgrade a shared FDDI backbone**—A FDDI backbone can be upgraded by replacing the FDDI concentrator or hub or Ethernet-to-FDDI router with a Gigabit Ethernet switch or repeater. The only upgrade required is the installation of new Gigabit Ethernet interfaces in the routers, switches, or repeaters.
- **Upgrade high performance desktops**—Gigabit Ethernet NICs can be used to upgrade high-performance desktop computers to Gigabit Ethernet. These desktop computers would be connected to Gigabit Ethernet switches or repeaters.

Layer 2 Devices

This section covers the following Layer 2 devices:

- Network interface cards
- Bridges
- Switches

Network Interface Cards

A *network interface card (NIC)* is a Layer 2 device that plugs into a motherboard and provides ports for network connection. This card can be designed as an Ethernet card, a Token Ring card, or an FDDI card. Network cards communicate with the network through serial connections and with the computer through parallel connections. They are the physical connections from workstations to the network. Network cards all require an IRQ, an I/O address, and upper memory addresses for DOS and Windows 95/98. When selecting a network card, consider the following three factors:

- Type of network (Ethernet, Token Ring, FDDI, or other)
- Type of media (twisted-pair, coaxial, or fiber-optic cable)
- Type of system bus (PCI or ISA)

NICs perform important Layer 2 data link layer functions, including the following:

- **Logical link control**—Communicates with upper layers in the computer
- **Addressing**—Provides a unique MAC address identifier

- **Framing**—Packages the bits for transport, as part of the encapsulation process
- **Media Access Control** (**MAC**)—Provides structured access to shared-access media
- **Signaling**—Creates signals and interfaces with the media by using built-in transceivers

Bridges

A bridge creates network segments and must make intelligent decisions about whether to pass on signals to the next segment. A bridge can improve network performance by eliminating unnecessary traffic and minimizing the chances of collisions. The bridge divides traffic into segments and filters traffic based on the station or MAC address (see Figure 7-16).

Bridges are not complicated devices. They analyze incoming frames, make forwarding decisions based on information contained in the frames, and either drop or forward the frames toward the destination. Bridges are concerned only with passing frames or not passing frames, based on their destination MAC address.

Bridges often pass frames between networks operating under different Layer 2 protocols.

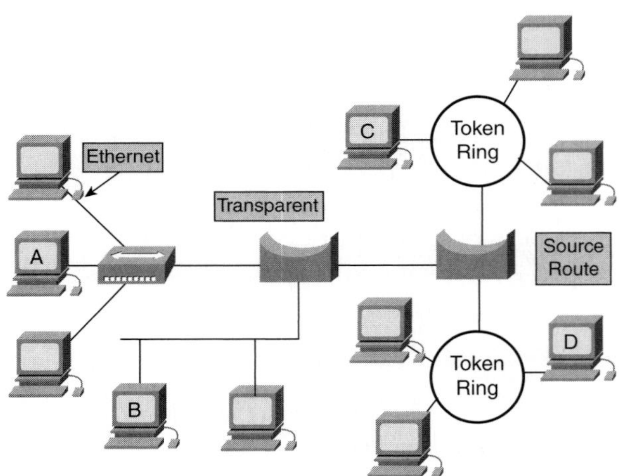

FIGURE 7-16 Installing a bridge between two LAN hubs results in two media access domains that share a common MAC broadcast domain.

Bridging occurs at the data link layer, which controls data flow, handles transmission errors, provides physical addressing, and manages access to the physical medium. Bridges provide these functions by using various link-layer protocols that dictate specific flow control, error handling, addressing, and media access algorithms. Examples of popular data link layer protocols include Ethernet, Token Ring, and FDDI.

Upper-layer protocol transparency is a primary advantage of bridging. Bridges are not required to examine upper-layer information because they operate at the data link layer or Layer 2 of the OSI model. Transparent bridges filter network traffic by looking at only the MAC address, not protocols. Because bridges look at only MAC addresses, they can rapidly forward traffic representing any network layer protocol. To filter or selectively deliver network traffic, a bridge builds tables of all MAC addresses located on their directly connected network segments.

If data comes along the network media, a bridge compares the destination MAC address carried by the data to MAC addresses contained in its tables. If the bridge determines that the destination MAC address of the data is from the same network segment as the source, it does not forward the data to other segments of the network. If the bridge determines that the destination MAC address of the data is not from the same network segment as the source, it forwards the data to the appropriate segment. By doing this, bridges can significantly reduce the amount of traffic between network segments by eliminating unnecessary traffic.

Bridges are networking devices that can be used to reduce large collision domains. Collision domains are areas where packets are likely to interfere with each other. Bridges do this by dividing the network into smaller segments and reducing the amount of traffic that must be passed between the segments. Bridges operate at Layer 2, or the data link layer, of the OSI model because they are concerned with only MAC addresses. As data is passed along the network on its way to a destination, it is picked up and examined by every device on the network, including bridges. Bridges work best where traffic is low from one segment of a network to other segments. When traffic between network segments becomes heavy, bridges can become a bottleneck and can slow communication.

Another potential problem exists with using a bridge: Bridges always spread and multiply a special kind of data packet. These data packets occur primarily when a device on a network wants to reach another device on the network but does not know the destination address of the device. When this occurs, the source frequently sends out a broadcast to all devices on a network. Because every device on the network must pay attention to such broadcasts, bridges always forward them. If too many broadcasts are sent out over the network, a broadcast storm can result. A broadcast storm can cause network timeouts and traffic slowdowns, and the network can operate at less than acceptable performance.

MORE INFORMATION

Transparent Bridges

Transparent bridges link together segments of the same type of LAN. The simplest transparent bridge contains just two ports, but transparent bridges may also contain more ports. Figure 7-17 illustrates how a transparent bridge isolates the traffic of two LAN segments by creating two media access domains.

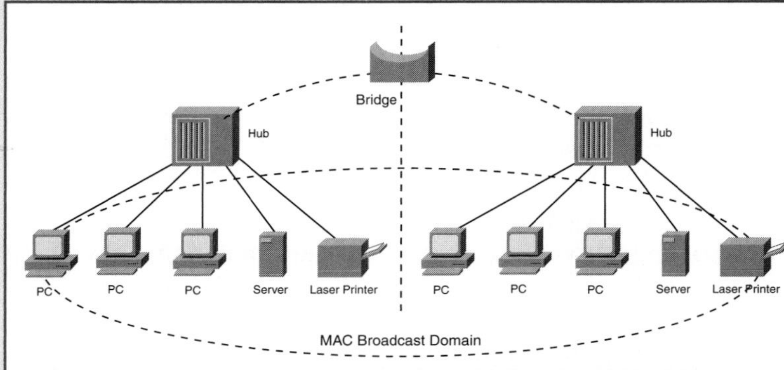

FIGURE 7-17 Transparent bridges segment the media access domain of a single LAN architecture.

The transparent bridge segments one LAN with one communications channel into two distinct communications channels within a common architecture. This is significant because it means that a bridge can reduce the number of devices in a media access domain by creating two such domains.

It is important to note that transparent bridges do not segment a LAN's MAC broadcast domain. Therefore, in Figure 7-17, MAC broadcasts are still carried throughout the entire LAN. Despite this, the LANs on each side of the bridge function as separate media access domains.

Switches

Like bridging, switching is a technology that alleviates congestion in Ethernet LANs by segmenting into multiple collision domains. This reduces traffic on each segment and increases available bandwidth. Switches, also referred to as LAN switches, often replace shared-media hubs and work with existing cable infrastructures to ensure that they are installed with minimal disruption of existing networks (see Figure 7-18).

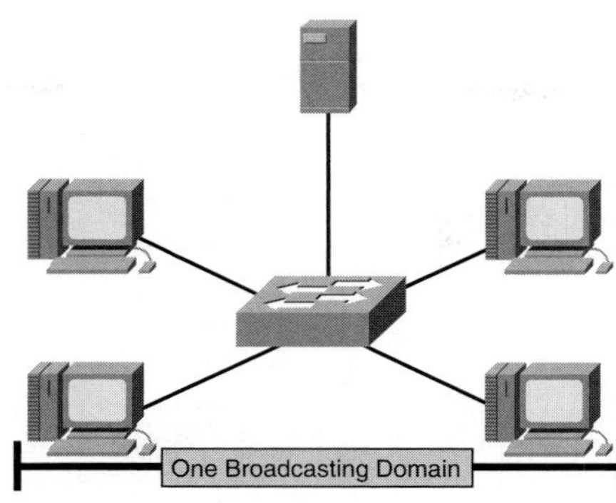

FIGURE 7-18
Switches use temporary but dedicated logical paths to interconnect LAN segments as needed.

In data communications today, all switching and routing equipment perform two basic operations:

- **Switching data frames**—A frame is received on an input medium and then is transmitted to an output medium.
- **Maintaining switching operations**—Switches build and maintain switching table and search for loops. Routers build and maintain both routing tables and service tables.

Like bridges, switches connect LAN segments, use a table of MAC addresses to determine the segment on which a frame needs to be transmitted, and reduce traffic. Switches operate at much higher speeds than bridges and can support new functionality, such as virtual LANs.

An Ethernet switch has many benefits. Among them, an Ethernet switch enables many users to communicate in parallel through the use of a dedicated connection that is temporarily switched between two ports and dedicated network segments in a collision-free environment (see Figure 7-19). This maximizes the bandwidth available on the shared medium. Another benefit is that moving to a switched LAN environment is very cost-effective because existing hardware and cabling can be reused. Finally, network administrators have great flexibility in managing the network through the power of the switch and the software to configure the LAN.

Data is exchanged at high speeds by switching the frame to its destination port. By reading the destination MAC address Layer 2 information, switches can achieve high-speed data transfers, much like a bridge does. The frame can be sent to the port of the receiving station before the entire frame enters the switch. This leads to low latency levels and a high rate of speed for frame forwarding. A switch can operate in store-and-forward mode, like a bridge, as well as in cut-through mode.

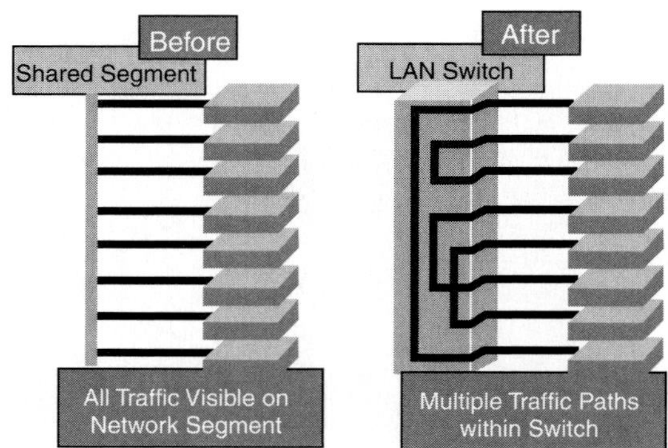

FIGURE 7-19 The number of ports and the capability to create and sustain temporary paths with their own dedicated bandwidth is what separates switches from bridges.

Ethernet switching increases the bandwidth available on a network. It does this by creating dedicated network segments, or point-to-point connections, and connecting these segments in a virtual network within the switch. A physical connection between two ports exists only when two nodes need to communicate.

Even though the LAN switch reduces the size of collision domains, all hosts connected to the switch are still in the same broadcast domain. Therefore, a broadcast from one node will still be seen by all other nodes connected through the LAN switch.

Switches are data link layer devices that, like bridges, enable multiple physical LAN segments to be interconnected into single larger network. Similar to bridges, switches forward and flood traffic based on MAC addresses. Because switching is performed in hardware instead of in software, it is significantly faster. You can think of each switch port as a microbridge; this process is called *microsegmentation*. Thus, each switch port acts as a separate bridge and gives the full bandwidth of the medium to each hub or individual host.

MORE INFORMATION

IP Switching

One form of switching is called Layer 3 switching, or Internet Protocol (IP) switching. Layer 3 switches are, essentially, a cross between a LAN switch and a router. Each port on the switch is a separate LAN port, but the forwarding engine actually calculates and stores routes based on IP addresses, not MAC addresses.

Layer 3 switches available today tend to only support IP or both IP and IPX, to the exclusion of other network layer protocols. Similarly, selection of LAN port technologies is frequently limited to either 10 or 100 or 1000 Mbps Ethernet.

Ethernet LAN Segmentation

The primary reason for segmenting a LAN is to isolate traffic between segments and to achieve more bandwidth per user by creating smaller collision domains. Without LAN segmentation, LANs larger than a small workgroup would quickly become clogged with traffic and collisions, and would deliver severely reduced bandwidth. The addition of devices such as bridges, switches, and routers segment the LAN as shown in Figure 7-20 into multiple collision domains.

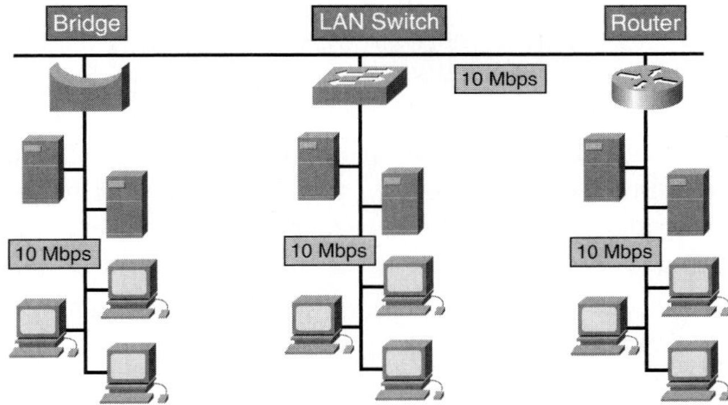

FIGURE 7-20
Some of the devices that could be used to segment a LAN are bridges, switches, and routers.

By dividing large networks into self-contained units, bridges and switches provide several advantages. A bridge or switch diminishes the traffic experienced by devices on all connected segments because only a certain percentage of traffic is forwarded. They also accommodate communication between a larger number of devices than would be supported on any single LAN connected to the bridge. Like repeaters, bridges and switches extend the effective length of a LAN, permitting the attachment of distant stations that were not previously permitted.

Although bridges and switches share most relevant attributes, several distinctions still exist between them. Switches are significantly faster because they switch in hardware, while bridges switch in software. A 10-Mbps Ethernet LAN and a 100-Mbps Ethernet LAN can be connected by using a switch. Switches can support higher port densities than bridges. Some switches support cut-through switching, which reduces latency and delays in the network, while bridges support only store-and-forward traffic switching. Finally, switches reduce collisions and increase bandwidth on network segments because they provide dedicated bandwidth to each network segment.

Segmentation by routers offers all these advantages and more. Each interface on the router connects to a separate network, so insertion of the router into a LAN creates smaller collision domains and smaller broadcast domains. This occurs because routers do not forward broadcasts unless programmed to do so. However, the router can perform bridging and switching functions, as well as perform best-path selection. The router also can be used to connect different networking media and different LAN technologies. Additionally, routers can connect LANs running different network layer protocols (IP vs. IPX vs. AppleTalk) and can have serial connections to WANs.

Bridge Segmentation of a Collision Domain

Ethernet LANs that use a bridge for segmenting the LAN provide more bandwidth per user because there are fewer users on the segments than when compared to the entire LAN (see Figure 7-21). The bridge allows only those frames that have destinations outside the segment to pass through. Bridges learn a network's segmentation by building address tables that contain the physical address of each network device, as well as the port to use to reach the device. Ethernet bridges pass on data frames, regardless of which Layer 3 protocol is used, and are transparent to the other devices on the network.

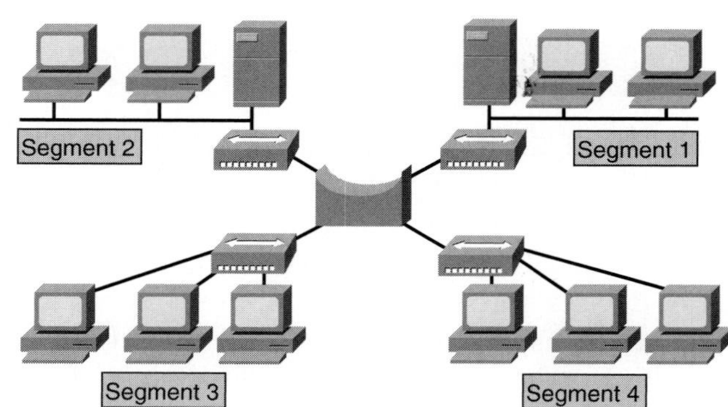

FIGURE 7-21 The bridging table maintains an up-to-date listing of every MAC address on the LAN, as well as the physical bridge port connected to the segment containing that address.

Bridges increase the latency (delay) in a network by 10 to 30 percent. This latency is a result of the decision making that is required of the bridge(s) when transmitting data to the correct segment. A bridge is considered a store-and-forward device because it must receive the entire frame and verify the cyclic redundancy check (CRC) before forwarding can take place. The time it takes to perform these tasks can slow network transmissions, causing delay.

Switch Segmentation of a Collision Domain

A LAN that uses a switched Ethernet topology with only one device on each port creates a network that performs as though it has only two nodes: the sending node and the receiving node (see Figure 7-22). These two nodes share 10 Mbps of bandwidth between them, which means that nearly all bandwidth is available for the transmission of data. A switched Ethernet LAN allows a LAN topology to work faster and more efficiently than a standard Ethernet LAN can because it uses bandwidth so efficiently. In a switched Ethernet implementation, the available bandwidth can reach close to 100 percent.

FIGURE 7-22 Segmentation with LAN Switches.

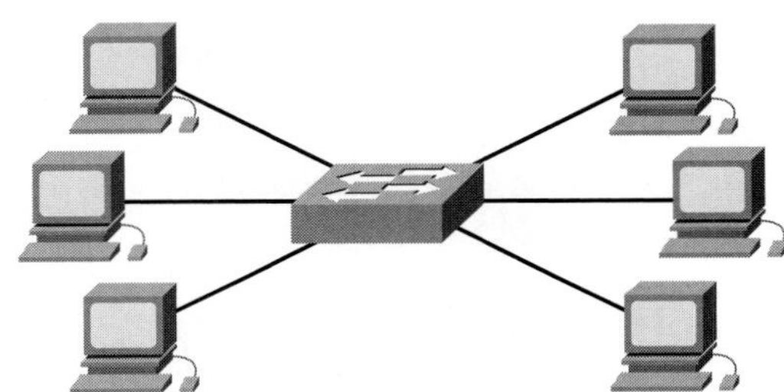

It is important to note that even though 100 percent of the bandwidth might be available, shared Ethernet networks perform best when kept to less than 30 to 40 percent of full capacity. This limitation is a result of Ethernet's media access method (CSMA/CD). Bandwidth usage that exceeds the recommended limitation results in increased collisions. The purpose of LAN switching is to ease bandwidth shortages and network bottlenecks, such as that occurring between a group of PCs and a remote file server. A LAN switch is a high-speed multiport bridge that has one port for each node or segment of the LAN. A switch segments a LAN into microsegments, thereby creating collision-free domains from one formerly larger collision domain.

Switched Ethernet is based on standard Ethernet. Each node is directly connected to one of its ports or to a segment that is connected to one of the switch's ports. This creates a 10-Mbps connection between each node and each segment on the switch. A computer connected directly to an Ethernet switch is its own collision domain and accesses the full 10 Mbps. As a frame enters a switch, it is read for the source or destination address. The switch then determines which switching action will take place based on what is learned from the information in the frame. If the destination address is located on another segment, the frame is then switched to its destination port.

Router Segmentation of a Collision Domain

Routers are more advanced than typical bridges. A bridge is transparent at the network layer and operates at the data link layer. A router operates at the network layer and bases all of its forwarding decisions on the Layer 3 protocol address. It accomplishes this by examining the destination address on the data packet and then looking in its routing table for forwarding instructions. Routers create the highest level of segmentation because of their capability to make exact determinations of where to send the data packet. Figure 7-23 illustrates a router being used to segment a LAN.

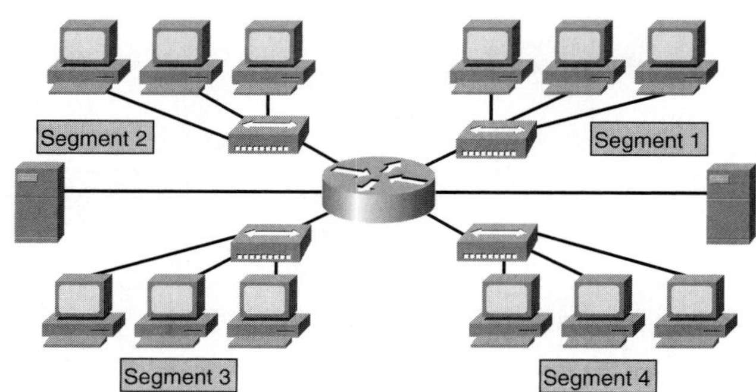

FIGURE 7-23 Routers, unlike bridges or switches, have the capability to operate at the first three layers of the OSI reference model—the physical, data link, and network layers.

Because routers perform more functions than bridges, they operate with a higher rate of latency. Routers must examine packets to determine the best path for forwarding them to their destinations. Unavoidably, this process takes time and introduces latency.

The topology in Figure 7-24 contains examples of segmentation by bridges, switches, and routers. The bridge divides the E1 Ethernet network into two segments. Traffic is filtered at the bridge, reducing potential collisions and the physical extent of the collision domain. Therefore, the bridge breaks the E1 Ethernet network into two segments: The first segment has the repeater and hosts K, L, M, and N on it; the second segment has hosts O and P on it. However, this remains a broadcast domain. The repeater extends the collision domain rather than segmenting it.

The main switch divides the E0 Ethernet network into multiple network segments, each having guaranteed full bandwidth. The workgroup switch divides the workgroup segment into more segments. Also note that the switches provide high connectivity to their unshared bandwidth. The hub and all the devices attached to it, all the way up to the main switch port, remain a single collision domain. The router segments the entire LAN into two Ethernet subnetworks, which are segmented, and a Token Ring and FDDI subnetwork, which by their nature have no collision domains. The router creates four broadcast domains.

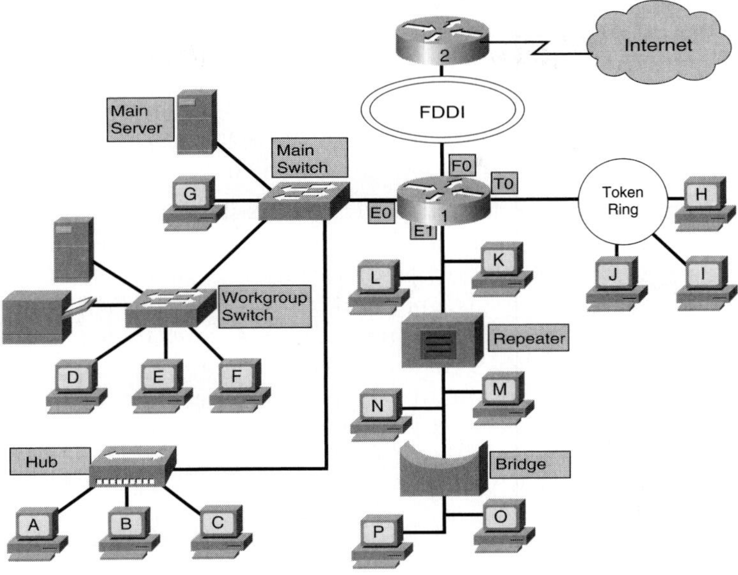

FIGURE 7-24 Many different parts of the network are brought together by the main router.

MORE INFORMATION

LAN Backbones

A LAN backbone is any mechanism or facility that interconnects all the LAN's hubs. There are many different ways to construct a LAN backbone. Some of these are clever and highly functional. Others are simplistic and shortsighted. Some are easy to scale, and some are not. Regardless of its components or topology, a LAN backbone unifies the disparate mini-LANs that would exist if the hubs were not interconnected.

The simplest of all LAN backbones is a hub that interconnects other hubs. As discussed earlier in the chapter, this creates large, flat LANs with singular media access and MAC broadcast domains. Although this may be, in fact, the most economical backbone for small LAN environments, it does not scale very well. Adding new users may require the addition of hubs. It doesn't take a great imagination to see that all the ports available on the backbone hub can quickly be consumed by connections to other hubs. When this happens, the solution, typically, is to just keep adding hubs to the backbone. This is known as a serial, or daisy-chained, backbone. Daisy-chained hubs can quickly become an administrative nightmare; it is difficult to maintain accurate records of the LAN's topology and wiring schemes over time.

Routers can be used to form a highly scalable LAN backbone in one of two main ways:

- Collapsed backbones
- Parallel backbones

continues

MORE INFORMATION (CONTINUED)

Collapsed Backbones

A collapsed backbone topology features a single, centralized router that interconnects all the LAN segments in a building. The router effectively creates multiple media access and broadcast domains, and thereby increases the performance of each of the LAN segments.

The simplest and most typical collapsed backbone topology segments a building according to its physical wire distribution—that is, all the computing or communications devices whose wiring is physically terminated in a single telephone closet become a segment. A single physical connection to this telephone closet (and its hubs and their computers, printers, and so on) runs back to a single port on a router. Therefore, they form a self-contained LAN segment, complete with their own media access domain, MAC broadcast domain, and IP network address. A LAN segmented with a router using a collapsed backbone topology is illustrated in Figure 7-25.

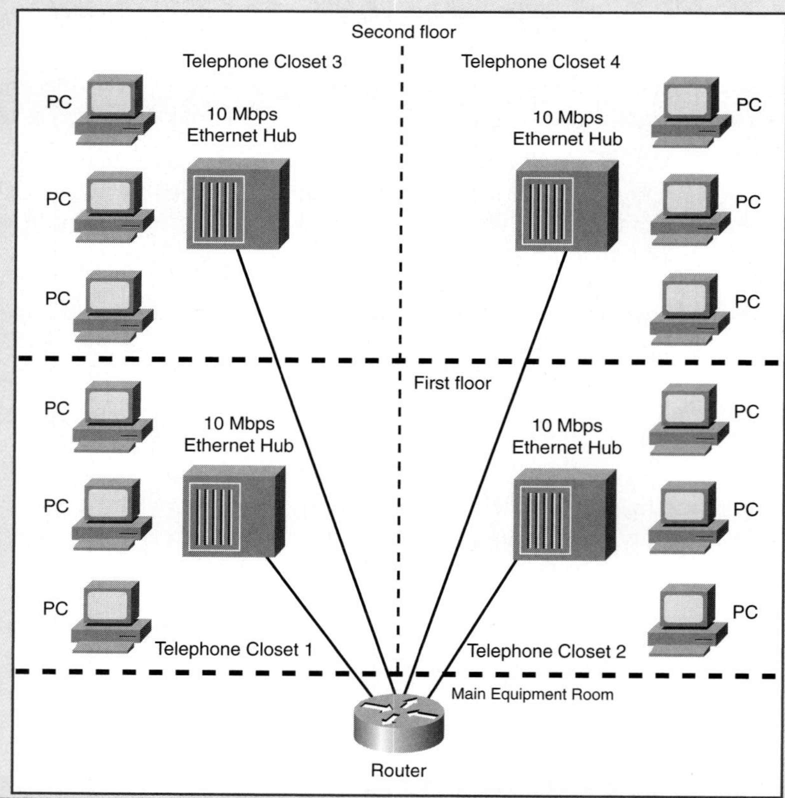

FIGURE 7-25 An example of a collapsed backbone.

MORE INFORMATION (CONTINUED)

An important consideration in collapsed backbone topologies is that user communities are seldom conveniently distributed throughout a building. Instead, the users are scattered far and wide, which means that there is a good chance that they will be found on different LANs interconnected via a collapsed backbone router. Subsequently, simple network tasks among the members of a workgroup are likely to traverse the router. As fast as routers might be, they are still software-driven. Therefore, in comparison to purely hardware devices, such as hubs and switches, routers are slow. Consequently, collapsed backbones might actually introduce a performance penalty not present with Layer 2-only LAN backbone solutions.

Today, Layer 3 LAN switches are available that duplicate the functionality of the router in a collapsed backbone without duplicating its slow performance. In other words, the IP switch performs inter-LAN routing at wire speeds.

Care should be taken when designing collapsed backbone LANs to absolutely minimize the amount of traffic that must cross the router. Use a collapsed backbone LAN as a traffic aggregator for LAN-level resources, such as WAN facilities, and do not use it indiscriminately.

Collapsed backbones, like the one shown in Figure 7-25, have another flaw: They introduce a single point of failure in the LAN. This is not necessarily a fatal flaw—in fact, many of the other LAN backbone topologies also introduce a single point of failure into the LAN. Nevertheless, that weakness must be considered when planning a network topology.

Parallel Backbones

In some cases in which collapsed backbones are untenable, a modified version might prove ideal. This modification is known as the parallel backbone. Many reasons exist for installing a parallel backbone. User communities can be widely dispersed throughout a building; some groups or applications might have stringent network security requirements, or high network availability might be required. Regardless of the reason, running parallel connections from a building's collapsed backbone router to the same telephone closet enables supporting multiple segments to be run from each closet, as shown in Figure 7-26.

continues

MORE INFORMATION (CONTINUED)

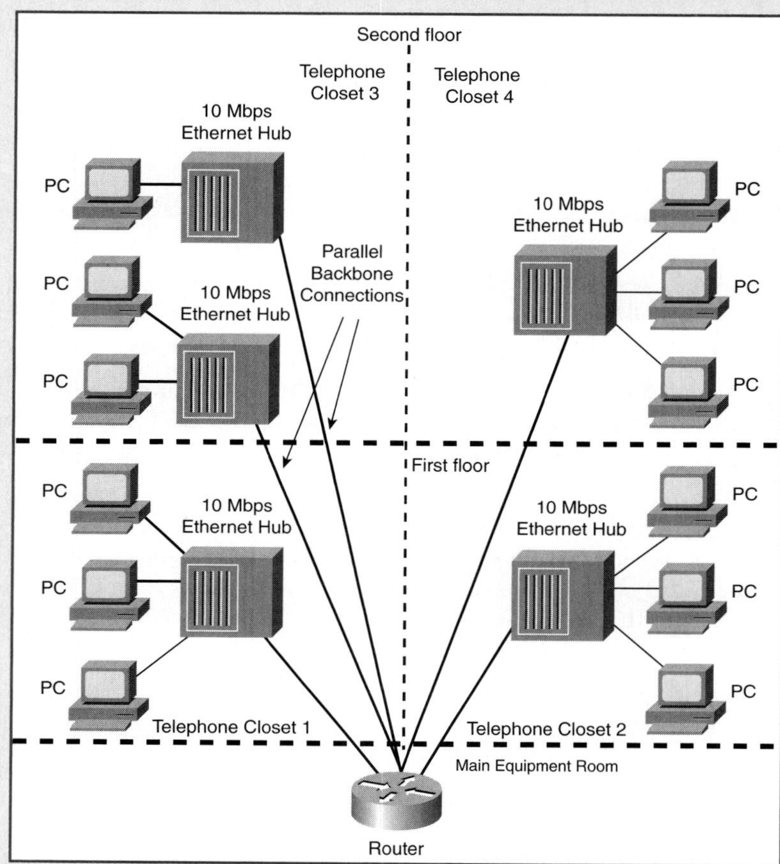

FIGURE 7-26 An example of parallel backbone topology.

The parallel backbone topology is a modification of the collapsed backbone. Much like the collapsed backbone, this backbone topology can create multiple media access and MAC broadcast domains. The key distinction is that this topology can achieve a finer degree of segmentation than a collapsed backbone can provide.

This approach marginally increases the cost of the network, but it can increase the performance of each segment and satisfy additional network criteria, such as security and fault tolerance.

Basic Ethernet 10BaseT Troubleshooting

Many approaches to network troubleshooting exist. The first is to work up through the layers of the OSI model. This method isolates problems that can masquerade as other problems. You can waste time troubleshooting a browser that does not function properly, only to find that the computer is not connected to the network. It is best to start troubleshooting at Layer 1. Ask yourself whether things are plugged in and connected before you go to the next higher level, with its more complicated issues.

SKILL BUILDERS

Lab Activity: Network Discovery

In this lab, you use the help menu, and the process of experimentation, to learn the basics of navigating within the Network Inspector (NI) environment.

Lab Activity: Network Inspector Problem Log

In this lab, you learn about the problems/symptoms that the NI program can detect.

Lab Activity: Protocol Inspector Frame Stats

In this lab, you work on a series of troubleshooting exercises that focus on problems, changes, and errors.

Summary

In this chapter, you learned the following:

- The term *Token Ring* refers both to IBM's Token Ring and to IEEEs 802.5 specification.
- FDDI has four specifications:
  1. Media Access Control (MAC)
  2. Physical Layer Protocol (PHY)
  3. Physical Layer Medium (PMD)
  4. Station Management (SMT)
- Ethernet and IEEE 802.3 currently maintain the greatest market share of any LAN protocol.
- The term *Ethernet* is often used to refer to all carrier sense multiple access collision detect (CSMA/CD) LANs that generally conform to Ethernet specifications, including IEEE 802.3.

Additionally, you learned about Layer 2 devices and their effects on data flow. Finally, you were introduced to basic Ethernet 10BaseT troubleshooting. In the next chapter, you are introduced to network design and documentation.

Check Your Understanding

1. In Token Ring and IEEE 802.5 networks, which one is true?

A. Individual stations are typically connected to form a physical ring.

B. Lobe cables are used to interconnect adjacent multistation access units (MSAUs).

C. Stations are connected to MSAUs.

D. Transceivers are used to connect cables to the physical media.

2. The token-passing process involves:

A. Listening for token traffic and transmitting when none is detected

B. Using possession of the token to grant the right to transmit

C. Attaching token frames to data frames to access the network

D. The token circulating a ring until it reaches the intended destination

3. ________, a Token Ring algorithm, detects and tries to repair network faults.

A. Beaconing

B. CSMA/DA

C. Token passing

D. Parity signaling

4. What are the primary advantages of fiber media over copper media?

A. Has higher data-carrying capacity at a lower cost

B. Uses installed cabling infrastructure and supports greater bandwidth

C. Uses the same MAC-layer and SMT specifications as CDDI

D. Provides greater security, immunity to interference, and better network distances

5. If a SAS that is attached to a concentrator on the primary ring fails, what happens?

A. The primary wraps onto the secondary, and network operation continues for all other stations.

B. The stations on either side of the concentrator wrap, bypassing the concentrator with the failed SAS.

C. The backup link is activated on the concentrator, and network operation is restored to the failed SAS.

D. The failed SAS is bypassed, and network operation continues for all other stations.

6. Ethernet uses what technique?

A. Token passing, to ensure that collisions do not occur on a network

B. Beaconing, to help networks recover from link failures

C. Carrier sense multiple access collision detect (CSMA/CD), to locate destinations

D. Broadcasting, to propagate traffic among network entities

7. With Ethernet, a transceiver is used for what purpose?

A. To make a network layer connection from a device to a server

B. To establish connections among network interface cards (NICs)

C. To attach a cable from an end station to the physical network medium

D. All of the above

8. In an Ethernet or IEEE 802.3 LAN, when do collisions occur?

A. When one node places a packet on a network without informing the other nodes

B. When two stations listen for a traffic, hear none, and transmit simultaneously

C. When two network nodes send packets to a node that is no longer broadcasting

D. When jitter is detected and traffic is disrupted during normal transmission

9. Network cards communicate with which of the following?

A. With the network through serial connections, and with the computer through parallel connections

B. With the network through parallel connections, and with the computer through serial connections

C. With the network through serial connections, and with the computer through serial connections

D. With the network through parallel connections, and with the computer through parallel connections

10. Which is an important Layer 2 data link layer function?

    A. Logical link control

    B. Addressing

    C. Media access control

    D. All of the above

11. Transparent bridges divide traffic into segments and filters traffic based on what?

    A. IP addresses

    B. MAC addresses

    C. Priority rules

    D. IPX addresses

12. Bridges use ________ to determine whether to forward data to other segments of the network.

    A. Maps

    B. Time-to-Live

    C. Tables

    D. None of the above

13. To filter or selectively deliver network traffic, bridges build tables of all ____ addresses located on a network and on which segment they are located.

    A. IP

    B. IPX

    C. MAC

    D. None of the above

14. To filter or selectively deliver network traffic, switches build tables of all ____ addresses located on a network and other networks and then map them.

    A. IP

    B. MAC

    C. NIC

    D. IPX

15. Which is true of switches?

A. They are considered multiport bridges.

B. They have no collision domains.

C. They increase bandwidth available on a network.

D. Both A and B.

16. Which is true of segmentation?

A. It merges traffic between segments.

B. It effectively creates more bandwidth by creating smaller collision domains.

C. It increases network broadcasts.

D. None of the above.

17. Which is not true of bridges?

A. Segmentation provides fewer users per segment.

B. Bridges store and then forward all frames based on Layer 2 address.

C. Bridges are Layer 3-independent.

D. None of the above.

18. Bridges increase the latency of cross-bridge traffic in a network by:

A. 10 to 30 percent

B. 5 to 20 percent

C. 10 to 20 percent

D. None of the above

19. Which is not true of switches?

A. A switch can eliminate the impact of collisions through microsegmentation.

B. A switch has high latency and high frame-forwarding rates at each interface port.

C. A switch works with existing 802.3 (CSMA/CD)–compliant NICs and cabling.

D. None of the above.

20. Which is *not* true of routers?

 A. More manageable, greater functionality, multiple active paths

 B. Smaller collision domains

 C. Operate at Layers 1, 2, and 3

 D. None of the above

Objectives

After reading this chapter, you will be able to

- Understand basic network design and documentation
- Describe wiring closet specifications
- Identify potential wiring closets
- Understand wiring closet selection
- Understand horizontal and backbone cabling
- Understand electricity and grounding
- Understand cabling and grounding
- Describe a wiring plan for an Ethernet star topology LAN
- Describe multiple earth ground problems
- Describe power line problems
- Describe surge suppressors and uninterruptible power supply (UPS) functions

Chapter 8

Design and Documentation

Introduction

Now that you have a firm understanding of data flow through the OSI model, along with Layer 1 and 2 concepts and technologies, you are ready to start learning how to design networks. Network design takes many technologies into consideration (Token Ring, FDDI, and Ethernet). For example, a Layer 1 LAN topology must be developed, the physical topology must be determined, and the type of cable must be chosen.

In this chapter, you learn how the network's physical and logical topologies should be designed and documented. You also learn to document brainstormed ideas, problem-solving matrices, and other notes used in making your decisions. In addition, you learn wiring closet specifications used in LANs, as well as wiring and electrical techniques used in building networks.

Basic Network Design and Documentation

This chapter includes a comprehensive list of the steps you must follow to design a network. Many of the decisions might have already been determined by the network administrator and the existing network design, but this process described here is the one you will follow.

Your network design could take into consideration many technologies such as Token Ring, FDDI, and Ethernet. This design focuses on Ethernet technology because that is the technology you will most likely encounter when you plan future designs. Ethernet has a logical bus topology, which leads to collision domains; however, you will try to keep the collision domains small by using a process called segmentation.

When you have settled on Ethernet, you must develop a Layer 1 LAN topology. You must determine the type of cable and the physical topology that you will use. The most common choice is Cat 5 UTP as the medium and an extended star topology as the physical topology. Then you must decide on which one of the several types of Ethernet topologies you want to use. Two common types of Ethernet are 10BaseT and 100BaseTX (Fast Ethernet). If you have the resources, you might run 100BaseTX throughout the network. If not, you might use Fast Ethernet to connect the main distribution facility (central control point of your

> **NOTE**
>
> As always, an important part of your design involves documenting your work.

network) to other intermediate distribution facilities. You might use hubs, repeaters, and transceivers in your design, along with other Layer 1 components such as plugs, cable, jacks, and patch panels. To finish the Layer 1 design, you must generate both a logical and a physical topology.

The next step is to develop a Layer 2 LAN topology—that is, to add Layer 2 devices to your topology to improve its capabilities. You could add switches to reduce congestion and collision domain size. In the future, you might be able to afford to replace hubs with switches and to upgrade other less intelligent Layer 1 devices to more intelligent Layer 2 devices. You could also integrate wireless equipment in your network to reduce the cabling requirements.

The next step, then, is to develop a Layer 3 topology—that is, to add Layer 3 devices that will add to the topology's capabilities. Layer 3 is where routing is implemented. You could use routers to build scalable internetworks such as LANs, WANs, or networks of networks. Routers will impose logical structure on the network you are designing. They can also be used for segmentation. Routers, unlike bridges, switches, and hubs, break up both collision and broadcast domains.

How the LANs link to WANs—the Internet, in particular—must be considered. As always, you should document your network design's physical and logical topologies. Your documentation should include any brainstormed ideas, problem-solving matrices, and any other notes involved in making your determinations.

Network Design Issues

For a LAN to be effective and serve the needs of its users, it should be implemented according to a systematic series of planned steps. While you are learning about the design process and creating your own designs, you should use your engineering journal extensively.

Your first step in the process is to gather information about the organization. This information should include the following:

1. The organization's history and current status
2. Projected growth
3. Operating policies and management procedures
4. Office systems and procedures
5. Viewpoints of the people who will be using the LAN

Hopefully, this step will also help you identify and define any issues or problems that need to be addressed (for example, you might find that a remote room in the building might not have network access).

The second step is to make a detailed analysis and assessment of the current and projected requirements of the people who will be using the network.

The third step is to identify the resources and constraints of the organization. Organization resources that can affect the implementation of a new LAN system fall into two main categories: computer hardware and software resources, and human resources. You must document an organization's existing computer hardware and software, and identify and define its projected hardware and software needs. The answers to some of these questions will also help you determine how much training will be required and how many people will be needed to support the LAN. The questions you ask should include the following:

1. What financial resources does the organization have available?
2. How are these resources currently linked and shared?
3. How many people will use the network?
4. What are the computer skill levels of the network users?
5. What are their attitudes toward computers and computer applications?

Following these steps and documenting the information in the framework of a formal report will help you estimate costs and develop a budget for the implementation of a LAN.

General Network Design Process

In technical fields, such as engineering, the design process resources include the following:

- **Designer**—Person doing the design
- **Client**—Person who has requested and is probably paying for the design
- **User(s)**—Person(s) who will use the product
- **Brainstorming**—Generation of creative ideas for the design
- **Specifications development**—Usually numbers that will measure how well the design works
- **Building and testing**—Process for meeting client objectives and satisfy certain standards

One of the methods you can use in the process of creating a design is the problem-solving cycle, as shown in Figure 8-1. You use this process repeatedly until you finish a design problem.

One of the methods that engineers use to organize their ideas and plans when doing a design is to use the problem-solving matrix. This matrix lists alternatives and various choices or options for your network.

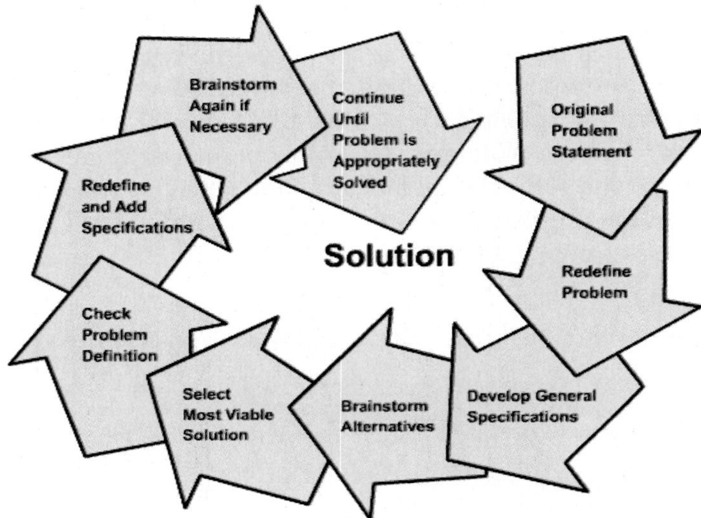

FIGURE 8-1 The Dartmouth problem-solving cycle.

Network Design Documents

The following list includes some of the documentation that you should create as you design a network:

- Engineering journal
- Logical topology
- Physical topology
- Cut sheets
- Problem-solving matrices
- Labeled outlets
- Labeled cable runs
- Summary of outlets and cable runs
- Summary of devices, MAC addresses, and IP addresses

You might also ask your instructor if any other documentation is relevant to your project. Perhaps the most important part of the network design process is designing according to the ANSI/EIA/TIA and ISO industry standards.

Planning Structured Cabling: Wiring Closet Specifications

One of the early decisions you must make when planning your network is where to place the wiring closet(s) because this will be where you have to install many of the networking cables and networking devices (see Figure 8-2). The most important decision is the selection of the main distribution facility (MDF). There are standards governing MDFs and IDFs, and you learn some of these while learning how to select the network wiring closet(s). If possible, tour the MDF/IDF of your own school or a local business. Finally, you learn how to plan your network so that you can avoid some of the problems related to negative effects caused by AC electricity.

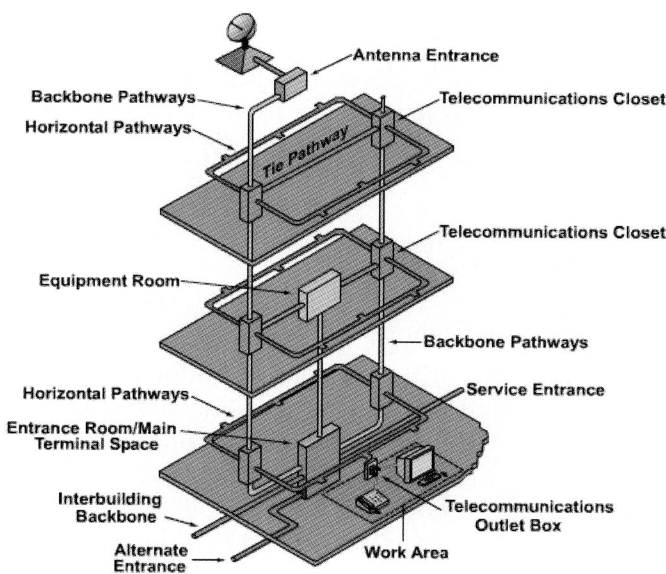

FIGURE 8-2
In an Ethernet LAN, the horizontal cabling runs must be attached to a central point in a star topology.

Wiring Closet Size

TIA/EIA-568-A specifies that, in an Ethernet LAN, the horizontal cabling runs must be attached to a central point in a star topology. The central point is the *wiring closet*, where the patch panel and the hub must be installed. The wiring closet must be large enough to accommodate all of the equipment and wiring that will be placed in it and account for future growth. Naturally, the size of the closet will vary with the size of the LAN and the types of equipment required to operate it. A small LAN needs only a space the size of a large filing cabinet, while a massive LAN requires a large room.

TIA/EIA-569 specifies that each floor must have a minimum of one wiring closet and that additional wiring closets should be provided for each 1000 m^2, when the area of the floor that is served exceeds 1000 m^2 or the horizontal cabling distance exceeds 90 m.

Environmental Specification

Any location that you select for a wiring closet must satisfy certain environmental requirements that include, but are not limited to, power supply and heating/ventilation/air conditioning (HVAC) issues. In addition, the location must be secure from unauthorized access and must meet all applicable building and safety codes.

Any room or closet that you choose to serve as a wiring closet should adhere to guidelines governing such items as the following:

- Materials for walls, floors, and ceilings
- Temperature and humidity
- Locations and types of lighting
- Power outlets
- Room and equipment access
- Cable access and support

Walls, Floors, and Ceilings

If there is only one wiring closet in a building, or if the wiring closet serves as the MDF, then the floor on which it is located must be capable of bearing the load specified by the installation instructions included with the equipment, with a minimum capability of 4.8 kPA (100 lb/ft^2). When the wiring closet serves as an IDF, the floor must be capable of bearing a minimum load of 2.4 kPA (50 lb/ft^2). Whenever possible, the room should have a raised floor to accommodate incoming horizontal cables that run from the work areas (see Figure 8-3). If this is not possible, it should have a 30.5 cm ladder rack installed in a configuration designed to support all proposed equipment and cable. Floor coverings should be tile or some other type of finished surface. This helps control dust and minimizes the exposure to equipment from static electricity.

FIGURE 8-3
A typical wiring closet.

A minimum of two walls should be covered with 20-mm A-C plywood that is at least 2.4 m high. If the wiring closet serves as the MDF for the building, then the telephone point of presence (POP) may be located inside the room. In such a case, the interior walls of the POP site, behind the PBX, should be covered from floor to ceiling with 20-mm plywood, with a minimum of 4.6 m of wall space provided for the terminations and related equipment. In addition, fire prevention materials that meet all applicable codes (fire-rated plywood, fire-retardant paint on all interior walls, and so on) should be used in the construction of the wiring closet. These rooms must not have a dropped, or false, ceiling. Failure to observe this specification could result in an insecure facility, allowing for possible unauthorized access.

Temperature and Humidity

The wiring closet should include sufficient HVAC to maintain a room temperature of approximately 21° C when all LAN equipment is in full operation. No water or steam pipes should be running through or above the room, with the exception of a sprinkler system, which may be required by local fire codes. Relative humidity should be maintained at a level between 30 and 50 percent. Failure to adhere to these particular specifications could result in serious corrosion of the copper wires that are contained within the UTP and STP cable. Such corrosion would diminish the efficient functioning of the network.

Lighting Fixtures and Power Outlets

If there is only one wiring closet in a building, or if the closet serves as the MDF, it should have a minimum of two dedicated, nonswitched AC duplex electrical outlet receptacles, each on a separate circuit. It should also have at least one duplex power outlet positioned every 1.8 m along each wall of the room, and it should be positioned 150 mm above the floor. A wall switch that controls the room's main lighting should be placed immediately inside the door.

Although fluorescent lighting should be avoided for cable pathways because of the outside interference that it generates, it can be used in wiring closets with proper installation. Lighting requirements for a telecommunications closet specify a minimum of 500 lx (brightness of light equal to 50-foot candles) and specify that light fixtures be mounted a minimum of 2.6 m above the floor.

Room and Equipment Access

The door of a wiring closet should be at least .9 m wide and should swing open out of the room, ensuring an easy exit for workers. The lock should allow anyone who is on the inside to exit at any time.

A wiring hub and patch panel may be mounted to a distribution rack or to a hinged swing-mount rack secured to a wall. If the choice is a hinged wall bracket, the bracket must be attached to the plywood that covers the underlying wall surface. The purpose of the hinge is to allow the assembly to swing out so that workers and repairmen can easily access the back side of the wall. Care must be taken, however, to allow 48 cm for the panel to swing out from the wall.

If the choice is a distribution rack, it must have a minimum 15.2 cm of wall clearance for the equipment, plus another 30.5 to 45.5 cm for physical access by workmen. A 55.9-cm floor plate used to mount the distribution rack will provide stability and will, in turn, determine the minimum distance from the wall for the rack's final position.

If the patch panel, hub, and other equipment are mounted in a full equipment cabinet, they require at least 76.2 cm of clearance in front, for the door to swing open. Typically, such cabinets are 1.8 m high × .74 m wide × .66 m deep.

Cable Access and Support

If a wiring closet serves as an MDF, all cable running from it to IDFs, computers, and communications rooms on other floors of the same building should be protected by 10.2-cm conduit or sleeved core, as shown in Figure 8-4. Likewise, all such cable running into the IDFs should be run through the same 10.2-cm conduit or sleeved cores. The exact amount of conduit required is determined by the amount of fiber-optic, UTP, and STP cable that must be supported in each wiring closet, computer, or communications room. Care should be taken to include additional lengths of conduit to provide for future growth. To meet this specification, a minimum of two excess sleeved cores or conduits should be kept in each wiring closet. Where construction permits, all conduit and sleeved core should be kept to within 15.2 cm of the walls.

FIGURE 8-4 Central wiring connections for a data or voice network are made in the wiring closet.

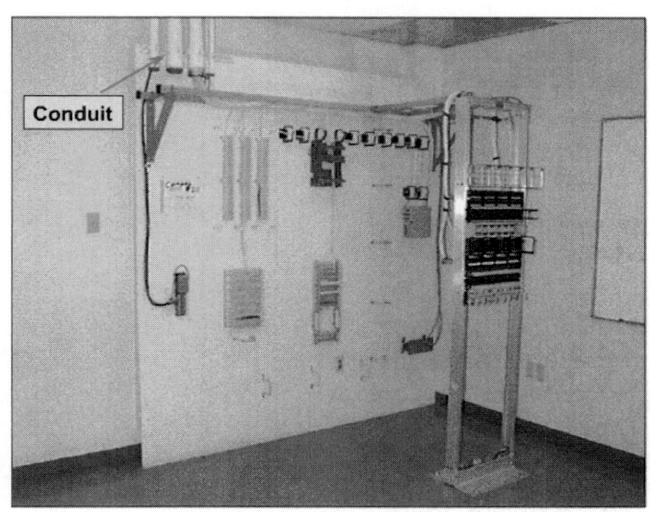

All horizontal cabling that runs from work areas to a wiring closet should be run under a raised floor. When this is not possible, the cabling should be run through 10.2-cm sleeves that are placed above door level. To ensure proper support, the cable should run from the sleeve directly onto a 30.5-cm ladder rack in the wiring closet. When used in this manner to support cable, the ladder rack should be installed in a configuration that supports the equipment layout. Finally, any wall/ceiling openings that provide access for the conduit or sleeved core must be sealed with smoke- and flame-retardant materials that meet all applicable codes.

Planning Structured Cabling: Identifying Potential Wiring Closets

TIA/EIA-568-A specifies that when using an Ethernet star topology, every device that is part of the network must be connected to the hub by a run of horizontal cabling (see Figure 8-5).

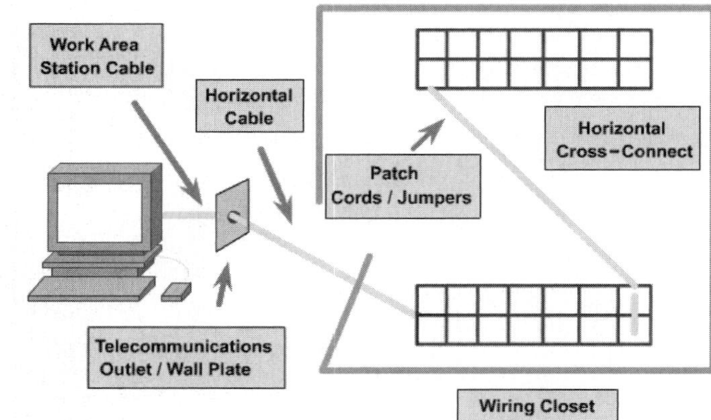

FIGURE 8-5
The central point of the star topology, where the hub is located, is called the wiring closet. It helps to think of the hub as the center point of a circle which has lines of horizontal cabling radiating from it, like spokes from the center of a wheel.

To determine the location of a wiring closet, begin by drawing a floor plan of the building (approximately to scale) and adding to it all the devices that will be connected to the network. As you do this, remember that computers are not the only devices that you will want to connect to the network; there are also printers and file servers to consider.

When you complete this process, you should have a floor plan that is similar to the one shown in the Figure 8-6.

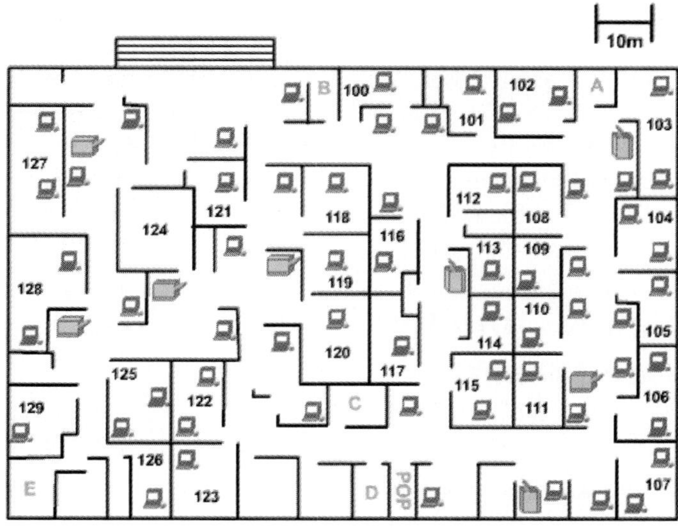

FIGURE 8-6
A floor plan.

Horizontal Cabling System Structure

The horizontal cabling system extends from the telecommunications outlet in the work area to the horizontal cross-connect in the telecommunications closet. It includes the telecommunications outlet, the horizontal cable, and the mechanical terminations and patch cords or jumpers that comprise the horizontal cross-connect.

Some points specified for the horizontal cabling subsystem include the following:

- Multipair and multiunit cables are allowed, provided that they satisfy the hybrid bundled cable requirements of TIA/EIA-568-A-3.
- Grounding must conform to applicable building codes, as well as ANSI/TIA/EIA-697.
- A minimum of two telecommunication outlets is required for each individual work area.
  - — First outlet: 100 _ UTP (Cat 5e recommended).
  - — Second outlet: 100 _ UTP (Cat 5e recommended).
  - — Two-fiber multimode optical fiber, either 62.5/125 µm or 50/125 µm.
- One transition point (TP) is allowed between different forms of the same cable type (for instance, where undercarpet cable connects to round cable).
- 50 Ω coax and 150 Ω STP cabling is not recommended for new installations.
- Additional outlets may be provided. These outlets are in addition to and may not replace the minimum requirements of the standard.
- Bridged taps and splices are not allowed for copper-based horizontal cabling. (Splices are allowed for fiber.)
- Application-specific components shall not be installed as part of the horizontal cabling. When needed, they must be placed external to the telecommunications outlet or horizontal cross-connect (splitters, baluns).
- The proximity of horizontal cabling to sources of electromagnetic interference (EMI) shall be taken into account.

NOTE

The definition provided for a "transition point" on ISO/IEC 11801 is broader than 568-A. It includes transitions to under carpet cabling as well as consolidations point connections.

NOTE

In ISO/IEC 11801, the equivalent cabling element to the horizontal cross-connect (HCC) is the *floor distributor* (FD).

Selecting Potential Locations

A good way to start looking for a potential wiring closet location is to identify secure locations that are close to the POP. The selected location can serve as either the sole wiring closet or the MDF (if IDFs are required). The POP is where telecommunications services provided by the telephone company connect to the building's communication facilities. It is essential that the hub be located near it, to facilitate wide-area networking and connection to the Internet. In the floor plan in Figure 8-7, five potential locations for wiring closets have been selected—they are marked as A, B, C, D, and E.

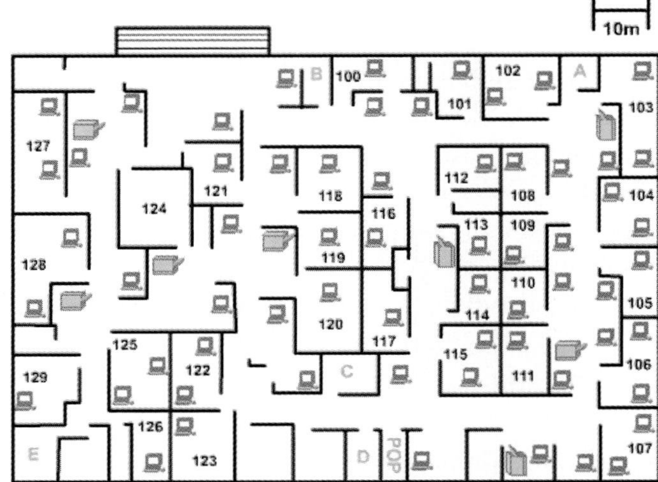

FIGURE 8-7 Potential location for wiring closets.

Determining Number of Wiring Closets

After all the devices that are to be connected to the network (floor plan) are documented in the site map, the next step is to determine how many wiring closets will be needed to serve the area covered by the network. You use your site map to do this.

Use your compass to draw circles that represent a radius of 50 m from each of the potential hub locations. Each of the network devices that you drew on your floor plan should fall within one such circle. However, if each horizontal cabling run can be 90 m in length, can you think of a reason why circles with a radius of only 50 m would be used?

MORE INFORMATION

Identification Exercise

Using the floor plan provided in this chapter, notice that there are five potential locations for wiring closets indicated on the floor plan: A, B, C, D, and E. Using the scale indicated on the floor plan, set the compass so that it will mark a circle that equals 50 m in diameter. Mark circles for each of the potential wiring closet sites. Then answer the following questions:

1. Do any of the circles overlap?
2. Can any of the potential wiring closet locations be eliminated?
3. Do any of the circles provide coverage for all the devices that will be connected to the network?
4. Which of the potential wiring closet locations seems to be the best?
5. Are there any circles in which only a few of the devices fall outside the catchment area?
6. Which potential wiring closet is closest to the POP?
7. Based on your findings, list the three best possible locations for wiring closets.
8. Based on your findings, how many wiring closets do you believe will be required for this network?
9. What are the advantages and disadvantages of each of the potential wiring closet locations shown on the floor plan?

Planning Structured Cabling: Selection Practice

The building in which you will install the LAN provides work stations for 71 workers and includes seven printers. The description of the building is as follows:

- The building occupies 669.8 m^2 of office space, all on a single floor.
- The building is 18.3 m wide × 36.6 m long.
- The ceiling height in all rooms, unless otherwise specified, is 3.7 m.
- All ceilings are dropped ceilings, unless otherwise specified.

- All floors are poured concrete covered with industrial carpet, unless indicated otherwise.
- All heating and cooling in the building is supplied by a forced air system.

Potential locations for wiring closets have already been identified. They are marked on the floor plan as A, B, C, D, E, F, G, H, I, and J (see Figure 8-8).

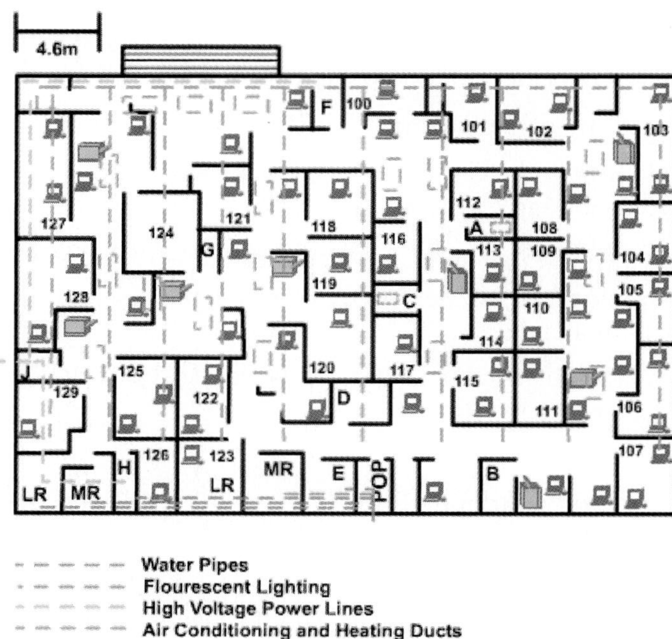

FIGURE 8-8
LAN floorplan.

The markings on the floor plan are as follows:

- The telephone company point of presence is labeled POP.
- Men's restrooms are labeled MR.
- Ladies' restrooms are labeled LR.

Closet A

Location A is a small closet approximately .9 m wide × 2.4 m deep (see Figure 8-9). It has a dropped ceiling with fluorescent lighting. The switch that turns the light on and off is located just inside the closet door. The floor is carpeted, and the walls are of concrete block construction. Only one electrical outlet is in the closet, located on the back wall. Currently, the room is used to store office supplies. Although a heating and cooling duct passes through the dropped ceiling space over the room, there is no vent into the room. The nearest thermostat for this section of the building is located in Room 113. The door swings outward when it opens and is approximately .9 m wide. However, because all the staff members must be able to access the storage area, no lock is on the door.

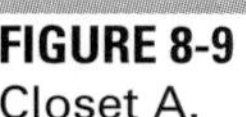

FIGURE 8-9
Closet A.

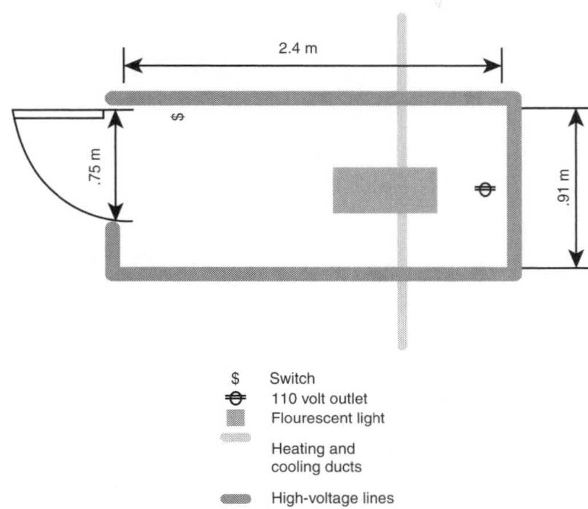

Closet B

Location B is slightly larger than location A (see Figure 8-10). Its dimensions measure approximately 1.8 m wide × 1.5 m deep. Like location A, location B has a dropped ceiling. The floor is covered with ceramic tile. The walls are made of concrete block construction covered by asbestos, which has been painted with a fire-retardant paint. No electrical outlets are in the room.

Lighting is provided by an incandescent fixture located in the ceiling; however, the switch that turns the light on and off is located on the wall across the corridor. There is no heating or cooling duct in the dropped ceiling space of this room, nor is there a heating or cooling duct into the room. The nearest thermostat for this section of the building is located on a wall along the corridor. Currently, the room is used to store toxic cleaning supplies. The door swings outward when it is opened and is approximately .9 m wide. Because it contains toxic materials, there is a lock on the door. The door can be unlocked from either inside or outside the room.

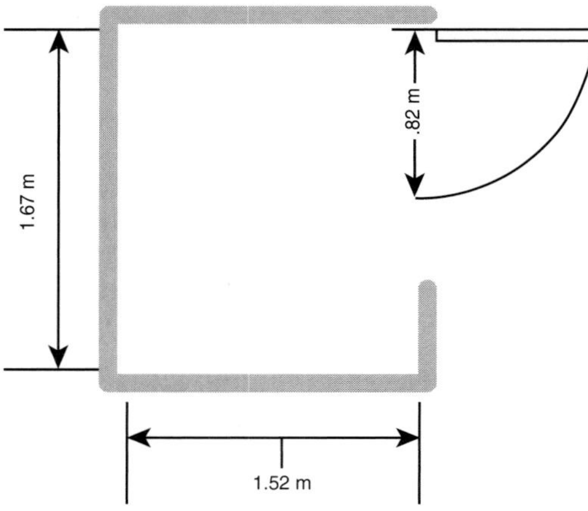

FIGURE 8-10
Closet B.

Closet C

Centrally located in the building, potential wiring closet C is larger than either A or B (see Figure 8-11). Its dimensions measure approximately 2.4 m wide × 2.4 m deep. There are five electrical outlets in the room, two along each side wall. One outlet is along the back wall. The floor is carpeted. Lighting is provided by a large fluorescent light fixture centered in the ceiling.

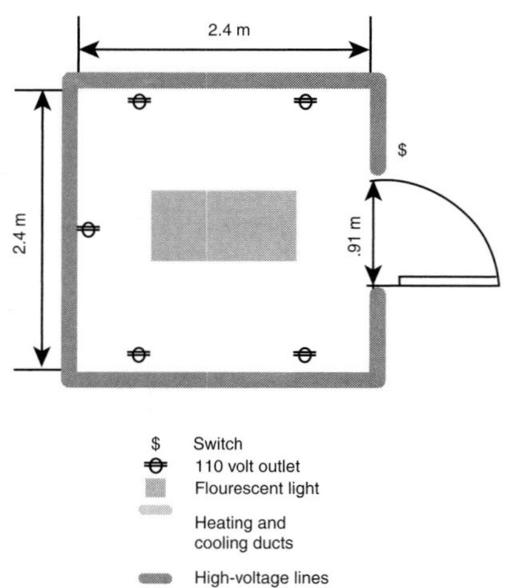

FIGURE 8-11
Closet C.

Immediately outside the room, in the corridor, are two additional large fluorescent lighting fixtures. The switch that turns all three fixtures on and off is located on the wall just outside Room C.

There is no heating or cooling duct in the dropped ceiling space of this room, nor is there a heating or cooling duct into the room. The nearest thermostat for this section of the building is located in Room 120. The walls are concrete block construction covered with asbestos. Although the room has a lock, it can be unlocked only from the outside. Currently, the room serves as the mail room for the building.

Closet D

Also centrally located, Room D is slightly larger than Room C (see Figure 8-12). Its dimensions are approximately 2.4 m wide × 3 m deep. In addition, Room D is near the POP. The room does not have a dropped ceiling. A heating and cooling duct that passes through the top of the room is also vented into the room. Temperatures inside the room are controlled by a thermostat that is located just inside the door. The exit door swings outward and is .91 m wide.

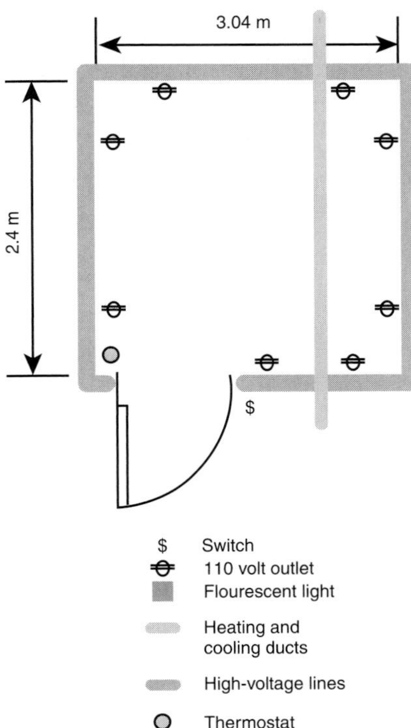

FIGURE 8-12
Closet D.

The floor is covered with ceramic tiles. Lighting is provided by an incandescent lighting fixture in the ceiling. The light switch that turns the light on and off is located just outside the door. There are eight electrical outlets in the room, two along each wall. The walls are of concrete block construction and are painted with a fire-retardant paint. Currently, the room is used to store extra office equipment and is kept locked. The door can be unlocked only from outside the room.

Closet E

Also centrally located in the building, Room E is adjacent to the POP. Room E is smaller than Room D (see Figure 8-13). Its dimensions are approximately 2.4 m wide × 1.5 m deep. A water pipe enters the building through Room E and travels from there to other locations throughout the building. There is also a hot water heater in Room E. In spite of repeated attempts to remedy the problem, the water pipes in Room E are heavily corroded. There is no false ceiling in the room. The floor is covered with ceramic tile. A heating and cooling duct that passes through the top of the room is also vented into the room. The nearest thermostat is located in the corridor outside the room.

Lighting is provided by an overhead incandescent light suspended from the ceiling. The switch that turns the light fixture on and off is located just inside the door to Room E. The door, which is approximately .9 m wide, swings into the room when it is opened. There are two electrical outlets in the room, located on opposite walls. Because of its contents, Room E is kept locked and can be unlocked from either inside or outside the room.

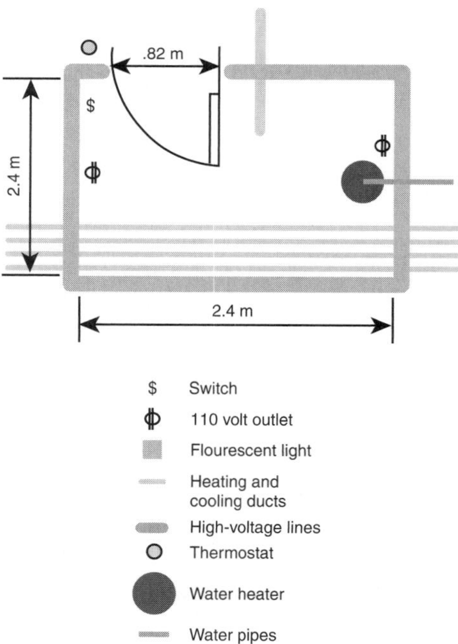

FIGURE 8-13
Closet E.

Closet F

Room F is centrally located near the front of the building, next to the main entry and behind the receptionist's desk. Currently, it is used as a cloak room. There are two doors into the room. Each door is approximately .9 m wide, and each swings out when opened (see Figure 8-14). Neither door has a lock. Lighting is provided by an incandescent light fixture. Two light switches turn the overhead light on and off, located just inside each door.

There are no heating or cooling vents into the room. The nearest thermostat is located along the corridor wall outside Room 118. The floor is carpeted. The room has one electrical outlet. It is located along the wall behind the receptionist's desk in the lobby. Also, Room F has high voltage power lines running through its outside walls.

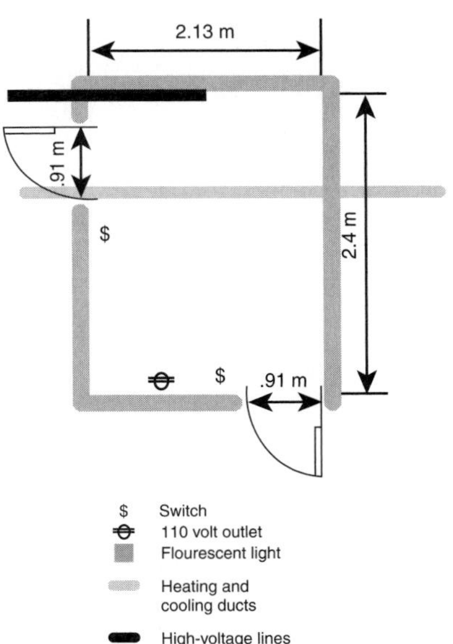

FIGURE 8-14
Closet F.

Closet G

Room G is relatively small. Its dimensions are approximately 1.8 m wide × .9 m deep (see Figure 8-15). The outside wall for Room G is only a partial wall: It does not reach all the way to the 3.7 m high dropped ceiling; it extends only from the floor and is of drywall construction. The two back walls do extend all the way to the dropped ceiling and are of concrete block construction.

One electrical outlet is located along the longer of the two back walls. Room G does not possess its own lighting fixture. Lighting is provided by fluorescent lighting fixtures in the corridor and in a shared work space. There is no door into Room G, but the entryway is about .9 m wide.

The floor is carpeted. There are no air vents from the heating and cooling duct into Room G. The nearest vent is located approximately 4.6 m away. The nearest thermostat is located on the wall opposite the entry into Room G. Currently, the space provided by Room G houses the water cooler, a small microwave, and a small refrigerator.

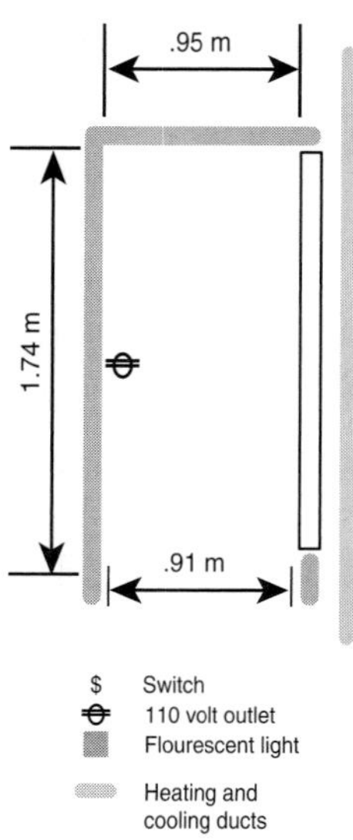

FIGURE 8-15
Closet G.

Closet H

Potential wiring closet H is a little larger than Room G. Its dimensions are approximately 2.4 m wide × .9 m deep (see Figure 8-16). Although its door is .9 m wide, entry into Room H is through a small narrow hallway. When the door opens, it swings into the room. Water pipes run through the dropped ceiling space of the room. High-voltage electrical conduits also pass through the room. Lighting is provided by an overhead incandescent light; however, the switch that turns the light on and off is located outside the doorway is in the room. The floor is carpeted. No heating or cooling vent is in the room, nor does any heating and cooling ductwork pass through the dropped ceiling space of this room. The nearest thermostat is located in the main corridor, around the corner. There is just one electrical outlet in Room H.

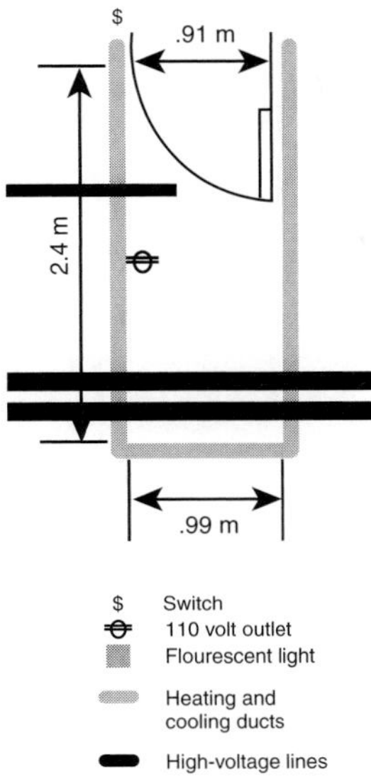

FIGURE 8-16
Closet H.

Closet I

Potential wiring closet I is located in the far corner of the building, next to the main entry. Its dimensions are approximately 2.4 m wide × 4.6 m deep (see Figure 8-17). Room I houses the heating and cooling equipment for the building. All heating and cooling ducts to other parts of the building lead from this room. High-voltage electrical conduit passes through this room along the outside walls. All walls are of concrete block construction and are covered with fire-retardant paint. The room does not have a dropped ceiling. The floor is covered with ceramic tile.

Lighting is provided by an overhead incandescent lighting fixture. The switch that turns the light on and off is located just inside the door. When the door is opened, it swings outward. Because the room houses potentially dangerous equipment, the door locks and unlocks from either inside or outside the room.

Closet J

Potential wiring closet J is located at one end of the building. Its dimensions are approximately .9 m wide × 2.4 m deep (see Figure 8-18). High-voltage power lines enter the building through Room J. High-voltage electrical conduit leads from Room J to other critical areas of the building. The floor is tiled, and there is a dropped ceiling. The door is .9 m wide and swings out when opened. Because the room is equipped with potentially dangerous equipment, the door to the room is kept locked; it can be unlocked from either inside or outside the room.

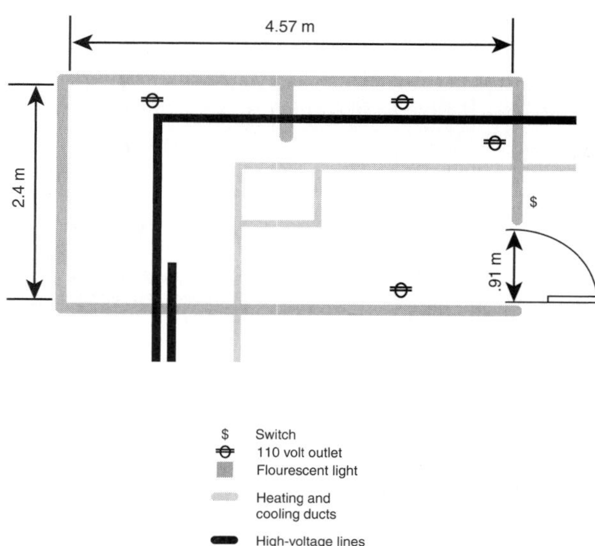

FIGURE 8-17
Closet I.

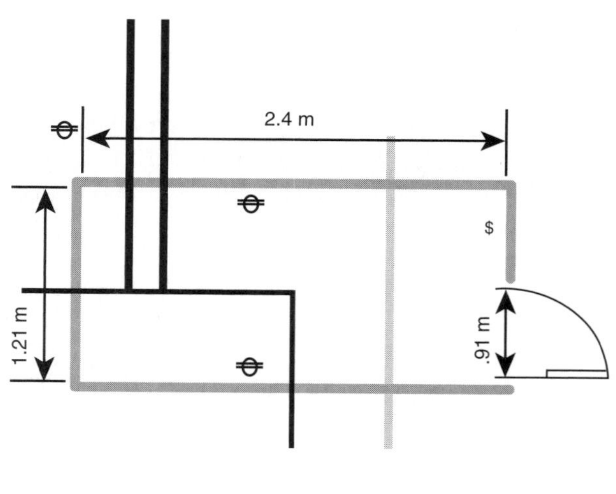

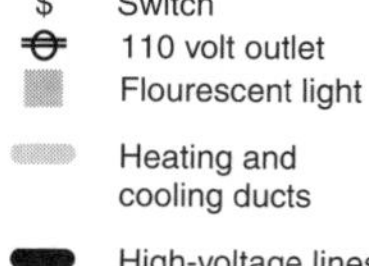

FIGURE 8-18
Closet J.

Lighting is provided by an overhead incandescent lighting fixture. The switch that turns the light on and off is located inside the doorway, on the right side. There are two electrical outlets in the room, located along opposite walls. All walls are of concrete block construction and are covered with fire-retardant paint. A heating and cooling duct passes through the dropped ceiling space above the room, but there is no vent outlet into the room.

Planning Structured Cabling: Horizontal and Backbone Cabling

If the 100-m catchment area of a simple star topology wiring closet cannot provide enough coverage for all the devices that need to be networked, the star topology can be extended by using repeaters or hubs. Repeaters or hubs are used to avoid the problem of signal attenuation. Generally speaking, when repeaters or hubs are used in this manner, they are located in additional wiring closets called IDFs (see Figure 8-19). These IDF closets are linked by networking media to a central hub located in another wiring closet, called the MDF. TIA/EIA-568-A specifies the use of one of the following types of networking media for backbone or vertical cabling:

- 100-ohm UTP (four pair)
- 150-ohm STP-A (two pair)
- Two-fiber (duplex) 62.5/125-µm optical fiber
- Multimode optical fiber

The TIA/EIA recommends the use of Cat 5 or 5E UTP for horizontal cabling when an Ethernet LAN uses a simple star topology.

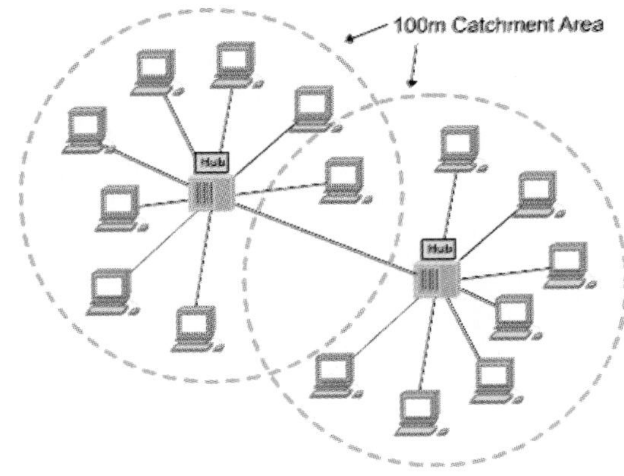

FIGURE 8-19
A hub or repeater can extend the total cable length to a host beyond a single catchment area.

MDF Location in a Multistory Building

The main hub or switch for an extended star topology (Ethernet LAN) is usually centrally located. This central location is so important that in a high-rise building, the MDF is usually located on one of the middle floors of the building, even though the POP might be located on the first floor, or in the basement.

Figure 8-20 illustrates where the backbone cabling and horizontal cabling would be used in an Ethernet LAN in a multistory building. The backbone cabling connects the POP to the MDF. Backbone cabling is also used to connect the MDF to the IDFs located on each floor. Horizontal cabling runs radiate out from the IDFs on each floor to the various work areas. Whenever the MDF is the only wiring closet on the floor, horizontal cabling radiates from it to the PCs on that floor.

FIGURE 8-20
Extended star topology in a multi-story building.

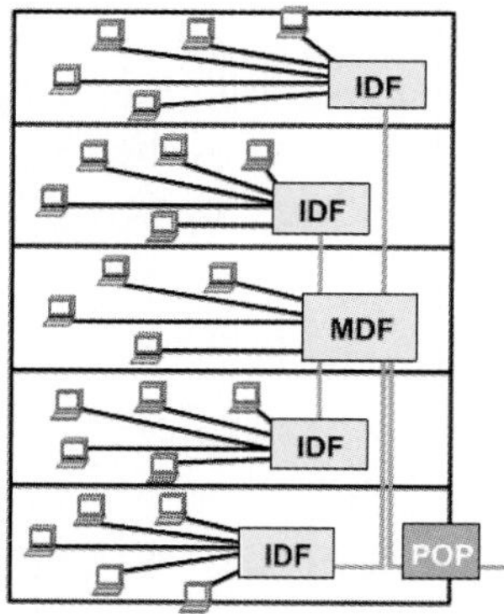

Multibuilding Campus

Another example of a LAN that would probably require more than one wiring closet is a multibuilding campus. Figure 8-21 illustrates locations where backbone and horizontal cabling have been placed in just such a multibuilding campus. This figure shows an MDF in the center of the campus. In this instance, the POP is located inside the MDF. The backbone cabling runs from the MDF to each of the IDFs. The IDFs are located in each of the campus buildings. In addition, the main building has an IDF as well as an MDF so that all computers fall within the catchment area. Horizontal cabling runs from the IDFs and MDFs to the work areas.

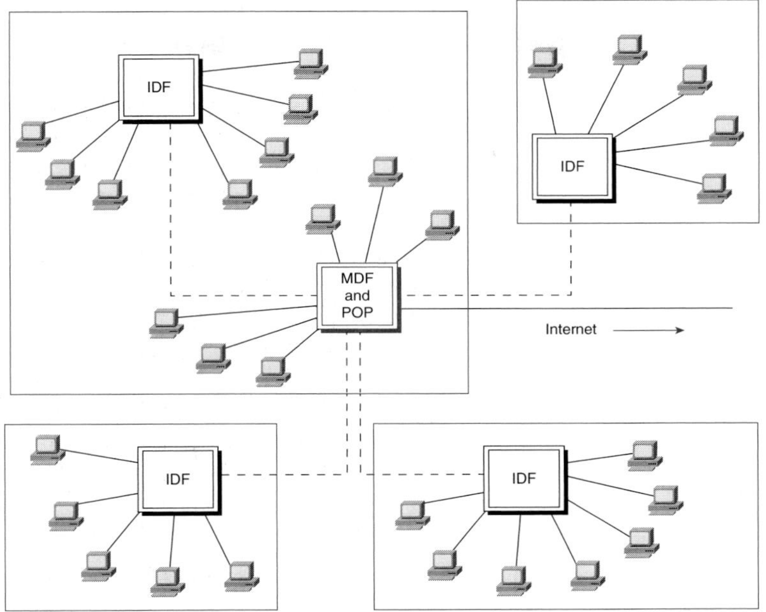

FIGURE 8-21
A central location on a campus is used for the MDF.

Cabling for MDF and IDF Connections

The type of cabling that TIA/EIA-568 specifies for connecting wiring closets to each other in an Ethernet LAN extended star topology is called backbone cabling. Sometimes, to differentiate it from horizontal cabling, you may see backbone cabling referred to as vertical cabling.

Backbone cabling consists of the following:

- Backbone cabling runs
- Intermediate and main cross-connects
- Mechanical terminations
- Patch cords used for backbone-to-backbone cross-connections
  - — Vertical networking media between wiring closets on different floors
  - — Networking media between the MDF and the POP
  - — Networking media used between buildings in a multibuilding campus

Backbone Cabling Media

TIA/EIA-568-A specifies four types of networking media that can be used for backbone cabling:

- 100-ohm UTP (four-pair)
- 150-ohm STP (two-pair)
- 62.5/125-µm multimode optical fiber
- Single-mode optical fiber

Although TIA/EIA-568-A recognizes 50-ohm coaxial cable, it is generally not recommended for new installations. It is anticipated that this cable will be removed as a choice the next time the standard is revised. Most installations today use the 62.5/125-µm fiber-optic cable for backbone cabling.

TIA/EIA-568-A Requirements for Backbone Cabling

The topology used when more than one wiring closet is required is the extended star topology (see Figure 8-22). Because more complex equipment is located at the most central point in an extended star topology, sometimes it is referred to as a hierarchical star topology.

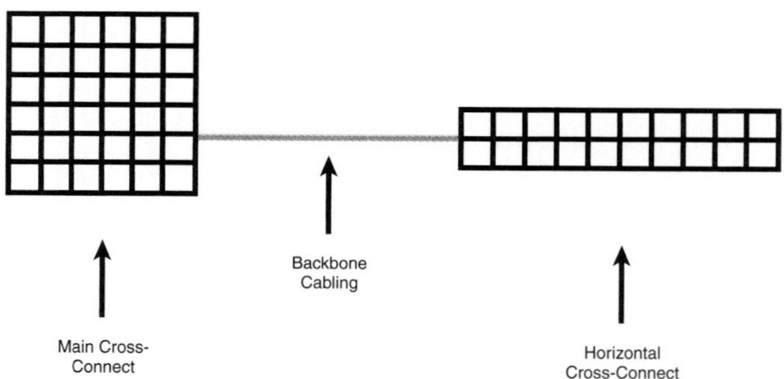

FIGURE 8-22 Extended star topology.

In the extended star topology, there are two ways in which an IDF can be connected to the MDF. In the first, each IDF can be connected directly to the main distribution facility. In this case, because the IDF is where the horizontal cabling connects to a patch panel in the wiring closet, whose backbone cabling then connects to the hub or switch in the MDF, the IDF is sometimes referred to as the horizontal cross-connect (HCC). The MDF is sometimes referred to as the main cross-connect (MCC) because it connects the backbone cabling of the LAN to the Internet (see Figure 8-23).

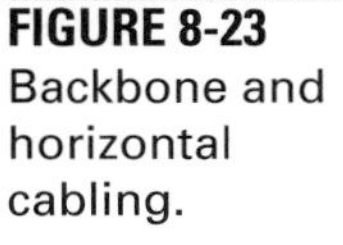

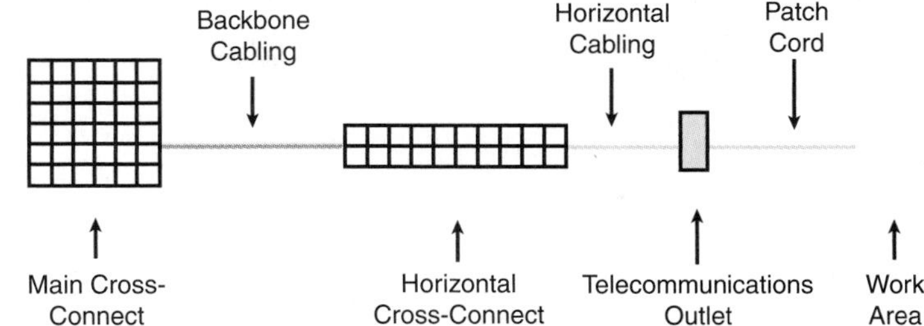

FIGURE 8-23
Backbone and horizontal cabling.

A second method of connecting an IDF to the central hub or switch uses a "first" IDF interconnected to a "second" IDF. The "second" IDF is then connected to the MDF. The IDF that connects to the work areas is called the horizontal cross-connect. The IDF that connects the horizontal cross-connect to the MDF is called the intermediate cross-connect (ICC). Note that no work areas or horizontal cabling connects to the intermediate cross-connect when this type of hierarchical star topology is used (see Figure 8-24).

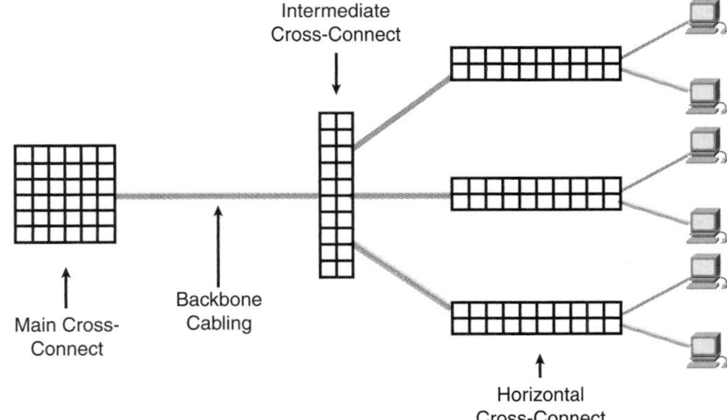

FIGURE 8-24
Type B backbone cabling.

When the second type of connection occurs, TIA/EIA-568-A specifies that no more than one ICC can be passed through to reach the MCC (see Figure 8-25).

Maximum Distances for Backbone Cabling

As you already learned, the maximum distances for cabling runs vary from one type of cable to another. For backbone cabling, the maximum distance for cabling runs can also be impacted by how the backbone cabling is to be used. To understand what this means, assume that a decision has been made to use single-mode fiber-optic cable for the backbone cabling. If the networking media is to be used to connect the HCC to the MCC, as described previously, then the maximum distance for the backbone cabling run would be 3000 m (see Figure 8-26).

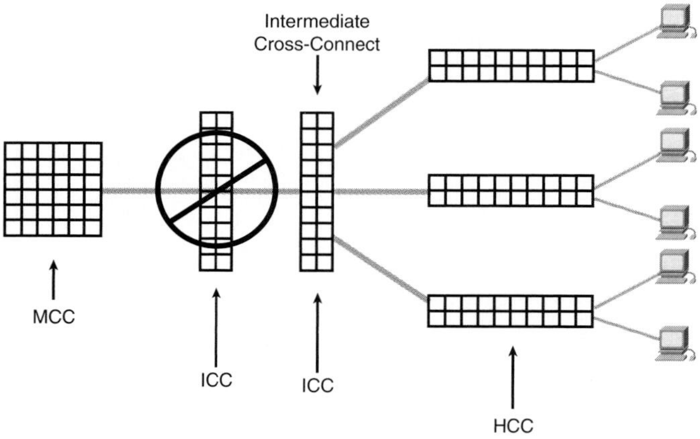

FIGURE 8-25
Extended star topology.

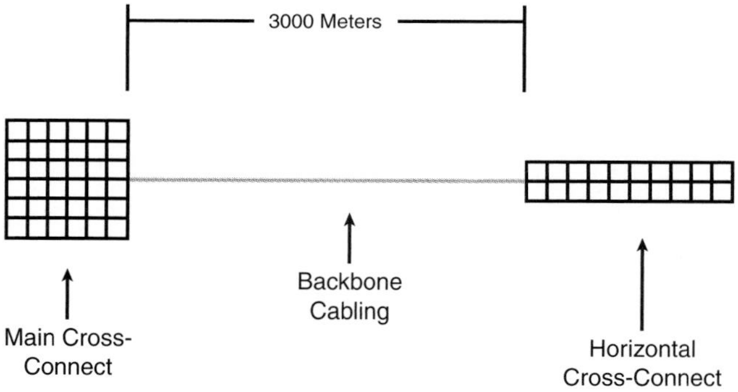

FIGURE 8-26
Type A cabling using single mode fiber-optic cable.

At times, the maximum distance of 3000 m for the backbone cabling run must be split between two sections. This occurs when the backbone cabling is to be used to connect an HCC to an ICC and then to connect that ICC to the MCC. When this occurs, the maximum distance for the backbone cabling run between the HCC and the ICC is 500 m. The maximum distance for the backbone cabling run between the ICC and the MCC is 2500 m (see Figure 8-27).

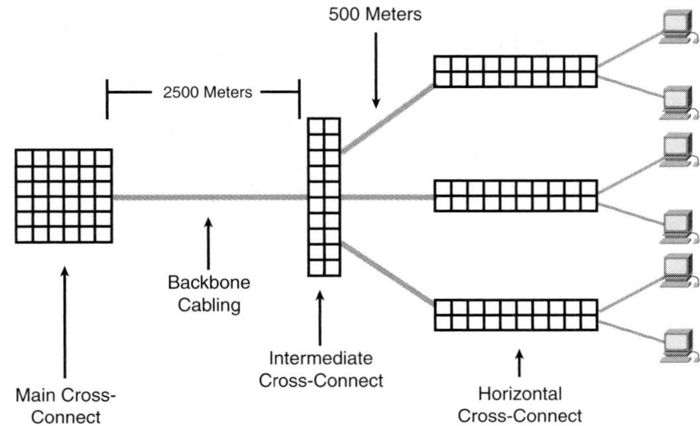

FIGURE 8-27
Type B cabling using single mode fiber-optic cable.

Planning Structured Cabling: Electricity and Grounding

Electricity is a fact of modern life. It is brought into our homes, schools, and offices by power lines that carry it in the form of *alternating current (AC)*. Another type of current, called *direct current (DC)*, is the kind found in a flashlight, in a car battery, or the motherboard of a computer. It is important to understand the difference between these two types of current flow. DC has a constant voltage.

AC Line Noise

After it reaches our homes, schools, and offices, electricity is carried to appliances and machines via wires concealed in walls, floors, and ceilings. Consequently, inside these buildings, AC power line noise is all around us. If not properly addressed, power line noise can present significant problems for a network.

In fact, you will discover as you work with networks that AC line noise coming from a nearby video monitor or hard disk drive can be enough to cause errors in a computer system. It does this by adding unwanted voltages to the desired signals and preventing a computer's logic gates from detecting the leading and trailing edges of the square signal waves. This problem can be further compounded when a computer has a poor ground connection.

Electrostatic Discharge

Electrostatic discharge (ESD), more commonly known as static electricity, is the most damaging and uncontrollable form of electricity. ESD must be dealt with to protect sensitive electronic equipment.

At one time or another, you have experienced what happens as you walk across a carpet. If the air is cool and dry, when you reach to touch another object a spark jumps from your fingertips and causes you to feel a small shock. You know from experience that such ESDs can sting momentarily, but in the case of a computer, such shocks can be disastrous. ESDs can randomly destroy semiconductors and data as they shoot through a computer. A solution that can help solve problems related to ESD is good grounding.

Grounding Electrical Current in Computer Equipment

The purpose of connecting the safety ground to the exposed metal parts of the computing equipment is to prevent such metal parts from becoming energized with a hazardous voltage that might occur as a result of a wiring fault inside the device. For AC and DC electrical systems, the flow of electrons is always from a negatively charged source to a positively charged source. However, for the controlled flow of electrons to occur, a complete circuit is required. Generally speaking, electrical current follows the path of least resistance. Because metals such as copper provide little resistance, they are frequently used as conductors for electrical current. Conversely, materials such as glass, rubber, and plastic provide more resistance. Therefore, they do not make good electrical conductors. Instead, these materials are frequently used as insulators and are used on conductors to prevent shock, fires, and short circuits.

Electrical power is usually delivered from the power company to a pole-mounted transformer. The transformer reduces the high voltages used in the transmission to the 120 or 240 volts used by typical consumer electrical appliances. In electrical equipment in which a safety ground connection is used, the safety ground wire is connected to any exposed metal part of the equipment. The motherboards and computing circuits in computing equipment are electrically connected to the chassis. This also connects them to the safety grounding wire, which is used to dissipate static electricity. The purpose of connecting the safety ground to exposed metal parts of the computing equipment is to prevent such metal parts from becoming energized with a hazardous voltage resulting from a wiring fault inside the device.

An accidental connection between the hot wire and the chassis is an example of a wiring fault that could occur in a network device. If such a fault occurred, the safety ground wire connected to the device would serve as a low resistance path to the earth ground. The safety ground connection provides a lower resistance path than your body.

When properly installed, the low-resistance path provided by the safety ground wire offers sufficiently low resistance and current-carrying capacity to prevent the buildup of hazardous high voltages. The circuit directly links the hot connection to the earth.

Whenever an electrical current is passed through this path into the ground, it causes protective devices such as circuit breakers and ground fault circuit interrupters (GFCIs) to activate. By interrupting the circuit, circuit breakers and GFCIs stop the flow of electrons and reduce the hazard of electrical shock. The circuit breakers protect you and your house wiring. Further protection, often in the form of surge suppressors, are required to protect computing and networking equipment.

Safety Ground Connections

Large buildings frequently require more than one earth ground. Separate earth grounds for each building are required in multibuilding campuses. Unfortunately, the earth ground between buildings is almost never the same. Separate earth grounds for the same building can also vary.

When ground wires in separate locations have slightly different potentials (voltages), the difference in voltages can present a serious problem. To understand this, assume that the ground wire for Building A has a slightly different potential than the ground wire for Building B. Because of this, the outside cases of computer devices located in Building A would have a different voltage (potential) than the outside cases of computer equipment located in Building B. If a circuit were established that linked computer devices in Building A to those in Building B, then electrical current would flow from the more negative source to the less negative source. This errant potential voltage could have the capability to severely damage delicate computer components.

Planning Structured Cabling: Cabling and Grounding

In the example previously outlined, can you explain why a person would have to simultaneously touch devices with different grounds for a shock to occur? As this theoretical example demonstrates, when devices with different ground potentials are linked in a circuit, they can produce hazardous shocks. In the real world, however, the chances of any such occurrence as described are very slight because in most instances, a person would have to have extremely long arms to complete the circuit. In some situations, however, such circuits can be created.

As illustrated in the previous example, the closed circuit produced by your body and the UTP cable would allow electrons to flow from the more negative source to the less negative source through your body. This is because the ground wires for the devices in one location have a slightly different potential to the ground wires for the devices in the second location. The closed circuit produced by the use of UTP cable would then allow electrical current to flow from the more negative source to the less negative source. Anyone touching the chassis of a device on the network would receive a nasty shock. A good way to avoid having current pass through the body—and through the heart—is to use the "one hand rule." Simply put, this rule says that you should not use more than one hand at a time to touch any electrical device. The second hand should remain in your pocket.

Faulty Ground Wiring Problems

When everything works correctly, according to IEEE standards, there should be no voltage difference between the networking media and the chassis of a networking device. This is because the standards separate LAN media connections from power connections. However, things don't always work as planned. For example, if there were a faulty ground wire connection to an outlet, there would be potentially fatal voltages between the LAN's UTP cabling and the chassis of a networking device.

To understand the potential consequences of such a situation, imagine what would happen if you placed your hand on the computer's case while simultaneously touching an Ethernet connector. By touching both the computer's case and the Ethernet connector, your body, acting as a closed circuit, would allow electrons to flow through you. As a result, you could receive a painful shock.

Avoiding Potentially Dangerous Circuits Between Buildings

TIA/EIA-568-A specifications for backbone cabling permit the use of fiber-optic cable and UTP cable. Because glass is an insulator rather than a conductor, electricity does not travel over fiber-optic cables. Therefore, when multiple buildings are to be networked, it is highly desirable to use fiber-optic cable as the backbone.

How Fiber-Optic Cable Can Prevent Electrical Shocks

Most network installers today recommend the use of fiber-optic cable for backbone cabling to link wiring closets that are on different floors of the same building, as well as between separate buildings. The reason for this is simple: It is not uncommon for floors of the same building to be fed by different power transformers. Different power transformers can have different earth grounds, thus causing the problems previously described. Nonconducting optical fibers eliminate the problem of different grounds.

Using UTP for Backbone Cabling Between Buildings

Although faulty wiring can present one type of electrical problem for a LAN that has UTP cable installed in a multibuilding environment, another type of problem can occur. Whenever copper is used for backbone cabling, it can provide a pathway for lighting strikes to enter a building. Such strikes are a common cause of damage to multibuilding LANs. For this reason, new installations of this type are moving toward the use of fiber-optic cable for the backbone cabling.

Wiring Plan for Ethernet Star Topology LAN

It is standard practice to develop a wiring plan for an Ethernet extended star topology LAN that uses both fiber-optic and Cat 5 UTP cabling. A description for a proposed network area is as follows (see Figure 8-28):

- The campus has three buildings.
- Each building is two stories tall.
- The dimensions of the main building are 40 m × 37 m.
- The dimensions of both the east building and the west building are 40 m × 23 m.
- Each building has a different earth ground.
- Each building has only a single earth ground.
- All floors are covered with ceramic tile, unless otherwise specified.

On the floor plans, the following locations have been indicated:

- MR = Men's restrooms
- WR = Women's restrooms
- POP, in the main building
- Power line entry into each building
- Water line entry into each building

You are asked to provide a plan to network the computing devices in all three buildings in an Ethernet extended star topology. As you develop your networking plan, assume that two computing devices are located in each numbered room. Your plan should show each of the following:

1. Location of the MDF
2. Location and number of IDFs
3. Identity of IDFs used as HCCs

4. Identity of IDFs used as ICCs
5. Location of all backbone cabling runs between the MDF and IDFs
6. Location of any backbone cabling runs between IDFs
7. Location of all horizontal cabling runs from IDFs to work areas

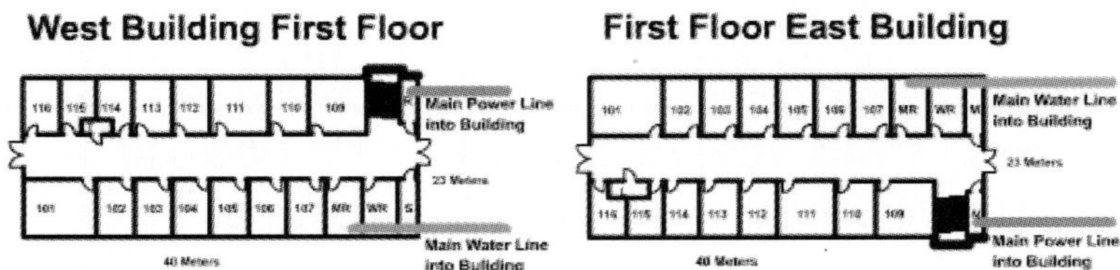

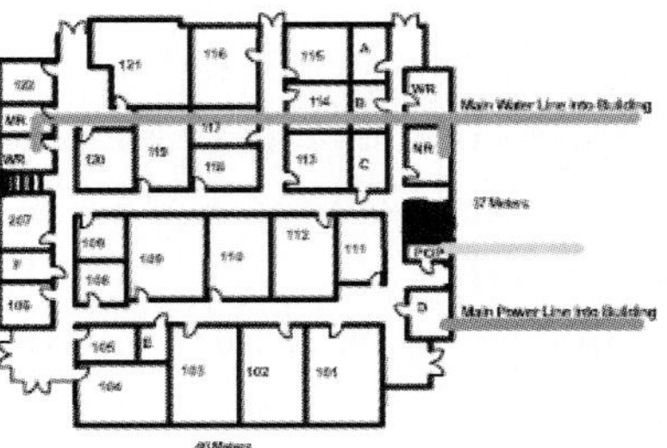

FIGURE 8-28 Floor plans for a campus with three buildings.

Don't forget to indicate on your floor plan the location of any backbone cabling runs between floors and between buildings. In addition, your plan should indicate what type of networking media you plan to use for the horizontal cabling and for the backbone cabling.

Main Building: First Floor

The dimensions of the main building are roughly 40 m × 37 m. A preliminary survey of the building has already been conducted, and six potential wiring closet locations have been identified for the first floor. On the floor plan shown in Figure 8-29, these are indicated by the letters A, B, C, D, E, and F.

Although the POP was considered as a possible location, it was determined during the preliminary survey of the building that the POP is too small to house all the equipment needed in an MDF.

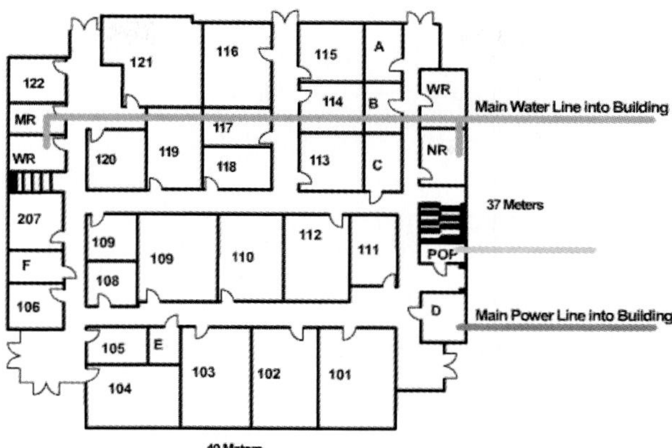

FIGURE 8-29
First floor of the main building.

1. Location A uses fluorescent lighting. The door opens into the room and has no lock. The light switch is located inside the door and to the right. The room has a dropped ceiling. The walls are of cinder block construction and are covered with fire-retardant paint. There are no electrical outlets in the room.

2. Location B also uses fluorescent lighting. The door opens into the room but can be secured with a lock. The light switch is located inside the door and to the left. The room has a dropped ceiling. Water lines pass through one side of the room. The walls are of cinder block construction and are covered with fire-retardant paint. There are two electrical outlets in the room.

3. Location C uses incandescent lighting. The door opens out of the room and can be secured with a lock. The light switch is located inside the door and to the right upon entering. There is no dropped ceiling in this room. The walls are of cinder block construction. They are painted with fire-retardant paint. The room is located close to the POP. There are four electrical outlets in the room.

4. Location D uses incandescent lighting. The door opens out of the room and can be secured with a lock. The light switch is located inside the door and to the right. There is no dropped ceiling in the room. Like Location C, the walls of this room are of cinder block construction and are painted with a fire-retardant paint. This room is also located in close proximity to the POP. There are four electrical outlets in the room.

5. Location E uses incandescent lighting. The door opens out of the room and can be secured with a lock. The light switch is located inside the door and to the right. Like rooms C and D, this room does not have a dropped ceiling. The walls are of cinder block construction and are painted with a fire-retardant paint. There are three electrical outlets in the room.

6. Location F uses incandescent lighting. The door opens out of the room and can be secured with a lock. The light switch is located inside the door and to the right. The room does not have a dropped ceiling. The walls are of cinder block construction and are painted with a fire-retardant paint. There are four electrical outlets in the room.

Main Building: Second Floor

Five additional potential wiring closet locations were identified for the second floor. Shown in Figure 8-30, they are marked on the plan of the second floor of the main building as G, H, I, J, and K.

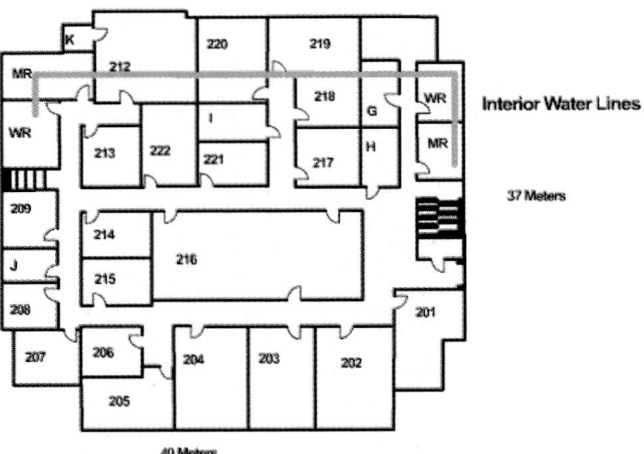

FIGURE 8-30 Second floor of the main building.

1. Location G uses incandescent lighting. The door opens into the room and is not secured with a lock. The light switch is to the left of the door. Interior water lines run through the dropped ceiling space along the right cinder block wall. Fire-retardant paint covers all walls. There are four electrical outlets in the room.

2. Location H uses fluorescent lighting. The door opens out of the room and can be secured with a lock. The light switch is to the right of the door. The room does not have a dropped ceiling. The walls are of cinder block construction and are painted with a fire-retardant paint. There are five electrical outlets in the room.

3. Location I uses incandescent lighting. The door opens out of the room and can be secured with a lock. The light switch is to the right of the door. The room does not have a dropped ceiling. The walls are of cinder block construction and are painted with a fire-retardant paint. There are six electrical outlets in the room.
4. Location J uses fluorescent lighting. The door opens into the room and cannot be locked. The light switch for this room is outside the room on the opposite wall of the hallway. There is a dropped ceiling in the room. The walls are of cinder block construction and are covered with a fire-retardant paint. There are two electrical outlets in the room.
5. Location K can be reached only by passing through Room 212. The room has incandescent lighting and is used to store toxic chemicals for experimental purposes. The door opens out of the room and can be secured with a lock. The light switch is to the left of the door. The room does not have a dropped ceiling. The walls are of cinder block construction and are covered with a fire-retardant paint. There is one electrical outlet in the room.

East Building: First Floor

The east building is located approximately 20 m from the main building. A preliminary survey of the building has been made. Three potential wiring closet locations have been identified for the first floor. As shown in Figure 8-31, they are marked on the floor plan as L, M, and N.

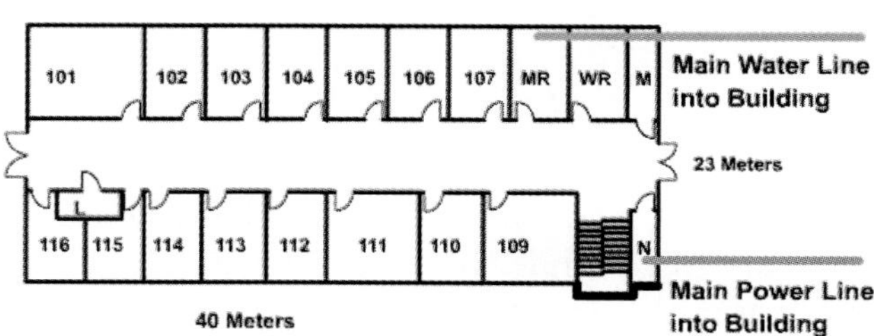

FIGURE 8-31
First floor of the east building.

1. Location L is near the front entry of the east building. The room uses incandescent lighting. The door opens out of the room and can be secured with a lock. The light switch is to the left of the door. There is no dropped ceiling in the room. The walls are of cinder block construction and are covered with a fire-retardant paint. There are three electrical outlets in the room.

2. Location M is where the main water line enters the east building. The room uses fluorescent lighting. The door opens out of the room and cannot be locked. The light switch for this room is outside the room to the left of the door. There is no dropped ceiling in the room. The walls are of cinder block construction and are covered with a fire-retardant paint. There are two electrical outlets in the room.

3. Location N is where the main power line enters the east building. The room uses incandescent lighting. The door opens out of the room and can be secured with a lock. The light switch is to the right of the door. There is no dropped ceiling in the room. The walls are of cinder block construction and are covered with a fire-retardant paint. There are four electrical outlets in the room.

East Building: Second Floor

During the preliminary survey, three potential wiring closet locations were identified for the second floor. Shown in Figure 8-32, they are marked on the floor plan as O, P, and Q.

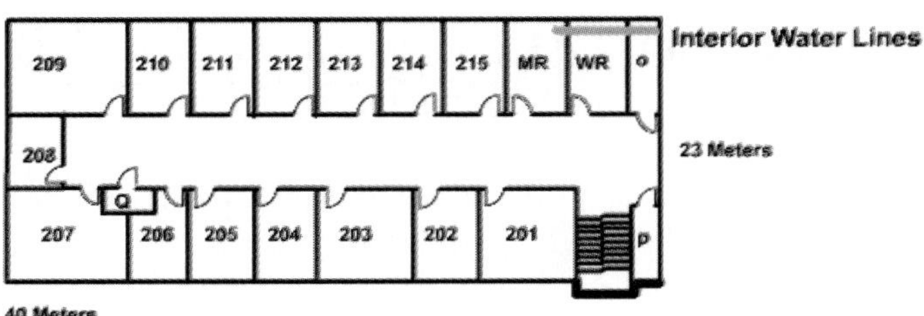

FIGURE 8-32
Second floor of the east building.

1. Interior water lines pass through the dropped ceiling space in Location O. The room uses incandescent lighting. The door opens out of the room and can be secured with a lock. The light switch is to the left of the door. The walls are of cinder block construction and are covered with a fire-retardant paint. There are four electrical outlets in the room.

2. Location P uses fluorescent lighting. The door opens out of the room and can be secured with a lock. The light switch is to the left of the door. The walls are of cinder block construction and are covered with a fire-retardant paint. There are four electrical outlets in the room.

3. Location Q is near the front of the building. The room uses incandescent lighting. The door opens out of the room and can be secured with a lock. The light switch is to the left of the door. The room does not have a dropped ceiling. The walls are of cinder block construction and are covered with a fire-retardant paint. There are four electrical outlets in the room.

West Building: First Floor

The west building is located approximately 17 m from the main building. A preliminary survey of the building has identified three potential locations for wiring closets on the first floor. As shown in Figure 8-33, they are marked on the floor plan as R, S, and T.

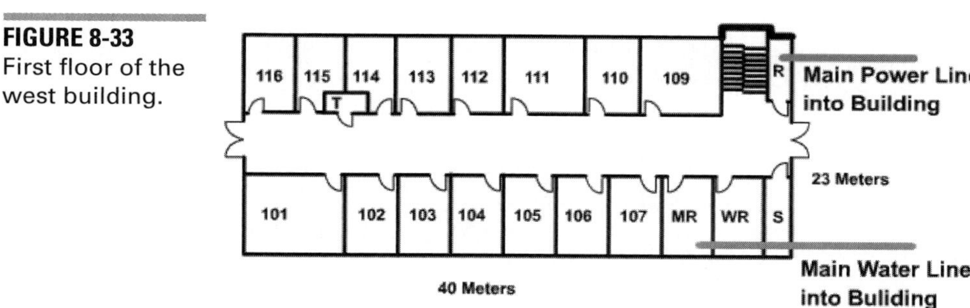

FIGURE 8-33 First floor of the west building.

1. Location R is where the main power line enters the building. The room uses incandescent lighting. The door opens out of the room and can be secured with a lock. The light switch is to the left of the door. The room does not have a dropped ceiling. The walls are of cinder block construction and are covered with a fire-retardant paint. There are four electrical outlets in the room.

2. Location S is where the main water line enters the building. Water lines pass through the dropped ceiling space and lead to adjacent men's and women's restrooms. Like Location R, this room uses incandescent lighting. The door opens out of the room and can be secured with a lock. The light switch for the room is just outside the door and to the right. The walls are of cinder block construction and are covered with a fire-retardant paint. There are three electrical outlets in the room.

3. Location T is near the front of the building. The room uses incandescent lighting. The door opens out of the room and can be secured with a lock. The light switch is to the left of the door upon entering the room. The room does not have a dropped ceiling. The walls are of cinder block construction and are covered with a fire-retardant paint. There are four electrical outlets in the room.

West Building: Second Floor

During the preliminary survey, three potential locations for wiring closets were identified for the second floor of the west building. As shown in Figure 8-33, they are identified on the floor plan as U, V, and W.

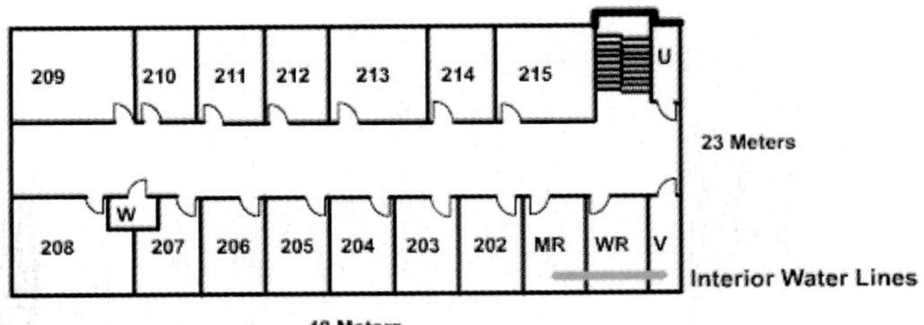

FIGURE 8-34 Second floor of the west building.

1. Location U uses fluorescent lighting. The door opens out of the room and can be secured with a lock. The light switch is to the left of the door. The room has a dropped ceiling. Walls are covered with an asbestos material. There are four electrical outlets in the room.
2. Location V has interior water lines that pass through its dropped ceiling space and lead into adjacent men's and women's restrooms. The room uses incandescent lighting. The door opens out of the room and can be secured with a lock. The light switch is to the right of the door. The walls are covered with an asbestos material. There are four electrical outlets in the room.
3. Location W is near the front of the building. The room uses incandescent lighting. The door opens out of the room and can be secured with a lock. The light switch is to the right of the door. The walls are covered in a fire-retardant paint. There are two electrical outlets in the room.

Preparing a Wiring Plan

Assume that you are asked to prepare a wiring plan for a 20-story building. Three companies occupy the building:

- Company A occupies the first 15 floors.
- Company B occupies the 16th, 17th, and 18th floors.
- Company C occupies the 19th and 10th floors.

The description of the building is as follows:

- The building has three separate supplies of power.
- Each company has its own earth ground (see Figure 8-35).
- None of the earth grounds is identical.
- The height of each story is 4.9 m.
- Only one wiring closet is needed on each floor to supply horizontal cabling runs to the work areas located there.
- The POP is located on the first floor.

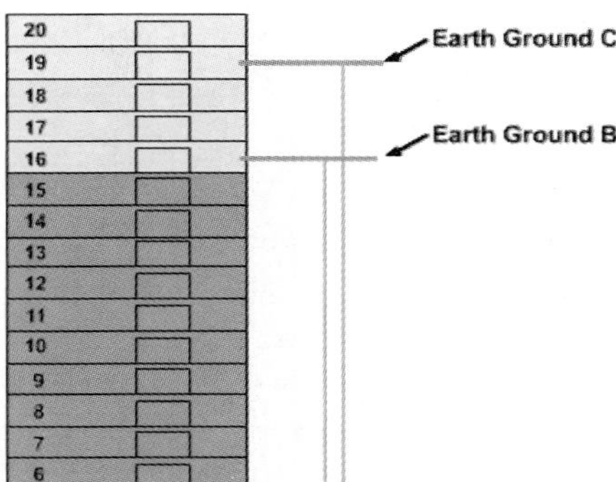

FIGURE 8-35
Location of earth grounds.

Company A: MDF Location

You have been directed to develop a wiring plan for Company A. A study has been conducted and all work areas have been mapped on a plan for each floor. The plans include the selections for the wiring closet on each floor. These are shown in the building profile in Figure 8-36.

In multistory buildings, the MDF is usually located on one of the middle floors of the building because it is the center of an Ethernet star topology. A middle floor is the best location even though the POP might be located on the first floor. On which floor would you locate the MDF? (See Figure 8-37).

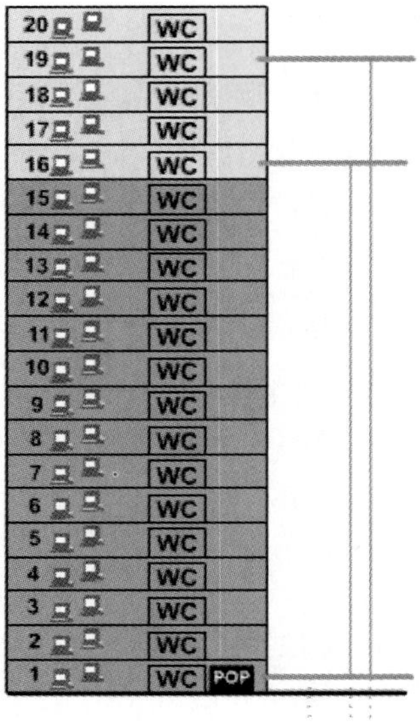

FIGURE 8-36
Wiring closet locations.

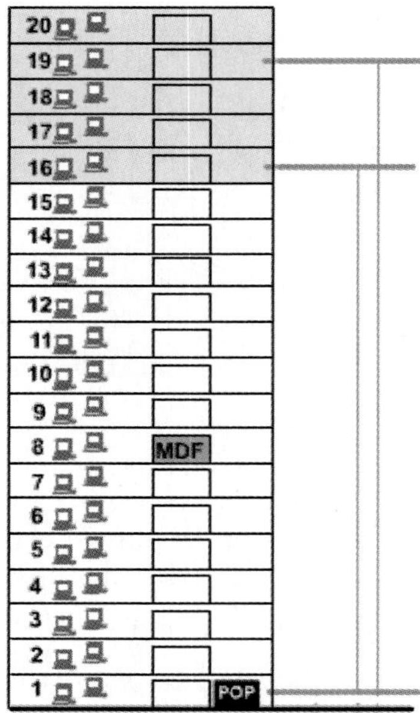

FIGURE 8-37
MDF Location for Company A.

Company A: Backbone Media

This will be a new installation; therefore, the networking media for the horizontal cabling will be Cat 5 UTP. Now you must determine which types of networking media you should use for the backbone cabling. After a preliminary study, you have narrowed the choices to two types: Cat 5 UTP and 62.6/125-µ fiber-optic cable. Because of the high cost of installation, you would like to avoid using fiber-optic cable unless absolutely necessary. Based on your preliminary study and projections, you have determined that it might not be necessary to use fiber-optic cable because UTP could sufficiently carry all anticipated network data for the next 10 years. However, two more factors could influence your decision: safety and distance. In light of this, you must consider the following points:

1. The building has three different earth grounds. Could this present any safety problems for Company A's network?
2. The maximum distance specified by TIA/EIA-568-A for Cat 5 cable is 100 m. Because the height of each floor is 4.9 m, you will need to exceed this distance if you use UTP for the backbone cabling. Can you think of a way to solve the problem of distance between the POP and the MDF?
3. Can you think of a way to solve the problem of distance between the MDF and the IDFs?

Exercises

Company A: IDFs and ICCs

To determine which IDFs will be ICCs, multiply each floor number by its height as you move away from the MDF. Assuming that the backbone cabling runs will all be vertical, from the MDF to the IDF on the ninth floor, the distance would be 4.9 m. The distance from the MDF to the 10th floor would be 9.8 m (see Figure 8-37). Then answer the following questions:

1. What would be the distance to the 11th-floor IDF from the MDF?
2. What would be the distance to the 12th-floor IDF from the MDF?
3. What would be the distance to the 13th-floor IDF from the MDF?
4. What would be the distance to the 14th-floor IDF from the MDF?

continues

5. What would be the distance to the 15th-floor IDF from the MDF? (*Note:* Backbone cabling must also run from the MDF to each of the floors below it.)

Company A: Determining HCC Locations

IDFs that are connected to the work areas by horizontal cabling runs are called horizontal cross-connects (HCCs). Can you determine where the HCCs for Company A's network will be located?

Company A: Drawing Horizontal Cabling Runs

Use blue ink or a blue pencil to draw the horizontal cabling runs on each floor. Use red ink or a red pencil to draw the backbone cabling for Company A's Ethernet star topology LAN.

Company B: MDF Location

You were directed to develop a wiring plan for Company B, which occupies the 16th, 17th, and 18th floors of the same building as Company A. A study has been conducted and all work areas have been mapped on a plan of each floor. The plans include the selections for the wiring closet on each floor. These are shown in the building profile in Figure 8-38.

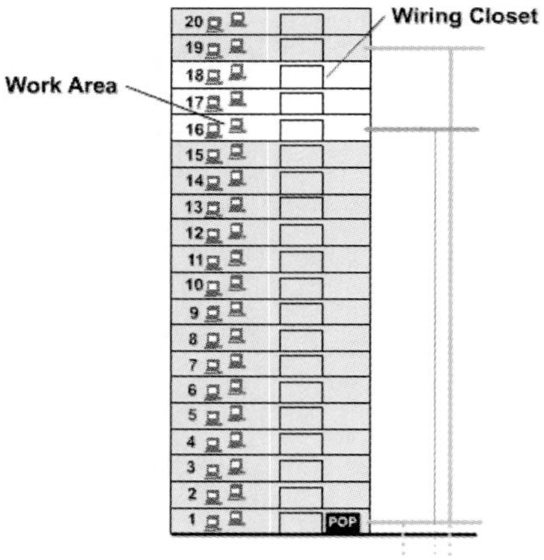

FIGURE 8-38
MDF location for Company B.

Because Company B occupies only three floors of the building, and because it is so far from the POP, you have made the decision to locate the MDF on the 16th floor. The remaining wiring closets, located on the 17th and 18th floors, will be IDFs.

Company B: Backbone Media

This will be a new installation; therefore, the networking media for the horizontal cabling will be Cat 5 UTP. Now you must determine which types of networking media you should use for the backbone cabling. After a preliminary study, you have narrowed the choices to two types: Cat 5 UTP and 62.5/125-µm fiber-optic cable. However, another factor could influence your decision: safety. In light of this, you must consider the following point:

> The building has three different earth grounds. Could this present any safety problems for Company B's network? (See Figure 8-39.)

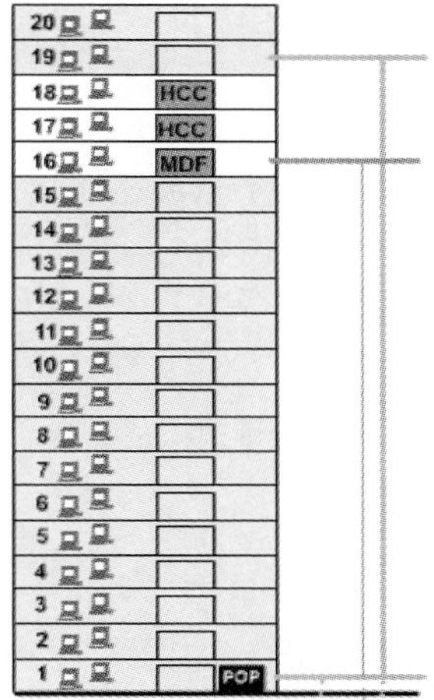

FIGURE 8-39
Network media for backbone cabling.

> **Exercise**
>
> **Company B: Drawing Horizontal Cabling Runs**
>
> Use blue ink or a blue pencil to draw the horizontal cabling runs on each floor. Use red ink or a red pencil to draw the backbone cabling for Company B's Ethernet star topology LAN.

Network Power Supply Issues: Power Line Problems

A power cable contains three wires, and problems that occur in the cable are labeled according to the particular wire(s) that are involved. If a problem exists between the hot and neutral wire, this is referred to as a normal-mode problem. If a situation involves either the hot or neutral wire and the safety ground wire, it is referred to as a common-mode problem.

Normal-mode problems do not ordinarily pose a hazard to you or to your computer. This is because they are usually intercepted by a computer's power supply, an uninterruptible power supply, or an AC power line filter. Common-mode problems, on the other hand, can go directly to a computer's chassis without an intervening filter. Therefore, they can do more damage to data signals than normal-mode problems. In addition, they are harder to detect.

Typical Power Line Problems

Unwanted voltage that is sent to electrical equipment is called a power disturbance. Typical power disturbances include voltage surges, sags, spikes, and oscillations. Total power loss is the extreme example of a power disturbance.

Surge

A *surge* is a voltage increase above 110 percent of the normal voltage carried by a power line. Typically, such incidents last only a few seconds; however, this type of power disruption is responsible for nearly all hardware damage that computer users experience. This is because most computer power supplies that run at 120 V are not built to handle more than 132 V for any length of time. Hubs are particularly vulnerable to electrical surges because of their sensitive low-voltage data lines.

Sag/Brownout

A *sag* is a brownout that lasts less than a second. These incidents occur when voltage on the power line falls below 80 percent of the normal voltage. Sometimes they are caused by overloaded circuits. Brownouts can also be caused intentionally by utility companies seeking to reduce the power drawn by users during peak demand periods. Like surges, sags and brownouts account for a large proportion of the power problems that affect networks and the computing devices that are attached to them.

Spike

A *spike* is an impulse that produces a voltage overload on the power line. Generally speaking, spikes last between .5 and 100 microseconds. In simple terms, when a spike occurs, it means that your power line has momentarily been struck with a powerful hit of at least 240 V on a power supply rated for 120 V (100 percent increase).

Oscillations and Noise

Oscillations are also sometimes referred to as harmonics, or noise. A common cause of oscillation is an excessively long electrical wiring run, which acts like an antenna.

Sources of Surges and Spikes

Numerous sources of electrical surges and spikes exist. Probably the most common one is a nearby lightning strike. Through induction, a nearby lightning strike can affect data lines. Utility switching operations performed by the local power company can also trigger electrical surges and spikes. Other sources of surges and spikes can be located inside your school, office, or building. For example, when equipment such as elevators, photocopiers, and air conditioners cycle on and off, they create momentary dips and surges in power.

Surge and Spike Damage

A spike or a surge can cause havoc on any type of sensitive electronic equipment, including networking devices. Consequences of electrical surges and spikes can be severe.

Possibilities include the following:

- Lockups
- Loss of memory
- Problems in retrieving data
- Altered data
- Garbling

Protection products can save your data equipment from damage caused by direct contact with lightning, power lines, or electrostatic discharge. Primary protection devices are designed to protect people and buildings, and are usually installed on the regulated side of a network by the local exchange carrier. Primary protection activates when lightning strikes, when power lines cross, or when other situations that create high voltage occur, triggering the device to divert the surge energy to ground. However, primary protection devices do not respond fast enough, and their clamping levels are not exact enough to protect today's sensitive electronic equipment. Secondary protection installed behind primary protection will stop any damaging surges or currents that get past your primary protection.

1. To protect the system equipment from surges introduced between the building entrance and the system equipment, install the inline surge protector between these two points and as close as possible to the equipment being protected.

2. To protect the system equipment from surges introduced between the system equipment and the work area, install the inline surge protector between these two points and as close as possible to the equipment being protected.

3. To protect the work area equipment that is connected to the local exchange carrier (LEC), campus backbone cabling, or system equipment. Install the inline surge protector as close as possible to the equipment being protected.

Surge and Spike Solutions

A common solution to the problem of surges and spikes is the use of surge suppressors. Theoretically, when surges or spikes come in, surge suppressors divert them to ground. In actual practice, however, it has been found that spot placement of surge suppressors can increase the incidence of electrical problems. For example, if equipment is not properly grounded when a surge suppressor channels a surge to ground, it actually elevates the ground potential. The resulting differences in ground voltages can create electrical current that flows in the ground circuit. Current flowing in a ground loop can damage unprotected devices; therefore, in any LAN installation, a good rule of thumb to follow is to protect all networking devices with surge suppressors.

If your network is attached to a telephone line for modem or fax use, it is important that the telephone line be surge-protected as well. This is because lighting strikes to telephone lines are not uncommon. Even lightning spikes across the telephone lines to unplugged networking devices have been known to destroy components. As a general rule, therefore, consider the telephone line to be part of the network. If you protect one networking device with a surge suppressor, then you should protect all devices, including the telephone line, in the same way.

Sag and Brownout Solutions

Although surge suppressors can help resolve problems presented by surges and spikes, they cannot prevent the occurrence of sags and brownouts. A drop in AC power might cause only the faintest flicker of your electric lights; however, the same drop in power can be devastating to your data. This is especially true if you happen to be updating a file directory when a power failure occurs. Such a brownout could cause the directory, all subdirectories, and files within its path to be lost.

The loss caused by power outages can be minimized by keeping current backups of all data, but this measure will not prevent the loss of working files that are open on network computers. Every network should have some type of uninterruptible power supply (UPS). An example is shown in Figure 8-40.

are open on network computers. Every network should have some type of uninterruptible power supply (UPS). An example is shown in Figure 8-40.

FIGURE 8-40
An example of a UPS.

Oscillation Solution

The best way to address the problem of oscillation is to rewire. Although this might seem to be an extreme and expensive solution, it is probably the only reliable way that you can ensure completely clean, direct power and reliable ground connections.

Network Power Supply Issues: Surge Suppressors and Uninterruptible Power Supply Functions

Surge suppressors are usually mounted on a wall power socket to which a networking device is connected (see Figure 8-41). These surge suppressors have circuitry that is designed to prevent surges and spikes from damaging the networking devices. A device called a metal oxide varistor (MOV) is most often used within this type of surge suppressor. An MOV protects the networking devices by redirecting excess voltages that occur during spikes and surges to a ground. Simply put, a varistor is a device that is capable of absorbing very large currents without damage. An MOV can hold voltage surges on a 120-V circuit to a level of approximately 330 V.

Unfortunately, an MOV might not be an effective means of protecting the networking device that is attached to it. This is because the ground also serves as the common reference point for data signals going into and out of the computer. Dumping excess voltages into the power line near the computer can create problems. Although this type of voltage diversion can avoid damage to the power supply, it can still result in garbled data.

FIGURE 8-41
An example of a surge suppressor.

When surge suppressors that are located close to networking devices divert large voltages onto the common ground, this can create a large voltage differential between network devices. As a result, these devices can experience loss of data or, in some instances, damaged circuits. You should also be aware that this type of surge suppressor has a limited lifetime, partly dependent on heat and usage. For all these reasons, this type of surge suppressor would not be the best choice for your network.

To avoid problems associated with surges, instead of installing individual surge suppressors at each work station, you could use a commercial-quality surge suppressor. This should be located at each power distribution panel rather than close to the networking devices. By placing a commercial-grade surge suppressor near the power panel, you can reduce the impact on the network of voltage surges and spikes diverted to ground.

UPS: For Certain LAN Devices

The problem of sags and brownouts can best be addressed with the use of uninterruptible power supplies (UPS). The extent to which UPS must be provided for a LAN depends on factors such as the budget, the types of services the LAN provides, the frequency of regional power outages, and the typical length and duration of power outages when they do occur. At a minimum, every network file server should have a source of backup power. If powered hubs or switches are required, they must also be supported with backup power. Finally, in extended star topology networks, where internetworking devices such as bridges and routers are used, power backup must be provided to them as well to avoid failures in the system. Where possible, power backup should also be provided for all work areas. As every network administrator knows, it does little good to have an operational server and cable plant if they cannot ensure that end-user computers will not go down before users can save their spreadsheets and word processing files.

UPS: For Certain Electrical Problems

Sags and brownouts are usually power reductions lasting for a short period of time, and are caused by something such as a lightning strike This creates a power overload and trips a circuit breaker. Because circuit breakers are designed to automatically reset, they can work from the surrounding power grid to where the source of a short is located to reestablish power. This usually occurs within seconds or minutes.

Longer power outages can occur, however, when an event such as a severe storm or flood causes physical disruption of the power transmission system. Unlike shorter power outages, this type of disruption in service usually depends on service crews for repair. An uninterruptible power source is designed to handle only short-duration power outages. If a LAN requires uninterrupted power during power outages that last several hours, a generator would be needed to supplement the backup provided by a UPS. Can you think of situations in which LANs might need the added backup of a generator?

UPS: Components

A UPS consists of batteries, a battery charger, and a power inverter, as shown in Figure 8-42.

FIGURE 8-42
Components of a UPS.

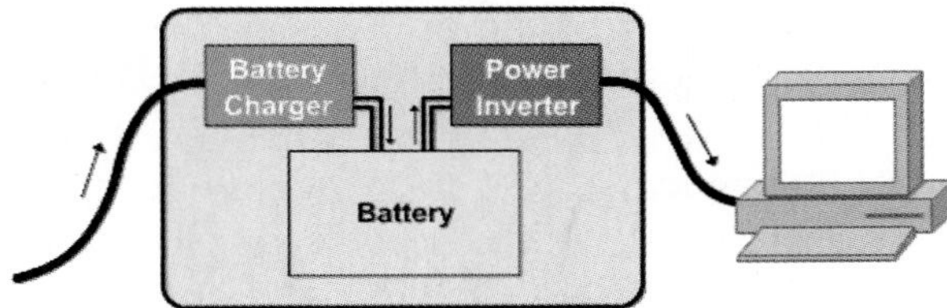

The functions of each are as follows:

- **Power inverter**—The inverter converts low-level direct current voltage of the batteries into AC voltage, normally supplied by the power line, to networking devices

- **Battery charger**—This component is designed to keep the batteries in peak condition during periods when the power line system is functioning normally
- **Batteries**—Generally, the bigger the batteries in a UPS, the longer the period of time it will be capable of supporting networking devices during power outages.

UPS: Differences in UPS Features

A number of vendors have developed UPS systems. You will find that they differ in the following ways: the power storage capacity of the batteries, the power delivery capability of the inverter, and the operational scheme (whether they operate continuously or only when the input voltage reaches a specific level). Also, the more features a UPS has, the more it costs.

Two UPS types exist, as shown in Figure 8-43—they are called *continuous* and *switched*.

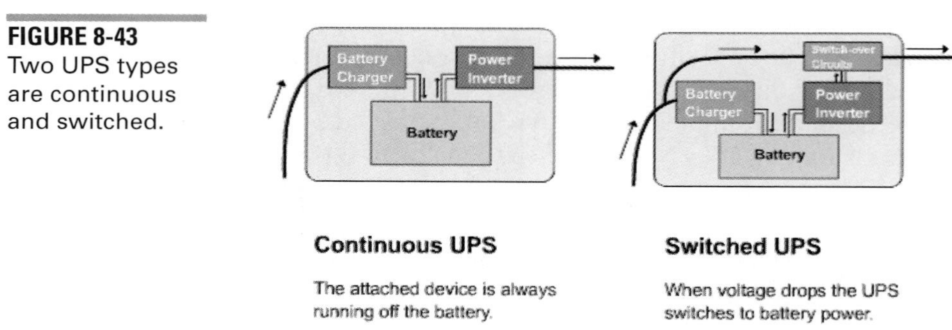

FIGURE 8-43
Two UPS types are continuous and switched.

UPS: Description and Operation

As a rule, UPS devices that offer fewer features and that cost less are used as standby power systems only. This means that they monitor power lines; if and when a problem occurs, the UPS switches over to the inverter, which is powered by its batteries. The time needed for this switch to occur is called the *transfer time*. Usually, the transfer time lasts for only a short time. This does not usually present a problem for most modern computers, which are designed to coast on their own power supplies for at least a hundred milliseconds.

UPS devices that offer more features and that cost more typically operate *online*. This means that they constantly supply power from inverters, which are powered by their batteries. While they do this, their batteries continue charging from the power line. Because their inverters supply freshly generated AC, such UPS devices have the added benefit of ensuring that no spikes from the power line reach the networking devices that they serve. If and when the AC power line goes down, however, the UPS batteries switch smoothly from recharging to providing power to the inverter. Consequently, this type of UPS effectively reduces the transfer time to zero.

Other UPS products fall into a hybrid category. Although they appear to be online systems, they do not run their inverters all the time. Because of these differences, be sure to investigate the features of any UPS you plan to incorporate as part of a LAN installation.

In any event, a good UPS should be designed to communicate with the file server. This is important so that the file server can be warned to shut down files when the UPS battery power nears its end. Additionally, a good UPS reports instances when the server starts to run on battery power and supplies this information to any work stations running on the network after the power outage has occurred.

Summary

The focus of this chapter was network design and documentation. You learned that

- Layer 1 components include plugs, cables, jacks, and patch panels.
- To finish Layer 1 design, both a logical and a physical topology must be generated.
- Layer 2 devices such as switches reduce congestion and collision domain size.
- Layer 3 devices such as routers are used to build scalable internetworks (larger LANs, WANs, networks of networks) or to impose a logical structure on the network.
- Databases and other shared resources, as well as LANs, link to WANs and to the Internet.
- Whenever you install cable, it is important to document what you have done.
- A wiring closet is a specially designed room used for wiring a data or voice network.
- Backbone cabling consists of the backbone cabling runs, intermediate and main cross-connects, mechanical terminations, and patch cords used for backbone-to-backbone cross-connections.

- Surge suppressors are an effective means of addressing the problems of surges and spikes.

Now that you have worked through this chapter, you are ready to begin the structured cabling project covered in the next chapter.

Check Your Understanding

1. Name some documentation that should be created when designing a network.
   - **A.** Engineering journal
   - **B.** Problem-solving matrices
   - **C.** Cut sheets
   - **D.** All of the above
2. MDF stands for what?
   - **A.** Main distribution facility
   - **B.** Metropolitan distribution facility
   - **C.** Metropolitan design facility
   - **D.** None of the above
3. EIA/TIA-569 specifies what?
   - **A.** Each floor must have a minimum of one wiring closet.
   - **B.** In an Ethernet LAN, the horizontal cabling runs must be attached to a central point in a star topology.
   - **C.** The wiring closet must be large enough to accommodate all of the equipment and wiring that will be placed in it.
   - **D.** None of the above.
4. Any room or closet chosen to serve as a wiring closet should adhere to guidelines governing the following items, except what?
   - **A.** Materials for walls, floors, and ceilings
   - **B.** Power outlets
   - **C.** Solar exposure
   - **D.** All of the above
5. EIA/TIA-568 specifies what?
   - **A.** Each floor must have a minimum of one wiring closet.
   - **B.** In an Ethernet LAN, the horizontal cabling runs must be attached to a central point in a star topology.

C. When using an Ethernet star topology, every device that is part of the network must be connected to the hub.

D. None of the above.

6. IDF stands for what?

A. Internal distribution facility

B. Intermediate distribution facility

C. Interim distribution facility

D. None of the above

7. What is the difference between an MDF and an IDF?

A. The MDF contains the primary network server and the major networking devices, and the IDF contains only the necessary additional routers and repeaters.

B. The MDF is on the lowest floor in a multifloor network, and the IDF is on upper floors.

C. The MDF has all the bridges, hubs, routers, and ports needed for the network, and the IDF holds any needed repeaters.

D. The MDF is the primary communications room and the central point in the network, and the IDF is the secondary communications room dependent on the MDF.

8. The type of cabling that EIA/TIA-568 specifies for connecting wiring closets to each other in an Ethernet LAN extended star topology is called what?

A. Pipeline

B. Cross-connection

C. Backbone

D. Horizontal

9. What is the primary purpose of grounding computing equipment?

A. To prevent metal parts from becoming energized with a hazardous voltage resulting from a wiring fault inside the device

B. To connect the safety ground to exposed metal parts of the computing equipment so that minor surges in power can be diverted

C. To forestall the possibility that a power surge may corrupt the motherboard or the RAM

D. To prevent any power surge from traveling through the computer that might harm the end user

10. In an extended star topology, a horizontal cross-connect is what?

A. Backbone cabling

B. MDF

C. IDF

D. Horizontal cabling

11. ESD stands for what?

A. Electromagnetic static disruption

B. Electrostatic disruption

C. Electrostatic discharge

D. Electromagnetic static discharge

12. EIA-TIA-568 specifications for backbone cabling permits ______ cable, which acts as an insulator between facilities.

A. Cat 5

B. Coaxial

C. Fiber optic

D. STP

13. What is another reason for using fiber-optic cable for the backbone?

A. Brownouts

B. Surges

C. Lightning

D. Sags

14. If a situation exists between the hot and neutral wire, this is referred to as what?

A. Common mode problem

B. Normal mode problem

C. Standard mode problem

D. Neutral mode problem

15. ______________ problems do not ordinarily pose a hazard to you or to your computer.

A. Normal mode

B. Common mode

C. Standard mode

D. Neutral mode

16. _________ is also sometimes referred to as harmonics, or noise.

A. Surge

B. Sag

C. Spike

D. Oscillation

17. Which problem cannot be helped by a surge suppressor?

A. Surge

B. Spike

C. Sag

D. Oscillation

18. A MOV in a surge suppressor stands for what?

A. Magnesium oxide varistor

B. Magnesium oxygen varistor

C. Metal oxide varistor

D. Metal oxygen varistor

19. UPS stands for what?

A. Uninterruptible power source

B. Uninterruptible power supply

C. Uninterruptible protection source

D. Uninterruptible protection supply

20. Which best describes a UPS?

A. It is a device that absorbs excess line voltage caused by lightning strikes.

B. It is a backup device that provides power during a power failure.

C. It is a device that enables you to avoid rewiring the network when power fluctuations are continual.

D. It is a device that powers the multipath connection between computers.

Objectives

After reading this chapter, you will be able to

- Understand project planning
- Describe RJ-45 jack and outlet installation
- Understand the basics of cable installation
- Describe structured cable run installation
- Describe how to string, run, and mount cable
- Understand the basics of wiring closets and patch panels
- Describe the range of equipment for testing structured cabling projects

Structured Cabling Project

Introduction

A network's performance is closely related to good connections. Therefore, the focus of this chapter is standards for networking media. These standards are developed and issued by the Institute of Electrical and Electronic Engineers (IEEE), the Underwriters Laboratories (UL), the Telecommunications Industry Association (TIA), and the Electrical Industries Association (EIA). The latter two organizations jointly issue a list of standards—frequently, you see them listed as the TIA/EIA standards. In addition to these groups and organizations, local, state, county, and national government agencies issue specifications and requirements that can affect the type of cable used in a LAN.

In this chapter, you learn how to use appropriate and recommended techniques for dressing and securing the cable. Included in this is the use of cable ties, cable support bars, wire-management panels, and releasable velcro straps. You learn that when RJ-45 jacks are used at the telecommunications outlet in a horizontal cabling scheme, the wiring sequence is critical for optimal network performance. A wiring closet serves as the center point of a star topology for the wiring and wiring equipment used for connecting devices in a network. With this in mind, you learn how a wiring closet should be designed for wiring a data or voice network. Lastly, you learn about the equipment found in a wiring closet, which can include patch panels, wiring hubs, bridges, switches, and routers.

Project Planning

This section discusses the following topics related to project planning:

- Network installation safety procedures
- Network documentation
- Network installation teams
- Work flow
- Scheduling of materials flow

Network Installation Safety Procedures

The process of installing a network requires constant awareness of safety procedures. You might think of building a network as the combination of activities performed by an electrician and a construction worker. In both cases, safety is the primary concern. The following lists contain safety procedures and general safety precautions that you must take while working with network building materials, both electrical and construction.

Electrical

The following list describes some of the precautions you should take when working with electrical materials:

- Never work on a device (hub, switch, router, or PC) with the case open and the line voltage (power cord) plugged in.
- Test electrical sockets with an appropriate voltage tester or multimeter.
- Locate all electrical conduits and power wires before trying to install any networking cable.
- Properly ground all networking equipment.
- Never cut or nick a live 120-V AC line.

Construction

The following list describes some of the precautions you should take when working with electrical materials:

- Wear safety glasses whenever you are drilling or cutting, and use care when handling bits and blades.
- Measure carefully before you cut, drill into, or permanently alter construction materials. "Measure twice; cut once."
- Investigate what you will drill or cut into before you begin. You do not want your power tools to come in contact with electrical wiring or other utilities in the wall.
- Follow practices of general cleanliness (for example, minimize dust that can affect sensitive networking devices).
- Follow proper ladder placement and safety procedures whenever you must use a ladder.

These are just some of the safety precautions that you must take when working with network building materials.

Network Documentation

Your structured cabling project will be done at the request of a client who wants you to wire a room (or a school). Your responsibility as the designer will include written documentation, including fact-finding assessments, work-in-progress reports, and final reports and test results. Your first task as the network designer will be to have your client specify, in writing, the desired outcome of the project.

The following list includes some of the documentation that you should create while you are in the process of planning/designing your network:

- Engineering journal
- Logical topology
- Physical topology
- Cut sheets
- Problem-solving matrices
- Labeled outlets
- Labeled cable runs
- Summary of outlets and cable runs
- Summary of devices, MAC addresses, and IP addresses

Perhaps the most important part of the network design process is designing according to the ANSI/TIA/EIA and ISO/IEC industry standards.

Network Installation Teams

One of the most efficient methods for working with a network installation team is to break the team into smaller groups consisting of one or more people. As a student, you might occasionally alternate or switch jobs with the other members of your installation team so that everyone in your team has the opportunity to perform a variety of tasks. This is one way that you can develop the required networking installation skills and at the same time learn how to work with others as a team member.

The following list describes some of the tasks that might be assigned to the small teams:

- **Project manager**—Responsible for the following:
  - Implementing safety procedures
  - Ensuring the documentation of materials and activities
  - Keeping other team members focused on their tasks
- **Materials and tools manager**—Responsible for tool kits, cable, connectors, and testers
- **Cable runner**—Responsible for planning and running cable safely and according to specifications, as well as for testing the cable run
- **Jack and patch panel terminator**—Responsible for performing quality punchdowns and for installing and testing jack installations

Work Flow

To ensure that your project is done thoroughly, accurately, and on time, you should create a flowchart. Your flowchart should include each of the tasks that must be completed and the order in which they should be tackled. Also included in this flowchart should be a timeline for each of these tasks.

The flowchart should include the following tasks:

1. Installing outlets
2. Installing jacks
3. Running cables
4. Punching cables into patch panels
5. Testing cables
6. Documenting cables
7. Installing NICs
8. Installing hubs, switches, bridges, and routers
9. Configuring routers
10. Installing and configuring PCs

You might not perform all these tasks as part of your structured cabling project, but likely someone (the local network administrator) will have to complete the list.

Scheduling Materials Flow

To build a network, you need to use a variety of materials. This includes such things as tools and the actual construction materials. You need some of these materials at the beginning of the project and some while the work is in progress. You should plan and then gather all the materials that you need well ahead of the projected start date.

Your plan should include the following:

1. Building and networking materials
2. Suppliers
3. Tools
4. Date and length of time tools required

RJ-45 Jack and Outlet Installation

You have learned which horizontal cabling, as defined by TIA/EIA-568-A, is the networking media that connects the telecommunications outlet to the horizontal cross-connect. In the following section, you learn how to install telecommunications outlets (wall jacks) and connect the networking medium (Category 5 UTP cable) to the wall jacks.

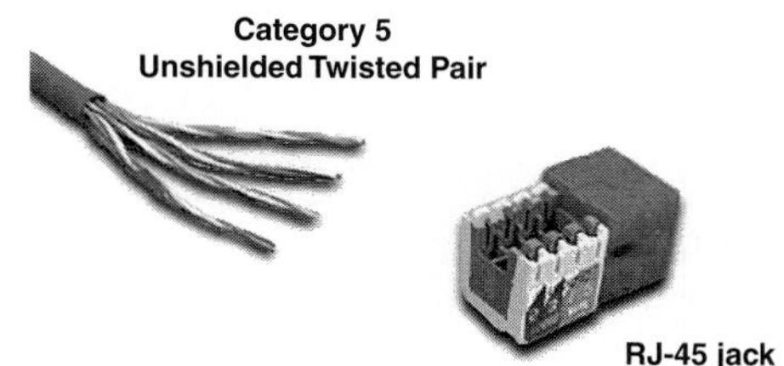

FIGURE 9-1
Category 5 UTP and an RJ-45 jack.

RJ-45 Jack

TIA/EIA-568-A specifies that, in a horizontal cabling scheme, you must use an RJ-45 jack for making the connection to a Cat 5 UTP cable, at the telecommunications outlet. One side of the RJ-45 jack contains eight color-coded slots. The individual Cat 5 wires are punched down into the slots according to color. A firm punchdown is required to make a good electrical connection. The other side of the jack is a female plug, which looks like a standard phone jack, except that the RJ-45 jack is larger and has eight pins.

The telecommunications outlet in a horizontal cabling scheme is usually mounted on a wall. TIA/EIA-568-A specifies two types of wall mounts that you can use to position an RJ-45 jack onto a wall: the surface mount and the flush mount.

Surface-Mounting an RJ-45 Jack

You can use two types of boxes to surface-mount RJ-45 jacks to a wall. The first is a screw-mounted box. The second is an adhesive-backed box. If you choose to use this method, be aware that after you have installed the box, it cannot be moved without patching the wall behind the box. This can be an important factor if you anticipate changes in the room's use or configuration.

To surface-mount an RJ-45 jack on a wall, you must follow these steps:

Step 1 Select the RJ-45 jack location.

Step 2 Run the wire to the location, either inside the wall or inside the surface-mounted raceway.

Step 3 Mount the box either with adhesive or screws at the desired location.

Step 4 Feed the wire into the box (from the top or the rear).

Step 5 Punch the wire down onto the RJ-45 jack.

Step 6 Insert the jack into a RJ-45 faceplate.

Step 7 Attach the faceplate to the box.

Many installers prefer to use surface-mounted RJ-45 jacks because they are easier to install. You do not need to cut into the wall; you simply mount the jacks onto the surface of the wall. This means that they are also faster to install. When labor costs are a factor in installing a LAN, this can become an important consideration. Surface-mounted jacks might also be the only choice in some situations.

Factors to Consider Before Flush-Mounting an RJ-45 Jack

You must take several factors into consideration before you decide to flush-mount an RJ-45 jack into a wall. For example, the techniques you use to cut into drywall differ from those that you use to cut into plaster. Therefore, it is important to determine first the type of wall material that you will have to work with.

Plaster can be a difficult material to work with because it crumbles easily. Also, it is not always possible for mounting screws to attach securely into the wood lath that is located behind the plaster wall. If this is a concern, you might want to surface-mount the jack instead.

If there are wide wood baseboards on the wall, you might want to install jacks there because this wood is a more solid material than the wall itself. If you do choose to place the jack on a wood baseboard, avoid cutting the opening into the bottom 5 cm of the baseboard. If you attempt to place the box in that location, the wall's bottom plate will block you from pushing it in. You should also avoid placing a jack anywhere that it might interfere with trim placed around doors or windows. Finally, the last step is to determine whether the jack is to be mounted in a box or whether it's to be mounted in a low-voltage mounting bracket.

Preparing a Drywall Surface for a Flush-Mounted Jack

To mount an RJ-45 jack in drywall, as shown in Figure 9-1, follow these steps:

Step 1 Select a position for the jack that will be 30 to 45 cm above the floor.

Step 2 Drill a small hole in the selected location.

Step 3 Check for any obstructions behind the hole by bending a piece of wire, inserting it into the hole, and rotating it in a circle.

Step 4 If the wire hits something, you know that there is an obstruction, and you must select a new location away from the first hole. Then you must do the last procedure again until you find an unobstructed location.

Step 5 Determine the size of the opening that you need for the box that will hold the jack by tracing an outline of the template that was included with the box or bracket.

Step 6 Before you cut into the wall, use a carpenter's level to make sure that the opening is straight.

Step 7 Use a utility knife to cut the opening. Push the knife through the drywall, inside the template outline, until you have an opening that is large enough to accommodate the blade of either a keyhole saw or a drywall saw.

Step 8 Insert the saw into the hole, and cut along the edge of the penciled outline. Continue cutting carefully along the line until you can pull out the piece of drywall.

Step 9 Make sure that the box or bracket fits the opening.

Step 10 If you're using a box to flush-mount the jack, do not secure the box until after you bring the cable to the opening.

Safety Procedure

Any time you are working in walls, ceilings, or attics, it is extremely important that you remember to turn off the power to all circuits that go to or pass through the work area! If you are not sure whether there are wires that pass through the section of the building in which you will be working, a good rule to follow is to shut off all power.

Preparing a Plaster Surface for a Flush-Mounted Jack

It is more difficult to cut into a plaster wall than it is to cut into drywall. To achieve the best results, follow these steps:

Step 1 Determine the appropriate location for the jack.

Step 2 Use a hammer and chisel to remove the plaster from the wall so that the lath behind the plaster is exposed.

Step 3 Use a utility knife to carefully trim plaster away from the lath.

Step 4 Place the template against the lathwork so that it overlaps three strips of lath equally at the top and bottom of the opening. Trace an outline around the template.

Step 5 Use an electric saw to cut away the full lath strip that is exposed in the center of the opening.

a. Make several small cuts on the full strip, first on one side and then on the other.

b. Proceed making these small cuts until you have completely cut through the center lath.

c. Be careful when you do this step. If you attempt to cut all the way through one side before cutting into the other side, the saw causes the lath to vibrate when you make the second cut. This can cause the plaster around the opening to crack and separate from the lath.

Step 6 Finish preparing the opening by sawing notches in the lath strips at the top and bottom.

Preparing a Wood Surface for a Flush-Mounted Jack

To prepare the wood for flush-mounting a jack, follow these steps:

Step 1 Select the position where you want to place the box. You have already learned that if you choose to place an RJ-45 jack on a wooden baseboard, you should avoid cutting the box opening into the bottom 5 cm of the baseboard.

Step 2 Use the box as a template, and trace around the outside.

Step 3 Drill a starter hole in each corner of the outline.

Step 4 Insert a keyhole saw or jigsaw into one of the holes, and saw along the outline until you reach the next hole. Turn the saw and continue cutting until you can remove the piece of wood.

Flush-Mounting a Jack in a Wall

After you prepare an opening in which to position the jack, you can then place it in the wall. If you are using a box for mounting the jack, hold the cable and feed it through one of the slots into the box; then push the box into the wall opening. Use the screws to secure the box to the wall's surface. As you tighten the screws, the box will be pulled tighter to the wall. If you are mounting the jack in a low-voltage mounting bracket, place the bracket against the wall opening, with the smooth side facing outward. Push the top and bottom flanges toward the back so that the bracket grips the wall. Then push one side up and the other down, to securely mount the bracket.

Procedure for Placing the Copper Wires into a Jack

A LAN's performance is closely linked to the quality of its connections. When you use RJ-45 jacks at the telecommunications outlet in a horizontal cabling scheme, the wiring sequence is critical to ensure the best possible network performance. Sequencing refers to the process of matching the wires of a cable to the proper terminals on the jack. To understand how this works, examine an RJ-45 jack closely. Notice that the jack is color-coded. The colors—blue, green, orange, and brown—correspond to the colors of the wires in each of the twisted pairs of Cat 5 UTP.

Following are the steps you must use to place the cable wires into the jack:

Step 1 Strip the jacket (coating) from the end of the cable that you want to connect to the jack. Try not to strip any more of the cable jacket than is necessary, approximately 2.5 cm. If you strip too much, data throughput will be reduced.

Step 2 Place the wires in the center of the jack, and keep them there while you work. Wires that are skewed can slow the rate of data transmission. Also make sure that you keep the portion of the cable, still covered by the jacket, within 3 mm of the jack.

Step 3 Separate out each pair of twisted wires.

Step 4 The first color that appears on the left side of the jack is blue. Find the pair of wires that contains the blue wire, and untwist them. Lay the blue wire on the slot on the left that is color-coded blue. Lay the second wire of this pair on the slot on the right that is color-coded blue and white.

Step 5 The color used to code the next slot on the right side of the jack is green. Locate the twisted pair that contains the green wire, and untwist them. Lay the green wire on the slot on the right that is color-coded green. Lay the second wire of this pair on the slot on the left that is color-coded green and white.

Step 6 Continue in this fashion until all the wires have been matched to their corresponding color-coded slots in the jack.

Step 7 After you complete these steps, you are ready to punch the wires down into the slots in the jack.

Procedure for Punching Wires Down into a Jack

To punch down the wires into the jack, you need to use a punch tool. A punch tool is a device that uses spring-loaded action to push wires between metal pins, while at the same time skinning the sheath away from the wire. This ensures that the wire makes a good electrical connection with the pins inside the jack. The punch tool also cuts off any extra wire.

When you use the punch tool, you must begin by positioning the blade on the outside of the jack. If you place the blade on the inside of the jack, you will cut the wire short of the connection point. If this happens, no electrical connection can occur. (If you tilt the handle of the punch tool a little to the outside, it will cut better.) If any wire remains attached after you have used the punch tool, simply twist the ends gently to remove them; then place the clips on the jack and tighten them. To snap the jack into its faceplate, push it in from the back side. Make sure that when you do this, the jack is right-side up. Then use the screws to attach the faceplate to either the box or the bracket.

If you have surface-mounted the box, keep in mind that it might hold 30 to 60 cm of excess cable. You need to either slide the cable through its tie-wraps, or pull back the raceway that covers it to push the rest of the excess cable back into the wall. If you have flush-mounted the jack, all you need to do is push the excess cable back into the wall.

SKILL BUILDER

Lab Activity: RJ-45 Jack Install

In this lab, you learn the correct process for terminating a RJ-45 jack as well as the correct procedure for installing the jack in a wall plate.

Basics of Cable Installation

This section covers the following topics:

- Basics of installing UTP cable
- How to document cable runs
- TIA/EIA-606 specifications for labeling cable
- Types of labels

- How to prepare cable for routing and labeling
- How to label cable ends

Basics of Installing UTP Cable

To connect cable to jacks, follow these steps:

Step 1 Strip back only as much of the cable's jacket as is required to terminate the wires. The more wire you expose, the poorer the connection and the greater the signal loss.

Step 2 Make sure that you maintain the twists in each pair of wires as much as possible, to the point of termination. This twisting of the wires produces the cancellation that is needed to prevent radio and electromagnetic interference. For Cat 4 UTP, the maximum amount of untwisted wire that is allowed is 25 mm. For Cat 5 UTP, the maximum amount of untwisted wire that is allowed is 13 mm.

Step 3 If you must bend the cable to route it, be sure to maintain a bend radius that is four times the diameter of the cable. Never bend cable to the extent that it is less than a 90° angle.

Step 4 Avoid stretching cable when you are handling it. If you exceed 11.3 kg of pull, the wires inside the cable can untwist—and, as you have already learned, that can lead to interference and crosstalk.

Step 5 If multiple cables must run over the same path, use cable ties to cinch them together. Position the ties at random intervals, and then tighten them carefully. Never tighten the ties too much because that can damage the cables.

Step 6 Minimize the twisting of the cable jackets. If you twist them too much, the jackets might tear. Never allow cables to be pinched or kinked. If this occurs, data throughput is reduced, and the LAN operates at less than optimal capacity.

Step 7 Never be stingy when determining the amount of cable that you will need for running cable. It is important to leave ample slack. Remember, a few feet of extra cable is a small price to pay to avoid having to redo a cable run because of problems caused by stretched cable. Most cable installers avoid this problem by leaving enough slack for the cable to reach the floor, and then they extend another 60 to 90 cm at both ends. Most installers follow the practice of leaving what is called a service coil, which is simply a couple of extra meters of cable left coiled up inside the ceiling or in another out-of-the-way location.

Step 8 When securing the cable, use appropriate and recommended techniques for using cable ties, cable support bars, wire-management panels, and releasable Velcro straps. Never use a staple gun to position cables. Staples can pierce the jacket, causing loss of connection.

Figure 9-2 shows a good example of well-installed cable.

FIGURE 9-2
You should use cable ties, cable support bars, wire management panels, releasable velcro straps before dressing and securing cable.

Documenting Cable Runs

Whenever you install cable, it is important that you document your actions. You can do this by using a cut sheet as you install the cable. A cut sheet is a rough diagram that shows the locations of the cable runs. It also indicates the numbers of the classrooms, offices, or other rooms to which the cables have been run. Later you can refer to this cut sheet to place corresponding numbers on all telecommunications outlets and at the patch panel in the wiring closet. You can use a page in your journal to document cable runs. By doing so, you will have an additional layer of documentation for any cable installation.

TIA/EIA-606 Specifications for Labeling Cable

TIA/EIA-606 specifies that each hardware termination unit must have some kind of unique identifier. This identifier must be marked on each termination hardware unit or on its label. When identifiers are used at the work area, station terminations must have a label on the faceplate, the housing, or the connector itself. Whether they are adhesive or insertable, all labels must meet legibility, defacement, and adhesion requirements.

Avoid labeling cables, telecommunications outlets, and patch panels with terms such as "Mr. Zimmerman's math class" or "Ms. Tuggle's art class." This can lead to confusion years later if someone who is unfamiliar with these locations needs to perform work involving the networking media that is located there. Instead, use labels that remain understandable to someone who might work on the system many years in the future.

Many network administrators incorporate room numbers in the label information. They assign letters to each cable that leads to a room. Some labeling systems, particularly those in very large networks, also incorporate color-coding. For example, a blue label might identify horizontal cabling at the wiring closet only, while a green label might identify cabling at the work area.

To understand how this works, imagine that four cables have been run to Room 1012. On a cut sheet, these cables would be labeled as 1012A, 1012B, 1012C, and 1012D, as shown in Figure 9-3.

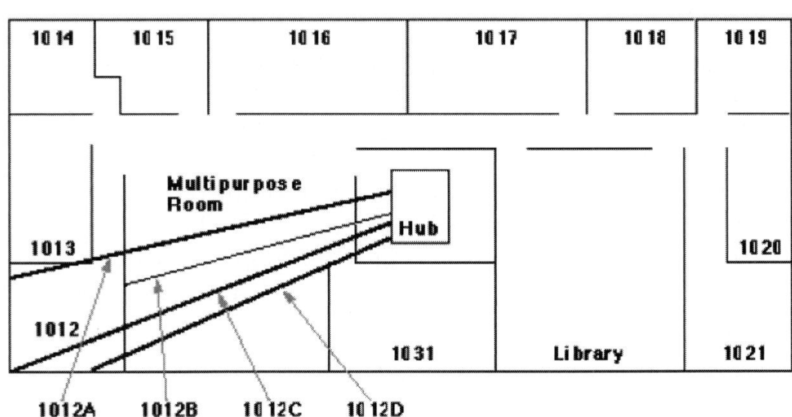

FIGURE 9-3 This cut sheet shows cables as labeled 1012A, 1012B, 1012C, and1012D.

The faceplates, where the cables 1012A, 1012B, 1012C, and 1012D connect to the work station patch cords, would also be labeled to correspond to each cable. You should label each cable connection at the patch panel in the wiring closet as well. Place the connections so that the labels are arranged in ascending order. This allows easy diagnosis and location of problems, if they occur later. Finally, label the cables at each end, as shown in Figure 9-4.

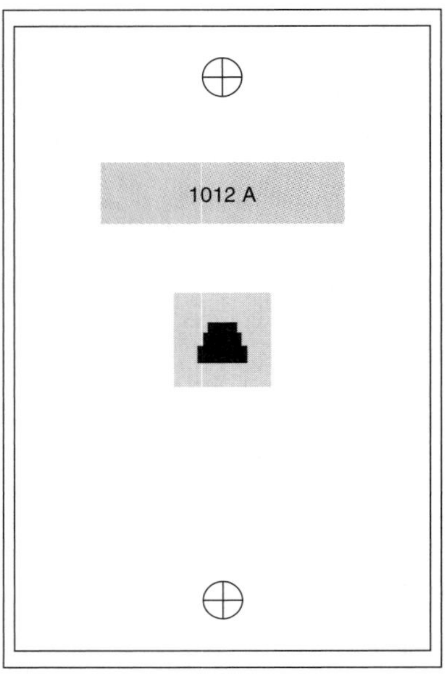

FIGURE 9-4
The properly labeled 1012A faceplate.

Preparing Cable for Routing and Labeling

After study and analysis, a determination has been made to run four cables to each room in your school. You have surveyed the routes that the cable will follow from the wiring closet to the classrooms. Now you are ready to run cable. Rather than run the cable four times over the same route, your work will be easier—and you will save time—if you route all four cables at the same time.

To do this, you need four spools of cable. Each spool holds 304.8 m of cable. For ease of handling and to prevent kinking, spools are usually packaged in boxes. The cable feeds from a hole in the side of the box, while the spool turns inside. If the spool you are working with ever becomes separated from the box in which it was packaged, never uncoil the cable. If you attempt to do so, the cable will twist and kink. Instead, lay the spool on its side and unroll the cable as you need it. This prevents the cable from kinking and becoming tangled.

To help you keep track of each cable as it comes off its spool, assign a letter to each spool. Place the spools at the central point or wiring closet. Unwind a short segment of cable from each spool. Use a permanent waterproof marker to mark the end of each cable so that it corresponds to the letter assigned to its spool. In this case, you know that the cable will run to classroom 1012, so include that number with each letter. When you finish, the four cables should be labeled 1012A, 1012B, 1012C, and 1012D.

To ensure that the labels do not rub off or get cut off (the end) later, mark the cable three times, approximately 60 cm apart. To keep all four cables tied securely together, use electrical tape. Bind the cable ends together along with the end of a pull string. You can ensure that the pull string does not come loose by tying some half-hitch knots around the cables with the pull string, before you tape the ends. Don't skimp on the tape. If the string or cables pull out later, it could cost you time and money.

Labeling Cable Ends

After you pull the cable along the route that you selected earlier, bring it into the classroom. (The following sections go into more detail regarding some of the techniques used to route cable along walls, inside walls, inside attics, and behind drop ceilings.) Allow enough cable for the ends to reach all the way to each jack location, plus enough excess or slack to reach the floor and extend another 60 to 90 cm.

Go back to the spools of cable at the central point or wiring closet. Use the labels on each spool as a reference; mark this end of each cable with the appropriate room number and letter. Do not cut the cables unless they have a label. For best results, cut the cable and the pull string with wire snips. This produces a clean cut that does not result in loss of signal. If you follow each of these steps, the networking media used for the horizontal cabling run should be labeled at both ends.

Structured Cable Run Installation

The easiest way to route cable is to mount it on a wall. However, this method should be used only in situations in which you are sure that the cable will not be bumped or pulled. Can you think of possible locations where this technique could be used?

To wall-mount cable, you need to select a device that will secure it to a wall. One such device is the tie-wrap. If it is unlikely that a tie-wrap will need to be removed, you can use an adhesive tie-wrap. Although this is easy to use, remember that it cannot be moved or repositioned later. If you think that the cable might have to be moved in the future, a tie-wrap with holes punched in it is a better choice. To use this type of tie-wrap, you need to drive screws into the wall.

To drive screws into a masonry wall, the first thing you must do is drill holes into the wall. However, this can present problems. If you need holes smaller

NOTE

By pushing the hammer drill firmly against your work, you can increase the hammering power and consequently the drilling speed.

than 9.5 mm in diameter, you can use an electric drill equipped with a carbide bit. Be prepared for the work to go slowly. If you need holes larger than 9.5 mm in diameter, the electric drill will probably overheat. For this task, you need to use a tool called a hammer drill. A hammer drill resembles an oversized electric drill, but unlike an electric drill, it hammers rapidly while the bit is turning. Never use staples to attach cable to walls; the use of staples to secure cable does not conform to TIA/EIA-568A specification.

Mounting Cable in Raceway

You can also route cable by mounting it in raceway, a wall-mounted channel that has a removable cover. Two types of raceway exist:

- **Decorative raceway**—Presents a more finished appearance. Decorative raceway is used to enclose cable on a wall inside a room where it might be visible.
- **Gutter raceway**—Is a less attractive alternative to decorative raceway. Its primary advantage is that it is big enough to hold several cables. Generally, the use of gutter raceway is restricted to spaces such as attics and spaces created by dropped ceilings.

Raceway can be made of either plastic or metal, and it can be mounted with adhesive backing or with screws. After you mount the raceway, lay the cable inside it and attach the top. This helps protect the cable.

Running Cable Through Existing Raceway

You might already be familiar with raceway because it is routinely used to hold other types of cable. It is not uncommon for raceway to exist in buildings in which LANs are being installed or expanded. Because that is often the case, people often wonder if cable can be routed in existing raceway. The answer depends on the type of cables that are currently contained within the raceway.

Personal Safety Precautions Before Installing Cable

Keep these safety rules in mind:

- Whenever you work on walls, ceilings, or in attics, the first thing you should do is turn off power to all circuits that might pass through those work areas! If you are not sure whether, or which, wires pass through the section of the building in which you are working, a good rule is to shut off all power. Never, ever touch power cables! Even if you think that you have cut all power to the area where you will be working, there is no way to know if these cables are "live."

- Before you begin work, learn the locations of all fire extinguishers in the area.
- Wear appropriate clothing. Long pants and sleeves help protect your arms and legs. Avoid wearing excessively loose or baggy clothing—if it is catches on something, you could be injured.
- If you anticipate working in a dropped-ceiling area, survey the area. You can do this by lifting a few of the ceiling tiles and looking around. This will help you locate electrical conduit, air ducts, mechanical equipment, and anything that might possibly cause problems later.
- If you need to cut or saw, protect your eyes with safety glasses. It's also a good idea to wear safety glasses when you work in a crawl space or above a dropped ceiling. If something falls from above, or if you lean into anything in the dark, your eyes will be protected.
- Consult with the building's maintenance engineer to find out if there is asbestos, lead, or PCB where you will be working. If so, follow all government regulations in dealing with that material.
- Keep your work area orderly and neat. Do not leave tools lying in places where someone might trip over them. Use caution with tools that have long extension cords—like tools, they are easy to trip over.

Building Safety

Always find out in advance what the local codes are. Some building codes might prohibit drilling or cutting holes in certain areas such as fire walls or ceilings. The site administrator or facility engineer will be able to help you determine which areas are off-limits.

When you install cable, if you find damaged insulation, do not run cable into that area. In some situations, if you drill through walls, you might have to fill holes completely with a noncombustible patching compound (meaning, one that cannot catch on fire). Again, the facility engineer will be able to help you identify where this will need to be done. Finally, if you find that you must route cable through spaces where air is circulated, you will need to use a fire-rated cable.

Supporting Horizontal Cabling

Many installers like to run cable in attics or dropped-ceiling spaces because it is out of sight. When running cable in a dropped-ceiling space, never lay the cable on top of the ceiling. You must provide some other means of support for the cable.

As mentioned earlier, wall-mounted gutter raceway offers one option for supporting the cable. Another option is to attach tie-wraps to the wires that suspend the dropped ceiling. If you use this option, string the cable from tie to tie. A third option for supporting the cable is to use a ladder rack. Ladder racks are hung from the ceiling and provide the best type of support for networking cable.

Stringing Cable in an Attic or a Room with a Dropped Ceiling

Attics and dropped ceiling spaces can be uncomfortable and difficult places in which to work. Often they are dark, dusty, and cramped spaces with poor air circulation. Temperatures can soar, particularly during the summer months in such spaces. A telepole offers an easy and simple solution to these problems. A telepole is nothing more than a telescoping pole with a hook at one end to hold the cable. It is used to string cable across a dropped ceiling or attic quickly.

Fishing Cable from the Basement to the First Floor

When you pull cable up through a wall—sometimes called fishing cable—you ordinarily work from an attic or dropped ceiling space. To fish cable through a wall, follow these steps:

Step 1 Locate the top plate of the wall, and drill a 19-mm hole through it.

Step 2 Slowly feed fish tape through the hole you drilled, down into the wall.

Step 3 Position another person (helper) next to the wall opening, below you. Tell your helper to signal you and to grab the hooked end of the fish tape when it reaches the wall opening.

Step 4 Your helper should strip back about 25 mm of the jacket from Cat 5 UTP cable, bend the wires around the hook of the fish tape, and use electrical tape to finish securing the cable.

Step 5 You can then pull the cable up through the wall to the wall plate.

Step 6 Be sure to leave enough excess cable at the jack end to reach the floor and extend another 60 to 90 cm.

Fishing Cable from Below a Wall

When you run horizontal cabling in a building that has a basement, you can fish cable from there to the work areas on the first floor. To do this, you must do the following:

Step 1 Drill a 3.2-mm hole at an angle through the floor, next to a baseboard.

Step 2 Push a coat hanger or stiff piece of wire into the hole to indicate the spot when you are in the basement.

Step 3 Go to the basement and locate the wire.

Step 4 Use a tape measure to mark a spot under the areas of the wall. This mark should be 57 mm from the hole.

Step 5 Drill a new hole in this spot, 19 mm in diameter. Unlike the first hole that was drilled at an angle, drill this hole straight up through the subfloor and wall plate.

Step 6 Push the cable up through this second hole, to the wall opening where the work area outlet is to be located.

Step 7 Be sure to allow enough excess cable so that it can reach the floor and extend another 60 to 90 cm.

Stringing, Running, and Mounting Cable

In this section, you demonstrate the following procedures/techniques:

1. Fish cable from above
2. Fish cable from below
3. String cable through a dropped-ceiling space
4. Wall-mount cable by using tie-wraps
5. Wall-mount cable by using decorative raceway
6. Wall-mount cable by using gutter
7. Mount cable by using a ladder rack
8. String cable by using a telepole
9. String cable by using fish tape
10. String cable using pull string

SKILL BUILDER

Lab Activity: Demo Cable Installation

In this lab, you learn three crucial cable installation skills: stringing, running, and mounting Cat 5.

Basics of Wiring Closets and Patch Panels

A wiring closet serves as a central junction point for the wiring and wiring equipment used to connect devices in a local-area network (LAN). It is the center point of a star topology. A wiring closest can be either a specially designed room or a cabinet. Normally, the equipment in a wiring closet, as shown in Figure 9-5, includes the following:

- Patch panels
- Wiring hubs
- Bridges
- Switches
- Routers

FIGURE 9-5
Central wiring connections for data or voice are in made in the wiring closet.

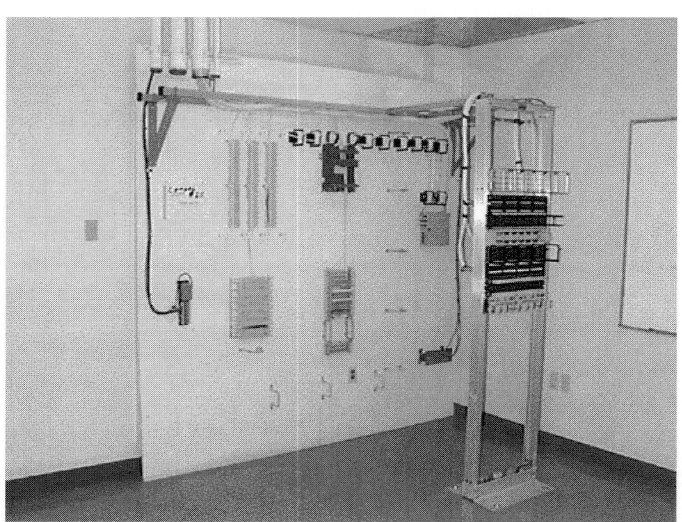

Reason for MDFs and IDFs

It is not unusual for large networks to have more than one wiring closet. Usually, when this occurs, one wiring closet is designated as the main distribution facility (MDF). All others, referred to as intermediate distribution facilities (IDFs), are dependent on it. A topology such as this is described as an extended star topology (see Figure 9-6).

Patch Panel

In an Ethernet LAN star topology, the horizontal cabling runs, which come from the work areas, usually terminate at a patch panel. A patch panel is an interconnecting device through which horizontal cabling runs can be connected to other networking devices, such as hubs and repeaters. More specifically, a patch panel is a gathering of pin locations and ports. A patch panel acts as a switchboard, where horizontal cables coming from workstations can connect to other workstations to form a LAN. In some instances, a patch panel can also provide locations for devices to connect to a WAN or to the Internet.

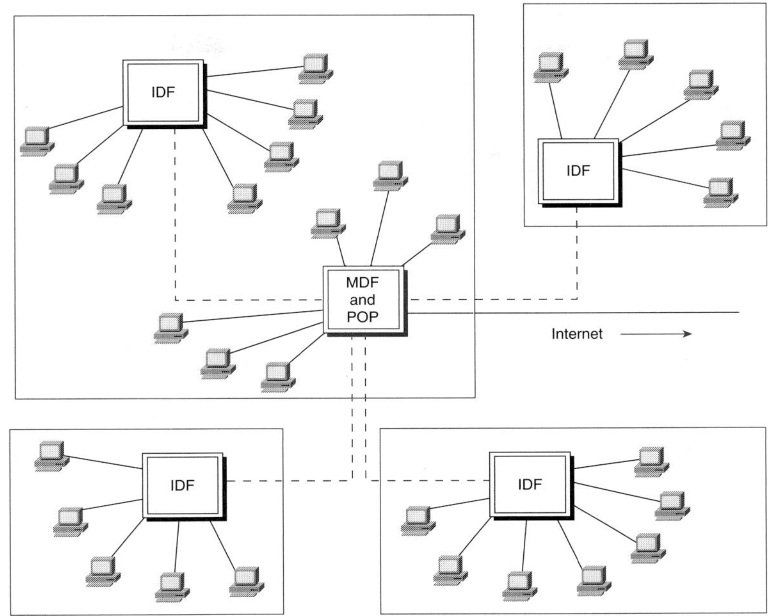

FIGURE 9-6 A central location on a campus is used for the MDF.

Structure of a Patch Panel

To understand how a patch panel provides for the interconnection of horizontal cabling runs with other networking devices, examine its structure. Rows of pins, much like those in an RJ-45 jack, are located on one side of a patch panel—and, just as they are on the jack, the pins are color-coded.

To make electrical connections to the pins, you must use a punch tool to punch down the wires. Keep in mind that proper wire sequence is critical for best network performance and operation. Therefore, when laying down the wires at the patch panel, make sure that the colors of the wires correspond exactly to the colors indicated on the pins. The wire and pin colors are not interchangeable.

On the opposite side of a patch panel are ports, as shown in Figure 9-7. They resemble the ports on faceplates of telecommunications outlets in the work area. Like the RJ-45 ports, the ports on patch panels take the same size plugs. Patch cords that connect to these ports make possible the interconnection of computers and other network devices (such as hubs, repeaters, and routers) that are also attached to the patch panel.

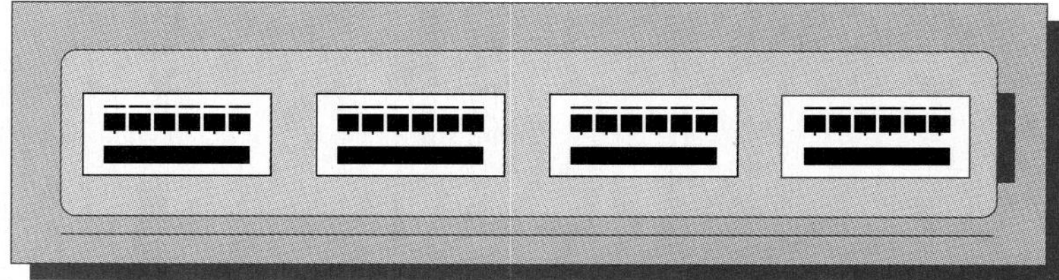

FIGURE 9-7
Ports are located on the front of a patch panel.

Laying Wires in a Patch Panel

In any LAN system, connectors are the weakest links. If not properly installed, connectors can create electrical noise and can cause intermittent electrical contact between wires and pins. When this occurs, transmission of data on the network can be disrupted or will occur at a reduced throughput; therefore, it pays to do it right.

To ensure that cable is installed correctly, you should follow the TIA/EIA standards:

1. When attaching several Cat 5 cable runs to the patch panel, you should lay down cable wires in ascending order, by cable number. Use the cut sheet that you prepared earlier to lay down the cable wires. Later, you can add the labels. Use the cable numbers that were assigned when it was run from the work area to the wiring closet. The cable numbers should correspond to the room numbers where the workstations are located. By laying the wires in ascending order at the patch panel, it becomes much easier to locate and diagnose any future problems.
2. As you work, it is important that you keep the ends of the cable centered above the pin locations. If you are not careful, the wires can become skewed, which will result in reduced data throughput when your LAN is fully connected.
3. Be sure to keep the jacket within 6.4 mm of the pin locations that you are working on, to avoid exposing too much wire. A good way to do this is to measure before you strip off the jacket—38 to 50 mm should be sufficient. If you expose too much wire, the consequence will be reduced data throughput on the network.
4. You must not untwist the wire pairs any more than necessary. Untwisted wires reduce data throughput and can lead to crosstalk.

Punch Tools

To punch the wires down in the jack, you need to use a punch tool. The patch panel type determines whether you use a 110-punch tool or a Krone punch tool. A punch tool has spring-loaded actions, which allows it to perform two functions at the same time. As it pushes the wire between two metal pins and skins the sheath from the wire (so that it can make an electrical connection with the pins), the punch tool's blade also cuts off any extra wire.

Occasionally, the punch tool might fail to make a clean cut. When this happens, twist the cut ends of the wires gently, and remove them after they are punched. When you use the punch tool, be sure to position it so that the blade faces away from where the wire enters each pin location. If you fail to take this precaution, you might cut the wire so that it falls short of its electrical connection point.

Mounting a Patch Panel

You can mount patch panels on walls (with the help of brackets), you can stand them in racks, or you can place them in cabinets (equipped with interior racks and doors). One of the most commonly used pieces of equipment is the distribution rack. A distribution rack is a simple skeletal frame that holds equipment such as patch panels, repeaters, hubs, and routers that are used in the wiring closet. It can range in height between 1 and 1.9 m.

The advantage of a distribution rack as shown in Figure 9-8 is that it allows easy access to both the front and the back of the equipment. To ensure stability, a floor plate attaches the distribution rack to the floor. Although a few companies currently market a rack that is .5 m wide, the standard since the 1940s has been the .48 m rack.

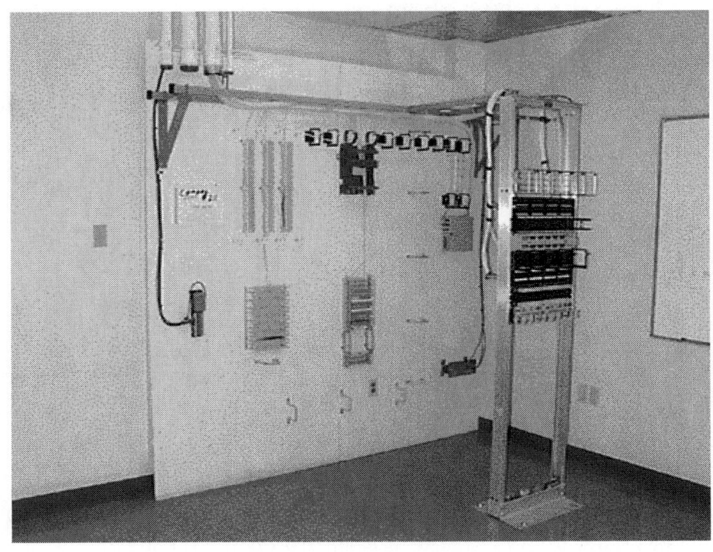

FIGURE 9-8
A distribution rack can hold patch panels and routers along with other equipment.

Range of Equipment for Testing Structured Cabling Projects

You already learned that networking media is the foundation of the OSI model and that every other layer of that model depends on and is supported by the networking media. You have also learned that a network is only as reliable as its cabling. In fact, many experts consider it the most important component of any network. Therefore, it is important that after you install the networking media, you determine the quality of the installation.

Even though a network might have been built with the best-quality cable, connectors, patch panels, and other equipment, poor installation practices can prevent it from operating at its best. When a network is in place, the entire installation should be tested. To test your network, follow these steps:

Step 1 Divide the network into smaller logical groups or elements.

Step 2 Test each group or element, one section at a time.

Step 3 Make a list of any problems you find.

Step 4 Use the list of problem(s) to help locate any nonfunctioning network element(s).

Step 5 Replace the bad element(s) or use additional testing to determine if the suspect element is, in fact, not working properly.

Step 6 If the first suspect element is not causing the problem, then proceed on to the next most likely element.

Step 7 Repair the bad or nonfunctioning element as soon as you find it.

Step 8 Replace the nonfunctioning element if you cannot repair it.

Network Operation Testing

The IEEE and the TIA/EIA have established standards that enable you to test whether your network is operating at an acceptable level. If your network passes this test and is certified as meeting the standards, you can use this measurement as an established baseline. The baseline is a record of your network's starting point or newly installed performance capabilities.

Knowing the baseline measurement is important. Testing does not end just because your network installation is certified as meeting the standards. You should continue to test your network on a regular basis to ensure that it performs at its peak. You can do this by comparing current measurements with recorded measurements that were taken when the system was known to be operating properly. If there is a significant change from the baseline measurement, it is an indication that something is wrong with the network. Repeated testing of your network and comparisons against its baseline will help you spot specific network problems that might be caused by aging, poor maintenance practices, weather, or other factors.

One example of an all-purpose tool for testing the baseline health of a network is Fluke Networks' NetTool (or other equivalent all-purpose handheld tester). NetTool provides insight into the cause of desktop-to-network connectivity problems, combining the capabilities of a network tester, a PC configuration tester, and a basic cable tester. NetTool (or the equivalent) connects between the PC and the wall jack. Once connected, the tool listens, collects, and organizes information regarding the following:

- Network resources available
- Network resources that the PC is configured to use
- The health of the network segment, including errors, collisions, utilization, and the health of the PC NIC and the local network

You can also use this tool to perform basic cable tests to detect opens, shorts, and split pairs; to determine the length to the open on any RJ-45–terminated cable; and to conduct pin-to-pin wire map tests on installed wiring or patch cables. Here's a summary of NetTool's capabilities:

1. **Service identification**—Identifies a jack as Ethernet, Token Ring, telco, or inactive
2. **Link reporting**—Discovers and reports the previously unseen PC hub/switch link negotiation
3. **Inline mode**—Concisely displays the PC's IP address and network resources used: default router, e-mail server, DNS, and Web servers accessed
4. **Basic cable testing**—Performs basic cable tests, showing opens, shorts, split pairs, length, and pin-to-pin wire mapping

Cable Testing Equipment

You might think that testing cable is simply a matter of substituting one cable for another. However, this does not provide certain proof of anything because a common problem can affect all cables on a LAN. For this reason, it is recommended that you use a cable tester to measure network performance.

A cable tester is a handheld device that can certify that installed cable meets the required IEEE and TIA/EIA standards. Cable testers vary in the types of testing functions they provide. Some can provide printouts; others can be attached to a PC to create a data file. Little or no special training is required to use the cable testers that are currently available on the market today. Most competent network administrators or installers find that the operating manuals supplied by the cable tester manufacturers provide sufficient instruction.

Cable Testers and Distance Measurements

It is important to measure the overall length of cable runs. Distance can affect the capability of devices on the network that share the networking media. As you have already learned, cable that exceeds the maximum length specified by TIA/EIA-568-A causes signal degradation.

Cable testers, sometimes referred to as time domain reflectometers (TDRs), measure the distance to open-ended, or shorted, cable. They do it by sending an electrical pulse through the cable. The devices then time the signal's reflection from the end of the cable. This test is called time domain reflectometry and can provide distance readings that are accurate to within 61 cm.

Time Domain Reflectometers

In LAN installations that use UTP cables, distance measurements can determine whether the connections at the patch panels and at the telecommunications outlets are good. To understand how this works, you must understand how a TDR works.

A TDR measures distance on a cable by sending an electrical signal through the cable. The signal is reflected when it encounters an open connection. For it to determine which connections in a cable run are faulty, you must attach the TDR to the patch cord at the patch panel. If the TDR reports the distance to the patch panel instead of a more distance point, then you know that there is a connection problem. You can use the same procedure at the opposite end of the cable to measure through the RJ-45 jack located at the telecommunications outlet.

Wire Maps

Cable testers use a feature called a wire map to indicate which wire pairs connect to which pins on lugs and sockets. The test indicates whether the installer properly connected the wires of a plug or jack, or whether these were connected in reverse order. When wires are connected in reversed order, they are referred to as crossed pairs. Unique to UTP cable installations, this is a common problem. When crossed pairs are detected in UTP LAN cabling systems, the connections are not good and must be redone.

Split Pairs

Visual inspection and crosstalk measurements are the only ways to detect a condition known as split pairs. As you know, the twisting in wire pairs shields them from external interference from signals that pass near other wire pairs. However, this shielding effect can occur only if the wires in the pair are part of the same circuit. When wires split, they are no longer part of the same circuit. Although current can flow in the circuit, making the system appear to work, no shielding is in effect. Consequently, the signals are not protected.

Eventually, near-end crosstalk will become a problem. A wire map cannot detect a split pair condition because, in split pairs, a circuit is still present.

Signal Attenuation

Various factors can reduce the power of a signal as it passes through the copper wires used in UTP cables. This reduction in the power of a signal is called *attenuation*. It occurs because a signal loses energy to a cable.

A cable tester can measure the reduction in power of a signal received from a device known as a signal injector, a small box approximately the size of a deck of playing cards that is attached to the far end of a cable. Cable testers generally measure attenuation at several frequencies. Cable testers for Cat 5 cable generally measure up to 100 MHz. Check the TIA/EIA-568-A specifications to see what amount of loss is allowed for the type of cable used in your LAN.

Causes of Near-End Crosstalk

Several factors can contribute to near-end crosstalk. The most common cause is crossed pairs. As mentioned earlier, you can detect these with the wire map feature of a cable tester. Near-end crosstalk can also be caused by twisted pairs that have become untwisted after being attached to cross-connect devices (such as patch panels) that have patch cords that are untwisted or by cables that have been pulled too tightly around sharp corners, causing pairs to change position inside the cable jacket.

If you measure near-end crosstalk, you should do a visual check of the horizontal cabling to rule out any of these possibilities. If you find nothing, then split pairs have most likely caused the problem. A cable tester measures for near-end crosstalk by measuring a series of frequencies up to 100 MHz. High numbers are good; low numbers indicate problems on the network.

Problems Detected by a Noise Level Test

Many outside factors can contribute to interference on the networking media. Some examples of sources that can produce outside signals that can impose themselves on wire pairs in UTP cable include the following:

- Fluorescent lights
- Heaters
- Radios
- Air cleaners
- Televisions

- Computers
- Motion sensors
- Radar
- Motors
- Switches
- Welders
- Auto ignitions
- Electronic devices of all kinds

Fortunately, signals produced by these outside sources often occupy specific frequencies. This enables an electrical noise level test not only to detect such outside interferences, but also to narrow the range of possible sources that produced them.

Using a Cable Tester to Locate Sources of Outside Interference

To use a cable tester to take a noise reading on a cable, you should disconnect all cables from the computer equipment. High reading levels usually indicate a problem. A simple way to locate the precise source is to unplug each electrical device until the source of the noise is found. Be aware, however, that this does not always work.

SKILL BUILDER

Lab Activity: Demo Cable Testing

In this lab, you use the Fluke 620 (or equivalent) to perform cable verification experiments on newly installed cable runs.

During the second half of the lab, you are asked to demonstrate your ability to use a star topology to set up a simple Ethernet LAN. You will be evaluated on your ability to handle the cable correctly, and to lay, and punch down wires, in a jack, and at a patch panel, so that there are good connections.

After you complete the connections for your star topology LAN, you are asked to test it. If tests indicate problems, you will be asked to diagnose and troubleshoot those problems. The goal in this series of lab exercises is to produce a completely functional star topology LAN that meets TIA/EIA and IEEE specifications.

Summary

In this chapter, you learned that to ensure that cabling is done thoroughly, accurately, and on time, you should create a flowchart that includes each of the tasks that must be completed and the order in which they should be performed. Additionally, your flowchart should also include a timeline for each of these tasks:

- Installing outlets
- Installing jacks
- Running cables
- Punching cables into patch panels
- Testing cables
- Documenting cables
- Installing NICs
- Installing hubs, switches, bridges, and routers
- Configuring routers
- Installing and configuring PCs

Your cabling plan should include the following:

- Building materials
- Suppliers
- Tools
- Date and length of time required

Lastly, you learned about how to install, string, and run cable; the basics of wiring closets and patch panels; and how to test cable. In the next chapter, you start to see how routing and addressing operate at the network layer.

Check Your Understanding

1. In a horizontal cabling scheme, an ______ jack be used for making the connection to a Cat 5 unshielded twisted-pair cable at the telecommunications outlet.

   A. RJ-69

   B. RJ-54

   C. RJ-45

   D. RJ-11

2. Which is not one of the two wall mounts that the TIA/EIA-568-A specifies?

   A. Surface mount

   B. Standard mount

   C. Flush mount

   D. A and B

3. What does sequencing refer to?

   A. Twisting the correct pair of wires

   B. The process of stripping the wire in the right order

   C. The process of matching the wires to the proper terminals

   D. Splitting the correct pair of wires

4. For Cat 5 UTP, what is the maximum length of untwisted wire?

   A. 1.3 cm

   B. 2.3 cm

   C. 1.4 cm

   D. 2.4 cm

5. When bending UTP cable, what is the bend radius that must be maintained?

   A. Three times the diameter of the cable

   B. Four times the diameter of the cable

C. Five times the diameter of the cable

D. Six times the diameter of the cable

6. What is a service coil?

A. A few extra feet of cable left coiled up inside the ceiling

B. Small coils left in strategic places to deter stretching

C. A small coil left at each jack to permit several punchdowns

D. All of the above

7. What does the EIA/TIA-606 specify?

A. On each end of the cable, a unique identifier must be attached.

B. Each jack must have a unique identifier attached to it.

C. Each hardware termination unit must have some kind of unique identifier.

D. None of the above.

8. What should be used to secure cable to a wall?

A. Staples

B. Tie-wraps

C. Square nails

D. Velcro

9. What is raceway?

A. A bundle of wires traveling in the same direction

B. A ceiling-mounted patch panel

C. A wall-mounted channel that has a removable cover

D. None of the above

10. What is a telepole?

A. A telescoping pole with a hook at one end to hold the cable

B. A telescoping pole that suspends cable from ceilings

C. A telescoping pole that aids in routing cable from ceiling to jack

D. All of the above

11. What are horizontal cabling runs connected to in a wiring closet?
    - A. LEDs
    - B. Patch panel
    - C. Patch cords
    - D. None of the above
12. What are located on the front of a patch panel?
    - A. Punchdown blocks
    - B. RJ-45 jacks
    - C. LEDs
    - D. RJ-11 jacks
13. Why shouldn't you install a jack in the bottom 5 cm of a wooded baseboard?
    - A. The bottom plate of the wall will prevent you from pushing the box into the baseboard.
    - B. Most floors have metal supports that produce electromagnetic interference when close to the jack.
    - C. Dust and dirt accumulate under it that can then get into the connection and affect network performance.
    - D. It's so close to the floor that there isn't enough space for most people to work and manipulate the wires.
14. How is a cable tester used to assist with an electrical noise level test?
    - A. The tester takes a noise reading on the cable while the cable is connected to computer equipment.
    - B. A decrease in levels read on the tester indicates a problem.
    - C. The source of the noise may be located by unplugging electrical devices.
    - D. A source of outside noise usually produces a wide range of frequencies.
15. Which is not a typical width of distribution racks?
    - A. 19 inches
    - B. 23 inches

C. 24 inches

D. All of the above

16. What does TDR stand for?

A. Time domain reflectometer

B. Time domain resistance

C. Time differential reflectometer

D. None of the above

17. When wires are connected in reversed order, they are referred to as

A. Critical pairs

B. Crossed pairs

C. Cancelled pairs

D. Split pairs

18. When a wire from one circuit is crossed with a wire from another circuit, it is called a

A. Crossed pair

B. Split pair

C. Cancelled pair

D. Critical pair

19. A reduction in power of a signal as it passes through copper wires used in UTP is called

A. Oscillation

B. Resistance

C. Attenuation

D. NEXT

20. Near-end crosstalk is caused by the following except

A. Crossed pairs

B. Twisted pairs that have become untwisted

C. Split pairs

D. All of the above

Objectives

After reading this chapter, you will be able to

- Understand the importance of the network layer
- Describe path determination
- Understand IP addresses
- Describe IP address classes
- Describe reserved address space
- Understand basics of subnetting
- Describe how to create subnets

Chapter 10

Layer 3: Routing and Addressing

Introduction

The network layer is responsible for navigating data through a network. The function of the network layer is to find the best path through a network. The network layer's addressing scheme is used by devices to determine the destination of data as it moves through the network. In this chapter, you learn about the router's role in performing the key internetworking function of Layer 3 of the Open System Interconnection (OSI) reference model: path determination.

In addition, you learn about IP addressing and the three classes of IP networks. You also learn that some IP addresses have been set aside by the American Registry for Internet Numbers (ARIN) and cannot be assigned to any network on the Internet. Finally, you learn about subnetworks and subnet masks, and their role in IP addressing schemes.

Importance of the Network Layer

The network layer defines how to transport traffic between devices that are not locally attached. Two pieces of information are used to achieve this:

- Logical addresses associated with the source and destination stations
- Paths through the network to reach desired destinations

The network layer moves data through a set of networks (internetwork). The network layer's addressing scheme is used by devices to determine the destination of data as it moves through the networks. As shown in Figure 10-1, without network layer services, Host B cannot determine where Host A is.

To determine what networks exist in an internetwork and where devices are in the context of those networks, logical addressing schemes are used. These schemes vary based on the network layer protocol that you use. IP is a common network layer protocol used in routed networks. Protocol stacks that have no network layer can be used on only small networks. These protocols usually use only a name or number (a character string) to identify a computer on a network. The problem with this approach is that, as the network grows in size, it becomes increasingly difficult to organize all the names/numbers.

FIGURE 10-1
The only way Host B can reach Host A is with an addressing scheme.

Protocols that support the network layer use a hierarchical addressing scheme that allows for unique addresses across network boundaries, along with a method for finding a path for data to travel between networks. MAC addresses use a flat addressing scheme that makes it difficult to locate devices on other networks. Hierarchical addressing, on the other hand, not only enables information flow through an internetwork, but it also provides an efficient means of doing so.

The telephone network is an example of a system that uses hierarchical addressing. The telephone system uses an area code that designates a geographical area for the call's first stop (or hop). The next three digits represent the local exchange (second hop). The final digits represent the individual destination telephone (the final hop).

Network devices need an addressing scheme that allows them to forward data packets through an internetwork (a set of networks composed of multiple segments using the same type of addressing). Several network layer protocols have different addressing schemes that allow devices to forward data throughout an internetwork, including IP and IPX.

A critical prerequisite to internetworking is having an efficient address architecture adhered to by all users of that internetwork. Address architectures can take many different forms. Network addresses are always numeric, but they can be expressed in base 2 (binary), base 10 (decimal), or even base 16 (hexadecimal). Address architectures can be highly scalable or designed to serve small communities of users. The next section examines the need for network segmentation in building scalable networks.

Segmentation and Autonomous Systems

Two primary factors affect the scale of a network: the growth in size of each network and the growth in the number of networks. When a LAN, MAN, or WAN grows, it might become necessary or desirable to break up the network into smaller pieces. This results in the network becoming a group of networks, each requiring a separate network address.

A vast number of networks already exist; separate computer networks are common in offices, schools, companies, businesses, and countries. It is convenient to have these separate networks (or *autonomous systems*, if each is managed by a single administration) communicate over the Internet. However, a sensible addressing schemes and appropriate internetworking devices are required. Otherwise, traffic flow would become severely restricted, and neither the local networks nor the Internet would function very well.

An analogy that might help you understand the need for network segmentation is to imagine a highway system and the number of vehicles that use it, as shown in Figure 10-2. As the population in the areas surrounding the highways increases, the roads become burdened with too many vehicles. Networks operate in much the same way. As networks grow, the amount of traffic grows. One solution is to increase the bandwidth; this is analogous to increasing the speed limit on the highway or adding lanes to the highway. Another solution might be to use devices that segment the network and control the flow of traffic, just as stoplights are used to control the flow of vehicle traffic on a street.

FIGURE 10-2
Network devices control flow just as streetlights do, and the network layer is responsible for decisions regarding which path to take.

Communication Between Separate Networks

The Internet is a collection of network segments tied together to facilitate the sharing of information. Again, a good analogy is the example of a highway system with multiple lanes constructed to interconnect geographical regions. Networks operate in much the same manner, with Internet service providers (ISPs) offering services that tie together multiple network segments.

MORE INFORMATION

The Internet's Address Architecture

The Internet's address architecture is implemented with the Internet Protocol (IP). IP's original addressing scheme dates back to the early days of network computing. At the time, the Internet itself was little more than a semi-public network that interconnected a few dozen universities, research organizations, and government agencies. Each of these entities that connected to the Internet had limited network computing infrastructures. Typically, these infrastructures consisted of little more than a mainframe computer or a handful of UNIX-based minicomputers. PCs had yet to play a role, and local-area networks (LANs) were in their infancy. Therefore, an internetwork did not require a complex architecture.

The Internet uses a two-level address hierarchy. Each of the hosts on the Internet needs to be uniquely identifiable. In the Internet's hierarchy, this requires an address with two parts:

- Network address
- Host address

Rather than calculating and tracking routes to each known host, the Internet propagates only network addresses. End systems that need to access hosts in other networks address their datagrams with the full address, including both network and host numbers, but the routers in the internetwork rely on routers in the destination network to deliver datagrams to the various end systems within its area. Therefore, the Internet's routers have to track routes only to every known network.

A router in the Internet's backbone would quickly become overwhelmed if it tracked paths through the Internet to each end system or host. Instead, the architects of the Internet and IP implemented a two-tier physical architecture. This was accompanied by a two-tier network address consisting of the network's address and a host address. The most practical implication of such a scheme was that routers in the Internet's backbone could greatly reduce their workload by just tracking routes to specific network segments (indicated by network addresses).

The greatly reduced size of the network-based routing tables did not compromise the capability of the Internet routers to forward datagrams to their destinations. (How routers build and use these routing tables is the essence of what you'll learn as you progress in the field of networking.) The more entries that exist in a router's routing table, the longer it takes to determine where to forward a datagram. A datagram must be buffered in a router's memory until this determination is made. Consequently, the larger a network's routing tables become, the greater the demands that are placed on the network routers' physical resources. These include random access memory (RAM) and central processing unit (CPU) cycles. It's important to keep in mind that the cost associated with more RAM and faster CPUs is one of the primary factors governing an organization's decision to purchase or upgrade networking equipment.

MORE INFORMATION (CONTINUED)

Closely related to performance—and just as significant—is scalability. Advertising networks enables an internetwork to be highly scalable. The Internet is a case in point. Without the capability to advertise network routes, the Internet's growth would have been severely constrained.

The Internet was aided in its scalability by its sophisticated addressing architecture. Its architects foresaw the potential for its growth and developed an addressing architecture that was both flexible and extensible. This architecture was manifested in the form of IP.

Layer 3 Network Devices and Path Determination

Routers are internetworking devices that operate at OSI Layer 3 (the network layer). They tie together, or interconnect, network segments or entire networks, as shown in Figure 10-3. They pass data packets between networks based on Layer 3 information.

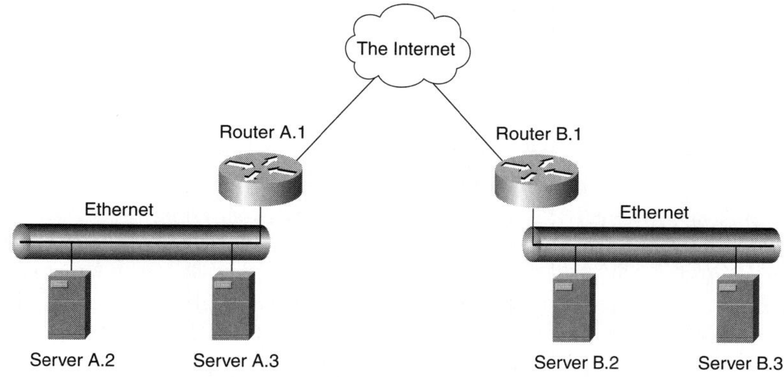

FIGURE 10-3
Unique addressing allows communication between end stations.

Routers make logical decisions regarding the best path for the delivery of data in an internetwork; these decisions are implemented by directing packets to the appropriate output ports and associated segments. Routers take packets from LAN devices (such as workstations) and, based on Layer 3 information, forward them through the network.

MORE INFORMATION

Understanding the Role of Routers in Networks

Routers provide physical connectivity between networks by virtue of their physical attachments to either local-area networks (LANs), such as Token Ring or Ethernet, or wide-area networks (WANs), such as Frame Relay or ISDN, as shown in Figure 10-4.

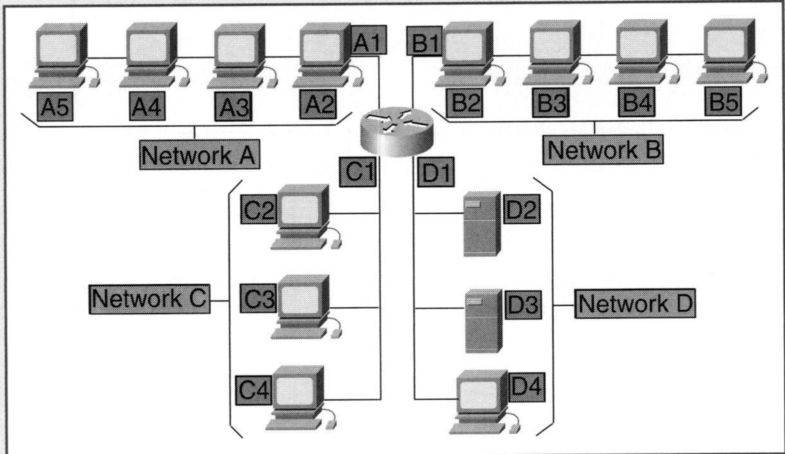

FIGURE 10-4 Cisco router configuration with multiple protocols is used to interconnect multiple media.

A router can be used to connect only LANs, only WANs, or any combination. The term physical connection should not be taken too literally. Many networks make use of microwave links for WAN connectivity. This means that no actual physical connection exists between two connected routers communicating over microwave links or any type of wireless point-to-point link.

The Router Interface

A router's attachment to a LAN or a WAN is usually referred to as an interface, but it might also be referred to as a port. For example, a connection to a Token Ring LAN is made at a Token Ring interface. When discussing a router's connections to a network, it is common to say something like, "We connect the finance department's Token Ring network to the corporate backbone via Bbone-1's first Token Ring interface." Bbone-1, in this case, is the logical name of a router in a corporate network. Routers are typically assigned names that provide some information about their location and function.

MORE INFORMATION (CONTINUED)

When a router is routing IP, each LAN or WAN that it is connected to must have a unique IP network or subnetwork address assigned to it. (In the case of some types of serial links, a router must "borrow" an address from another interface—the process of implementing this type of serial link on a router is called *IP unnumbered* because no additional IP network addresses are used. The interface on the router must have a valid IP host address for the subnet it is attached to. In most cases, a router can have only one connection to any single subnet.

IP unnumbered refers to using the network or subnet address of a local LAN interface as the router's network or subnetwork address for a point-to-point serial link. The term *point-to-point* means that only two devices are on the link, as is the case with a T1 connection between two routers or between two point-to-point subinterfaces in a Frame Relay network. Normally, a serial link has its own unique network or subnetwork address. IP unnumbered enables a network administrator to conserve network or subnetwork addresses. IP unnumbered is especially valuable for networks running IP routing protocols such as RIP V1 and IGRP, which do not support variable-length subnet masking (VLSM). Without VLSM support, a network must use the same subnet mask on its serial (WAN) interfaces as it does on its LAN interfaces. For a company using an 8-bit (255.255.255.0) subnet mask on a Class B network address, this means using a subnet capable of supporting 254 hosts on a WAN link with only two hosts.

Datagrams

In addition to providing physical connectivity between networks, routers also possess the capability to move information across multiple networks by forwarding datagrams based on their network layer addresses.

The users indicate via their Telnet application that they want to log in to a server. The Telnet application passes this request to the next-lower layer in the protocol stack—TCP, in this case—and waits for a response from the remote system.

The TCP layer adds its own information to what it received from the Telnet application and hands this combined message to the IP layer—the network layer—of the protocol stack. TCP holds on to the request that it received from Telnet in case the first attempt to contact the remote host fails. The term *packet* is often used interchangeably with *datagram*.

It is important to understand that IP datagrams are nonreliable. This means that they are delivered once by the originator's IP layer and then are discarded. If the destination host does not receive the datagram, some higher-layer protocol or application on the host that created the datagram must try again or give up.

If the destination host had not received the original IP datagram in the previous example, TCP would have made at least one more attempt. TCP would have handed another copy of its information to the IP layer, and IP would have attempted to deliver the datagram again.

continues

MORE INFORMATION (CONTINUED)

Note: Using the example of users attempting to log in to a remote server with Telnet to explain datagrams necessarily omits many of the actual details involved in establishing a Telnet session.

When routers forward datagrams based on their Layer 3 addresses, all Layer 2 information that arrived with the packet is discarded. The router creates the required Layer 2 information for the next link before forwarding the datagram to the next router, which allows routers to connect networks with different Layer 2 frame and addressing formats.

As Figure 10-5 illustrates, routers track route update information by keeping a routing table. The table includes this information:

- **Network address**—A network address is protocol-specific. If a router supports more than one protocol, it has a unique table of network addresses for each protocol.
- **INT**—This refers to the interface used to reach a given network. The router lists the interface or interfaces through which it forwards packets destined for a specific network.
- **Metric**—This refers to the distance to the target network. How distance is measured depends on the protocol being used. Common metrics include the number of internetworking devices that a packet must cross (hop count), the time it takes to get from the source to the destination (delay), or a value associated with the speed of a link.

FIGURE 10-5
Routers use configured information to identify paths to destination networks.

Routing Table		
NET	INT	Metric
1	E0	0
2	S0	0
4	S0	1

Path Determination

Path determination occurs at Layer 3 (network layer). It enables a router to evaluate the available paths to a destination and to establish the preferred handling of a packet. Routing services use network topology information when evaluating network paths (see Figure 10-6). Path determination is the process that a router uses to choose the next hop in a path toward a packet's ultimate destination. This process is also called *routing* the packet.

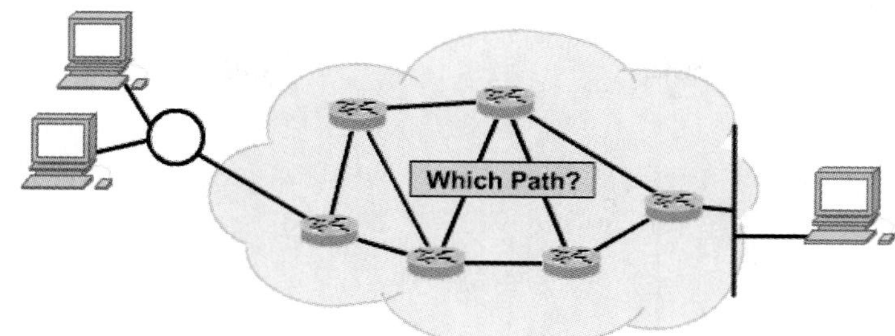

FIGURE 10-6
The path determination function enables a router to evaluate available paths to a destination to best handle a packet.

Path determination for a packet can be compared to a person driving a car from one side of a city to another. The driver has a map that shows the streets to take to get to the destination. The drive from one intersection to another is a hop. Similarly, a router uses a map that shows the available paths to a destination. Routers can also make their decisions based on the traffic density and the speed of the link (bandwidth), just as a driver might choose a faster path (a highway) or use less crowded back streets. In this section, you see how a router determines the best path for packets traveling from one network to another.

Network Layer Addressing

A network address helps the router identify a path within the network cloud. The router uses the network address to identify the destination network of a packet within an internetwork. In addition to the network address, network protocols use some form of host, or node, address. For some network layer protocols, a network administrator assigns host addresses according to some predetermined network addressing plan. For other network layer protocols, assigning host addresses is partially or completely dynamic or automatic. Figure 10-7 shows three devices in Network 1 (two workstations and a router), each with its own unique host address. (The figure also shows that the router is connected to two other networks, networks 2 and 3.)

Logical addressing occurs at the network layer. The telephone company analogy of a network address includes the first portions (area code and first three digits) of a telephone number. The remaining (last four) digits of a phone number tell the phone company equipment which specific phone to ring. This is similar to the function of the host portion of an address. The host portion tells the router the specific device to which it should deliver a packet.

Without network layer addressing, routing cannot take place. Routers require network addresses to ensure proper delivery of packets. Without some hierarchical addressing structure, packets would not be capable of traveling across an internetwork. Similarly, without some hierarchical structure to telephone numbers, postal addresses, or transportation systems, there would be no smooth delivery of goods and services.

FIGURE 10-7
A network address consists of a network portion and a host portion.

Network	Host
1	1 2 3
2	1
3	1

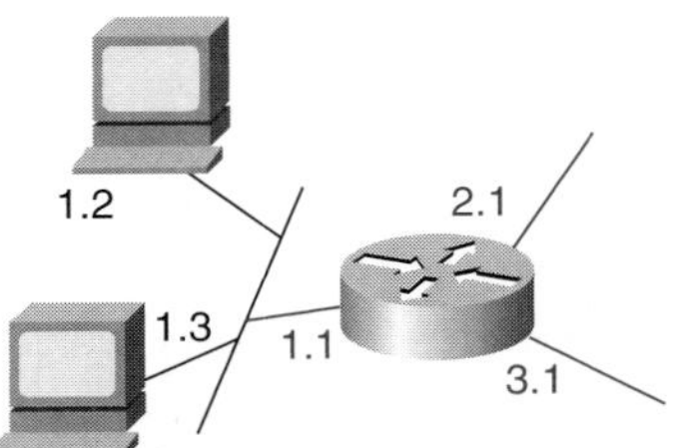

A MAC address can be compared to your name, and the network layer address can be compared to your mailing address (network and host address). For example, if you were to move to another town, your name would remain unchanged, but your mailing address would indicate your new location. Network devices (routers as well as individual computers) have both a MAC address and a protocol (network layer) address. When you physically move a computer to a different network, the computer maintains the same MAC address, but you must assign it a new network layer address.

The Communication Path

The function of the network layer is to find the best path through the network. To be truly practical, a network must consistently represent the paths available between routers. As Figure 10-8 shows, each line between the routers has a number that the routers use as a network address. These addresses must convey information that can be used by a routing process. This means that an address must have information about the path of media connections that the routing process uses to pass packets from a source toward a destination.

Using these addresses, the network layer can provide a relay connection that interconnects independent networks. The consistency of Layer 3 addresses across the entire internetwork also improves the use of bandwidth by preventing unnecessary broadcasts. Broadcasts invoke unnecessary process overhead and waste capacity on any devices or links that do not need to receive the broadcast. By using consistent end-to-end addressing to represent the path of media connections, the network layer can find a path to the destination without unnecessarily burdening the devices or links on the internetwork with broadcasts.

FIGURE 10-8 Network addresses logically represent media connections.

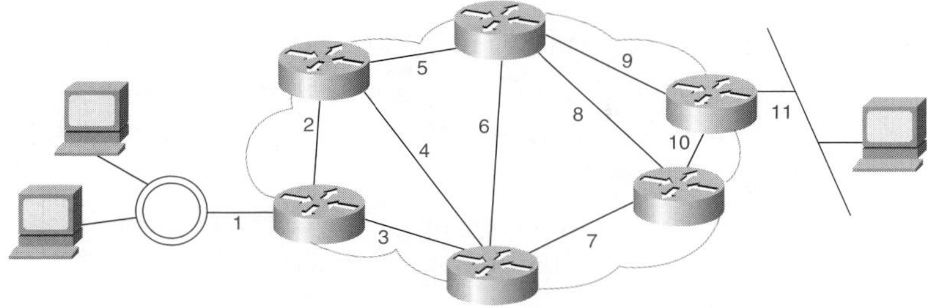

IP Addresses Within the IP Header

The Internet Protocol (IP) is the most popular implementation of a hierarchical network addressing scheme. IP is the network protocol the Internet uses. As information flows down the layers of the OSI model, the data is encapsulated at each layer. At the network layer, the data is encapsulated within packets (also known as datagrams). IP determines the form of the IP packet header (which includes addressing and other control information), but it does not concern itself with the actual data; it accepts whatever is passed down from the higher layers.

Network Layer Fields

The Layer 3 packet/datagram becomes the Layer 2 data, which is then encapsulated into frames (as previously discussed). Similarly, the IP packet consists of the data from upper layers plus an IP header, which consists of the following fields (see Figure 10-9):

- **Version**—Indicates the version of IP currently used (4 bits).
- IP Header Length (HLEN)—Indicates the datagram header length in 32-bit words (4 bits).
- **Type of Service**—Specifies the level of precedence of the packet that has been assigned by a particular upper-layer protocol (8 bits).
- **Total Length**—Specifies the length of the entire IP packet, including data and header, in bytes (16 bits).
- **Identification**—Contains an integer that identifies the current datagram (16 bits).
- **Flags**—Is a 3-bit field in which the 2 low-order bits control fragmentation. One bit specifies whether the packet can be fragmented, and the second bit

specifies whether the packet is the last fragment in a series of fragmented packets (3 bits).

- **Fragment Offset**—Helps piece together datagram fragments (13 bits).
- **Time-to-Live**—Maintains a counter that gradually decrements to zero, at which point the datagram is discarded, keeping the packets from looping endlessly (8 bits).
- **Protocol**—Indicates which upper-layer protocol receives incoming packets after IP processing has been completed (8 bits).
- **Header Checksum**—Helps ensure IP header integrity (16 bits).
- **Source Address**—Specifies the sending node IP address (32 bits).
- **Destination Address**—Specifies the receiving node IP address (32 bits).
- **Options**—Allows IP to support various options, such as security (variable length)
- **Data**—Contains upper-layer information (variable length, maximum 64 KB)
- **Padding**—Adds extra zeros to ensure that the IP header is always a multiple of 32 bits

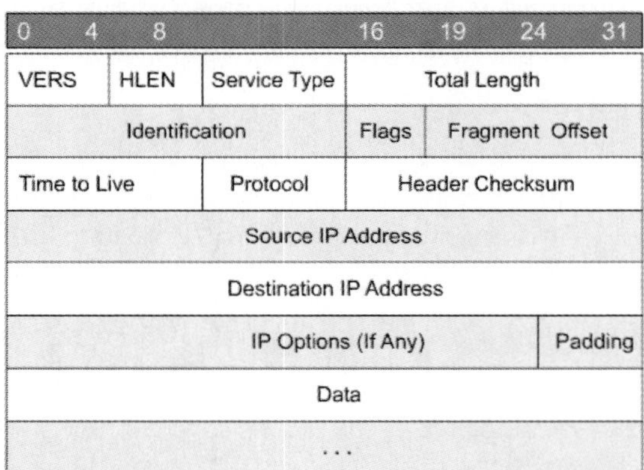

FIGURE 10-9
The IP network header fields.

The IP header contains the information that is necessary to route a packet through the network. Each source and destination address field contains a 32-bit address. The source address field contains the IP address of the device that sends the packet. The destination field contains the IP address of the device that receives the packet.

IP Address as a 32-Bit Binary Number

An IP address can be represented by a 32-bit binary number written as four octets, as shown in Figure 10-10. As a quick review, remember that each binary digit (bit) can be only 0 or 1. In a binary number, the value of the right-most bit (also called the least significant bit) is either 0 or 1. The corresponding decimal value of each bit doubles as you move left in the binary number. So, the decimal value of the second bit from the right is either 0 or 2. The third bit is either 0 or 4, the fourth bit 0 or 8, and so on.

Octet (8 bits) • Octet (8 bits) • Octet (8 bits) • Octet (8 bits)
$2^7 2^6 2^5 2^4 2^3 2^2 2^1 2^0 . 2^7 2^6 2^5 2^4 2^3 2^2 2^1 2^0 . 2^7 2^6 2^5 2^4 2^3 2^2 2^1 2^0 . 2^7 2^6 2^5 2^4 2^3 2^2 2^1 2^0$
11000000 00000101 00100010 00001011
EQUALS
192 • 5 • 34 • 11

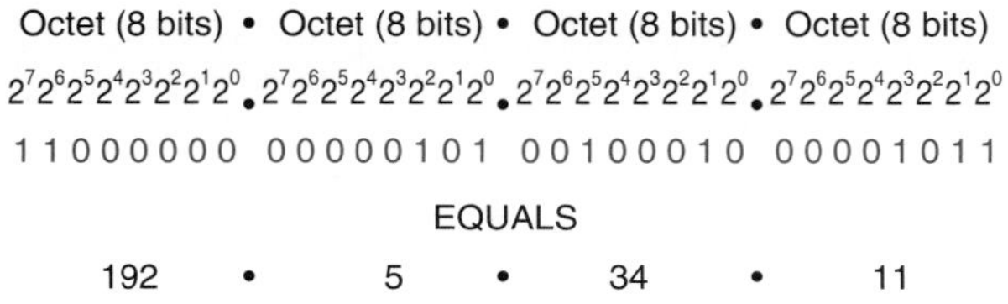

FIGURE 10-10
IP addresses can be expressed as binary numbers consisting of 1s and 0s.

IP addresses are often expressed as dotted-decimal numbers—the 32 bits of the address are broken into four octets (an octet is a group of 8 bits), as shown in Figure 10-11. The maximum decimal value of each octet is 255. The largest 8-bit binary number is 11111111. Those bits, from left to right, have decimal values of 128, 64, 32, 16, 8, 4, 2, and 1. Added, they total 255.

1 byte
8 bits
1 byte
8 bits
1 byte
8 bits
1 byte
8 bits
192 • 5 • 34 • 11

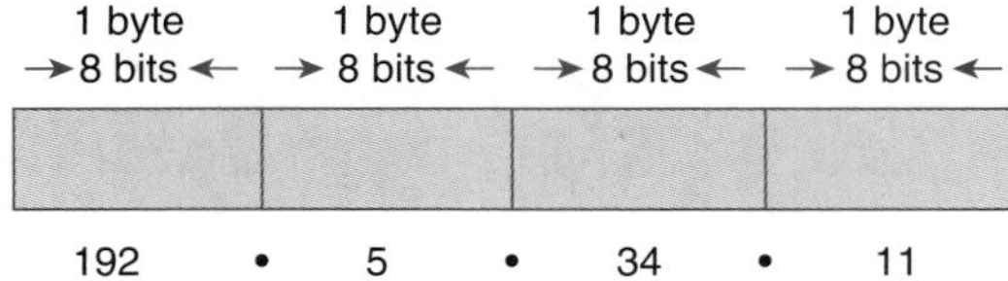

FIGURE 10-11
A 4-byte IP address containing four 1-byte octets.

The network number of an IP address identifies the network to which a device is attached (see Figure 10-12). The host portion of an IP address identifies a specific device on a network. Because IP addresses consist of four octets separated by dots, one, two, or three of these octets might be used to identify the network number. Similarly, up to three of these octets might be used to identify the host portion of an IP address.

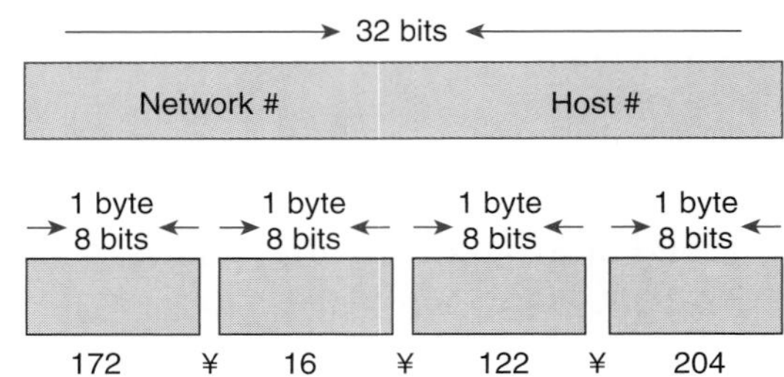

FIGURE 10-12
The network number and the host number make up the IP address.

MOVIE 10.1

IP Addressing Format

An IP address has a network number and a host number, and uses dotted-decimal notation.

IP Address Classes

An organization can receive three classes of IP addresses from the American Registry for Internet Numbers (ARIN) (or the organization's ISP) (see Figure 10-13): Class A, B, and C. ARIN now reserves Class A addresses for governments throughout the world (although a few large companies, such as Hewlett-Packard, have received one in the past) and reserves Class B addresses for medium-sized companies. All other requestors are issued Class C addresses.

FIGURE 10-13
ARIN assigns three classes of IP addresses.

Class A:	N	H	H	H
Class B:	N	N	H	H
Class C:	N	N	N	H

Class D: for multicast
Class E: for research

N = Network number assigned by ARIN
H = Host number assigned by network administrator

MOVIE 10.2

IP Address Classes

Five classes of addresses explained.

SKILL BUILDER

Lab Activity: IP Addressing

In this lab, you learn different classes of IP addresses and how TCP/IP networks operate.

MOVIE 10.3

Where to Get an IP Address

You can get IP addresses from an ISP and InterNIC.

Class A

The Class A address was designed to support extremely large networks. Because the need for very large-scale networks was perceived to be minimal, an architecture was developed that maximized the possible number of host addresses but severely limited the number of possible Class A networks that could be defined.

When written in a binary format, the first (left-most) bit of a Class A address is always 0 (see Figure 10-14). An example of a Class A IP address is 124.95.44.15. The first octet, 124, identifies the network number assigned by ARIN. The internal administrators of the network assign the remaining 24 bits. An easy way to recognize whether a device is part of a Class A network is to look at the first octet of its IP address, which can range from 1 to 126. (127 does start with a 0 bit, but it has been reserved for special purposes.)

All Class A IP addresses use only the first 8 bits to identify the network part of the address. The remaining three octets (24 bit) can be used for the host portion of the address. Every network that uses a Class A IP address can be

address. Every network that uses a Class A IP address can be assigned up to $2^{24} - 2$ = 16,777,214 possible IP addresses to devices attached to the network.

MORE INFORMATION

The IP Loopback Address

It's easy to imagine why the network 0.0.0.0 is not used to address Internet hosts. Null values can confuse systems and are often reserved for special purposes. But what's special about 127.0.0.0? The entire Class A network 127.0.0.0 (which contains more than 16 million possible host addresses) has been "reserved" to accommodate one special address: 127.0.0.1. This address is used as a loopback. Data sent to 127.0.0.1 loops back to the sender, without traversing the network or even going through the network interface card. By sending test data (such as a **ping**) to 127.0.0.1, a host can test whether its IP software is working. This basic test should be performed:

```
Router>ping 127.0.0.1
Type escape sequence to abort.
Sending 5, 100-byte ICMP Echos to 127.0.0.1, timeout is 2 seconds:
!!!!!
Success rate is 100 percent (5/5), round-trip min/avg/max = 1/3/8 ms
```

Note that the last 3 octets can have any value except 0.0.0 or 255.255.255 for this test to work.

All TCP/IP hosts use this address to refer to themselves, the localhost. Because every IP-enabled device believes that it is connected to the 127.0.0.0 network, routing to that network is problematic. For this reason, this entire range of IP addresses has not been assigned for Internet use.

Class B

Class B addresses were designed to support the needs of moderate- to large-sized networks. The first 2 bits of a Class B address are always 10 (1 and 0) (see Figure 10-15). An example of a Class B IP address is 151.10.13.28. The first two octets identify the network number assigned by ARIN. The internal administrators of the network assign the remaining 16 bits. An easy way to recognize whether a device is part of a Class B network is to look at the first octet of its IP address. Class B IP network addresses always have values ranging from 128.0.0.0 to 191.255.0.0.

All Class B IP addresses use the first 16 bits to identify the network part of the address. The two remaining octets of the IP address can be used for the host portion of the address. Every network that uses a Class B IP address can have assigned up to $2^{16} - 2 = 65{,}534$ possible IP addresses to devices attached to the network.

MOVIE 10.4

IP Address Classes

Class B addresses explained.

Class C

The Class C address space is, by far, the most commonly used of the original IPv4 address classes. This address space was intended to support a small network. The first 3 bits of a Class C address are always 110 (1, 1, and 0) (see Figure 10-14). An example of a Class C IP address is 201.110.213.28. The first three octets identify the network number assigned by ARIN. The internal administrators of the network assign the remaining 8 bits. An easy way to recognize whether a device is part of a Class C network is to look at the first octet of its IP address. Class C IP network addresses always have values ranging from 192.0.0.0 to 223.255.255.0.

All Class C IP addresses use the first 24 bits to identify the network part of the address. Only the last octet of a Class C IP address can be used for the host portion of the address. Every network that uses a Class C IP address can have assigned up to $2^8 - 2 = 254$ possible IP addresses to devices attached to the network.

FIGURE 10-14 Specific IP address bit patterns are associated with Class A, Class B, and Class C IP addresses.

# bits	1	7			24
Class A:	0	Network #			Host #
# bits	1	1	14		16
Class B:	1	0	Network #		Host #
# bits	1	1	1	21	8
Class C:	1	1	0	Network #	Host #

IP Addresses as Decimal Numbers

IP addresses identify a device on a network and the network to which it is attached. To make them easy to remember, IP addresses are usually written in dotted-decimal notation. Therefore, IP addresses are four decimal numbers separated by dots. An example of this is the address 166.122.23.130. Keep in mind that a decimal number is a base 10 number, the type you use in everyday life.

Binary and Decimal Conversion Review

Each place in an octet represents a different power of 2. As in the base 10 number system, the powers increase from right to left (see Figure 10-15).

128	64	32	16	8	4	2	1
2^7	2^6	2^5	2^4	2^3	2^2	2^1	2^0
1	1	1	1	1	1	1	1

128 + 64 + 32 + 16 + 8 + 4 + 2 + 1 = 255

FIGURE 10-15 Each octet in an IP address can total a number less than or equal to 255.

Example:

10010000 (work from right to left)

$0 \times 2^0 = 0$

$0 \times 2^1 = 0$

$0 \times 2^2 = 0$

$0 \times 2^3 = 0$

$1 \times 2^4 = 16$

$0 \times 2^5 = 0$

$0 \times 2^6 = 0$

$1 \times 2^7 = 128$

Total = 144

In this example, there are 0 values of 2^0, 0 values of 2^1, 0 values of 2^2, 0 values of 2^3, 1 value of 2^4, 0 values of 2^5, 0 values of 2^6, and 1 value of 2^7. There are no 1s, no 2s, no 4s, no 8s, one 16, no 32s, no 64s, and one 128. Added, the values total 144; therefore, the binary number 10010000 equals the decimal number 144.

Converting Decimal IP Addresses to Binary Equivalents

To convert decimal IP addresses to binary numbers, you must know the decimal values of each of the 8 bits in each octet. Starting with the bit that is on the left side of the octet, the values start at 128 and are reduced by half each time you move 1 bit to the right, continuing to a value of 1 on the far right of the octet. The following conversion illustrates the first octet only.

Example:

Convert the first octet of 192.57.30.224 to a binary format.

128+	64+	0+	0+	0+	0+	0+	0= 192
2^7	2^6	2^5	2^4	2^3	2^2	2^1	2^0
1	1	0	0	0	0	0	0= 11000000

The first step is to select the octet on the far left and to determine whether the value is greater than 128. In this instance (192), it is. Then place a 1 in the first bit and subtract 128 from 192. The remainder is 64. The decimal value represented by the next bit is 64, which is equal to the value of the remainder, so that bit is 1 as well. Subtract 64 from 64. The remainder is 0, so the remaining bits are all 0. The binary number for the first octet is 11000000.

Exercise: Convert the remaining octets (57, 30, 224) in the IP address to binary format.

Converting Binary IP Addresses to Decimal Equivalents

To convert binary IP addresses to decimal numbers, use the opposite approach that you used to convert decimal numbers to binary numbers.

Example: Convert the first octet of the binary IP address 10101010.11111111.00000000.11001101 to a dotted-decimal number.

1	0	1	0	1	0	1	0	
2^7	2^6	2^5	2^4	2^3	2^2	2^1	2^0	
128	0	32	0	8	0	2	0	128 + 32 + 8 + 2 = 170

To convert this IP address, start with the bit that is on the far left side in the first octet—it is 1.

You know that the decimal value represented by a bit in that position is 128, so the decimal number starts with a value of 128. The next value is 0, so skip it. The third value is 1; a 1-bit in that position represents 32; therefore, you add 32 to 128 to get 160. The fourth bit is 0, so skip it. The fifth bit is 1, which means that you add 8 to the current total of 160, giving you a new total of 168. The sixth bit is also 0, so skip it; the seventh bit is 1, which means that you add 2 to the current total of 168. The last bit is 0, so you can skip it. Hence, 170 is the decimal value.

Reserved Address Space

If your computer wanted to communicate with of the devices on a network, it would be quite unmanageable to write out the IP address for each device. You might try two hyphenated addresses, indicating that you are referring to all devices within a range of numbers, but that, too, would be quite unmanageable. Fortunately, there is a shorter method.

An IP address that has binary 0s in all host bit positions is reserved for the network address (sometimes called the wire address). Therefore, as a Class A network example, 113.0.0.0 is the IP address of the network containing the host 113.1.2.3. A router uses a network's IP address when it forwards data on the Internet. As a Class B network example, the IP address 176.10.0.0 is a network address, as shown in Figure 10-16.

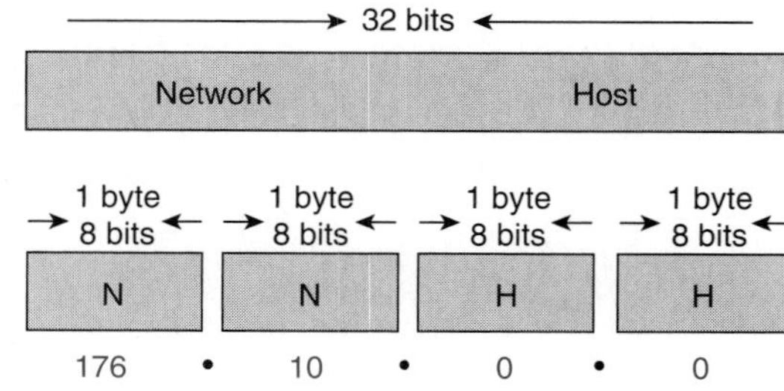

FIGURE 10-16
A network address, such as 176.10.0.0 is never used as an IP address for a device attached to the network.

The decimal numbers that fill the first two octets in a Class B network address are assigned. The last two octets contain 0s because those 16 bits are for host numbers and are used for devices that are attached to the network. The IP address in the example (176.10.0.0) is reserved for the network address; it is never be used as an address for any device that is attached to it.

If you wanted to send data to all the devices on a network, you would need to use a *broadcast address*. A broadcast occurs when a source sends out data to all devices on a network. To ensure that all of the devices on the network pay attention to the broadcast, the sender must use a destination IP address that all of them can recognize and pick up.

Broadcast IP addresses end with binary 1s in the entire host part of the address (the host field).

For the network in the example (176.10.0.0), in which the last 16 bits make up the host field (or host part of the address), the broadcast that would be sent out to all devices on that network would include a destination address of 176.10.255.255 (because 255 is the decimal value of an octet containing 11111111).

MOVIE 10.6

IP Reserved Addresses

Extensions explained.

Network ID

It is important to understand the significance of the network portion of an IP address, which is referred to as the network ID. Hosts on a network can communicate directly only with devices that have the same network ID. They might share the same physical segment, but if they have different network numbers, they usually cannot communicate with each other—unless there is another device that can make a connection between the networks.

ZIP codes and network IDs are quite similar in how they work. A ZIP code enables the postal system to direct your mail to your local post office and to your neighborhood. From there, the street address directs the carrier to the proper destination. A network ID enables a router to put a packet onto the appropriate network segment. The host ID helps the router deliver the Layer 2 frame encapsulating the packet to a specific host on the network. As a result, the host ID is mapped to the correct MAC address, which is needed by the Layer 2 process on the router to create the frame.

Broadcast Address

As stated earlier, a broadcast address is an address that has all 1s in the host field. When you send a broadcast packet on a network, all devices on the network process it. For example, on a network with an ID of 176.10.0.0, a broadcast that would reach all hosts would have the IP address 176.10.255.255 and the MAC address FFFF FFFF FFFF.

A broadcast address is quite similar to a bulk postal mailing. The ZIP code directs the mail to the appropriate area, and the broadcast address of "Current Resident" further directs the mail to every address. An IP broadcast address uses the same concept. The network number designates the segment, and the rest of the address tells every IP host in that network that this is a broadcast message and that the device needs to pay attention to the message. All devices on a network recognize their own host IP address (and MAC address) as well as the broadcast address for their network (and the MAC broadcast address).

Hosts for Classes of IP Addresses

Each class of network allows a fixed number of hosts. In a Class A network, the first octet is assigned, leaving the last three octets (24 bits) to be assigned to hosts. The maximum number of hosts in a Class A network is $2^{24} - 2$ (subtracting the network and broadcast reserved addresses), or 16,777,214 hosts.

In a Class B network, the first two octets are assigned, leaving the final two octets (16 bits) to be assigned to hosts. The maximum number of hosts in a Class B network is $2^{16} - 2$, or 65,534 hosts. In a Class C network, the first three octets are assigned. This leaves the final octet (8 bits) to assign to hosts, so the maximum number of hosts is $2^{8} - 2$, or 254 hosts. Remember that the first host address in each network (all 0s) is reserved for the actual network address (or network number), and the final host address in each network (all 1s) is reserved for broadcasts.

MORE INFORMATION

Inefficiencies in the System

The address classes have wasted a considerable number of potential addresses over the years. Consider, for example, a medium-sized company that requires 300 IP addresses. A single Class C address (254 addresses) is inadequate. Using two Class C addresses provides more than enough addresses but results in two separate domains within the company. This increases the size of the routing tables across the Internet: One table entry is required for each of the address spaces, even though they belong to the same organization.

MORE INFORMATION (CONTINUED)

Alternatively, stepping up to a Class B address provides all the needed addresses within a single domain but wastes 65,234 addresses. Too frequently, a Class B address was handed out whenever a network supported needed more than 254 hosts. Therefore, the Class B address space approached depletion more rapidly than the other classes.

Perhaps the most wasteful practice was that address spaces were handed out upon request. Any organization that wanted an address space just requested one; no attempts to verify need were made. Consequently, many organizations locked up substantial portions of the IPv4 address space as a hedge against some unseen, unspecified future need.

Fortunately, this is no longer the case. Numerous extensions to IP have been developed that are specifically designed to improve the efficiency with which the 32-bit address space can be used. Three of the more important of these are the following:

- Subnet masks
- Variable-length subnet masks (VLSM)
- Classless interdomain routing (CIDR)

Different mechanisms were designed to solve different problems. Subnet masks, both fixed and of variable length, were developed to accommodate the multiple logical networks that might exist within a physical site that connects to the Internet. CIDR was developed to eliminate the inefficiency inherent in the original rigid address classes. This enabled routers in the Internet to more efficiently aggregate many different network addresses into a single routing table entry. It is important to note that these two mechanisms are not mutually exclusive; they can and should be used together. For example, the two Class C addresses mentioned in the example can be represented with a single entry in the routing tables when CIDR is used.

Basics of Subnetting

The Internet's original two-level hierarchy assumed that each site would have only a single network. Therefore, each site would need only a single connection to the Internet. Initially, these were safe assumptions. Over time, however, network computing matured and expanded. By 1985, it was no longer safe to assume that an organization would have only a single network, nor that it would be satisfied with a single connection to the Internet.

MOVIE 10.7

Addressing Without Subnets

An explanation of addressing without subnets.

As sites began to develop multiple networks, it became obvious to the IETF that some mechanism was needed to differentiate among the multiple logical networks that were emerging as subsets of the Internet's second tier. Otherwise, there could be no efficient way to route data to specific end systems in sites with multiple networks. This is illustrated in Figure 10-17.

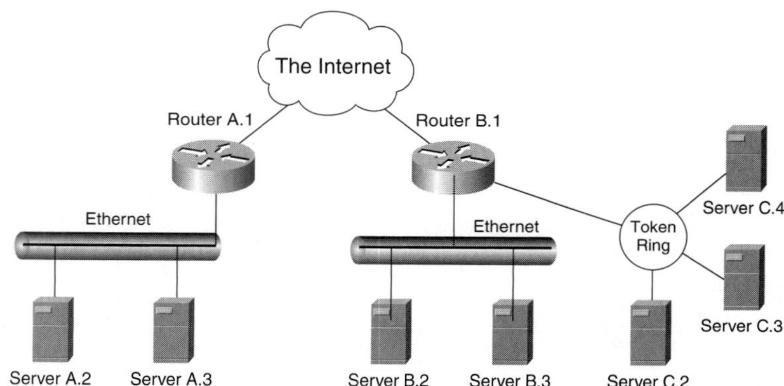

FIGURE 10-17
The emergence of multiple networks per site violated the Internet two-level hierarchy.

One answer was to give each logical network, or subnetwork, its own IP address range. This would work but would be a tremendously inefficient use of the IP address space. It wouldn't take very long for this approach to completely consume the remaining unassigned IP address ranges. A more immediate impact was the expansion of routing tables in the Internet's routers. Each network would require its own routing table entry. Clearly, a better approach was needed.

The answer was to organize these logical networks hierarchically and to route between them. From the Internet's perspective, sites with multiple logical networks should be treated as a single network. Therefore, they would share a common IP address range. However, they would need their own unique range of subnetwork numbers.

Classical IP Addressing

Network administrators sometimes need to divide networks, especially large ones, into smaller networks. These smaller divisions are called *subnetworks* and provide addressing flexibility. Normally, subnetworks are simply referred to as subnets. The concept of *subnetting* is based on the need for a third level in the Internet's addressing hierarchy. As internetworking technologies matured, their acceptance and use increased dramatically. As a result, it became common for moderate- and large-sized organizations to have multiple networks. Frequently, these networks were LANs. Each LAN might be treated as a subnet.

In such multiple-network environments, each subnetwork connected to the Internet via a common point: a router (see Figure 10-18). The actual details of the internal network environment are inconsequential to the Internet. They comprise a private network that is (or should be) capable of delivering its own datagrams. Therefore, the Internet must concern itself only with how to reach that network's gateway router to the Internet. Inside the private network, the host portion of the IP address can be subdivided to create subnetworks.

FIGURE 10-18
Four subnets make up network 172.16.0.0.

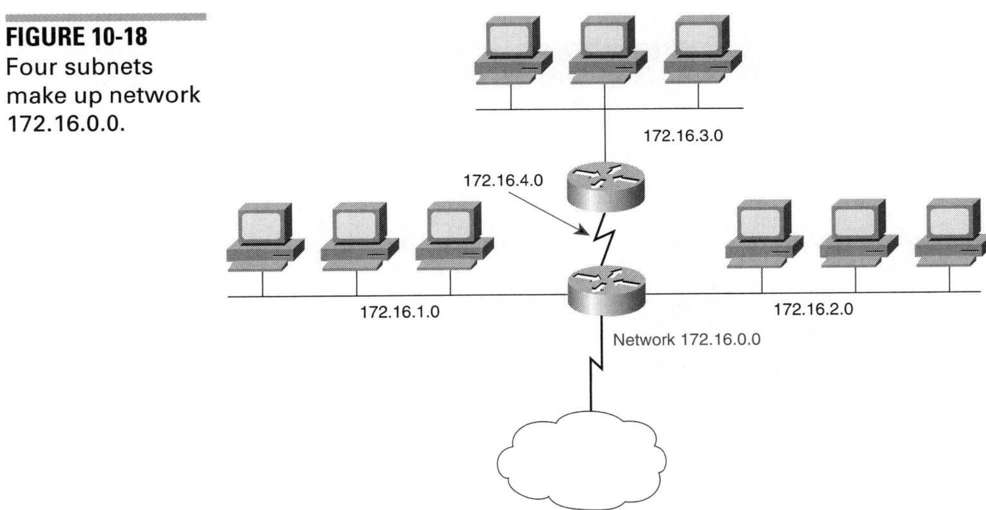

Because the subnet address is taken from the host number portion of Class A, Class B, and Class C addresses, it is assigned locally, usually by the network administrator. Also, like the other portions of IP addresses, each subnet address must be unique within its scope (see Figure 10-19).

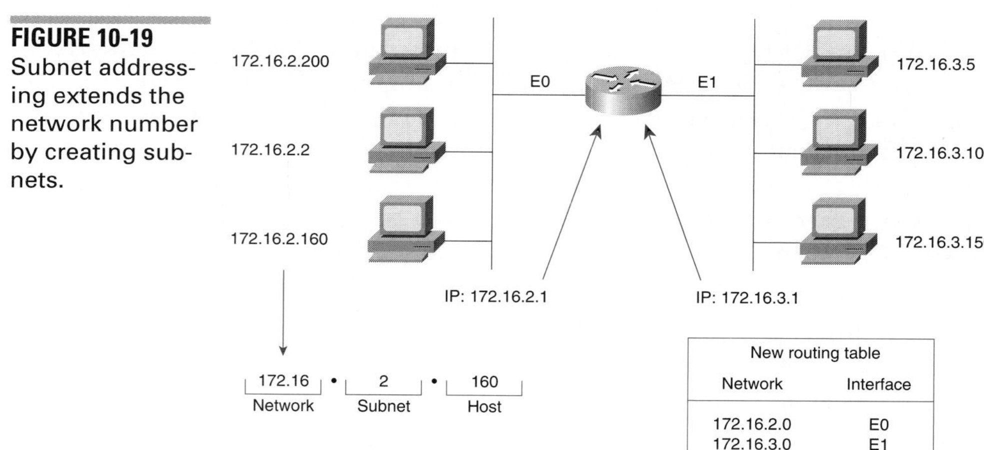

FIGURE 10-19 Subnet addressing extends the network number by creating subnets.

A primary reason for using subnets is to reduce the size of a broadcast domain. Broadcasts are sent to all hosts on a network or subnetwork. When broadcast traffic begins to consume too much of the available bandwidth, network administrators might choose to reduce the size of the broadcast domain.

MOVIE 10.8

Addressing With Subnets

An explanation of addressing with subnets.

MORE INFORMATION

Classless Interdomain Routing

A relatively recent functional addition to IP addressing is classless interdomain routing (CIDR). CIDR was born of the crisis that accompanied the Internet's explosive growth during the early 1990s. As early as 1992, the IETF became concerned with the Internet's capability to continue to scale upward in response to demand for Internet use. Its specific concerns were as follows:

- Exhaustion of the remaining unassigned IPv4 network addresses. The Class B space was in particular danger of depletion.
- The rapid and substantial increase in the size of the Internet's routing tables as a result of its growth.

MORE INFORMATION (CONTINUED)

To avoid the collapse of the Internet, the IETF decided that both short- and long-term solutions were needed. In the long term, the only viable solution was a completely new version of IP, with greatly expanded address space and address architectures. Ultimately, this solution became known as Internet Protocol: The Next Generation (IPng) or, more formally, as IP Version 6 (IPv6). The more pressing, short-term needs were to slow the rate of depletion of the remaining unassigned addresses. Part of the answer was to eliminate the inefficient classes of addresses in favor of a more flexible addressing architecture. The result was CIDR.

In September 1993, the plans for CIDR were released in RFCs 1517, 1518, 1519, and 1520. CIDR had key features that were invaluable in staving off depletion of the IPv4 address space:

- The elimination of classful addressing
- Enhanced route aggregation
- Supernetting
- Classless addressing

Mathematically, the IPv4 address space still held a substantial number of available addresses. Unfortunately, many of these potential addresses were squandered because they were locked into assigned blocks, or classes, of assigned addresses. Eliminating classes wouldn't necessarily recover the addresses locked into those address spaces that were already assigned, but it would enable the remaining addresses to be assigned much more efficiently. Ostensibly, this stop-gap effort would buy the time needed for IPv6 to be developed and deployed.

Enhanced Route Aggregation

CIDR enables Internet routers (or any CIDR-compliant router) to more efficiently aggregate routing information. In other words, a single entry in a routing table can represent the address spaces of many networks. This can greatly reduce the size of the routing tables that are needed in any given internetwork and directly translates to increased scalability.

CIDR was implemented initially on the Internet in 1994 and 1995. It was immediately effective in containing the expansion of the Internet routers' routing tables. It is doubtful that the Internet would have continued to grow if CIDR had not been implemented.

Supernetting

Supernetting is nothing more than using contiguous blocks of Class C address spaces to simulate a single—albeit larger—address space. If you obtained enough contiguous Class C addresses, you could redefine the allocation of bits between network and host identification fields and simulate a Class B address.

continues

MORE INFORMATION (CONTINUED)

Supernetting is designed to alleviate the pressure on the rapidly depleting Class B address space by offering a more flexible alternative. Supernetting is also designed to help reduce the routing table size. The previous class-based address architecture suffered from a tremendous disparity between its Class B and C networks. Networks that required more than the 254 hosts offered by a Class C network had the following two choices, neither of which was highly desirable:

1. Using multiple Class C addresses (which would have necessitated routing between the network domains)
2. Stepping up to a Class B address with its 65,534 usable host addresses

Frequently, the simpler solution was to use the Class B address, even though it wasted tens of thousands of IP addresses.

How CIDR Works

CIDR represented a dramatic break from tradition in that it completely abandoned the rigid classes of IP addresses. The original IPv4 address architecture used an 8-bit network number for Class A addresses, a 16-bit network number for Class B addresses, and a 24-bit number for Class C addresses. CIDR replaced these categories with a more generalized *network prefix*. This prefix could be of any length, rather than just 8, 16, or 24 bits. This allows CIDR to craft network address spaces according to the size of a network instead of force-fitting networks into presized network address spaces.

Each CIDR-compliant network address is advertised with a specific bit mask. This mask identifies the length of the network prefix. For example, 192.125.61.8/20 identifies a CIDR address with a 20-bit network address. The IP address can be any mathematically valid address, regardless of whether that address was originally part of the Class A, B, or C range! CIDR-compliant routers look at the number after the slash (/) to determine the network number. Therefore, the former Class C address 192.125.61.8 previously had a network number of 192.125.61 and a host number of 8. With a Class C address, you could provide addresses for a maximum of 254 hosts within the network. Using CIDR, the architectural limitations of the 8-bit boundaries between address components is eliminated. To better understand how this works, it is necessary to translate the decimal number to binary.

In binary, the network portion of this address is 11000000.01111101.00111101. The first 20 bits of this example identify the network number.

MORE INFORMATION (CONTINUED)

The split between the network and host portions of the address falls in the middle of the third octet. The bits that aren't allocated to the network number are used to identify hosts. Therefore, an IPv4 address with a 20-bit network prefix has 12 bits left for host identification. Mathematically, this translates to 4094 usable host addresses. Because none of the left-most bits is preset (which previously established the address class), virtually the entire range of addresses can be used in a CIDR network. Therefore, a 20-bit network prefix can be associated with Class A, B, or C networks.

Subnetworks

Subnet addresses include the Class A, Class B, or Class C network portion, plus a subnet field and a host field. The subnet field and the host field are created from the original host portion for the entire network. The capability to decide how to divide the original host portion into the new subnet and host fields provides addressing flexibility for the network administrator. To create a subnet address, a network administrator borrows bits from the original host portion and designates them as the subnet field. The minimum number of bits that can be borrowed is 2.

MOVIE 10.9

Subnet Addresses

A subnet address includes the network number, subnet number and host number.

If you borrowed only 1 bit to create a subnet, you would have only a network number, the 0.0 network, and the broadcast number, the 0.1 network. The maximum number of bits that can be borrowed can be any number that leaves at least 2 bits remaining for the host number (see Figure 10-20). In this example of a Class C IP address, bits from the host field for the subnet field have been borrowed.

MOVIE 10.10

Creating Subnet Addresses

Bits explained.

FIGURE 10-20
If a 1-bit is in the subnet mask under any field in the IP address, that bit is part of the network or subnetwork field.

Network • Network • Network • Subnet mask host
Octet (8 bits) • Octet (8 bits) • Octet (8 bits) • Octet (8 bits)
$2^7\ 2^6\ 2^5\ 2^4\ 2^3\ 2^2\ 2^1\ 2^0 . 2^7\ 2^6\ 2^5\ 2^4\ 2^3\ 2^2\ 2^1\ 2^0 . 2^7\ 2^6\ 2^5\ 2^4\ 2^3\ 2^2\ 2^1\ 2^0 . 2^7\ 2^6\ 2^5\ 2^4\ 2^3\ 2^2\ 2^1\ 2^0$
1 1 1 1 1 1 1 1 1 1 1 1 1 1 1 1 1 1 1 1 1 1 1 1 1 1 1 0 0 0 0 0
Subnet field
New host field

Subnet Mask

> **NOTE**
> The extended network prefix includes the Class A, B, or C network number, plus the subnet field (or subnet number) that is being used to extend the routing information (which is otherwise just the network number).

The subnet mask (formal term: extended network prefix) is not an address, but it determines which part of an IP address is the network field and which part is the host field. A subnet mask is 32 bits long and has four octets, just like an IP address.

To determine the subnet mask for a particular subnetwork IP address, follow these steps:

Step 1 Express the subnetwork IP address in binary form.

Step 2 Replace the network and subnet portion of the address with all 1s.

Step 3 Replace the host portion of the address with all 0s.

Step 4 Convert the binary expression back to dotted-decimal notation.

Boolean Operations: AND, OR, and NOT

The term *operations* in mathematics refers to rules that define how one number combines with other numbers or how a single number is affected. Decimal number operations include addition, subtraction, multiplication, and division. There are related but different operations for working with binary numbers. The basic Boolean operations are AND, OR, and NOT.

- AND is like multiplication.
- OR is like addition.
- NOT changes 1 to 0, and 0 to 1.

Performing the AND Function

The network or subnet address has all 0s in the host portion. To route a data packet, the router must first determine the destination network/subnet address by performing a logical AND using the destination host's IP address and the subnet mask. The result is the network/subnet address.

SKILL BUILDER

Lab Activity: Subnet Mask 1—Class C with 2 Subnets

In this lab, you learn the basics of IP subnet masks and their use with TCP/IP networks.

In Figure 10-21, the router has received a packet for host 131.108.2.2; it uses the AND operation to learn that this packet should be routed to subnet 131.108.2.0.

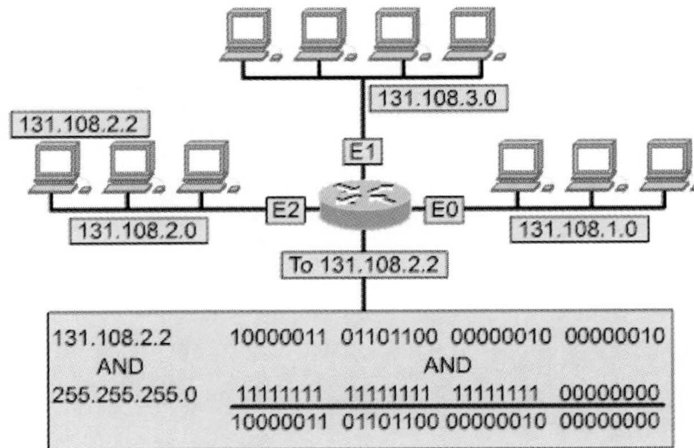

FIGURE 10-21 The AND function.

Creating a Subnet

To create subnets, you must extend the routing portion of the address. The Internet "knows" your network as a whole, identified by the Class A, B, or C address, which defines 8, 16, or 24 routing bits (the network number). The subnet field represents additional routing bits so that the routers within your organization can recognize different locations, or subnets, within the whole network.

Subnet masks use the same format as IP addresses. In other words, each is 32 bits long and is divided into four octets. Subnet masks have all 1s in the network and subnetwork portion, and all 0s in the host portion. By default, if no bits are borrowed, the subnet mask for a Class B network is 255.255.0.0. However, if 8 bits were borrowed, the subnet mask for the same Class B network would be 255.255.255.0, as shown in Figure 10-22 and Figure 10-23. However, because there are two octets in the host field of a Class B network, up to 14 bits can be borrowed to create subnetworks. A Class C network has only one octet in the host field. Therefore, only up to 6 bits can be borrowed in Class C networks to create subnetworks.

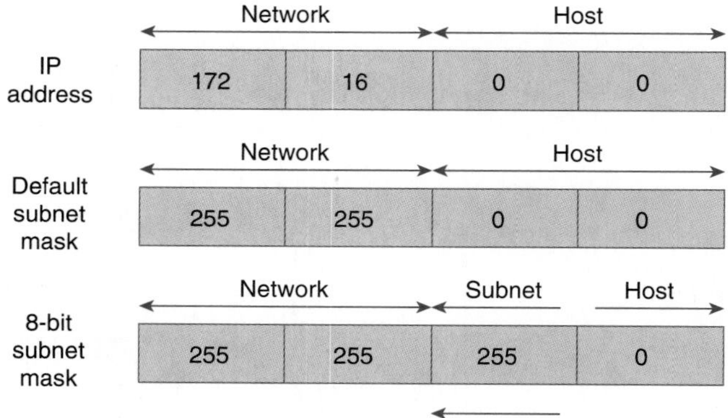

FIGURE 10-22 If you borrow bits for a subnet mask, use host bits starting at the high-order bit position.

FIGURE 10-23 The decimal equivalent of the binary is typically used in an IP address.

128	64	32	16	8	4	2	1		
1	0	0	0	0	0	0	0	=	128
1	1	0	0	0	0	0	0	=	192
1	1	1	0	0	0	0	0	=	224
1	1	1	1	0	0	0	0	=	240
1	1	1	1	1	0	0	0	=	248
1	1	1	1	1	1	0	0	=	252
1	1	1	1	1	1	1	0	=	254
1	1	1	1	1	1	1	1	=	255

Question: In the address 131.108.0.0, which are the routing bits?

Answer: 131.108. That's the 16-bit Class B network number.

Question: What are the other two octets (16 bits) of the address 131.108.0.0 used for?

Answer: Well, as far as the Internet knows, that's just a 16-bit host field because that's what a Class B address is: a 16-bit network number and a 16-bit host number.

Question: What part of the address 131.108.0.0 is the subnet field?

Answer: When you decide to create subnets, you must divide the original host field (16 bits, in the case of Class B) into two parts: the subnet field and the host field. This is sometimes referred to as "borrowing" some of the original host bits to create the subnet field. The other networks in the Internet won't care—they look at the address the same—because all they see is the Class A, B, or C network number. The minimum number of bits that you can borrow is 2, regardless of whether you're working with a Class A, B, or C network. Because at least 2 bits must remain for host numbers, the maximum number of bits borrowed varies by address class. (See Table 10-1.)

TABLE 10-1 Subnets

Address Class	Size of Default Host Field	Maximum Number of Subnet Bits
A	24	22
B	16	14
C	8	6

The subnet field always immediately follows the network number. That is, the borrowed bits must be the first n bits of the default host field, where *n* is the desired size of the new subnet field (see Figure 10-24). The subnet mask is the tool used by the router to determine which bits are routing bits and which bits are host bits.

FIGURE 10-24 A subnet address is created by borrowing bits from the host field and designating them as subnet bits.

Class B

NETWORK	HOST

Before Subnetting

NETWORK	SUBNET	HOST

After Subnetting

MORE INFORMATION

Enabling the Use of Subnet 0

The benefits of subnetting come at a price—each time you subnet, some of your addresses become unusable and are therefore wasted. For example, a 26-bit mask applied to the Class C network 192.168.1.0 yields the following four subnets:

- 192.168.1.0
- 192.168.1.64
- 192.168.1.128
- 192.168.1.192

A 26-bit mask means that the first three octets comprise the network number, and the first two bits of the last octet comprise the subnet field. Note that the subnets have the first three octets in common (192.168.1). The "action" is in the fourth octet. In this case, the first 2 bits of the fourth octet determine what subnet an address belongs to.

Decimal Range	Subnet No.#	Subnet Address	Broadcast
0 to 63	Subnet 0	00000000	00111111
64 to 127	Subnet 1	01000000	01111111
128 to 191	Subnet 2	10000000	10111111

You might have been taught that the first subnet, subnet 0, should not be used because its subnet address can be confused with the major network number. For example, if network 192.168.1.0 is subnetted with subnet mask 255.255.255.192, subnet 0 would be written as 192.168.1.0, which is identical to the major network address.

The last subnet presents a similar problem, but with its subnet broadcast address, which is identical to the network broadcast address (192.168.1.255). If both of these subnets were discarded, half of the previous addresses (0 to 63 and 192 to 255) would be lost.

MORE INFORMATION (CONTINUED)

One way to reduce the waste caused by subnetting is to borrow more bits from the host field, thereby increasing the size of the subnet field. By borrowing just one more bit, the lost address space is cut in half.

Decimal Range	Subnet No.	Subnet Address	Broadcast
0 to 31	Subnet 0	00000000	00011111
32 to 63	Subnet 1	00100000	00111111
64 to 95	Subnet 2	01000000	01011111
96 to 127	Subnet 3	01100000	01111111
128 to 159	Subnet 4	10000000	10011111
160 to 191	Subnet 5	10100000	10111111
192 to 223	Subnet 6	11000000	11011111
224 to 255	Subnet 7	11100000	11111111

In this example, only the ranges 0 to 31 and 224 to 255 are lost. But wouldn't it be great to "reclaim" those lost ranges (subnet 0 and subnet 7)? The Cisco IOS enables an administrator to reclaim the IP space lost to subnet 0. This can create problems with older TCP/IP software, but the practice of using subnet 0 has become common enough that, since IOS 12.0, Cisco routers use subnet 0 by default. If you're not using IOS 12.0 or later, you can enable the use of subnet 0 with the following global configuration command:

```
RTA(config)#ip subnet-zero
```

If you ever need to turn off this feature, add a "no" in front of the command:

```
RTA(config)#no ip subnet-zero
```

Determining Subnet Mask Size

Again, subnet masks contain all 1s in the network bit positions (determined by the address class) as well as the subnet bit positions, and they contain all 0s in the remaining bit positions, designating them as the host portion of an address.

By default, if you borrow no bits, the subnet mask for a Class B network would be 255.255.0.0, which is the dotted-decimal equivalent of 1s in the 16 bits corresponding to the Class B network number and 0s in the other 16 bits. If 8 bits were borrowed for the subnet field, the subnet mask would include 8 additional 1-bits and would become 255.255.255.0.

For example, if the subnet mask 255.255.255.0 were associated with the Class B address 130.5.2.144 (8 bits borrowed for subnetting), the router would know to route this packet to subnet 130.5.2.0 rather than just to network 130.5.0.0 (see Figure 10-25).

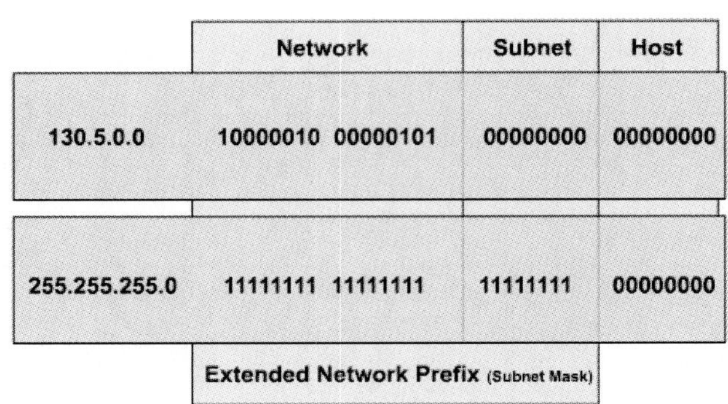

Network
Subnet
Host
130.5.0.0
10000010 00000101
00000000
00000000
255.255.255.0
11111111 11111111
11111111
00000000
Extended Network Prefix (Subnet Mask)

FIGURE 10-25
Subnet masking example.

Another example is the Class C address 197.15.22.131 with a subnet mask of 255.255.255.224. With a value of 224 in the final octet (11100000, in binary), the 24-bit Class C network portion has been extended by 3 bits, to make the total 27 bits. The 131 in the last octet now presents the third usable host address in the subnet 197.15.22.128 (see Figure 10-26). The routers in the Internet (that don't know the subnet mask) worry about only routing to the Class C network 197.15.22.0, while the routers inside that network, knowing the subnet mask, will be looking at 27 bits to make a routing decision.

FIGURE 10-26
Subnet masking example.

11000101	00001111	00010110	10000011
Network Field		Subnetwork Field	Host Field

Computing Subnet Mask and IP Address

Whenever you borrow bits from the host field, it is important to note the number of additional subnets that are being created each time you borrow one more bit. You have already learned that you cannot borrow only 1 bit; the fewest you can borrow is 2 bits.

Borrowing 2 bits creates four possible subnets (2 × 2) (but you must remember that there are two reserved/unusable subnets). Each time you borrow another bit from the host field, the number of subnets created increases by a power of 2.

Eight possible subnets are created by borrowing 3 bits (2 × 2 × 2). Sixteen possible subnets are created by borrowing 4 bits (2 × 2 × 2 × 2). From these examples, it is easy to see that each time you borrow another bit from the host field, the number of possible subnets doubles.

Question: How many bits are being borrowed (how long is the subnet field) for a Class B network using a subnet mask of 255.255.240.0?

Answer: The first two octets of the mask (255.255) correspond with the 16 bits in a Class B network number. Remember that the subnet field is represented by all the additional 1-bits beyond that. The number 240 decimal is 11110000 in binary, so you see that 4 bits are borrowed for the subnet field.

Question: How many possible subnets are there with a 4-bit subnet field?

Answer: Start with finding the smallest 4-bit number—0000 (0)—and then the largest 4-bit number—1111 (15). So, there are 16 possible subnets (0 to 15). However, you know that you cannot use subnet 0 (it's part of the network address), and you cannot use subnet 15 (part of the network broadcast address). So, this 4-bit subnet field gives you 14 usable subnets (1 to 14).

Computing Hosts Per Subnetwork

Each time you borrow 1 bit from a host field, there is 1 less bit remaining that can be used for host numbers. Specifically, each time you borrow another bit from the host field, the number of host addresses that you can assign decreases by a power of 2 (gets cut in half).

To help you understand how this works, use a Class C network address as an example. If there is no subnet mask, all 8 bits in the last octet are used for the host field. Therefore, there are 256 (2^8) possible addresses available to assign to hosts (254 usable addresses, after you subtract the 2 that you know you can't use). Now, imagine that this Class C network is divided into subnets. If you borrow 2 bits from the default 8-bit host field, the host field decreases in size to 6 bits. If you wrote out all the possible combinations of 0s and 1s that could occur in the remaining 6 bits, you would discover that the total number of possible hosts that could be assigned in each subnet would be reduced to 64 (26^6). The number of usable host numbers would be reduced to 62.

In the same Class C network, if you borrow 3 bits, the size of the host field decreases to 5 bits, and the total number of hosts that you could assign to each subnet would be reduced to 32 (2^5). The number of usable host numbers would be reduced to 30.

The number of possible host addresses that can be assigned to a subnet is related to the number of subnets that have been created. In a Class C network, for example, if a subnet mask of 255.255.255.224 has been applied, then 3 bits (224 in decimal = 11100000 in binary) would have been borrowed from the host field. Six usable subnets are created (8 – 2), each having 30 (32 – 2) useable host addresses.

Boolean AND Operation

As mentioned earlier, the network or subnet address has all 0s in the host portion. To route a data packet, the router must first determine the destination network/subnet address. To accomplish this, the router performs a logical AND using the destination host's IP address and the subnet mask for that network.

SKILL BUILDER

Lab Activity; Subnet Mask 2—Class B with Three Subnets

This lab focuses on a Class B network with three subnets. It helps you develop a better understanding of IP subnet masks.

Imagine that you have a Class B network with the network number 172.16.0.0. After assessing the needs of your network, you decide to borrow 8 bits to create subnets. As you learned earlier, when you borrow 8 bits with a Class B network, the subnet mask is 255.255.255.0 (see Figure 10-27).

FIGURE 10-27
Eight bits of subnetting.

	Network	Subnet	Host
IP Host Address 172.16.2.120	10101100 00010000	00000010	01111000
Subnet Mask 255.255.255.0 or /24	11111111 11111111	11111111	00000000
Subnet	10101100 00010000 172 16	00000010 2	00000000 0

Someone outside the network sends data to the IP address 172.16.2.120. To determine where to deliver the data, the router ANDs this address with the subnet mask.

When the two numbers are ANDed, the host portion of the result is always 0. What is left is the network number, including the subnet. Thus, the data is sent to subnet 172.16.2.0, and only the final router notices that the packet should be delivered to host 120 in that subnet.

Now, imagine that you have the same network, 172.16.0.0. This time, however, you decide to borrow only 7 bits for the subnet field. The binary subnet mask for this would be 11111111.11111111.11111110.00000000. What would this be in dotted-decimal notation?

Again, someone outside the network sends data to host 172.16.2.120. To determine where to send the data, the router again ANDs this address with the subnet mask. As before, when the two numbers are ANDed, the host portion of the result is 0. So what is different in this second example? Everything looks the same—at least, in decimal. The difference is in the number of subnets available and the number of hosts available per subnet. You can see this only by comparing the two different subnet masks (see Figure 10-28).

FIGURE 10-28
Network number extended by 7 bits.

	Network	Subnet	Host
IP Host Address 172.16.2.120	10101100 00010000	00000010	01111000
Subnet Mask 255.255.254.0 or /23	11111111 11111111	11111110	00000000
Subnet	10101100 00010000 172 16	00000010 2	00000000 0

With 7 bits in the subnet field, there can be only 126 subnets. How many hosts can there be in each subnet? How long is the host field? With 9 bits for host numbers, there can be 510 hosts in each of those 126 subnets.

Figure 10-27 and Figure 10-28 include something you'll learn more about later: an alternate way to express the subnet mask. You learned that the 1s of the mask represent the routing bits—the network plus the subnet. 255.255.255.0 indicates that there are 24 total routing bits. This is sometimes indicated by following an IP address with "/24", as in 131.108.3.1/24—this says the same thing as the longer subnet mask.

MORE INFORMATION

Variable-Length Subnet Masking

Although subnetting proved a valuable addition to the Internet addressing architecture, it did suffer from one fundamental limitation: You were limited to a single subnet mask for an entire network. Therefore, after you selected a subnet mask (which dictated the number of hosts that you could support per subnet), you couldn't support subnets of a different size. Any requirement for larger-sized subnets meant that you had to change the size of the subnet mask for the entire network. Needless to say, this could be a complicated and time-consuming affair.

A solution to this problem arose in 1987. The IETF published RFC 1009, which specified how a subnetted network could use more than one subnet mask. Ostensibly, each subnet mask could be a different size. The new subnetting technique, therefore, was called VLSM.

VLSM enables a more efficient use of an organization's IP address space by enabling the network's administrator(s) to customize the size of a subnet mask to the specific requirements of each subnet. To illustrate this point, assume a base IP address of 172.16.0.0. This is a Class B address, which uses a 16-bit network number. Extending the network prefix by 6 bits results in a 22-bit extended network prefix. Mathematically, there are 62 usable subnet addresses and 1022 usable host addresses per subnet.

This subnetting scheme would make sense if the organization needed more than 30 subnets populated with more than 500 hosts per subnet. However, if the organization consisted of a few large suborganizations with more than 500 hosts each and many smaller suborganizations with just 40 or 50 host devices each, the majority of possible IP addresses would be wasted. Each organization, regardless of need, would be allocated a subnet with 1022 host addresses. The smaller organizations would each waste approximately 950 host addresses. Given that a subnetted network could use only a single mask of fixed and predetermined length, such address waste could not be avoided.

Recall that the size of an extended network prefix can be identified by using a / followed by the number of bits used for the network and subnetwork addressing. Therefore, 193.168.125.0/27 identifies a specific Class C address, with 27 bits used for the extended network prefix.

As a purely mathematical exercise, subnetting was an ideal solution to a vexing problem: the rapid depletion of the finite IP address space. Enabling private networks to redefine the host field of an IP address into subnetwork and host addresses greatly reduces the amount of wasted IP addresses.

MORE INFORMATION (CONTINUED)

Unfortunately, in a real-world setting, the need for subnets is not homogeneous. It is not realistic to expect an organization or its networks to be divided into uniformly sized subcomponents. It is much more likely that there will be organizations (and subnetworks) of all sizes. Therefore, using a fixed-length subnet mask would still result in wasted IP host addresses in each subnet defined.

The solution to this dilemma was to allow an IP address space to be subnetted flexibly using different-sized subnet masks. Using the preceding example, a network administrator could carve a base IP address into different-sized subnets. The few large organizations could continue to use the 22-bit extended network prefix, whereas the smaller organizations could be given a 25- or 26-bit extended network prefix. The 25-bit prefix would enable the creation of 126-host subnets, and the 26-bit prefix would permit subnets with up to 62 hosts each. This solution is VLSM.

IP Configuration on a Network Diagram

When you configure routers, you must connect each interface to a different network segment. Then, each of these segments become a separate subnet. You must select an address from each different subnet to assign to the interface of the router that connects to that subnet. Each segment of a network—the actual wires and links—must have different network/subnet numbers. Figure 10-29 shows what a network diagram might look like using a subnetted Class B network.

NOTE

The number of subnets required in turn determines the number of hosts available. For example, if you borrow 3 bits with a Class C network, only 5 bits remain for hosts.

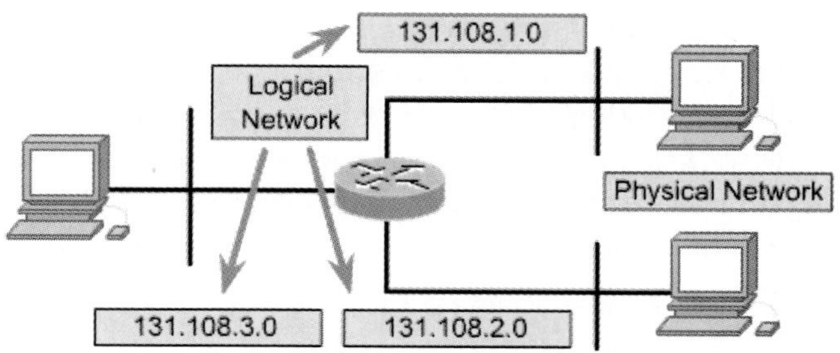

FIGURE 10-29 The router connects subnets and networks.

Host and Subnet Schemes

One of the decisions that you must make whenever you create subnets is to determine the optimal number of subnets and hosts. (See Figure 10-30.)

When you create subnets, you lose quite a few potential addresses. For this reason, network administrators must pay close attention to the percentage of addresses that they lose by creating subnets.

FIGURE 10-30
The number of lost IP addresses with a Class C network depends on the number of bits borrowed for subnetting.

Number of Bits Borrowed	Number of Subnets Created	Number of Hosts Per Subnet	Total Number of Hosts	Percent Used
2	2	62	124	49%
3	6	30	180	71%
4	14	14	196	77%
5	30	6	180	71%
6	62	2	124	49%

SKILL BUILDER

Lab Activity: Subnet Mask C—Class C with Three Subnets

This lab focuses on a Class C network with three subnets and using a custom subnet mask. It helps you develop a better understanding of IP subnet masks.

Here's an example: If you borrow 2 bits with a Class C network, you create 4 subnets, each with 64 hosts. Only 2 of the subnets are usable, and only 62 hosts are usable per subnet, giving 124 usable hosts out of 254 that were possible before you chose to use subnets. This means that you are losing 51 percent of your addresses.

Imagine, this time, that you borrow 3 bits. You now have 8 subnets, of which only 6 are usable, with 30 usable hosts per subnet. This gives you a total of 180 usable hosts, down from 254, but now you are losing only 29 percent of your addresses. Whenever you create subnets, you need to take into consideration future network growth and the percentage of addresses that you lose by creating subnets. It turns out that by borrowing half of the maximum possible number of bits, you lose the least number of host addresses (refer to Figure 10-30).

Private Addresses

Certain addresses in each class of IP address are not assigned. These addresses are called *private addresses* (see Figure 10-31). Private addresses might be used by hosts that use network address translation (NAT) or a proxy server to connect to the Internet, or by hosts that do not connect to the Internet at all.

FIGURE 10-31
Private address space.

The following ranges are available for private addressing

10.0.0.0 - 10.255.255.255

172.16.0.0 - 172.31.255.255

192.168.0.0 - 192.168.255.255

Many applications require connectivity within only one network and do not need external connectivity. In large networks, TCP/IP is often used even when network layer connectivity outside the network isn't needed. Banks are good examples: They might use TCP/IP to connect to automatic teller machines (ATMs). These machines do not connect to the public network, so private addresses are ideal for them. Private addresses can also be used on a network on which there are not enough public addresses available.

The private addresses can be used together with a network address translation (NAT) server. Either a NAT server or a proxy server is needed to provide connectivity to all hosts in a network that has relatively few public addresses available. By agreement, any traffic with a destination address within one of the private address ranges will not be routed on the Internet.

MORE INFORMATION

Network Address Translation

Network address translation (NAT), as defined by RFC 1631, is the process of swapping one address for another in the IP packet header. In practice, NAT is used to allow hosts that are privately addressed to access the Internet.

A NAT-enabled device, such as a UNIX box or a Cisco router, operates at the border of a stub domain (an internetwork that has a single connection to the outside world). When a host inside the stub domain wants to transmit to a host on the outside, it forwards the packet to the NAT box. The NAT process then looks inside the IP header and, if appropriate, replaces the local IP (inside) address with a globally unique IP address. When an outside host sends a response, the NAT process receives it, checks the current table of network address translations, and replaces the destination address with the original inside source address.

continues

MORE INFORMATION (CONTINUED)

In Figure 10-32, the host 10.4.4.5 transmits a packet to an Internet host. Because a private address can't be routed on the Internet, this host uses the services of a router running NAT. The NAT router alters the IP packet by removing the original source address, 10.4.4.5, and replacing it with a globally unique address from a pool defined by an administrator (in this case, 2.2.2.3). The NAT box keeps a record of this address swap in a NAT table. When the Internet host's reply packet is sent to 2.2.2.3, it arrives at the NAT router, which checks its NAT table for the mapping to the inside address. The NAT router then replaces the destination address with the original inside address, 10.4.4.5.

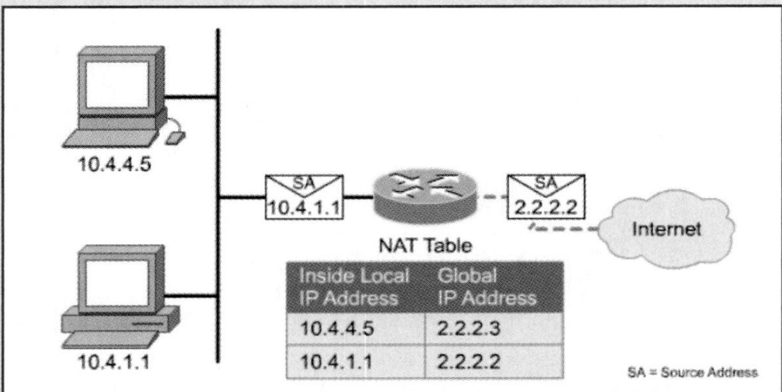

FIGURE 10-32 NAT routers keep a table that maps global IP addresses to private, internal addresses.

Why would Company XYZ use private addresses instead of "real" IP address to access the Internet? One advantage of NAT is that because not every inside host needs outside access at the same time, Company XYZ can get away with using a small pool of globally unique addresses to serve a relatively large number of privately addressed hosts.

NAT comes as a great relief to organizations that outgrow their address space. For instance, if a school with a Class C address suddenly finds that more than 500 nodes on campus need occasional Internet access, NAT might provide a convenient solution.

NAT has the effect of hiding the inside structure of a network. Although NAT is not a security firewall, it can prevent outsiders from connecting directly to inside hosts, unless a permanent global address mapping exists in the NAT table. If Company XYZ actually wants outside users to access an internally addressed Web server, an administrator can statically map a global address (2.2.2.3) to an inside address (10.0.0.1). Internet hosts and DNS can use the global address to access the privately addressed Web server.

MORE INFORMATION (CONTINUED)

A powerful NAT feature enables administrators to map one global address to multiple inside addresses for the purpose of distributing conversations among multiple (usually mirrored) hosts. In Figure 10-33, Company XYZ has configured its NAT router to rotate conversations between two inside Web servers at 10.0.0.1 and 10.0.0.2 when an outside host requests Web services at 2.2.2.3.

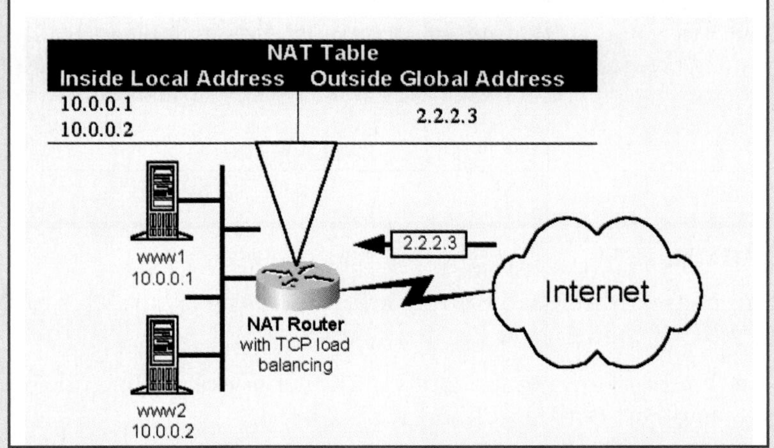

FIGURE 10-33 Assignment of multiple addresses to a single outside address.

The capability to create static mappings makes NAT a useful tool if Company XYZ ever changed providers. Because CIDR places the authority to assign addresses at the ISP level, if Company XYZ moved from one ISP to another, it might have to completely readdress its systems with the new ISP's CIDR block. Instead of readdressing, NAT can be deployed to temporarily translate the old addresses to new ones, with static mappings in place to keep Web and other public services available to the outside world. In fact, some organizations opt to use RFC 1918 addressing and NAT permanently to avoid ever having to renumber hosts. If such a company changes ISPs, it can just configure NAT to translate to the new address pool.

MORE INFORMATION

NAT for the Home User

The advent of broadband Internet connections in the home has had an interesting side effect: Average home users are networking their own computers with the goal of sharing a single high-speed Internet connection. Recognizing this new market, vendors have quickly packaged affordable NAT solutions for the home. Some products are stand-alone solutions or appliances that provide "many-to-one" NAT along with DHCP services—all with little or no configuration. Other products are software solutions that run on a computer with multiple logical addresses. Notable among these software solutions is Internet Connection Sharing, which ships with Microsoft's latest versions of Windows. With NAT now built into the world's most ubiquitous operating system, you can bet that its popularity will increase.

Summary

This chapter discussed routing and addressing as it relates to the network layer of the OSI model. You learned that

- Internetworking functions of the network layer include network addressing and best-path selection for data traffic.
- Two addressing methods exist: flat and hierarchical.
- An organization can receive three classes of IP addresses from ARIN: Class A, B, and C.
- ARIN reserves Class A addresses for governments throughout the world, Class B addresses for medium-size to large companies, and Class C addresses for all other entities.
- When written in a binary format, the first bit of a Class A address is always 0, the first 2 bits of a Class B address are always 10, and the first 3 bits of a Class C address are always 110.
- To provide extra flexibility for the network administrator, networks—particularly large ones—are often divided into smaller networks called subnetworks or subnets.
- Subnets are concealed from outside networks by using masks referred to as subnet masks.

In the next chapter, you see how devices and routing protocols operate at the network layer.

Check Your Understanding

1. How do MAC addresses differ from that of the network layer?
   - **A.** The network layer requires a hierarchical addressing scheme as opposed to the MAC's flat addressing scheme.
   - **B.** The network layer uses addresses in the binary format, whereas the MAC's addresses are hexadecimal.
   - **C.** The network layer uses a transferable unique address.
   - **D.** None of the above.
2. How many bits are in an IP address?
   - **A.** 16
   - **B.** 32
   - **C.** 64
   - **D.** None of the above
3. What is the maximum value of each octet in an IP address?
   - **A.** 128
   - **B.** 255
   - **C.** 256
   - **D.** None of the above
4. The network number plays what part in an IP address?
   - **A.** It specifies the network to which the host belongs.
   - **B.** It specifies the identity of the computer on the network.
   - **C.** It specifies which node on the subnetwork is being addressed.
   - **D.** It specifies which networks the device can communicate with.
5. The host number plays what part in an IP address?
   - **A.** It designates the identity of the computer on the network.
   - **B.** It designates which node on the subnetwork is being addressed.
   - **C.** It designates the network to which the host belongs.
   - **D.** It designates which hosts the device can communicate with.

6. What is the decimal equivalent to the binary number 101101?

   A. 32

   B. 35

   C. 45

   D. 44

7. Convert the following decimal number to its binary form: 192.5.34.11.

   A. 11000000.00000101.00100010.00001011

   B. 11000101.01010111.00011000.10111000

   C. 01001011.10010011.00111001.00110111

   D. 11000000.00001010.01000010.00001011

8. Convert the following binary IP address to its decimal form: 11000000.00000101.00100010.00001011.

   A. 190.4.34.11

   B. 192.4.34.10

   C. 192.4.32.11

   D. None of the above

9. What portion of the following Class B address is the network address: 154.19.2.7?

   A. 154

   B. 154.19

   C. 154.19.2

   D. 154.19.2.7

10. Which portion of the IP address 129.219.51.18 represents the network?

    A. 129.219

    B. 129

    C. 14.1

    D. 1

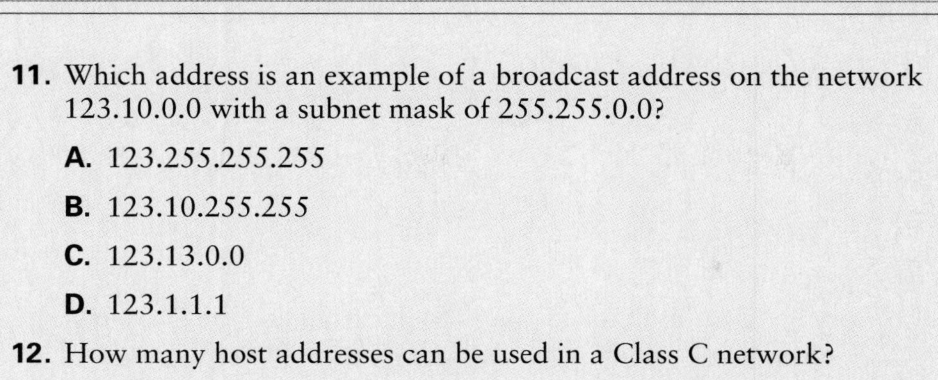

11. Which address is an example of a broadcast address on the network 123.10.0.0 with a subnet mask of 255.255.0.0?

A. 123.255.255.255

B. 123.10.255.255

C. 123.13.0.0

D. 123.1.1.1

12. How many host addresses can be used in a Class C network?

A. 253

B. 254

C. 255

D. 256

13. How many subnets can a Class B network have?

A. 16

B. 256

C. 128

D. None of the above

14. What is the minimum number of bits that can be borrowed to form a subnet?

A. 1

B. 2

C. 4

D. None of the above

15. What is the primary reason for using subnets?

A. To reduce the size of the collision domain

B. To increase the number of host addresses

C. To reduce the size of the broadcast domain

D. None of the above

16. How many bits are in a subnet mask?

    A. 16

    B. 32

    C. 64

    D. None of the above

17. Performing the Boolean function as a router would on the IP addresses 131.8.2.5 AND 255.0.0.0, what is the network/subnetwork address?

    A. 131.8.1.0

    B. 131.8.0.0

    C. 131.8.2.0

    D. None of the above

18. How many bits can be borrowed to create a subnet for a Class C network?

    A. 2

    B. 4

    C. 6

    D. None of the above

19. With a Class C address of 197.15.22.31 and a subnet mask of 255.255.255.224, how many bits have been borrowed to create a subnet?

    A. 1

    B. 2

    C. 3

    D. None of the above

20. Performing the Boolean function as a router would on the IP addresses 172.16.2.120 AND 255.255.255.0, what is the subnet address?

    A. 172.0.0.0

    B. 172.16.0.0

    C. 172.16.2.0

    D. None of the above

Objectives

After reading this chapter, you will be able to

- Understand Layer 3 basics
- Describe methods for assigning an IP address
- Understand advanced ARP concepts
- Explain routed versus routing protocols
- Describe connectionless, non-reliable network services and connection-oriented, reliable network services
- Describe ARP tables
- Understand Interior Gateway Protocols (IGPs) and Exterior Gateway Protocols (EGPs)
- Explain static versus dynamic routes

Layer 3: Protocols

Introduction

A router is a type of internetworking device that passes data packets between networks based on Layer 3 addresses. A router has the capability to make intelligent decisions regarding the best path for delivery of data on the network. In this chapter, you learn how routers use a Layer 3 addressing scheme and routing tables to make forwarding decisions.

In addition, you learn how devices on local-area networks (LANs) use the Address Resolution Protocol (ARP) before forwarding data to a destination. You learn what happens when a device on one network does not know the MAC address of a device on another network. You learn that the Reverse Address Resolution Protocol (RARP) is the protocol that a device uses when it does not know its own IP address. You also learn the difference between routing and routed protocols, and how routers track cost between locations. Finally, you learn about distance-vector, link-state, and hybrid routing approaches and how each resolves common routing problems.

Layer 3 Basics

Layer 3, or the network layer, provides end-to-end packet delivery services to its user, the transport layer. The network layer sends packets from the source network to the destination network. In this section, you learn about the general performance of the network layer, including how routers operate at this layer to determine and select the chosen path(s) to a destination, and how addressing schemes work and vary at this layer.

Routers

Although routers are often thought of as wide-area network (WAN) devices, they can be equally useful in local-area networks (LANs). By virtue of their capability to communicate at both the data link layer and the network layer, routers can provide LAN administrators with a multitude of options for managing LANs and bolstering their performance.

Typically, routers are required to support multiple protocol stacks, each with its own routing protocols, and to allow these different environments to operate in parallel. In practice, modern routers also incorporate bridging functions. In addition, routers can implement a variety of value-added features that help to improve the cost-effectiveness of the network. These features include sequencing traffic based on priority and traffic filtering.

Routers provide interfaces for a wide range of links and subnetworks at a wide range of speeds. Routers manage networks by providing dynamic control over resources and supporting the tasks and goals for networks: connectivity, reliable performance, management control, and flexibility. Routers are active and intelligent network nodes and, thus, can participate in managing the network. A router is an internetworking device that passes data packets between networks based on Layer 3 addresses. A router has the capability to make intelligent decisions regarding the best path for delivery of data on the network (see Figure 11-1).

MORE INFORMATION

Router Operation at the Network Layer

Because routers function at the network layer of the OSI model, they are used to separate segments into unique collision and broadcast domains. The segments are referred to as networks. Not only is each network its own collision and broadcast domain, but each network also has its own logical network address. In addition, each station on the network has a logical address that indicates what network it is on and what its unique node identifier is.

In addition, the following is true:

- Routers do not forward broadcast or multicast frames by default.
- Routers forward packets based on the Layer 3 header information. Routers view the Layer 3 control information and determine the next network point to which the packet should be forwarded.
- Because routers map a single Layer 3 logical address to a single network device, routers can limit or secure network traffic based on identifiable attributes within each packet. These options can be applied to inbound or outbound packets on any router interface. Generally, these controls are called access lists or access control lists (ACLs).
- Routers can perform bridging and routing, depending on their configuration.
- In a Layer 2 switched network that uses virtual LANs (VLANs), routers provide connectivity between different VLANs.
- Routers can be used to deploy security measures and quality of service parameters for specified types of network traffic.

In addition to its benefits in the campus, routers are used to connect remote locations to the main office. Routers support a variety of physical layer connectivity standards that enable you to build WANs. Finally, routers are capable of providing the security and access control that are needed when interconnecting remote locations.

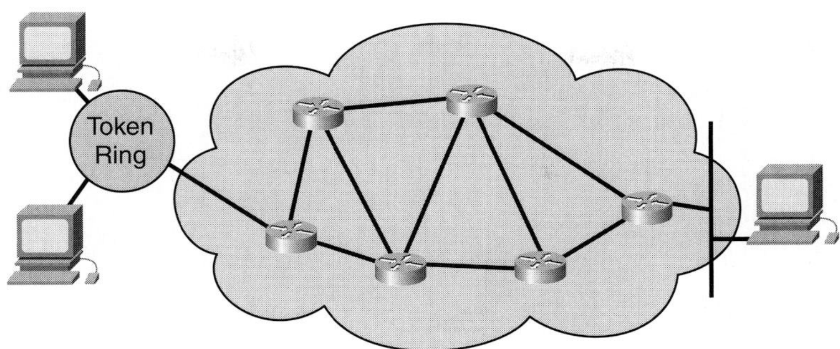

FIGURE 11-1 Routers are active and intelligent network nodes and, thus, can find the best path through an internetwork.

Layer 3 Addresses

In networking, two addressing schemes are used: One uses the MAC address, a data link (Layer 2) address; the other uses an address located at the network layer (Layer 3) of the OSI model. An example of a Layer 3 address is an IP address. Bridges and switches use physical addresses, or MAC addresses, to make data forwarding decisions. Routers use a Layer 3 addressing scheme to make forwarding decisions; they use IP addresses, or logical addresses, rather than MAC addresses. Because IP addresses are implemented in software and refer to the network on which a device is located, sometimes these Layer 3 addresses are referred to as protocol addresses, or network addresses.

Physical addresses, or MAC addresses, are assigned by the NIC manufacturer and are hard-coded into the NIC. The network administrator usually assigns IP addresses. In fact, it is not unusual for a network administrator to group devices in the IP addressing scheme according to their geographical location, department, or floor within a building. Because they are implemented in software, IP addresses are fairly easy to change. Finally, bridges and switches are primarily used to connect segments of a network. Routers are used to connect separate networks and to access the worldwide Internet. They do this by providing end-to-end routing.

Unique Network Numbers

Routers connect two or more networks, each of which must have a unique network number for routing to be successful. The example in Figure 11-2 shows how a unique network layer address (network number and node number) is assigned to each device attached to that network.

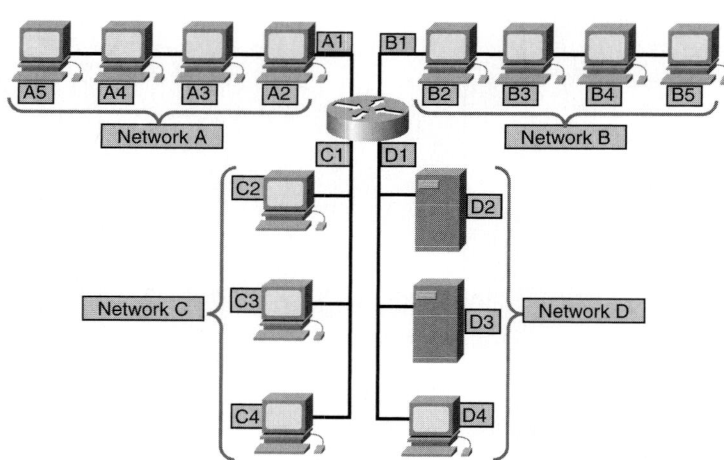

FIGURE 11-2 The network number is incorporated into the IP address that is assigned to each device attached to that network.

In the example shown in Figure 11-2, a network has a unique network number: A. It has four devices attached to it, in addition to the router. The IP addresses of the devices are A2, A3, A4, and A5. Because the interface where the router connects to a network is considered to be part of that network, the interface where the router connects to Network A has an IP address of A1.

Another network with a unique network number (B) has four devices besides the router attached to it. This network is also attached to the same router, but at a different interface. The IP addresses of the devices on this second network are B2, B3, B4, and B5. The IP address of the router's second interface is B1.

Now, imagine that you want to send data from one network to another. The source network is A, the destination network is B, and a router is connected to networks A, B, C, and D. When data (frames) coming from Network A reaches the router, the router performs the following functions:

1. It strips off the data link header, carried by the frame. (The data link header contains the MAC addresses of the source and destination.)
2. It examines the network layer address to determine the destination network.
3. It consults its routing tables to determine which of its interfaces it will use to send the data for it to reach its destination network.

The router determines that it should send the data from Network A to Network B from its interface with address B1. Before actually sending the data out interface B1, the router encapsulates the data in the appropriate data link frame, addressed with the MAC address of the destination.

Router Interface/Port

Routers generally relay a packet from one data link to another. To relay a packet, a router uses two basic functions: a path selection function and a switching function. A router is responsible for passing the packet to the next network along the path. The router uses the network portion of the address to make path selections.

A router's attachment to a network is called an interface; it can also be referred to as a port. In IP routing, each interface must have a separate, unique network (or subnetwork) address, as shown in Figure 11-3. The switching function allows a router to accept a packet on one interface and forward it on a second interface. The path selection function enables the router to select the most appropriate interface for forwarding a packet. The node portion of the address refers to a specific port on the router that leads to an adjacent router on that network/subnetwork.

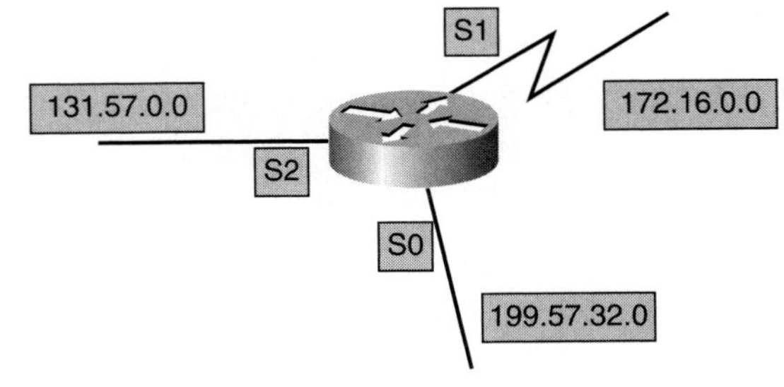

FIGURE 11-3 The network portion of the address is used to make path selections, and the node portion of the address refers to the router port on that network or subnetwork.

Network-to-Network Communications

To be truly practical, a network must consistently represent the paths available between routers to enable communication between networks. These paths consist of addresses that convey information that can be used by a router. This means that an address must have information about the path, which the router uses to pass packets from a source toward a destination. In this section, you learn how communication between networks is enabled. This section covers the following topics:

- Methods for assigning an IP address
- DHCP
- Function of the Address Resolution Protocol (ARP)
- ARP operation within a subnet

Methods for Assigning an IP Address

After you determine the addressing scheme for a network, you must choose the method for assigning addresses to hosts. Essentially, two methods exist for assigning IP addresses: static addressing and dynamic addressing. Regardless of which addressing method you use, no two interfaces can have the same IP address.

Static Addressing

If you assign IP addresses statically, you must go to each individual device and configure it with an IP address. This method requires you to keep very meticulous records because problems can occur on the network if you use duplicate IP addresses. Some operating systems, such as Windows 95 and Windows NT, send an ARP request to check for a duplicate IP address when they attempt to initialize TCP/IP. If they discover a duplicate, the operating systems do not initialize TCP/IP and generate an error message. Record keeping is important, too, because not all operating systems identify duplicate IP addresses.

Dynamic Addressing

You can use a few different methods to assign IP addresses dynamically:

- **Reverse Address Resolution Protocol (RARP)**—RARP binds MAC addresses to IP addresses. This binding allows network devices to encapsulate data before sending them out on the network. A network device, such as a diskless workstation, might know its MAC address but not its IP address. Devices using RARP require that a RARP server be present on the network to answer RARP requests.

  Figure 11-4 illustrates an example in which a source device wants to send data to another device. In the example, the source knows its own MAC address, but is incapable of locating its own IP address in its ARP table. For the destination device to retrieve the data, pass it to higher layers of the OSI model, and respond to the originating device, the source must include both its MAC address and its IP address. Therefore, the source initiates a process called a *RARP request*, which helps it detect its own IP address. The device builds a RARP request packet and sends it out on the network. To ensure that all devices (in particular, the RARP server) see the RARP request on the network, it uses a broadcast frame. As shown in Figure 11-4, devices using RARP require that a RARP server be present on the network to answer RARP requests.

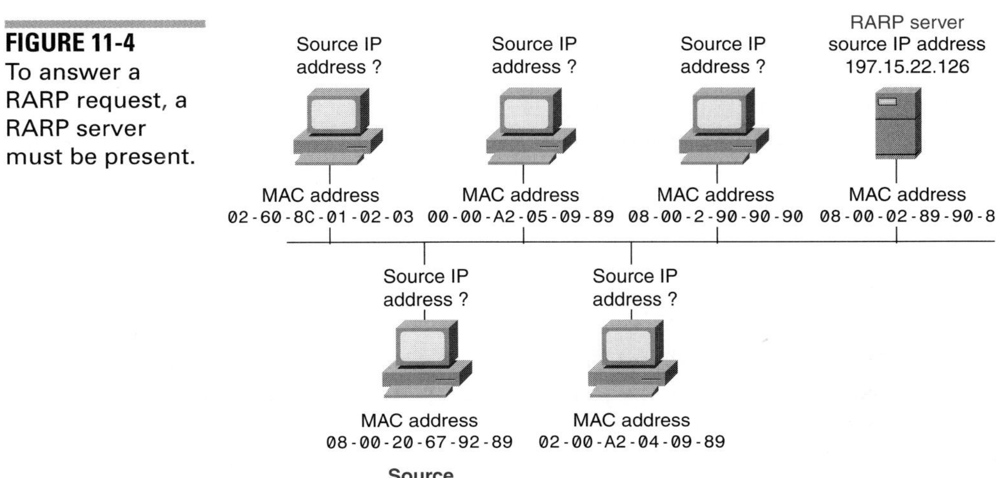

FIGURE 11-4 To answer a RARP request, a RARP server must be present.

As shown in Figure 11-5, RARP uses the same packet format as ARP, but with different operation codes. Like the ARP message format, the RARP packet format contains places for MAC and IP addresses of both the target and the source. Both the source and target MAC address fields are set to the sender's MAC address. The IP address fields are empty (undefined). The message is sent as a broadcast frame, which goes to all devices on the network; therefore, the destination MAC address is set to all binary 1s. Workstations running RARP have codes in ROM that direct them to start the RARP process and locate the RARP server.

MAC header		IP header		RARP request message
Destination	Source	Destination	Source	What is my IP address?
00-40-33-2B-35-77	01-60-8C-01-02-03	11111111	?????????	

FIGURE 11-5 Structurally, RARP and ARP requests are the same.

- **BOOTstrap Protocol (BOOTP)**—A device uses the BOOTstrap protocol (BOOTP) when it starts up to obtain an IP address. BOOTP uses UDP to carry messages; the UDP message is encapsulated in an IP datagram. A computer uses BOOTP to send a broadcast IP datagram (using a destination IP address of all 1s—255.255.255.255). If the server's address is known, that address is used instead of the broadcast address. A BOOTP server receives the request and then sends a broadcast in response. The client receives this datagram and checks the MAC address. If it finds its own MAC address in the client hardware address field, then it takes the IP address in the IP address field. Like RARP, BOOTP operates in a client/server environment and requires only a single packet exchange. However, unlike RARP, which sends back only a four-octet IP address, BOOTP datagrams can include the IP address, the address of a router (default gateway), the address of a server, and a vendor-specific field. One of the problems with BOOTP is that it was not designed to provide dynamic address assignment. With BOOTP, you can create a configuration file that specifies the parameters for each device.

Dynamic Host Configuration Protocol

The Dynamic Host Configuration Protocol (DHCP) has been proposed as a successor to BOOTP. Unlike BOOTP, DHCP allows a host to obtain an IP address quickly and dynamically. All that is required using DHCP is a defined range of IP addresses on a DHCP server. As hosts come online, they contact the DHCP server and request an address. The DHCP server chooses an address and allocates it to that host. With DHCP, the entire computer's configuration can be obtained in one message (along with the IP address, the server can also send a subnet mask, default gateway, DNS server, and other TCP/IP configuration settings).

DHCP Initialization Sequence

When a DHCP client boots, it enters an initialize state. It sends DHCPDISCOVER broadcast messages, which are UDP packets with the port number set to the BOOTP port.

After sending the DHCPDISCOVER packets, the client moves into the select state and collects DHCPOFFER responses from DHCP server.

The client then selects the first response that it receives and negotiates the lease time (the length of time that it can keep the address without renewing it) with the DHCP server by sending a DHCPREQUEST packet.

Next, the DHCP server acknowledges a client request with a DHCPACK packet. The client can now enter the bound state and begin using the address.

Function of the Address Resolution Protocol

For devices to communicate, the sending devices need both the IP addresses and the MAC addresses of the destination devices. When they try to communicate with devices whose IP addresses they know, they must determine the MAC addresses. The TCP/IP suite has a protocol called ARP that can automatically obtain the MAC address. ARP enables a computer to find the MAC address of the computer that is associated with an IP address (see Figure 11-6).

> **NOTE**
>
> The basic unit of data transfer in IP is the IP packet or datagram. Packet processing occurs in software, which means that content and format are not hardware-dependent. A packet is divided into two major components: the header, which includes source and destination IP addresses and more; and the data. Other protocols have their own packet formats. The IP packet format is unique to IP.

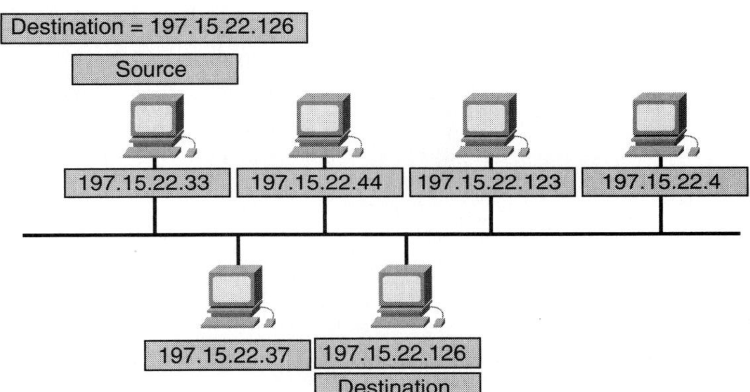

FIGURE 11-6 The source looks at its ARP table after it has determined the IP address for the destination.

MOVIE 11.1

Address Resolution

MAC addresses and ARP explained.

Some devices keep tables that contain the MAC addresses and IP addresses of other devices that are connected to the same LAN. Called *Address Resolution Protocol (ARP) tables*, they map IP addresses to the corresponding MAC addresses. ARP tables are sections of RAM memory in which the cached memory is maintained automatically on each of the devices. It is rare that you must make an ARP table entry manually. Each computer on a network maintains its own ARP table.

Whenever a network device wants to send data across a network, it uses information provided by its ARP table. In the example shown in Figure 11-7, a source device wants to send data to another device.

> **NOTE**
>
> Another major component of IP is *Internet Control Message Protocol (ICMP)*. This protocol is used by a device to report a problem to the sender of a message. For example, if a router receives a packet that it cannot deliver, ICMP sends a message back to the sender of the packet. One of the many features of ICMP is echo-request/echo-reply, which is a component that tests whether a packet can reach a destination. This is called **ping**ing the destination.

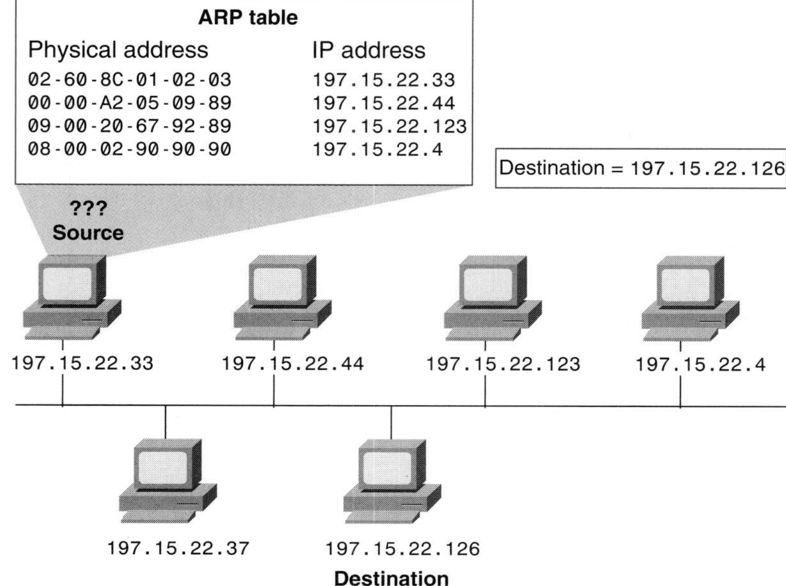

FIGURE 11-7
The source cannot locate a MAC address for the destination in its ARP table.

ARP Operation Within a Subnet

If a host wants to send data to another host, it must know the destination IP and MAC addresses. If it is cannot locate a MAC address for the destination IP address in its ARP table, the host initiates a process called an ARP request (see Figure 11-8). An ARP request enables it to discover the destination MAC address.

A host builds an ARP request packet and sends it to all devices on the network. As shown in Figure 11-9, this ARP request packet is divided into two parts: the frame header and the ARP message.

To ensure that all devices see the ARP request, the source uses a broadcast MAC address. The broadcast address in a MAC addressing scheme has all places set to hexadecimal F. Thus, a MAC broadcast address would have the form FF-FF-FF-FF-FF-FF.

Because ARP request packets travel in a broadcast mode, all devices on the local network receive the packets and pass them up to the network layer for further examination. If the IP address of a device matches the destination IP address in the ARP request, that device responds by sending the source its MAC address. This is known as the ARP reply.

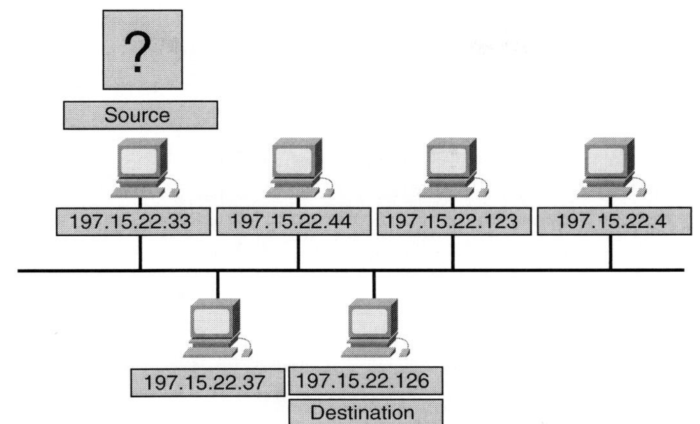

FIGURE 11-8 The device initiates a process called an ARP request that is designed to help it discover the destination MAC address.

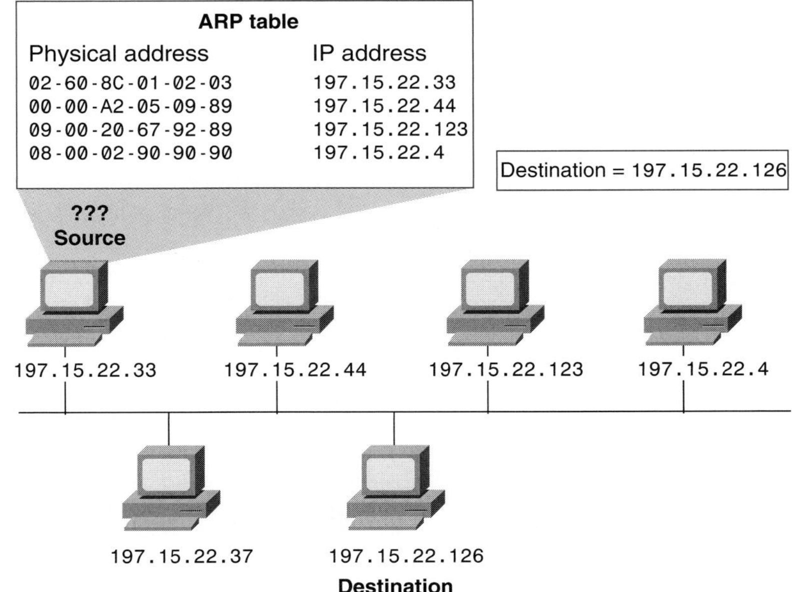

FIGURE 11-9 The ARP request packet is divided into the frame header and the ARP message.

When the originating device receives the ARP reply, it extracts the MAC address from the sender hardware address field and updates its ARP table. The originating device can then properly address its data with both a destination MAC address and a destination IP address. It uses this new information to perform Layer 2 and Layer 3 encapsulations of the data before it sends them out over the network.

When the data arrives at the destination, the data link layer makes a match, strips off the MAC header, and transfers the data up to the network layer. The network layer examines the data and finds that its IP address matches the destination IP address carried in the IP header. The network layer strips off the IP header and transfers the encapsulated data to the next-highest layer in the OSI model, the transport layer (Layer 4). This process is repeated until the rest of the packet's partially de-encapsulated data reaches the application, where the user data can be read.

Advanced ARP Concepts

One of the major problems in networking is how to communicate with devices that are not on the same physical network segment. There are two parts to the problem. The first is obtaining the MAC address of the destination host or of a router that can forward the packet toward the destination host. The second part is transferring the data packets from one network segment to another, to get to the destination host. In this section, you learn how devices on different networks communicate.

Default Gateway

A *default gateway* is the IP address of the interface on the router that connects to the network segment on which the source host is located. The default gateway's IP address must be in the same network segment as the source host, as shown in Figure 11-10.

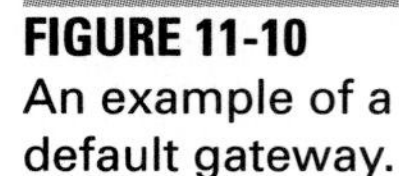

FIGURE 11-10
An example of a default gateway.

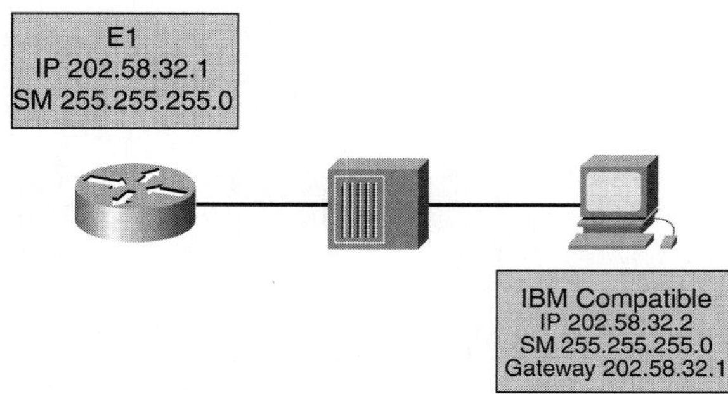

MORE INFORMATION

Three Ways to Communicate with a Device on Another Network

To communicate with a device on another network, you have three options.

One option is the default gateway. When a device has been configured with the address of a default gateway (also called default network or default route) and after it is determined that a packet is for a device on another network, that packet is addressed to the MAC address of the gateway router. An ARP request might need to be sent to get the router's MAC address. The IP address, of course, is the final destination.

In the second option, devices listen for router advertisements and save this information. Then a packet destined for a different network is sent to the appropriate router's MAC address. Again, an ARP can be sent first.

Third is the proxy ARP situation, discussed next. In this case, a device sends an ARP regardless of the destination, and a router responds with its MAC address in response to the ARP.

If there are no default gateway, no router advertisements, and no response to an ARP, the packet cannot be sent.

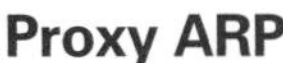

Proxy ARP

Proxy ARP is a variation of the ARP protocol. In this case, an intermediate device (such as a router) sends an ARP response on behalf of an end node to the requesting host (see Figure 11-11). Routers running proxy ARP capture ARP packets. They respond with their MAC addresses for those requests in which the IP address is not in the range of addresses of the local subnet. For example, in Figure 11-12, if Machine A sends an ARP requests to Machine F, the router would process the request and reply to A with its MAC address to be mapped to the IP address of Machine F.

In the previous description of how data is sent to a host on a different subnet, the default gateway is configured. If the source host does not have a default gateway configured, it sends an ARP request. All hosts on the segment, including the router, receive the ARP request. The router compares the IP destination address with the IP subnet address to determine if the destination IP address is on the same subnet as the source host.

If the subnet address is the same, the router discards the packet. The packet is discarded because the destination IP address is on the same segment as the source's IP address. This means that the destination device on the segment should respond to the ARP request. The exception to this is that the destination IP address is not currently assigned, which generates an error response on the source host.

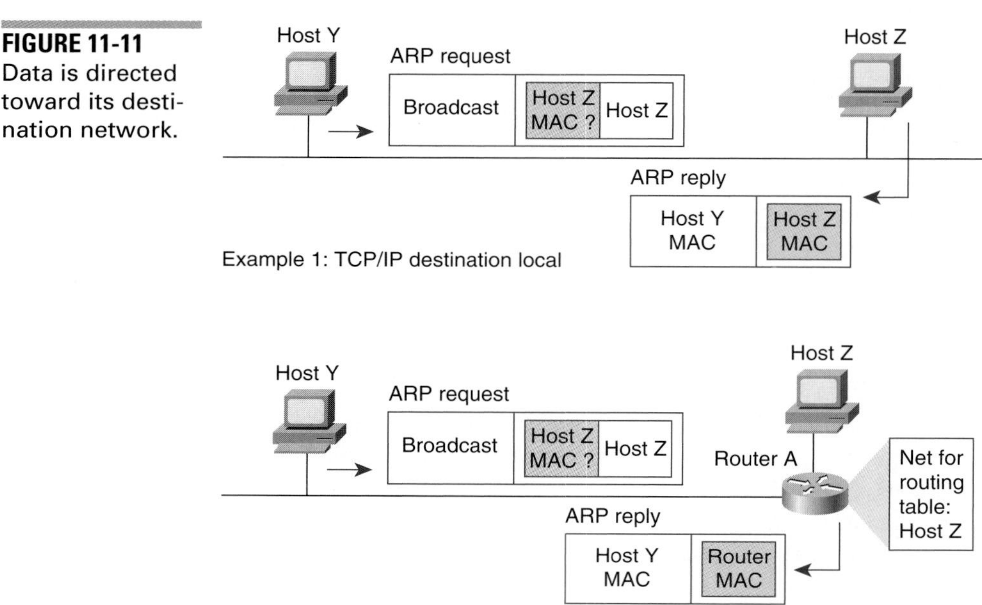

FIGURE 11-11 Data is directed toward its destination network.

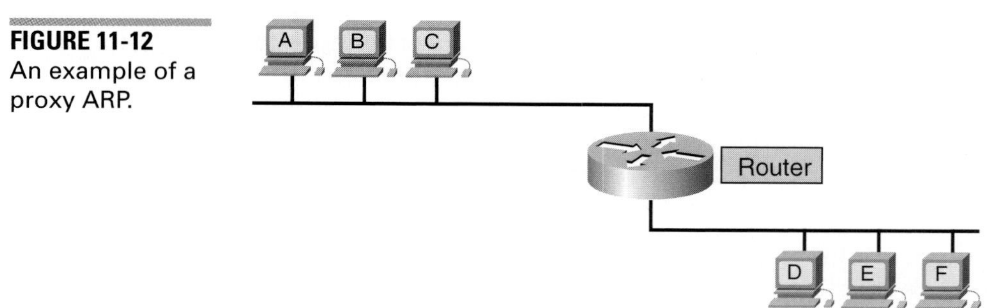

FIGURE 11-12 An example of a proxy ARP.

If the subnet address is different, the router responds with its own MAC address for the interface that is directly connected to the segment on which the source host is located. This is the proxy ARP. Because the MAC address is unavailable for the destination host, the router supplies its MAC address to get the packet. Then the router can forward the ARP request (based on the destination IP address) to the proper subnet for delivery.

Routed Versus Routing Protocols

Confusion often exists between the similar terms *routing protocol* and *routed protocol*. This section provides some clarification.

- **Routed protocol**—Any network protocol that provides enough information in its network layer address to allow a packet to be forwarded from host to host based on the addressing scheme. Routed protocols define the format and use of the fields within a packet. Packets generally are conveyed from end system to end system. The Internet Protocol (IP) is an example of a routed protocol.
- **Routing protocol**—Protocol that supports a routed protocol by providing mechanisms for sharing routing information. Routing protocol messages move between routers. A routing protocol allows the routers to communicate with other routers to update and maintain tables. Examples of routing protocols are the Routing Information Protocol (RIP), the Interior Gateway Routing Protocol (IGRP), the Enhanced Interior Gateway Routing Protocol (EIGRP), and Open Shortest Path First (OSPF).

Routed Protocols

The Internet Protocol (IP) is a network layer protocol; as a result, it can be routed over an internetwork, which is a network of networks. Protocols that provide support for the network layer are called routed or routable protocols. The focus of this book is on the most commonly used routable protocol, IP. Even though you concentrate on IP, it is important to know that there are other routable protocols. Two of them are Novell's Internetwork Packet eXchange (IPX) and the AppleTalk Datagram Delivery Protocol (DDP).

Protocols such as IP, IPX, and AppleTalk DDP provide Layer 3 support and, therefore, are routable. However, some protocols do not support Layer 3; these are classed as nonroutable protocols. The most common of these nonroutable protocols is NetBEUI. NetBEUI is a small, fast, and efficient protocol that is limited to running on one segment.

For a protocol to be routable, it must provide the capability to assign a network number, as well as a host or node number, to each individual device. Some protocols, such as IPX, require only that you assign a network number because they use a host's MAC address for the physical address. Other protocols, such as IP, require that you provide a complete address and a subnet mask. The network address is obtained by ANDing the address with the subnet mask (see Figure 11-13).

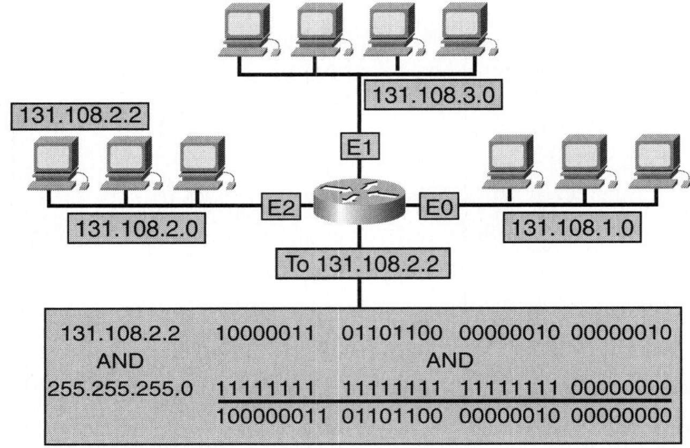

FIGURE 11-13 Obtaining an address takes place by ANDing the address with the subnet mask.

Routing Protocols

Routing protocols determine the paths that routed protocols follow to their destinations. Examples of routing protocols include the Routing Information Protocol (RIP), the Interior Gateway Routing Protocol (IGRP), the Enhanced Interior Gateway Routing Protocol (EIGRP), and Open Shortest Path First (OSPF). Routing protocols enable routers that are connected to create a map internally of other routers in the network or on the Internet. This allows routing (selecting the best path) and switching to occur.

Routers use routing protocols to exchange routing information. Within a domain or autonomous system, the most common protocol used to transfer routing information between routers is the Routing Information Protocol (RIP). This Interior Gateway Protocol (IGP) calculates distances to a destination host in terms of how many hops (that is, how many routers) a packet must pass through. RIP enables routers to update their routing tables at programmable intervals, usually every 30 seconds. One disadvantage of routers that use RIP is that they are constantly connecting to neighboring routers to update their routing tables, thus creating large amounts of network traffic in a complex environment.

RIP allows routers to determine which path to use to send data. It does so by using a concept known as *distance-vector routing*. Whenever data goes through a router—and, thus, through a new network number—this is considered to be equal to one hop. A path that has a hop count of 4 indicates that data traveling along that path have to pass through four routers before reaching the final destination on the network. If there are multiple paths to a destination, the path with the least number of hops is the path chosen by the router.

Because hop count is the only routing metric used by RIP, it doesn't necessarily select the fastest path to a destination. A metric is a measurement for making decisions. You soon learn that other routing protocols use many other metrics besides hop count to find the best path for data to travel. Nevertheless, RIP remains very popular and is still widely implemented. This might be primarily because it was one of the earliest routing protocols developed.

One other problem posed by the use of RIP is that sometimes a destination can be located too far away to be reachable. When using RIP, the maximum number of hops that data can be forwarded through is 15. The destination network is considered unreachable if it is more than 15 router hops away.

Routing Encapsulation Sequence

At the data link layer, an IP datagram is encapsulated into a frame. The datagram, including the IP header, is treated as data. A router receives the frame, strips off the frame header and trailer, and checks the destination IP address in the IP header. The router then looks for that destination IP network address in its routing table, encapsulates the data in a data link layer frame, and sends it out to the appropriate interface for the next hop. If it does not find the destination IP network address, it drops the packet if no default network is defined.

Multiprotocol Routing

Routers are capable of concurrently supporting multiple independent routing protocols and of maintaining routing tables for several routed protocols. This capability allows a router to deliver packets from several routed protocols over the same data links (see Figure 11-14).

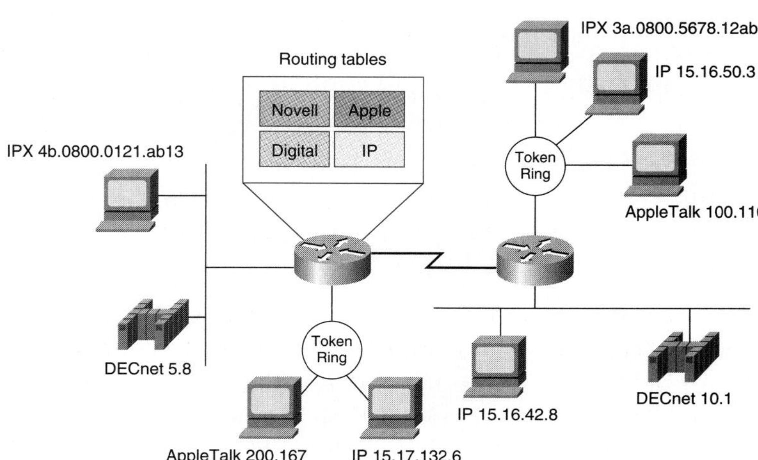

FIGURE 11-14 Routers pass traffic from all routed protocols over the network.

Connectionless and Connection-Oriented Network Services

Most network services use a connectionless delivery system (see Figure 11-15). They treat each packet separately and send it on its way through the network. The packets might take different paths to get through the network, but they are reassembled when they arrive at the destination. In a connectionless system, the destination is not contacted before a packet is sent. A good analogy for a connectionless system is a postal system. The recipient is not contacted before a letter is sent from one destination to another. The letter is sent on its way, and the recipient learns of the letter when it arrives.

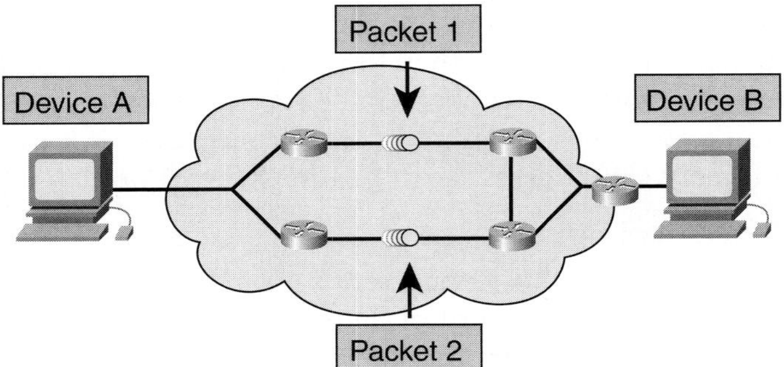

FIGURE 11-15
Connectionless network services.

Connectionless network processes are often referred to as being packet-switched. In these processes, as the packets pass from source to destination, they can switch to different paths, as well as (possibly) arrive out of order. Devices make the path determination for each packet based on a variety of criteria. Some of the criteria (such as available bandwidth) might differ from packet to packet.

The Internet is a huge connectionless internetwork in which all packet deliveries are handled by IP. TCP (Layer 4) adds connection-oriented and reliable services on top of IP (Layer 3). TCP segments are encapsulated into IP packets for transport across the Internet.

IP is a connectionless system; it treats each packet independently. For example, if you use an FTP program to download a file, IP does not send the file in one long stream of data; it treats each packet independently. Each packet can travel different paths; some can even get lost. IP relies on the transport layer protocol to determine whether packets have been lost and to request retransmission. The transport layer is also responsible for reordering the packets.

In connection-oriented systems, a connection is established between the sender and the recipient before any data is transferred (see Figure 11-16). An example of a connection-oriented network is the telephone system. You place a call, a connection is established, and then communication occurs.

Connection-oriented network processes establish a connection with the recipient first and then begin the data transfer. All packets travel sequentially across the same physical circuit—or, more commonly, across the same virtual circuit.

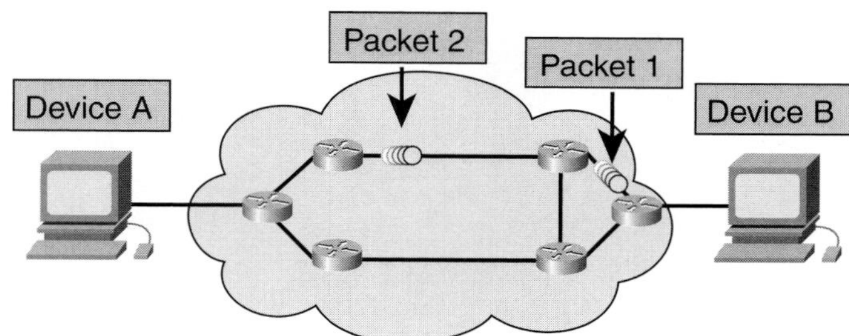

FIGURE 11-16 Connection-oriented network services.

ARP Tables

You have learned that the port, or interface, where a router connects to a network is considered part of that network; therefore, the router interface connected to the network has an IP address for that network. Just like every other device on the network, routers send and receive data on the network and build ARP tables that map IP addresses to MAC addresses, as shown in Figure 11-17.

Physical address	IP address
02-60-8C-01-02-03	197.15.22.33
00-00-A2-05-09-89	197.15.22.44
09-00-20-67-92-89	197.15.22.123
08-00-02-90-90-90	197.15.22.4

FIGURE 11-17 Each computer on a network maintains an ARP table.

Routers can be connected to multiple networks or subnetworks. Generally speaking, network devices map the IP addresses and MAC addresses for devices with which they communicate. This means that a typical device contains mapping information pertaining only to devices on its own network. It knows very little about devices beyond its LAN. However, routers build tables that describe all networks connected to them. As a result, as shown in Figure 11-18, ARP tables kept by routers can contain IP addresses and MAC addresses of devices that are located on more than one network.

FIGURE 11-18
ARP tables are built by routers.

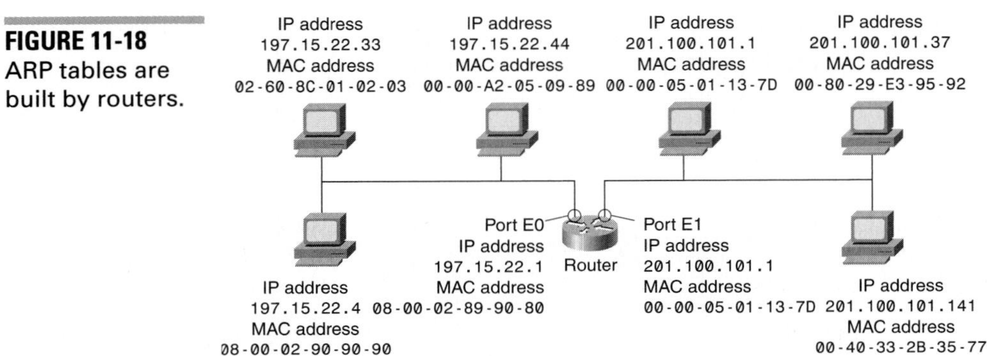

Routers build tables that describe all networks connected to them. ARP tables kept by routers can contain IP addresses and MAC addresses of devices located on more than one network.

In addition to mapping IP addresses to MAC addresses, router tables also map ports, as shown in Figure 11-19.

FIGURE 11-19
Ports are mapped by router tables.

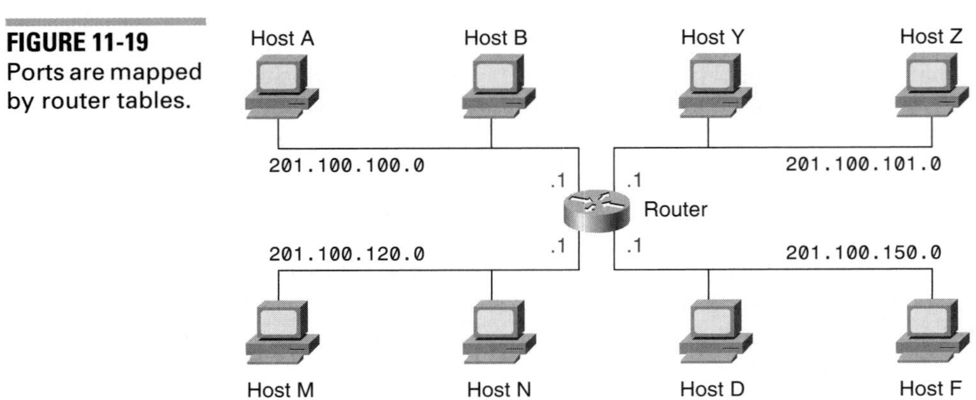

In addition to IP addresses and MAC addresses of devices located on networks to which it connects, a router also possesses IP addresses and MAC addresses of other routers. It uses these addresses to direct data toward its final destination. If a router receives a packet whose destination address is not in its routing table, it forwards it to a default network, if it is defined. Otherwise, it drops the packet.

ARP Requests and ARP Replies

ARP is used only on a local network. When a router does not know the MAC address of the next-hop router, the source router (the router that has the data to be sent on) issues an ARP request. A router that is connected to the same segment as the source router receives the ARP request. This router issues an ARP reply to the router that originated the ARP request. The reply contains the MAC address of the replying router.

When a router picks up data, it strips off the data link layer information that is used in the encapsulation. It then passes the data up to the network layer, where the router examines the destination IP address. It compares the destination IP address with information contained in its routing tables. If the router locates the mapped destination IP address and the MAC address, and learns that the location of the destination network is attached to one of its ports, it encapsulates the data with the new MAC address information and forwards it to the correct destination. If the router cannot locate the mapped destination IP address and MAC address of the final target device, it either sends an ARP or locates the MAC address of another router that can perform this function (the default router) and forwards the data to that router. If there is no default or advertised router and no ARP reply, the packet is dropped.

Interior Gateway Protocols and Exterior Gateway Protocols

Routers use routing protocols to exchange routing information. In other words, routing protocols determine how routed protocols are routed. Two types of routing protocols are the Exterior Gateway Protocols (EGPs) and the Interior Gateway Protocols (IGPs).

IGPs route data within an autonomous system (AS), also called a domain. An AS is a network or set of networks that are under the administrative control of a single entity, such as the cisco.com domain. Examples of IGPs are listed here:

- Routing Information Protocol (RIP)
- Interior Gateway Routing Protocol (IGRP)
- Enhanced Interior Gateway Routing Protocol (EIGRP)
- Open Shortest Path First (OSPF)

EGPs route data between autonomous systems. Autonomous systems are collections of networks that create a single internetwork.An example of an EGP is the Border Gateway Protocol (BGP), the primary exterior routing protocol of the Internet.

Network Layer Protocol Operations

The network layer examines the header to determine the destination network and then references the routing table that associates networks to outgoing interfaces. Each router provides its services to support upper-layer function, as shown in Figure 11-20.

FIGURE 11-20
Each router provides its services to support upper-layer function.

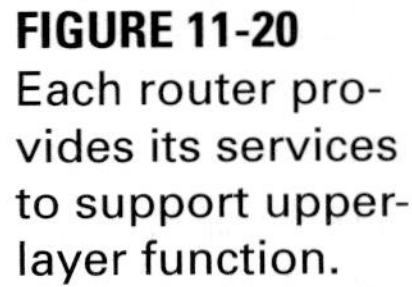

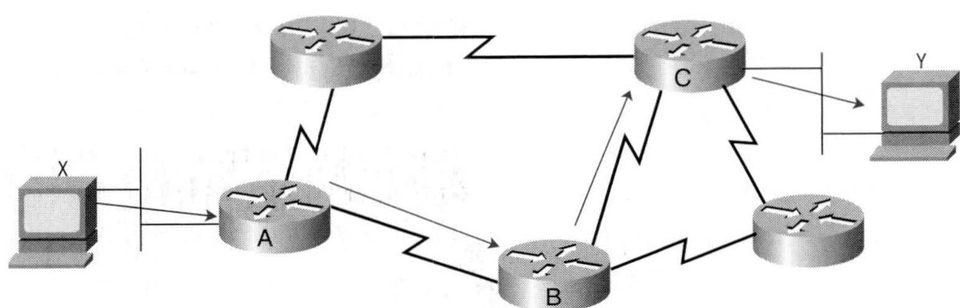

The packet is again encapsulated in the data link frame for the selected interface and is queued for delivery to the next hop in the path. This process occurs each time the packet switches through another router. At the router connected to the network containing the destination host, the packet is again encapsulated in the destination LAN's data link frame type and is delivered to the destination host.

MORE INFORMATION

Representing Distance with Metrics

When a routing algorithm updates the routing table, its primary objective is to determine the best information to include in the table. Each routing algorithm interprets best in its own way. The algorithm generates a number—called the *metric*—for each path through the network. Typically, the smaller the metric number, the better the path.

Metrics can be calculated based on a single characteristic of a path. You can calculate more complex metrics by combining several characteristics. Several path characteristics are used in metric calculations.

The metrics most commonly used by routers follow:

- **Hop count**—The number of routers that a packet must go through to reach a destination. The lower the hop count, the better the path. Path length is used to indicate the sum of hops to a destination.
- **Bandwidth**—The data capacity of a link. For instance, normally a T1 link at 1.544 Mbps is preferable to a 64-kbps leased line.
- **Delay**—The length of time required to move a packet from source to destination.
- **Load**—The amount of activity on a network resource such as a router or a link.
- **Reliability**—The error rate of each network link.
- **Ticks**—The delay on a data link using IBM PC clock ticks (approximately 55 milliseconds). Novell NetWare's RIP uses this metric in addition to hop count.
- **Cost**—The generic term, based on bandwidth, dollar expense, or other measurement or metric, that is used to represent the desirability of a path. In some cases, cost is assigned by a network administrator.

RIP

The most common routing protocol used to transfer routing information between routers that are located in the same domain is RIP. This Interior Gateway protocol calculates distances (hop counts) to a destination. RIP allows routers that use this protocol to update their routing tables at programmable intervals, typically every 30 seconds. However, the routers exchange routing tables so frequently (every 30 seconds) that it can consume significant network bandwidth in a complex environment. In a simple network environment, RIP can actually use less bandwidth than link state protocols.

RIP allows the router to determine which path it will use to send data, based on a concept known as distance-vector routing. Whenever data travels on a router, and thus through a new network number, it is considered to have traveled one hop. A path that has a hop count of 4 indicates that data traveling along that path must have passed through four routers before reaching its final destination on the network.

If there are multiple paths to a destination, the router (using RIP) selects the path with the least number of hops. However, because hop count is the only routing metric used by RIP in determining best path, it is not necessarily the fastest path. Nevertheless, RIP remains very popular and is widely implemented. This is primarily because it was one of the earliest routing protocols to be developed, which means that it is well understood; it is much simpler than link-state routing protocols.

Another problem with using RIP is that a destination might be located too far away for the data to reach it. With RIP, the maximum number of hops that data can travel is 15. Because of this, if the destination network is more than 15 routers away, it is considered unreachable.

IGRP and EIGRP

IGRP and EIGRP are routing protocols that were developed by Cisco Systems, Inc. Therefore, they are considered proprietary routing protocols. IGRP was developed specifically to address problems associated with routing in large multivendor networks that were beyond the scope of protocols such as RIP. Like RIP, IGRP is a distance-vector protocol; however, when determining the best path, it also takes into consideration such things as bandwidth, load, delay, and reliability. Network administrators can determine the importance given to any one of these metrics or allow IGRP to automatically calculate the optimal path. EIGRP is an advanced version of IGRP. Specifically, EIGRP provides superior operating efficiency and combines the advantages of link-state protocols with those of distance-vector protocols.

Open Shortest Path First

Open Shortest Path First (OSPF) is a link-state routing protocol based on open standards. A better description, however, might be "determination of optimum path" because this Interior Gateway Protocol actually uses several criteria to determine the best route to a destination. These criteria include cost metrics, which factor in such things as route speed, traffic, reliability, and security.

Static Versus Dynamic Routes

So how does route information get into a routing table in the first place? The network administrator can manually enter the information in the router. Routers can learn the information from each other on the fly. Manual entries in routing tables are called *static routes*. Routes learned automatically via routing protocols are called *dynamic routes*.

A Static Route Example

If routers can learn routing information automatically, it might seem pointless to manually enter information into a router's routing table. However, such manual entries can be useful whenever a network administrator wants to control which path a router selects. For example, routing tables that are based on static information could be used to test a particular link in the network or to conserve wide-area bandwidth. Static routing is also the preferred method for maintaining routing tables when there is only one path to a destination network, as shown in Figure 11-21. This type of network is referred to as a stub network. There is only one way to get to this network, so it is important to indicate this situation to prevent routers from trying to find another way to this stub network if its connection fails. In addition, this saves bandwidth, particularly on a WAN link, because there is no point in sending routing updates to a stub network; it has only one way in (better served with a static route) and one way out (best served with a default route).

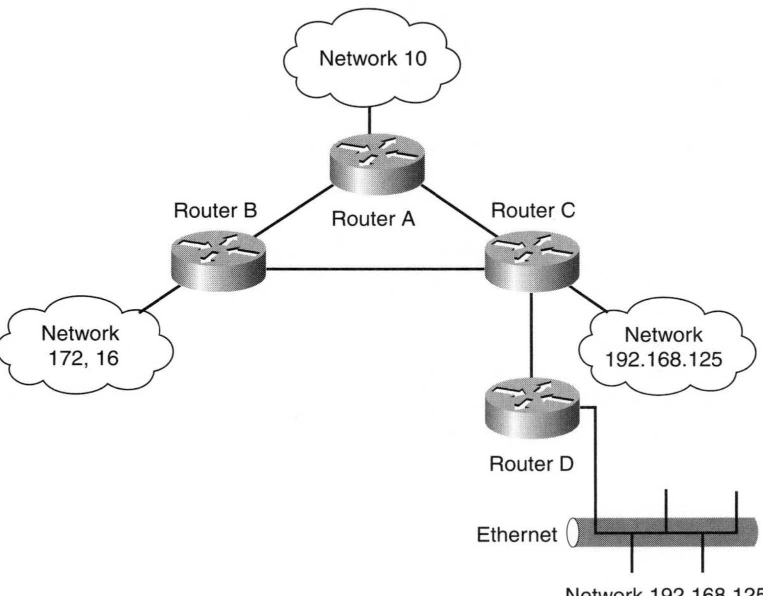

FIGURE 11-21 Static routing entries can eliminate the need to allow route updates across the WAN link.

MORE INFORMATION

A Default Route Example

Figure 11-22 shows a use for a default route—a routing table entry that is used to direct frames for which the next hop is not explicitly listed in the routing table. Default routes can be set as the result of the administrator's static configuration.

In this example, Company X routers possess specific knowledge of the topology of the Company X network but not of other networks. Maintaining knowledge of every other internetwork accessible by way of the Internet cloud is unnecessary and unreasonable, if not impossible.

Instead of maintaining specific network knowledge, each router in Company X is informed by the default route that it can reach any unknown destination by directing the packet to the Internet.

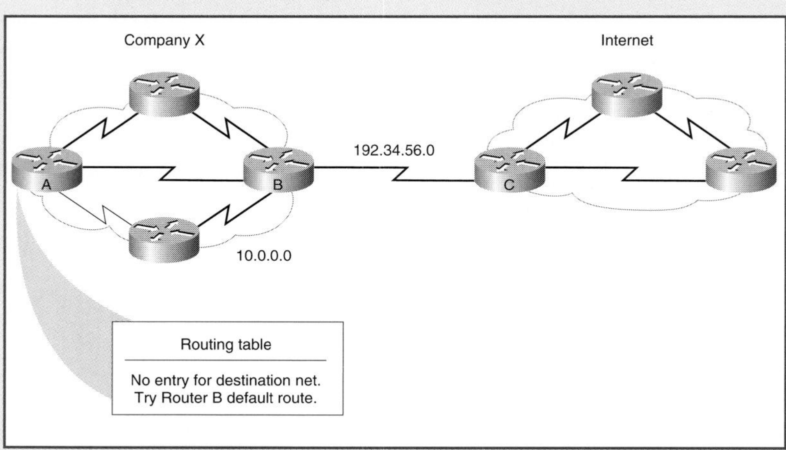

FIGURE 11-22 A default route is used if the next hop is not explicitly listed in the routing table.

Dynamic Routing

Adaptive, or dynamic, routing occurs when routers send periodic routing update messages to each other. Each time a router receives a routing update containing new information, it recalculates the new best route and sends the new updated information to other routers. By using dynamic routing, routers can adjust to changing network conditions (see Figure 11-23).

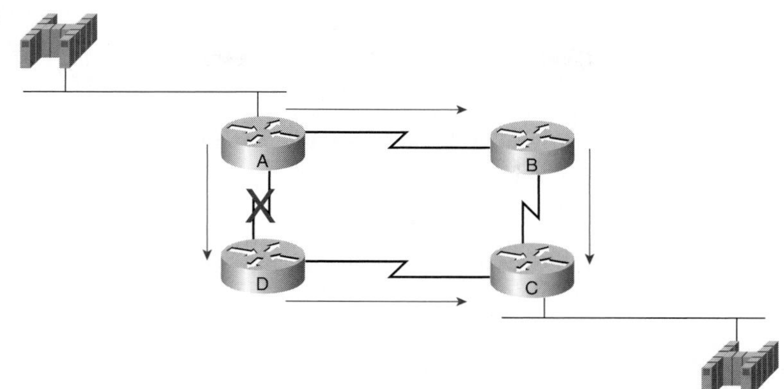

FIGURE 11-23 Dynamic routing enables routers to automatically use backup routes whenever necessary.

Static routing allows the routers to properly route a packet from network to network. The router refers to its routing table and follows the static knowledge there to relay the packet to Router D. Router D uses a default route and relays packets to Router C. Router C delivers the packet to the destination host.

But what happens if the path between Router A and Router C fails? Obviously, Router A is not capable of relaying the packet to Router D with a static route. Until Router A is manually reconfigured to relay packets by way of Router B, communication with the destination network is impossible.

Dynamic routing offers more automatic flexibility. According to the routing table generated by Router A, a packet can reach its destination over the preferred route through Router C. However, a second path to the destination is available by way of Router B. When Router A recognizes that the link to Router D is down, it adjusts its routing table, making the path through Router B the preferred path to the destination. The routers continue sending packets over this link.

When the path between Routers A and C is restored to service, Router A can once again change its routing table to indicate a preference for the path through Router C to the destination network.

The success of dynamic routing depends on two basic router functions:

- Maintenance of a routing table
- Timely distribution of knowledge—in the form of routing updates—to other routers

Dynamic routing relies on a routing protocol to share knowledge. A routing protocol defines the set of rules used by a router when it communicates with neighboring routers. For example, a routing protocol describes the following:

- How updates are sent
- What knowledge is contained in these updates
- When to send this knowledge
- How to locate recipients of the updates

Before the advent of dynamic updating of routing tables, most vendors had to maintain router tables for their clients. This meant that vendors had to manually enter network numbers, their associated distances, and port numbers into the router tables of all the equipment they sold or leased. As networks grew larger, this became an increasingly cumbersome, time-consuming, and expensive task. Dynamic routing eliminates the need for network administrators or vendors to manually enter information into routing tables. It works best when bandwidth and large amounts of network traffic are not issues. RIP, IGRP, EIGRP, and OSPF are all examples of dynamic routing protocols because they allow this process to occur. Without dynamic routing protocols, the Internet would be impossible.

Using RIP to Route Data Through a Network

Figure 11-24 illustrates a Class B network that is divided into eight subnetworks that are connected by three routers. Host A has data that it wants to send to Host Z. It passes the data down through the OSI model from the application layer to the data link layer, where Host A encapsulates the data with information provided by each layer. When the data reaches the network layer, Source A uses its own IP address and the destination IP address of Host Z because that is where it wants to send the data. Then Host A passes the data to the data link layer.

At the data link layer, Source A places the destination MAC address of the router, to which it is connected, and its own MAC address as the source in the MAC header. Source A does this because it sees Subnetwork 8 as a separate network. It knows that it cannot send data directly to a different network, but it must pass such data through a default gateway. In this example, the default gateway for Source A is Router 1.

The data packet travels along Subnetwork 1. The hosts do not copy the frame because the destination MAC address in the MAC header does not match their own. The data packet continues along Subnetwork 1 until it reaches Router 1. Like the other devices on Subnetwork 1, Router 1 sees the data packet and picks it up because it recognizes that its own MAC address is the same as the destination MAC address.

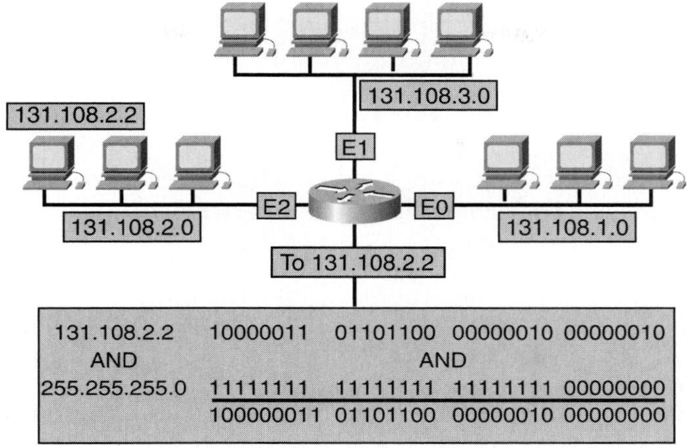

FIGURE 11-24
How routers use RIP to route data through a network.

Router 1 strips off the MAC header of the data and passes the data up to the network layer, where it looks at the destination IP address in the IP header. The router then searches its routing tables to map a route for the network address of the destination to the MAC address of the next router in the path to Subnetwork 8. The router is using RIP as its routing protocol; therefore, it determines that the best path for the data is one that places the destination only three hops away. Then the router determines that it must send the data packet through the port attached to Subnetwork 4 for the data packet to reach its destination via the selected path. The router passes the data down to the data link layer, where it places a new MAC header on the data packet. The new MAC header contains the destination MAC address of Router 2 on Subnetwork 4 and the MAC address of the first router that became the new source. The IP header remains unchanged. The first router passes the data packet through the port that it selects and on to Subnetwork 4.

The data passes along Subnetwork 4. The hosts do not copy the frame because the destination MAC address in the MAC header does not match their own. The data packet continues along Subnetwork 4 until it reaches Router 2. Like the other devices on Subnetwork 4, Router 2 sees the data packet. This time, it picks up the packet because it recognizes that its own MAC address is the same as the destination MAC address.

At the data link layer, the router strips off the MAC header and passes the data up to the network layer. There, it examines the destination network IP address and looks in its routing table. Using RIP as its routing protocol, the router determines that the best path for the data is one that places the destination only two hops away. Then the router determines that it must send the data packet through the port attached to Subnetwork 5 for the data packet to reach its destination via the selected path. The router passes the data down to the data link layer, where it places a new MAC header on the data packet. The new MAC header contains the destination MAC address of Router 3 on Subnetwork 5, and the MAC address of Router 2 becomes the new source MAC address.

The IP header remains unchanged. The router passes the data packet through the port that it selects and on to Subnetwork 5.

The data passes along Subnetwork 5. The data packet continues along Subnetwork 5 until it reaches Router 3. Like the other devices on Subnetwork 5, Router 3 sees the data packet. This time, it picks it up because it recognizes that its own MAC address is the same as the destination MAC address.

At the data link layer, the router strips off the MAC header and passes it up to the network layer. There, it sees that the destination IP address in the IP header matches that of a host that is located on one of the subnetworks to which it is attached. Then the router determines that it must send the data packet through the port attached to Subnetwork 8 for the data packet to reach its destination address. It places a new MAC header on the data. This time, the new MAC header contains the destination MAC address of Host Z and the source MAC address of Router 3. As before, the IP header remains unchanged. Router 3 sends the data through the port that is attached to Subnetwork 8.

The data packet travels along Subnetwork 8. The hosts do not copy the frame because the destination MAC address in the MAC header does not match their own. Finally, the packet reaches Host Z, which picks it up because it sees that its MAC address matches the destination MAC address carried in the MAC header of the data packet. Host Z strips off the MAC header and passes the data to the network layer. At the network layer, Host Z sees that its IP address and the destination IP address carried in the IP header match. Host Z strips off the IP header and passes the data up to the transport layer of the OSI model. Host Z continues to strip off the layers that encapsulate the data packet and then passes the data to the next layer of the OSI model. This continues until the data finally arrives at the application layer of the OSI model.

SKILL BUILDER

Lab Activity: Protocol Inspector and ARP

In this lab, you use Protocol Inspector (or its equivalent) software to view the many mini-conversations that occur on a network, including ARPs and broadcasts.

Summary

In this chapter, you learned that

- Internetworking functions of the network layer include network addressing and best-path determination and selection for traffic.
- All devices on the LAN are required to look at an ARP request, but only the device whose IP address matches the destination IP address carried in the ARP request must respond by providing its MAC address to the device that originated the request.
- When a source cannot locate the destination MAC address in its ARP table, it issues an ARP request in broadcast mode to all devices on the local network.
- When a device does not know its own IP address, it uses RARP, BootP, or DHCP. When a device that originated a RARP request receives a RARP reply, it copies its IP address into its memory cache, where it resides until the system is rebooted.
- Like every other device on the network, routers send and receive data on the network and build ARP tables that map IP addresses to MAC addresses.
- If the source resides on a network that has a different network number than the desired destination, and if the source does not know the MAC address of the destination, it must use the router as a default gateway for its data to reach the destination.
- Routed protocols forward user traffic, whereas routing protocols work between routers to maintain path tables for the routed protocols.
- Network discovery for distance-vector routing involves the exchange of routing tables.

The next chapter discusses the functions of the transport layer.

Check Your Understanding

1. Which of the following best describes one function of Layer 3, the network layer, in the OSI model?
   - **A.** It is responsible for reliable network communication between nodes.
   - **B.** It is concerned with physical addressing and network topology.
   - **C.** It determines the best path for traffic to take through the network.
   - **D.** It manages data exchange between presentation layer entities.
2. What function allows routers to evaluate available routes to a destination and to establish the preferred handling of a packet?
   - **A.** Data linkage
   - **B.** Path determination
   - **C.** SDLC interface protocol
   - **D.** Frame Relay
3. What is a router's attachment to a network called?
   - **A.** Segment
   - **B.** AUI
   - **C.** Interface
   - **D.** None of the above
4. What is the first thing that happens when a DHCP clients boots?
   - **A.** DHCPREQUEST
   - **B.** DHCPBOOT
   - **C.** DHCPDISCOVER
   - **D.** None of the above
5. How does the network layer forward packets from the source toward the destination?
   - **A.** By using a routing table
   - **B.** By using ARP responses
   - **C.** By referring to a name server
   - **D.** By referring to the bridge

6. What are the two parts of an IP?
   - **A.** Network address and host address
   - **B.** Network address and MAC address
   - **C.** Host address and MAC address
   - **D.** MAC address and subnet mask
7. What Internet protocol is used to map an IP address to a MAC address?
   - **A.** UDP
   - **B.** ICMP
   - **C.** ARP
   - **D.** RARP
8. Pinging is a function of what TCP/IP protocol?
   - **A.** UDP
   - **B.** ICMP
   - **C.** ARP
   - **D.** RARP
9. Which of the following initiates an ARP request?
   - **A.** A device that cannot locate the destination IP address in its ARP table
   - **B.** The RARP server, in response to a malfunctioning device
   - **C.** A diskless workstation with an empty cache
   - **D.** A device that cannot locate the destination MAC address in its ARP table
10. Which of the following best describes an ARP table?
   - **A.** A method to reduce network traffic by providing lists of shortcuts and routes to common destinations
   - **B.** A way to route data within networks that are divided into subnetworks
   - **C.** A protocol that performs an application layer conversion of information from one stack to another
   - **D.** A section of RAM on each device that maps IP addresses to MAC addresses

11. Which of the following best describes the ARP reply?
    A. The process of a device sending its MAC address to a source in response to an ARP request
    B. The route of the shortest path between the source and the destination
    C. The updating of ARP tables through intercepting and reading messages traveling on the network
    D. The method of finding IP addresses based on the MAC address, used primarily by RARP servers
12. What are the two parts of the frame header called?
    A. The MAC header and the IP header
    B. The source address and the ARP message
    C. The destination address and the RARP message
    D. D.The request and the data packet
13. Why are current, updated ARP tables important?
    A. For testing links in the network
    B. For limiting the amount of broadcast
    C. For reducing network administrator maintenance time
    D. For resolving addressing conflicts
14. Why is a RARP request made?
    A. A source knows its MAC address but not its IP address.
    B. The data packet needs to find the shortest route between the destination and the source.
    C. The administrator needs to manually configure the system.
    D. A link in the network faults, and a redundant system must be activated.
15. What is in a RARP request?
    A. A MAC header and the RARP request message
    B. A MAC header, a RARP header, and a data packet
    C. A RARP header and MAC and IP addresses
    D. A RARP header and an ARP trailer

16. Which of the following functions is unique to routers?
    - **A.** They bind MAC and IP addresses.
    - **B.** They receive broadcast messages and supply the requested information.
    - **C.** They build ARP tables that describe all networks connected to them.
    - **D.** They reply to ARP requests.
17. If a device doesn't know the MAC address of a device on an adjacent network, it sends an ARP request to:
    - **A.** The default gateway
    - **B.** The closest router
    - **C.** The router interface
    - **D.** All of the above
18. An example of an IGP is:
    - **A.** OSPF
    - **B.** IGRP
    - **C.** RIP
    - **D.** All of the above
19. An example of an EGP is:
    - **A.** OSPF
    - **B.** EIGRP
    - **C.** RIPv2
    - **D.** BGP
20. When is static routing advisable?
    - **A.** To test a particular link
    - **B.** To conserve wide-area bandwidth
    - **C.** Whenever there is only one path to a destination
    - **D.** All of the above

Objectives

After reading this chapter, you will be able to

- Describe the transport layer functions
- Understand TCP and the TCP/IP protocol stack
- Understand Layer 4 protocols
- Describe TCP connection methods

Layer 4: The Transport Layer

Introduction

The transport layer uses the services provided by the network layer, such as best path selection and logical addressing, to provide end-to-end communication between source and destination. This chapter describes how the transport layer regulates the flow of information from source to destination reliably and accurately. The primary features of the transport layer are discussed, including the following:

- The transport-layer data stream is a logical connection between the endpoints of a network.
- End-to-end control is provided by sliding windows and reliability in sequencing numbers and acknowledgments.
- Layer 4 protocols TCP and UDP use port numbers to keep track of different conversations that cross the network at the same time, and to pass information to the upper layers.

The Transport Layer Functions

The transport layer defines end-to-end connectivity between host applications. Transport services include four basic services:

- Segmenting upper-layer application data
- Establishing end-to-end operations
- Sending segments from one end host to another end host
- Ensuring data reliability
- Providing flow control

The transport layer, Layer 4, assumes that it can use the network as a "cloud," as shown in Figure 12-1, to send data packets from the sender source to the receiver destination. The cloud deals with issues such as "Which of several paths is best for a given route?" You can start to see the role that routers perform in this process.

FIGURE 12-1
The network is used as a cloud to send data packets.

The transport layer provides transport services from the source host to the destination host. Services such as these are sometimes referred to as end-to-end services. The transport layer data stream is a logical connection between the endpoints of a network. Its primary duties are to transport and regulate the flow of information from source to destination reliably and accurately. End-to-end control, provided by sliding windows and reliability in sequencing numbers and acknowledgments, is the primary duty of Layer 4.

Flow Control

As the transport layer sends its data segments, it can also ensure the integrity of the data. One method of doing this is called *flow control*. Flow control avoids the problem of a host at one side of the connection overflowing the buffers in the host at the other side. Overflows can present serious problems because they can result in the loss of data.

Transport layer services also enable users to request reliable data transport between hosts and destinations. To obtain such reliable transport of data, a connection-oriented relationship is used between the communicating end systems. Reliable transport can accomplish the following:

- Ensure that segments delivered will be acknowledged to the sender
- Provide for retransmission of any segments that are not acknowledged
- Put segments back into their correct sequence at the destination
- Provide congestion avoidance and control

Establishing a Connection with a Peer System

In the OSI reference model, multiple applications can share the same transport connection. As shown in Figure 12-2, transport functionality is accomplished segment by segment. This means that different applications can send data segments on a first-come, first-served basis. Such segments can be intended for the same destination or for many different destinations. This is sometimes referred to as the multiplexing of upper-layer conversations.

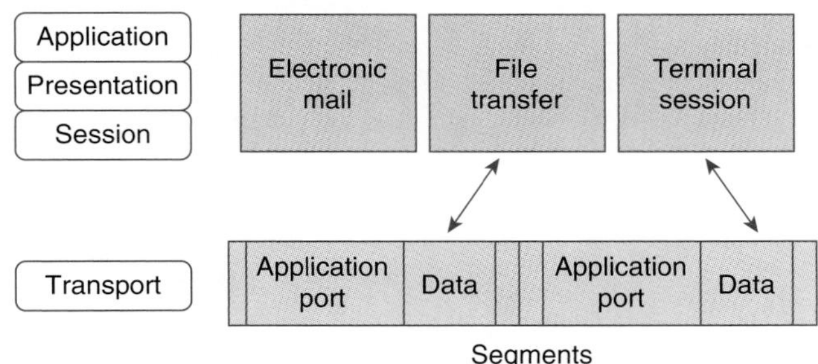

FIGURE 12-2 Multiple applications can share the same transport connection.

One user of the transport layer must establish a connection-oriented session with its peer system. For data transfer to begin, both the sending and the receiving applications inform their respective operating systems that a connection will be initiated. One machine initiates a connection that must be accepted by the other. Protocol software modules in the two operating systems communicate by sending messages across the network to verify that the transfer is authorized and that both sides are ready.

After all synchronization has occurred, a connection is said to be established and the transfer of data begins. During transfer, the two machines continue to communicate with their protocol software to verify that data is received correctly.

Figure 12-3 shows a typical connection between sending and receiving systems. The first handshake requests synchronization. The second and third handshakes acknowledge the initial synchronization request, as well as synchronize connection parameters in the opposite direction. The final handshake segment is an acknowledgment used to inform the destination that both sides agree that a connection has been established. After the connection has been established, data transfer begins.

When data transfer is in progress, congestion can occur for two reasons. First, a high-speed computer might be capable of generating traffic faster than a network can transfer it. Second, if many computers simultaneously need to send datagrams to a single destination, that destination can experience congestion, although no single source caused the problem.

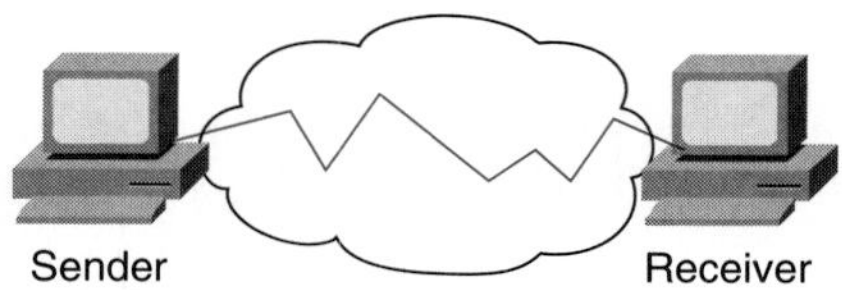

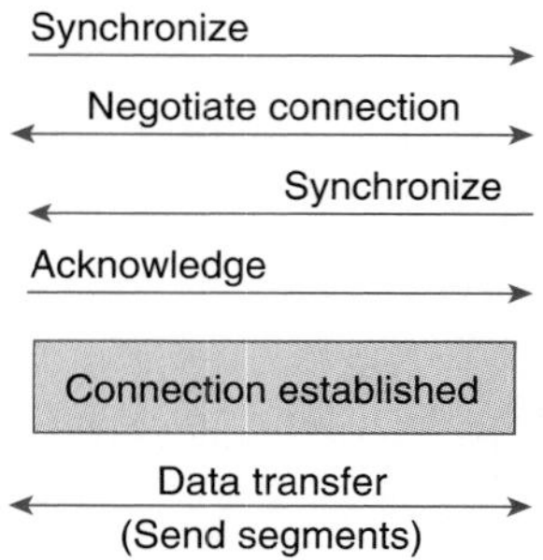

FIGURE 12-3
A typical connection between sending and receiving systems.

When datagrams arrive too quickly for a host or gateway to process, they are stored in memory temporarily. If the traffic continues, the host or gateway eventually exhausts its memory and must discard additional datagrams that arrive.

Instead of allowing data to be lost, the transport function can issue a "not ready" indicator to the sender. Acting like a stop sign, this indicator signals the sender to stop sending data. When the receiver can handle additional data, the receiver sends a "ready" transport indicator, which is like a go signal. As shown in Figure 12-4, when it receives this indicator, the sender can resume segment transmission.

Windowing

In the most basic form of reliable connection-oriented data transfer, data packets must be delivered to the recipient in the same order in which they were transmitted. The protocol fails if any data packets are lost, damaged, duplicated, or received in a different order. The basic solution is to have a recipient acknowledge the receipt of each and every data segment.

If the sender must wait for an acknowledgment after sending each segment, throughput is low. Therefore, most connection-oriented, reliable protocols allow more than one frame or segment to be outstanding at a time. Because time is available after the sender finishes transmitting the data packet and before the sender finishes processing any received acknowledgment, the interval is used for transmitting more data. The number of data packets the sender is allowed to have outstanding without having received an acknowledgment is known as the *window*.

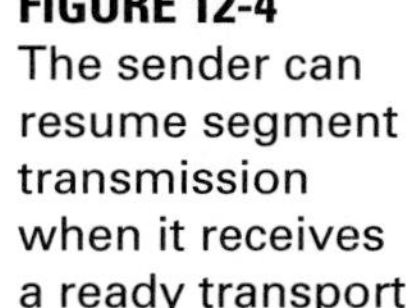

FIGURE 12-4
The sender can resume segment transmission when it receives a ready transport indicator from the receiver.

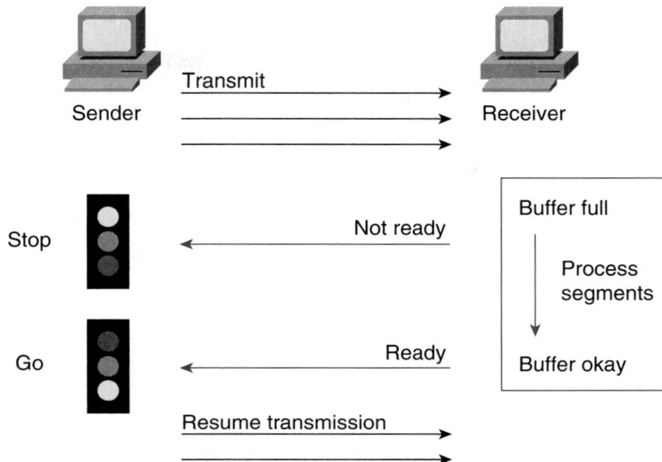

Windowing is a method of controlling the amount of information transferred end to end. Some protocols measure information in terms of the number of packets; others, such as TCP, measure information in terms of the number of bytes.

In Figure 12-5, the sender and receiver are workstations. With a window size of 2, the sender waits for an acknowledgment for every data packet transmitted. With a window size of 3, the sender can transmit three data packets before expecting an acknowledgment.

Acknowledgment

Reliable delivery guarantees that a stream of data sent from one machine will be delivered through a data link to another machine without duplication or data loss. Positive acknowledgment with retransmission is one technique that guarantees reliable delivery of data. Positive acknowledgment requires a recipient to communicate with the source, sending back an acknowledgment message when it receives data. The sender keeps a record of each data packet (TCP segment) that it sends and expects an acknowledgment. The sender also starts a timer when it sends a segment, and it retransmits a segment if the timer expires before an acknowledgment arrives.

Figure 12-6 shows the sender transmitting data packets 1, 2, and 3. The receiver acknowledges receipt of the packets by requesting packet 4. Upon receiving the acknowledgment, the sender sends packets 4, 5, and 6. If packet 5 does not arrive at the destination, the receiver acknowledges with a request to resend packet 5. The sender resends packet 5 and then receives an acknowledgment to continue with the transmission of packet 7.

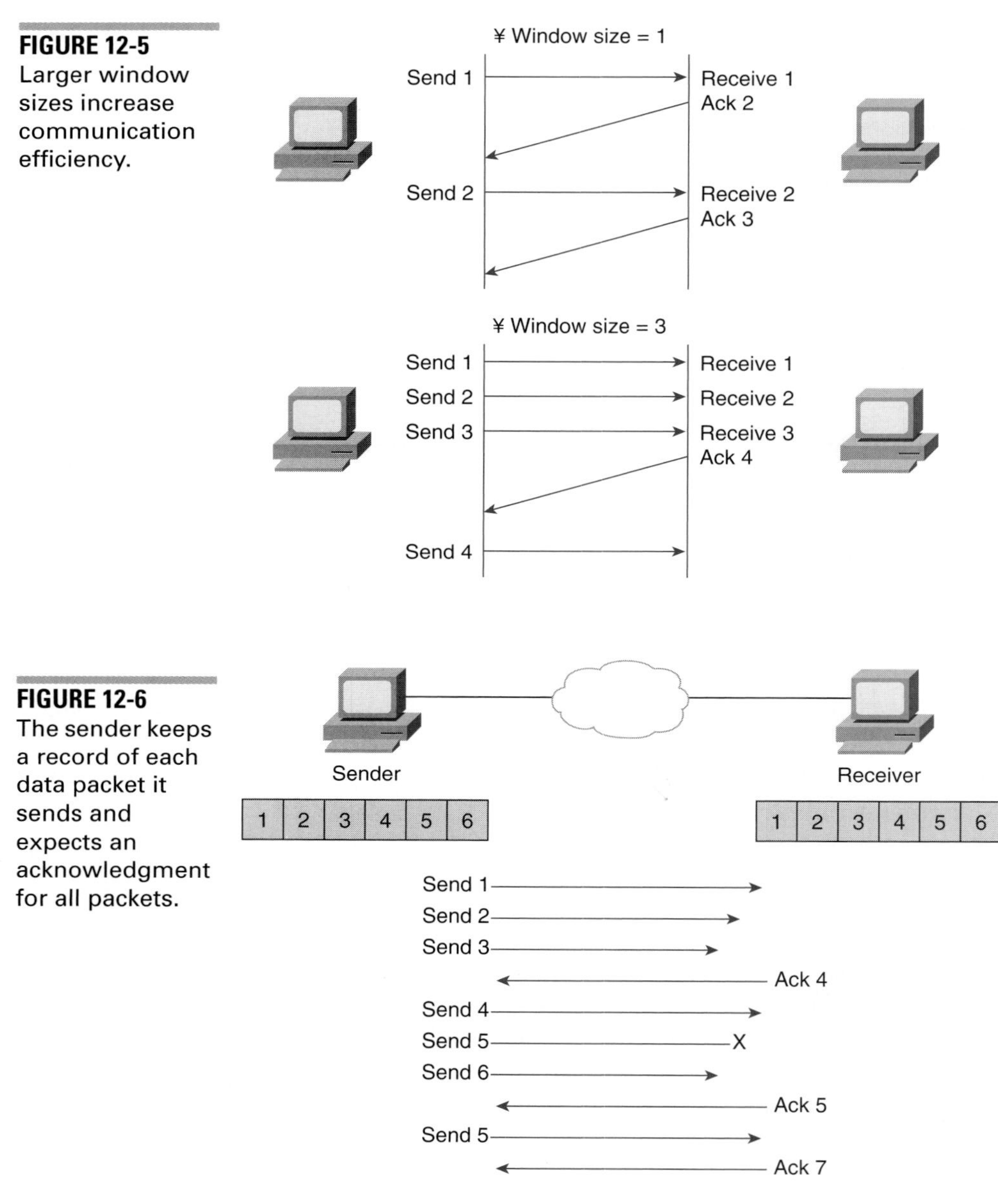

FIGURE 12-5 Larger window sizes increase communication efficiency.

FIGURE 12-6 The sender keeps a record of each data packet it sends and expects an acknowledgment for all packets.

The TCP/IP Protocol Stack

TCP/IP is a combination of two individual protocols: TCP and IP. IP is a Layer 3 protocol, a connectionless service that provides best-effort (nonreliable) delivery across a network. TCP is a Layer 4 protocol, a connection-oriented service that provides flow control as well as reliability. Pairing the protocols enables them to provide a wider range of services. TCP/IP is also used to refer to the entire suite of protocols. These protocols, working together, provide the basis for much of the Internet.

The TCP/IP suite of protocols was developed as part of the research done by the Defense Advanced Research Projects Agency (DARPA). It was originally developed to provide communication through DARPA. Now, TCP/IP is the de facto standard for internetwork communications and serves as the transport protocols for the Internet, enabling millions of computers to communicate globally.

This book focuses on TCP/IP for these reasons:

- TCP/IP is a universally available protocol suite that you likely will use at work.
- TCP/IP is a useful reference for understanding other protocols because it includes elements that are representative of other protocols.

Internet protocols can be used to communicate across any set of interconnected networks. They are equally well suited for LAN and WAN communication. The Internet Protocol suite includes not only Layers 3 and 4 specifications (such as IP and TCP), but also specifications for supporting such common applications as e-mail, remote login, terminal emulation, and file transfer.

The TCP/IP protocol stack maps closely to the lower layers of the Open System Interconnection (OSI) reference model, as shown in Figure 12-7. TCP/IP supports all standard physical and data-link protocols. TCP/IP information is transferred in a sequence of datagrams. One message might be transmitted as a series of datagrams that are reassembled into the message at the receiving location.

SKILL BUILDER

Lab Activity: Protocol Inspector and TCP

In this lab, you use Protocol Inspector (or equivalent) software to view dynamic TCP operations.

As shown in Figure 12-8, application layer protocols exist for file transfer, e-mail, and remote login. Network management is also supported at the application or process layer of the Internet protocol suite.

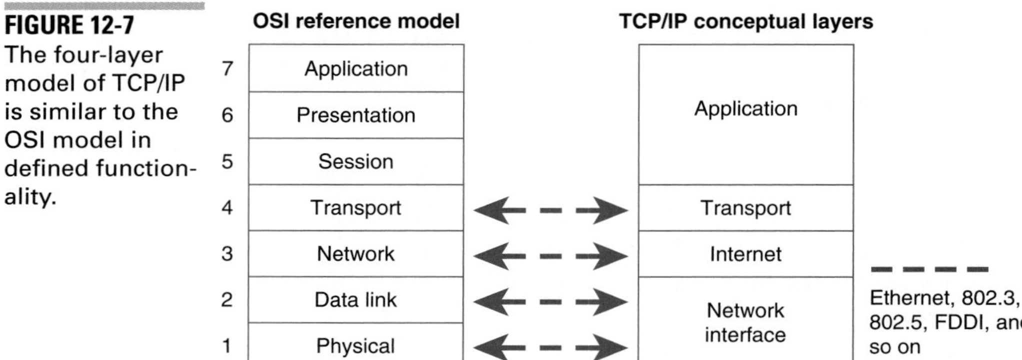

FIGURE 12-7
The four-layer model of TCP/IP is similar to the OSI model in defined functionality.

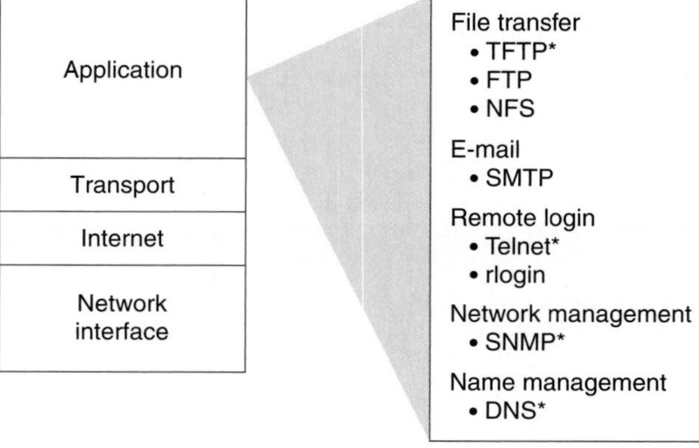

FIGURE 12-8
Some applications, such as Trivial File Transfer Protocol (TFTP) and Simple Network Management Protocol (SNMP), can reside on routers.

Layer 4 Protocols

The emphasis of this book is on TCP/IP Ethernet networks. The TCP/IP protocol suite, at OSI model Layer 4 (transport layer), has two protocols: TCP and UDP (see Figure 12-9).

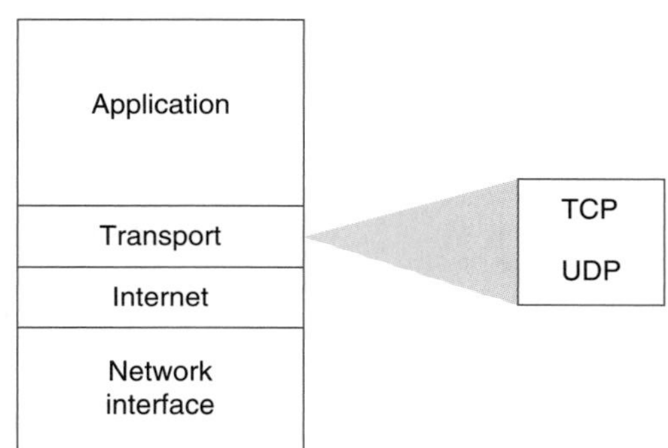

FIGURE 12-9 Application developers can select a connection-oriented and reliable transport (TCP) or a connectionless and nonreliable (UDP) transport.

TCP sets up a connection sometimes called a virtual circuit between end-user applications. These are its characteristics:

- Is connection-oriented
- Is reliable
- Divides outgoing messages into segments
- Reassembles messages at the destination station from incoming segments
- Resends anything not received

UDP transports data unreliably between hosts. The characteristics of UDP are the following:

- Connectionless
- Unreliable
- Transmits messages (called user datagrams)
- Provides no software checking for message delivery (unreliable)
- Does not reassemble incoming messages
- Uses no acknowledgments
- Provides no flow control

TCP Segment Format

Transmission Control Protocol (TCP) is a connection-oriented Layer 4 (transport layer) protocol that provides reliable full-duplex data transmission. TCP is part of the TCP/IP protocol stack.

The following are the definitions of the fields in the TCP segment (see Figure 12-10):

- **Source port**—Number of the calling port. This identifies the upper-layer process at the source end of this segment, which may or may not be the end that initiated the connection.
- **Destination port**—Number of the called port. Likewise, this is the port assigned at the destination end for this segment.
- **Sequence number**—Number used to ensure correct sequencing of the arriving data. This is the sequence number for the first octet in the user data field.
- **Acknowledgment number**—The next expected TCP octet.
- **HLEN**—Number of 32-bit words in the header. The term *HLEN* is not used to name this field in the TCP header, although it is applied to a similar field in the IP header. The term usually used is "data offset."
- **Reserved**—Set to zero.
- **Code bits**—Control functions (such as setup and termination of a session). This set of bits is typically documented as "flags," not "code bits."
- **Window**—Number of octets that the device is willing to accept.
- **Checksum**—Calculated checksum of the header and data fields.
- **Urgent pointer**—Indicator for the end of the urgent data.
- **Options**—Maximum TCP segment size.
- **Data**—Upper-layer protocol data.

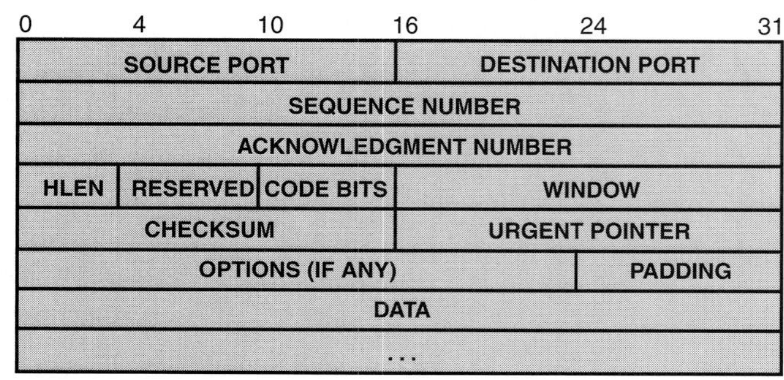

FIGURE 12-10
The TCP segment format includes 12 fields.

UDP Segment Format

User Datagram Protocol (UDP) is the connectionless transport protocol in the TCP/IP protocol stack. UDP is a simple protocol that exchanges datagrams, without acknowledgments or guaranteed delivery. Error processing and retransmission must be handled by other protocols.

UDP uses no windowing or acknowledgments; therefore, application layer protocols provide the reliability. UDP is designed for applications that do not need to put sequences of segments together. As you can see in Figure 12-11, a UDP header is relatively small.

FIGURE 12-11
UDP has no sequence or acknowledgment fields.

Number of bits	16	16	16	16	
	Source Port	Destination Port	Length	Checksum	Data...

Protocols that use UDP include the following:

- Trivial File Transfer Protocol (TFTP)
- Simple Network Management Protocol (SNMP)
- Dynamic Host Control Protocol (DHCP)
- Domain Name System (DNS)
- BOOTP

TCP Connection Methods

Both TCP and UDP use port numbers to pass information to the upper layers. Port numbers are used to keep track of different conversations that cross the network at the same time. Application software developers have agreed to use the well-known port numbers that are defined in RFC 1700. For example, any conversation bound for the FTP application uses the standard port number 21 (see Figure 12-12). Conversations that do not involve applications with well-known port numbers are assigned port numbers that have been randomly selected from within a specific range. These port numbers are used as source and destination addresses in the TCP segment.

Some ports are reserved in both TCP and UDP, although applications might not be written to support them (see Table 12-1). Port numbers have the following assigned ranges:

- Numbers below 255 are used for public applications.
- Numbers from 255 to 1023 are assigned to companies for marketable applications.

- Numbers above 1023 are unregulated.

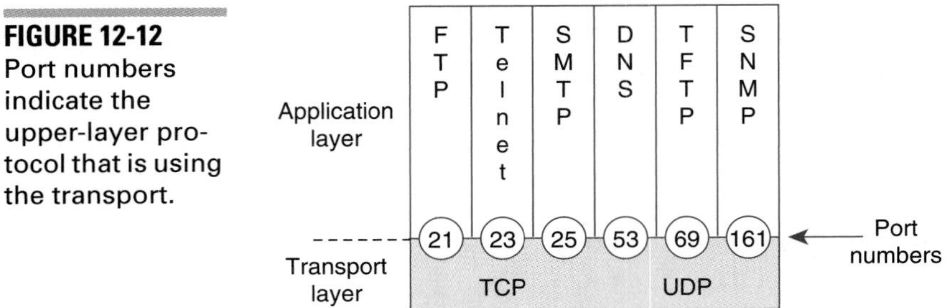

FIGURE 12-12 Port numbers indicate the upper-layer protocol that is using the transport.

TABLE 12-1 Reserved TCP and UDP Port Numbers

Decimal	Keyword	Description
0	—	Reserved
1–4	—	Unassigned
5	rje	Remote job entry
7	echo	Echo
9	discard	Discard
11	users	Active users
13	daytime	Daytime
15	netstat	Who is up or netstat
17	quote	Quote of the day
19	chargen	Character generator
20	ftp-data	File Transfer Protocol (data)
21	ftp	File Transfer Protocol
23	telnet	Terminal connection
25	smtp	Simple Mail Transfer Protocol
37	time	Time of day
39	rlp	Resource Location Protocol
42	nameserver	Hostname server

TABLE 12-1 Reserved TCP and UDP Port Numbers (Continued)

Decimal	Keyword	Description
43	nicname	Who is
53	domain	Domain Name Server
67	bootps	Bootstrap protocol server
68	bootpc	Bootstrap protocol client
69	tftp	Trivial File Transfer Protocol
75	—	Any private dial-out service
77	—	Any private RJE service
79	finger	Finger
123	ntp	Network Time Protocol
133–159	—	Unassigned
160–223	—	Reserved
224–241	—	Unassigned
242–255	—	Unassigned

As shown in Figure 12-13, end systems use port numbers to select proper applications. Originating source port numbers are dynamically assigned by the source host; usually, it is a number larger than 1023.

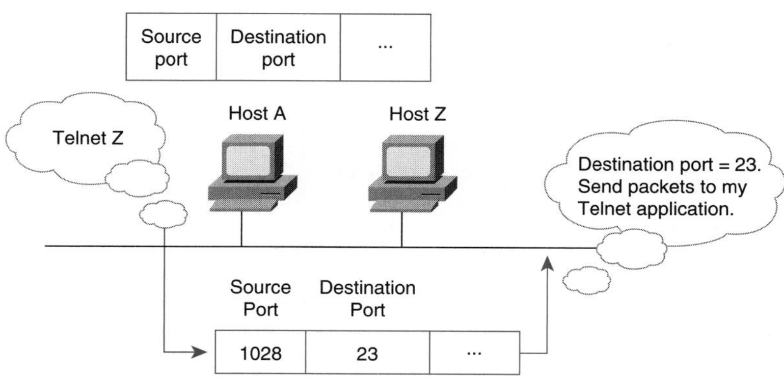

FIGURE 12-13 The source port and destination is typically not the same.

Three-Way Handshake/Open Connection

Connection-oriented services involve three phases: connection establishment phase, data tranfer phase, and connection termination phase. In the connection establishment phase, a connection or session is set up between the source and the destination. Resources are typically reserved at this time to ensure a consistent grade of service. During the data transfer phase, data is transmitted sequentially over the established path, arriving at the destination in the order in which it was sent. The connection termination phase consists of terminating the connection between the source and destination when it is no longer needed.

TCP hosts establish a connection-oriented session with one another using a three-way handshake. A three-way handshake/open connection sequence synchronizes a connection at both ends before data is transferred. This exchange of introductory sequence numbers during the connection sequence is important because it ensures that any data that is lost due to transmission problems can be recovered.

First, one host initiates a connection by sending a packet indicating its initial sequence number of x with a certain bit in the header set to indicate a connection request. Second, the other host receives the packet, records the sequence number of x, replies with an acknowledgment of x + 1, and includes its own initial sequence number of y. The acknowledgment number of x + 1 means that the host has received all octets up to and including x and is expecting x + 1 next. As illustrated in Figure 12-14, both ends of a connection are synchronized with a three-way handshake/open connection sequence.

FIGURE 12-14 Data cannot be exchanged until the three-way handshake has been successfully completed.

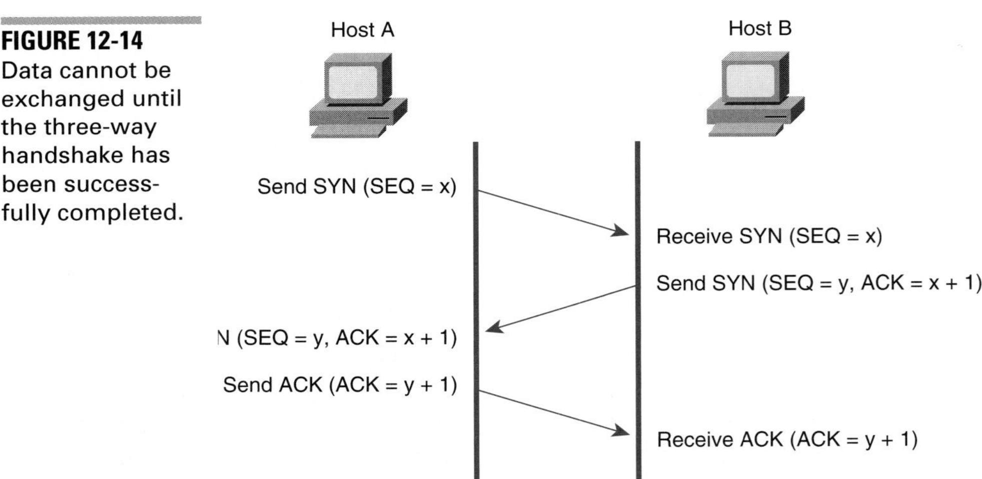

Positive acknowledgment and retransmission is a common technique that many protocols use to provide reliability. With positive acknowledgement and retransmission, the source sends a packet, starts a timer, and waits for an acknowledgment, if the entire "window size" has been transmitted. If the timer expires before the source receives an acknowledgment, the source retransmits the packet and starts the timer over again.

Window size determines the amount of data that you can transmit at one time before stopping transmission and waiting for an acknowledgment from the destination. The larger the window size number (in bytes, for TCP), the greater the amount of data that the host can transmit before stopping. After a host transmits the window-sized number of bytes, (window size = 1 when acknowledging frames) the host must receive an acknowledgment that the data has been received before it can send any more messages. For example, with a window size of 2, each individual (1) segment must be acknowledged before you can send the next segment (see Figure 12-15).

FIGURE 12-15 With a window size of 2, the sender must wait for an acknowledgment after each segment sent before sending more data.

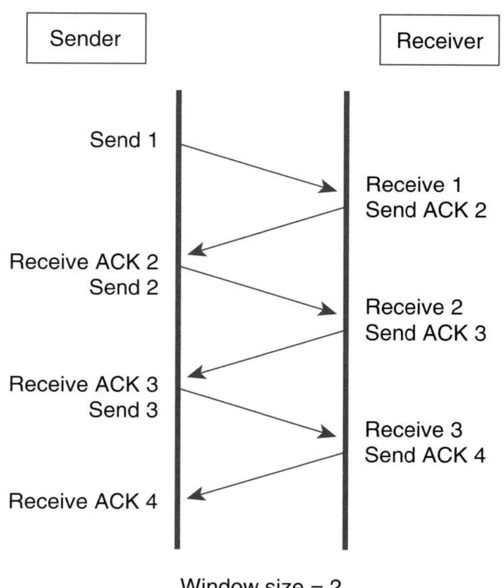

TCP uses expectational acknowledgments, meaning that the acknowledgment number refers to the segment that is next expected. The "sliding" part of sliding window refers to the fact that the window size is negotiated dynamically during the TCP session. This results in efficient use of bandwith by the hosts.

TCP provides sequencing of bytes with a forward reference acknowledgment. The sequence number in the TCP header is associated with the first byte in the user data area. At the receiving station, TCP reassembles the segments into a complete message. Segments that are not acknowledged within a given time period result in retransmission.

Summary

In this chapter, you learned about the functions of the transport layer and the different processes that occur as data packets travel through this layer. More specifically, you learned that

- The transport layer regulates information flow to ensure end-to-end connectivity between host applications reliably and accurately.
- The TCP/IP protocol suite has two primary protocols at Layer 4 (transport layer): TCP and UDP.
- TCP and UDP use port numbers to keep track of different conversations that cross the network at the same time, to pass information to the upper layers.
- The three-way handshake sequence synchronizes a logical connection between the endpoints of a TCP connection.

Now that you have completed this chapter, you should have a firm understanding of how the transport layer provides transport services from the host to the destination, often referred to as end-to-end services. In the next chapter, you examine what happens to data packets as they travel through the session layer or Layer 5 of the OSI model.

Check Your Understanding

1. When conversing with an individual whose primary language is different than yours, you might need to repeat your words and speak more slowly. Repeating your words can be compared to ______, and the need to speak slowly can be compared to the ______ functions of the transport layer.

   A. Reliability; flow control

   B. Flow control; reliability

   C. Transport; acknowledgment

   D. Flow control; transport

2. When you mail a registered package through the standard mail system, you make an assumption that the person to which it is addressed receives it. This is analogous to which protocol?

   A. UDP

   B. TCP

   C. IPX

   D. IP

3. The following characteristics describe what TCP/IP protocol: connection-oriented; resends anything not received; divides outgoing messages into segments.

   A. IPX

   B. TCP

   C. UDP

   D. SPS

4. What does the window field in a TCP segment indicate?

   A. Number of 32-bit words in the header

   B. Number of the called port

   C. Number used to ensure correct sequencing of the arriving data

   D. Number of octets that the device is willing to accept

5. What transport protocol exchanges datagrams without acknowledgments or guaranteed delivery?

   A. UDP

   B. TCP

   C. IRQ

   D. LLC

6. What do TCP and UDP use to keep track of different conversations crossing a network at the same time?

   A. Port numbers

   B. IP addresses

   C. MAC addresses

   D. Route numbers

7. How does TCP synchronize a connection between the source and the destination before data transmission?

   A. Two-way handshake

   B. Three-way handshake

   C. Four-way handshake

   D. Holton functions

8. Which of the following is initially true when the TCP window size is 4?

   A. The host must receive an ACK 4 acknowledgement before sending more messages.

   B. Bandwidth is used less efficiently than with a window size of 1.

   C. The host must receive an ACK 2 acknowledgement before sending more messages.

   D. TCP does not use windowing.

9. Which range of port numbers is unregulated?

   A. Below 255

   B. Between 256 and 512

   C. Between 256 and 1023

   D. Above 1023

10. With TCP transmission, what occurs if a segment is not acknowledged in a certain time period?
    A. UDP takes over the transmission.
    B. The virtual circuit is terminated.
    C. Nothing happens.
    D. Retransmission occurs.
11. Which best describes flow control?
    A. A method to manage limited bandwidth
    B. A method of connecting two hosts synchronously
    C. A method to prevent buffer overrun
    D. A method to check data for viruses before transmission
12. Which of the following best describes the purpose of the TCP/IP protocol stack?
    A. Maps closely to the OSI reference model's upper layers
    B. Supports all standard physical and data link protocols
    C. Transfers information from one host to another in a sequence of datagrams
    D. Reassembles datagrams into complete messages at the receiving location
13. Which of the following is one of the protocols found in the transport layer?
    A. UCP
    B. UDP
    C. TDP
    D. TDC
14. What is the purpose of port numbers?
    A. They keep track of different upper-layer conversations crossing the network at the same time.
    B. Source systems use them to keep a session organized.

C. End systems use them to dynamically assign end users to a particular session, depending on their application use.

D. Source systems generate them to predict destination addresses.

15. Why are TCP three-way handshake/open connections used?

A. To ensure that lost data can be recovered if problems occur later

B. To determine how much data the receiving station can accept at one time

C. To provide efficient use of bandwidth by users

D. To change binary **ping** responses into information in the upper layers

16. What does a dynamic TCP sliding window do?

A. It makes the window larger so that more data can come through at once, which results in more efficient use of bandwidth.

B. The window size slides to each section of the datagram to receive data, which results in more efficient use of bandwidth.

C. It allows the window size to be negotiated dynamically during the TCP session, which results in more efficient use of bandwidth.

D. It limits the incoming data so that each segment must be sent one by one, which is an inefficient use of bandwidth.

17. UDP segments use what protocols to provide reliability?

A. Network layer protocols

B. Application layer protocols

C. Internet protocols

D. Transmission control protocols

18. What is one purpose of ICMP testing?

A. To determine whether messages reach their destination and, if they don't, to determine possible reasons why they did not

B. To make sure that all activity on the network is being monitored

C. To determine whether the network was set up according to the model

D. To determine whether the network is in control mode or user mode

19. Assuming that the MAC is not in the ARP table, how does a sender find the destination's MAC address?

A. It consults its routing table.

B. It sends a message to all the addresses, searching for the address.

C. It sends out a broadcast message to the entire LAN.

D. It sends out a broadcast message to the entire internetwork.

20. Which of the following best describes window size?

A. The maximum size of the window that software can have and still process data rapidly

B. The number of messages or bytes that can be transmitted before stopping and awaiting an acknowledgment

C. The size of the window, in picas, that must be set ahead of time so that data can be sent

D. The size of the window opening on a monitor, which is not always equal to the monitor size

Objectives

After reading this chapter, you will be able to

- Describe the session layer
- Understand dialog control
- Understand dialog separation
- Identify Layer 5 protocols

Chapter 13

Layer 5: The Session Layer

Introduction

In this chapter, you learn more about the control mechanisms provided by the session layer (Layer 5) of the OSI model. Included are accounting control, conversation control (that is, determining who can talk when), and session parameter negotiation.

This chapter also describes how the session layer coordinates service requests and responses, which occur when applications communicate between different hosts. You also learn about the processes that take place as data travels through the session layer, including dialog control and dialog separation that enable applications to communicate between the source and the destination.

Session Layer Functions

Layer 5 of the OSI model is the session layer, as shown in Figure 13-1. The session layer allows two applications to synchronize their communications and exchange of data. This layer breaks the communication between two systems into dialog units and provides major and minor synchronization points during that communication. For example, a large distributed database transaction among multiple systems might use session layer protocols to ensure that a transaction either is completed fully or is "rolled back" to a known checkpoint on all systems.

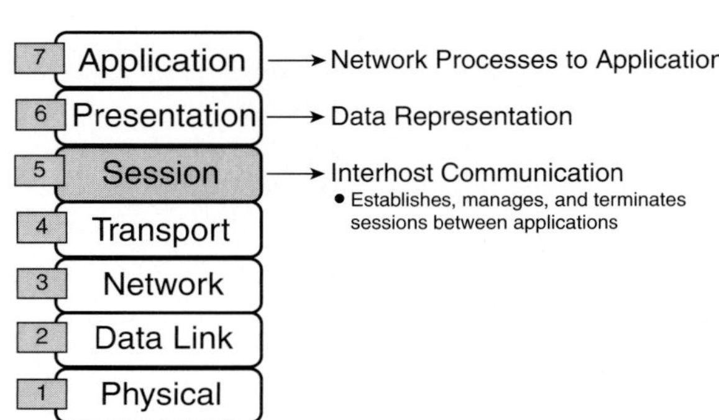

FIGURE 13-1
Session layer functions.

MORE INFORMATION

Session Layer Analogies

Networking processes often occur in less than a second, making them difficult to "see." By using analogies, you can understand more clearly what happens during these processes. The following analogy helps explain the session layer:

You just had an argument with a friend. You are now communicating (referred to here as a "session") with this friend to discuss the state of your friendship. You are using the Instant Mail feature on America Online (AOL) or an Internet Relay Chat (IRC). However, two problems may interfere with your session. The first problem is that your messages may cross during your conversation. You may both type messages at exactly the same time, thus interrupting each other. The second problem is that you need to pause (to save your current conversation as a file) or to check each other's previous conversation (for clues to the cause of the argument) or resynchronize your communication after an interruption.

To solve the first problem, you should establish a protocol (or set of protocols) that dictates rules for communicating with each other. This means that each of you agree to a set of guidelines to use during the conversation (such as taking turns sending messages to avoid interrupting each other). This two-way alternate communication is referred to as *half-duplex communication*. Another solution is for each person to type whenever he wants to, regardless of who is transmitting; assume that more information is always on the way. This two-way simultaneous communication is called *full-duplex communication*.

To solve the second problem, you should send a checkpoint to each other, which means that each person should save the conversation as a file. Then each person should reread the last part of his conversation and check the time on the clock. This is referred to as *synchronization*.

Two important checkpoints are how the conversation starts and how it ends. This is referred to as orderly initiation and termination of the conversation. For example, when you use Instant Mail or Internet Relay Chat, good-byes are usually exchanged before terminating a session. The other person then realizes that you are ending the session.

To help understand what the session layer does, let's use the same analogy in another way. Imagine that you are communicating with a pen pal via the postal service. The same problems might occur. Messages could pass each other because you haven't agreed to use full-duplex communication rather than half-duplex communication. Or you could experience poor communication because you haven't synchronized the subjects of your conversations.

MORE INFORMATION

Common Session Layer Implementations

Many protocols bundle this layer's functionality into their transport layers. A couple specific examples of session layer services are Remote Procedure Calls (RPCs) and quality of service protocols, such as RSVP, the bandwidth reservation protocol.

The session layer establishes, manages, and terminates communication sessions between application layer entities. Communication sessions consist of service requests and service responses that occur between applications located in different network devices. These requests and responses are coordinated by protocols implemented at the session layer. Some examples of session layer implementations include Zone Information Protocol (ZIP), the AppleTalk protocol that coordinates the name-binding process; and Session Control Protocol (SCP), the DECnet Phase IV session layer protocol.

The Zone Information Protocol (ZIP) is a session layer protocol in the AppleTalk protocol suite that maintains network number-to-zone name mappings in AppleTalk routers. ZIP is used primarily by AppleTalk routers. However, other network nodes use ZIP services at startup to choose their zone. ZIP maintains a zone information table (ZIT) in each router. ZITs are lists maintained by ZIP that map more specific network numbers to a zone name. Each ZIT contains a network number-to-zone name mapping for every network in the internetwork. Figure 13-2 shows a basic ZIT.

FIGURE 13-2
A ZIT maps a network number-to-zone name for every network in the internetwork.

Network Number	Zones
10	Marketing
20-25	Documentation, Training
50	Finance
100-120	Engineering
100-120	Facilities, Administration

MORE INFORMATION (CONTINUED)

The Session Control Protocol (SCP) is the DECnet Phase IV session control layer protocol. SCP performs a number of functions, including the following:

- Requesting a logical link from an end device
- Receiving logical link requests from end devices
- Accepting or rejecting logical link requests
- Translating names to addresses
- Terminating logical links

Figure 13-3 shows how the DECnet Phase IV upper-layer protocols map to the layers of the Phase IV DNA.

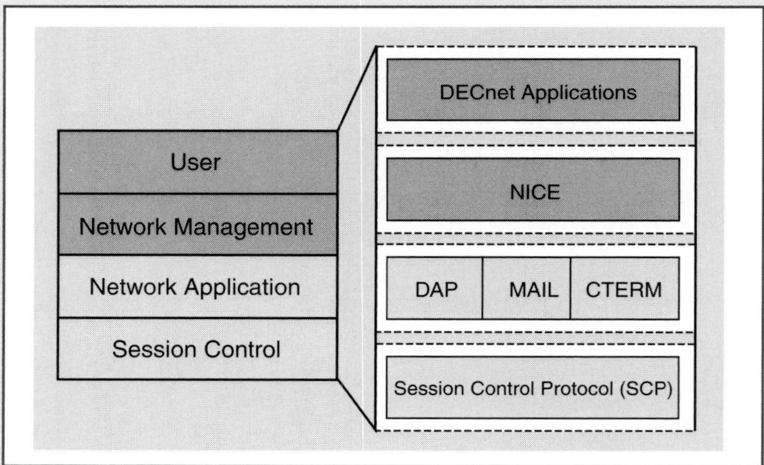

FIGURE 13-3 The DECnet Phase IV session layer protocol.

Dialog Control

The session layer establishes, manages, and terminates sessions between application layer protocols. This includes starting, stopping, and resynchronizing on two computers communication between applications. The session layer coordinates applications as they interact on two communicating hosts. Data communications travel on packet-switched networks, not like telephone calls that travel on circuit-switched networks.

Communication between two computers involves many mini-conversations, thus ensuring that the two computers can communicate effectively. One requirement of these mini-conversations is that each host plays dual roles: requesting service, like a client, and replying with service, like a server.

service, like a server. Determining which role they are playing at any given moment is part of dialog control.

The session layer decides whether to use full-duplex or half-duplex conversation. This is also part of dialog control. If two-way simultaneous (full-duplex) communication is allowed, the session layer does little in the way of managing the conversation. In these cases, other layers of the communicating computers manage the conversation. It is possible to have session layer collisions, although these are very different from the media collisions that occur in Layer 1. At this level, collisions can occur only as two messages pass each other and cause confusion in either or both of the communicating hosts.

If these session layer collisions are intolerable, then dialog control has another option: half-duplex (two-way alternate) communication. Half-duplex communication can involve the use of a session layer data token that allows each host to take turns. This is similar to the way a Layer 2 Token Ring handles permission to transmit. There are other methods for determining whose turn it is to talk as well.

Dialog Separation

Dialog separation is the orderly initiation, termination, and management of communication in which a transaction is tracked through completion. A transaction is defined as an atomic or indivisible unit of work—that is, it is a unit of work that either must fully complete or must be rolled back to some known state, as though it never began. An example of such a transaction is a bank withdrawal. If the transaction begins, it must complete and the customer must receive the money; otherwise, the customer's account should not be debited for the amount.

Figure 13-4 illustrates a minor synchronization. At "Time Axis t = checkpoint," the Host A session layer sends a synchronization message to Host B, at which time both hosts perform the following routine:

1. Back up the particular files.
2. Save the network settings.
3. Save the clock settings.
4. Make note of the endpoint in the conversation.

A major synchronization would involve more back-and-forth steps and conversation than what is shown in Figure 13-4.

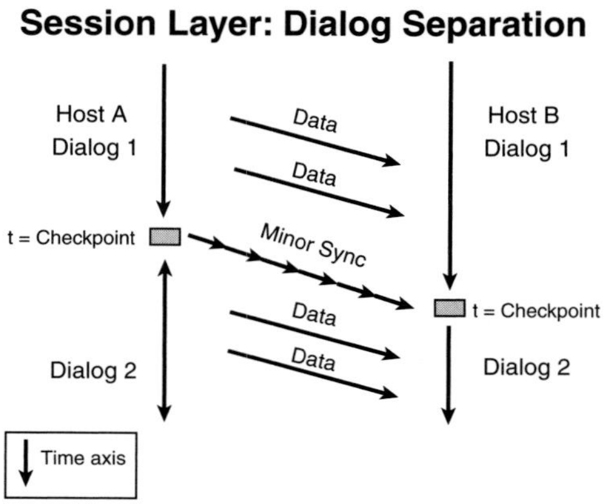

FIGURE 13-4
Session layer: dialog separation.

Checkpointing is similar to the way a word processor on a stand-alone computer pauses for a second when it performs an AutoSave of the current document. However, these checkpoints are used instead to separate parts of a session, sometimes referred to as dialogs, to ensure that the transaction either completes or doesn't begin.

Layer 5 Protocols

Layer 5 involves a number of important protocols. You should be able to recognize these protocols when they appear in a login procedure or in an application. Examples of Layer 5 protocols are the following:

- Structured Query Language (SQL)
- Remote Procedure Call (RPC)
- X Window System
- AppleTalk Session Protocol (ASP)
- Digital Network Architecture Session Control Protocol (DNA SCP)

Summary

In this chapter, you learned about the functions of the session layer and the different processes that occur as data packets travel through this layer. More specifically, you learned that

- The session layer establishes, manages, and terminates sessions between applications.
- Communication sessions consist of mini-conversations that occur between applications located in different network devices.
- Requests and responses are coordinated by protocols implemented at the session layer.
- The session layer decides whether to use full-duplex (two-way simultaneous) communication or half-duplex (two-way alternate) communication by using dialog control.
- The session layer uses dialog separation to initiate, terminate, and manage communication in an orderly fashion.

Now that you have completed this chapter, you should have a firm understanding of how the session layer provides orderly communication between applications on hosts. In the next chapter, you examine what happens to data packets as they travel through the presentation layer of the OSI model.

Check Your Understanding

1. The session layer of the OSI model handles such functions as
   - **A.** Physical addressing, sequencing of frames, flow control, and error notification
   - **B.** Data compression and encryption
   - **C.** Flow control, multiplexing, virtual circuit management, and error handling
   - **D.** Establishes, manages, and terminates sessions between applications
2. Half-duplex communication often involves the use of ______.
   - **A.** MAC addresses
   - **B.** Handshakes
   - **C.** A session-layer data token
   - **D.** Full-duplex connection
3. What is the term for the session layer dialog-control option that uses a data token?
   - **A.** Two-way simultaneous
   - **B.** Two-way continuous
   - **C.** Two-way alternate
   - **D.** One-way alternate
4. What are used to separate the parts of a session?
   - **A.** Checkpoints
   - **B.** Spacers
   - **C.** Pointers
   - **D.** Sequence numbers
5. Which of the following are session layer protocols?
   - **A.** ASP, SQL, RPC
   - **B.** SQL, RPG, SCO
   - **C.** TCP, CFM, ISP
   - **D.** UDP, IPX, ARP

6. Which of the following is considered a Layer 5 protocol?
   - **A.** TCP
   - **B.** PPP
   - **C.** UDP
   - **D.** SQL
7. Determining which role mini-conversations are playing at any given moment is called:
   - **A.** Dialog control
   - **B.** Communication control
   - **C.** Order control
   - **D.** None of the above
8. A minor synchronization consists of the following, except:
   - **A.** Back up the particular files
   - **B.** Save the network settings
   - **C.** Make note of the endpoint in the conversation
   - **D.** None of the above
9. Which is not a Layer 5 protocol?
   - **A.** SCP
   - **B.** RPC
   - **C.** SQL
   - **D.** None of the above
10. The Zone Information Protocol (ZIP) is a session layer protocol in the:
    - **A.** DECnet protocol suite
    - **B.** IPX protocol suite
    - **C.** AppleTalk protocol suite
    - **D.** TCP/IP protocol suite

Objectives

After reading this chapter, you will be able to

- Describe presentation layer functions and standards
- Describe file formats handled by the presentation layer
- Understand data encryption and compression functions at the presentation layer

Chapter 14

Layer 6: The Presentation Layer

Introduction

This chapter looks at Layer 6, the presentation layer. This layer provides services that allow communication betwwen applications on diverse computer systems in a manner that is transparent to the applications.

The presentation layer is concerned with the format and representation of data. If necessary, this layer can translate among different data formats. In this chapter, you learn how the presentation layer provides code formatting and conversion, which is used to make sure that applications have meaningful information to process. Layer 6 is also concerned with the data structures that are used by applications. To better understand this, you learn how Layer 6 arranges and organizes data before it is transferred.

Presentation Layer Functions and Standards

The presentation layer presents data in a form that the receiving device can understand. To better understand the concept, use the analogy of two people speaking different languages. The only way for them to understand each other is to have another person translate. The presentation layer serves as the translator for devices that need to communicate over a network.

Layer 6, the presentation layer, provides functions related to the format of user data (see Figure 14-1).

As shown in Figure 14-2, these functions are as follows:

- Data formatting (presentation)
- Data encryption
- Data compression

After receiving data from the application layer, the presentation layer performs one or all of its functions on the data before it sends it to the session layer. At the receiving station, the presentation layer takes the data from the session layer and performs the required functions before passing it to the application layer.

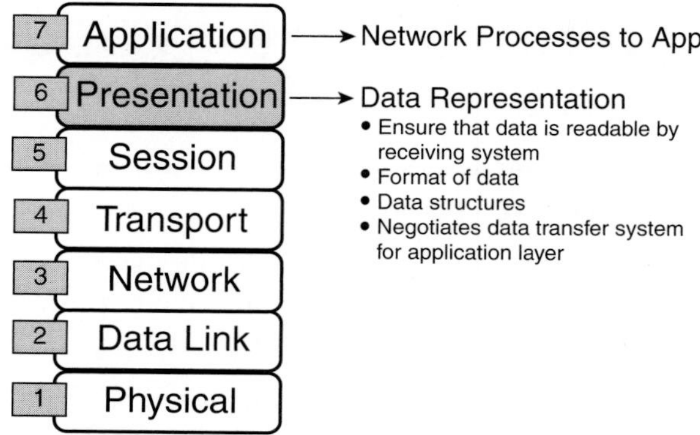

FIGURE 14-1
Presentation layer functions.

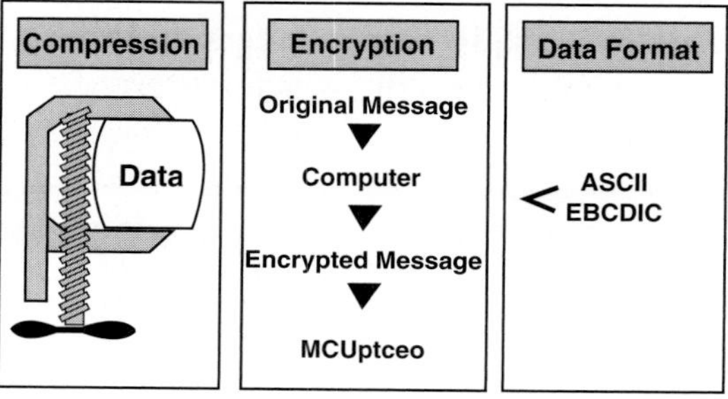

FIGURE 14-2
Presentation layer formatting, encryption, and compression functions.

NOTE

Most personal computers use ASCII, while mainframe computers traditionally use EBCDIC.

To understand how data formatting works, imagine two dissimilar systems. The first system uses Extended Binary Coded Decimal Interchange Code (EBCDIC) to represent characters onscreen. The second system uses ASCII for the same function. Layer 6 provides the translation between these two different types of codes.

Layer 6 standards also determine how graphic images are presented. Three of these standards are as follows:

- **PICT**—A picture format used to transfer QuickDraw graphics between programs on the MAC operating system
- **Tagged Image File Format** (**TIFF**)—A format for high-resolution, bitmapped images

- **Joint Photographic Experts Group (JPEG)**—A graphic format used most often to compress still images of complex pictures and photographs

Other Layer 6 standards guide the presentation of sound and movies. Included in these standards are the following:

- **Musical Instrument Digital Interface (MIDI)**——Standard for digitized music
- **Motion Picture Experts Group (MPEG)**—Standard for the compression and coding of motion video for CDs and digital storage
- **QuickTime**—Standard that handles audio and video for programs on both MAC and PC operating systems

File Formats

ASCII and EBCDIC are character codes used to represent text. Each ASCII or EBCDIC bit pattern represents a single character. Simple ASCII text files contain simple character data and lack any sophisticated formatting commands, such as boldface or underline. Notepad is an example of an application that uses and creates text files, which usually have the extension .txt. EBCDIC is very similar to ASCII in that it also does not use any sophisticated formatting. The main difference between the two is that EBCDIC is an 8-bit code and is primarily used on mainframes; ASCII is a 7-bit code used on personal computers.

Another common file format is binary. Binary files contain special coded data that can be read by only specific software applications. Programs such as FTP use the binary file type to transfer files. Networks use many different types of files. The previous section briefly touched on graphic file formats. The Internet uses two binary file formats to display images: Graphic Interchange Format (GIF) and Joint Photographic Experts Group (JPEG). Any computer with a reader for the GIF and JPEG file formats can read these file types, regardless of the type of computer. Readers are software programs designed to display an image of a particular file type.

Some programs can read multiple image types as well as convert files from one type to another. Web browsers have the capability to display graphic files in either of these two formats without any additional software.

The multimedia file format is another type of binary file that stores sounds, music, and video. Sound files generally operate in one of two ways. They can be completely downloaded first, and then played, or they can download while they are playing. The latter method is referred to as streaming audio. Windows uses the WAV format for sound and the AVI format for animation files. A few of the more common video formats are MPEG, MPEG2, and Macintosh QuickTime.

Another type of file format is markup language. This format acts as a set of directions that tell a Web browser how to display and manage documents. Hypertext Markup Language (HTML), the language of the Internet, tells a browser whether to display text or to provide a hyperlink to another URL. HTML is not a programming language, but it is a set of directions for displaying a page.

Data Encryption and Compression

Layer 6 is also responsible for data encryption. Data encryption protects information during its transmission. Financial transactions (such as credit card information) use encryption to protect sensitive information as it traverses the Internet. An encryption key is used to encrypt the data at its source and then to decrypt the data at its destination (see Figure 14-3).

FIGURE 14-3
Data encryption.

The presentation layer is also responsible for the compression of files. Compression works by using algorithms (complex mathematical formulas) to shrink the size of the files (see Figure 14-4). The algorithm searches each file for repeating bit patterns and then replaces them with a token. A token is a much shorter bit pattern that represents the long pattern. A simple analogy might be the name Cathy (the nickname), the token, to refer to anyone whose full name is Catherine.

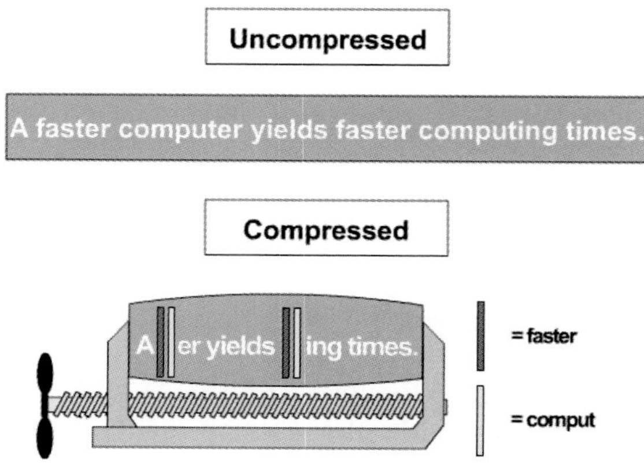

FIGURE 14-4
File compression.

Summary

In this chapter, you learned that when two differing systems need to communicate, the presentation layer is needed to convert and translate between the two different formats. In addition, you learned that the presentation layer does these tasks:

- Determines how graphic images, sound, and movies are presented
- Provides encryption of data
- Compresses text
- Converts graphic images into bit streams so that they can be transmitted across a network

Now that you have a firm understanding of the functions that occur at the presentation layer, you are ready to look at the processes that occur at the application layer, covered in the next chapter.

Check Your Understanding

1. What are the three main functions of the presentation layer?
   A. Data formatting, data encryption, and data compression
   B. Data formatting, data encryption, and data defragmentation
   C. Data encryption, data compression, and data encapsulation
   D. Data compression, data queries, and data formatting
2. Which sequence is accurate for data moving toward the physical layer?
   A. Application layer, transport layer, session layer
   B. Session layer, presentation layer, application layer
   C. Application layer, presentation layer, session layer
   D. Application layer, presentation layer, transport layer
3. Which are examples of sound or movie formats?
   A. QuickTime, AVI, TIFF
   B. QuickTime, MPEG, JPEG
   C. QuickTime, MPEG, MIDI
   D. MPEG, TIFF, AVI
4. Which is an example of a graphic image format?
   A. QuickTime
   B. MIDI
   C. JPEG
   D. MPEG
5. Which of the following is used to format text?
   A. ASCII
   B. JPEG
   C. AVI
   D. TIFF

6. What general term describes the binary file format used to store sounds, music, and video?

   A. Media

   B. Multimedia

   C. Extramedia

   D. Intermedia

7. The method by which sound files are downloaded while they are playing is referred to as what?

   A. Filtering

   B. MIDI

   C. Streaming audio

   D. MP3

8. Which of the following is a set of directions for displaying a Web page?

   A. HTTP

   B. HTML

   C. HDLC

   D. URL

9. Which function of Layer 6 protects data during transmission?

   A. Data formatting

   B. Data compression

   C. Data encryption

   D. Data protection

10. The process of replacing repeating bit patterns with a shorter "token" is referred to as ______.

    A. Compression

    B. Condensing

    C. Shrinking

    D. Encryption

Objectives

After reading this chapter, you will be able to

- Understand application layer basics
- Describe the Domain Name System
- Describe network applications
- Provide application layer examples

Layer 7: The Application Layer

Introduction

Now that you have seen what happens to data packets as they travel through the presentation layer, it's time to look at the last layer that data packets traverse before reaching their final destination. The last layer, or Layer 7, of the OSI model is referred to as the application layer. The application layer is the closest to the end user when interacting with software applications such as sending and receiving e-mail over a network. You see how the application layer deals with data packets from client/server applications, domain name services, and network applications by examining the following elements:

- Client/server
- Redirectors
- Domain Name System
- E-mail
- Telnet
- FTP
- HTTP

Basics of the Application Layer

In the context of the OSI reference model, the application layer (Layer 7) supports the communicating component of an application (see Figure 15-1). The application layer is responsible for the following:

- Identifying and establishing the availability of intended communication partners
- Synchronizing cooperating applications
- Establishing agreement on procedures for error recovery
- Controlling data integrity

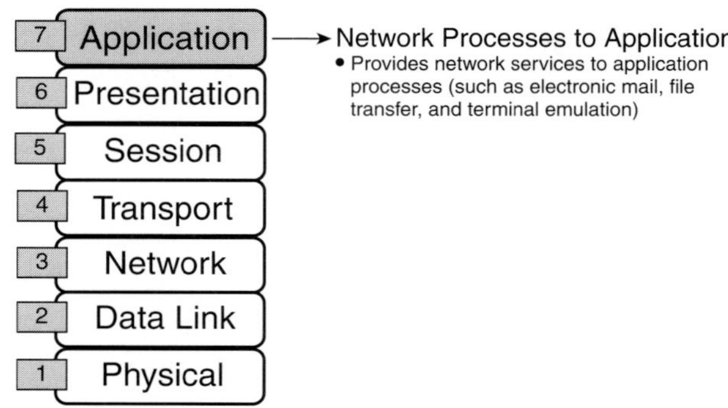

FIGURE 15-1
Application layer processes.

The application layer is the OSI layer closest to the end user. This determines whether sufficient resources exist for communication between systems. Without the application layer, there would be no network communication support. The application layer does not provide services to any other OSI layer, but it does provide services to application processes lying outside the scope of the OSI model, such as spreadsheet programs, word processing programs, and banking terminal programs. Additionally, the application layer provides a direct interface to the rest of the OSI model for network applications (such as browser, e-mail, FTP, and Telnet) or an indirect interface for stand-alone applications (such as word processors, spreadsheets, and presentation managers) with a network redirector.

Direct Network Applications

Most applications that work in a networked environment are classified as client/server applications. These applications, such as FTP, Web browsers, and e-mail, all have two components that allow them to function: the client side and the server side. The client side is located on the local computer and is the requestor of the services. The server side is located on a remote computer and provides services in response to the client's requests.

A client/server application works by constantly repeating the following looped routine: client request, server response; client request, server response. For example, a Web browser accesses a Web page by requesting a uniform resource locator (URL), or Web address, on a remote Web server. After it locates the URL, the Web server that is identified by that URL responds to the request. Then, based on the information received from the Web server, the client can request more information from the same Web server or can access another Web page from a different Web server.

Netscape Navigator and Internet Explorer are probably the most commonly used network applications. An easy way to understand a Web browser is to compare it to a television remote control. A remote control gives you the ability to directly control a TV's functions: volume, channels, brightness, and so on. For the remote control to function properly, you do not need to understand how the remote control functions electronically. The same is true of a Web browser; the browser gives you the ability to navigate through the Web by clicking hyperlinks. For the Web browser to function properly, it is not necessary for you to understand how the lower-layer OSI protocols work and interact.

Indirect Network Support

Within a LAN environment, indirect-application network support is also a client/server function. If a client wants to save a file from a word processor to a network server, the redirector enables the word processing application to do so transparently. Remember that this transparency is supplied by the session layer RPC functionality.

A redirector is an OSI model session layer function that works with computer operating systems and network clients instead of specific application programs.

Examples of protocols that use redirectors are listed here:

- AppleTalk Filing Protocol
- NetBIOS Extended User Interface (NetBEUI)
- Novell IPX/SPX protocols
- Network File System (NFS) of the TCP/IP protocol suite

A redirector enables a network administrator to assign remote resources to logical names on the local client. When you select one of these logical names to perform an operation such as saving a file or printing a file, the network redirector sends the selected file to the proper remote resource on the network for processing. If the resource is on a local computer, the redirector ignores the request and allows the local operating system to process the request.

The advantage of using a network redirector on a local client is that the applications on the client never have to recognize the network. In addition, the application that requests service is located on the local computer, and the redirector reroutes the request to the proper network resource, while the application treats it as a local request.

Redirectors expand the capabilities of non-network software. They also enable users to share documents, templates, databases, printers, and many other resource types without having to use special application software.

Networking has had a great influence on the development of programs such as word processors, spreadsheets, presentation managers, database programs, graphics, and productivity software. Many of these software packages are now network-integrated or network-aware; they have the capabilities of launching integrated Web browsers or Internet tools and publishing their output to HTML for easy Web integration.

Making and Breaking a Connection

It is important to note that in each of the previous examples, the connection to the server was maintained only long enough to complete a single task. In the Web example, the connection was maintained just long enough to download the current Web page. In the printer example, the connection was maintained just long enough to send the document to the print server. After the processing was completed, the connection was broken and had to be re-established for the next processing request to take place. This is one of the two ways that communication sessions take place.

Later in this chapter, you learn about the second method in which communication sessions take place. This is illustrated by the Telnet and FTP examples, in which a connection to the server is established and maintained until all processing has been performed. The client computer terminates the connection when the user determines that he or she has finished. All communication activity falls into one of these two categories. In the next section, you learn about the Domain Name System, which is supported by the application layer processes.

Domain Name System

The Internet is built on a hierarchical addressing scheme. This allows for routing that is based on groups of addresses rather than individual addresses. The problem this creates for the user is associating the correct address with the Internet site. The only difference between the addresses 198.151.11.12 and 198.151.11.21 is one transposed digit. It is very easy to forget an address to a particular site, because there is nothing to associate the contents of the site with its address.

A domain-naming system was developed to eliminate this problem. A domain name is a string of characters or numbers, usually a name or abbreviation, that represents the numeric address of an Internet site. More than 200 top-level domains exist on the Internet, examples of which include the following:

- **.us**—United States
- **.uk**—United Kingdom

Generic top-level domain names also exist, examples of which include the following:

- **.edu**—Educational sites
- **.com**—Commercial sites
- **.gov**—Government sites
- **.org**—Nonprofit sites
- **.net**—Network service

The Domain Name System Server

The Domain Name System server (DNS server) server is a device on a network that responds to requests from clients to translate a domain name into the associated IP address. The DNS system is set up in a hierarchy that creates different levels of DNS servers.

If a local DNS server is capable of translating a domain name into its associated IP address, it does so and returns the result to the client. If it cannot translate the address, it passes the request up to the next higher-level DNS server on the system, which then tries to translate the address. If the DNS server at this level is capable of translating the domain name into an associated IP address, it does so and returns the result to the client. If not, it sends the request to the next higher level. This process repeats itself until the domain name has been translated or until the top-level DNS server has been reached. If the domain name cannot be found on the top-level DNS server, it is considered to be an error and the corresponding error message is returned. Any type of application that uses domain names to represent IP addresses uses the DNS server to translate that name into its corresponding IP address (see Figure 15-2).

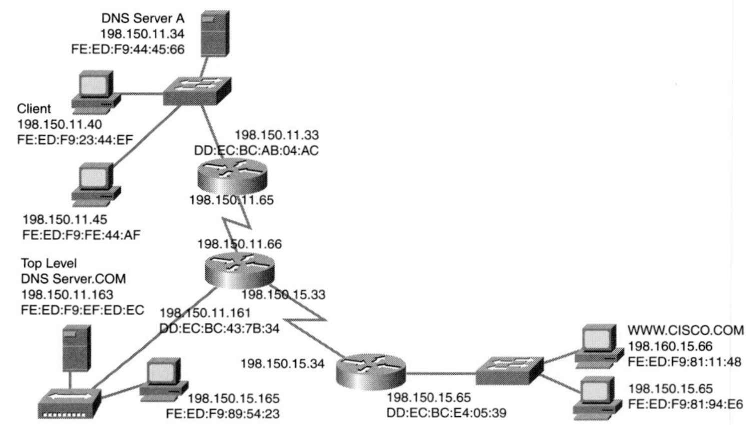

FIGURE 15-2
The DNS lookup sequence.

Network Applications

You select network applications based on the type of work you need to accomplish. A complete set of application layer programs is available to interface with the Internet. Each application program type is associated with its own application protocol. Although more programs and protocol types are available, the following are the main focus of this chapter:

- The World Wide Web uses the Hypertext Transfer Protocol (HTTP).
- Remote access programs use the Telnet protocol for directly connecting to remote resources.
- E-mail programs support the POP3 application layer protocol for electronic mail.
- File utility programs use the FTP protocol for copying and moving files between remote sites.
- Network data gathering and monitoring use the SNMP protocol.

It is important to re-emphasize that the application layer is just another protocol layer in the OSI or TCP/IP models. The user programs interface with application layer protocols.

E-mail client applications (Eudora, Microsoft Mail, Pegasus, and Netscape Mail) work with the POP3 protocol. The same is true with Web browsers. The two most popular Web browsers are Microsoft Internet Explorer and Netscape Communicator. The appearance and operation of these two programs is very different, but they both work with the Internet's application layer HTTP protocol.

E-Mail Messages

Electronic mail (e-mail) enables you to send messages between connected computers. The procedure for sending an e-mail document involves three separate processes. The first is to send the e-mail to the sending user's post office. The second is to forward the e-mail from that post office to the recipient's post office, and the third is to deliver the e-mail to the user's e-mail client (the recipient).

The following steps help you understand the process of sending an e-mail:

1. Start your e-mail program.
2. Type in a recipient's e-mail address.
3. Type in a subject.
4. Type a letter.

Now examine the e-mail address. This is an example of what it might look like: JJones@bigsky.com. The address consists of two parts: the recipient's name (located before the @ sign) and the recipient's post office address (after the @ sign). The recipient's name is important only after the message arrives at the destination post office address, which is a DNS entry that represents the IP address of the post office server.

DNS Function

Whenever e-mail clients send letters, they request that a DNS server connected to the network translate the domain names into their associated IP addresses. If the DNS server is capable of translating the names, it returns the IP addresses to the clients, thus enabling proper transport layer segmentation and encapsulation. If the DNS server cannot translate the names, the requests are passed on until the names can be translated.

The part of the e-mail address that contains the recipient's name becomes important at the destination post office. The server extracts it from the e-mail message and checks to see if the recipient is a member of its post office. If the recipient is a member, the server stores the message in his or her mailbox until someone retrieves it. If the recipient is not a member, the post office generates an error message and sends the e-mail back to the sender.

The third part of the e-mailing process is the receiving process. E-mail message recipients must use the e-mail client software on their computers to establish requests to the e-mail post offices. When message recipients click the Get Mail or Retrieve Mail buttons on the e-mail client, they are usually prompted for a password. After they enter the password and click OK, the e-mail software builds a request for the post office servers. It then extracts the post office addresses from the configuration data that was entered when the e-mail software was configured. The process then uses another DNS search to find the IP addresses of the servers.

Finally, the requests are segmented and sequenced by the transport layer. Data packets travel through the rest of the OSI model layers (network layer, data link layer, physical layer) and are then transmitted across the Internet to the destination e-mail post office. At this post office, the packets are reassembled in the proper sequence and are checked for any data transmission errors.

At the post office, requests are examined and usernames and passwords are verified. If everything is correct, the post office server transmits all e-mail messages to the user's computers. Here the messages are again segmented, sequenced, and encapsulated as data frames to be sent to the client's or recipient's computer.

After e-mail messages arrive at a computer, the recipient might open them and read them. If the recipient clicks the Reply button or the Forward button to send a response to a message, the whole process starts over again. E-mail messages themselves are normally sent as ASCII text, but the attachments that are sometimes included with them can be audio, video, graphic, or many other types of data. To correctly send and receive attachments, the encoding schemes must be the same on both the sending and the receiving computers. The two most common formats for e-mail attachments are the Multipurpose Internet Mail Extension (MIME) and uuencode (a UNIX utility program).

Application Layer Examples

In this section, you learn about the following TCP/IP application layer examples:

- Telnet
- File Transfer Protocol
- Hypertext Transfer Protocol

Telnet

Terminal emulation (Telnet) software provides the capability to remotely access another computer. It enables a user to log in to an Internet host and execute commands. A Telnet client is referred to as a local host; a Telnet server, which uses special software called a *daemon*, is referred to as a remote host.

To make a connection from a Telnet client, you must select a connection option. A dialog box prompts you for a host name and the terminal type. The host name is mapped to the IP address or DNS name of the remote computer to which you connect. The terminal type describes the type of terminal emulation that you want the computer to perform. The Telnet operation uses none of the transmitting computer's processing power. Instead, it transmits the keystrokes to the remote host and sends the resulting screen output back to the local monitor. All processing and storage take place on the remote computer.

Telnet begins in the same way that e-mail does. When you enter a DNS name for a Telnet location, the name must be translated into its associated IP address before a connection can be established. The Telnet application works mainly at the top three layers of the OSI model: the application layer (commands), the presentation layer (formats, usually ASCII), and the session layer (transmission).

The data then passes to the transport layer, where it is segmented and the port address and error checking are added. The data then passes to the network layer, where the IP header (containing the source and destination IP addresses) is added. Next, the packet travels to the data link layer, which encapsulates the packet in a data frame and adds the source and destination MAC address and a frame trailer. If the source computer doesn't have the MAC address of the destination computer, it performs an ARP request. When the MAC address has been determined, the frame travels across the physical medium (in binary form) to the next device.

When the data reaches the remote host computer, the data link, network, and transport layers de-encapsulate the message with the commands. The remote host computer executes the commands and transmits the results back to the local client computer using the same process of encapsulation that delivered the original commands. This whole process repeats itself, sending commands and receiving results until the local client has completed the work that needs to be done. When the work is done, the client terminates the session.

File Transfer Protocol

File Transfer Protocol (FTP) is designed to download files (receive or get from the Internet) and upload files (send or put to the Internet). The capability to upload and download files is one of the most valuable features of the Internet. This is especially helpful for people who rely on computers for many purposes and who might need software drivers and upgrades immediately. Network administrators can rarely wait even a few days to get the necessary drivers that enable their network servers to function again. The Internet can provide these files immediately by using FTP. FTP, like e-mail and Telnet, is a client/server application. It requires server software running on a host that can be accessed by client software.

An FTP session is established the same way in which a Telnet session is established. Just like Telnet, the FTP session is maintained until the client terminates it or until there is some sort of communication error. When you establish a connection to an FTP process or daemon, you must supply a login ID and a password. Normally, you use Anonymous as the login ID and your e-mail address as the password. This type of connection is known as anonymous FTP. After your identity is established, a command link opens between your client machine and the FTP server. This is similar to a Telnet session, in which commands are sent and executed on the server and the results are returned to the client. This feature enables you to create and change folders, erase and rename files, and execute many other functions associated with file management.

The main purpose of FTP is to transfer files from one computer to another by copying and moving files from servers to clients and from clients to servers. When you copy files from a server, FTP establishes a second connection, a data link between the computers, across which the data is transferred. Data transfer can occur in ASCII mode or binary mode. These two modes determine how the data file is to be transferred between the stations. After the file transfer has ended, the data connection terminates automatically. After you complete the entire session of copying and moving files, you might log off, thus closing the command link and ending the session.

Another protocol that has the capability to download files is Hypertext Transfer Protocol (HTTP), which you learn about in the next section. One limitation of HTTP is that you can use it only to download files, not upload them.

Hypertext Transfer Protocol

Hypertext Transfer Protocol (HTTP) works with the World Wide Web, which is the fastest-growing and most-used part of the Internet. One of the main reasons for the extraordinary growth of the Web is the ease with which it allows access to information. A Web browser (along with all the other network applications covered in this chapter) is a client/server application, which means that it requires both a client and a server component to function. A Web browser presents data in multimedia formats on Web pages that use text, graphics, sound, and video. The Web pages are created with a format language called Hypertext Markup Language (HTML). HTML directs a Web browser on a particular Web page to produce the appearance of the page in a specific manner. In addition, HTML specifies locations for the placement of text, files, and objects that are to be transferred from the Web server to the Web browser.

Hyperlinks make the World Wide Web easy to navigate. A hyperlink is an object (word, phrase, or picture) on a Web page that, when clicked, transfers you to a new Web page. The Web page contains (often hidden within its HTML description) an address location known as a *uniform resource locator (URL)*.

In the following example, http:// tells the browser which protocol to use. The second part, www, tells the browser the name of the server to contact. In many cases, "www" is used as the server name because the server's primary function is the delivery of Web resources. The third part, cisco.com, identifies the domain of the Web server IP address. The last part, edu, identifies the specific folder location (on the server) that contains the Web page.

http://www.cisco.com/edu/

When you open a Web browser, the first thing you usually see is a starting page, or home page. The URL of the home page has already been stored in the configuration area of your Web browser and can be changed at any time. From the starting page, you can click one of the Web page hyperlinks or type a URL in the browser's address bar. The Web browser then examines the protocol to determine whether it needs to open another program and then determines the IP address of the Web server. After that, the transport layer, network layer, folder name of the Web page location. (Note: The data can also contain a specific filename for an HTML page.) If no name is given, the server uses a default name (as specified in the server's configuration).

The server responds to the request by sending all the text, audio, video, and graphic files, as specified in the HTML instructions, to the Web client. The client browser reassembles all the files to create a view of the Web page and then terminates the session. If you click another page that is located on the same server or a different server, the whole process begins again.

Summary

In this chapter, you learned about the functions of the OSI application layer and about the Internet model's application or process layer. You also learned about the different processes that occur as data packets travel through this layer. More specifically, you learned that the application layer is responsible for these actions:

- Identifies and establishes the availability of intended communication partners
- Synchronizes cooperating applications
- Establishes agreement on procedures for error recovery
- Controls data integrity

In addition, you learned that the application layer supports the following:

- Direct and indirect network applications
- The Domain Name System
- Telnet, FTP, and HTTP

Now that you have completed this chapter, you should have a firm understanding of how the application layer provides services from the host to the destination.

Check Your Understanding

1. A network redirector enables data to travel ______.

A. Only to a network print server

B. Only to a network file server

C. In a single direction

D. None of the above

2. An example of a client/server application is ______.

A. E-mail

B. A spreadsheet

C. A NIC

D. Hard drive utilities

3. The client side of the client/server relationship is ______.

A. Located on the remote computer

B. The requestor of services

C. The most important

D. Always located on the server

4. Which of the following best describes a domain name?

A. It represents the numeric address of an Internet site.

B. It is the same as the name you give your primary server.

C. It represents the specific location where your LAN is located.

D. It is an IP address used to represent a print server.

5. com is the domain typically assigned to ______.

A. Client machines

B. Customers

C. Network provider companies

D. Corporations

6. During a Telnet connection, the remote computer is responsible for ______.
   - A. Nothing
   - B. Processing
   - C. Client-side Telnet application
   - D. Client-side printing
7. At which three layers of the OSI model does Telnet primarily work?
   - A. Application layer, session layer, transport layer
   - B. Presentation layer, session layer, transport layer
   - C. Data link layer, transport layer, presentation layer
   - D. Application layer, presentation layer, session layer
8. Typical anonymous FTP sessions use ______ as the login ID and ______ as the password.
   - A. Anonymous; user e-mail address
   - B. User e-mail address; FTP
   - C. FTP; FTP
   - D. Guest; anonymous
9. What is used to specify the placement of text, files, and objects that are to be transferred from the Web server to the Web?
   - A. HTTP
   - B. HTML
   - C. HDLC
   - D. URL
10. Instead of working with specific application programs, redirectors work with ______.
    - A. Computer operating systems
    - B. Spreadsheets
    - C. E-mail
    - D. Web browsers

Objectives

After reading this chapter, you will be able to

- Describe WAN devices, standards, and technologies
- Describe the function of a router in a WAN

Chapter 16

WANs and Routers

Introduction

Now that you have a firm understanding of the OSI reference model, LANs, and IP addressing, you are ready to learn about and use the Cisco Internetwork Operating System (IOS). However, before using the IOS, it is important to have a firm grasp of WAN and router basics. Therefore, in this chapter, you learn about WAN devices, technologies, and standards. In addition, you learn about the function of a router in a WAN. Lastly, you perform lab activities related to particular router setup.

WANs

A *wide-area network (WAN)* operates at the physical layer and the data link layer of the OSI reference model. It interconnects *local-area networks (LANs)*, usually separated by large geographic areas. WANs provide for the exchange of data packets/frames between routers/bridges and the LANs they support.

The major characteristics of WANs are the following:

- They operate beyond the local LAN's geographic scope. They use the services of carriers such as Regional Bell Operating Companies (RBOCs) and Sprint and MCI Worldcom.
- They use serial connections of various types to access network bandwidth.

MORE INFORMATION

WAN Performance Criteria

Component Uptime

Each physical component of the WAN can be monitored and measured for its availability using uptime. *Uptime* is the opposite of downtime: It is the amount of time that the device is functional and in service relative to the users' requirements for its availability. It is quite common for uptime to be statistically overstated by measuring it on a 7 × 24 basis, even though the users' requirements may be for only 5 × 12. Remember to tailor this and every other metric as closely as possible to your users' stated requirements for network performance.

Although electronic devices are highly reliable, they eventually fail. Most manufacturers provide a *mean time between failures (MTBF)* rating for their equipment as a reassurance of how reliable their products really are. Typically, MTBF ratings are in the tens of thousands of hours. This could conceivably translate into years of trouble-free service. Unfortunately, these ratings are statistically derived. The actual time between failures of any given device depends greatly on a number of factors, including the following:

- Ambient temperature ranges of the operating environment
- Cleanliness of the commercial electric power
- How well devices are handled before and during operation

Monitoring and tracking uptime of individual components enables you to demonstrate to your user community how well you are satisfying their requirements for the network's availability. Component uptime data can also be charted over time to identify potentially problematic components in your network infrastructure. Such trends can provide information about the general reliability of a given type or brand of hardware, which then can be used to identify individual components that may be at risk of failure.

Note that the term *availability* is sometimes used to generically describe aggregate network uptime. Unfortunately, it is not a good metric. In theory, network availability provides a quantified synopsis of the network's readiness. In practice, availability is so nebulous that it is virtually meaningless. To illustrate this point, if a router at a premise location fails, the entire network is unavailable to the users at that location. The network, however, is available to users at every other location. They will not be able to access hosts at the affected location, but they will also not be impeded from accessing every other host in the network. The extent to which the network is available varies greatly by location and by usage requirements. Therefore, quantifying network availability can be more onerous than it is valuable.

MORE INFORMATION (CONTINUED)

Traffic Volumes

One of the more important metrics for any WAN is the volume of traffic that it is expected to support. Volume is almost always volatile; it varies with time, business cycles, seasons, and so on. In other words, you can count on traffic volumes being anything but constant. Given this volatility, it is important to measure volumes in two different ways, maximum volumes and average volumes:

- The *maximum volume* that you expect the network to support is known as the peak volume. As its name implies, this is the greatest amount of traffic that you expect the network to have to support.
- *Average volumes* are the traffic loads that you can reasonably expect during the course of a business day from any given work location.

Establishing these two traffic volumes is critical to sizing the WAN's transmission facilities as well as its routers. If you expect any given location to generate a traffic load of 100 kbps during the course of a business day, for example, it is clear that a 56-kbps transmission facility will be inadequate.

Delay

Delay is one of the more common metrics that can be used to measure network performance. Delay is the time that elapses between two events. In data communications, these two events are typically the transmission and reception of data. Therefore, delay is the total amount of time that is required by the network to transport a packet from its point of origin to its destination. Given this definition, delay is an aggregate phenomenon with many potential causes. Three of the more common causes are the following:

- **Propagation delay**—Propagation delay is the cumulative amount of time required to transmit, or propagate, the data across an end-to-end transmission path. The network infrastructure within each transmission facility in the network path directly contributes to the aggregate forwarding delay of any given transmission. An additional factor in propagation delay is traffic volume. The more traffic that is flowing across a given facility, the less bandwidth that is available for new transmissions. Propagation delay is inherent in terrestrial circuits, regardless of whether they traverse glass or copper media or are transmitted through the air using microwave radio frequencies.
- **Satellite uplink/downlink delays**—Some transmission facilities are satellite-based. These require the signal to be transmitted up to the satellite and then transmitted back down from the satellite. Because of the great distances between the terrestrial transmission facilities and the satellite, these delays can be quite noticeable.

continues

MORE INFORMATION (CONTINUED)

- **Forwarding delay**—Forwarding delay in a network is the amount of time that a physical device needs to receive, buffer, process, and forward data. The actual forwarding delay of any given device may vary over time. Individual devices operating at or near capacity will likely experience a greater forwarding delay than comparable devices that are less utilized. Additionally, forwarding delay can be exacerbated by heavy traffic or error conditions in the network. Forwarding delay can be described as *latency* within individual components.

WAN Devices

By definition, WANs connect devices that are separated by wide geographic areas. As shown in Figure 16-1, such devices include the following:

- **Routers**—Offer many services, including LAN internetworking and WAN interface ports
- **Switches**—Connect to WAN bandwidth for voice, data, and video communication
- **Modems**—Interface with voice-grade services, channel service units/digital service units (CSU/DSUs) that interface with T1/E1 services, and Terminal Adapters/Network Termination 1 (TA/NT1s) that interface with Integrated Services Digital Network (ISDN) services
- **Communication servers**—Concentrate dial-in and dial-out user connections

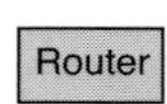

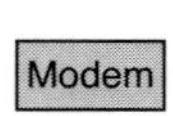

FIGURE 16-1 Common WAN devices include routers, WAN switches, modems, and communication servers.

WAN Standards

WAN physical layer protocols describe how to provide electrical, mechanical, operational, and functional connections for WAN services. These services are most often obtained from WAN service providers such as RBOCs, alternate carriers, and post-telephone and telegraph (PTT) agencies.

WAN data link protocols describe how frames are carried between systems on a single data link. They include protocols designed to operate over dedicated point-to-point, multipoint, and multiaccess switched services such as Frame Relay. WAN standards are defined and managed by a number of recognized authorities, including the following agencies:

- International Telecommunication Union–Telecommunication Standardization Sector (ITU-T), formerly the Consultative Committee for International Telegraph and Telephone (CCITT)
- International Organization for Standardization (ISO)
- Internet Engineering Task Force (IETF)
- Electronic Industries Association (EIA)

WAN standards typically describe both physical layer and data link layer requirements. The WAN physical layer describes the interface between the data terminal equipment (DTE) and the data circuit-terminating equipment (DCE). Typically, a DCE device is service provider equipment and a DTE device is an attached customer device. In this model, the services offered to the DTE are made available through a modem or a CSU/DSU (see Figure 16-2).

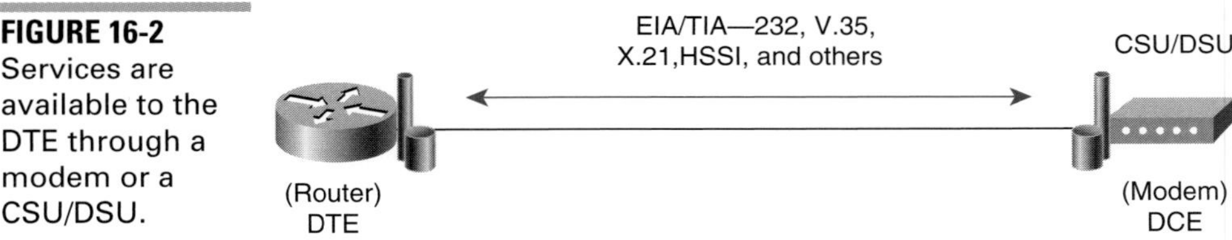

FIGURE 16-2 Services are available to the DTE through a modem or a CSU/DSU.

Several physical layer standards are implemented on WAN equipment:

- EIA/TIA-232
- EIA/TIA-449
- V.24
- V.35
- X.21
- G.703
- EIA-530

The common data link encapsulations, which are shown in Figure 16-3, are associated with synchronous serial lines:

- **High-Level Data Link Control (HDLC)**—HDLC is an IEEE standard that may not be compatible with different vendors because of the way each vendor has chosen to implement this transmission protocol. HDLC supports both point-to-point and multipoint configurations with minimal overhead.

- **Frame Relay**—Frame Relay uses high-quality digital facilities and utilizes simplified framing with no error correction mechanisms; this means that it can send Layer 2 information much more rapidly than other WAN protocols. Frame Relay is connection-oriented with no built-in error-correction mechanism.
- **Point-to-Point Protocol (PPP)**—PPP is much like HDLC, with an added field to specify the upper-layer protocol. PPP contains a protocol field to identify the network layer protocol. PPP can also be used for asynchronous transmission. In fact, the default is a connection-oriented but unreliable byte-oriented connection in which unnumbered frames are used. PPP can also operate in a bit-oriented (HDLC) mode that is reliable.

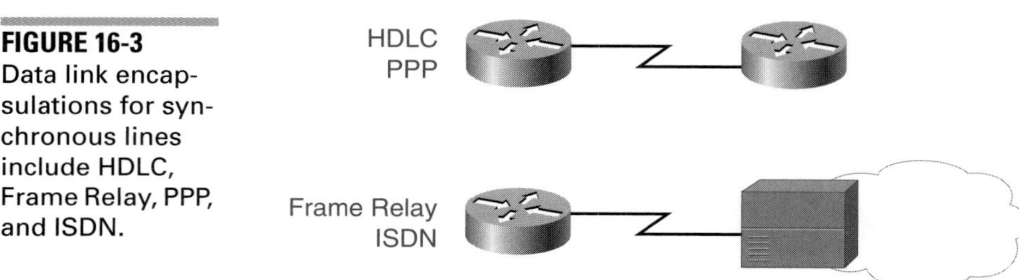

FIGURE 16-3 Data link encapsulations for synchronous lines include HDLC, Frame Relay, PPP, and ISDN.

Because this subsection focuses on synchronous serial lines, these also should be mentioned:

- **Synchronous Data Link Control Protocol (SDLC)**—An IBM-designed WAN data link protocol for System Network Architecture (SNA) environments.
- **Serial Line Interface Protocol (SLIP)**—An extremely popular WAN data link protocol for carrying IP packets; it is being replaced in many applications by the more versatile PPP. Like PPP, SLIP was designed primarily for dialup connections and is connection-oriented but unreliable. It provided only an encapsulation method, and many incompatible implementations exist.
- **Link Access Procedure Balanced (LAPB)**—A data link protocol now used by X.25 that is both connection-oriented and reliable. Like SDLC and HDLC, LAPB is reliable, carrying sequence and acknowledgment numbers.
- **Link Access Procedure D channel (LAPD)**—The WAN data link protocol used for signaling and call setup on an ISDN D channel. Data transmissions

take place on the ISDN B channels. This protocol is both connection-oriented and reliable.

- **Link Access Procedure Frame** (LAPF)—For Frame-Mode Bearer Services, a WAN data link protocol, similar to LAPD, used with Frame Relay technologies. This protocol is unreliable.

In this model, the services offered to the router are made available through a modem or a CSU/DSU (see Figure 16-4).

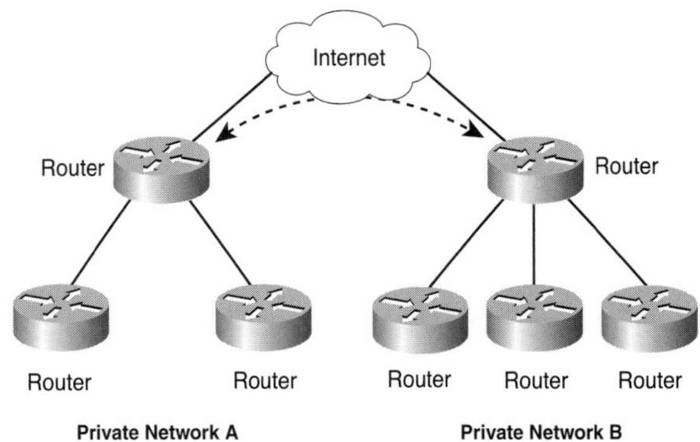

FIGURE 16-4
CSU/DSU is a DCE connected to a router that is a DTE.

WAN Technologies

The following subsections give a brief description of the most common WAN technologies. They have been grouped into the categories of circuit-switched services, packet-switched services, cell-switched services, dedicated digital services, and analog services.

> **NOTE**
> POTS and ISDN are dialup services, which means that when the call is made, an end-to-end physical path is set up and the bandwidth is reserved end to end. Both POTS and ISDN use straight time-division multiplexing (TDM), which is sometimes referred to as synchronous transfer mode (STM).

Circuit-Switched Services

Two circuit-switched services exist: POTS and narrowband ISDN. They are briefly described in the following list:

- **Plain Old Telephone Service** (POTS)—Not a computer data service, this is included for two reasons: Many of its technologies are part of the growing data infrastructure, and it is a model of an incredibly easy-to-use wide-area communications network. The typical medium is twisted-pair copper wire. This is the service used with a standard dial-in connection and is still the most common way for a home PC user to connect to the Internet.
- **Narrowband Integrated Services Digital Network** (Narrowband ISDN)—A versatile, widespread, historically important technology, this was the first all-digital dialup service. Usage varies greatly from country to country. Cost is moderate; maximum bandwidth is 128 kbps for the lower-cost Basic

Rate Interface (BRI) and about 3 Mbps for the Primary Rate Interface (PRI). The typical medium is twisted-pair copper wire.

Packet-Switched Services

> **NOTE**
> X.25 is both connection-oriented and reliable at both Layers 2 and 3, which is a big part of why it is so much slower than Frame Relay.

With these packet-switched services, the physical path is always in place. Data formatted in packets is sent along these physical paths, from node to node. In the typical LAN packet-switching environment, each packet is dynamically switched (routed) to the next link—that is, the protocols are connectionless. In general, WAN packet-switching services are connection-oriented, although X.25 is reliable and Frame Relay is not.

- **X.25**—An older technology, X.25 is still widely used. It has extensive error-checking capabilities from the days when WAN links were more prone to errors, which makes it reliable but limits its bandwidth. Bandwidth may be as high as about 2 Mbps. Usage is fairly extensive; cost is moderate. The typical medium is twisted-pair copper wire.
- **Frame Relay**—An extremely popular WAN technology in its own right, Frame Relay is more efficient than X.25 but offers similar services. Maximum bandwidth is 44.736 Mbps; 56 kbps and 384 kbps are extremely popular in the United States. Usage is widespread; cost is moderate to low. Typical media include twisted-pair copper wire and optical fiber.

> **NOTE**
> Frame Relay is typically regarded as a much faster, sleeker version of X.25; it has no defined Layer 3 protocol, nor is it reliable. However, it is connection-oriented. Circuit-switched services use TDM and are said to be synchronous (they use STM), so packet switching is said to use statistical TDM and is sometimes said to be asynchronous (similar to ATM).

Cell-Switched Services

A cell is the same as a packet. The real difference is that a packet is of variable size and a cell is a fixed size. Cell-switched services include the following:

- **Asynchronous Transfer Mode (ATM)**—Debatably becoming an increasingly important WAN (and even LAN) technology, ATM uses small, fixed-length (53 byte) frames to carry data. Maximum bandwidth is currently 622 Mbps, although support for higher speeds is being developed. Typical media are twisted-pair copper wire or optical fiber. Usage is widespread, and cost is high.
- **Switched Multimegabit Data Service (SMDS)**—Closely related to ATM, SMDS typically is used in metropolitan-area networks (MANs). Maximum bandwidth is 44.736 Mbps. The typical media are twisted-pair copper wire or optical fiber. Usage is not very widespread; cost is relatively high.

Dedicated Digital Services

The following dedicated digital services are also circuit-switched, but the connection is an "always-up" connection:

- **T1, T3, E1, E3**—The T series of services in the United States and the E series of services in Europe are extremely important WAN technologies. Like dialup service, they use time division multiplexing to "slice up" and assign time slots for data transmission; bandwidth is shown here (other bandwidths are available):

— **T1**—1.544 Mbps
— **T3**—44.736 Mbps
— **E1**—2.048 Mbps
— **E3**—34.368 Mbps

The media used are typically twisted-pair copper wire and optical fiber. Usage is extremely widespread; cost is moderate.

- **xDSL**—DSL stands for Digital Subscriber Line, and x indicates a family of technologies. This relatively new and developing WAN technology intended for home use has a bandwidth that decreases with increasing distance from the phone company's equipment. Top speeds of 51.84 Mbps are possible near a phone company office, but more common are much lower bandwidths (from hundreds of kilobits per second to several megabits per second). Usage is small but increasing rapidly; cost is moderate and decreasing. x indicates the entire family of DSL technologies, including the following:

  — **HDSL**—High bit-rate DSL
  — **SDSL**—Single-line DSL
  — **ADSL**—Asymmetric DSL
  — **VDSL**—Very-high-bit-rate DSL
  — **RADSL**—Rate-adaptive DSL

- **Synchronous Optical Network (SONET)**—A family of high-speed physical layer technologies, SONET was designed for optical fiber but can also run on copper cables. A series of data rates are available with special designations. SONET is implemented at different optical carrier (OC) levels, ranging from 51.84 Mbps (OC-1) to 9952 Mbps (OC-192). Usage is widespread among Internet backbone entities; cost is expensive (it's not a technology that connects to your house).

MORE INFORMATION

Costs of the WAN

Tempering the various performance criteria is cost. The costs of owning and operating a WAN include the initial startup costs as well as the monthly recurring expenses. Not surprisingly, the larger and more powerful network components are much more expensive than smaller, less-robust components. Therefore, designing a WAN becomes an economic exercise in which a careful balance of performance and cost is achieved.

continues

MORE INFORMATION (CONTINUED)

Achieving this balance can be painful. No one wants to design a WAN that disappoints the users with its performance, but no one wants to design a WAN that blows the budget, either! Fortunately, the following truisms can help guide the design of a WAN that satisfies existing requirements, provides flexibility for future growth, and doesn't exceed the budget:

- The capital investments in routers and other network hardware become a fixed part of the network. After the hardware components are placed in operation, the logistics of replacing hardware become quite complicated. And, depending on your depreciation schedule for capital equipment, you might find yourself obligated to use it for five or more years! It might behoove you to purchase a larger router that is relatively low in port density. You can add hardware (memory, CPUs, and interfaces) in the future as the need for them arises. This allows future expansion at modest incremental costs and little (if any) operational downtime.
- The transmission facilities are relatively easy to replace with other transmission facilities. They are an expense item, not a capital investment, so there is no depreciation expense to retire. These can be replaced with other facilities as often as your lease agreement with the carrier permits. Therefore, you might want to explore your options for meeting performance requirements with the various available transmission facilities and technologies.

Other WAN Services

Other WAN services that are used include the following:

- **Dialup modems (switched analog)**—Limited in speed but quite versatile, these modems works with the existing phone network. Maximum bandwidth is approximately 56 kbps. Cost is low, and usage is still very widespread. The typical medium is the twisted-pair phone line.
- **Cable modems (shared analog)**—Cable modems put data signals on the same cable as television signals. They're increasing in popularity in regions that have large amounts of existing cable TV coaxial cable (90 percent of homes in the United States). Maximum bandwidth can be 10 Mbps, although this degrades as more users attach to a given network segment (behaving like an unswitched LAN). Cost is relatively low; usage is small but increasing. The medium is coaxial cable.
- **Wireless**—No medium (other than air) is required, because the signals are electromagnetic waves. A variety of wireless WAN links exist, two types of which are discussed here:
  - **Terrestrial**—Bandwidth typically is in the range of 11 Mbps or less (for example, microwave). Cost is relatively low; usage is moderate. Line-of-sight is usually required.

— **Satellite**—Satellite can serve mobile users (as in a cellular telephone network) and remote users (who are too far from any wires or cables). Usage is widespread; cost is high.

MORE INFORMATION

Resource Utilization Rates

The degree to which the various physical resources of the WAN are being utilized is also a good indicator of how well, or how poorly, the WAN is performing relative to the performance requirements. Two main categories of resource utilization rates should be monitored carefully:

- Router CPU and memory utilization rates
- Transmission facility utilization rates

Router Physical Resource Rates

Routers are one of the most vital components of any WAN. And, unlike the transmission facilities, they are outside the view of the telecommunications carrier. Therefore, they are distinctly the responsibility of the customer. Fortunately, routers are intelligent devices that contain their own CPU and memory. These physical resources are indispensable in the calculation of WAN routes and the forwarding of packets. They can also be used to monitor the performance of the router.

If either CPU or memory utilization rates approach 100 percent, performance suffers. Numerous conditions can result in either utilization rate temporarily spiking upward with subsequent performance degradation. One example is a sudden increase in transmissions from the LAN to the WAN. LANs can operate at speeds of up to 1 Gbps, but they usually operate only at 10, 16, or 100 Mbps. Any of these speeds is a gross mismatch against the typical WAN transmission facility, which offers a paltry 1.544 Mbps of bandwidth. This mismatch in bandwidth must be buffered by the router's memory. It won't take long for a router to become resource-constricted given a sustained period of heavy LAN transmissions.

If such situations are rarely experienced, they should be considered aberrations. Aberrations should be monitored, but they shouldn't drive physical upgrades. If these resource constrictions recur or constitute a trend, however, something needs to be done. Usually this requires an upgrade, either to the next-larger router or via an expansion of memory. If a router is chronically at or near 100 percent of capacity with its memory, it is time to purchase additional memory.

Responding to chronically high CPU utilization rates might not be as simple as a memory upgrade. Really, only three options exist for improving high CPU utilization rates:

- If possible, add another CPU to the router.
- Upgrade to a more powerful router.

continues

MORE INFORMATION (CONTINUED)

- Investigate the WAN's traffic patterns to see whether the load on the problematic router can be reduced.

Manipulating traffic patterns is really only a viable option in larger WANs with complex topologies that can afford route redundancy.

Transmission Facility Rates

Transmission facilities can also be monitored for utilization. Typically, this utilization rate is expressed in terms of the percentage of consumed bandwidth. If you are using a T1, for example, a given sample might indicate that 30 percent of its 1.544 Mbps of available bandwidth is currently being utilized.

These rates can be tricky to analyze and may even be misleading. It is not uncommon, for example, for network-management software packages to capture utilization data in time intervals. These can be 1 hour, 5 minutes, or just about any other interval. If set too coarsely, the sampling frequency can miss short-duration fluctuations in bandwidth consumption. If the sampling is too frequent, you could find yourself mired in a meaningless morass of data points. The trick is finding the right frequency that provides meaningful data about how the network is performing relative to the users' expectations.

Beyond merely selecting the sampling rate is the issue of sampling window. The sampling window should be determined by the users' requirements for WAN availability. If the utilization samples are spread over a 24-hour day and a 7-day week, whereas the users work only 10 hours per day, 5 days per week, the statistical data is not indicative of how well the users' requirements are being met.

Utilization rates are a wonderful statistical tool for monitoring and measuring the status of transmission facilities. However, they are not the only metric for assessing a network's performance. The network is successful only if it satisfies the users' requirements. Therefore, a combination of performance metrics that provides a multifaceted, composite perspective is likely to provide a better assessment of the network's success.

WANs and Routers

Computers have four basic components: a CPU, memory, interfaces, and a bus. A router also has these components; therefore, it can be called a computer. However, it is a special-purpose computer. Instead of having components that are dedicated to video and audio output devices, keyboard and mouse input, and all of the typical easy-to-use graphical user interface (GUI) software of a modern multimedia computer, the router is dedicated to routing.

Just as computers need operating systems to run software applications, Cisco routers need the Internetworking Operating Software (IOS) to run the processes defined by the configuration files. These configuration files define the control of flow of traffic in the internetwork. Specifically, by using routing protocols and routing tables to direct routed protocols, routers make decisions regarding the best paths for packets. To control these protocols and these decisions, the router must be configured.

You will learn how to build configuration files from IOS commands to get the router to perform the network functions that you desire. Although at first glance, the router configuration file might look complex, by the end of the course you will be able to read and completely understand it, as well as write your own configurations.

The router is a computer that selects the best paths and manages the switching of packets between two or more networks. Internal components of a router include the following:

- **RAM/DRAM**—Stores routing tables, the ARP cache, the fast-switching cache, packet buffering (shared RAM), and packet hold queues. RAM also provides running memory for the router's configuration file while the router is powered on. RAM content is lost when you power down or restart.
- **NVRAM**—Nonvolatile RAM; stores a router's backup/startup configuration file. Content remains when you power down or restart.
- **Flash memory**—Erasable, reprogrammable ROM; holds the operating system image and microcode. Flash memory enables you to update software without removing and replacing chips on the processor. Content remains when you power down or restart. Multiple versions of IOS software can be stored in Flash memory.
- **ROM**—Contains power-on diagnostics, a bootstrap program, and operating system software. Software upgrades in ROM require replacing pluggable chips on the CPU.
- **Interface**—Network connection through which packets enter and exit a router. It can be on the motherboard or on a separate interface module.

MORE INFORMATION

A Closer Look at Routers

Routers are designed to interconnect multiple networks. This interconnection enables machines on different networks to communicate with each other. Interconnected networks can be colocated or geographically dispersed. Networks that are geographically dispersed are usually interconnected via a WAN. WANs are constructed of numerous different technologies, including routers, transmission facilities, and line drivers. It is the router's capability to interconnect networks in a WAN that has made it indispensable.

continues

MORE INFORMATION (CONTINUED)

A router is an intelligent network device that operates predominantly at the first three layers of the OSI reference model. Routers, like any host, are actually capable of operating at all seven layers of the OSI reference model. Depending on your particular configuration, you may or may not use all seven layers of functionality. However, the need for the first three layers is virtually universal. Communication across the first two layers allows routers to communicate directly with LANs (data link layer constructs). More importantly, routers can identify routes through networks based on Layer 3 addresses. This enables routers to internetwork multiple networks by using network layer addressing, regardless of how near or far they may be relative to each other.

Understanding routers and routing requires examining a router from two different perspectives: physical and logical. From a physical perspective, routers contain myriad parts, each of which has a specific function. From a logical perspective, routers perform many functions, including finding other routers in the network, learning about potential destination networks and hosts, discovering and tracking potential routes, and forwarding datagrams toward their specified destination. Together, these physical components and logical functions enable you to build and use internetworks, including WANs.

Physical Components

A router is a remarkably complex device. Its complexity lies in its routing engine—logic that enables the physical device to perform the various routing functions. The complexity of routing logic is hidden by the relative simplicity of the router's physical form. The most common type of router is actually a highly specialized type of computer; it contains the same basic components as any other computer. These include the following:

- A central processing unit (CPU)
- Random access memory (RAM)
- A Basic Input/Output System (BIOS)
- An operating system (OS)
- A motherboard
- Physical input/output (I/O) ports
- A power supply, chassis, and sheet-metal skin

The vast majority of a router's components will remain forever shielded from the eyes of network administrators by the chassis's sheet-metal skin. These components are extremely reliable and, under normal operating conditions, shouldn't see the light of day. The obvious exceptions to this general statement are born of expansion. Any time you need to add more resources to the router, you may have to take off its cover. Such resources usually include either memory or I/O ports.

MORE INFORMATION (CONTINUED)

The components that a network administrator will encounter most often are the operating system and the I/O ports. A router's operating system (in Cisco Systems' case, the *Internetwork Operating System*—IOS) is the software that controls the various hardware components and makes them usable. Network administrators mostly use a command-line interface to develop a logical configuration. The configuration is a profile of the system: the numbers, the locations, the types of each I/O port, and details such as addressing and bandwidth information. A router's configuration can also include security information such as which users are permitted access to specific I/O ports and configuration modes.

The I/O ports are the one physical router component that network administrators see on a routine basis. These bear out the router's unique capability to interconnect seemingly endless combinations of LAN and WAN transmission technologies. Each one of these, whether LAN or WAN, must have its own I/O port on the router. These ports function like a network interface card (NIC) in a LAN-attached computer; they are related to the medium and framing mechanisms expected and provide the appropriate physical interfaces. Many of these physical interfaces appear quite similar to each other. This physical similarity belies the differences between the higher-layer functions of those technologies. Therefore, it is more useful to examine transmission technologies than to examine specific physical interfaces.

Router Functions

Equally important as providing physical interconnectivity for multiple networks are the logical functions that a router performs. These functions make the physical interconnections usable. For example, internetworked communications require that at least one physical path interconnect the source and destination machines. However, having and using a physical path are two very different things. Specifically, the source and destination machines must speak a common language (a *routed protocol*). It also helps if the routers that lie between them also speak a common language (a *routing protocol*) and agree on which specific physical path is the best one to use.

Therefore, some of the more salient functions that a router provides are listed here:

Physical interconnectivity

Logical interconnectivity

Route calculation and maintenance

Security

Physical Interconnectivity

A router has a minimum of two (and frequently many more) physical I/O ports. I/O ports, or *interfaces*, as they are better known, are used to physically connect network transmission facilities to a router. Each port is connected to a circuit board that is attached to the router's motherboard. Thus, the motherboard actually provides the interconnectivity among multiple networks.

continues

MORE INFORMATION (CONTINUED)

The network administrator must configure each interface via the router's console. Configuration includes defining the interface's port number in the router, the specific transmission technology and bandwidth available on the network connected to that interface, and the types of protocols that will be used through that interface. The actual parameters that must be defined vary based on the type of network interface.

Note that, on the higher-end platforms (7500 and 12000), the interfaces (VIP2 or line card) can forward packets without interrupting the main CPU.

Logical Interconnectivity

As soon as a router interface is configured, it can be activated. The interface's configuration identifies the type of transmission facility that it connects to, the interface's IP address, and the address of the network that it connects to. Upon activation of a port, the router immediately begins monitoring all the packets that are being transmitted on the network attached to the newly activated port. This allows it to "learn" about network and host IP addresses that reside on the networks that can be reached via that port. These addresses are stored in tables called *routing tables*. Routing tables correlate the port number of each interface in the router with the network layer addresses that can be reached (either directly or indirectly) via that port.

A router can also be configured with a *default route*. A default route associates a specific router interface with all unknown destination addresses. This allows a router to forward a datagram to destinations that it has not yet learned of. Default routes can be useful in other ways, too. Default routes can be used to minimize the growth of routing tables, for example, or can be used to reduce the amount of traffic generated between routers as they exchange routing information.

Route Calculation and Maintenance

Routers communicate with each other using a predetermined protocol, a *routing protocol*. Routing protocols enable routers to do the following:

- Identify potential routes to specific destination networks
- Perform a mathematical calculation, based on the routing protocol's algorithm, to determine the best path to each destination
- Continuously monitor the network to detect any topology changes that may render known routes invalid

MORE INFORMATION (CONTINUED)

Many different types of routing protocols exist. Some, such as the Routing Information Protocol (RIP), are quite simple. Others, such as Open Shortest Path First (OSPF), are remarkably powerful and feature-rich but complicated. In general, routing protocols can use two approaches to make routing decisions: distance vectors and link states. A distance-vector routing protocol makes its decisions based on some measurement of the distance between source and destination machines. A link-state protocol bases its decisions on various states of the links, or transmission facilities, that interconnect the source and destination machines. Neither one is right or wrong: They are just different ways of making the same decisions. However, they result in different levels of performance, including convergence times.

You can evaluate routing protocols using numerous, more-specific criteria than just which approaches they use. Some of the more meaningful criteria include the following:

- **Optimality**—Optimality describes a routing protocol's capability to select the best available route. Unfortunately, the word *best* is ambiguous. Many different ways exist to evaluate different routes to any given destination. Each way could result in the selection of a different "best" route depending on the criteria used. The criteria used by routing protocols to calculate and evaluate routes are known as *routing metrics*. A wide variety of metrics are used, and they vary widely by routing protocol. A simple metric is *hop count*, the number of hops, or routers, that lie between the source and destination machines.
- **Efficiency**—Another criterion to consider when evaluating routing protocols is their operational efficiency. Operational efficiency can be measured by examining the physical resources, including router RAM and CPU time, and network bandwidth required by a given routing protocol. You may need to consult your router manufacturer or vendor to determine the relative efficiencies of any protocols you are considering.
- **Robustness**—A routing protocol should perform reliably at all times, not just when the network is stable. Error conditions, including hardware or transmission-facility failures, router configuration errors, and even heavy traffic loads, adversely affect a network. Therefore, it is critical that a routing protocol function properly during periods of network failure or instability.
- **Convergence**—Because they are intelligent devices, routers can automatically detect changes in the internetwork. When a change is detected, all the routers involved must converge on a new agreement of the network's topology and recalculate the routes to known destinations accordingly. This process of reaching mutual agreement is called *convergence*. Each routing protocol uses different mechanisms for detecting and communicating network changes. Therefore, each one converges at a different rate. In general, the slower a routing protocol converges, the greater the potential is for disrupting service across the internetwork.

continues

MORE INFORMATION (CONTINUED)

- **Scalability**—A network's scalability is its capability to grow. Although growth isn't a requirement in every organization, the routing protocol that you select should be capable of scaling upward to meet your network's projected growth.

The Function of a Router in a WAN

Routers are useful for segmenting LANs into separate broadcast domains, and they must be used when connecting these LANs over a wide area (see Figure 16-5). Routers have both LAN and WAN interfaces. WAN technologies are frequently used to connect routers. They communicate with each other over WAN connections, and they connect networks within autonomous systems as well as the backbone of the Internet. Routers operate at Layer 3 of the OSI model, making decisions based on network addresses (on the Internet by using the Internet Protocol, or IP).

FIGURE 16-5
Routers connected by WAN technologies.

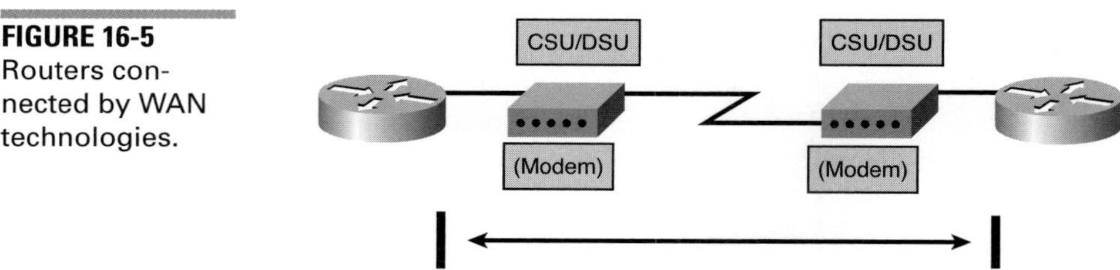

The two main functions of routers are the determination of best paths for incoming data packets and the switching of packets to the proper outgoing interface. Routers accomplish this by building routing tables and exchanging the network information contained within these routing tables with other routers. You can configure routing tables, but generally they are maintained dynamically by using a routing protocol that exchanges network topology (path) information with other routers.

For example, if you want any computer (x) to be capable of communicating with any other computer (y) anywhere on Earth, and with any other computer (z) anywhere in the moon-Earth system, you must include a routing feature for information flow and redundant paths for reliability. Many network design decisions and technologies can be traced to this desire for computers x, y, and z to be capable of communicating, or internetworking. Any internetwork also typically includes the following:

- Consistent end-to-end addressing
- Addresses that represent network topologies

- Best-path selection
- Dynamic routing
- Switching/forwarding

SKILL BUILDER

Lab Activity: Router Characteristics

In this lab, you examine a Cisco router to gather information about its physical characteristics and begin to relate Cisco router products to their function. You determine the model number and features of a specific Cisco router, including which interfaces are present and to which cabling and devices they are connected.

MORE INFORMATION

Roles of the Router in WANs

More often than not, internetworks are quite extensive in terms of the number of routers, transmission facilities, and attached end systems. In an extensive internetwork, such as the Internet or even large private networks, it would be virtually impossible for any given machine to know about every other machine. Therefore, some semblance of hierarchy is needed. Hierarchical organization of internetworked machines creates the need for specialized routing functions.

Routers can specialize in learning about and distributing routing information within their domain. These routers are called *interior gateways*. Alternatively, routers can specialize in collecting routing information about networks that lie beyond their domain. These routers are known as *exterior gateways*.

Networking is often used as a generic or universal term. However, networked machines communicate in tremendously different ways. Routers can function in different capacities in an internetwork—for example, as interior, exterior, or border routers.

Note that it is not uncommon to find interior routers, exterior routers, and border routers described as *interior gateways, exterior gateways*, and *border gateways*, respectively. The term *gateway* is as old as routing itself. Over time, this term has lost some of its descriptive value. Consequently, both sets of terms are technically correct, except in the presence of technological purists. Then you have to determine which terminology they consider correct!

continues

MORE INFORMATION (CONTINUED)

These functional specializations are more than merely academic. Understanding the differences among them requires examining them in the context of a WAN. Therefore, a logical starting point is an examination of the context. The terms *WAN*, *network*, *internetwork*, and *autonomous system* are all used interchangeably, yet each has a slightly different meaning:

- **WAN**—A *WAN* is a collection of related LANs linked via routers and serial transmission facilities such as leased lines or Frame Relay circuits. Implicit in this definition is that the LANs in the WAN may be geographically dispersed, but they still fall under the auspices of a single organization such as a company or school.
- **Network**—*Network* is a more nebulous term that defies specificity. Everything from LANs to WANs can be classified as a network. Consequently, for the purposes of this book, a network identifies a generic collection of related networking mechanisms. Therefore, a network may be a LAN or a WAN, but it must belong to a single organization and feature a consistent addressing architecture. This term is sometimes used to indicate an internetwork or even the Internet.
- **Internetwork**—*Internetwork* is only slightly more concrete than network. An internetwork is a collection of loosely related networks that are interconnected. The interconnected networks can belong to different organizations. For example, two companies can use the Internet to interconnect their private WANs. The resulting internetwork consists of one public network and two private networks linked together. The most common definition of internetwork is a set of networks linked by routers. This is not necessarily a loosely related set of networks, although the term is applied to both a single domain or autonomous system (AS) internetwork or an internetwork comprised of separate ASes.
- **Autonomous system**—An autonomous system (AS) is a network or internetwork (either LAN or WAN) that is relatively self-contained. It is administered by a single person (or organization), features a single routed protocol, has an address architecture, and usually involves just one routing protocol. An autonomous system may support connections to other autonomous systems owned and operated by the same organization. Alternatively, an AS may have connections to other networks, such as the Internet, yet it retains autonomy of operation. This term is usually used in conjunction with specific routing protocols, such as OSPF or BGP, that enable a network to be carved into numbered subsections.

Given these definitions, it is possible to better define the functional classes of routers. An *interior router* is one that can be used by end systems in a network to access other end systems within the same network. The interior router supports no connections to any other network. Figure 16-6 illustrates a small network and identifies those devices that function as interior routers.

MORE INFORMATION (CONTINUED)

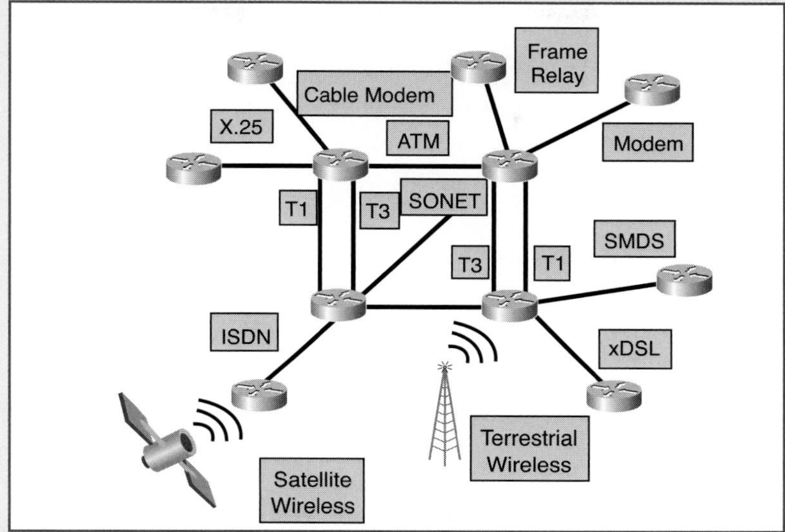

FIGURE 16-6
Interior routers in a network.

An exterior router is one that lies beyond the boundaries of any given network. Figure 16-7, although not pretending to depict the Internet's actual topology, presents a highly simplified Internet topology that is solely intended to demonstrate what an exterior router is.

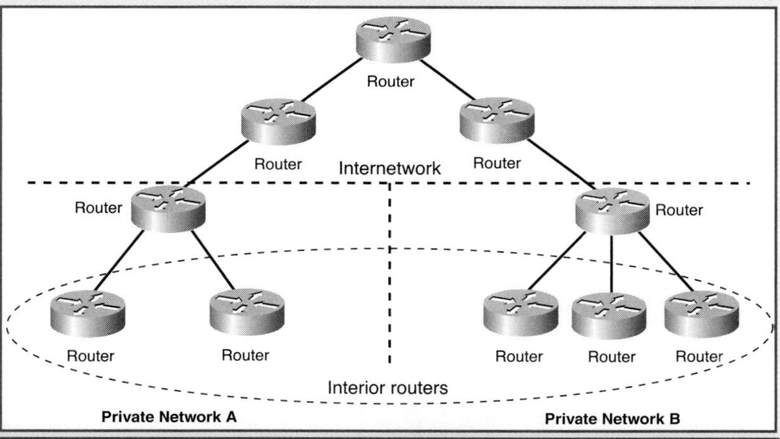

FIGURE 16-7
Exterior routers from the perspective of private networks.

continues

MORE INFORMATION (CONTINUED)

The last functional class of router is the *border router.* As the name implies, border routers interconnect a network with other networks. It is important to note that a single entity may own and operate multiple autonomous systems. Therefore, a border router may denote the boundary between two autonomous systems rather than the border between a private network and some other network. Figure 16-8 identifies the border routers in the sample network that were used in Figure 16-6 and Figure 16-7.

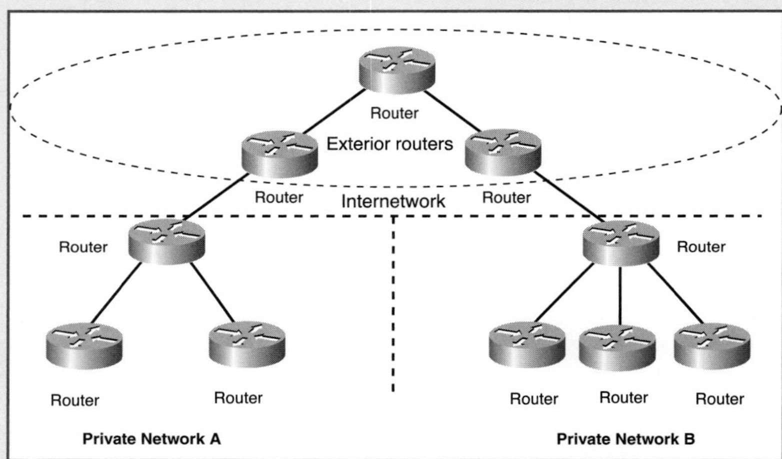

FIGURE 16-8 The border routers from the perspective of the private networks.

Lab Topology

The lab topology in Figure 16-9 should be thought of as an enterprise WAN for a medium-sized company with offices around the world. It is not connected to the Internet; it is the company's private network.

Figure 16-10 provides interface configurations for the router lab, along with password information.

Also, the topology, as shown, is not redundant—a failure of any router along the chain breaks the network. This network of networks under a common administration (the company) is called an *autonomous system*.

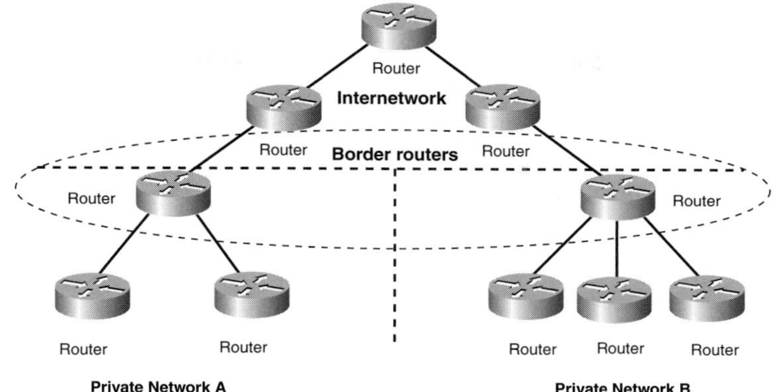

FIGURE 16-9
Router lab topology.

The Internet is a network of autonomous systems, each of which has routers that typically play one of four roles, as shown in Figure 16-11:

- **Internal routers**—Stay internal to one area
- **Area Border Routers**—Connect two or more areas
- **Backbone routers**—Serve as primary paths for traffic that is most often sourced from and destined for other networks
- **Autonomous System (AS) Boundary Routers**—Communicate with routers in other autonomous systems

MORE INFORMATION

Although the lab topology used in your CCNA studies is not a model of the Internet, it is a model of one topology that might represent an autonomous system. The protocol that is routed almost universally is IP; the routing protocol Border Gateway Protocol (BGP) is widely used between Internet routers.

Router A is in Kuala Lumpur, Router B is in San Francisco, Router C is in New York City, and Routers D and E are in Paris. Each of the routers connects to an office or campus LAN. The connections from A to B, B to C, and C to D are leased T1/E1 lines that are attached to the routers' serial interfaces.

Note that each router has an Ethernet LAN attached to it. Hosts are typical devices on Ethernet LANs; they're shown along with their console cables to allow configuration and display of the routers' contents. Also note that four of the routers have wide-area serial connections between them.

FIGURE 16-10
Router configuration.

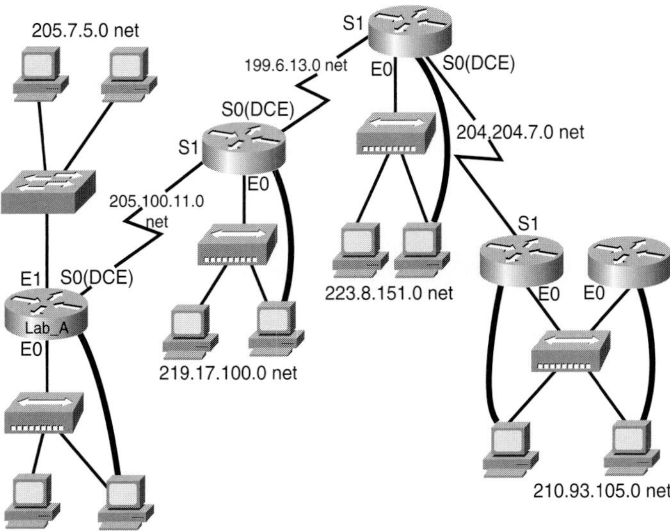

Router Name	Router Type	E0	E1	S0	S1	SM	Enable Password	Vty Password
Lab_A	2514	192.5.5.1	205.7.5.1	201.100.11.1	--	255.255.255.0	class	cisco
Lab_B	2501	219.17.100.1	--	199.6.13.1	201.100.11.2	255.255.255.0	class	cisco
Lab_C	2501	223.8.151.1	--	204.204.7.1	199.6.13.2	255.255.255.0	class	cisco
Lab_D	2501	210.93.105.1	--	--	204.204.7.2	255.255.255.0	class	cisco
Lab_E	2501	210.93.105.2	--	--	--	255.255.255.0	class	cisco

e-LAB ACTIVITY 16.1

Setting Up Cisco Lab Equipment

In this activity, you demonstrate an understanding of how the Cisco lab routers are set up and connected for the Semester 2 topology.

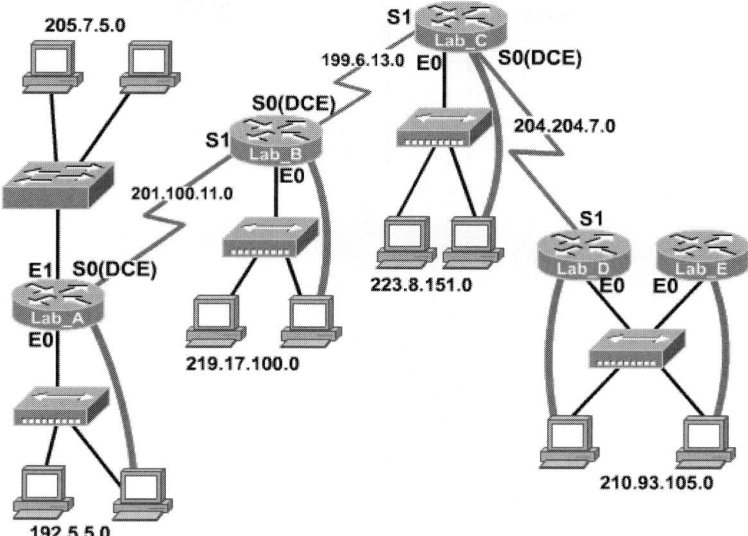

FIGURE 16-11 OSPF view of the Internet.

SKILL BUILDER

Lab Activity: Router Lab Setup

This lab helps you develop an understanding of how the Cisco lab routers are set up and connected for the Semester 2 topology. You examine and document the physical connections between these routers and the other lab hardware components, such as hubs, switches, and workstations.

e-LAB ACTIVITY 16.2

Router and Workstation Configuration

In this activity, you demonstrate an understanding of how the Cisco lab routers and workstations are configured for the Semester 2 topology.

SKILL BUILDER

Lab Activity: Router Lab Configuration

This lab helps you develop an understanding of how the Cisco lab routers and workstations are configured for the Semester 2 topology. You use IOS commands to examine and document the IP network configurations of each router.

MORE INFORMATION

Internetworking Scenarios

Having examined the concepts underlying routing and internetworking, as well as some of the terminology inherent with these topics, you can see how they are used by examining three internetworking scenarios. Each scenario demonstrates some of the issues that need to be addressed in any network or internetwork:

- Routing within a network
- Routing between adjacent networks
- Routing between nonadjacent networks

These three generic aspects encompass virtually every form of internetworking that you are likely to encounter. Each one holds different implications for the network administrator, including such routing aspects as route calculation and distribution, convergence, and security. The following sections provide an overview of each internetworking scenario and highlight the areas of concern for a network administrator. The various potential resolutions to these routing concerns are presented throughout this book.

Routing Within an Autonomous System

The simplest form of routing is routing within the confines of a single autonomous system. Such a network contains just interior routers. In theory, this form of network would use just one routed protocol, one address architecture, and a minimum number of destinations. This would greatly reduce the workload of each router and maximize potential network performance. Therefore, the routing issues in intranetwork routing are more closely related to the network's size and topology rather than its address architectures and routing protocols. The topology must be carefully selected to match the requirements of the user community.

If the network were small enough, it might be feasible for the administrator to preprogram all the possible routes statically rather than introduce the complexity of a dynamic routing protocol. Statically programmed routes, however, can become an onerous burden in a growing or constantly changing network.

MORE INFORMATION (CONTINUED)

Routing Between Adjacent Autonomous Systems

A small step up in complexity from intranetwork routing is internetwork routing, between adjacent ASes. Physical adjacency means that the two networks are directly connected to each other. Such an adjacency may have been designed to promote rapid convergence, improve security, or satisfy any number of other performance criteria.

The logical separation of the multiple networks implies that the border routers must summarize and redistribute routing information between them. In this fashion, the end systems of one network can directly address the end systems in another network. Figure 16-12 illustrates this type of routing.

FIGURE 16-12 Routing between adjacent networks.

Router Name	Router Type	E0	E1	S0	S1	SM	Enable Password	Vty Password
Lab_A	2514	192.5.5.1	205.7.5.1	201.100.11.1	--	255.255.255.0	class	cisco
Lab_B	2501	219.17.100.1	--	199.6.13.1	201.100.11.2	255.255.255.0	class	cisco
Lab_C	2501	223.8.151.1	--	204.204.7.1	199.6.13.2	255.255.255.0	class	cisco
Lab_D	2501	210.93.105.1	--	--	204.204.7.2	255.255.255.0	class	cisco
Lab_E	2501	210.93.105.2	--	--	--	255.255.255.0	class	cisco

The routing issues that need to be addressed in this type of internetwork arise from the differences between the two networks. Some of the potential differences that must be identified include the following:

- Do the networks belong to the same organization? If not, the border routers need to secure the network's perimeter.
- Do the networks use the same routing protocol? If not, some mutually acceptable metric must be found.
- Do the networks use the same routed protocol? If not, you may have to support a second routed protocol in your network to facilitate internetworking.

continues

MORE INFORMATION (CONTINUED)

Additionally, topology can affect routing between adjacent networks. Using a single point of interconnection between the two networks, for example, makes it easy to control the calculation and redistribution of routing information between the networks. This convenience introduces a single point of failure; however, it might not be acceptable to your users. Introducing a second (or even more) interconnection point solves the single point of failure problem but can create the opportunity for infinite routing loops to occur. Resolving such a dilemma requires an understanding of your users' tolerance for downtime and risk. Armed with this understanding, you can evaluate specific routing protocols for their capabilities to converge quickly and compensate for potential routing problems.

Internetworking Nonadjacent Networks

Routing between nonadjacent networks is simultaneously the most complicated and useful type of routing. Two networks can use a third network as an intermediary. It is highly likely that the three different networks will use different routing protocols, routed protocols, and address architectures. Therefore, the boundary router's job is to overcome these obstacles to communication while also guarding the border of its network. Figure 16-13 illustrates routing between nonadjacent small networks.

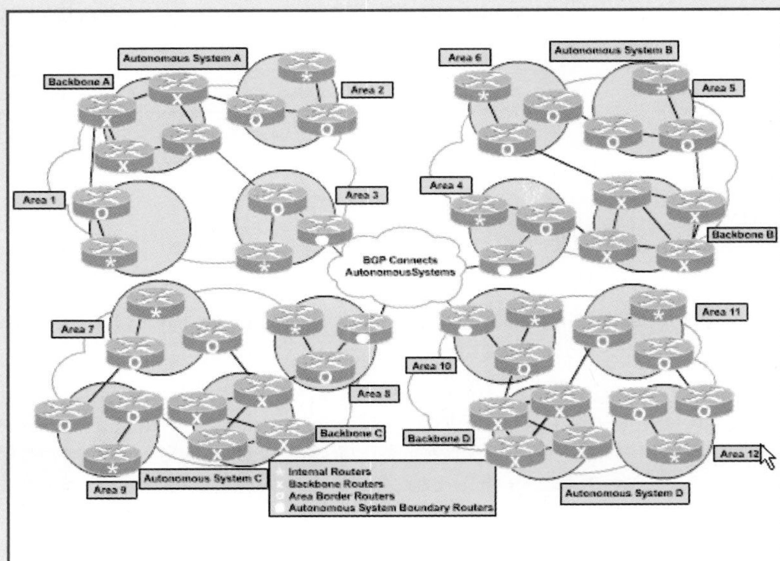

FIGURE 16-13 Routing between nonadjacent networks.

MORE INFORMATION (CONTINUED)

The border router of each private network in this illustration needs to protect the border of its network from unwanted intrusion. Because the two networks that need to communicate aren't adjacent and the intermediary network is beyond their control, the risks of unwanted intrusion are much higher than if the networks were directly internetworked. Therefore, the network administrators must develop a set of criteria for allowing specific external users into their network, while disallowing access to everyone else. The border router would implement these criteria in an access control list.

Another responsibility of the border router is to summarize the internal routes and redistribute this information to the networks beyond. This enables users outside the bounds of the private network to access its end systems. If this routing information isn't distributed, no one outside that private network would be able to access its end systems.

Finally, it is highly likely that the border routers will have to be configured to use multiple routing protocols. An interior gateway protocol will likely be selected for intranetwork routing purposes. Calculating routes across the internetwork, however, might require a different protocol—one that features stronger support for route summarization.

Summary

Now that you have completed this chapter, you should have an understanding of the following:

- WAN characteristics
- WAN devices such as the following:
  — Routers
  — Switches
  — Modems
  — Communication servers
- WAN standards such as the following:
  — EIA/TIA-232
  — EIA/TIA-449
  — V.24
  — V.35
  — X.21

- G.703
- EIA-530

- WAN technologies such as the following:
  - Circuit-switched services
  - Packet-switched services
  - Cell-switched services
  - Dedicated digital services
- How routers function in a WAN

Check Your Understanding

1. Which of the following best describes a WAN?
   - **A.** Connects LANs that are separated by a large geographic area
   - **B.** Connects workstations, terminals, and other devices in a metropolitan area
   - **C.** Connects LANs within a large building
   - **D.** Connects workstations, terminals, and other devices within a building
2. How do WANs differ from LANs?
   - **A.** WANs emphasize access over serial interfaces operating at lower speeds.
   - **B.** WANs provide high-speed multiple access services.
   - **C.** WANs typically exist in small geographic areas.
   - **D.** WANs use tokens to regulate network traffic.
3. Which of the following are examples of WAN technologies?
   - **A.** Token Ring, ARCNet
   - **B.** Frame Relay, ISDN
   - **C.** Star, Banyan VINES
   - **D.** CSU/DSU, ARCView
4. Which layers of the OSI model do WAN standards describe?
   - **A.** Data link and network
   - **B.** Data link and presentation
   - **C.** Physical and application
   - **D.** Physical and data link
5. Which best describes data circuit-terminating equipment (DCE)?
   - **A.** Consists of the user device at the end of a network
   - **B.** Serves as the data source or destination
   - **C.** Consists of physical devices such as protocol translators and multiplexors
   - **D.** Consists of physical devices at the end of a WAN connection

6. Which of the following components provide interface voice-grade services, channel service units/digital service units (CSU/DSUs) that interface T1/E1 services, and Terminal Adapters/Network Termination 1 (TA/NT1s) that interface Integrated Services Digital Network (ISDN) services?

   A. Switches

   B. Routers

   C. Modems

   D. Communication servers

7. Which of the following concentrates the dial-in and dial-out user connections?

   A. Switches

   B. Routers

   C. Modems

   D. Communication servers

8. Some WAN physical and data link layer standards are:

   A. EIA/TIA-232

   B. PPP

   C. Frame Relay

   D. All of the above

9. Match the functions with the components.

   1. RAM/DRAM
   2. NVRAM
   3. ROM
   4. Flash memory
   5. Interface

   a. Stores a router's backup/startup configuration file

   b. Stores routing tables, the ARP cache, the fast-switching cache, packet buffering (shared RAM), and packet hold queues

c. Contains power-on diagnostics, a bootstrap program, and operating system software

d. Serves as a network connection through which packets enter and exit a router

e. Holds the operating system image and microcode; enables you to update software without removing and replacing chips on the processor

A. 1-b, 2-a, 3-c, 4-e, 5-d

B. 1-a, 2-b, 3-c, 4-e, 5-d

C. 1-b, 2-a, 3-e, 4-c, 5-d

D. 1-b, 2-a, 3-c, 4-d, 5-e

10. Any internetwork will probably include the following:

A. Consistent end-to-end addressing and priority-level bandwidth allocation capabilities

B. Addresses that represent network topologies and assurance of quality of service

C. Best-path selection and dynamic routing

D. All of the above

11. Which of the following are data link encapsulations for WAN?

A. High-Level Data Link Control (HDLC)

B. Frame Relay

C. Point-to-Point Protocol (PPP)

D. All of the above

12. What are the main functions of routers?

A. The determination of best paths for incoming data packets, and the switching of packets to the proper outgoing interface

B. Replying to ARP requests when two nodes are on different LANs

C. Building routing tables and exchanging the network information contained within them with other routers

D. Both A and B

13. Which is an IBM-designed WAN data link for Systems Network Architecture (SNA) environments, largely being replaced by the more versatile HDLC?

    A. Serial Line Interface Protocol

    B. Point-to-Point Protocol

    C. Synchronous Data Link Control Protocol

    D. Simple Data Level Control Protocol

14. Which WAN data link protocol is used for signaling and call setup on an ISDN D channel?

    A. LAPD

    B. LAPF

    C. LAPB

    D. LAPR

15. Identify the WAN circuit-switched service(s):

    A. Plain old telephone services (POTS)

    B. Narrowband ISDN with a maximum bandwidth of 1.544 Mbps

    C. Narrowband ISDN with a maximum bandwidth of 128 kbps

    D. Both A and C

16. Which service has become an extremely popular WAN technology in its own right, more efficient than X.25 but with similar services, maximum bandwidth of 44.736 Mbps, and popular 56-kbps and 384-kbps implementations extremely popular in the United States?

    A. Frame Relay

    B. X.25

    C. POTS

    D. ATM

17. Identify the cell-switched technology/technologies:

    A. ATM

    B. Switched Multimegabit Data Service

    C. T1

    D. Both A and B

18. Identify the common type(s) of DSL technology/technologies:

A. High bit-rate DSL (HDSL)

B. Single-line DSL (SDSL)

C. Asymmetric DSL (ADSL)

D. All of the above

19. Which is a family of very high-speed physical layer technologies with a series of data rates available with special designations, implemented at different optical carrier (OC) levels ranging from 51.84 Mbps (OC-1) to 9952 Mbps(OC-192), that can achieve these amazing data rates by using wavelength division multiplexing (WDM)?

A. SONET

B. HDSL

C. ATM

D. SMDS

20. Which are the kind of routers that form the primary paths for traffic that is sourced from and destined to other networks?

A. Internal routers

B. Area Border Routers

C. Backbone routers

D. Autonomous System (AS) Boundary Routers

Objectives

After reading this chapter, you will be able to

- Describe user and privileged modes
- Use router help functions
- Use IOS editing commands
- Use IOS command history

Chapter 17

Router CLI

Introduction

In this chapter, you learn about operating a router to ensure delivery of data on a network with routers. You also become familiar with the Cisco command-line interface and learn how to accomplish these actions:

- Log in with the user password
- Enter privileged mode with the enable password
- Disable or quit

In addition, you learn how to use the following advanced help features:

- Command completion and prompting
- Syntax checking

Lastly, you learn how to use the following advanced editing features:

- Automatic line scrolling
- Cursor controls
- History buffer with command recall
- Copy and paste, which are available on most computers

An Overview of the Router User Interface

To configure Cisco routers, you must either access the user interface via the console port on the router with a terminal or access the router remotely through a Telnet session. When accessing a router, you must log in to the router before you enter any other commands.

For security purposes, the router has two levels of access to commands:

- **User mode**—Typical tasks include those that check the router status. In this mode, router configuration changes are not allowed.
- **Privileged mode**—Typical tasks include those that change the router configuration.

e-LAB ACTIVITY 17.1

User and Privileged Modes

In this activity, you demonstrate how to use the command that allows you to access the privileged mode of a router.

MORE INFORMATION

Logging In to a Router: The Cisco Internetwork Operating System (IOS)

When you first log in to a router, you see a user mode prompt:

```
Router>
```

Commands available at this user level are a subset of the commands available at the privileged level. These commands enable you to display information (**show**) but do not allow any changes to the router configuration settings.

To access the full set of commands, you must first access privileged mode. At the > prompt, type **enable**, as shown in Listing 17-1, At the password prompt, enter the password that has been set with the **enable secret** command. When you have completed the login steps, the prompt changes to a pound sign (#) because you are now in privileged mode. From privileged mode, you can access modes such as global configuration mode and other specific configuration modes, including the following:

- Interface
- Subinterface
- Line
- Router
- Route-map
- Several additional configuration modes

Listing 17-1 Logging In to and Out of the Router

```
Router con0 is now available.

Press RETURN to get started.

User Access Verification
Password:
Router>
Router> enable
Password:
Router#
Router# disable
```

MORE INFORMATION (CONTINUED)

```
Router>
Router> exit
```

To log out of the router, type **exit**.

Note that screen output varies with the specific Cisco IOS software level and router configuration.

MORE INFORMATION

Basic Operation of Cisco IOS Software

Cisco's Internetwork Operating System (IOS) software platform is implemented on the various hardware used in this course. It is the embedded software architecture in all the Cisco routers.

Cisco IOS software enables network services in these products, including the following:

- Features to carry the chosen network protocols and functions
- Connectivity for high-speed traffic between devices
- Security to control access and discourage unauthorized network use
- Scalability to add interfaces and capability as needed for network growth
- Reliability to ensure dependable access to networked resources

The Cisco IOS command-line interface can be accessed through a console connection, a modem connection, or a Telnet session. Regardless of which connection method is used, access to the IOS command-line interface is generally referred to as an EXEC session.

User Mode Command List

Typing a question mark (?) at the user mode prompt or the privileged mode prompt displays a handy list of commonly used commands (see Table 17-1). When you are logged into a Cisco router, you might notice "–More–" at the bottom of the router's output. The screen displays 22 lines at one time, so sometimes you get this prompt at the bottom of the display. The –More– prompt indicates that multiple screens are available as output—that is, more output follows. Here, or anywhere else in Cisco IOS software, whenever a –More– prompt appears, you can continue viewing the next available screen by pressing the Spacebar. To display just the next line, press the Return key (or, on some keyboards, the Enter key). Press any other key to return to the router prompt.

e-LAB ACTIVITY 17.2

User Mode Command List

In this activity, you demonstrate the use of the command that allows you to display the list of commands in user mode.

NOTE

At this point, the list of commands displayed is context-sensitive. You see a different list when you are in user mode versus enable mode, and when in global configuration versus configure interface modes.

TABLE 17-1 User Mode Commands

Command	Description
access-enable	Creates a temporary access list entry
atmsig	Executes ATM signaling commands
cd	Changes current device
clear	Resets functions
connect	Opens a terminal connection
dir	Lists files on a given device
disable	Turns off privileged commands
disconnect	Disconnects an existing network connection
enable	Turns on privileged commands
exit	Exits EXEC
help	Gets a description of the interactive help system
lat	Opens a LAT connection
lock	Locks the terminal
login	Logs in as a particular user
logout	Exits from EXEC mode
mrinfo	Requests neighbor and version information from a multicast router
mstat	Shows statistics after multiple multicast traceroutes
mtrace	Traces the reverse multicast path from destination to source
name-connection	Names an existing network connection
pad	Opens an X.29 PAD connection

TABLE 17-1 User Mode Commands (Continued)

Command	Description
ping	Sends echo messages
ppp	Starts IETF Point-to-Point Protocol (PPP)
pwd	Displays current device
resume	Resumes an active network connection
rlogin	Opens an rlogin connection
show	Shows running system information
slip	Starts Serial-Line IP (SLIP)
systat	Displays information about terminal lines
telnet	Opens a Telnet connection
terminal	Sets terminal line parameters
tn3270	Opens a TN3270 connection
traceroute	Sets a traceroute to the destination
tunnel	Opens a tunnel connection
where	Lists active connections
x3	Sets X.3 parameters on PAD
xremote	Enters Xremote mode

Privileged Mode Command List

To access privileged mode, type **enable** (or the abbreviation **ena**).

```
Router> ena
Password:
```

You are prompted for a password. If you type a question mark (?) at the privileged mode prompt Router# ?, the screen displays a longer list of commands than it would at the user mode prompt (see Table 17-2).

TABLE 17-2 Privileged Mode Commands

Command	Description
access-enable	Creates a temporary access list entry
access-template	Creates a temporary access list entry
appn	Sends a command to the APPN subsystem
atmsig	Executes ATM signaling commands
bfe	Sets manual emergency modes
calendar	Manages the hardware calendar
cd	Changes the current device
clear	Resets functions
clock	Manages the system clock
cmt	Starts or stops FDDI connection management functions
configure	Enters configuration mode
connect	Opens a terminal connection
copy	Copies configuration or image data
debug	Uses debugging functions (see also **undebug**)
delete	Deletes a file
dir	Lists files on a given device
disable	Turns off privileged commands
disconnect	Disconnects an existing network connection
enable	Turn on privileged commands
erase	Erases Flash or configuration memory
exit	Exits from EXEC mode
format	Formats a device
help	Gets a description of the interactive help system
lat	Opens a LAT connection

TABLE 17-2 Privileged Mode Commands (Continued)

Command	Description
lock	Locks the terminal
login	Logs in as a particular user
logout	Exits EXEC mode
mbranch	Traces the multicast route down the tree branch
mrbranch	Traces the reverse multicast up the tree branch
mrinfo	Requests neighbor and version information from a multicast router
mstat	Shows statistics after multiple multicast traceroutes
mtrace	Traces reverse multicast path from destination source
name-connection	Names an existing network connection
ncia	Starts/stops NCIA server
pad	Opens an X.29 PAD connection
ping	Sends echo messages
PPP	Starts IETF Point-to-Point Protocol (PPP)
pwd	Displays current device
reload	Halts and performs a cold return
resume	Resumes an active network connection
rlogin	Opens an rlogin connection
rsh	Executes a remote command
sdlc	Sends SDLC test frames
send	Sends a message over tty lines
setup	Runs the setup command facility
show	Shows running system information
slip	Starts Serial-Line IP (SLIP)
squeeze	Squeezes a device

continues

TABLE 17-2 Privileged Mode Commands (Continued)

Command	Description
start-chat	Starts a chat script on a line
systat	Displays information about terminal lines
tarp	Targets ID Resolution Process (TARP) commands
telnet	Opens a Telnet connection
terminal	Sets terminal line parameters
test	Tests subsystems, memory, and interfaces
tn3270	Opens a TN3270 connection
traceroute	Sets a traceroute to the destination
tunnel	Opens a tunnel connection
undebug	Disables debugging functions (see also **debug**)
undelete	Undeletes a file
verify	Verifies the checksum of a Flash file
where	Lists active connections
which-route	Does an OSI route table lookup and displays results
write	Writes running-configuration to memory, network, or terminal
x3	Sets X.3 parameters on PAD
xremote	Enters Xremote mode

e-LAB ACTIVITY 17.3

Privileged Command List

In this activity, you demonstrate the use of the command that allows you to display the list of commands in user mode.

Using Router Help Functions

The following exercise illustrates one of the many functions of the **help** command. Your task is to set the router clock. Assuming that you do not know the command, proceed using the following seven steps:

Step 1 Use the **help** command to check the syntax for setting the clock. The **help** output shows that the clock command is required (see Listing 17-2).

Step 2 Check the syntax for changing the time.

Step 3 The system indicates that you need to provide additional information to complete the command. The **help** output shows that the **set** keyword is required.

Step 4 Check the syntax for entering the time, and enter the current time using hours, minutes, and seconds. The system indicates that you need to provide additional information to complete the command (see Listing 17-3).

Step 5 Press Ctrl-P (or the up arrow) to repeat the previous command entry automatically. Then add a space and a question mark (?) to reveal the additional arguments. Now you can complete the command entry.

Step 6 The caret symbol (^) and **help** response indicate an error. The placement of the caret symbol shows you where the possible problem is located. To input the correct syntax, re-enter the command up to the point where the caret symbol is located, and then enter a correction for the error. A question mark (?) following the correction will return **help** information about the next item needed.

Step 7 Enter the year, using the correct syntax, and press Return to execute the command.

The user interface provides syntax checking by placing a ^ where the error occurred. The ^ appears at the point in the command string where you have entered an incorrect command, keyword, or argument. The error location indicator and interactive help system enable you to find and correct syntax errors easily.

Listing 17-2 Help Functions

```
Router# clok
Translating "CLOK"
% Unknown command or computer name, or unable to find computer address
```

continues

Listing 17-2 Help Functions (Continued)

```
Router# cl?
clear   clock

Router# clock
% Incomplete command.

Router# clock ?
set     Set the time and date

Router# clock set
% Incomplete command

Router# clock set ?
Current Time ( hh : mm : ss )
```

Listing 17-3 Syntax Checking and Command Prompting

```
Router# clock set 19:56:00% Incomplete command.

Router# clock set 19:56:00 ?
<1-31>      Day of the month
MONTH       Month of the year

Router# clock set 19:56:00 04 8
                              ^
% Invalid input detected at the '^' marker

Router# clock set 19:56:00 04 August
% Incomplete command.

Router# clock set 19:56:00 04 August ?
<1993-2035>   Year
```

e-LAB ACTIVITY 17.4

Setting the Router Clock

In this activity, you demonstrate how to use the command that allows you to set the router clock.

MORE INFORMATION

Keyboard Help in Switch Command-Line Interface

The Catalyst OS has a command-line input help facility. For example, the Catalyst 1900 series switches OS CLI offers context-sensitive help.

Any time during an EXEC session, you can type a question mark (?) to get help. Two types of context-sensitive help are available: word help and command syntax help.

MORE INFORMATION (CONTINUED)

- Enter ? to get word help for a list of commands that begin with a particular character sequence. Type in the character sequence followed immediately by the ?. Do not include a space before the question mark. The switch then displays a list of commands that start with the characters that were entered.
- Enter ? to get command syntax help so that you can see how to complete a command. Enter ? in the place of a keyword or argument. Include a space before the ?. The network device then displays a list of available command options, with <cr> standing for carriage return.

Using IOS Editing Commands

The user interface includes an enhanced editing mode that provides a set of editing key functions that enable you to edit a command line as it is being typed. Use the key sequences indicated in Table 17-3 to move the cursor around on the command line for corrections or changes. Although enhanced editing mode is automatically enabled with the current software release, you can disable it if you have written scripts that do not interact well while enhanced editing is enabled. To disable enhanced editing mode, type **terminal no editing** at the privileged mode prompt.

TABLE 17-3 Editing Commands

Command	Description
Ctrl-A	Moves to the beginning of the command line
Ctrl-E	Moves to the end of the command line
Esc-B	Moves back one word
Ctrl-F	Moves forward one character
Ctrl-B	Moves back one character
Esc-F	Moves forward one word

The editing command set provides a horizontal scrolling feature for commands that extend beyond a single line on the screen. When the cursor reaches the right margin, the command line shifts 10 spaces to the left. The dollar sign ($) indicates that the line has been scrolled to the left. Each time the cursor reaches the end of the line, the line is again shifted 10 spaces to the left.

You cannot see the first 10 characters of the line, but you can scroll back and check the syntax at the beginning of the command. To scroll back, press Ctrl-B or the left arrow key repeatedly until you are at the beginning of the command entry, or press Ctrl-A to return directly to the beginning of the line.

Using IOS Command History

The user interface provides a history, or record, of commands that you have entered. This feature is particularly useful for recalling long or complex commands or entries. With the command history feature, you can complete the following tasks (see Table 17-4):

- Set the command history buffer size.
- Recall commands.
- Disable the command history feature.

TABLE 17-4 Command History Commands

Command	Description
Ctrl-P or up arrow key	Recalls last (previous) command
Ctrl-N or down arrow key	Recalls most recent command
show history	Shows command buffer
terminal history [**size** *number-of-lines*]	Sets command buffer size
no terminal editing	Disables advanced editing features
terminal editing	Reenables advanced editing features
Tab	Completes the entry

By default, the command history is enabled and the system records 10 command lines in its history buffer. To change the number of command lines that the system records during a terminal session, use the **terminal history size** or **history size** commands. The maximum number of commands is 256.

To recall commands in the history buffer, beginning with the most recent command, press Ctrl-P or the up arrow key repeatedly to recall successively older commands. To return to more recent commands in the history buffer after recalling commands with Ctrl-P or the up arrow, press Ctrl-N or the down arrow key repeatedly to recall successively more recent commands.

When typing commands, as a shortcut, you can enter the unique beginning characters for a command and press the Tab key—EXEC finishes the entry for you. The unique letters identify the command, the Tab key simply returns the entire command text that the router has extrapolated from your shortcut. The key is to use enough characters to ensure that there is only one IOS command beginning with that string of characters.

e-LAB ACTIVITY 17.5

Using IOS Command History

In this activity, you demonstrate how to use the IOS command history.

e-LAB ACTIVITY 17.6

Command-line User Interface

In this activity, you demonstrate how to use different commands in user mode and privileged mode.

SKILL BUILDER

Lab Activity: Router User Interface

This lab introduces the Cisco Internetwork Operating System (IOS) command-line user interface. You log on to the router and use different levels of access to enter commands in user mode and privileged mode.

SKILL BUILDER

Lab Activity: Router User Interface Modes

When using router operating systems such as the Cisco IOS, you have to know each of the different user modes that a router has and what each one of them is used for. Memorizing every command in all of the user modes would be time-consuming and pointless. Try to develop an understanding of what commands and functions are available within each of the modes. In this lab, you work with the lab topology and the six main modes available with most routers:

1. User EXEC mode
2. Privileged EXEC mode (also known as enable mode)
3. Global configuration mode

continues

SKILL BUILDER (CONTINUED)

4. Router configuration mode
5. Interface configuration mode
6. Subinterface configuration mode

Summary

You can configure Cisco routers from the user interface running on the router console or via a terminal connection. For security purposes, Cisco routers have two levels of access to commands: user mode and privileged mode.

Using a user interface to a router, you can do the following:

- Log in with a user password
- Enter privileged mode with the enable password
- Quit the user interface

You can use advanced help features to perform the following:

- Command completion and prompting
- Syntax checking

The user interface includes an enhanced editing mode that provides a set of editing key functions.

The user interface provides a history, or record, of commands you have entered.

Check Your Understanding

1. What is the acronym used to describe a Cisco router's text-based user interface?

   A. CLI

   B. TCP/IP

   C. OSPF

   D. OSI

2. What two modes of access to router commands exist for Cisco routers?

   A. User and privileged

   B. User and guest

   C. Privileged and guest

   D. Guest and anonymous

3. Which mode do you use to make router configuration changes on Cisco routers?

   A. User

   B. Privileged

   C. Administrator

   D. Root

4. In what mode can you do typical tasks, including those that check the router status? (In this mode, router configuration changes are not allowed.)

   A. User mode

   B. Privileged mode

   C. Access privileged mode

   D. Enable configuration mode

5. What does it mean if you see a greater-than symbol (>) on a Cisco router user interface?

   A. You are in login mode.

   B. You are in help mode.

   C. You are in user mode.

   D. You are in privileged mode.

6. Which of the following is the privileged mode prompt for Cisco router user interfaces?

   A. #

   B. >

   C. <

   D. l#

7. Which mode gives you access to a list of commonly used commands if ? is typed on a Cisco router user interface?

   A. Guest

   B. Privileged only

   C. User only

   D. User and privileged

8. What does the –More– prompt at the bottom of a screen on a Cisco router user interface mean?

   A. Multiple screens are available as output.

   B. Additional detail is available in the manual pages.

   C. Multiple entries are required in the command.

   D. Additional conditions must be stated.

9. Which keystroke(s) automatically repeat(s) the previous command entry on a Cisco router user interface?

   A. Left arrow

   B. Right arrow

   C. Ctrl-R

   D. Ctrl-P

10. What happens if you press the up arrow key in a Cisco router user interface?

    A. You see a list of all users logged in to the router.

    B. You list the last command you typed.

    C. You print the screen.

    D. You pause the current process.

11. What happens if you type ? in a Cisco router user interface?

    A. You see a list of all users logged in to the router.

    B. You list the last command you typed.

    C. You see the list of commands available.

    D. You find out which mode you are currently in.

12. What happens if you type **show ?** at the router prompt?

    A. You get a list of the users currently on the router.

    B. You get a list of all active connections and their status.

    C. You get a list of the most recent router table.

    D. You get a list of the subcommands that are available within the **show** command.

13. The maximum number of commands that can be stored in the history buffer is:

    A. 256

    B. 64

    C. 128

    D. 32

14. What command is used to change the size of the history buffer?
    A. **terminal history size**
    B. **history size**
    C. **history buffer value**
    D. Both A and B
15. What key is used to complete incomplete commands or keywords by entering some unique characters from the beginning of the command or keyword?
    A. Spacebar
    B. Esc
    C. Tab
    D. Enter
16. How do you get to the next screen if "More" is indicated at the bottom of the current screen on a Cisco router user interface?
    A. Press the Page Down key.
    B. Press the Spacebar.
    C. Press the End key.
    D. Press the Tab key.
17. How do you switch from user to privileged mode on Cisco routers?
    A. Type **admin** and enter a password at the next prompt.
    B. Type **root** and enter a password at the next prompt.
    C. Type **enable** and enter a password at the next prompt.
    D. Type **privileged** and enter a password at the next prompt.

18. What does it mean if you see a caret symbol (^) after entering a command on a Cisco router?

A. It indicates the location of an error in a command string.

B. It indicates that you are in help mode.

C. It indicates that more information must be entered to complete the command.

D. It indicates that you are in privileged mode.

19. Match the different router modes with their appropriate prompts (for example: 1-a, 2-b, and so on).

1. User EXEC mode	a. Router #
2. Privileged EXEC mode	b. Router >
3. Global configuration mode	c. Router (config-router) #
4. Router configuration mode	d. Router (config)#

A. 1-b, 2-a, 3-c, 4-d

B. 1-b, 2-a, 3-d, 4-c

C. 1-c, 2-a, 3-b, 4-d

D. 1-a, 2-c, 3-b, 4-d

20. Show the hierarchy of the router modes with the initial mode on the top and the most specific mode at the bottom. If two or more modes have equal priority, choose any order.

1. Global configuration mode
2. Subinterface configuration mode.
3. User EXEC mode
4. Interface configuration mode
5. Router configuration mode
6. Privileged EXEC mode

A. 3, 6, 1, 5, 4, 2

B. 3, 1, 6, 5, 2, 4

C. 1, 3, 6, 5, 4, 2

D. 3, 6, 4, 1, 2, 5

Objectives

After reading this chapter, you will be able to

- Describe external router configuration sources
- Describe internal router configuration components
- Describe router modes
- Use router **show** Commands
- Describe how to access other routers by using the Cisco Discovery Protocol
- Use basic network testing commands

Router Components

Introduction

Now that you have an understanding of the router command-line interface, it is time to examine the router components that ensure efficient and effective delivery of data on a network. In this chapter, you learn the correct procedures and commands to access a router, examine and maintain its components, and test its network connectivity.

Router Configuration Components and Router Modes

In this section, you learn about the router components that play a key role in the configuration process. Knowing which components are involved in the configuration process gives you a better understanding of how the router stores and uses your configuration commands. Being aware of the steps that take place during router initialization helps you determine what problems can occur where when you start up your router.

As shown in Figure 18-1, you can configure a router from many external locations, including the following:

- From the console terminal (a computer connected to the router through a console port) during its installation
- Via modem by using the auxiliary port
- From virtual terminals, after the router has been installed on the network
- From a TFTP server on the network

Internal Router Configuration Components

The internal architecture of the Cisco router supports components that play an important role in the startup process, as shown in Figure 18-2. Internal router configuration components are as follows:

- **RAM/DRAM**—Stores routing tables, the ARP cache, the fast-switching cache, packet buffering (shared RAM), and packet hold queues. RAM also provides running memory for a router's configuration file while the router is powered. RAM content is lost during a powerdown or restart.

- **Nonvolatile RAM (NVRAM)**—Nonvolatile RAM stores the router's backup/startup configuration file. NVRAM content is retained during a powerdown or restart.
- **Flash memory**—Acts as erasable, reprogrammable ROM that holds the operating system image and microcode. Flash memory enables software updates without removing and replacing processor chips. Flash memory content is retained during power down or restart. Flash memory also can store multiple versions of IOS software.
- **ROM**—Contains power-on diagnostics, a bootstrap program, and minimal operating system software. Software upgrades in ROM require removing and replacing pluggable chips on the motherboard.

Interfaces are network connections on the motherboard or on separate interface modules, through which packets enter and exit a router. When configuring the router, you must go through one of these external interfaces. Examples of these external interfaces include console, auxiliary, Ethernet, and serial interfaces.

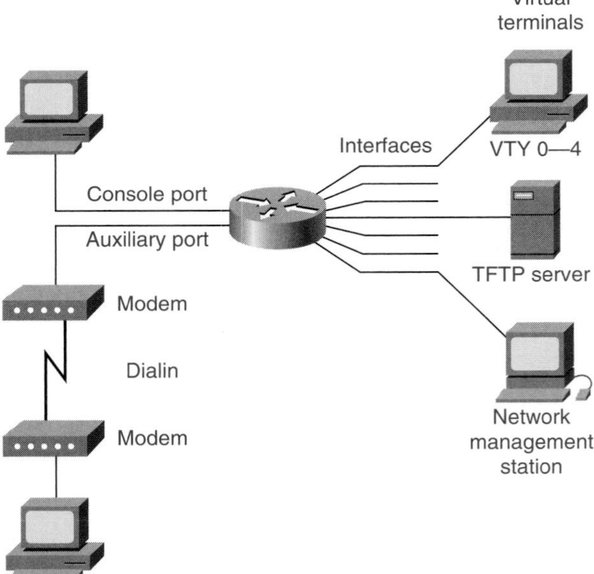

FIGURE 18-1 Configuration information can come from many sources.

RAM—Working Storage for the Router

RAM is the working storage area for a router. When you turn on a router, the ROM executes a bootstrap program. This program performs some tests and then loads the Cisco IOS software into memory. The command executive, or EXEC, is one part of the Cisco IOS software. EXEC receives and executes commands that you enter for the router.

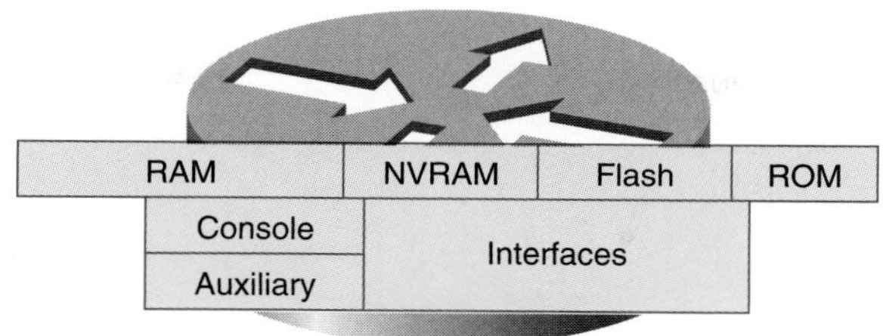

FIGURE 18-2
The internal configuration components include several parts.

As shown in Figure 18-3, a router also uses RAM to store an active configuration file and tables of network maps and routing address lists. You can display the configuration file on a remote or console terminal. A saved version of this file is stored in NVRAM; it is accessed and loaded into main memory each time a router initializes. The configuration file contains global, process, and interface information that directly affects the operation of a router and its interface ports.

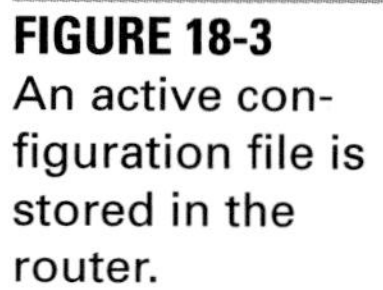

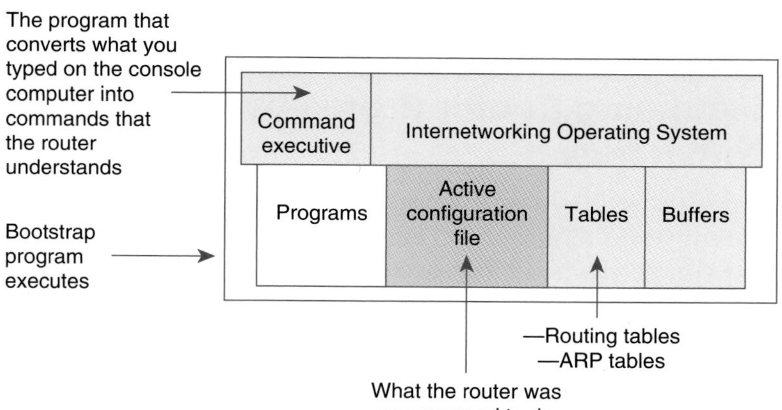

FIGURE 18-3
An active configuration file is stored in the router.

An operating system image cannot be displayed on a terminal screen. An image is usually executed from the main RAM and is loaded from one of several input sources. The operating software is organized into routines that handle the tasks associated with different protocols, such as data movement, table and buffer management, routing updates, and user command execution.

Router Modes

Whether accessed from the console or by a Telnet session through a vty port, a router can be placed in several modes. Each mode provides different functions:

- **User EXEC mode**—This is a view-only mode in which the user can view some information about the router but cannot make changes.
- **Privileged EXEC mode**—This mode supports the debugging and testing commands, detailed examination of the router, manipulation of configuration files, and access to configuration modes.
- **Setup mode**—This mode presents an interactive prompted dialog box at the console that helps the new user create a first-time basic configuration.
- **Global configuration mode**—This mode implements powerful one-line commands that perform simple configuration tasks or puts the user into a more specific configuration mode.
- **Other configuration modes**—These modes provide more detailed multiple-line configurations.
- **RXBOOT mode**—This is the maintenance mode that you can use, among other things, to recover from lost passwords.

Examining Router Status by Using Router Status Commands

In this section, you learn basic commands that you can issue to determine the current status of a router. These commands help you obtain vital information that you need when monitoring and troubleshooting router operations.

It is important to be able to monitor the health and state of your router at any given time. As shown in Figure 18-4, Cisco routers have a series of commands that enable you to determine whether the router is functioning correctly or where problems exist. Router status commands and their descriptions are shown in Table 18-1.

TABLE 18-1 Router Status Commands

Command	Description
show version	Displays the configuration of the system hardware, the software version, the names and sources of configuration files, and the boot images, and displays the reason for the last system reboot.
show processes	Displays information about the active processes.

TABLE 18-1 Router Status Commands (Continued)

Command	Description
show protocols	Displays the configured protocols. This command shows the status of any configured Layer 3 (network layer) protocol.
show memory	Shows statistics about the router's memory, including memory-free pool statistics.
show stacks	Monitors the stack use of processes and interrupt routines.
show buffers	Provides statistics for the buffer pools on the router.
show flash	Shows information about the Flash memory device.
show running-config (**write term** on Cisco IOS Release 10.3 or earlier)	Displays the active configuration file.
show startup-config (**show config** on Cisco IOS Release 10.3 or earlier)	Displays the backup configuration file.
show interface	Displays statistics for all interfaces configured on the router.

NOTE

The commands **write term** and **show config**, used with Cisco IOS Release 10.3 and earlier, have been replaced with new commands. The commands that have been replaced continue to perform their normal functions in the current release but are no longer documented. Support for these commands will cease in a future release.

e-LAB ACTIVITY 18.1

Examining Router Status

In this activity, you demonstrate how to use the command that allows you to examine router status.

The show running-config and show startup-config Commands

Among the most used Cisco IOS software EXEC commands are **show running-config** and **show startup-config** (see Listing 18-1 and Listing 18-2). These commands enable an administrator to see the current running configuration on the router or the startup configuration commands that the router will use on the next restart.

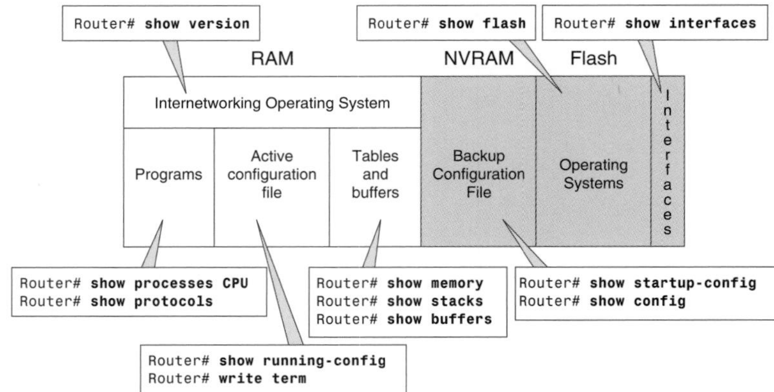

FIGURE 18-4 Many commands are available to monitor router configuration.

Listing 18-1 The show running-config Command

```
Router# show running-config
Building configuration...

Current configuration:
!
Version 11.1
!
    --More--
```

Listing 18-2 The show startup-config Command

```
Router# show startup-config
Using 1108 out of 130048 bytes
!
version 11.2
!
Hostname router

   --More--
```

You can recognize an active configuration file by the words "Current configuration" at the top. You can recognize a backup configuration file when you see a message at the top that tells you how much nonvolatile memory you have used.

e-LAB ACTIVITY 18.2

Show Running and Startup Configurations

In this activity, you demonstrate how to use the command that allows you to see the active configuration file on a router.

The show interfaces Command

The **show interfaces** command displays configurable parameters and real-time statistics related to all interfaces configured on the router (see Listing 18-3).

Listing 18-3 The show interfaces Command

```
Router# show interfaces
Serial0 is up, line protocol is up
Hardware is MK5025
Internet address is 183.8.64.129, subnet mask is 255.255.255.128
MTU 1500 bytes, BW 56 kbit, DLY 20000 usec, rely 255/255. load 9/255
Encapsulation HDLC, loopback not set, keepalive set (10 sec)
Last input 0:00:00, output 0:00:01, output hang never
Last clearing of show interfaces counters never
Output queue 0/40, 0 drops, input queue 0/75, 0 drops
Five minute input rate 1000 bits/sec, 0 packets/sec
331885 packets input, 62400237 bytes, no buffer
Received 230457 broadcasts, 0 runts, 0 giants
3 input errors, 3 CRC, 0 frame, 0 overrun, 0ignored, 0 abort
403591 packets output, 66717279 bytes, 0 underruns
0 output errors, 0 collisions, 8 interface resets, 0 restarts
45 carrier transitions
```

The show version Command

The **show version** command displays information about the Cisco IOS software version that is currently running on the router (see Listing 18-4).

Listing 18-4 The show version Command

```
Router# show version
Cisco Internetwork Operating System Software
IOS (tm) 4500 Software (C4500-J-M). Version 11.2
Copyright (c) 1986-1996 by Cisco Systems, Inc.
Compiled Fri 28-Jun-96  16:32 by rbeach
Image text-base: 0x600088A0, data-base: 0x6076E000

ROM: System Bootstrap, Version 5.1(1) RELEASE SOFTWARE (fc1)
ROM: 4500-XBOOT Bootstrap Software, Version 10.1(1) RELEASE SOFTWARE (fc1)

router uptime is 1 week, 3 days, 32 minutes
System restarted by reload
System image file is c4500-j-mz, booted via tftp from 171.69.1.129

--More--
```

The show protocols Command

You use the **show protocols** command to display the protocols configured on the router. This command shows the global and interface-specific status of any configured Level 3 protocols (for example, IP, DECnet, IPX, and AppleTalk) (see Listing 18-5).

Listing 18-5 The show protocols Command

```
Router# show protocols
Global values:
Internet Protocol routing is enabled
DECnet routing is enabled
XNS routing is enabled

Vines routing is enabled
AppleTalk routing is enabled
Novell routing is enabled
--More--
Ethernet0 is up, line protocol is up
Internet address is 183.8.126.2, subnet mask is 255.255.255.128
DECnet cost is 5
XNS address is 3010.aa00.0400.0284
CLNS enabled
Vines metric is 32
AppleTalk address is 3012.93, zone ld-e0
Novell address is 3010.aa00.0400.0284
--More--
```

e-LAB ACTIVITY 18.3

show interfaces, show version, and show protocols

In this activity, you demonstrate how to use the **show interfaces, show version**, and **show protocols** commands.

e-LAB ACTIVITY 18.4

Router show Commands

In this activity, you demonstrate how to use the router **show** commands, which are the most important information-gathering commands available for the router.

SKILL BUILDER

Lab Activity: Router show Commands

This lab helps you become familiar with the router show commands. The **show** commands are the most important information-gathering commands available for the router. The **show running-config** (or **show run**) command is probably the single most valuable command to help determine the current status of a router because it displays the active configuration file running in RAM. The **show startup-config** (or **show start**) command displays the backup configuration file that is stored in NVRAM. This is the file that will be used to configure the router when it is first started or rebooted with the **reload** command. All the detailed router interface settings are contained in this file.

SKILL BUILDER (CONTINUED)

The **show flash** command is used to view the amount of available and used Flash memory, where the Cisco Internetwork Operating System (IOS) file or image is stored. The **show arp** command displays the router's IP to MAC-to-interface address mapping. The **show interface** command displays statistics for all interfaces configured on the router. The **show protocol** command displays the global and interface-specific status of configured Layer 3 protocols (IP, IPX, and so on).

Gaining Access to Other Routers by Using the Cisco Discovery Protocol

The *Cisco Discovery Protocol (CDP)* provides a single proprietary command that enables network administrators to access a summary of what the configurations look like on other directly connected routers. CDP runs over a data link layer that connects lower physical media and upper network layer protocols, as shown in Figure 18-5. Because it operates at this level, CDP devices that support different network layer protocols can learn about each other. (Remember that a data link address is the same as a MAC address.)

When a Cisco device that is running Cisco IOS (Release 10.3 or later) boots up, CDP starts up automatically, which then allows the device to detect neighboring Cisco devices that are also running CDP. Such devices extend beyond those using TCP/IP and include directly connected Cisco devices, regardless of which Layer 3 and 4 protocol suite they are running.

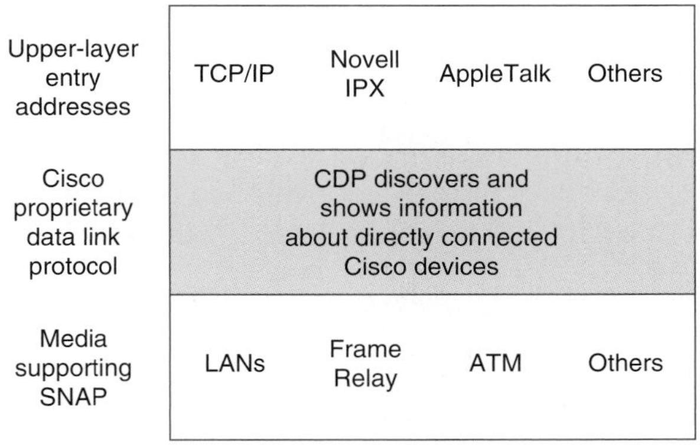

FIGURE 18-5 CDP enables discovery on multiprotocol networks.

Upper-layer entry addresses	TCP/IP	Novell IPX	AppleTalk	Others
Cisco proprietary data link protocol	CDP discovers and shows information about directly connected Cisco devices			
Media supporting SNAP	LANs	Frame Relay	ATM	Others

Showing CDP Neighbor Entries

The primary use of CDP is to discover platforms and protocols on your neighboring devices. Use the **show cdp neighbors** command to display the CDP updates on the local router.

Figure 18-6 displays an example of how CDP delivers its collection of information to a network administrator. Each router that is running CDP exchanges information regarding any protocol entries with its neighbors. The administrator can display the results of this CDP information exchange on a console that is connected to a router configured to run CDP on its interfaces.

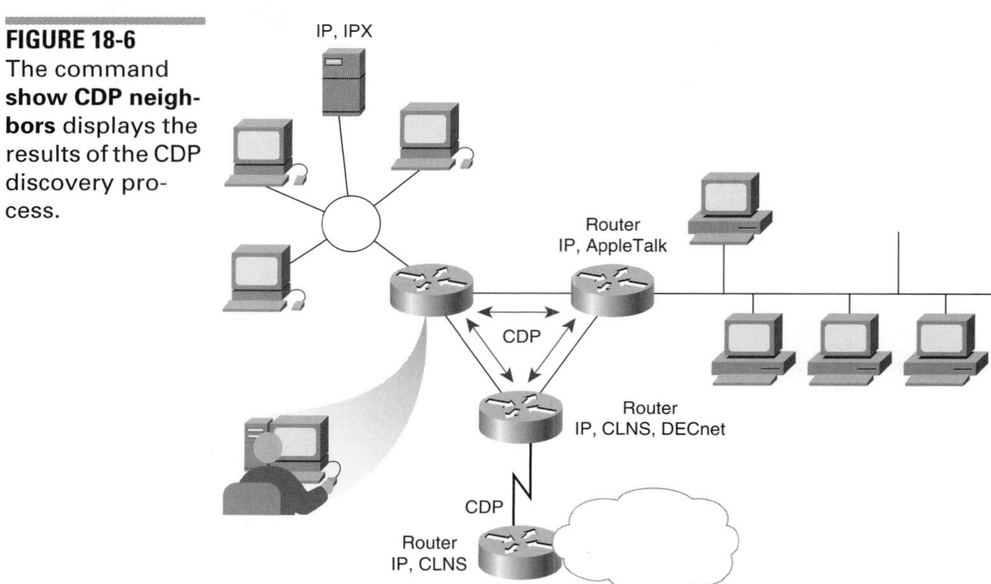

FIGURE 18-6 The command **show CDP neighbors** displays the results of the CDP discovery process.

The network administrator uses a **show** command to display information about the networks directly connected to the router. CDP provides information about each CDP neighbor device. Values include the following:

- **Device identifiers**—The router's configured hostname and domain name (if any)
- **Address list**—At least one address for SNMP, and up to one address for each supported protocol

- **Port identifier**—For example, Ethernet 0, Ethernet 1, and Serial 0
- **Capabilities list**—For example, information on whether the device acts as a source route bridge as well as a router
- **Version**—Information such as that provided by the local command show version
- **Platform**—The device's hardware platform, such as Cisco 7000

Notice that the lowest router in the Figure 18-16 is not directly connected to the administrator's console router. To obtain CDP information about this device, the administrator must Telnet to a router that is directly connected to this target.

e-LAB ACTIVITY 18.5

show CDP neighbors

In this activity, you demonstrate how to use the **show CDP neighbors** command to display information about neighboring devices.

A CDP Configuration Example

CDP begins automatically upon a device's system startup. The CDP function normally starts by default when a Cisco product boots up with Cisco IOS Release 10.3 or later.

Although CDP runs by default, you must explicitly enable it on each of the device's interfaces by using the command **cdp enable**. For example, Figure 18-7 shows the **cdp enable** command that you use on the E0 and S0 interfaces on the router named Router A. This command begins CDP's dynamic discovery function on the device's interfaces.

Only directly connected neighbors exchange CDP frames. A router caches any information that it receives from its CDP neighbors. If a subsequent CDP frame indicates that any of the information about a neighbor has changed, the router discards the older information and replaces it with the new information.

Use the command **show cdp interface**, as shown in Listing 18-6, to display the values of the CDP timers, the interface status, and the encapsulation used by CDP for its advertisement and discovery frame transmission. Default values for timers set the frequency for CDP updates and for aging CDP entries. These timers are set automatically at 60 seconds and 180 seconds, respectively. If the device receives a more recent update, or if this hold-time value expires, the device must discard the CDP entry.

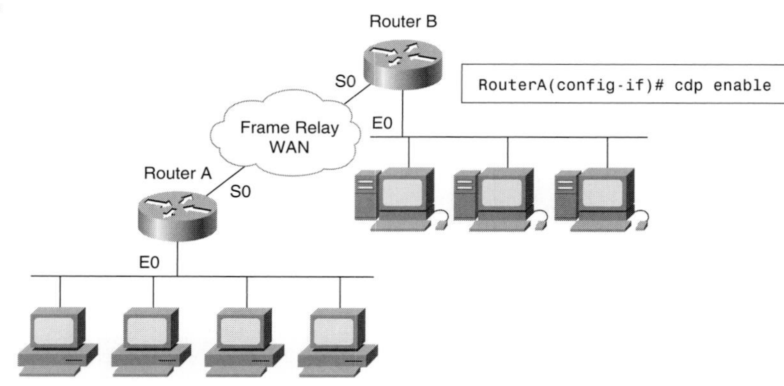

FIGURE 18-7
The **cdp enable** command enables CDP on each interface.

Listing 18-6

```
routerA# show cdp interface
Serial 0 is up, line protocol is up, encapsulation is Frame Relay
  Sending CDP packets every 60 seconds
  Holdtime is 180 seconds
Ethernet0 is up, line protocol is up, encapsulation is ARPA
  Sending CDP packets every 60 seconds
  Holdtime is 180 seconds
```

e-LAB ACTIVITY 18.6

CDP Configuration

In this activity, you demonstrate how to enable CDP on a router interface.

Showing CDP Entries for a Device

CDP was designed and implemented as a simple, low-overhead protocol. A CDP frame can be small yet can retrieve a lot of useful information about neighboring routers and switches. You use the command **show cdp entry {device name}**, as shown in Listing 18-7, to display a single cached CDP entry. Notice that the output from this command includes all the Layer 3 addresses present in the neighbor router, Router B. An administrator can view the IP addresses of the targeted CDP neighbor (Router B) with the single command entry on Router A. The hold-time value indicates the amount of elapsed time since the CDP frame arrived with this information. The command includes abbreviated version information about Router B.

Listing 18-7 The show cdp entry device-name Command

```
routerA# show cdp entry routerB
-----------------------------
Device ID: routerB
Entry address(es):
  IP address: 198.92.68.18
Platform: 2501. Capabilities: Router
Interface: Ethernet), Port ID (outgoing port): Ethernet0
Holdtime: 155 sec

Version
IOS (tm) GS Software (GS3), 11.2(13337)[asastry 161]
Copyright (c) 1986-1996 by Cisco Systems, Inc.
Compiled Tue 14-May-96 1:04
```

e-LAB ACTIVITY 18.7

show cdp

In this activity, you demonstrate how to use the **show cdp** command to check general CDP settings.

Showing CDP Neighbors

You use the command **show cdp neighbors**, as shown in Listing 18-8, to display the CDP updates received on the local router. Notice that for each local port, the display shows the following:

- Neighbor device ID
- Local port type and number
- Decremental hold-time value, in seconds
- Neighbor device capability code
- Neighbor hardware platform
- Neighbor remote port type and number

To display this information as well as information like that from **show cdp entry**, you use the optional **show cdp neighbors detail** command.

Listing 18-8 The show cdp neighbors Command

```
routerA#show cdp neighbors
Capability Codes: R - Router, T - Trans Bridge,
                  B - Source Route Bridge,
                  S - Switch, H - Host, I - IGMP

Device ID    Local Interface   Holdtime   Capability   Platform   Port ID
routerB      Eth 0             151        R            2501       Eth 0
routerB      Ser 0             165        R            2501       Ser 0

routerA#show cdp neighbors detail
----------------
```

continues

Listing 18-8 The show cdp neighbors Command (Continued)

```
Device ID: routerB
Entry address(es):
  IP address: 198.92.68.18
Platform: 2501, Capabilities: Router
Interface: Ethernet0, Port ID (outgoing port): Ethernet0
Holdtime: 143 sec
```

e-LAB ACTIVITY 18.8

cdp neighbors

In this activity, you demonstrate how to use the **show cdp** command to discover and show information about directly connected Cisco devices (routers and switches).

SKILL BUILDER

Lab Activity: CDP Neighbors

In this lab, you use the **show cdp** command. The Cisco Discovery Protocol (CDP) discovers and shows information about directly connected Cisco devices (routers and switches). CDP is a Cisco proprietary protocol that runs at the data link layer (Layer 2) of the OSI model. This allows devices that might be running different network Layer 3 protocols, such as IP or IPX, to learn about each other. CDP begins automatically upon a device's system startup, if you are using Cisco IOS Release 10.3 or a newer version of IOS; however, you must enable it on each of the device's interfaces by using the **cdp enable** command.

Using the command **show cdp interface**, you gather information that CDP uses for its advertisement and discovery frame transmission. Use the **show cdp neighbors** and **show cdp neighbors** detail commands to display the CDP updates received on the local router.

Basic Network Testing

The most common problems that occur on IP networks result from errors in the addressing scheme. It is important to test your address configuration before continuing with further configuration steps. Basic testing of a network should proceed in sequence from one OSI reference model layer to the next. Each test presented in this section focuses on network operations at a specific layer of the OSI model. As shown in Figure 18-8, **telnet, ping, trace, show ip route, show interfaces**, and **debug** are commands that enable you to test your network.

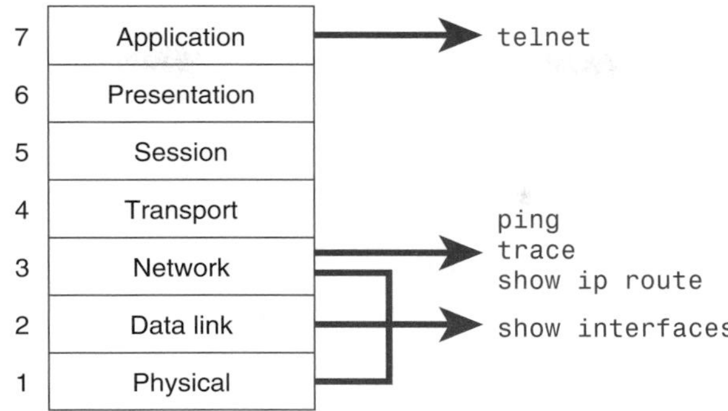

FIGURE 18-8 You use the **telnet**, **ping**, and **trace** commands to verify your configuration.

e-LAB ACTIVITY 18.9

Testing Process that Uses the OSI Model

In this activity, you demonstrate how use the telnet command to test a connection between two routers.

Testing the Application Layer by Using the telnet Command

Another way to learn about a remote router is to connect to it. Telnet, a virtual terminal protocol that is part of the TCP/IP protocol suite, allows connections to be made to hosts. You can set up a connection between a router and a connected device running Telnet. Telnet also enables you to verify the application layer connectivity between source and destination stations, which implicitly verifies all lower layers at the same time. This is the most complete test mechanism available. Most routers can have up to five simultaneous incoming Telnet sessions.

As shown in Figure 18-9, the **telnet** command provides a virtual terminal so that administrators can use Telnet operations to connect with other routers running TCP/IP. With Cisco's implementation of TCP/IP, you do not need to enter the command **connect** or **telnet** to establish a Telnet connection. If you prefer, you can just enter the router's hostname or one of its IP addresses. To end a Telnet session, use the EXEC commands **exit** or **logout**.

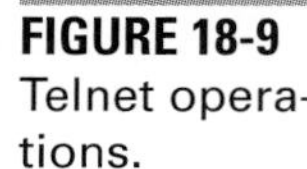

FIGURE 18-9
Telnet operations.

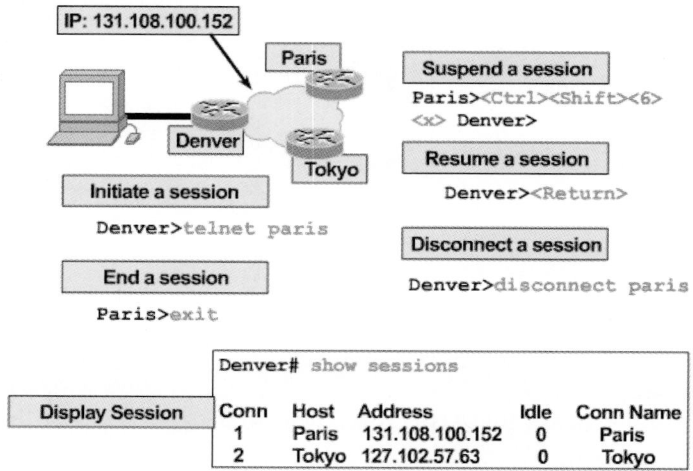

The following shows alternative commands for the operations listed in Figure 18-9. These are three different commands to initiate a session from Denver to Paris:

```
Denver> connect paris    - or
Denver> paris        - or
Denver> 131.108.100.152
Paris>

Resume a session (enter session number or name):
Denver>1
Paris>

End a session:
Paris> exit
```

You can use Telnet to perform a test to determine whether you can access a remote router. As shown in Figure 18-10, if you can successfully use Telnet to connect the York router to the Paris router, you have performed a basic test of the network connection.

If you can remotely access another router through Telnet, you know that at least one TCP/IP application can reach the remote router. A successful Telnet connection indicates that the seven layers of the OSI model are functioning properly for the associated source and destination.

FIGURE 18-10
You can test all layers up to the application layer by using Telnet.

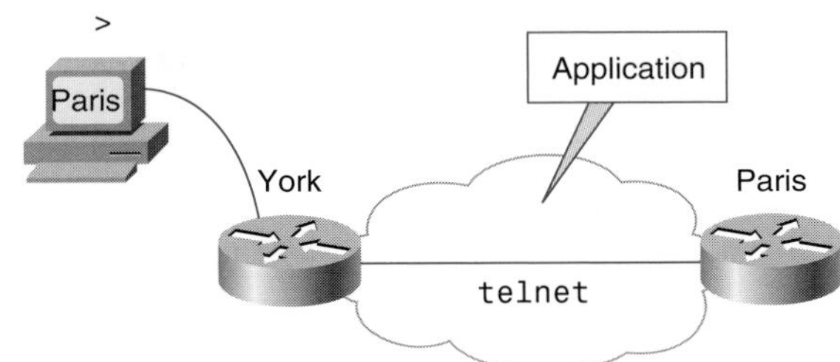

If you can Telnet to one router but not to another router, the Telnet failure likely is caused by specific addressing, naming, or access permission problems. These problems can exist on your router or on the router that failed as a Telnet target. The next step is to try the **ping** command, which is covered next. **ping** lets you test end to end at the network layer.

e-LAB ACTIVITY 18.10

Testing the Application Layer by Using telnet

In this activity, you demonstrate how to log on to a remote router and gather information about that router.

e-LAB ACTIVITY 18.11

Remote Telnet Access

In this activity, you demonstrate how to use **telnet** command to log on to a remote router and gather information about it using the **show interfaces**, **show protocols**, **show running-config**, and **show startup-config** commands.

SKILL BUILDER

Lab Activity: Remote Telnet Access

In this lab, you work with the Telnet (remote terminal) utility to access routers remotely. You Telnet from your "local" router into another "remote" router to simulate being at the console on the remote router.

Testing the Network Layer by Using the ping Command

As an aid to diagnosing basic network connectivity, many network protocols support an echo protocol. Echo protocols are used to test whether protocol packets are being routed. The **ping** command sends a packet to the destination host and then waits for a reply packet from that host, as shown in Figure 18-11. Results from this echo protocol can help evaluate the path-to-host reliability, identify delays over the path, and determine whether the host can be reached or is functioning.

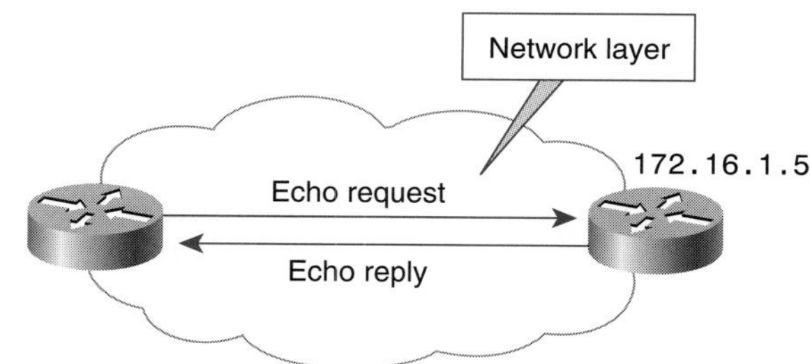

FIGURE 18-11
The **ping** command tests IP network connectivity.

In Listing 18-9, the **ping** target 172.16.1.5 responded successfully to all five datagrams sent. The exclamation points (!) indicate each successful echo. If you receive one or more periods (.) instead of exclamation marks on your display, the application on your router timed out waiting for a given packet echo reply from the **ping** target. You can use the **ping** user EXEC command to diagnose basic network connectivity. **ping** uses the Internet Control Message Protocol (ICMP).

Listing 18-9 The ping Command

```
Router> ping 172.16.1.5
Type escape sequence to abort.
Sending 5, 100 byte ICMP Echos to 172.16.1.5, timeout is 2 seconds:
!!!!!
Success rate is 100 percent, round-trip min/avg/max - 1/3/4 ms
Router>
```

e-LAB ACTIVITY 18.12

Testing the Network Layer Using the ping Command

In this activity, you demonstrate how use the ping command to test network connectivity.

SKILL BUILDER

Lab Activity: ICMP ping

In this lab, you use the Internet Control Message Protocol (ICMP). ICMP gives you the capability to diagnose basic network connectivity. Using **ping xxx.xxx.xxx.xxx** sends an ICMP packet to the specified host whose IP address is *xxx.xxx.xxx.xxx*; it then waits for a reply packet from that host. You can **ping** the hostname of a router, but you must have a static host lookup table in the router or a DNS server for resolving names to IP addresses.

Testing the Network Layer with the trace Command

The **trace** command is the ideal tool for finding where data is being sent in your network. The **trace** command is similar to the **ping** command, except that, instead of testing end-to-end connectivity, **trace** tests each step along the way, as shown in Figure 18-12. This operation can be performed at either the user or the privileged EXEC levels.

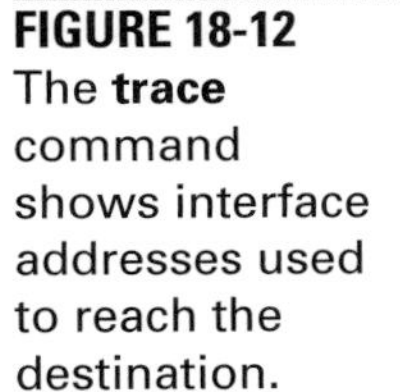

FIGURE 18-12 The **trace** command shows interface addresses used to reach the destination.

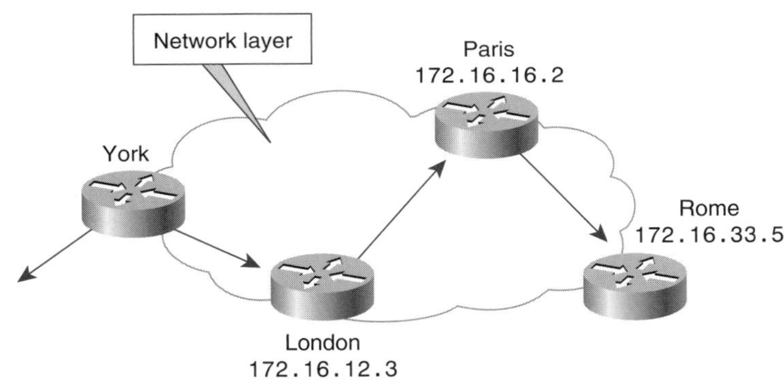

The **trace** command takes advantage of the error messages generated by routers when a packet exceeds its Time-To-Live (TTL) or hop count value. The **trace** command sends several **ping** packets with an incrementing TTL value and displays the round-trip time for each. Because the TTL value is incremented each time a **ping** is sent, each successive **ping** gets closer to the destination. The benefit of the **trace** command is that it also tells which router in the path was the last one to be reached. This allows for *fault isolation*.

In Listing 18-10, you are tracing the path from York to Rome. Along the way, the path must go through London and Paris. If one of these routers had been unreachable, you would have seen three asterisks (*) instead of the name of the router. The **trace** command would continue attempting to reach the destination until it is reached, until the hop count limit is reached, or until you terminate the command using the Ctrl-Shift-6 escape sequence.

Listing 18-10 The trace Command

```
York# trace ROME
Type escape to abort.
Tracing the route to Rome (172.16.33.5)
  1 LONDON (172.16.12.3) 1000 msec 8 msec 4 msec
  2 PARIS (172.16.16.2) 8 msec 8 msec 8 msec
  3 ROME (172.16.35.5) 8 msec 8 msec 4 msec

York#
```

e-LAB ACTIVITY 18.13

Testing the Network Layer Using the traceroute Command

In this activity, you demonstrate how to use **traceroute** command to see how data is being routed between the two routers each step along the network.

SKILL BUILDER

Lab Activity: traceroute Command

In this lab, you use the IOS **traceroute** command. The **traceroute** command uses ICMP packets and the error message generated by routers when the packet exceeds its Time-To-Live (TTL).

Testing the Network Layer with the show ip route Command

The router offers some powerful tools at this point in the search. You can actually look at the routing table, which contains directions that the router uses to determine how it will direct traffic across the network.

The next basic test also focuses on the network layer. Use the **show ip route** command to determine whether a routing table entry exists for the target network. Listing 18-11 shows that Rome (131.108.33.0) is reachable by Paris (131.108.16.2) via the Ethernet1 interface.

Listing 18-11 The show ip route Command

```
Paris# show ip route

Codes: I - IGRP derived, R - RIP derived, O - OSPF derived
       C - connected, S - static, E - EGP derived, B - BGP derived
       i - IS-IS derived, D - EIGRP derived
       * - candidate default route, IA - OSPF inter area route
      E1 - OSPF external type 1 route, E2 - OSPF external type 2 route
      L1 - IS-IS level-1 route, L2 - IS-IS level-2 route
      EX - EIGRP external route
```

Listing 18-11 The show ip route Command (Continued)

```
Gateway of last resort is not set

I    144.253.0.0 [100/1300] via 133.3.32.2 0:00:22 Ethernet1
     131.108.0.0 is subnetted (mask is 255.255.255.0), 3 subnets
I       131.108.33.0 [100/180771] via 131.108.16.2, 0:01:29, Ethernet1
C       131.108.12.0 is directly connected, Ethernet1
C       101.108.16.0 is directly connected, Ethernet0
I    219.100.103.0 [100/1200]via 133.3.32.2, 0:00:22, Ethernet1
```

e-LAB ACTIVITY 18.14

Testing the Network Layer Using show ip route

In this activity, you demonstrate how to use the **show ip route** command to display the router's routing table.

Using the show interfaces serial Command to Test the Physical and Data Link Layers

Figure 18-13 shows a serial connection between two router interfaces. The interface has two pieces, physical (hardware) and logical (software):

- The hardware—including cables, connectors, and interfaces—must make the actual connection between the devices.
- The software is responsible for the messages such as keepalive messages, control information, and user information that are passed between adjacent devices. This data is being passed between the two connected router interfaces.

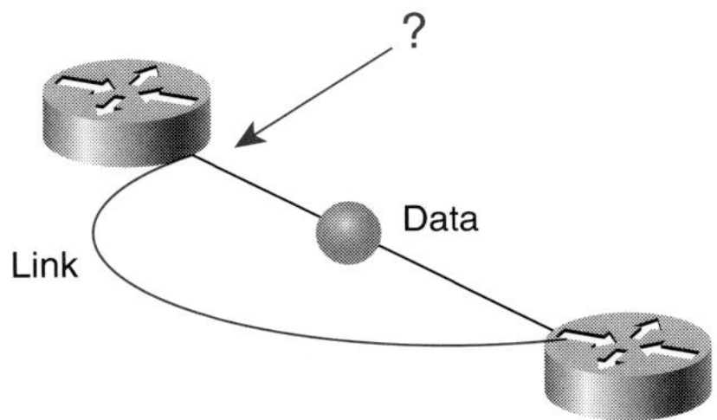

FIGURE 18-13 You use the **show interfaces serial** command to test the physical and data link layers.

When you test the physical and data link layers, you ask these questions:

- Is there a carrier detect signal?
- Is the physical link between devices good?
- Are the keepalive messages being received?
- Can data packets be sent across the physical link?

One of the most important elements of the **show interfaces serial** command output is the display of the line and data link protocol status. Figure 18-14 indicates the key summary line used to check the status of the line and the data link protocol.

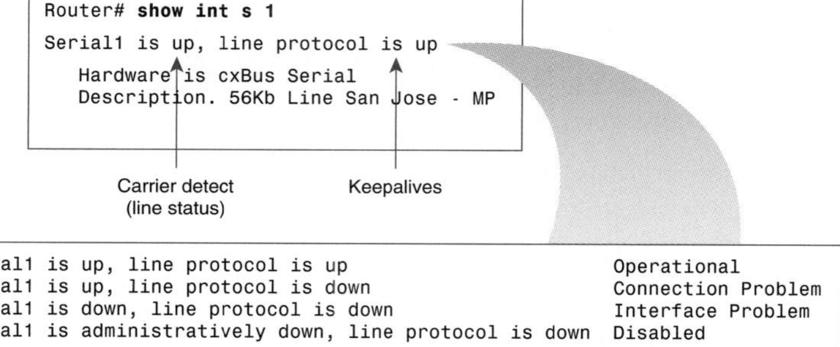

FIGURE 18-14 You use the **show interfaces serial** command to identify line and protocol problems.

The line status in this example is triggered by a carrier detect signal and refers to the physical layer status. However, the line protocol, triggered by keepalive frames, refers to data link framing (a Layer 2 function).

e-LAB ACTIVITY 18.15

Testing the Physical and Data Link Layers

In this activity, you demonstrate how to check the status of the physical and data link layers of your network by displaying information about serial interfaces configured.

The show interfaces and clear counters Commands

The router tracks statistics that provide information about the interfaces. You use the show interfaces command to display the statistics, as shown in Listing 18-12. The statistics reflect router operation since the last time the counters were cleared. Use the clear counters command to reset the counters to 0. By starting from 0, you get a better picture of the current status of the network.

Listing 18-12 The show interfaces Command

```
Router# show interfaces serial 1

Serial1 is up, line protocol is up

  Hardware is cxBus Serial
  Description: 56Kb Line San Jose - MP
  Internet address is 150.136.190.203, subnet mask is 255.255.255.0
  MTU 1500 bytes, BW 56 Kbit, DLY 20000 usec, rely 255/255, load 1/255
  Encapsulation HDLC, loopback not set, keepalive set (10 sec)
```

Listing 18-12 The show interfaces Command (Continued)

```
Last input 0:00:07, output 0:00:)), output hang never
  Last clearing of show interfaces counters 2w4d
  Output queue 0/40, 0 drops; input queue 0/75, 0 drops
  Five minute input rate 0 bits/sec, 0 packets/sec
  Five minute output rate 0 bits/sec, 0 packets/sec
      16263 packets input, 1347238 bytes, no buffer
      Received 13983 broadcasts, 0 runts, 0 giants
      2 input errors, 0 CRC, 0 frame, 0 overrun, 0 ignored, 2 abort
      0 input packets with dribble condition detected
      22146 packets output, 2383680 bytes, 0 underruns
      0 output errors, 0 collisions, 2 interface resets, 0 restarts
      1 carrier transitions
```

e-LAB ACTIVITY 18.16

Displaying Information about Interfaces

In this activity, you demonstrate how to display information about all interfaces configured on the router.

e-LAB ACTIVITY 18.17

Using show interfaces and clear counters

In this activity, you demonstrate how to use **show interfaces** and **clear counters.**

SKILL BUILDER

Lab Activity: show interfaces and clear counters Commands

In this lab, you use **show interfaces** and **clear counters.** The router keeps very detailed statistics about data traffic that it has sent and received on its interfaces. This is very important in troubleshooting a network problem. The **clear counters** command resets the counters that are displayed when you issue the **show interfaces** command. By clearing the counters, you get a clearer picture of the current status of the network.

Checking Real-Time Traffic with the debug Command

The router includes hardware and software to aid it in tracking down problems on it or on other hosts in the network. The **debug** privileged EXEC command starts the console display of the network events specified in the command parameter. Use the **terminal monitor** command to forward **debug** output to your Telnet session terminal.

> **NOTE**
>
> Be careful with the **debug** command on a live network. Substantial debugging on a busy network slows the network significantly. Do not leave debugging turned on; use it to diagnose a problem, and then turn it off. Excessive debugging on routers with minimal RAM can cause the router to force a reload.

In Figure 18-15, the data link broadcasts received by the router are displayed. Use the **undebug all** (or **no debug all**) command to turn off debugging when you no longer need it. Debugging is really intended for solving problems.

FIGURE 18-15
Checking real-time traffic with the **debug** command.

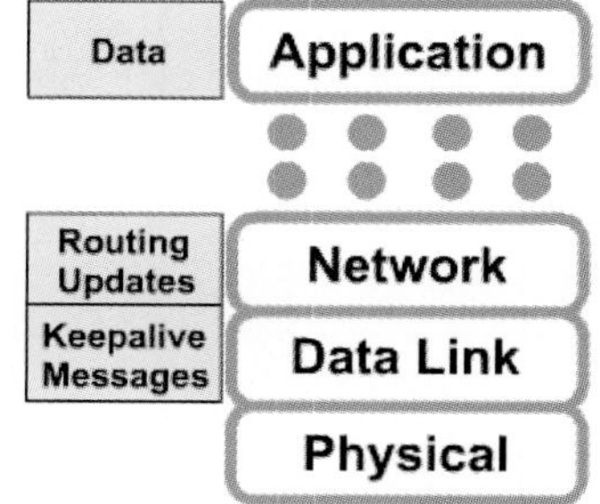


```
Router#debug broadcast
broadcast debugging is on

Ethernet0: Broadcast ARPA, src 0000.00c0.5fa4, dat ffff.ffff.ffff
type 0x0800, data 4500002800000000FF11EA7B, len 60
Serial3: Broadcast HDLC, size 64, type 0x80, fkags 0x8F00
```

By default, the router sends system error messages and output from the **debug** EXEC command to the console terminal. Messages can be redirected to a UNIX host or to an internal buffer. The terminal monitor command gives you the capability to redirect these messages to a terminal.

e-LAB ACTIVITY 18.18

Checking Real-Time Traffic with debug

In this activity, you demonstrate how to check all possible router traffic as it happens.

SKILL BUILDER

Lab Activity: Troubleshooting Tools Challenge

Knowing the topology of a network is extremely useful. It enables a network administrator to know exactly what equipment he or she has in what area (for bandwidth needs), how many devices are on the network, and what the physical layout of the network is. In this lab, you need to figure out what a particular topology looks like based on the information that you gather while navigating through the network using IOS commands.

SKILL BUILDER (CONTINUED)

Through the use of **show** commands, you should be able to see which interfaces are up (using **show interface**), what devices the router is connected to (using **show CDP neighbors**), and how the user can get there (using **show protocols**). With the information received from the **show** commands, you should be able to remotely access the neighboring routers (using **telnet**). Applying troubleshooting commands (such as **ping** and **trace**), you should be able to see which devices are connected.

Your final goal is to construct a logical topology drawing of the network by making use of all these commands without referring to any diagrams ahead of time.

Summary

In this chapter, you learned that

- The router is made up of configurable components, and it has modes that facilitate examining, maintaining, and changing of components.
- **show** commands are used for examination.
- You use CDP to show Layer 2 and 3 information about neighbors.
- You can gain access to other routers by using Telnet.
- You should test network connectivity layer by layer.
- Testing commands include **telnet**, **ping**, **trace**, and **debug**.

Check Your Understanding

1. When a router is turned on, what is the first thing that happens?
   - **A.** The ROM executes a bootstrap program.
   - **B.** The Cisco IOS software is loaded into memory.
   - **C.** The command executive, or EXEC, receives and executes commands that you enter for the router.
   - **D.** The configuration file is loaded into memory from NVRAM.
2. Which of the following router components has these characteristics: holds the operating system and microcode, retains its contents when you power down or restart, and allows software updates without replacing chips?
   - **A.** NVRAM
   - **B.** RAM/DRAM
   - **C.** Flash memory
   - **D.** ROM
3. Which command displays the configuration of the system hardware, the software version, the names and sources of configuration files, and the boot image?
   - **A.** **show version**
   - **B.** **show running-config**
   - **C.** **show active-config**
   - **D.** **show mem**
4. What information does testing a network by using the **show interfaces serial** command provide?
   - **A.** It displays line and data link protocol status.
   - **B.** It displays how the router directs traffic across the network.
   - **C.** It displays the path that packets follow across the network.
   - **D.** It displays the names of routers on the network.

5. Which command is entered to display the router's active configuration file?

   A. **show running-config**

   B. **show config term**

   C. **show version**

   D. **show backup-config**

6. What information does the **show CDP neighbors** command provide for each CDP neighbor?

   A. Device identifiers

   B. Address list

   C. Port identifier

   D. All of the above

7. The **show cdp interface** command is used to display which of the following?

   A. The values of the CDP timers and the interface status

   B. The encapsulation used by CDP for its advertisement and discovery frame transmission

   C. The interface configuration of the neighboring routers

   D. Both A and B

8. Which of these is true for the output of the command **show cdp entry** **{device name}**?

   A. It displays all the Layer 3 addresses present in the neighbor router.

   B. It displays the value of neighbors that the router has.

   C. It displays the list of the device numbers of all the neighboring routers.

   D. It displays all the Layer 2 addresses on the interfaces of the neighbor router.

9. To display the information that is obtained both from the **show cdp neighbors** and **show cdp entry {device name}** commands, which of the following commands is used?

   A. **show cdp neighbors detail**

   B. **show cdp interface entry**

C. **show cdp neighbors entry**

D. **show cdp details**

10. What information is displayed by the **show cdp neighbors** command?

A. Neighbor device ID

B. Local port type and number

C. Decremental hold-time value, in seconds

D. All of the above

11. What four important pieces of information do you receive after issuing a **ping** command?

A. The size and quantity of ICMP packets; the timeout duration; the success rate; and the minimum, average, and maximum round-trip times

B. The size and quantity of ICMP packets; the MAC address; the success rate; and the minimum, average, and maximum round-trip times

C. All of the above

D. None of the above

12. What information does testing a network by using the **trace** command provide?

A. It determines whether the line protocol is operational.

B. It determines whether a routing table entry exists for the target network.

C. It maps every router that a packet goes through to reach its destination.

D. It determines whether upper-layer applications are functioning properly.

13. As an aid to diagnosing basic network connectivity, many network protocols support ____________________, which is used to test whether a destination is reachable.

A. An echo protocol

B. A trial protocol

C. A test protocol

D. A packet-testing protocol

14. In reply to the **ping** command, the exclamation points (!) indicate which of these?

A. The number of successful echos

B. The number of unsuccessful echos

C. The number of hops before reaching the destination

D. All of the above

15. What is true of the router **debug** commands?

A. The **debug** privileged EXEC command starts the console display of the network events specified in the command parameter.

B. The **undebug all** command (or no debug all) turns off debugging.

C. The **buffer debug** command is used to buffer the login.

D. Both A and B.

Objectives

After reading this chapter, you will be able to

- Understand router boot sequence
- Understand setup mode
- Use commands related to router startup
- Use the **setup** command
- Set up global parameters
- Set up interface parameters
- Set up script review and use

Chapter 19

Router Startup and Setup

Introduction

In Chapter 18, "Router Components," you learned the correct procedures and commands to access a router, examine and maintain its components, and test its network connectivity. In this chapter, you learn how to start a router for the first time by using the correct commands and startup sequence to do an initial configuration of the router. In addition, this chapter explains the startup sequence of a router and the setup dialog that the router uses to create an initial configuration file.

Router Boot Sequence and Setup Mode

When a Cisco router powers up, it performs a power-on self-test (POST). During this self-test, the router executes diagnostics from ROM on all hardware modules. These diagnostics verify the basic operation of the CPU, memory, and network interface ports. After verifying the hardware functions, the router proceeds with software initialization.

A router initializes by loading the bootstrap, the operating system, and a configuration file.

The goal of the startup routines for Cisco IOS software is to start the router operations. The router must deliver reliable performance in its job of connecting the user networks that it was configured to serve. To do this, the startup routines must do the following:

- Make sure that the router starts with all its hardware tested
- Find and load the Cisco IOS software that the router uses for its operating system
- Find the startup-config file and apply the configuration statements, including protocol functions and interface addresses

If you choose to save the new configuration from setup mode, the router stores a backup copy in NVRAM.

If the router cannot find a configuration file, it then enters setup mode. The router stores in NVRAM a backup copy of the new configuration from setup mode.

Router Startup Sequence

After the power-on self-test on the router, the following events occur as the router initializes (see Figure 19-1):

Step 1 The generic bootstrap loader in ROM executes on the CPU card. A bootstrap is a simple, preset operation to load instructions that, in turn, cause other instructions to be loaded into memory or that affect entry into other configuration modes.

Step 2 The operating system (Cisco IOS) can be found in one of several places (Flash, TFTP, server, or ROM). The location is disclosed in the boot field of the configuration register. If the boot field indicates a Flash, or network (TFTP server) load, boot system commands in the configuration file indicate the exact location of the image.

Step 3 The operating system image is loaded. After it is loaded and operational, the operating system locates the hardware and software components and lists the results on the console terminal.

Step 4 The configuration file saved in NVRAM or a TFTP server is loaded into main memory and is executed one line at a time. These configuration commands start routing processes, supply addresses for interfaces, set media characteristics, and so on.

Step 5 If no valid configuration file exists in NVRAM or a TFTP server, the operating system executes a question-driven initial configuration routine referred to as the system configuration dialog or the initial configuration dialog, also called setup mode.

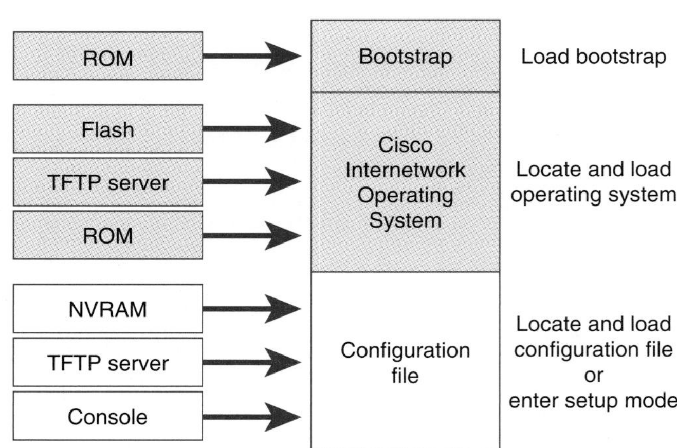

FIGURE 19-1 After the power-up self-test on the router, a start-up sequence is initiated.

Setup is not intended as the mode for configuring complex protocol features in the router. You should use setup to bring up a minimal configuration, and then use various configuration-mode commands rather than setup for most router configuration tasks.

MORE INFORMATION

What Happens When You Start a Switch

Initial start up of a Catalyst switch includes the following steps:

1. Before you start the switch, verify the following:
   — All network cable connections are secure.
   — Your terminal is connected to the console port.
   — Your console terminal application is selected.
2. Attach the power cable plug to the switch power supply socket. The switch starts (there is no on/off switch).
3. Observe the boot sequence.
   — Look at the light-emitting diodes (LEDs) on the switch chassis.
   — Observe the Cisco IOS software output text on the console.

Catalyst Switches Status LEDs

The Catalyst switches have several status LEDs that are generally lighted green when the switch is functioning normally, but turn amber when there is a malfunction. The LED functions are explained in Table 19-1.

TABLE 19-1 Catalyst Switch Systems and RPS LED Status Descriptions

Switch LED	Description
System LED	Green—System powered and operational Amber—System malfunction
Redundant power supply (RPS)	Green—RPS operational Amber—RPS installed but not operational Flashing amber—Internal power supply and RPS are powered up, and the internal power supply is powering the switch

Catalyst switch port LEDs have several modes of operation. As you see later, the initial startup routines use LEDs to display power-on self-test (POST) status.

If the switch is up and running, you press the mode button and toggle through other LED display modes. The three modes indicate the following:

- Port status
- Bandwidth utilization for the switch
- Full-duplex support

Table 19-2 lists the port LED display modes and the information provided with the various LED colors or lighting.

TABLE 19-2 Catalyst Switch Systems and RPS LED Status Descriptions

Port LED Display Mode	Description
Port status (STAT LED on)	Green—Link present; flashing green—activity Alternating green and amber—Link fault Amber—Port not forwarding
Bandwidth utilization (UTL LED on)	1 to 8 LEDs on—0.1 to < 6 Mbps 9 to 16 LEDs on—6 to < 120 Mbps 17 to 24 LEDs on—120 to 280 Mbps *Note:* The values shown are for a 24-port switch. For a 12-port switch, the values are: 1 to 4 = 0.1 to < 1.5; 5 to 8 = 1.5 to < 20; 9 to 12 = 20 to 120 Mbps
Full-duplex mode (FDUP LED on)	Green—Ports are configured in full-duplex mode Off—Ports are in half-duplex mode

The Catalyst POST is executed only when the switch is powered up. The POST uses the switch's port LEDs to indicate test progress and status. Initially, all port LEDs light green. This condition indicates the start of POST and that the LEDs are functioning properly. Each of the first 16 port LEDs (1x through 16x) is associated with one of the POST tests, as shown in Table 19-3.

TABLE 19-3 Catalyst Switch Systems and RPS LED Status Descriptions

LED	Component Tested—Failure Type
LED 16x	ECU DRAM—Fatal
LED 15x	Not used
LED 14x	Not used
LED 13x	Not used
LED 12x	Forwarding engine—Fatal

TABLE 19-3 Catalyst Switch Systems and RPS LED Status Descriptions (Continued)

LED	Component Tested—Failure Type
LED 11x	Forwarding engine SRAM—Fatal
LED 10x	Packet DRAM—Fatal
LED 9x	ISLT ASIC—Fatal
LED 8x	Port control/status—Fatal
LED 7x	System timer interrupt—Fatal
LED 6x	Content-addressable (CAM) SRAM—Fatal
LED 5x	Real-time clock—Nonfatal (If this test failed, the switch forwards packets. However, if the switch unexpectedly shuts down, it cannot restart itself automatically.)
LED 4x	Console port—Nonfatal (If this test failed, you cannot access the management console through the console port. You can still Telnet to the management console.)
LED 3x	CAM—Fatal
LED 2x	Burned-in address—Nonfatal (If this test failed, the switch uses the default Ethernet address of the switch and begins forwarding packets.)
LED 1x	Port loopback—Nonfatal (If this test failed, some functionality to one or more ports is lost. The switch disables any port(s) that failed this test, and the failure message on the menu console logon screen indicates which port(s) did not pass this test. Connect only to ports that passed this test.)

After each POST test, the LED for that test indicates the test results in the following manner:

- If the test completes without failure, the LED for that test turns off.
- If the test turns up a failure, the LED for that test turns amber and the system LED also turns amber.

On successful POST completion, the port LEDs blink and then turn off.

If fatal failures occur, as indicated in Table 19-3, the switch is not operational. The switch is still operational with nonfatal failures, but it might have limited functionality.

During initial startup, if POST test failures are detected, they are reported to the console. If POST completes successfully, the first display shown is that of the menu console logon screen.

From the logon screen, you initially have three choices:

- Type **M** to enter menu mode.
- Type **K** to enter command-line mode.
- Type **I** to enter IP configuration mode.

Commands Related to Router Startup

The top two commands in Listing 19-1—show **startup-config** and **show running-config**—display the backup and active configuration files. The **erase startup-config** command deletes the backup configuration file in NVRAM. The **reload** (**reboot**) command reloads the router, causing it to run through the entire startup process. The last command, **setup**, is used to enter setup mode from the privileged EXEC prompt.

NOTE

The commands show config, write term, and write erase, used with Cisco IOS Release 10.3 and earlier, have been replaced with new commands. The old commands, shown in parentheses in Listing 19-1, continue to perform their normal functions in the current release, but they are no longer documented. Support for these commands will cease in a future release.

Listing 19-1 Startup Commands

```
Router# show startup-config
         (show config) *


Router# show running-config
         (write term) *


Router# erase startup-config
          (write erase) *


Router# reload


Router# setup
```

e-LAB ACTIVITY 19.1

Commands Related to Router Startup

In this activity, you demonstrate how to reconfigure a router from scratch.

System Configuration Dialog

One of the routines for initial configuration is setup mode. The main purpose of setup mode is to quickly bring up a minimal configuration for any router that cannot find its configuration from some other source (see Listing 19-2).

Listing 19-2 Setup Mode

```
#setup
-- System Configuration Dialog --
At any port you may enter a question mark '?' for help.
Use Ctrl-c to abort configuration dialog at any prompt.
Default settings are in square brackets '[]'.
Continue with configuration dialog? [yes].
First, would you like to see the current interface summary? [yes]
Interface       IP-Address    OK?   Methord    Status   Protocol
TokenRing0      unassigned    NO    not set    down     down
Ethernet0       unassigned    NO    not set    down     down
Serial0         unassigned    NO    not set    down     down
Fddi0           unassigned    NO    not set    down     down
```

For many of the prompts in the system configuration dialog of the setup command facility, default answers appear in square brackets ([ ]) following the question. Press the Return key to use these defaults. If the system has been previously configured, the defaults that appear are the currently configured values. If you are configuring the system for the first time, the factory defaults are provided. If there is no factory default, as in the case of passwords, nothing is displayed after the question mark (?). During the setup process, you can press Control-C at any time to terminate the process. When setup is terminated, all interfaces are administratively shut down. This is done to prevent false data on the networks until all configuration is complete.

When you complete the configuration process in setup mode, the screen displays the configuration that you have just created. You then are asked whether you want to use this configuration. If you enter "yes," the configuration is executed and saved to NVRAM. If you answer "no," the configuration is not saved and the process begins again. If a –More– prompt appears, press the Spacebar to continue.

You enter setup mode from the global configuration prompt **Router# setup**. The router responds with the current router interface configuration.

Setting Up Global Parameters

After viewing the current interface summary, a prompt appears on your monitor, indicating that you are to enter the global parameters for your router. These parameters are the configuration values you select.

A prompt appears on your monitor, as illustrated in Listing 19-3. The first statement indicates that you are configuring the global parameters in the router. The first global parameter enables you to set the router host name. This hostname will be part of the Cisco IOS prompts for all EXEC modes. At initial configuration, the router name default is displayed between square brackets as [Router]. Use "Configuring global parameters", shown in Listing 19-3, to set the various passwords used on the router.

Listing 19-3 The Prompts at Which You Enter the Global Parameters for Your Router

```
Configuring global parameters:

  Enter host name [Router]

The enable secret is a one-way cryptographic secret used
instead of the enable password when it exists.

  Enter enable secret[<Use current secret>]

  Enter enable password[san-fran]:
 %Please choose a password that is different from the enable secret
  Enter enable password[san-fran].
  Enter virtual terminal password [san-fran]:
  Configure SNMP Network Management? [no]:
```

You must enter an enable password. When you enter a string of password characters for the prompt "Enter enable secret," the characters are processed by Cisco proprietary encryption. This enhances the security of the password string. Whenever anyone lists the contents of the router configuration file, this enable password appears as a meaningless string of characters.

Setup recommends, but does not require, that the "enable password" be different from the "enable secret word." The enable secret word is a one-way cryptographic secret word that is used instead of the enable password, when it exists. The enable password is used when no enable secret word exists.

It is also used when using older versions of the IOS. All passwords are case-sensitive and can be alphanumeric.

After the password for the various ports are entered, the router asks you to enter the routing protocols that are to be used, as shown in Listing 19-4. When you are prompted for parameters for each protocol, as shown in Listing 19-4, use the configuration values that you have selected for your router. Whenever you answer "yes" to a prompt, additional questions might appear regarding the protocol.

Listing 19-4 The Prompts for Global Parameters at the Console

```
Configure IP? [yes]:
  Configure IGRP routing? [yes]:
    Your IGRP autonomous system number [1]: 200
Configure DECnet? [no]:
Configure XNS? [no]:
Configure Novell? [no]: yes
Configure Apollo? [no]:
Configure AppleTalk? [no]: yes
    Multizone networks? [no]: yes
Configure Vines? [no]:
Configure bridging? [no]:
```

Setting Up Interface Parameters

When you are prompted for parameters for each installed interface, as shown in Listing 19-5, you need to use the configuration values that you have determined for your interface to enter the interface parameters at the prompts.

Listing 19-5 The Prompts for Parameters for Each Installed Interface

```
Configuring interface parameters:

Configuring interface TokenRing0:
Is this interface in use? [yes]:
Tokenning ring speed (4 or 16)? [16]:
Configure IP on this interface? [no]: yes
IP address for this interface: 172.16.92.67
Number of bits in subnet field [0]:
Class B network is 172.16.0.0, 0 subnet bit; mask is 255.255.0.0
Configure Novell on this interface? [no]: yes
Novell network number [1]:

Configure interface Serial0:'
Is this interface in use? [yes]:
Configure IP on this interface? [yes]
Configure IP unnumbered on this interface? [no]:
IP address for this interface: 172.16.97.67
Number of bits in subnet field [0]:
Class B network is 172.16.0.0, 0 subnet bits; mask is 255.255.0.0
Configure Novell on this interface? [yes]: no

Configuring Interface Serial 1:
Is this interface in use? [yes]: no
```

e-LAB ACTIVITY 19.2

Using the setup Command

In this activity, you demonstrate how to enter router setup mode.

SKILL BUILDER

Lab Activity: Router setup Command

In this lab, you use the command **setup** to enter setup mode. Setup is a Cisco IOS utility (program) that can help get some of the basic router configuration parameters established. Setup is not intended as a mode for entering complex protocol features in the router. Rather, the purpose of setup mode is to bring up a minimal configuration for any router that cannot find its configuration from some other source.

Setting Up Script Review and Use

After you complete the configuration process for all installed interfaces on your router, the **setup** command program displays the configuration script that you have created (see Listing 19-6). The setup process then asks if you want to use this configuration. If you answer "yes," the configuration is executed and saved to NVRAM. If you answer "no," the configuration is not saved, and the process begins again. There is no default for this prompt; you must answer either "yes" or "no." After you answer yes to the last question, your system is ready to use. If you want to modify the configuration that you have just established, you must do the configuration manually.

After displaying the setup configuration, the script tells you to use the configuration mode to change any commands after setup has been used. The script file generated by setup is additive; you can turn on features with setup, but you cannot turn them off. Also, setup does not support many of the advanced features of the router or features that require a more complex configuration.

Listing 19-6 The setup Command Program Displaying the Configuration That Was Created

```
The following configuration command script was created:
hostname router
enable secret 5 $ 1Sg772S
enable password san-fran
enable password san-fran
line vty 0 4
password san-fran
```

Listing 19-6 The setup Command Program Displaying the Configuration That Was Created (Continued)

```
snmp-server community
!
ip routing
no decnet routing
no xns routing
no apollo routing
appletalk routing
no cins routing
no vines
no bridge
no mop enabled
Interface Ethernet
IP address 172.16.92.67 255.255.0.0
network 1
no mop enabled

!
interface Serial0
IP address 172.16.97.67 255.255.0.0

Interface Serial1
shutdown
!
end

Use this configuration? [yes/no]: yes
[OK]
Use the enable mode 'configure' command to modify this configuration.
```

SKILL BUILDER

Lab Activity: Router Setup Challenge

When you first start a router and the operating system is loaded, you must go through the process of the initial setup. In this scenario, you have just received a shipment of new routers, and you need to set up a basic configuration. You have a Class B IP network address of 156.1.0.0, and you need to subnet your Class B address using 5 bits for your subnets. Use the standard five-router diagram to determine which subnetwork numbers and which IP addresses you will use for the eight networks that you will need to define. For this lab, set up all five routers.

Summary

In this chapter, you learned that

- The router initializes by loading a bootstrap, the operating system, and a configuration file.
- If the router cannot find a configuration file, the router enters setup mode.
- The router stores a backup copy of the new configuration from setup mode in NVRAM.

Check Your Understanding

1. Which of the following is the correct order of steps in the Cisco router system startup routine?

   A. Locate and load operating system, load bootstrap, test hardware, locate and load configuration file

   B. Test hardware, load bootstrap, locate and load operating system, locate and load configuration file

   C. Load bootstrap, locate and load configuration file, test hardware, locate and load operating system

   D. Test hardware, load bootstrap, locate and load configuration file, locate and load operating system

2. Which of the following is an important function of the power-up self-test?

   A. To determine the router hardware and software components and list them on the console terminal

   B. To cause other instructions to be loaded into memory

   C. To execute diagnostics that verify the basic operation of router hardware

   D. To start routing processes, supply addresses for interfaces, and set up media characteristics

3. Which of the following is an important result of the Cisco IOS software loading onto a router?

   A. Determining the router hardware and software components and listing them on the console terminal

   B. Causing other instructions to be loaded into memory

   C. Executing diagnostics that verify the basic operation of router hardware

   D. Starting routing processes, supplying addresses for interfaces, and setting up media characteristics

4. Which of the following is an important result of the configuration file loading onto a router?

   A. Determining the router hardware and software components and listing them on the console terminal

   B. Causing other instructions to be loaded into memory

   C. Executing diagnostics that verify the basic operation of router hardware

   D. Start routing processes, supply addresses for interfaces, and set up media characteristics

5. If the router cannot find the configuration file after the operating system is loaded, what does the router do?

   A. Enters setup mode

   B. Looks for the file on another server

   C. Loads the bootstrap

   D. Waits for a reset

6. After the bootstrap program is loaded, the router tries to locate Cisco IOS from which of the following?

   A. Flash memory

   B. ROM

   C. NVRAM

   D. Both A and B

7. At what position can the operating system (Cisco IOS) be found?

   A. It is disclosed in the boot field of the configuration register.

   B. It is found only on the ROM.

   C. It is accepted as input from the console.

   D. It is found only on the TFTP server.

8. The configuration file saved in NVRAM is loaded into main memory and is executed one line at a time. The configuration commands from the file:

   A. Start routing processes.

   B. Supply addresses for interfaces.

C. Reset all the media characteristics.

D. Both A and B.

9. The command **show running config**

A. Displays the configuration file that is located in RAM

B. Displays the configuration files that are located in NVRAM

C. Displays the configuration of an interface on the router

D. Both A and B

10. The **reload** (**reboot**) command

A. Reloads the router, causing it to run through the entire startup process

B. Resets all the interfaces

C. Loads the configuration file once again

D. All of the above

11. The setup ...

A. Mode can be reached directly from the privileged EXEC prompt

B. Dialog is also called system configuration dialog

C. Command is the same as the **write term** command

D. Both A and B

12. The enable secret password:

A. Is a one-way encrypted password by Cisco proprietary encryption

B. May be same as the enable password

C. Is displayed in ASCII when the configuration file contents are listed

D. Both A and B

13. Which of the following parameters are configured when an interfaced is configured on a router?

A. Token Ring speed

B. IP address

C. Number of subnet bits

D. All of the above

14. The features that are set during the setup process:

    A. Can be added to

    B. Can be turned off

    C. Can be displayed using some commands

    D. All of the above

15. What is the function of the **erase startup-config** command?

    A. It deletes the backup configuration file in NVRAM.

    B. It deletes the bootstrap image from Flash memory.

    C. It deletes the current Cisco IOS software from NVRAM.

    D. It deletes the current running configuration from Flash memory.

16. What is the function of the **reload** command?

    A. It loads a backup configuration file from a TFTP server.

    B. It saves the new Cisco IOS software to Flash memory.

    C. It reboots the router.

    D. It loads the new configuration file in NVRAM.

17. When is router setup mode executed?

    A. After the saved configuration file is loaded into main memory

    B. When the network administrator needs to enter complex protocol features on the router

    C. When the router begins software initialization

    D. When the router cannot find a valid configuration file

18. Which of the following correctly describes a procedure for setup of router global and interface parameters on a router?

    A. A default parameter is shown in square brackets at every prompt.

    B. The router host name is required to be set.

    C. An enable secret password can be set but is not required.

    D. None of the above.

19. Why might you want to issue **show startup-config** and **show running-config** commands?

A. It's time to update the Cisco IOS software, and you need to kill certain router processes before proceeding.

B. You need to determine the time since the router booted and to determine the current register setting.

C. The router suddenly isn't working right, and you want to compare the initial state to the present state.

D. You need to find out where the Cisco IOS software booted from and which version is being used.

20. What file(s) would you find in NVRAM?

A. Cisco IOS software and configuration files

B. Configuration files

C. A backup copy of Cisco IOS software

D. A limited version of Cisco IOS software and registry files

Objectives

After reading this chapter, you will be able to

- Work with router configuration files
- Use various router configuration modes
- Use various configuration methods

Chapter 20

Router Configuration 1

Introduction

In Chapter 19, "Router Startup and Setup," you learned how to start a router for the first time by using the correct commands and startup sequence to do an initial configuration of a router. In this chapter, you learn how to use router modes and configuration methods to update a router's configuration file using current and older versions of Cisco Internetwork Operating System (IOS) software.

Router Configuration Files

In this section, you learn how to work with configuration files originated from the console, from NVRAM, or from TFTP servers. A router uses the following information from the configuration file when it starts up:

- Cisco IOS software version
- Router identification
- Boot file locations
- Protocol information
- Interface configurations

The configuration file contains commands to customize router operation. The router uses this information when it starts up. If no configuration file is available, the system configuration dialog setup guides you through the process of creating one.

Working with Release 11.x Configuration Files

Router configuration information can be generated by several means. You can use the privileged EXEC **configure** command to configure from a virtual (remote) terminal, a modem connection, or a console terminal. This enables you to enter changes to an existing configuration at any time.

You can also use the privileged EXEC **copy** command to load a configuration from a network TFTP server, which enables you to maintain and store configuration information at a central site.

Figure 20-1 illustrates the configuration command summary, which consists of the commands shown in Table 20-1.

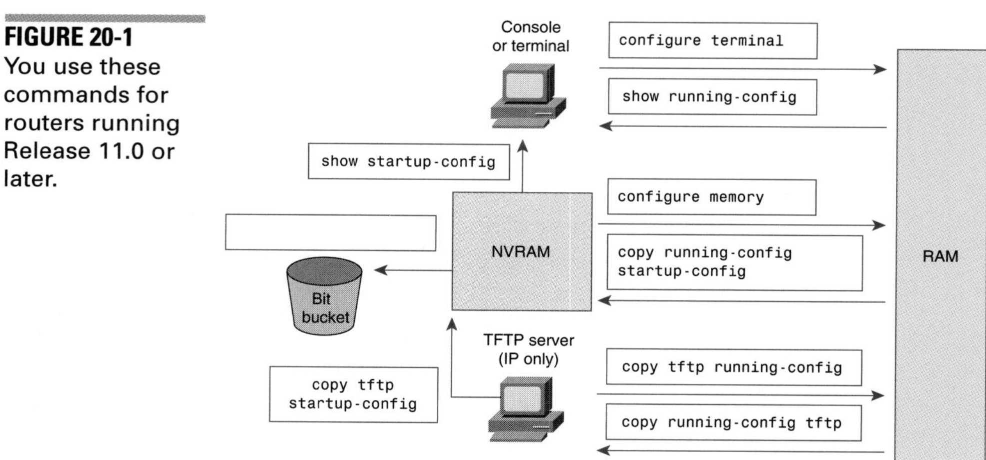

FIGURE 20-1
You use these commands for routers running Release 11.0 or later.

TABLE 20-1 The Configuration Command Summary for Routers Running Release 11.0 or Later

Command	Description
configure terminal	Configures the router manually from the console terminal.
configure memory	Loads configuration information from nonvolatile random-access memory (NVRAM).
copy tftp running-config	Loads configuration information from a network TFTP server.
show running-config	Displays the current configuration in RAM.
copy running-config startup-config	Stores the current configuration in RAM into NVRAM.
copy running-config tftp	Stores the current configuration in RAM on a network TFTP server.
show startup-config	Displays the saved configuration, which is the contents of NVRAM.
erase startup-config	Erases the contents of NVRAM.

SKILL BUILDER

Lab Activity: Router Configuration with HyperTerminal

In this lab, you use the Windows terminal emulation program HyperTerminal to capture and upload a router configuration as an ASCII text file.

Working with Pre-Release 11.0 Configuration Files

The commands shown in Figure 20-2 are used with Cisco IOS, Release 10.3 and earlier. They have been replaced with new commands. The old commands that have been replaced continue to perform their normal functions in the current release, but are no longer documented. Support for these commands will cease in a future release.

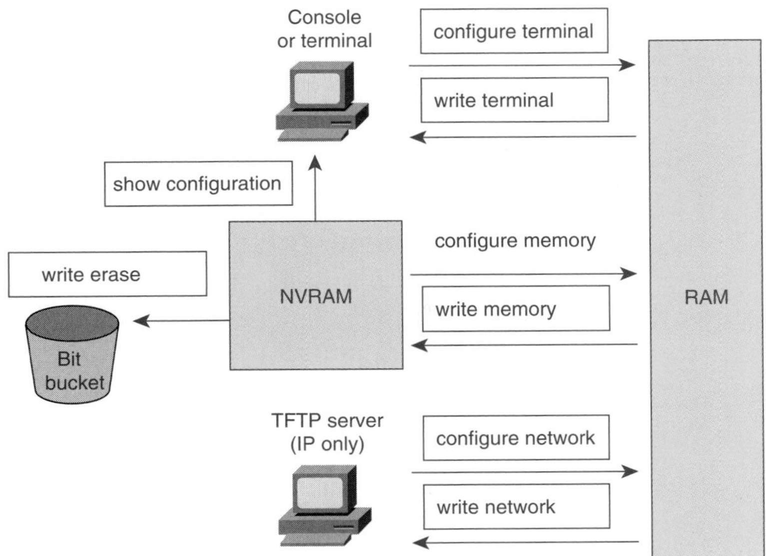

FIGURE 20-2
The configuration commands used with Cisco IOS Release 10.3 and earlier.

Using a TFTP Server

You can store a current copy of the configuration on a TFTP server. You use the **copy running-config tftp** command, as shown in Listing 20-1, to store the current configuration file on a TFTP server. To do so, complete the following tasks:

Step 1 Enter the **copy running-config tftp** command.

Step 2 Enter the IP address of the TFTP server that you want to use to store the configuration file.

Step 3 Enter the name that you want to assign to the configuration file.

Step 4 Confirm your choices by answering "yes" each time.

Listing 20-1 The copy running-config tftp Command

```
tokyo# copy running-config tftp
Remote host []? 131.108.2.155
Name of configuration file to write [tokyo-config]? tokyo.2
Write file tokyo.2 to 131.108.2.155? [confirm] y
Writing tokyo.2 !!!!!! [OK]
tokyo#
```

You can configure the router by loading the configuration file stored on one of your network servers. To do so, complete the following tasks:

Step 1 Enter the **copy tftp running-config** command, as shown in Listing 20-2.

Step 2 At the system prompt, select a host or network configuration file. The network configuration file contains commands that apply to all routers and terminal servers on the network. The host configuration file contains commands that apply to one router in particular. At the system prompt, enter the IP address of the remote host from which you are retrieving the configuration file. In this example, the router is configured from the TFTP server at IP address 131.108.2.155.

Step 3 At the system prompt, either enter the name of the configuration file or accept the default name. The filename convention is UNIX-based. The default filename is Router-config for the host file and network-config for the network configuration file. In the DOS environment, the server filenames are limited to eight characters plus a three-character extension (for example, router.cfg). Notice that the router prompt changes to tokyo immediately. Assuming that the router's hostname is set in the file, this is evidence that the reconfiguration happens as soon as the new file is downloaded.

Listing 20-2 The copy tftp running-config Command

```
Router# copy tftp running-config
Host or network configuration file [host]?
IP address of remote hose [255.255.255.255]? 131.108.2.155
Name of configuration file [Router-config]? tokyo.2
Configure using tokyo.2 from 131.108.2.155? [confirm] y
Booting tokyo.2 from 131.108.2.155:!! [OK-874/16000 bytes]
tokyo#
```

e-LAB ACTIVITY 20.1

Copying Configuration Files to and From a TFTP Server

In this activity, you demonstrate how to store a current copy of the configuration on a tftp server.

e-LAB ACTIVITY 20.2

Router config: TFTP

In this activity, you demonstrate how to use a Trivial File Transfer Protocol (TFTP) server to save a copy of the router's configuration file.

SKILL BUILDER

Lab Activity: Router Configuration with TFTP

In this lab, you use a Trivial File Transfer Protocol (TFTP) server to save a copy of the router's configuration file.

Using NVRAM with Release 11.x and Higher

The commands shown in Listing 20-3 manage the contents of NVRAM (see Table 20-2).

Listing 20-3 Release 11.x Commands That Manage the Contents of NVRAM

```
Router# configure memory
[OK]
Router#


Router# erase startup-config
[OK]
Router#


Router# copy running-config startup-config
[OK]
Router#


Router# show startup-config
Using 5057 out of 32768 bytes
!
enable-password san-fran
!
interface Ethernet 0
ip address 131.108.100.5 255.255.255.0
!
 --More--
```

TABLE 20-2 Commands Used to Manage the Contents of NVRAM in Cisco IOS Release 11.x and Above

Command	Description
configure memory	Loads configuration information from NVRAM.
erase startup-config	Erases the contents of NVRAM.
copy running-config startup-config	Stores the current configuration in RAM (that is, the running configuration) into NVRAM (as the startup configuration).
show startup-config	Displays the saved configuration, which is the contents of NVRAM.

e-LAB ACTIVITY 20.3

Using NVRAM Configuration Commands

In this activity, you demonstrate how to load a configuration from NVRAM.

Using NVRAM with Pre-11.0 IOS Software

The commands shown in Listing 20-4 are used with Cisco IOS, Release 10.3 and earlier. These commands have been replaced with new commands. The commands that have been replaced continue to perform their normal function in the current release, but they are no longer documented. Support for these commands will cease in a future release.

Listing 20-4 NVRAM Commands That Are Used with Cisco IOS Release 10.3 and Earlier

```
Router# configure memory
[OK]
Router#


Router# write erase
[OK]
Router#


Router# write memory
[OK]
Router#


Router# show configuration


Using 5057 out of 32768 bytes
!
enable-password san-fran
!
interface Ethernet 0
ip address 131.108.100.5 255.255.255.0
!
 --More--
```

Router Configuration Modes

EXEC mode interprets the commands that you type and carries out the corresponding operations. You must log in to the router before you can enter an EXEC command. Two EXEC modes exist. The EXEC commands available in user mode are a subset of the EXEC commands available in privileged mode. From the privileged level, you can also access global configuration mode and specific configuration modes, some of which are shown in Figure 20-3 and listed in Table 20-3.

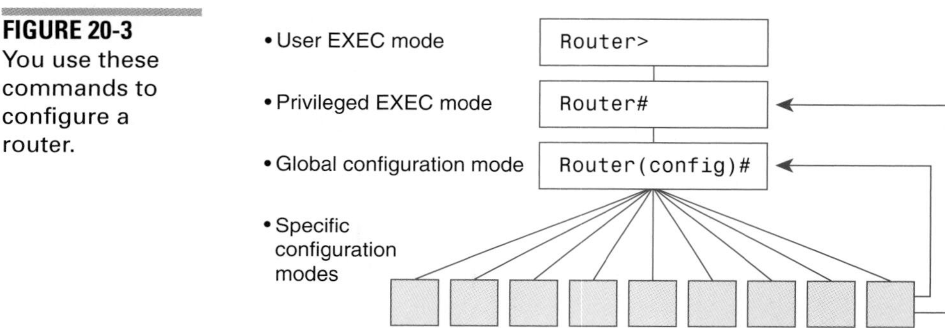

FIGURE 20-3 You use these commands to configure a router.

TABLE 20-3 Configuration Modes and Prompts

Configuration Mode	Prompt
Interface	Router(config-if)#
Subinterface	Router(config-subif)#
Controller	Router(config-controller)#
Map-list	Router(config-map list)#
Map-class	Router(config-map-class)#
Line	Router(config-line)#
Router	Router(config-router)#

If you type **exit** from within a configuration mode, the router backs out one level, eventually enabling you to log out. In general, typing **exit** from one of the specific configuration modes returns you to global configuration mode. Typing

exit from global configuration mode returns you to privileged mode. Typing **exit** from user mode or privileged mode completely logs you out of the router. Pressing Ctrl-Z leaves configuration mode completely and returns the router to privileged EXEC mode; typing **end** has the same effect as pressing Ctrl-Z.

e-LAB ACTIVITY 20.4

Basic Router Configuration

In this activity, you demonstrate how to use the router's global configuration mode and enter one-line commands that change the entire router.

SKILL BUILDER

Lab Activity: Basic Router Configuration

In this lab, you use the router's global configuration mode and enter one-line commands that have global significance to the router.

Global Configuration Modes

Global configuration commands apply to features that affect the system as a whole. You use the privileged EXEC command configure to enter global configuration mode. When you enter this command, EXEC prompts you for the source of the configuration commands (see Listing 20-5).

Listing 20-5 The Privileged EXEC Command configure

```
Router# configure terminal
Router(config)# (commands)
Router(config)# exit
Router#


Router# configure terminal
Router(config)# router protocol
Router(config-router)# (commands)
Router(config-router)# exit
Router(config)# interface type port
Router(config-if)# (commands)
Router(config-if)# exit
Router(config)# exit
Router#
```

You must specify the terminal, NVRAM, or a file stored on a network server as the source. The default is to type in commands from the terminal console. Pressing the Return key begins this configuration method. Or, you can type **configure terminal**, as shown in Listing 20-5, to go directly to this mode.

Commands enabling a particular routing or interface function begin with global configuration commands:

- To configure a routing protocol (indicated by the prompt config-router), you first enter a global **router** *protocol* command (see Listing 20-6).

  For example:

  ```
  Router(config)#router rip
  ```

Listing 20-6 Configuring a Routing Protocol

```
Router# configure terminal
Router(config)# router protocol


Router(config-router)# (commands)
Router(config-router)#
```

- To configure an interface (indicated by the prompt config-if), you first enter the global interface type and number command. After entering commands in any of these modes, you finish with the command **exit**, Ctrl-Z, or **end** (see Listing 20-7).

  For example:

  ```
  Router(config)# int e0
  ```

Listing 20-7 Configuring an Interface

```
Router# configure terminal
Router(config)# interface type port
Router(config-if)# (commands)
Router(config-if)# exit
```

e-LAB ACTIVITY 20.5

Entering Terminal Configuration Mode

In this activity, you demonstrate how to enter the global configuration mode.

Configuring Routing Protocols

After a routing protocol is enabled by a global command, the router configuration mode prompt Router(config-router)# is displayed as shown in Listing 20-8. You type ? (a question mark) to list the routing protocol configuration subcommands.

Listing 20-8 Router Configuration Mode Prompt After a Routing Protocol Is Enabled

```
Router(config)# router?
bgp        Border Gateway Protocol (BGP)
egp        Exterior Gateway Protocol (EGP)
eigrp      Enhanced Interior Gateway Routing Protocol (EIGRP)
igrp       Interior Gateway Routing Protocol (IGRP)
isis       ISO IS-IS
iso-igrp   IGRP for OSI networks
mobile     Mobile routes
odr        On Demand stub Routes
ospf       Open Shortest Path First (OSPF)
rip        Routing Information Protocol (RIP)
static     Static routes


Router(config)# router rip
Router(config-router)# ?
Router configuration commands
default-information    Control distribution of default information
default-metric         Set metric of redistributed routes
distance               Define an administrative distance
distribute-list        Filter networks in routing updates
exit                   Exit from routing protocol configuration mode

--More--
```

Interface Configuration Commands

Interface configuration commands modify the operation of an Ethernet, Token Ring, or serial port. In addition, interface subcommands always follow an interface command, such as the **ip address** subcommand.

In the following command, the *type* argument includes **serial, ethernet, token ring**, and others:

```
Router(config)# interface type port
Router(config)# interface type slot/port
```

The following command is used to administratively turn off the interface:

```
Router(config-if)# shutdown
```

The following command is used to turn on an interface that has been shut down:

```
Router(config-if)# no shutdown
```

The following command is used to quit the current interface configuration mode:

```
Router(config-if)# exit
```

Configuring a Specific Interface

On serial links, one side must provide a clocking signal on the DCE end of a cable; the other side is a DTE. By default, Cisco routers are DTE devices, but in some cases, they can be used as DCE devices.

If you are using an interface to provide clocking, you must specify a rate with the **clockrate** command. The **bandwidth** command overrides the default bandwidth that is displayed in the **show interfaces** command and is used by some routing protocols, such as IGRP.

The following commands are examples of interface configuration:

```
Router(config)# interface serial 1/0
Router(config-if)# bandwidth 56
Router(config-if)# clockrate 56000
```

The following command is used to configure an interface:

```
Router(config)# interface serial 0
Router(config-if)# int & 0.1 point-to-point
Router(config-if)# int & 0.2 point-to-point
```

The following commands are associated with Cisco 4000 series routers:

```
Router(config)# interface ethernet 2
Router(config-if)# media-type 10baset
```

The third set of commands is associated with the Cisco 4000 series routers. On the Cisco 4000, there are two connections on the outside of the box for Ethernet interfaces—an attachment unit interface (AUI) connector and a 10BaseT connector. The default is AUI, so you must specify media type 10BaseT if you want to use the other connection.

e-LAB ACTIVITY 20.6

Router Interface Configuration Challenge

In this activity, you demonstrate how to use the router's interface configuration mode to configure an IP address and subnet mask for each router interface.

e-LAB ACTIVITY 20.7

Defining an Interfaces Physical Properties

In this activity, you demonstrate how to set the clock rate to 56,000 so that it can be used.

SKILL BUILDER

Lab Activity: Router Interface Configuration

In this lab, you use the router's interface configuration mode to configure an IP address and subnet mask for each router interface.

Configuration Methods

In this section, you learn more commands associated with Cisco IOS configuration methods:

- Release 11.x configuration
- Pre-11.0 release configuration
- Password configuration
- Router identification configuration

Release 11.x Configuration Methods

The commands shown in Figure 20-4 are used with Cisco IOS Release 11.0 and later. Figure 20-4 shows you a way to do the following:

- Enter configuration statements
- Examine the changes you have made
- If necessary, modify or remove configuration statements
- Save the changes to a backup in NVRAM that the router uses when it starts up

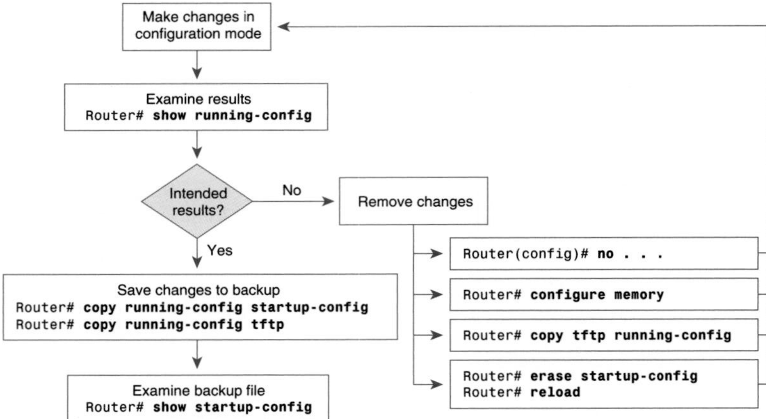

FIGURE 20-4
You use these configuration commands with 11.x configuration methods.

Pre-Release 11.0 Configuration Methods

The commands shown in Figure 20-5 are used with Cisco IOS Release 10.3 and earlier. They have been replaced with new commands. The old commands that have been replaced continue to perform their normal function in the current release, but they are no longer documented. Support for these commands will cease in a future release.

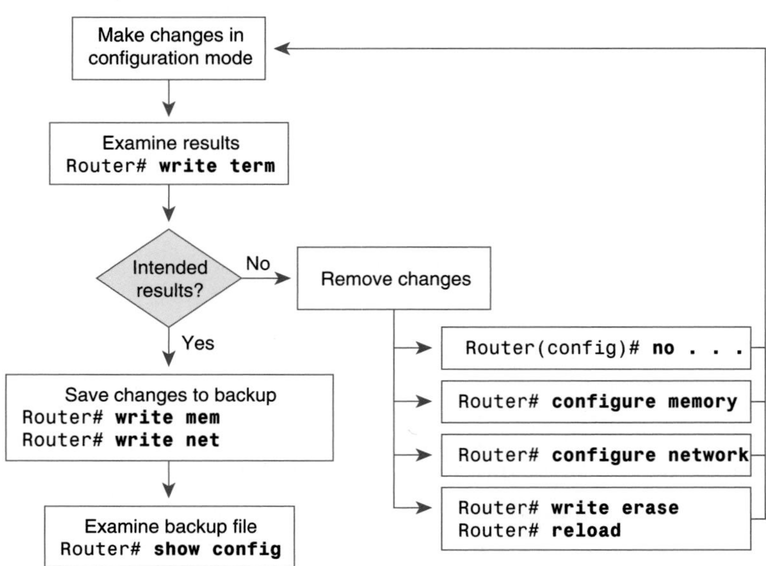

FIGURE 20-5
You use these configuration commands for routers running Cisco IOS Release 10.3 and earlier.

Password Configuration Methods

You can secure your system by using passwords to restrict access. Passwords can be established both on individual lines and in privileged EXEC mode:

- The **line console** 0 command establishes a password on the console terminal:

```
Router(config)# line console 0
Router(config-line)# login
Router(config-line)# password cisco
```

- The **line vty** 0 4 command establishes password protection on incoming Telnet sessions:

```
Router(config)# line vty 0 4
Router(config-line)# login
Router(config-line)# password cisco
```

- The **enable password** command restricts access to privileged EXEC mode:

```
Router(config)# enable password san-fran
```

The **enable secret** password from the system configuration dialog uses a Cisco-proprietary encryption process to alter the password character string. Passwords can be further protected from display through the use of the **service password-encryption** command. The encryption algorithm does not match the Data Encryption Standard (DES):

```
Router(config)# service password-encryption
        (set passwords here)
Router(config)# no service password-encryption
```

e-LAB ACTIVITY 20.8

Router Password Recovery

In this activity, you demonstrate how to use the password recovery procedure on a router.

Router Identification Configuration

The configuration of network devices determines the network's behavior. To manage device configurations, you need to list and compare configuration files on running devices, store configuration files on network servers for shared access, and perform software installations and upgrades.

One of your first basic tasks is to name your router. The name of the router is referred to as the hostname and is the name displayed by the system prompt. If you do not configure a name, the system default router name will be Router. You can name the router in global configuration mode. In the example shown in Figure 20-6, the router name is Tokyo.

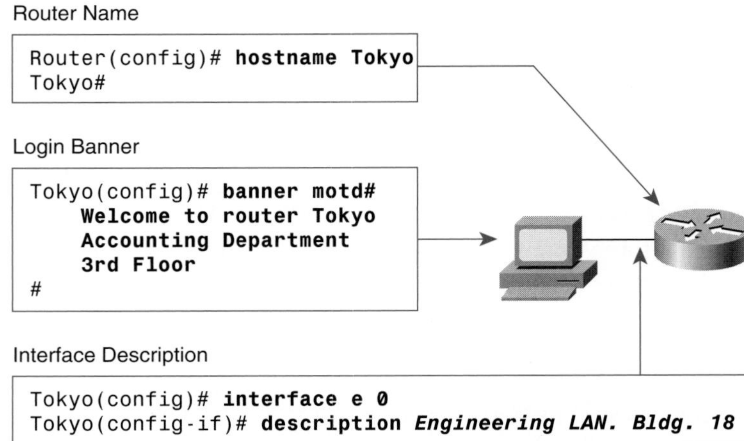

Router Name
Router(config)# hostname Tokyo
Tokyo#
Login Banner
Tokyo(config)# banner motd#
Welcome to router Tokyo
Accounting Department
3rd Floor
#
Interface Description
Tokyo(config)# interface e 0
Tokyo(config-if)# description Engineering LAN. Bldg. 18

FIGURE 20-6
The identification of the router can be set in global configuration mode.

You can configure a message-of-the-day banner to be displayed on all connected terminals. This banner is displayed at login and is useful for conveying messages that affect all router users (such as impending system shutdowns). To configure this message, use the **banner motd** command in global configuration mode.

MORE INFORMATION

Configuring a Switch from the Command Line

The Catalyst 1900 switch IOS has various configuration modes. To configure global switch parameters, such as the switch hostname or IP address, use global configuration mode. To configure a particular port (interface), use interface configuration mode.

One of the first tasks in configuring your switch is to name it. Naming your switch helps you to better manage your network by being able to uniquely identify each switch within the network. The name of the switch is considered to be the hostname and is the name displayed at the system prompt. You assign the switch name in global configuration mode.

To configure an IP address and subnet mask on the switch, use the **ip address** global configuration command. An IP address is required on the switch for management purposes.

For example, an IP address must be assigned if you plan to use Telnet from the switch, if you plan to use Telnet to the switch, or if you plan to use the Simple Network Management Protocol (SNMP) to manage the switch.

e-LAB ACTIVITY 20.9

USING THE line con 0 COMMAND

In this activity, you demonstrate how to go into console line configuration mode so others can set the password and log on.

e-LAB ACTIVITY 20.10

Using the Message of the Day Command

In this activity, you demonstrate how to start a message of the day.

SKILL BUILDER

Lab Activity: Router Configuration Challenge

You and your group are administrators of a LAN. Because of the rapid expansion of this company, you need to link the headquarters (your group's router) to the rest of the network. You must link up the networks via the serial ports, which means that your group is responsible for only your router's connections. Before starting this lab, the lab assistant or the instructor should erase the running configuration and the startup configuration for Lab-A only, and make sure that the rest of the routers are configured with the standard lab setup.

You also need to verify your workstation IP configuration so that you can test the connectivity between workstations and routers.

SKILL BUILDER

Lab Activity: Cisco ConfigMaker

This lab helps you become familiar with Cisco ConfigMaker. Cisco ConfigMaker is an easy-to-use Windows 95/98/NT application that configures Cisco routers, switches, hubs, and other devices.

SKILL BUILDER

Lab Activity: Router Configuration with a Web Browser

With Cisco IOS version 11.0, the **ip http server** command allows the router to act as a limited Hypertext Transfer Protocol (HTTP) Web server.

Summary

Configuration files can originate from the console, from NVRAM, or from a TFTP server. The router has several modes:

- **Privileged mode**—Used for copying and managing entire configuration files
- **Global configuration mode**—Used for one-line commands and commands that make global changes to the router configuration
- **Other configuration modes**—Used for multiple command lines and detailed configurations

The router can be configured with a hostname and a banner that aid in identification.

Check Your Understanding

1. Which of the following is not a function of the privileged EXEC **configure** command?
   - **A.** To configure a router from a virtual terminal
   - **B.** To configure a TFTP server from a virtual terminal
   - **C.** To configure a router from the console terminal
   - **D.** To load a configuration from a network TFTP server
2. What is the function of the **copy running-config startup-config** router command?
   - **A.** It loads configuration information from NVRAM.
   - **B.** It erases the contents of NVRAM.
   - **C.** It stores in NVRAM the current configuration in RAM.
   - **D.** It displays the configuration saved in NVRAM.
3. If you want to completely back out of configuration mode, which of the following must you enter?
   - **A.** **exit**
   - **B.** **no config-mode**
   - **C.** Ctrl-E
   - **D.** Ctrl-Z
4. If you are planning to configure an interface, what prompt should be on the router?
   - **A.** router(config)#
   - **B.** router(config-in)#
   - **C.** router(config-intf)#
   - **D.** router(config-if)#

5. Which of the following is the correct order for the process of configuring a router? (Assume that you have already made router changes in configuration mode.)

   A. Save changes to backup, decide whether the changes are your intended results, examine the results, and examine the backup file.

   B. Examine the results, decide whether the changes are your intended results, save the changes to backup, and examine the backup file.

   C. Decide whether the changes are your intended results, examine the backup file, save the changes to backup, and examine the results.

   D. Examine the results, save the changes to backup, decide whether the changes are your intended results, and examine the backup file.

6. Which of the following is a command that can be used to save router configuration changes to a backup?

   A. Router# **copy running-config tftp**

   B. Router# **show running-config**

   C. Router# **config mem**

   D. Router# **copy tftp running-config**

7. Which of the following correctly describes password configuration on routers?

   A. All passwords are established in privileged EXEC mode.

   B. All passwords alter the password character string.

   C. A password can be established on all incoming Telnet sessions.

   D. The **enable password** command restricts access to user EXEC mode.

8. Which of the following does not describe password configuration on routers?

   A. Passwords can be established in every configuration mode.

   B. A password can be established on any console terminal.

   C. The enable secret password uses an encryption process to alter the password character string.

   D. All password establishment begins in global configuration mode.

9. What is used for one-line commands that change the entire router?
   - A. Global configuration mode
   - B. Privileged mode
   - C. User EXEC mode
   - D. Interface mode
10. The **erase startup-config** command erases the contents of
    - A. NVRAM
    - B. RAM
    - C. ROM
    - D. TFTP server
    - E. Flash memory
11. What does the command **configure terminal** mean?
    - A. Configure manually from the console.
    - B. Configure the router manually from a console, virtual terminal, or modem.
    - C. Configure the router from the console or modem.
    - D. Configure the router from the TFTP server.
12. What is the default filename for a remote configuration file on a TFTP server?
    - A. hostname-config
    - B. hostname.configure
    - C. router.cfg
    - D. ttfp.cfq
13. What is the prompt for the interface configuration mode?
    - A. Router(config-if)#
    - B. Router(config-interface)#
    - C. Router(config-int)#
    - D. Router(configure-if)#

14. When the command **no shutdown** is typed on the prompt Router (config-if)#, what does this do?

    A. It turns on an interface that is shut down.

    B. It does not allow anyone to shut down that interface in the future by mistake.

    C. It turns off an interface.

    D. It shuts off the display of configuration settings while shutting down the routing.

15. What does the **exit** command do in a configuration mode having the prompt Router(config-if)#?

    A. It quits the current configuration interface mode.

    B. It reaches the privileged EXEC prompt.

    C. It exits the router.

    D. It switches to the user EXEC prompt.

Objectives

After reading this chapter, you will be able to

- Describe the process used to locate Cisco Internetwork Operating System (IOS) software
- Identify the commands to locate information about Cisco IOS software
- Describe bootstrap options in Cisco IOS software
- Describe the process and commands for creating and loading a software image backup
- Describe Cisco IOS naming conventions

IOS Images

Introduction

In Chapter 20, "Router Configuration 1," you learned how to use router modes and configuration methods to update a router's configuration file, using both current and older versions of Cisco IOS software. In this chapter, you learn how to use a variety of Cisco IOS software source options, execute commands to load Cisco IOS software onto the router, maintain backup files, and upgrade Cisco IOS software. In addition, you learn about the functions of the configuration register and how to determine which version of the IOS file you have. This chapter also describes how to use a TFTP server as a software source. Multiple source options provide flexibility and fallback alternatives. Routers boot Cisco IOS software from the following sources:

- Flash memory
- TFTP server
- ROM (not full Cisco IOS software)

Locating the Cisco IOS Software

The default source for Cisco IOS software startup depends on the hardware platform, but most commonly, the router looks to the boot system commands saved in NVRAM. However, Cisco IOS software does allow you to use several alternatives. You can specify other sources for the router to look for software, or the router can use its own fallback sequence, as necessary, to load the software.

As depicted in Figure 21-1, the default settings in the configuration register enable the following alternatives: You can specify global configuration-mode boot system commands to enter fallback sources for the router to use in sequence. Save these statements in NVRAM to use during the next startup with the command **copy running-config startup-config**. The router uses these commands as needed, in sequence, when it restarts. If NVRAM lacks boot system commands that the router can use, the system has its own fallback sequence. It can use default Cisco IOS in Flash memory. If Flash memory is empty, the router can try its next alternative: TFTP.

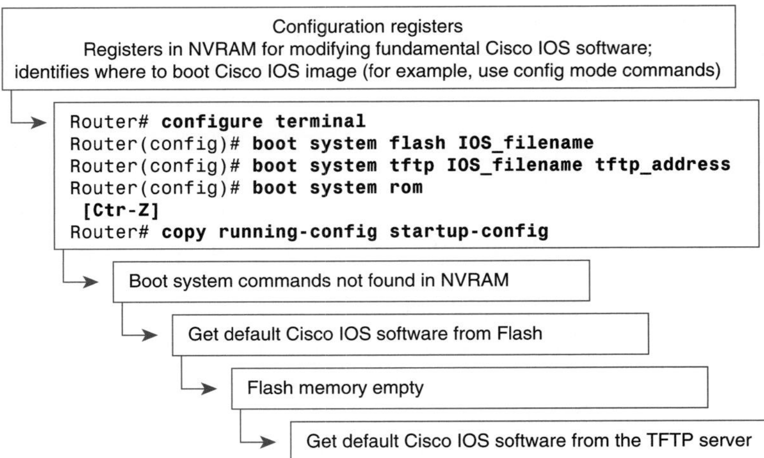

FIGURE 21-1 Settings in the configuration register enable alternatives for where the router will bootstrap Cisco IOS software.

Configuration Register Values

The order in which the router looks for IOS images to load depends on the boot field setting in the configuration register. You can change the default configuration register setting with the global configuration command **config-register.** Use a hexadecimal number as the argument for this command in the following example:

```
Router# configure terminal
Router(config)# config-register 0x10F
   [Ctrl - Z]
```

In this example, the configuration register is set so that the router will examine the startup file in NVRAM for boot system options. The configuration register is a 16-bit register in NVRAM. The lowest 4 bits of the configuration register (bits 3, 2, 1, and 0) form the boot field. To change the boot field and leave all other bits set at their original values, follow these guidelines (see Table 21-1):

- Set the configuration register value to 0x100 if you need to enter the ROM monitor (primarily a programmer's environment). From ROM monitor, boot the operating system manually by using the **b** command at the ROM monitor prompt. (This sets the boot field bits to 0-0-0-0.)
- Set the configuration register to 0x101 to configure the system to boot automatically from ROM. (This sets the boot field bits to 0-0-0-1.)
- Set the configuration register to any value from 0x102 to 0x10F to configure the system to use the boot system commands in NVRAM. This is the default. (This sets the boot field bits to between 0-0-1-0 and 1-1-1-1.)

TABLE 21-1 config-register Values

Value	Description
0x100	Use ROM monitor mode (manually boot using the **b** command).
0x101	Automatically boot from ROM (default if router has no Flash memory).
0x102 to 0x10F	Examine NVRAM for boot system commands (0x102 is the default if the router has Flash memory).

To check the boot field setting, and to verify the **config-register** command, use the **show version** command.

e-LAB ACTIVITY 21.1

Setting the Configuration Register

In this activity, you demonstrate how to set the router to boot from ROM.

The show version Command

The **show version** command displays information about the Cisco IOS software version that is currently running on the router. This includes the configuration register and the boot field setting. In the example illustrated in Listing 21-1, the Cisco IOS version and descriptive information is highlighted on the second output line. The screen captured shows an experimental version of Release 11.2. This line shows the system image name:

```
System image file is "c4500-f-mz", booted via tftp from 171.69.1.129
```

You learn about Cisco IOS software Release 11.2 image-naming conventions later in this chapter. For now, notice the portion of the filename that indicates that this image is for a Cisco 4500 platform.

In addition, the **show version** command displays information about the type of platform on which the version of Cisco IOS software is currently running.

Listing 21-1 The show version Command

```
Router# show version
Cisco Internetwork Operating System Software
IOS (tm) 4500 Software (C4500-J-M),
     Experimental Version 11.2 (19960626:214907)  ]
Copyright (c)1986-1006 by Cisco Systems, Inc.
Compiled Fri 28-Jun-96  16.32 by rbeach
Image text-base: 0x600088A0, data-base: 0x6076E000
```

continues

Listing 21-1 The show version Command (Continued)

```
ROM: System Bootstrap, Version 5.1(1) [daveu 1], RELEASE SOFTWARE (fc1)
ROM: 4500-XBOOT Bootstrap Software, Version 10.1(1), RELEASE SOFTWARE (fc1)


router uptime is 1 week, 3 days, 32 minutes
System restarted by reload
System image file is "c4500-f-mz", booted via tftp from 171.69.1.129


Cisco 4500 (R4K) processor (revision 0x00) with 32768K/16384K bytes of memory
Processor board ID 01217941
R4600 processor, implementation 32, Revision 1.0
G.703/E1 software, Version 1.0
Bridging software
SuperLAT software copyright 1990 by Meridian Technology Corp.
X.25 software, Version 2.0 NET2, BFE and GOSIP compliant
TN3270 Emulation software (copyright 1994 by TGV Inc.)
Primary Rate ISDN software, Version 1.0
2 Ethernet/IEEE 802.3 interfaces.
48 Serial network interfaces.
2 Channelized t1/PRI ports.
128K bytes of non-volatile configuration memory.
8192 bytes of processor board System flash (Read/Write)
4096K bytes of processor board Boot flash (Read/Write)


Configuration register is 0x0 ( will be 0x10F at next reload )
```

NOTE

You do not see evidence of any config-register setting in output from either the **show running-config** or **show startup-config** commands.

e-LAB ACTIVITY 21.2

Identifying the IOS Version Number

In this activity, you demonstrate how to verify the IOS version.

e-LAB ACTIVITY 21.3

IOS Image Boot

In this activity, you demonstrate how to gather information on the version of IOS software that is currently running on the router.

SKILL BUILDER

Lab Activity: IOS Boot Image

In this lab, you gather information on the version of IOS software that is currently running on the router. You also check the configuration register value to see where the router is currently configured to boot from.

Bootstrap Options in Software

The following examples show how you can enter multiple boot system commands to specify the fallback sequence for booting Cisco IOS software. The three examples show boot system entries that specify that a Cisco IOS image will load first from Flash memory, then from a network server, and finally from ROM:

- **Flash memory**—You can load a system image from electrically erasable programmable read-only memory (EEPROM). The advantage is that information stored in Flash memory is not vulnerable to network failures that can occur when loading system images from TFTP servers:

```
Router# configure terminal
Router(config)# boot system flash gsnew-image
 [Ctrl-Z]
   Router# copy running-config startup-config
network server -- In case Flash memory becomes corrupted, you provide for a
  backup by specifying that a system image should be loaded from a TFTP server:
Router# configure terminal
Router(config)# boot system tftp test exe 172.16.13.111
 [Ctrl-Z]
   Router# copy running-config startup-config
```

- **ROM**—If Flash memory is corrupted and the network server fails to load the image, booting from ROM is the final bootstrap option in software. However, the system image in ROM is a subset of Cisco IOS software that lacks the protocols, features, and configurations of the full Cisco IOS software. Also, if you have updated the software since you purchased the router, it is likely an older version of Cisco IOS software:

```
Router# configure terminal
Router(config)# boot system rom
 [Ctrl-Z]
   Router# copy running-config startup-config
```

The command **copy running-config startup-config** saves the commands in NVRAM. The router will execute the boot system commands as needed in the order in which they were originally entered into configuration mode.

Preparing for the Use of TFTP

Production internetworks usually span wide areas and contain multiple routers. These geographically distributed routers need a source or backup location for software images. A TFTP server enables image and configuration uploads and downloads over the network. The TFTP server can be another router, or it can be a host system. The TFTP host can be any system that has TFTP server software loaded and operating and that is capable of receiving files from the TCP/IP network. You will be copying software between the TFTP server and Flash memory in the router. However, before you do this, you must prepare by checking the following preliminary conditions:

- From the router, check to make sure that you can access the TFTP server over the TCP/IP network. The **ping** command is one method that can help you do this:

```
Router# ping tftp-address
...
  !!!!!
```

- Verify that the router has sufficient room in Flash memory to accommodate the Cisco IOS software image:

```
Router# show flash
4096 kbytes of flash memory on embedded flash (in XX).

file      offset      length         name
 0         0x40       1204637       xk09140z
  [903848/2097152 bytes free]
```

- On the UNIX TFTP server, check to make sure that you know the filename and location for the Cisco IOS software image. For upload and download operations, you need to specify a path or filename:

```
ls gs7-j-mz.112-0.11
```

These steps help ensure a successful file copy. If you rush into the file copy, the copy could fail and you will have to begin troubleshooting the cause of the copy failure.

The show flash Command

Use the **show flash** command to verify that you have sufficient memory on your system for the Cisco IOS software that you want to load. The following example shows the router has 4 MB of Flash memory, all of which is free:

```
Router# show flash
4096K bytes of flash memory sized on embedded flash
File name/status
 0  mater/California//i11/bin/gs7-j-mz.112-0.11 [deleted]
 [0/4194304 bytes free/total]
```

Compare this with the length of the Cisco IOS software image. Sources for the image size might include the software order document or information on the IOS software information at the Cisco Connection Online (CCO) World Wide Web site, or output from a command such as **dir** or **ls** issued on your TFTP server.

If there is insufficient free memory, you cannot copy or load the image, which means that you can either try to obtain a smaller Cisco IOS software image or increase the available Flash memory on the router. It is a good idea to keep a backup copy of the IOS image file for each router. You will also want to always back up your current IOS before upgrading to a newer version.

e-LAB ACTIVITY 21.4

Checking an IOS Image in Flash

In this activity, you demonstrate how to check an IOS image in Flash.

Cisco's IOS Naming Conventions

Cisco products have expanded beyond the generic router to include many platforms at many points within the networking product spectrum. To optimize how Cisco IOS software operates on these various platforms, Cisco is working to develop many different Cisco IOS software images. These images accommodate the various platforms, available memory resources, and feature set needs that customers have for their network devices. The naming convention for Cisco IOS Release 11.2 contains three parts, which are depicted in Table 21-2:

1. The platform on which the image runs
2. A letter or series of letters that identifies the special capabilities and feature sets supported in the image
3. Specifics on where the image runs and whether it has been zipped or compressed

The Cisco IOS software naming conventions, image content, and other details are subject to change. Refer to your sales representative, distribution channel, or the CCO for updated details. Also, see the book *Cisco IOS Releases: The Complete Reference* (published by Cisco Press).

TABLE 21-2 Naming Conventions for Cisco IOS Release 11.2

Naming Example	Hardware Product Platform	Feature Cabaility	Run Location Compressed Status
cpa25-cg-1	CiscoPro 2500 (cpa25)	Comm-server/ Remote Access Server, ISDN (cg)	Relocatable, not compressed (1)
igs-inr-1	Cisco ICG, 25xx, and 3xxx (igs)	IP subset, Novell IPX, and IBM base option (inr)	Relocatable, not compressed (1)
c4500-aj-m	Cisco 4500 and 4700 (c4500)	APPN and Enterprise subset for low-end/ midrange (aj)	RAM, not compressed (m)
gs7-k-mz	Cisco 7000 and 7010 (gs7)	Enterprise for high-end range (k)	RAM, zip compressed (mz)

Creating a Software Image Backup

You should copy a system image back to a network server. This copy of the system image can serve as a backup copy. Figure 21-2 and Listing 21-2 use the **show flash** command to learn the name of the system image file (xk09140z), and the **copy flash tftp** command to copy the system image to a TFTP server. The files can be renamed during transfer.

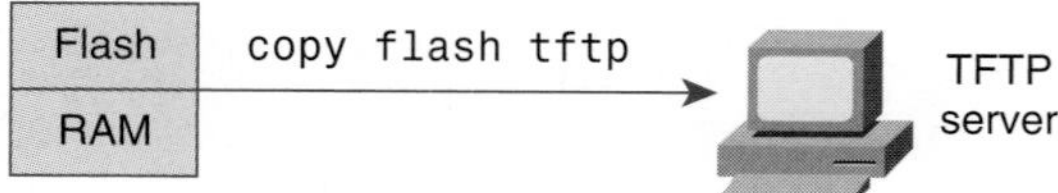

FIGURE 21-2 Use the **show flash** command to learn the name of the system image file (xk09140z), and the **copy flash tftp** command to copy the system image to a TFTP server.

Listing 21-2 The show flash and copy flash tftp Commands

```
Router# show flash
4096 bytes of flash memory on embedded flash (in XX).


file     offset      length        name
 0       0x40        1204637       xk09140z
  [903848/2097152 bytes free]


Router# copy flash tftp
IP address of remote host [255.255.255.255]? 172.16.13.111
filename to write on tftp hose? c4500-i
writing C4500-1 !!!!!!!!!!!!!!!!!!!!!!!!!!!!!!!!!!!!!!!!!
successful tftp write.
Router#
```

One reason for this upload to the server would be to provide a fallback copy of the current image before updating the image with a new version. Then, if problems develop with the new version, the administrator can download the backup image and return to the previous image.

e-LAB ACTIVITY 21.5

Using copy flash tftp

In this activity, you demonstrate how to do a back up to a tftp server.

The copy tftp flash Command

After you have a backup copy of the current Cisco IOS software image, you can load a new image. You download the new image from the TFTP server by using the command **copy tftp flash**. Figure 21-3 and Listing 21-3 show that this command begins by requesting the IP address of the remote host that will act as the TFTP server. Next, the prompt asks for the filename of the new IOS image. You need to enter the correct filename of the update image (as it is named on the TFTP server).

Following a confirmation to your entries, the procedure asks if you are willing to erase Flash memory. This makes room for the new image. Often, there is insufficient Flash memory for more than a single Cisco IOS image.

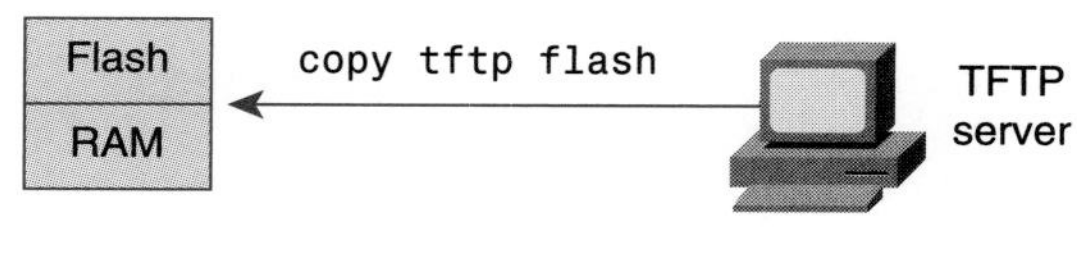

FIGURE 21-3 The **copy tftp flash** command begins operation by requesting the IP address of the remote host that will act as a TFTP server.

Listing 21-3 The copy tftp flash Command

```
Router# copy tftp flash
IP address or name of remote host [255.255.255.255]? 172.16.13.111
Name of tftp filename to copy into flash []? c4500-aj-m
copy C4500-AJ-M from 172.16.13.111 into flash memory? [confirm] <Return>
xxxxxxxx bytes available for writing without erasure.
erase flash before writing? [confirm] <Return>
Clearing and initializing flash memory [please wait] ####...##
Loading from 172.16.13.111: !!!!!!!!!!!!!!!!!!!!!!!!!!
!!!!!!! (text omitted) [OK - 324572/524212 bytes]
Verifying checksum...
VVVVVVVVVVVVVVVVVVVVVVVVVVVVVVVVVVVVVVVVVVVVVVVVVVVVV
VVVVVVVVV (text omitted)
Flash verification successful. Length = 1804637, checksum = 0xA5D3
```

You have the option of erasing the existing Flash memory before writing onto it. If no free Flash memory space is available, or if the Flash memory has never been written to, the erase routine is usually required before new files can be copied. The system informs you of these conditions and prompts you for a response. Note that the Flash memory is erased at the factory before shipment. Each exclamation point (!) means that one User Datagram Protocol (UDP) segment has successfully transferred. A series of V's indicates successful checksum verification.

Use the **show flash** command to view the file information and to compare its size with that of the original on the server before changing the boot system commands to use the updated image. Following a successful load, the **reload** command reboots the router using the updated image.

e-LAB ACTIVITY 21.6

Loading a New Flash Image

In this activity, you demonstrate how to start the process of getting the IOS on the router upgraded.

How to Load a Software Image Backup

If you need to load the backup Cisco IOS version, again use the copy command **copy tftp flash**, which will enable you to download the image that you previously uploaded to the TFTP server. After you enter the **copy tftp flash** command, as shown in Listing 21-4, the system prompts you for the IP address (or name) of the TFTP server. This can be another router serving ROM or Flash software images. The system then prompts you for the filename of the software image. Listing 21-4 shows sample output from copying a system image, named C4500-I, into Flash memory.

Listing 21-4 The copy tftp flash Command

```
Router# copy tftp flash
ILP address or name of remote host [255.255.255.255]? 172.16.13.111
Name of tftp filename to copy into flash []? c4500-I
copy C4500-I already exists; it will be invalidated!
Copy C4500-I from 172.16.13.111 into flash memory? [confirm] <Return>
xxxxxxxx bytes available for writing without erasure.
erase flash before writing? [confirm] <Return>
Clearing and initializing flash memory [please wait] ####...##
Loading from 172.16.13.111: !!!!!!!!!!!!!!!!!!!!!!!!!!!
!!!!!!! (text omitted) [OK - 324572/524212 bytes]
Verifying checksum...
VVVVVVVVVVVVVVVVVVVVVVVVVVVVVVVVVVVVVVVVVVVVVVVVVVVVVVVVV
VVVVVVVVV (text omitted)
Flash verification successful. Length = 1204637, checksum = 0x95D9
```

If you attempt to copy into Flash memory a file that is already there, a prompt tells you that a file with the same name already exists. This file is deleted when you copy the new file into Flash memory. If there is room for both copies in Flash memory, the first copy of the file still resides within Flash memory, but is rendered unusable in favor of the newest version; it will be listed with the [deleted] tag when you use the **show flash** command.

If you abort the copy process, the newer file will be marked (deleted) because the entire file was not copied and is therefore not valid. In this case, the original file still resides within Flash memory and is available to the system.

Summary

In this chapter, you learned that

- The default source for Cisco IOS software depends on the hardware platform, but, most commonly, the router looks to the configuration commands saved in NVRAM.
- The **show version** command displays information about the Cisco IOS software version that is currently running on the router.
- You can enter multiple boot system commands to specify the fallback sequence for booting Cisco IOS software. Routers can boot Cisco IOS software from Flash memory, from a TFTP server, and from ROM.
- You use the **show flash** command to verify that you have sufficient memory on your system for the Cisco IOS software that you want to load.
- With Cisco IOS Release 11.2 and above, the naming convention for Cisco IOS contains the following three parts:
  - The platform on which the image runs
  - The special capabilities of the image
  - Where the image runs and whether it has been zipped or compressed
- You can copy a system image back to a network server. This copy of the system image can serve as a backup copy and can be used to verify that the copy in Flash memory is the same as the original file.
- If you need to load the backup Cisco IOS version, you can use a variation of the copy command, **copy tftp flash**, to download the image which you previously uploaded to the TFTP server.

Check Your Understanding

1. Which of the following correctly describes a method for specifying how a router loads the Cisco IOS software?

   A. Designate fallback sources for the router to use in sequence from NVRAM.

   B. Configure the Cisco IOS software image for the location where it will bootstrap.

   C. Manually boot a default system image at a virtual terminal.

   D. Manually boot a default system image at the network server.

2. Which of the following is not a boot option that can be set with the configuration register boot field?

   A. IOS boots in ROM monitor mode.

   B. IOS automatically boots from ROM.

   C. IOS automatically boots from a TFTP server.

   D. NVRAM is examined for boot system commands.

3. Which of the following is information displayed by the Cisco IOS **show version** command?

   A. Detailed statistics about each page of the router's memory

   B. The name of the system image

   C. The names and sizes of all files in Flash memory

   D. The status of configured network protocols

4. Which command is used to discover the configuration register setting?

   A. **show register**

   B. **show running-config**

   C. **show version**

   D. **show startup-config**

5. Which of the following does not describe the procedure to verify sufficient room in Flash memory for copying software?

   A. Use the **show flash** command.

   B. Verify that the configuration register is set properly.

C. Compare the available memory with the length of the Cisco IOS software image to be copied.

D. If there is not enough available memory, you may have to load a smaller Cisco IOS software image.

6. What information is not provided in the Cisco image filename system?

A. The capabilities of the image

B. The platform on which the image runs

C. Where the image runs

D. The size of the image

7. Which of the following is not part of the recommended procedure for loading a new Cisco IOS software image to Flash memory from a TFTP server? (The procedures are listed in correct order.)

A. Back up a copy of the current software image to the TFTP server.

B. Enter the **copy flash tftp** command to start downloading the new image from the server.

C. The procedure asks if you are willing to erase Flash memory.

D. A series of Vs on the display indicates successful checksum verification.

8. What is the initial boot attempt if the router configuration register is set to Ox101?

A. Setup mode

B. TFTP server

C. ROM

D. Flash memory

9. Which of the following has a limited version of router IOS?

A. ROM

B. Flash memory

C. TFTP server

D. Bootstrap

10. What is the initial boot attempt if the router config-register is set to Ox102?
    - **A.** Flash memory
    - **B.** TFTP server
    - **C.** ROM
    - **D.** Check for boot system commands
11. Which of the following is the sequence used by the router for automatic fallback to locate the Cisco IOS software?
    - **A.** Flash memory, (2) NVRAM, (3) TFTP server
    - **B.** NVRAM, (2) TFTP server, (3) Flash memory
    - **C.** NVRAM, (2) Flash memory, (3) TFTP server
    - **D.** TFTP server, (2) Flash memory, (3) NVRAM
12. Which of the following does not describe configuration register settings for Cisco IOS bootstrapping?
    - **A.** The order in which the router looks for system bootstrap information depends on the boot field setting.
    - **B.** You change the configuration register setting with the command **config-register**.
    - **C.** You use a hexadecimal number when setting the configuration register boot field.
    - **D.** Use the **show running-config** command to check the boot field setting.
13. Which of the following is not displayed by the Cisco IOS **show version** command?
    - **A.** Statistics for configured interfaces
    - **B.** The type of platform running the Cisco IOS software
    - **C.** The configuration register setting
    - **D.** The Cisco IOS version
14. Which of the following is *not* part of specifying the fallback sequence to boot the Cisco IOS software?
    - **A.** Boot system commands are entered from global configuration mode.
    - **B.** One boot system command is used to specify the entire fallback sequence.

C. The command **copy running-config startup-config** saves boot system commands to NVRAM.

D. Boot system commands are executed as needed during fallback in the order in which they were entered.

15. Which of the following correctly describes preparing to use a TFTP server to copy software to Flash memory?

A. The TFTP server must be a connected router or a host system, such as a UNIX workstation or a laptop computer.

B. The TFTP server must be a system connected to an Ethernet network.

C. The name of the router containing the Flash memory must be identified.

D. The Flash memory must be enabled.

16. Which of the following is the fastest way to make sure that the TFTP server is reachable before trying to transfer a Cisco IOS image file?

A. **trace** the TFTP server.

B. **ping** the TFTP server.

C. **telnet** to the TFTP server.

D. Call the TFTP server administrator.

17. Why do you need to determine the file size of the Cisco IOS image on the TFTP server before transferring it to your router?

A. To check that there is enough space in Flash memory to store the file

B. To verify that the file is the correct Cisco IOS version for your router

C. To complete a TFTP operation

D. To calculate the download time for the file and, thus, the amount of time the router will be out of service

18. Why do you create a Cisco IOS software image backup?

A. To verify that the copy in Flash memory is the same as the copy in ROM

B. To provide a fallback copy of the current image before copying the image to a new router

C. To create a fallback copy of the current image as part of the procedures during recovery from system failure

D. To create a fallback copy of the current image before updating with a new version

19. Which of the following has a limited version of Cisco IOS software?

A. ROM

B. Flash memory

C. TFTP server

D. ROM monitor

20. What is the command you need to issue if you want to upgrade an old version of the Cisco IOS by downloading a new image from the TFTP server?

A. **boot system tftp 131.21.11.3**

B. **copy tftp flash**

C. **show flash**

D. **tftp ios.exe**

\Objectives

After reading this chapter, you will be able to

- Configure a router from the CLI after startup config has been erased
- Perform password recovery tasks

Chapter 22

Router Configuration 2

Introduction

One way to begin understanding the way the Internet works is to configure a router. Router configuration is also one of the primary topics on the CCNA exam and one of the most important and sought-after skills by employers. Routers are complex devices that can have a wide variety of possible configurations.

In this chapter, you practice configuring a router. You spend a great deal of time configuring routers. Practice with simulations and actual routers is the only way to learn this extremely important skill. Although the actual configuration is fairly simple, repeating it many times makes it "second nature" for you.

Configuring a Router from the CLI After Startup Config Has Been Erased

Just as the router configuration file has different parts to it, the router configuration process also has different parts (see Figure 22-1 and Figure 22-2).

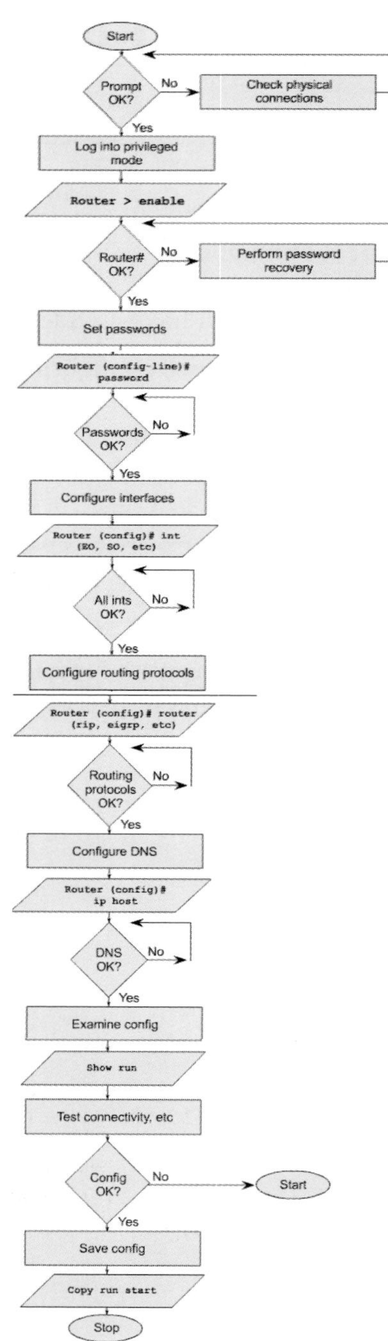

FIGURE 22-1
Router configuration process.

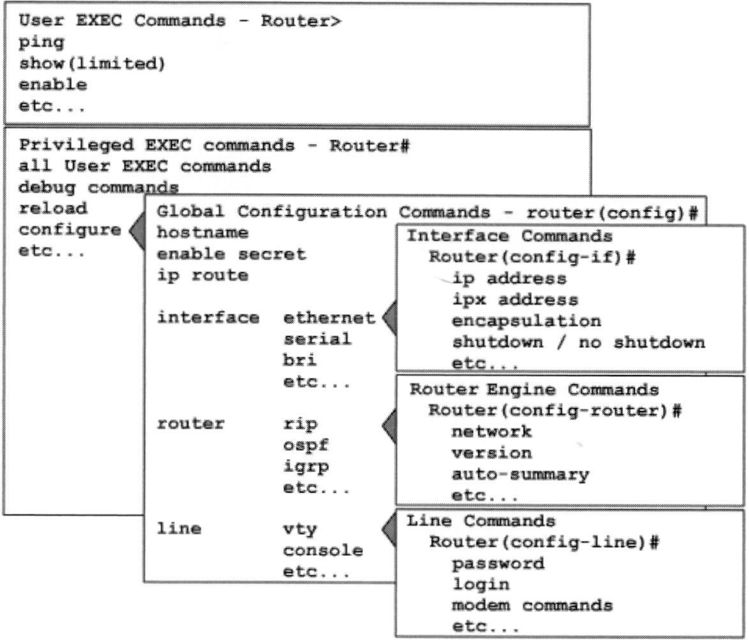

User EXEC Commands - Router>
ping
show(limited)
enable
etc...
Privileged EXEC commands - Router#
all User EXEC commands
debug commands
reload
configure
etc...
Global Configuration Commands - router(config)#
hostname
enable secret
ip route
interface
ethernet
serial
bri
etc...
router
rip
ospf
igrp
etc...
line
vty
console
etc...
Interface Commands
Router(config-if)#
ip address
ipx address
encapsulation
shutdown / no shutdown
etc...
Router Engine Commands
Router(config-router)#
network
version
auto-summary
etc...
Line Commands
Router(config-line)#
password
login
modem commands
etc...

FIGURE 22-2
Router configuration commands.

Password Recovery

This section explains several password recovery techniques for Cisco routers and Catalyst switches. You can perform password recovery on most of the platforms without changing hardware jumpers, but all platforms require the router to be rebooted. Password recovery can be done only from the console port (physically attached to the router).

Overview of Password Recovery

Three ways exist to restore access to a router when the password is lost. You can view the password, change the password, or erase the configuration and start over as if the box was new.

Each procedure follows these basic steps:

Step 1 Configure the router to start up without reading the configuration memory (NVRAM). This is done from what is sometimes called test system mode, ROM mode, or boot mode.

Step 2 Reboot the system.

Step 3 Access enable mode (which can be done without a password if you set the configuration register correctly in Step 1).

Step 4 View or change the password, or erase the configuration.

Step 5 Reconfigure the router to boot up and read the NVRAM as it normally does.

Step 6 Reboot the system.

Some password recovery requires a terminal to issue a **BREAK** signal; you must be familiar with how your terminal or PC terminal emulator issues this signal. In ProComm, for example, the keys Alt-B generate the **BREAK** signal by default; in Windows Terminal, you press Break or Ctrl-Break. Windows Terminal also allows you to define a function key as **BREAK**. From the terminal window, select Function Keys and define one as Break by filling in the characters **^$B** (Shift 6, Shift 4, and uppercase B). Several free terminal emulation packages also are available for download on the Internet, which you might find preferable.

The following sections contain detailed instructions for specific Cisco routers. Locate your product at the beginning of each section to determine which technique to use.

Password Recovery Technique 1

The following are the relevant devices for this technique:

- Cisco 2500 series
- Cisco 3000 series
- Cisco 7000 series running Cisco IOS 10.0 or later in ROMs

This technique can be used on the Cisco 7000 and Cisco 7010 series only if the router has Cisco IOS 10.0 ROMs installed on the Route Processor (RP) card. It might be booting Flash Cisco IOS 10.0 software, but it needs the actual ROMs on the processor card as well. The following steps outline password recovery technique 1:

Step 1 Attach a terminal or PC with terminal emulation to the console port of the router. To connect a PC to the console port, attach a null modem adapter (Tandy Null Modem Adapter No. 26-1496 has been tested) to the console port, and then attach a straight-through modem cable to the null modem adapter.

Step 2 Type **show version** and record the setting of the configuration register. It is usually 0x2102 or 0x102. If you do not get the router prompt to do a **show version**, look on a similar router to obtain the configuration register number, or try using 0x2102.

Step 3 Power-cycle the router.

Step 4 Press the Break key on the terminal within 60 seconds of the powerup. You see the > prompt with no router name. If you don't see this, the terminal is not sending the correct **BREAK** signal. In that case, check the terminal or terminal emulation setup.

Step 5 Type **o/r 0x42** at the > prompt to boot from Flash memory, or type **o/r 0x41** to boot from the boot ROMs. (Note that this is the letter o, not the numeral zero.) If you have Flash memory and it is intact, 0x42 is the best setting because it is the default. Use 0x41 only if the Flash memory is erased or not installed. If you use 0x41, you can either view or erase the configuration. You cannot change the password.

Step 6 Type **i** at the > prompt. The router reboots, but ignores its saved configuration.

Step 7 Answer **no** to all the setup questions, or type Ctrl-C.

Step 8 Type **enable** at the Router> prompt. You'll be in enable mode and will see the Router# prompt.

Step 9 Choose one of the following three options:

— To view the password, type **show start.**

— To change the password (in case it is encrypted, for example), do the following:

a. Type **copy start run** to copy the NVRAM into memory.

b. Type **show run.**

c. If you have **enable secret** password **set,** perform the following:

— Type **config term** and make the changes.

— Type **enable secret** <*new_password*>.

— Press Ctrl-Z.

d. If you do not have **enable secret xxxx**, type **enable password** <*new_password*> and press Ctrl-Z.

e. Type **copy run start** to commit the changes.

— To erase the config, type **erase start.**

Step 10 Type **config term** at the prompt.

Step 11 Type **config-register 0x2102**, or whatever value you recorded in Step 2.

Step 12 Press Ctrl-Z to return to privileged EXEC mode.

Step 13 Type **reload** at the prompt. You do not need to write memory.

Password Recovery Technique 2

The relevant devices for this password recovery technique are as follows:

- Cisco 1003
- Cisco 4500

Follow these steps:

Step 1 Attach a terminal or PC with terminal emulation to the console port of the router.

Step 2 Type **show version** and record the setting of the configuration register. It is usually 0x2102 or 0x102.

Step 3 Power-cycle the router.

Step 4 Press the Break key on the terminal within 60 seconds of the power-up. You will see the rommon> prompt. If you don't see this, the terminal is not sending the correct **BREAK** signal. In that case, check the terminal or terminal emulation setup.

Step 5 Type **confreg** at the rommon> prompt.

Step 6 Answer **y** to the question "Do you wish to change configuration [y/n]?"

Step 7 Answer **n** to all the questions that appear until you reach this question: Ignore system config info[y/n]? There, answer **y**.

Step 8 Answer **n** to the remaining questions until you reach the question "Change boot characteristics[y/n]?" There, answer **y**.

Step 9 At the enter to boot: prompt, type **2** followed by a carriage return. If Flash memory is erased, type **1**. If all Flash memory is erased, the 4500 must be returned to Cisco for service. If you use 1, you can either view or erase the configuration. You cannot change the password.

Step 10 A configuration summary is displayed. Answer **no** to the question "Do you wish to change configuration[y/n]?"

Step 11 Type **reset** at the rommon> prompt, or power-cycle your 4500 or 7500.

Step 12 After it boots up, answer **no** to all the setup questions.

Step 13 Type **enable** at the Router> prompt. You'll be in enable mode and will see the Router# prompt.

Step 14 Choose one of these three options:

— To view the password, type **show start**.

— To change the password (in case it is encrypted, for example), perform the following:

a.Type **copy run start** to copy the NVRAM into memory.

b.Type **show run**.

If you have the enable secret password set, perform the following:

— Type **config term** and make the changes.

— Type **enable secret** <*password*>.

— Press Ctrl-Z.

If you do not have the enable secret password set, perform the following:

— Type **enable password** <*password*>.

— Press Ctrl-Z.

— Type **copy run start** to commit the changes.

— To erase the config, type **erase start**.

Step 15 Type **config term** at the prompt.

Step 16 Type **config-register 0x2102**, or whatever value you recorded in Step 2.

Step 17 Press Ctrl-Z to return to privileged EXEC mode.

Step 18 Type **reload** at the prompt. You do not need to write to memory.

SKILL BUILDER

Lab Activity: Router Password Recovery

In some circumstances, the password for a router needs to be reset. The password might have been forgotten, or the previous administrator might have left the employment of the company that owns the router. The technique described requires physical access to the router. Because this technique is well known, it is vital that routers are in a secured location, with limited physical access.

e-LAB ACTIVITY 22.1

Router Configuration

In this activity, you demonstrate how to configure a router from the command line.

e-LAB ACTIVITY 22.2

Individual Router Configuration Challenge

In this activity, you demonstrate how to do a step-by-step configuration of a router.

SKILL BUILDER

Lab Activity: Individual Router Configuration

In this lab, you configure one of the five lab routers from the command line by yourself without the use of any notes, using only the network topology. You can use the router Help facility. Your goal is to configure the router as quickly as possible without errors. You also configure the IP settings for one of the corresponding Ethernet attached workstations.

Summary

Now that you have completed this chapter, you should be able to do the following:

- Configure a router from the CLI after the startup configuration has been erased
- Perform tasks related to the router configuration process
- Perform the router password recovery procedure on various routers

Check Your Understanding

1. What are the major elements of a typical router configuration?

   A. Passwords, interfaces, routing protocols, DNS

   B. Boot sequence, interfaces, TFTP server, NVRAM

   C. NVRAM, ROM, DRAM, interfaces

   D. Interfaces, routing protocols, configuration register, Flash memory

2. In a password recovery procedure, immediately after issuing a Ctrl-BREAK upon router startup, what should be the config register setting?

   A. 0x2102

   B. 0x2142

   C. 0x0000

   D. 0x10F

3. In a password recovery procedure, just before saving the running config and after you have enabled a new secret password, what should be the config register setting?

   A. 0x2102

   B. 0x2142

   C. 0x0000

   D. 0x10F

4. What is the correct syntax to enable RIP on Router A in the lab topology?

   A.
   ```
   config t
   router rip
   int e0
   ip address 192.5.5.1 255.255.255.0
   no shutdown
   description this is the first Ethernet Interface
   CNTRL/Z
   copy run start
   ```

   B.
   ```
   config t
   router rip
   network 192.5.5.0
   network 205.7.5.0
   network 201.100.11.0
   CNTRL/Z
   copy run start
   ```

C.
```
config t
router rip
ip host LAB-A 192.5.5.1 207.5.1 201.100.11.1
ip host LAB-B 201.100.11.2 219.17.100.1 199.6.13.1
ip host LAB-C 199.6.13.2 223.8.151.1 204.204.7.1
ip host LAB-D 204.204.7.2 210.93.105.1
ip host LAB-E 210.93.105.2
CNTRL/Z
copy run start
```

D. None of the above

5. What is the correct syntax for completely configuring Ethernet and serial interfaces?

A.
```
config t
int e0
ip host LAB-A 192.5.5.1 207.5.1 201.100.11.1
ip host LAB-B 201.100.11.2 219.17.100.1 199.6.13.1
ip host LAB-C 199.6.13.2 223.8.151.1 204.204.7.1
ip host LAB-D 204.204.7.2 210.93.105.1
ip host LAB-E 210.93.105.2
CNTRL/Z
copy run start
```

B.
```
config t
int e0
network 192.5.5.0
network 205.7.5.0
network 201.100.11.0
CNTRL/Z
copy run start
```

C.
```
config t
int e0
ip address 192.5.5.1 255.255.255.0
no shutdown
description this is the first Ethernet Interface
CNTRL/Z
copy run start
```

D. None of the above

Objectives

After reading this chapter, you will be able to

- Describe the TCP/IP protocol suite
- Describe the TCP/IP Internet layer

Chapter 23

TCP/IP

Introduction

Now that you have learned about the router configuration process, it's time to review the Transmission Control Protocol/Internet Protocol (TCP/IP). In this chapter, you learn about TCP/IP operation to ensure communication across any set of interconnected networks. In addition, you learn about the TCP/IP protocol stack components, such as protocols to support file transfer, e-mail, remote login, and other applications. Also, you learn about reliable and unreliable transport layer protocols and about connectionless datagram (packet) delivery at the network layer. Lastly, you learn how ICMP provides control and message functions at the network layer and how ARP and RARP work.

The TCP/IP Protocol Suite

The TCP/IP suite of protocols was developed as part of the research done by the Defense Advanced Research Projects Agency (DARPA). It was originally developed to provide communication within DARPA. Later, TCP/IP was included with the Berkeley Software Distribution of UNIX. Now, TCP/IP is the de facto standard for internetwork communications and serves as the transport protocol stack for the Internet, enabling millions of computers to communicate globally.

This book focuses on TCP/IP for several reasons:

- TCP/IP is a universally available protocol that you likely will use at work.
- TCP/IP is a useful reference for understanding other protocols because it includes elements that are representative of other protocols.
- TCP/IP is important because the router uses it as a configuration tool.

The function of the TCP/IP protocol stack is to transfer information from one network device to another. In doing so, it closely maps the OSI reference model in the lower layers and supports all standard physical and data link protocols (see Figure 23-1).

The OSI layers most closely related to TCP/IP are Layer 7 (application layer), Layer 4 (transport layer), and Layer 3 (network layer). Included in these layers are various types of protocols with a variety of purposes/functions, all of which are related to the transfer of information. The TCP/IP layers map quite well to the OSI model: TCP (at the transport or host-to-host layer) maps to the OSI transport layer, and the Internet layer maps to the OSI network layer.

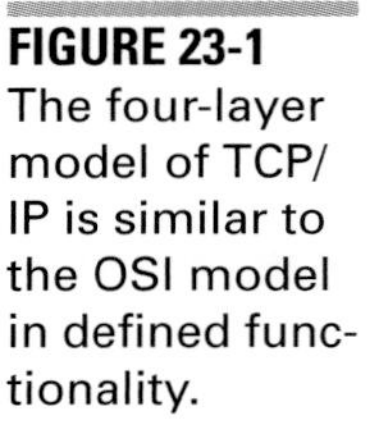

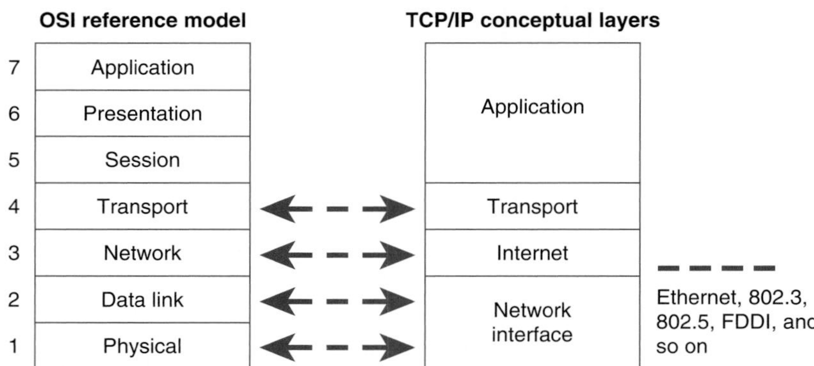

FIGURE 23-1 The four-layer model of TCP/IP is similar to the OSI model in defined functionality.

TCP/IP enables communication among any set of interconnected networks and is equally well suited for both LAN and WAN communication. TCP/IP includes not only Layer 3 and 4 specifications (such as IP and TCP), but also specifications to support such common applications as e-mail, remote login, terminal emulation, and file transfer.

TCP/IP Protocol Stack and the Application Layer

The application layer of the TCP/IP or Internet protocols combines the functionality found in the OSI session and the presentation and application layers. TCP/IP has protocols to support file transfer, e-mail, and remote login, including the following (see Figure 23-2):

- Domain Name System (DNS) is a system used on the Internet for translating names of domains and their publicly advertised network nodes into IP addresses.

  Note: This is considered to be Transport Layer functionality because it provides services to the layer above (application layer) and receives services from the layer below (Internetwork layer).
- Windows Internet Naming Service (WINS) is a Microsoft-developed standard for Microsoft Windows NT that automatically associates NT workstations with Internet domain names.
- HOSTS is a file created by network administrators and maintained on servers. The file is used to provide static mappings between IP addresses and computer names.

- Post Office Protocol (POP3) is an Internet standard for storing e-mail on a mail server until you can access it and download it to your computer. It enables users to receive mail from their inboxes using various levels of security.
- Simple Mail Transfer Protocol (SMTP) governs the transmission of e-mail over computer networks. It does not provide support for transmission of data other than plain text.
- Simple Network Management Protocol (SNMP) is a protocol that provides a means to monitor and control network devices, and to manage configurations, statistics collection, performance, and security.
- File Transfer Protocol (FTP) is a reliable, connection-oriented service that uses TCP to transfer files between systems that support FTP. It supports bidirectional binary file and ASCII file transfers.
- Trivial File Transfer Protocol (TFTP) is a connectionless service that uses UDP. TFTP is used on the router to transfer configuration files and IOS images, and to transfer files between systems that support TFTP. It is useful in some LANs because it operates faster than FTP in a stable environment.
- Hypertext Transfer Protocol (HTTP) is the Internet standard that supports the exchange of information on the World Wide Web as well as on internal networks. It supports many different file types, including text, graphics, sound, and video. It defines the process by which Web browsers originate requests for information to send to Web servers.

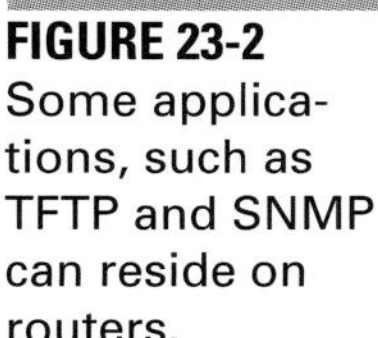

FIGURE 23-2 Some applications, such as TFTP and SNMP can reside on routers.

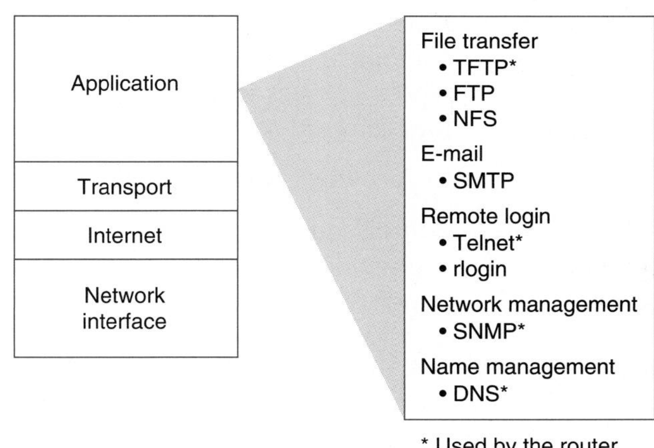

The TCP/IP protocols include many application layer protocols.

The following list provides an overview of some troubleshooting protocols:

- Telnet is a standard terminal emulation protocol used by clients to make remote terminal connections to Telnet server services. It enables users to remotely connect to routers to enter configuration commands.
- Packet Internet Groper (PING) is used to determine whether a computer is reachable. PING uses the ICMP echo request and reply messages.
- The traceroute program is available on many systems and is similar to PING, except that traceroute provides more information than PING. Traceroute traces the path that a packet takes to a destination and is used to debug routing problems.

You also should be familiar with a few Windows-based utilities:

- **NBSTAT**—A utility used to troubleshoot NetBIOS name resolution; used to view and remove entries from the name cache
- **NETSTAT**—A utility that provides information about TCP/IP statistics; can be used to provide information about the status of TCP/IP connections and summaries of ICMP, TCP, and UDP
- **ipconfig/winipcfg**—Utilities used to view current network settings for all network adapters (NICs) on a device; can be used to view the MAC address, IP address, and gateway

TCP/IP Protocol Stack and the Transport Layer

The transport layer enables a user's device to segment data from several upper-layer applications for placement on the same Layer 4 data stream, and enables a receiving device to reassemble the upper-layer application segments. The Layer 4 data stream is a logical connection between the endpoints of a network; it provides transport services from a source host to a destination host. This service is sometimes referred to as an *end-to-end service*.

The transport layer also provides two protocols (see Figure 23-3):

- **TCP**—A connection-oriented, reliable protocol that provides flow control by providing sliding windows and offers reliability by providing sequence numbers and acknowledgments. TCP resends anything that is not acknowledged and supplies a virtual circuit between end-user applications. The advantage of TCP is that it provides guaranteed delivery of segments.
- **UDP**—A connectionless and unreliable protocol that is responsible for transmitting messages but provides no software checking for segment delivery. The advantage that UDP provides is speed. Because UDP provides no acknowledgments, less control traffic is sent across the network, making the transfer faster.

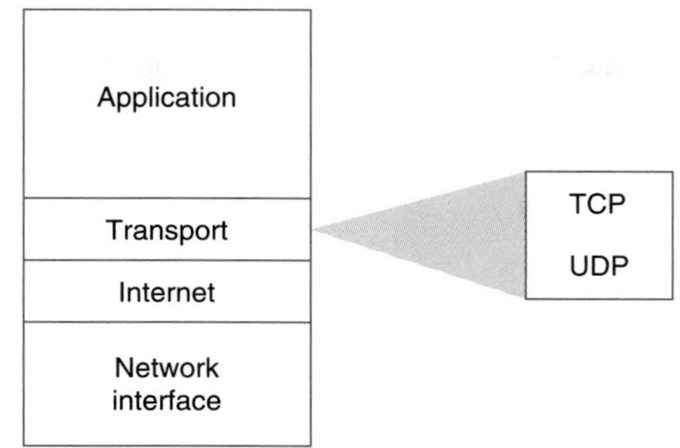

FIGURE 23-3 Application developers can select a connection-oriented (TCP) or connection-less (UDP) transport.

TCP and UDP Segment Format

The TCP segment contains the following fields (see Figure 23-4):

- **Source Port**—The number of the source (port) for this segment.
- **Destination port**—The number of the destination (port) for this segment.
- **Sequence Number**—The number used to ensure correct sequencing of the arriving data. It is the number assigned to the first octet in the user data field.
- **Acknowledgment Number**—The next expected TCP octet.
- **HLEN**—The number of 32-bit words in the header.
- **Reserved**—Set to 0.
- **Code Bits**—The control functions (for example, setup and termination of a session).
- **Window**—The number of octets that the sender is willing to accept.
- **Checksum**—The calculated checksum of the header and data fields.
- **Urgent Pointer**—Indicator of the end of the urgent data.
- **Option**—One currently defined: maximum TCP segment size.
- **Data**—Upper-layer protocol data.

When using UDP, application layer protocols must provide for reliability if it is necessary. UDP uses no windowing or acknowledgments. It is designed for applications that do not need to put sequences of segments together. As you can see in Figure 23-5, a UDP header is relatively small.

FIGURE 23-4
The TCP segment format includes 12 fields.

Number of bits	16	16	32	32	4	6	6
	Source Port	Destination Port	Sequence Number	Acknowledgment Number	HLEN	Reserved	Code Bits

16	16	16	0 or 32	
Window	Checksum	Urgent Pointer	Option	Data

FIGURE 23-5
UDP has no sequence or acknowledgment fields.

Number of bits	16	16	16	16	
	Source Port	Destination Port	Length	Checksum	Data...

Protocols that use UDP include the following:

- TFTP
- SNMP
- Network File System (NFS)
- Domain Name System (DNS)

TCP and UDP Port Numbers

Both TCP and UDP use port numbers to pass information to the upper layers. Port numbers are used to keep track of the different conversations that cross the network at the same time (see Figure 23-6).

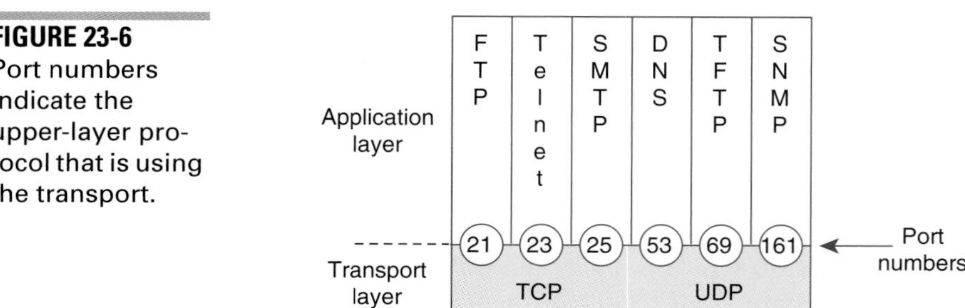

FIGURE 23-6
Port numbers indicate the upper-layer protocol that is using the transport.

Application software developers have agreed to use the well-known port numbers that are defined in RFC 1700. For example, any conversation bound for an FTP application uses the standard port number 21.

Conversations that do not involve an application with a well-known port number are instead assigned port numbers that are randomly selected from within a specific range. These port numbers are used as source and destination addresses in the TCP segment (see Table 23-1).

TABLE 23-1 Reserved TCP and UDP Port Numbers

Decimal	Keyword	Description
0	—	Reserved
1–4	—	Unassigned
5	rje	Remote job entry
7	echo	Echo
9	discard	Discard
11	users	Active users
13	daytime	Daytime
15	netstat	Who is up or netstat
17	quote	Quote of the day
19	chargen	Character generator
20	ftp-data	File Transfer Protocol (data)
21	ftp	File Transfer Protocol
23	telnet	Terminal connection
25	smtp	Simple Mail Transfer Protocol
37	time	Time of day
39	rlp	Resource Location Protocol
42	nameserver	Hostname server
43	nicname	Who is
53	domain	Domain Name Server
67	bootps	Bootstrap protocol server
68	bootpc	Bootstrap protocol client
69	tftp	Trivial File Transfer Protocol

continues

TABLE 23-1 Reserved TCP and UDP Port Numbers (Continued)

Decimal	Keyword	Description
75	—	Any private dial-out service
77	—	Any private RJE service
79	finger	Finger
123	ntp	Network Time Protocol
133–159	—	Unassigned
160–223	—	Reserved
224–241	—	Unassigned
242–255	—	Unassigned

Some ports are reserved in both TCP and UDP, although applications might not be written to support them. Port numbers have the following assigned ranges:

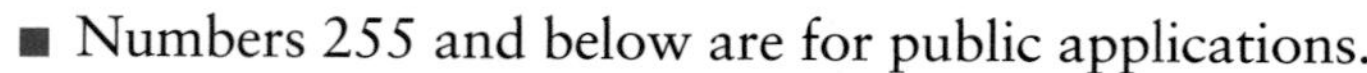

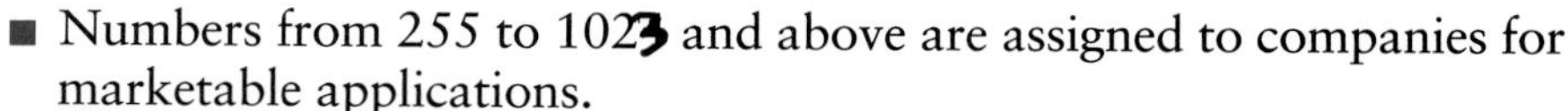

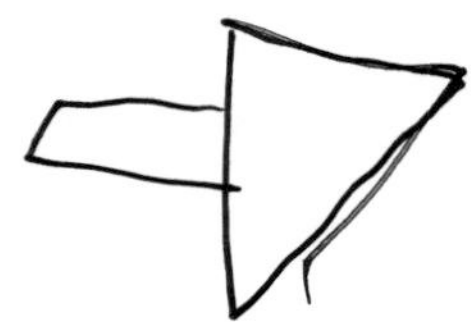

- Numbers 255 and below are for public applications.
- Numbers from 255 to 1023 and above are assigned to companies for marketable applications.
- Numbers 1024 and above are unregulated.

End systems use port numbers to select the proper application. As shown in Figure 23-7, an originating source port number (usually some number larger than 1023) is dynamically assigned by the source host.

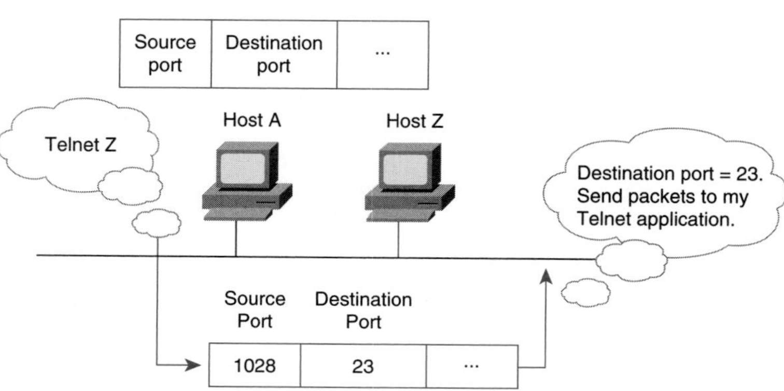

FIGURE 23-7 The source port and destination do not need to be the same.

TCP Three-Way Handshake/Open Connection

For a connection to be established, the two end stations must synchronize on each other's initial TCP sequence numbers (ISNs). Sequence numbers are used to track the order of packets and to ensure that no packets are lost in transmission. The initial sequence number is the starting number used when a TCP connection is established. Exchanging initial sequence numbers during the connection sequence ensures that lost data can be recovered.

Synchronization is accomplished by exchanging packets carrying the ISNs and a control bit called SYN, which stands for *synchronize*. (Packets carrying the SYN bit are also called SYNs.) Successful connection requires a suitable mechanism for choosing an initial sequence and a slightly involved handshake to exchange the ISNs. Synchronization requires that each side send its own ISN and receive a confirmation and ISN from the other side of the connection. Each side must receive the other side's ISN and send a confirming acknowledgment (ACK) in a specific order, outlined in the following steps:

1. A→B SYN—My sequence number is X.
2. A←B ACK—Your sequence number is X – I; expect X + 1 next.
3. A←B SYN—My sequence number is Y.
4. A→B ACK—Your sequence number is Y – I; expect Y + 1 next.

Because the second and third steps are combined in a single message, the exchange is called a three-way handshake/open connection. As illustrated in Figure 23-8, both ends of a connection are synchronized with a three-way handshake/open connection sequence.

FIGURE 23-8 Data cannot be exchanged until the three-way handshake has been successfully completed.

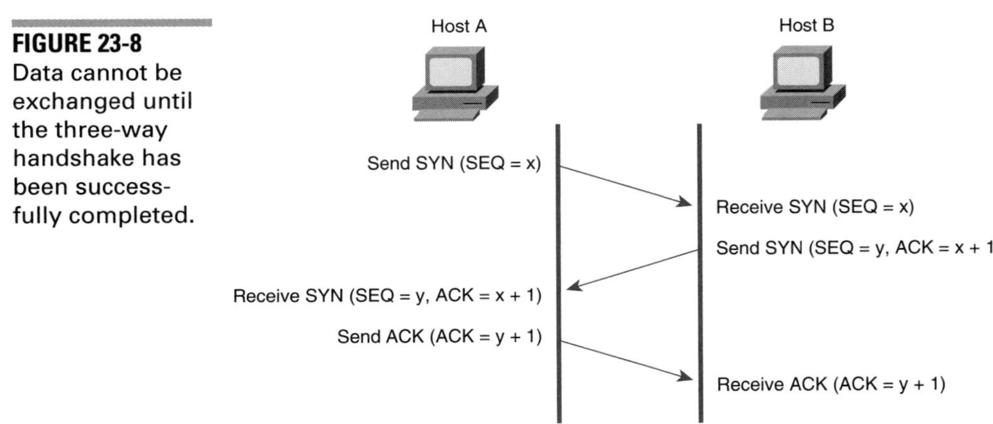

A three-way handshake is necessary because TCPs may use different mechanisms for picking the ISN. The receiver of the first SYN has no way of knowing if the segment was an old delayed one unless it remembers the last sequence number used on the connection. This is not always possible, so it must ask the sender to verify this SYN.

At this point, either side can begin communicating, and either side can break the communication because TCP is a peer-to-peer (balanced) communication method.

TCP Simple Acknowledgment and Windowing

To govern the flow of data between devices, TCP uses a peer-to-peer flow control mechanism. The receiving host's TCP layer reports a window size to the sending host's TCP layer. This window size specifies the number of packets, starting with the acknowledgment number, that the receiving host's TCP layer is currently prepared to receive.

Window size refers to the number of packets that can be transmitted before receiving an acknowledgment. After a host transmits the window size number of packets, it must receive an acknowledgment before any more data can be sent.

The window size determines how many packets the receiving station can accept at one time. With a window size of 1, each packet carries only 1 byte of data and must receive an acknowledgment before another packet is transmitted.

The purpose of windowing is to improve flow control and reliability. Unfortunately, with a window size of 1, you see very inefficient use of bandwidth, as shown in Figure 23-9.

TCP Sliding Window

TCP uses expectational acknowledgments, meaning that the acknowledgment number refers to the packets expected next, which implicitly acknowledges all preceding bytes. The *sliding part of sliding window* refers to the fact that the window size is negotiated dynamically during the TCP session. A sliding window results in more efficient use of bandwidth because a larger window size allows more packets to be transmitted pending acknowledgment (see Figure 23-10).

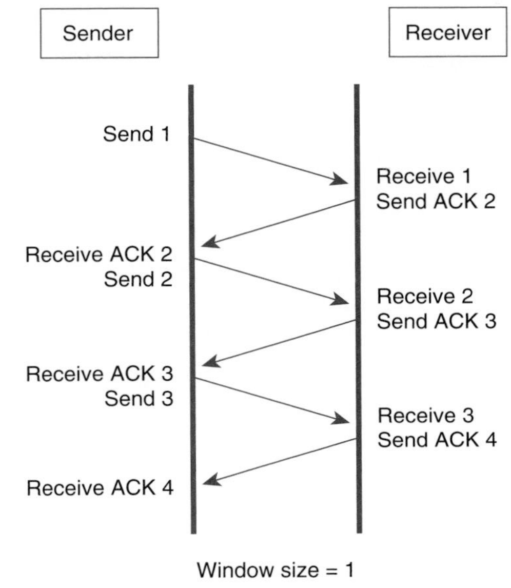

FIGURE 23-9 With a window size of 1, the sender must wait for an acknowledgment before sending more data.

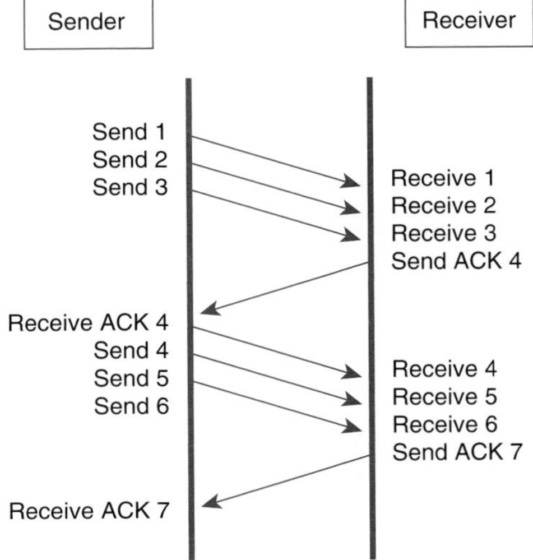

FIGURE 23-10 A larger window increases flow efficiency.

MOVIE 12.1

TCP Sliding Window

Flow control explained.

TCP Sequence and Acknowledgment Numbers

TCP provides sequencing of packets with a forward reference (next expected) acknowledgment. The first packet of each segment is numbered before transmission. At the receiving station, TCP reassembles the packets into a complete message. If a sequence number is missing in the series, that packet will be retransmitted. If packets are not acknowledged within a given time period, retransmission occurs as well.

The sequence and acknowledgment numbers are directional, which means that the communication occurs in both directions. Figure 23-11 illustrates the communication going in one direction. The sequence and acknowledgments take place with the receiver on the right.

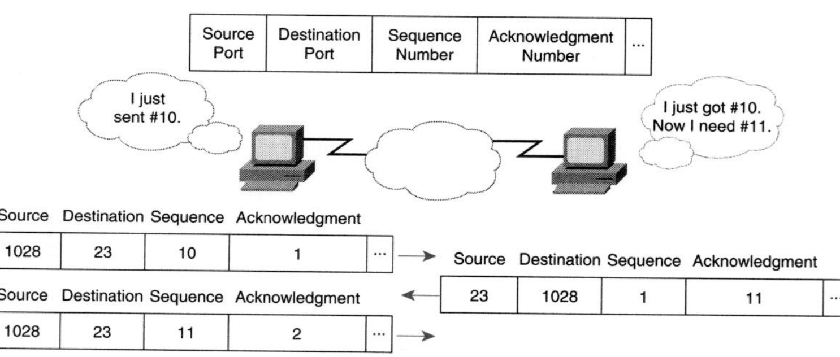

FIGURE 23-11
The receiver asks for the next datagram in the sequence.

TCP/IP and the Internet Layer

The Internet layer of the TCP/IP stack corresponds to the network layer of the OSI model. The network layer is responsible for getting packets through a network using software addressing.

As shown in the Figure 23-12, several protocols operate at the TCP/IP Internet layer, corresponding to the OSI network layer:

- **IP**—Provides connectionless, best-effort delivery routing of datagrams; is not concerned with the content of the datagrams; looks for a way to move the datagrams to their destination
- **ICMP**—Provides control and messaging capabilities
- **ARP**—Determines the data link layer (MAC) addresses for known IP addresses
- **RARP**—Determines network addresses when data link layer addresses are known

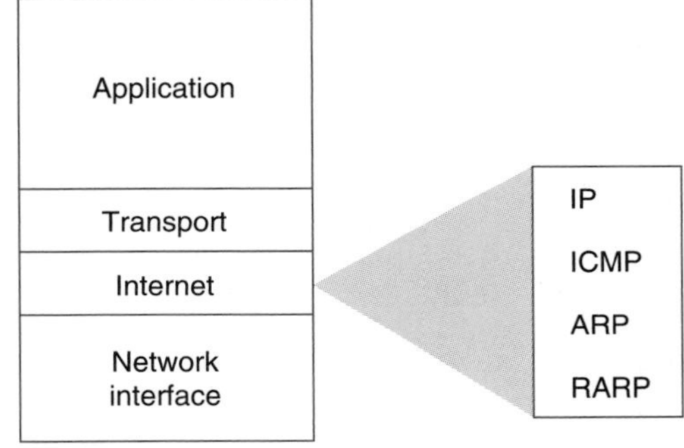

FIGURE 23-12
The OSI network layer corresponds to the TCP/IP Internet layer.

MOVIE 12.2

Reachability

The TCP/IP host sends an ICMP echo request.

IP Datagram

Figure 23-13 illustrates the format of an IP datagram. An IP datagram contains an IP header and data, and is surrounded by the Media Access Control (MAC)–layer header and MAC-layer trailer. One segment may be transmitted as a series of datagrams that are reassembled into the segment at the receiving location. The fields in this IP datagram are as follows:

- **VERS**—Version number
- **HLEN**—Header length, in 32-bit words
- **Type of Service**—How the datagram should be handled
- **Total Length**—Total length (header + data)
- **Identification, Flags, Frag Offset**—Provides fragmentation of datagrams to allow differing MTUs in the internetwork

- **TTL**—Time-To-Live
- **Protocol**—The upper-layer (Layer 4) protocol sending and receiving the datagram
- **Header Checksum**—In integrity check on the header
- **Source IP Address and Destination IP Address**—32-bit IP addresses
- **IP Options**—Network testing, debugging, security, and other options

FIGURE 23-13
The IP header is variable in length because of the IP Options field.

Number of bits	4	4	8	16	16	3	13	8
	VERS	HLEN	Type of Service	Total Length	Identification	Flags	Frag Offset	TTL

Number of bits	8	16	32	32	var	
	Protocol	Header Checksum	Source IP Address	Destination IP Address	IP Options	Data...

The Protocol field determines the Layer 4 protocol being carried within an IP datagram. Although most IP traffic is TCP, other protocols can also use IP. Each IP header must identify the destination Layer 4 protocol for the datagram. Transport layer protocols are numbered, similarly to port numbers. IP includes the protocol number in the Protocol field (see Figure 23-14).

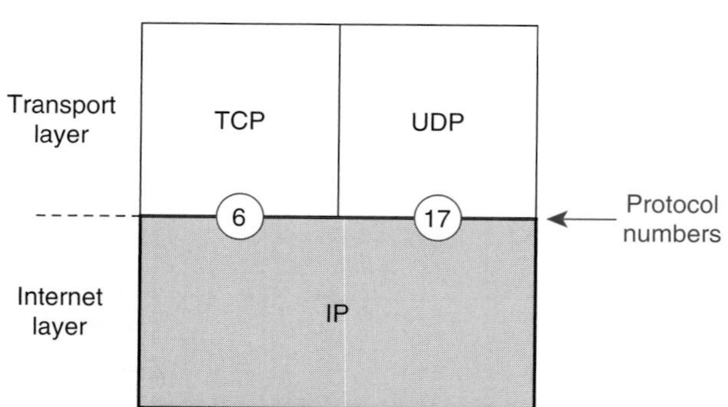

FIGURE 23-14
The Protocol field determines the destination upper-layer protocol.

Internet Control Message Protocol

All TCP/IP hosts implement Internet Control Message Protocol (ICMP). ICMP messages are carried in IP datagrams and are used to send error and control messages. ICMP uses the following types of defined messages (see Figure 23-15):

- Destination unreachable
- Time-To-Live exceeded

- Parameter problem
- Source quench
- Redirect
- Echo request
- Echo reply
- Timestamp request
- Timestamp reply
- Information request
- Information reply
- Address mask request
- Address mask reply

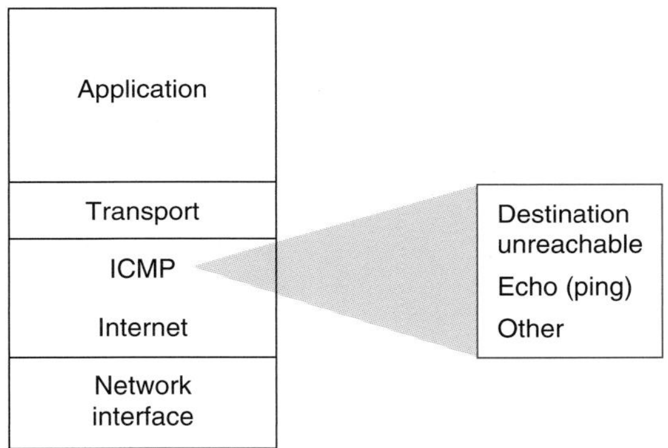

FIGURE 23-15
ICMP provides error and control mechanisms.

MOVIE 12.3

ICMP Time Exceeded Message

Time-To-Live field.

How ICMP Testing Works

If a router receives a packet that it is incapable of delivering to its final destination, the router sends an ICMP unreachable message to the source, as shown in Figure 23-16 and Figure 23-17. The message might be undeliverable because there is no known route to the destination. In Figure 23-17, an echo reply is a successful reply to a **ping** command. However, results could include other ICMP messages, such as destination unreachable and timeout messages.

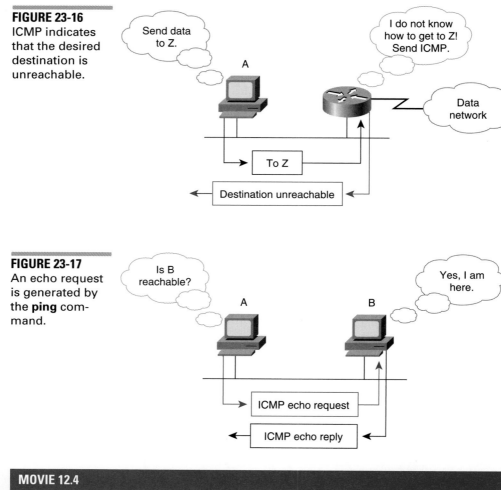

FIGURE 23-16 ICMP indicates that the desired destination is unreachable.

FIGURE 23-17 An echo request is generated by the **ping** command.

MOVIE 12.4

Router Can't Deliver

ICMP destination unreachable message.

How ARP Works

ARP is used to resolve or map a known IP address to a MAC sublayer address. This allows for communication because the data link hardware will not accept a frame unless the MAC address in the frame matches the hardware MAC address (or it is a broadcast MAC address). To determine a destination MAC

is checked. If the address is not in the table, ARP sends a broadcast that is received by every station on the network, looking for the destination station.

The term *local ARP* is used to describe the search for an address when the requesting host and the destination host share the same medium or wire. As shown in Figure 23-18, before issuing the ARP, the subnet mask must be consulted. In this case, the mask determines that the nodes are on the same subnet.

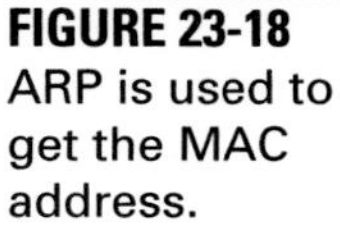

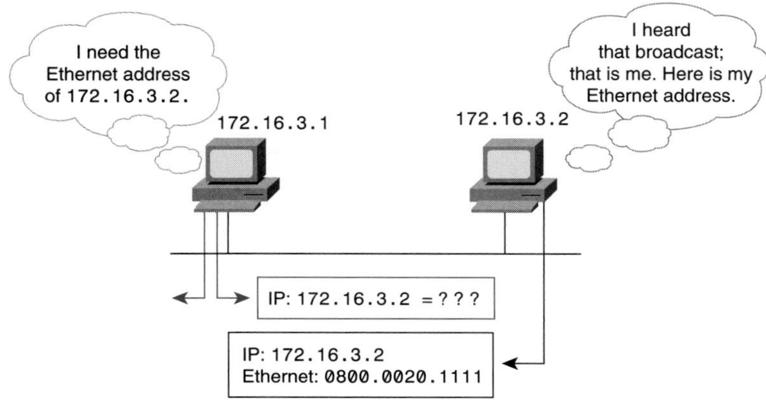

FIGURE 23-18
ARP is used to get the MAC address.

MOVIE 12.5

Broadcast Transmission

Source node to network transmission.

e-LAB ACTIVITY 23.1

ARP Challenge

In this activity, you demonstrate how to identify the MAC addresses of each Ethernet interface.

SKILL BUILDERS

Lab Activity: show ARP and clear ARP

In this lab, you view the ARP table stored in the router and clear the router's ARP table. These two commands are very important in troubleshooting a network problem.

Lab Activity: ARP Challenge

You and your group have been assigned to help a system administrator of a network for XYZ Company. The system administrator of this network would like to know the MAC addresses of each of the Ethernet interfaces on the routers.

Summary

In this chapter, you learned that

- The TCP/IP protocol stack maps closely to the lower layers of the OSI reference model and has the following components:
  - Protocols to support file transfer, e-mail, remote login, and other applications
  - Reliable and unreliable transports
  - Connectionless datagram delivery at the network layer
- Application protocols exist for file transfer, e-mail, and remote login. Network management is also supported at the application layer.
- The transport layer performs two functions:
  - Flow control, which is provided by sliding windows
  - Reliability, which is provided by sequence numbers and acknowledgments
- The TCP/IP Internet layer corresponds to the OSI network layer.
- ICMP provides control and message functions at the network layer. ICMP is implemented by all TCP/IP hosts.
- ARP is used to resolve or map a known IP address to a MAC sublayer address to allow communication on a multiaccess medium, such as Ethernet.

Check Your Understanding

1. Which of the following best describes TCP/IP?

   A. It is a suite of protocols that can be used to communicate across any set of interconnected networks.

   B. It is a suite of protocols that allows LANs to connect into WANs.

   C. It is a suite of protocols that allows for data transmission across a multitude of networks.

   D. It is a suite of protocols that allows different devices to be shared by interconnected networks.

2. Which of the following does not describe the TCP/IP protocol stack?

   A. It maps closely to the OSI reference model's upper layers.

   B. It supports all standard physical and data link protocols.

   C. It transfers information in a sequence of datagrams.

   D. It reassembles datagrams into complete messages at the receiving location.

3. The TCP/IP protocol suite has specifications for which layer(s) of the OSI model?

   A. 1 through 3

   B. 1 through 4 and 7

   C. 3, 4, and 5 through 7

   D. 1, 3, and 4

4. Which of the following is not a function of the network layer?

   A. RARP determines network addresses when data link layer addresses are known.

   B. ICMP provides control and messaging capabilities.

   C. ARP determines the data link layer address for known IP addresses.

   D. UDP provides connectionless exchanges of datagrams without acknowledgments.

5. Which of the following is one of the protocols found at the transport layer?

   A. UCP

   B. UDP

   C. TDP

   D. TDC

6. What is the purpose of port numbers?

   A. They keep track of different conversations crossing the network at the same time.

   B. Source systems use them to keep a session organized and to select the proper application.

   C. End systems use them to dynamically assign end users to a particular session, depending on their application use.

   D. Source systems generate them to predict destination addresses.

7. Which of the following best describes UDP?

   A. A protocol that acknowledges flawed or intact datagrams

   B. A protocol that detects errors and requests retransmissions from the source

   C. A protocol that processes datagrams and requests retransmissions when necessary

   D. A protocol that exchanges datagrams without acknowledgments or guaranteed delivery

8. Which of the following TCP/IP layers includes file transfer, e-mail, remote login, and network management?

   A. Transport

   B. Application

   C. Internet

   D. Network

9. Why are TCP three-way handshake/open connections used?

   A. To ensure that lost data can be recovered if problems occur later

   B. To determine how much data the receiving station can accept at one time

C. To provide efficient use of bandwidth by users

D. To change binary **ping** responses into information in the upper layers

10. What does a TCP sliding window do?

A. It makes the window larger so that more data can come through at once, which results in more efficient use of bandwidth.

B. The window size slides to each section of the datagram to receive data, which results in more efficient use of bandwidth.

C. It allows the window size to be negotiated dynamically during the TCP session, which results in more efficient use of bandwidth.

D. It limits the incoming data so that each segment must be sent one by one, which is an inefficient use of bandwidth.

11. UDP segments use what protocols to provide reliability?

A. Network layer protocols

B. Application layer protocols

C. Internet protocols

D. Transmission Control Protocols

12. What is the purpose of ICMP testing?

A. To determine whether messages reach their destination and, if they don't, to determine possible reasons why they did not

B. To make sure that all activity on the network is being monitored

C. To determine whether the network was set up according to the model

D. To determine whether the network is in control mode or user mode

13. Assuming that the MAC is not in the ARP table, how does a sender find out the destination's MAC address?

A. It sends a message to all the addresses, searching for the address.

B. It sends out a broadcast message to the entire LAN.

C. It sends out a broadcast message to the entire network.

D. All of the above

14. Which of the following best describes window size?
   - **A.** The maximum size of the window that software can have and still process data rapidly
   - **B.** The number of messages or bytes that can be transmitted while awaiting an acknowledgment
   - **C.** The size of the window, in picas, that must be set ahead of time so that data can be sent
   - **D.** The size of the window opening on a monitor, which is not always equal to the monitor size
15. If I am Host A in the process of setting up a three-way handshake with Host B, and I send a segment with sequence number n to Host B, what will B send back to me as an acknowledgment?
   - **A.** n
   - **B.** $n1$
   - **C.** $n + n$
   - **D.** $n + 1$
16. If the source is using a window size of 512 bytes to send data and it does not get a response back from the destination, what will the source do?
   - **A.** Stop sending data
   - **B.** Query the destination to see if the line is still up
   - **C.** Resend the data
   - **D.** Confirm the window size with the destination
17. What does the following describe: Provides sequencing of segments with a forward reference acknowledgment, numbers the first bytes of each segment before transmission, and reassembles the segments into a complete message.
   - **A.** Header checksums and data protocol checksums
   - **B.** TCP sequence and acknowledgment numbers
   - **C.** Expectational acknowledgments
   - **D.** Simple UDP acknowledgment

18. What is the purpose of the Protocol field in an IP datagram?

A. It numbers the Layer 3 protocol and makes it similar to a port number.

B. It determines the Layer 4 protocol being carried within an IP datagram.

C. It changes other protocols so that they can be used by IP.

D. It allows dynamic generation of source protocols.

19. What is the purpose of ICMP messages?

A. They put the internetwork in control mode so that protocols can be set up.

B. They are messages that the network uses to monitor connection protocols.

C. They are standard binary messages that act as model internetwork protocols.

D. They are messages carried in IP datagrams and are used to send error and control messages.

20. What is the function of ARP?

A. It completes research for a Layer 3 destination address.

B. It is used to develop a cached Layer 4 address resource table.

C. It is used to map an IP address to a MAC address.

D. It sends a broadcast message looking for the router IP address.

Objectives

After reading this chapter, you will be able to

- Describe IP addressing and subnetting
- Describe IP address configuration
- Verify address configuration
- Assign new subnet numbers to the topology

IP Addressing

Introduction

In Chapter 23, "TCP/IP," you learned about the Transmission Control Protocol/ Internet Protocol (TCP/IP) and its operation to ensure communication across any set of interconnected networks. In this chapter, you review the details of IP address classes, network and node addresses, and subnet masking. In addition, you learn the concepts that you need to understand before configuring an IP address on a router. Lastly, you learn how to configure IP addresses.

IP Addressing and Subnetting

In a TCP/IP environment, end stations communicate with servers or other end stations. This can occur because each node using the TCP/IP protocol suite has a unique 32-bit logical address. This address is known as the *IP address* and is specified in 32-bit dotted-decimal format. Each router interface must be configured with an IP address if IP is to be routed to or from the interface. **ping** and **trace** commands can be used to verify IP address configuration.

Each company or organization listed on the Internet is viewed as a single unique network that must be reached before an individual host within that company can be contacted. Each company network has a network address; the hosts on the network share the same network address, but each host is identified by a unique host address on the network (see Figure 24-1).

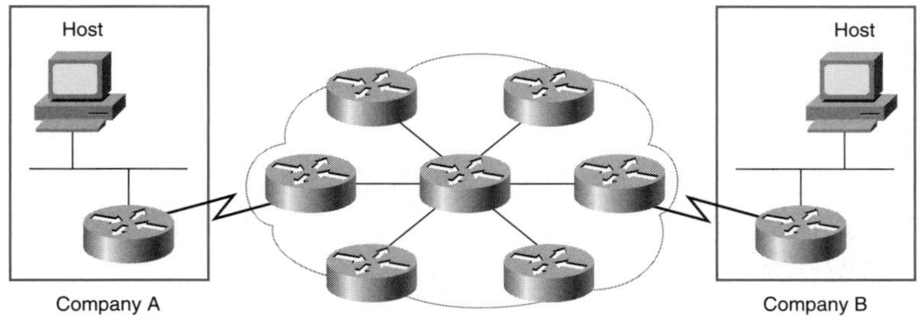

FIGURE 24-1 The network portion of the (unique) 32-bit logical address must be reached before an individual host within a company can be contacted.

The Role of the Host Network on a Routed Network

In this section, you learn the basic concepts that you need to understand before configuring an IP address. By examining various network requirements, you can select the correct class of address and define how to establish IP subnets. Each device or interface must have an IP address that does not have all 0s in the host field. A host address of all 1s is reserved for an IP broadcast into the network, as shown in Figure 24-2. A host value of 0 means "this network" or "the wire itself" (as in 172.16.0.0). The routing table (shown in Table 24-1) contains entries for network or wire addresses; it usually contains no information about hosts.

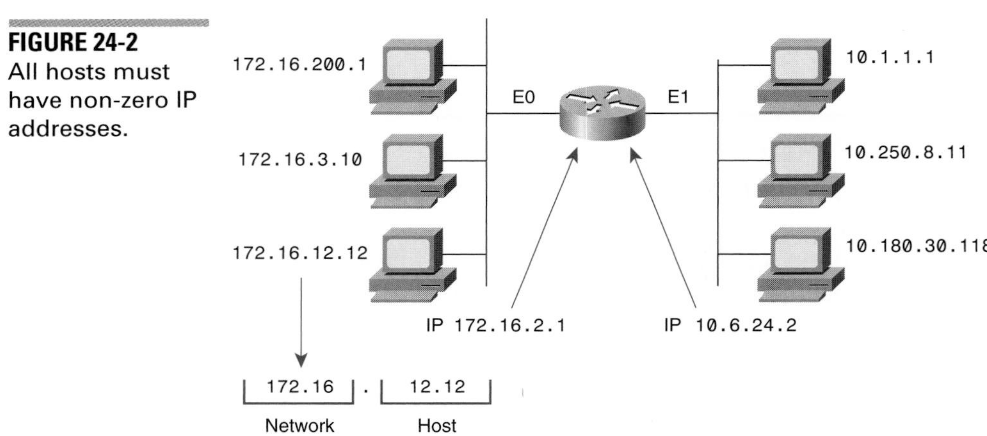

FIGURE 24-2
All hosts must have non-zero IP addresses.

TABLE 24-1 A Routing Table that Contains Entries for Network Addresses

Network	Interface
172.16.0.0	E0
10.0.0.0	E1

An IP address and a subnet mask in an IP network host address achieve three purposes:

- They enable the host to process the receipt and transmission of packets.
- They specify the host's local IP address.
- They specify a range of IP addresses that share the cable with the host.

The Role of Broadcast Addresses on a Routed Network

Broadcasting is supported by IP. Broadcast messages are intended to be seen by every host on a network. The broadcast address is formed by using all 1s within a portion or all of the IP address.

Cisco IOS software supports two kinds of broadcasts: directed broadcasts and flooded broadcasts. Broadcasts directed into a specific network/subnet are allowed and are forwarded by the router if it is configured to transmit such broadcasts. These directed broadcasts contain all 1s only in the host portion of the address. Flooded broadcasts (255.255.255.255) are not propagated, but are considered local broadcasts, as illustrated in Figure 24-3.

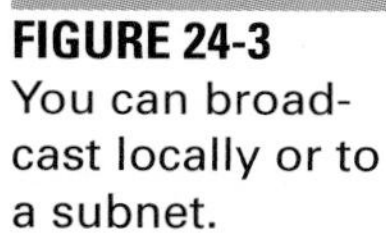

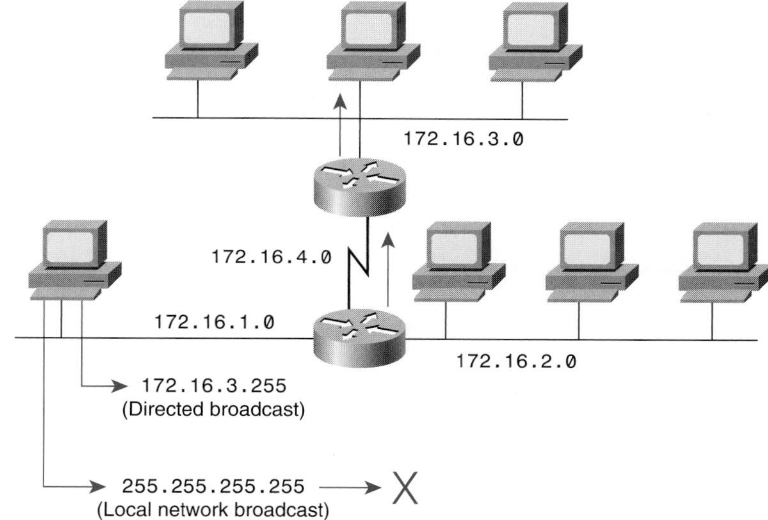

FIGURE 24-3
You can broadcast locally or to a subnet.

The Assignment of Router Interface and Network IP Addresses

Figure 24-4 and Table 24-2 show a small network with assigned interface addresses, subnet masks, and resulting subnet numbers. The number of routing bits (network and subnet bits) in each subnet mask is indicated by the "/24" (Classless Inter-Domain [CIDR] notation) following the mask.

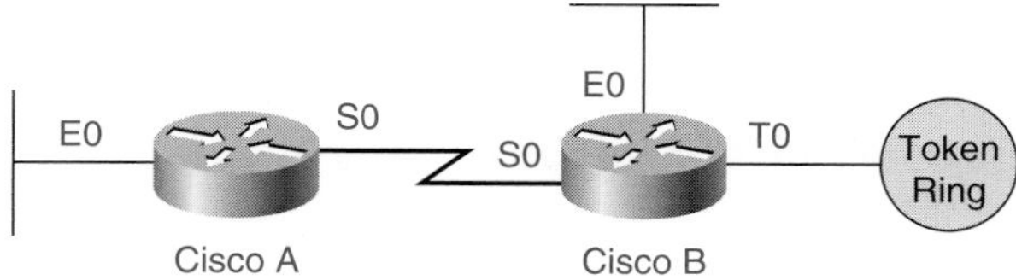

FIGURE 24-4
Interface addresses, subnet masks, and the resulting subnet numbers are assigned to a network.

TABLE 24-2 Network Assignment

Interface Address	Subnet Mask	Subnet Number
Cisco A		
E0: 172.16.2.1	255.255.255.0/24	172.16.2.0
S0: 172.16.1.1	255.255.255.0/24	172.16.1.0
Cisco B		
S0: 172.16.1.2	255.255.255.0/24	172.16.1.0
E0: 172.31.4.1	255.255.255.0/24	172.31.4.0
T0: 172.31.16.1	255.255.255.0/24	172.31.16.0

SKILL BUILDER

Lab Activity: IP Addressing and Subnets Challenge

In this lab, you work with other group members to design a five-router network topology and an IP addressing scheme.

IP Address Configuration

Use the **ip address** command to establish the logical IP address of an interface:

```
Router(config-if)# ip address ip-address subnet-mask
```

Here, ip-address is a 32-bit dotted-decimal number and subnet-mask is a 32-bit dotted-decimal number; 1s indicate positions that must match, and 0s indicate positions that do not match. The **ip address** command assigns an address and a subnet mask and starts IP processing on an interface.

Use the **term ip** *netmask-format* command as follows to specify the format of network masks on all interfaces for the current session:

```
Router(config)# term ip netmask-format
```

This command sets the format of the network mask (see Table 24-3). Format options for the network mask are as follows:

- Bit count
- Dotted decimal (the default)
- Hexadecimal

TABLE 24-3 IP Address Commands

Command Level	Command	Purpose
Router(config-if)	**ip address** *ip-address subnet mask*	Assigns an address and subnet to an interface; starts IP processing.
Router#	**term ip** *netmask-format* {bit-count/decimal/hexadecimal}	Sets format of network mask for current session.
Router(confi-if)#	**ip** *netmask-format* {bit-count/decimal/hexadecimal}	Sets format of network mask for a specific line.

S-LAB ACTIVITY 24.1

Assigning an IP Address to a Router Interface

In this activity, you demonstrate how to assign an IP address with the subnet mask to an interface.

The ip host Command

The Cisco IOS software maintains a table of hostnames and their corresponding IP addresses. Telnet uses hostnames to identify network devices (hosts). The router and other network devices must be capable of associating hostnames with IP addresses to communicate with other IP devices by name.

The **ip host** command makes a static name-to-address entry in the router's configuration file (see Table 24-4).

TABLE 24-4 The ip host Command

ip host Command	Description
name	Any name you prefer to describe the destination.
tcp-port-number	An optional number that identfies the TCP port to use when using the host name with an EXEC connect or Telnet command. The default is port 23 for Telnet.
address	An IP address (or addresses) where the device can be reached.

The following command defines a static hostname-to-IP address mapping:

```
Router(config)# ip host name [tcp-port-number] address [address]...
ip host tokyo 1.0.0.5 2.0.0.8
ip host kyoto 1.0.0.4
```

1.0.0.5 2.0.0.8 defines two network addresses for the host tokyo, and 1.0.0.4 defines kyoto as a name equivalent for the address 1.0.0.4.

e-LAB ACTIVITY 24.2

Creating an IP Host Table Entry

In this activity, you demonstrate how to set up a static name-to-address entry on a router.

The ip name-server Command

The **ip name-server** command defines which hosts can provide the name service. You can specify a maximum of six IP addresses as name servers in a single command:

```
Router(config)# ip name-server server-address1 [[server-address2]
  ...server-address6]
```

To map domain names to IP addresses, you must identify the host names, specify a name server, and enable DNS. Any time the operating system software receives a hostname that it does not recognize, it refers to DNS for the IP address of that host.

e-LAB ACTIVITY 24.3

Setting up an IP-Name Server

In this activity, you demonstrate how to set up a router to recognize a new name server.

How to Enable and Disable DNS on a Router

Each unique IP address can have a host name associated with it. The Cisco IOS software maintains a cache of hostname-to-IP address mappings for use by EXEC commands. This cache speeds the process of converting names to addresses.

IP defines a naming scheme that allows a device to be identified by its location. A name such as ftp.cisco.com identifies the domain of the File Transfer Protocol (FTP) for Cisco. To keep track of domain names, IP identifies a name server that manages the name cache. Domain Name Service (DNS) is enabled by default with a server address of 255.255.255.255, which is a local broadcast.

The **router(config)# no ip domain-lookup** command turns off name-to-address translation in the router. This means that the router will not generate or forward name system broadcast packets.

This command is strongly recommended if hostname resolution is not required, especially in a lab setting; otherwise, when you mistype something on the command line, the router takes considerable time trying to discover the identity of a host that doesn't exist.

e-LAB ACTIVITY 24.4

Using no ip domain-lookup

In this activity, you demonstrate how to turn off **ip domain-lookup**.

Displaying Hostnames

The show hosts command, which is shown in Listing 24-1, is used to display a cached list of hostnames and addresses.

Listing 24-1 The show hosts Command (Continued)

```
Router# show hosts
Default domain is not set
Name/address lookup uses static mappings
Host       Flags        Age     Type     Address(es)
TOKYO      (perm, OK)   5       IP       144.253.100.200 133.3.13.2
                                         133.3.5.1   133.3.10.1
S          (perm, OK)   **      IP       172.16.100.156
LUBROCK    (perm, OK)   5       IP       183.8.128.12  153.50.3.2
AMARILLO   (perm, OK)   **      IP       153.50.129.200  153.50.3.1
BELLEVUE   (perm, OK)   **      IP       144.253.100.201  153.50.193.2
153.50.33.1
BOSTON     (perm, OK)   **      IP       144.253.100.203  192.3.63.129
192.3.63.65
CHICAGO    (perm, OK)   5       IP       183.8.0.129  183.8.128.130
                                         183.8.64.130
Router     (perm, OK)   **      IP       144.253.100.202  183.8.128.2
183.8.64.129
FARGO      (perm, OK)   **      IP       183.8.0.130  183.8.64.100
HARTFORD   (perm, OK)   **      IP       192.3.63.196  192.3.63.34
                                         192.3.63.66
HOUSTON    (perm, OK)   **      IP       153.50.129.1  153.50.65.2
 --More--
```

Table 24-5 shows the fields and description from the **show hosts** command, which you can use to obtain specific information about a hostname entry.

TABLE 24-5 show hosts Command Output

show hosts Fields	Description
Host	Names of learned hosts.
Flag	Descriptions of how information was learned and its current status.
perm	Manually configured in a static host table.
temp	Acquired from DNS use.
OK	Entry is current.
EX	Entry has aged out or expired.
Age	Time, measured in hours, since software referred to the entry.
Type	Protocol field.
Address(es)	Logical addresses associated with the name of the host.

e-LAB ACTIVITY 24.5

Discovering Hostnames

In this activity, you demonstrate how to determine whether or not any hostnames are linked to IP addresses.

Verifying Address Configuration

Addressing problems are the most common problems that occur on IP networks. It is important to verify your address configuration before continuing with further configuration steps.

Three commands enable you to verify address configuration in your internetwork:

- **telnet**—Verifies the application layer software between source and destination stations. This command is the most complete testing mechanism available.
- **ping**—Uses the ICMP protocol to verify the hardware connection and the logical address at the Internet layer. This command is a very basic testing mechanism and is the most common means of testing IP connectivity.
- **trace**—Uses TTL values to generate messages from each router used along the path. This command is very powerful in its capability to locate failures in the path from the source to the destination.

The telnet and ping Commands

The **telnet** command is a simple command that you use to see whether you can connect to the router. If you cannot Telnet to the router but you can **ping** the router, you know the problem lies in the upper-layer functionality at the router.

The **ping** command sends ICMP echo packets and is supported in both user and privileged EXEC modes. In the following example, one **ping** timed out, as reported by the dot (.), and four were successfully received, as shown by the exclamation points (!):

```
Router> ping 172.16.101.1
Type escape sequence to abort.
Sending 5 100-byte ICMP echoes to 172.16.10.1. timeout is 2 seconds:
.!!!!
Success rate is 80 percent, round-trip min/avg/max = 6/6/6 ms
Router>
```

The responses in Table 24-6 might be returned by the **ping** test.

TABLE 24-6 The ping Command for Testing IP Network Connectivity

Character	Definition
!	Successful receipt of an echo reply
.	Timed out waiting for datagram reply
U	Destination unreachable error
C	Congestion-experienced packet
I	ping interrupted (for example, Ctrl-Shift-6 X)
?	Packet type unknown
&	Packet TTL exceeded

The extended **ping** command is supported only from privileged EXEC mode. As shown in Listing 17-2, you can use the extended command mode of the **ping** command to specify the supported Internet header options. To enter the extended mode, enter **ping <return>** and then **Y** at the extended commands prompt. These options are valuable for advanced troubleshooting.

Listing 24-2 The Extended ping Command, Which Is Supported Only from Privileged EXEC Mode

```
Router# ping
Protocol [ip]:
Target IP address: 192.168.101.162
Repeat count [5]:
Datagram size [100]:
Timeout in seconds [2]:
Extended commands [n]: y
Source address:
Type of service [0]:
Set DF bit in IP header? [no]: yes
Data pattern [0xABCD]:
Loose, Strict, Record, Timestamp, Verbose [non]:
Sweep range of sizes [n]:
Type escape sequence to abort.
Sending 5 100-byte ICMP echoes to 192.168.101.162. timeout is 2 seconds:
!!!!!
Success rate is 100 percent (5/5), roundrobin min/avg/max = 24/26/28 ms
Router#
```

e-LAB ACTIVITY 24.6

Using the telnet Command

In this activity, you demonstrate how to **telnet** to the Serial 0 interface of a remote router.

The trace Command

When you use the **trace** command, as shown in Listing 24-3 (output), hostnames are shown if the addresses are translated dynamically or via static host table entries. The times listed represent the time required for each of three probes to return.

Listing 24-3 The trace Command

```
Router# trace aba.nyc.mil
Type escape sequence to abort.
Tracing the route to aba.nyc.mil (26.0.0.73)

debris.cisco.com (172.16.1.6) 1000 msec 8 msec 4 msec
barmet-gw.cisco.com (172.16.16.2) 8 msec 4 msec 4 msec
external-a-gateway.stanford.edu (192.42.110.225) 8 msec 4 msec 4 msec
bb2.su.barmet.net (131.119.254.6) 8 msec 8 msec 8 msec
```

```
su.arc.barmet.net (131.119.3.8) 12 msec 12 msec 8 msec
moffett-fld-mb.in.mil (192.52.195.1) 216 msec 120 msec 132 msec
aba.nyc.mil (26.0.0.73) 412 msec * 664 msec
```

NOTE

trace is supported by IP, CLNS, VINES, and AppleTalk.

When the **trace** command reaches the target destination, an asterisk (*) is reported at the display. In other cases, the asterisk indicates a timeout in response to one of the probe packets. Other responses include those shown in Table 24-7.

TABLE 24-7 trace Command Responses

Response	Definition
!H	The probe was received by the router but not forwarded, which is usually due to an access list.
P	The protocol was unreachable.
N	The network was unreachable.
U	The port was unreachable.
*	Timed out.

- Timed out.

E-LAB ACTIVITY 24.7: USING THE TRACE COMMAND

In this activity, you demonstrate how to trace to a workstation.

SKILL BUILDER

Lab Activity: Semester 2 Topology Challenge

You and your group members have just received your Cisco certification. Your first job is to work with other group members in designing a topology and IP addressing scheme. It will be a five-router topology similar to the standard five-router lab diagram as shown, but with a few changes. Refer to the modified five-router lab diagram shown in the worksheet. You must come up with a proper IP addressing scheme using multiple Class C addresses that are different from those of the standard lab setup. You then use ConfigMaker to do your own diagram of the network.

Summary

In this chapter, you learned that

- In a TCP/IP environment, end stations communicate with servers or other end stations. This occurs because each node using the TCP/IP protocol suite has a unique 32-bit logical address known as the IP address.
- An IP address with a subnet mask on an interface achieves three purposes:
  - It enables the system to process the receipt and transmission of packets.
  - It specifies the device's local address.
  - It specifies a range of addresses that share the cable with the device.
- Broadcast messages are messages that you want every host on the network to see.
- You use the **ip address** command to establish the logical network address of this interface.
- The **ip host** command makes a static name-to-address entry in the router's configuration file.
- The **ip name-server** command defines which hosts can provide the name service.
- The **show hosts** command is used to display a cached list of host names and addresses.
- **telnet, ping,** and **trace** commands can be used to verify IP address configuration.

Check Your Understanding

1. If a router receives a packet with destination address 192.16.1.2, assuming a subnet mask of 255.255.255.0, what is the subnet address for the actual subnet where that host is located? That is, what would a router look for in its routing table to forward a packet to host 192.16.1.2?

   A. 192.16.1.0

   B. 192.31.4.0

   C. 192.31.16.0

   D. 192.31.12.0

2. If a router has a serial interface S0, with IP address 172.16.1.2 and using a subnet mask of 255.255.255.0, what is the subnet address? (What will be put in the routing table for S0?)

   A. 172.31.4.0

   B. 172.31.16.0

   C. 172.31.12.0

   D. 172.16.1.0

3. If you want to associate a name with an IP address, such as asu 129.219.2.1, what command structure would you use?

   A. **ip host asu 129.219.2.1**

   B. **ip name asu 129.219.2.1**

   C. **ip host name asu 129.219.2.1**

   D. **ip host address asu 129.219.2.1**

4. Which of the commands enable you to verify address configuration in your internetwork?

   A. **ping**

   B. **telnet**

   C. **trace**

   D. All of the above

5. What is the purpose of **tcp-port-number** in the **ip host** commands?
   - **A.** It identifies which IP address to use when using the hostname with an EXEC connect or Telnet command.
   - **B.** It sets the default port of any device to port 23.
   - **C.** It sets the port of the source device in the router table.
   - **D.** It identifies which TCP port to use when using the hostname with an EXEC connect or Telnet command.
6. If you typed **show host** at the router prompt, what would an entry of **temp** in the resulting table mean?
   - **A.** It shows that the entry has expired.
   - **B.** It identifies the entries that were manually configured in a static host table.
   - **C.** It lets the user know that the entry was acquired from DNS use.
   - **D.** It alerts the administrator that the entry is not current.
7. Which is true of an IP address for a device or interface?
   - **A.** It has a network number and then all 0s.
   - **B.** It has a network number and then all 1s.
   - **C.** It has a nonzero network number with 0 in the host field.
   - **D.** It has a nonzero host number.
8. Which of the following best describes the function of a broadcast address?
   - **A.** It sends a message to a single network destination.
   - **B.** It copies messages and sends them to a specific subset of network addresses.
   - **C.** It sends a message to all nodes on a network.
   - **D.** It sends a message to every node to which the router has access.
9. What is the purpose of using the **trace** command?
   - **A.** It is the most complete test mechanism available.
   - **B.** It is a very basic testing mechanism.
   - **C.** It adds the IP address and the DNS to the router table.
   - **D.** It locates failures in the path from the source to the destination.

10. What is the purpose of the **ip name-server** command?

A. It defines which hosts can provide the name service.

B. It defines a naming scheme that allows a device to be identified by its location.

C. It identifies which TCP port to use when using the hostname.

D. It generates messages from each router used along a datagram's path.

11. If you want to map a domain name to an IP address, what is the first thing you must do?

A. Identify the hostnames

B. Specify a name server

C. Enable the DNS

D. Refer to the DNS for the IP address of that device

12. What is the purpose of the **no ip domain-lookup** command?

A. It defines which hosts can provide the name service.

B. It defines a naming scheme that allows a device to be identified by its location.

C. It turns on name-to-address translation in the router.

D. It turns off name-to-address translation in the router.

13. Which of the following best describes the function of the **show hosts** command?

A. It identifies the subnet mask being used at the destination site.

B. It maintains a cache of host name-to-IP address mappings for use by EXEC commands.

C. It is used to display a cached list of hostnames and addresses.

D. It shows the host name for the IP address.

14. What is the function of the **telnet** command?

A. It verifies the application layer software between source and destination stations.

B. It verifies the hardware connection and the logical address of the network layer.

C. It generates messages from each router used along the path.

D. It shows how many hours have passed since the software referred to the entry.

15. What is the function of the **ping** command?

A. It verifies the application layer software between source and destination stations.

B. It uses ICMP to verify the hardware connection and the logical address of the network layer.

C. It assigns values to generate messages from each router used along the path.

D. It gives descriptions of how information was sent and its current status.

16. Which command would you use to set up static name-to-address entries in the router's configuration file?

A. **ip perm**

B. **ip route**

C. **ip name**

D. **ip host**

17. Which of the following best describes the function of the extended command mode of the **ping** command?

A. It is used to specify the supported Internet header options.

B. It is used to specify the time frame for the **ping** return.

C. It is used to diagnose why a **ping** was delayed or not returned.

D. It is used to trace the datagram as it passes through each router.

18. What does it mean when you use the **ping** command and get a result of **!**?

A. Successful receipt of an echo reply

B. A timeout waiting for an echo reply

C. A destination unreachable message received

D. A congestion-experienced message received

19. How do you enter the extended mode of the **ping** command?

A. ping x

B. ping e

C. ping [return key]

D. eping

20. What does the response * mean when it comes in response to the **trace** command?

A. The destination device refused the trace.

B. The system timed out waiting for the trace reply.

C. The network refused the trace.

D. The source used a trace that was not supported by the network protocol.

Objectives

After reading this chapter, you will be able to

- Understand routing basics
- Describe why routing protocols are necessary
- Describe distance-vector routing
- Describe link-state routing
- Understand how to use different routing protocols in context

Chapter 25

Routing

Introduction

In Chapter 24, "IP Addressing," you learned the process of configuring Internet Protocol (IP) addresses. In this chapter, you learn more about the router's use and operations in performing the key internetworking function of the Open System Interconnection (OSI) reference model's network layer, Layer 3. In addition, you review the difference between routing and routed protocols and how routers track distance between locations. Finally, you learn more about distance-vector, link-state, and hybrid routing approaches and how each resolves common routing problems.

Routing Basics

Path determination for traffic going through a network cloud occurs at the network layer (Layer 3). The path determination function enables a router to evaluate the available paths to a destination and to establish the preferred handling of a packet. Routing services use network topology information when evaluating network paths. This information can be configured by the network administrator or can be collected through dynamic processes running in the network.

The network layer provides best-effort end-to-end packet delivery across interconnected networks. The network layer uses the IP routing table to send packets from the source network to the destination network. After the router determines which path to use, it proceeds with forwarding the packet. It takes the packet that it accepted on one interface and forwards it to another interface or port that reflects the best path to the packet's destination.

How Routers Route Packets from Source to Destination

To be truly practical, a network must consistently represent the paths available between routers. As Figure 25-1 shows, each line between the routers has a number that the routers use as a network address. These addresses must convey information that can be used by a routing process to pass packets from a source toward a destination. Using these addresses, the network layer can provide a relay connection that interconnects independent networks.

FIGURE 25-1
Addresses represent the path of media connections.

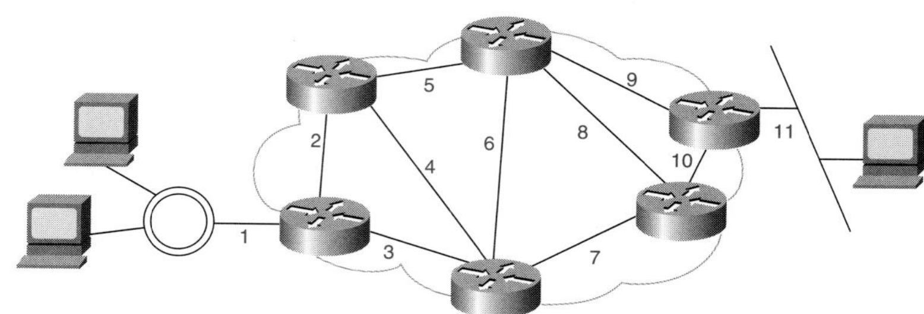

The consistency of Layer 3 addresses across the entire internetwork also improves the use of bandwidth by preventing unnecessary broadcasts. Broadcasts invoke unnecessary process overhead and waste capacity on any devices or links that do not need to receive the broadcasts. By using consistent end-to-end addressing to represent the path of media connections, the network layer can find a path to the destination without unnecessarily burdening the devices or links on the internetwork with broadcasts.

Network and Host Addressing

The router uses the network address to identify the destination network of a packet within an internetwork. Figure 25-2 shows three network numbers identifying segments connected to the router.

FIGURE 25-2
A network address consists of a network portion and a host portion.

Network	Host
1	1 2 3
2	1
3	1

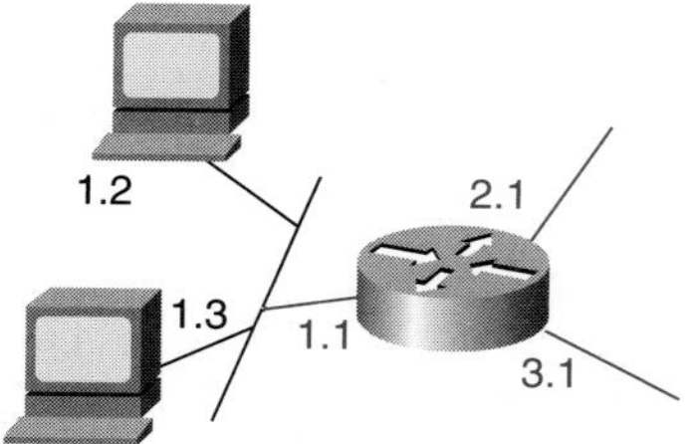

Most network protocol-addressing schemes use some form of host or node address. For some network layer protocols, a network administrator assigns network host addresses according to a predetermined internetwork addressing plan. For other network layer protocols, assignment of host addresses is partially or completely dynamic. In Figure 25-2, three hosts share the network number 1.

Path Selection and Packet Switching

A router generally relays a packet from one data link to another, using two basic functions:

- A path-determination function
- A switching function

Figure 25-3 illustrates how routers use addressing for these routing and switching functions. The router uses the network portion of the address to make path selections to pass the packet to the next router along the path.

FIGURE 25-3
The network portion of the address is used to make path selections.

Destination network	Direction and router port
1.0	← 1.1
2.0	→ 2.1
3.0	→ 3.1

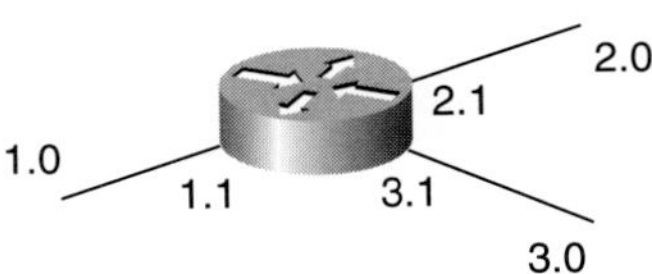

The switching function allows a router to accept a packet on one interface and forward it through a second interface. The path-determination function enables the router to select the most appropriate interface for forwarding a packet. The node portion of the address is used by the final router (the router connected to the destination network) to deliver the packet to the correct host.

Routed Protocols Versus Routing Protocols

Because of the similarity of the two terms, confusion often exists between the routed protocol and the routing protocol (see Figure 25-4). The following provides some clarification:

- **Routed protocol**—Any network protocol that provides enough information in its network layer address to allow a packet to be forwarded from one host to another host based on the addressing scheme. Routed protocols define the field formats within a packet. Packets are generally conveyed from end system to end system. A routed protocol uses the routing table to forward packets. The Internet Protocol (IP) is an example of a routed protocol.
- **Routing protocol**—Support a routed protocol by providing mechanisms for sharing routing information. Routing protocol messages move between the routers. A routing protocol allows the routers to communicate with other routers to update and maintain tables. TCP/IP examples of routing protocols are the following:
  - — Routing Information Protocol (RIP)
  - — Interior Gateway Routing Protocol (IGRP)
  - — Enhanced Interior Gateway Routing Protocol (EIGRP)
  - — Open Shortest Path First (OSPF)

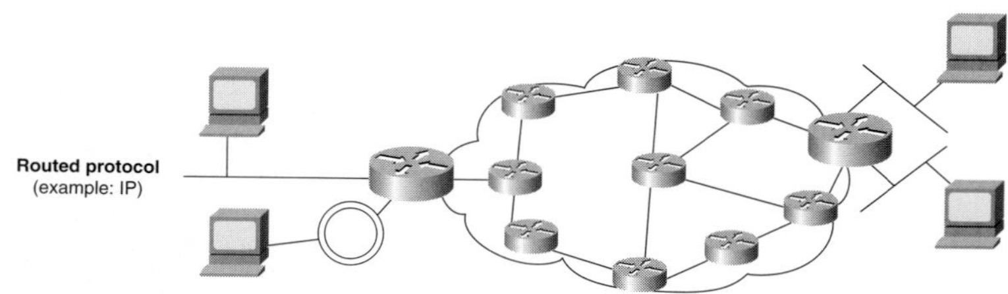

Network protocol	Destination network	Exit port to use
Protocol name	1.0	1.1
	2.0	2.1
	3.0	3.1

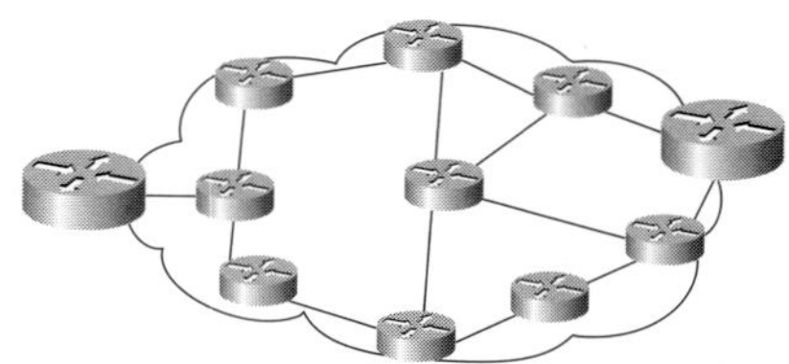

FIGURE 25-4
A routed protocol is used to direct traffic and a routing protocol is used between routers to maintain tables.

Network Layer Protocol Operations

Suppose that a host application needs to send a packet to a destination on a different network. The host addresses the data link frame to the router, using the address of one of the router's interfaces. The router's network layer process examines the incoming packet's Layer 3 header to determine the destination network and then references the routing table, which associates networks to outgoing interfaces (see Figure 25-5). The packet is encapsulated again in the data link frame that is appropriate for the selected interface and is queued for delivery to the next hop in the path.

FIGURE 25-5
Each router provides its services to support upper-layer functions.

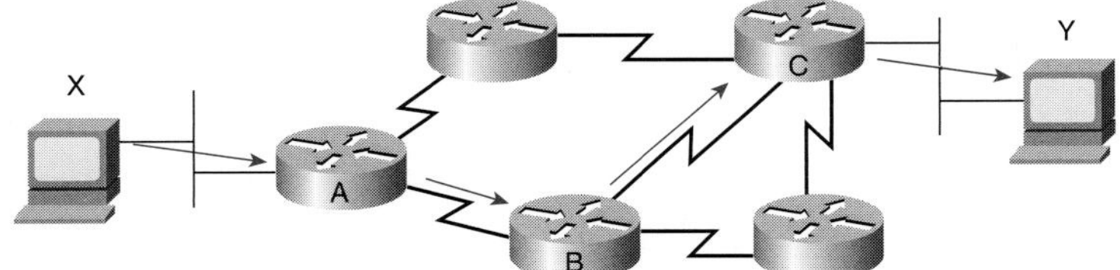

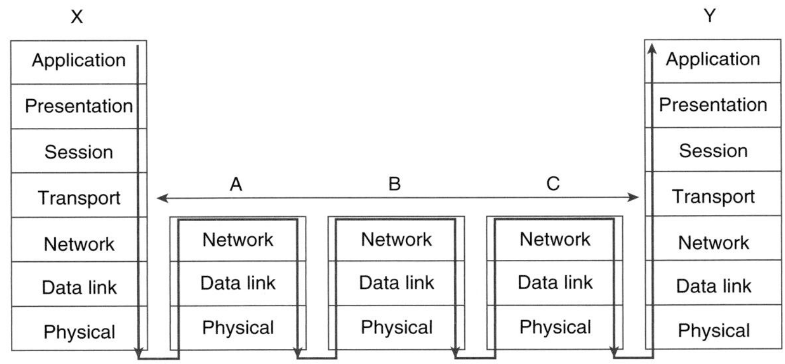

This process occurs each time that the packet is forwarded through another router. When the packet reaches the router that is connected to the destination host's network, it is encapsulated in the destination LAN's data link frame type and is delivered to the destination host.

Multiprotocol Routing

Routers are capable of supporting multiple independent routing protocols and maintaining routing tables for several routed protocols. This capability allows a router to deliver packets from several routed protocols over the same data links (see Figure 25-6).

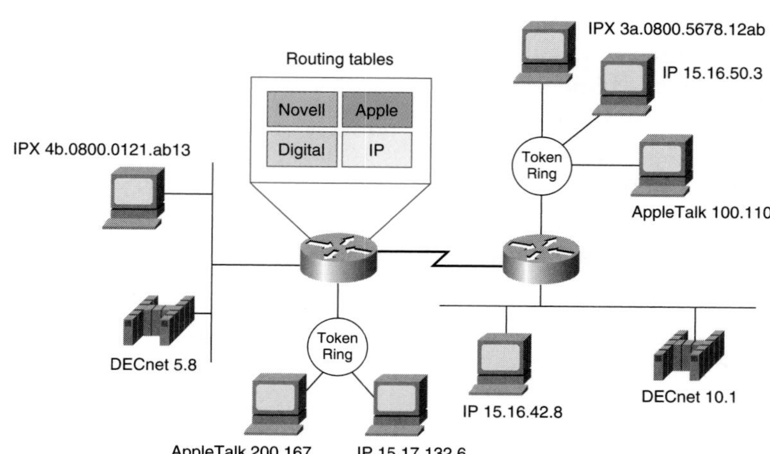

FIGURE 25-6 Routers pass traffic from all routed protocols over the network.

Static Versus Dynamic Routes

Static route knowledge is administered manually by a network administrator who enters it into a router's configuration. The administrator must manually update this static route entry whenever an internetwork topology change requires an update.

Dynamic route knowledge works differently. After a network administrator enters configuration commands to start dynamic routing, the route knowledge is automatically updated by a routing process whenever new information is received from the internetwork. Changes in dynamic knowledge are exchanged between routers as part of the update process.

The Purpose of a Static Route

Static routing has several useful applications. Dynamic routing tends to reveal everything known about an internetwork that, for security reasons, you might want to hide parts of an internetwork. Static routing enables you to specify the information that you want to reveal about restricted networks.

When a network is accessible by only one path, a static route to the network can be sufficient. This type of network is called a stub network. Configuring static routing to a stub network avoids the overhead of dynamic routing (see Figure 25-7).

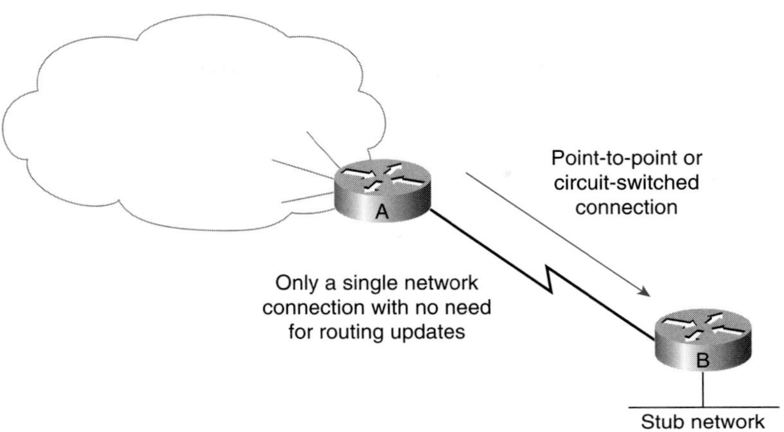

FIGURE 25-7
Static routing entries can eliminate the need to allow route updates across the WAN link.

How a Default Route Is Used

Figure 25-8 shows a use for a default route, a routing table entry that directs packets to the next hop when that hop is not explicitly listed in the routing table. You can set default routes as part of the static configuration.

In this example, the Company X routers possess specific knowledge of the topology of the Company X network, but not of other networks. Maintaining knowledge of every other network accessible by way of the Internet cloud is unnecessary and unreasonable, if not impossible.

Instead of maintaining specific network knowledge, each router in Company X is informed of the default route that it can use to reach any unknown destination by directing the packet to the Internet.

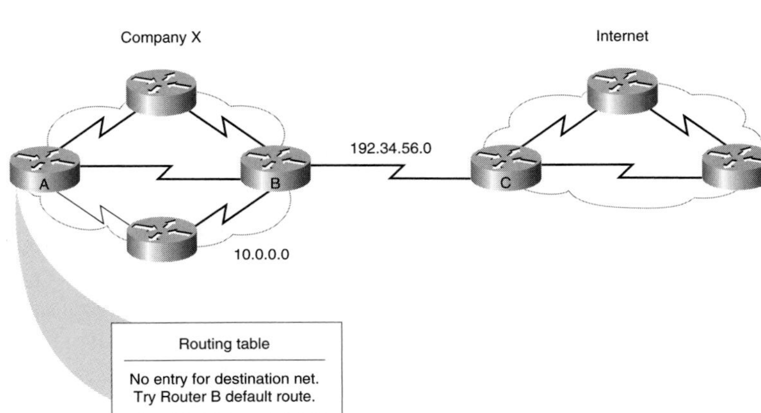

FIGURE 25-8
A default route is used if the next hop is not explicitly listed in the routing table.

Why Dynamic Routing Is Necessary

The network shown in Figure 25-9 adapts differently to topology changes depending on whether it uses statically or dynamically configured routing information.

FIGURE 25-9
Dynamic routing enables routers to automatically use backup routes whenever necessary.

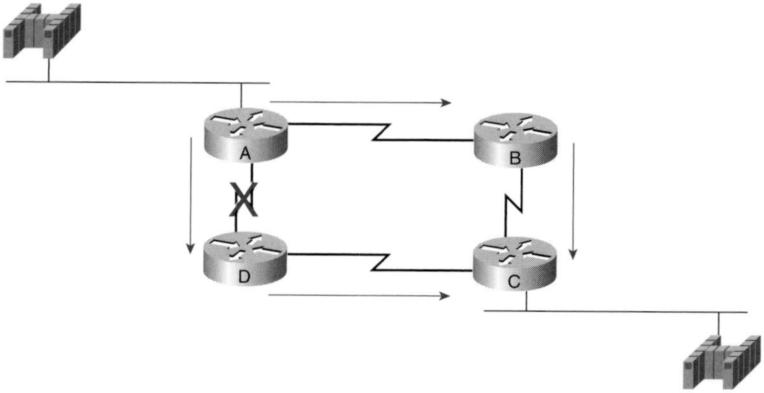

Static routing allows routers to properly route a packet from network to network based on manually configured information. In the example, Router A always sends traffic destined for Router C to Router D. The router refers to its routing table and follows the static knowledge residing there to relay the packet to Router D. Router D does the same and relays the packet to Router C. Router C delivers the packet to the destination host.

If the path between Router A and Router D fails, Router A is not capable of relaying the packet to Router D using that static route. Until Router A is manually reconfigured to relay packets by way of Router B, communication with the destination network is impossible. Dynamic routing offers more flexibility. According to the routing table generated by Router A, a packet can reach its destination over the preferred route through Router D.

However, a second path to the destination is available by way of Router B. When Router A recognizes that the link to Router D is down, it adjusts its routing table, making the path through Router B the preferred path to the destination. The routers continue sending packets over this link.

When the path between Routers A and D is restored to service, Router A can once again change its routing table to indicate a preference for the counter-clockwise path through routers D and C to the destination network. Dynamic routing protocols can also direct traffic from the same session over different paths in a network for better performance. This is known as *load sharing*.

Dynamic Routing Operations

The success of dynamic routing depends on two basic router functions:

- Maintenance of a routing table
- Timely distribution of knowledge, in the form of routing updates, to other routers (see Figure 25-10)

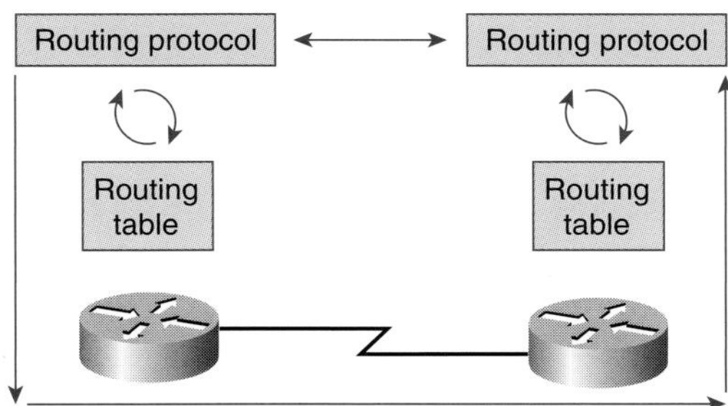

FIGURE 25-10 Routing protocols maintain and distribute routing information.

Dynamic routing relies on a routing protocol to share knowledge among routers. A routing protocol defines the set of rules used by a router when it communicates with neighboring routers. For example, a routing protocol describes the following:

- How to send updates
- What knowledge is contained in these updates
- When to send this knowledge
- How to locate recipients of the updates

How Distances on Network Paths Are Determined by Various Metrics

When a routing algorithm updates a routing table, its primary objective is to determine the best information to include in the table. Each routing algorithm interprets what is best in its own way. The algorithm generates a number, called the metric value, for each path through the network. Typically, the smaller the metric number is, the better the path (see Figure 25-11).

You can calculate metrics based on a single characteristic of a path; you can calculate more complex metrics by combining several characteristics. As shown in Figure 25-12, the metrics that are most commonly used by routers are as follows:

- **Bandwidth**—The data capacity of a link. (Normally, a 10-Mbps Ethernet link is preferable to a 64-kbps leased line.)

- **Delay**—The length of time required to move a packet along each link from source to destination.
- **Load**—The amount of activity on a network resource such as a router or a link.
- **Reliability**—Usually a reference to the error rate of each network link.
- **Hop count**—The number of routers that a packet must travel through before reaching its destination.
- **Ticks**—The delay on a data link using IBM PC clock ticks (approximately 55 milliseconds or 1/18 second).
- **Cost**—An arbitrary value, usually based on bandwidth, monetary expense, or other measurement, that is assigned by a network administrator.

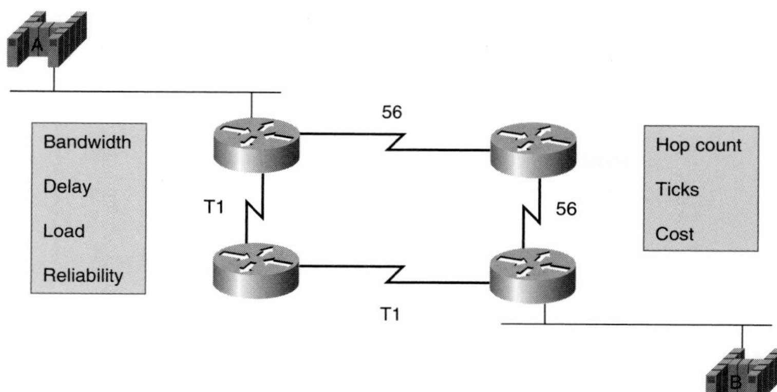

FIGURE 25-11
A variety of metrics can be used to define the best path.

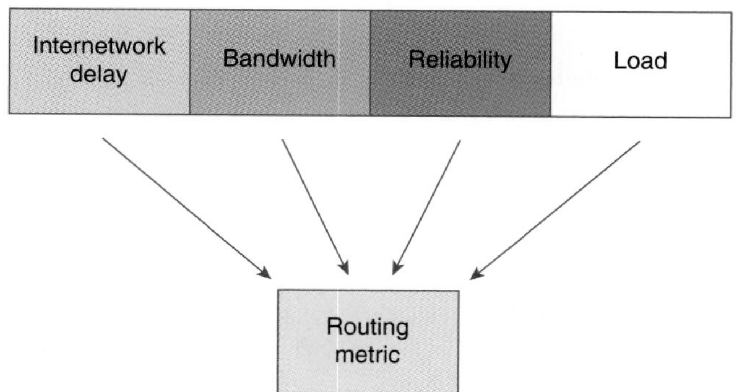

FIGURE 25-12
In order to calculate metrics, several path characteristics are used.

Classes of Routing Protocols

Most routing algorithms can be classified as one of three basic algorithms:

- Distance-vector algorithms
- Link-state algorithms
- Hybrid algorithms (see Figure 25-13)

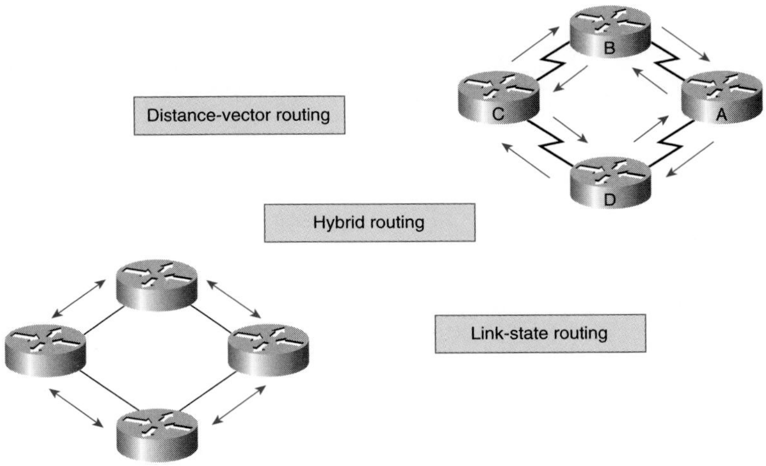

FIGURE 25-13
Distance-vector, link-state, and hybrid routing represent most routing algorithms.

The distance-vector routing algorithm approach determines the direction (vector) and distance to any link in the internetwork. The link-state (also called shortest path first) algorithm approach recreates the exact topology of the entire internetwork (or at least the portion in which the router is situated).

The balanced hybrid approach combines aspects of the link-state and distance-vector algorithms. The next several pages cover procedures and problems for each of these routing algorithms and present techniques for minimizing the problems.

Time for Convergence

The routing algorithm is fundamental to dynamic routing. Whenever the topology of a network changes because of growth, reconfiguration, or failure, the network knowledge base must also change. The knowledge needs to reflect an accurate, consistent view of the new topology. This view or state is called *convergence*.

When all routers in an internetwork are operating with the same knowledge, the internetwork is said to have converged. Fast convergence is a desirable network feature because it reduces the period of time in which routers continue to make incorrect/wasteful routing decisions after a topology change.

Distance-Vector Routing Basics

Distance vector-based routing algorithms pass periodic copies of a routing table from router to router. These regular updates between routers communicate topology changes.

MOVIE 25.1

Distance-Vector Algorithms

Routing updates explained.

Routing Updates Explained

Each router receives a routing table from its directly connected neighboring routers. For example, in Figure 25-14, Router B receives information from Router A. Router B adds a distance-vector number (such as a number of hops), which increases the distance vector and passes this new routing table to its other neighbor, Router C. This same step-by-step process occurs in all directions between direct-neighbor routers.

FIGURE 25-14
Distance-vector routers periodically pass copies of their routing table to neighbor routers and accumulate distance vectors.

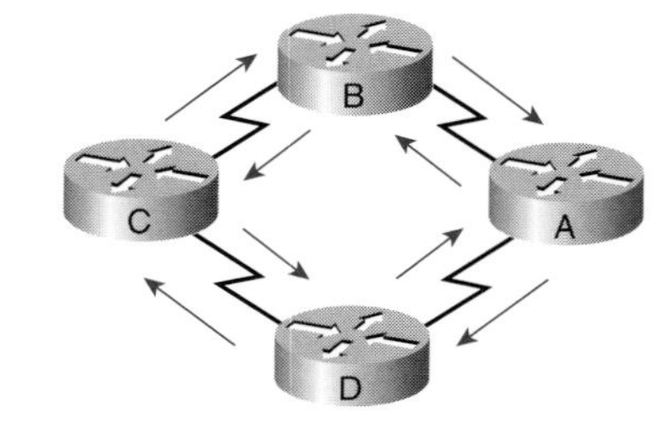

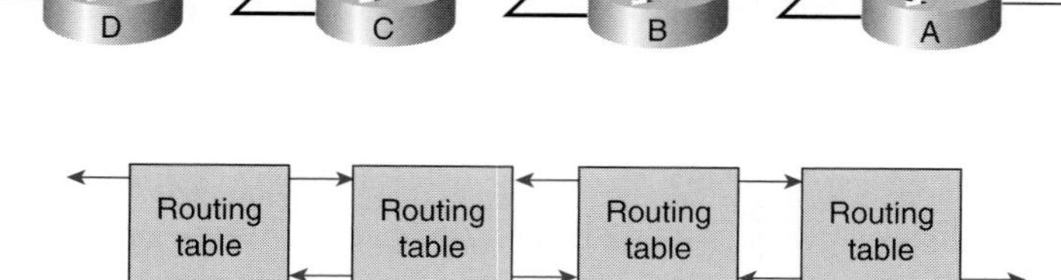

The router eventually accumulates network distances so that it can maintain a database of network topology information. Distance-vector algorithms, however, do not allow a router to know the exact topology of an internetwork.

How Distance-Vector Protocols Exchange Routing Tables

Each router that uses distance-vector routing begins by identifying its own neighbors. In Figure 25-15, the interface that leads to each directly connected network is shown as having a distance of 0. As the distance-vector network discovery process proceeds, routers discover the best path to destination networks based on the information they receive from each neighbor. For example, Router A learns about other networks based on the information that it receives from Router B. Each of the other network entries in the routing table has an accumulated distance vector to show how far away that network is in a given direction.

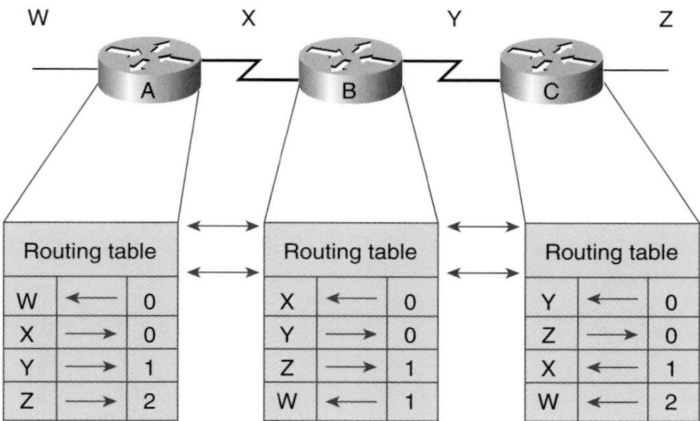

FIGURE 25-15 Distance-vector routers discover the best path to the destination from each neighbor.

How Topology Changes Propagate Through the Network of Routers

When the topology in a distance-vector protocol network changes, routing table updates must occur. As with the network discovery process, topology change updates proceed step by step from router to router, as shown in Figure 25-16. Distance-vector algorithms call for each router to send its entire routing table to each of its adjacent neighbors. The routing tables include information about the total path cost (defined by its metric) and the logical address of the first router on the path to each network contained in the table.

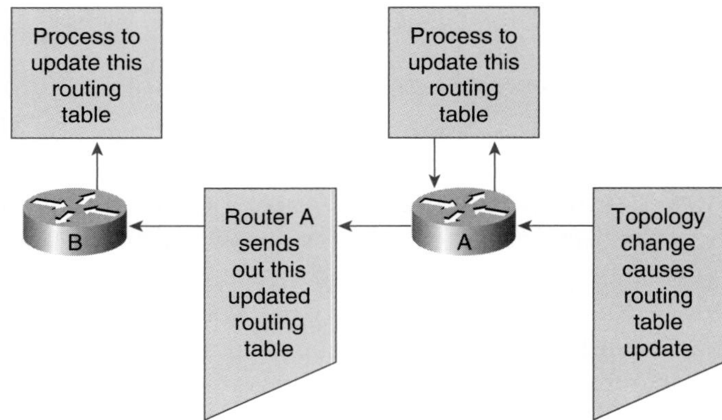

FIGURE 25-16
Updates proceed step-by-step from router to router.

The Problem of Routing Loops

Routing loops can occur if a network's slow convergence on a new configuration causes inconsistent routing entries. Figure 25-17 illustrates how a routing loop can occur:

1. Just before the failure of Network 1, all routers have consistent knowledge and correct routing tables. The network is said to have converged. Assume for the remainder of this example that Router C's preferred path to Network 1 is by way of Router B, and the distance from Router C to Network 1 is 3.
2. When Network 1 fails, Router E sends an update to Router A. Router A stops routing packets to Network 1, but routers B, C, and D continue to do so because they have not yet been informed of the failure. When Router A sends out its update, routers B and D stop routing to Network 1; however, Router C has not received an update. To Router C, Network 1 is still reachable via Router B.
3. Now Router C sends a periodic update to Router D, indicating a path to Network 1 by way of Router B. Router D changes its routing table to reflect this new but incorrect information, and propagates the information to Router A. Router A propagates the information to routers B and E, and so on. Any packet destined for Network 1 now loops from Router C to B to A to D and back again to C.

The Problem of Counting to Infinity

Continuing the previous example, the invalid updates of Network 1 continue to loop until some other process stops the looping. This condition, called *count to infinity*, loops packets continuously around the network in spite of the fundamental fact that the destination network, Network 1, is down. While the routers are counting to infinity, the invalid information allows a routing loop to exist.

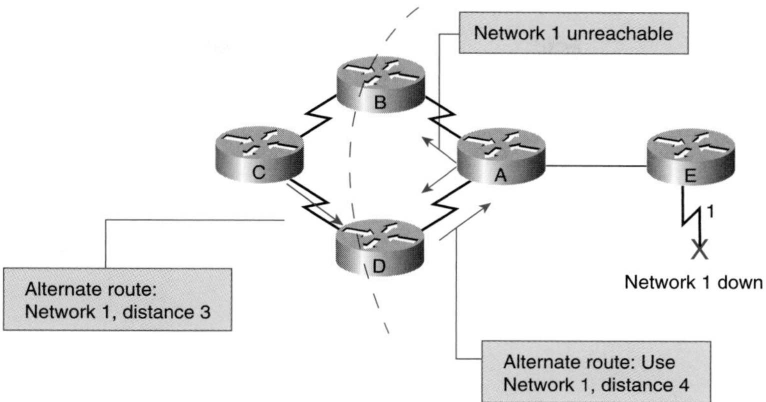

FIGURE 25-17
Router A updates its table to reflect the new, but erroneous, hop count.

Without countermeasures to stop the process, the distance vector (metric) of hop count increments each time the packet passes through another router (see Figure 25-18). These packets loop through the network because of wrong information in the routing tables.

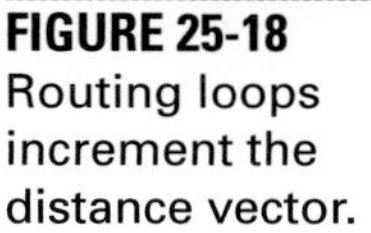

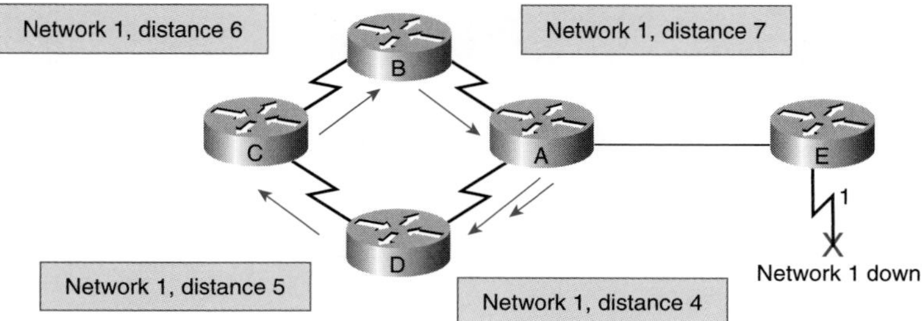

FIGURE 25-18
Routing loops increment the distance vector.

The Solution of Defining a Maximum

In order to keep a routing protocol from truly counting to infinity, or as close to infinity as a router's circuitry allows it to get, distance-vector protocols define infinity as a specific arbitrary maximum number. This number refers to a routing metric (for example, a simple hop count).

With this approach, the routing protocol permits the routing loop to continue until the metric exceeds its maximum allowed value. Figure 25-19 shows the metric value as 16 hops, which exceeds the distance-vector default maximum of 15 hops, and the packet is discarded by the router. In any case, when the metric value exceeds the maximum value, Network 1 is considered unreachable.

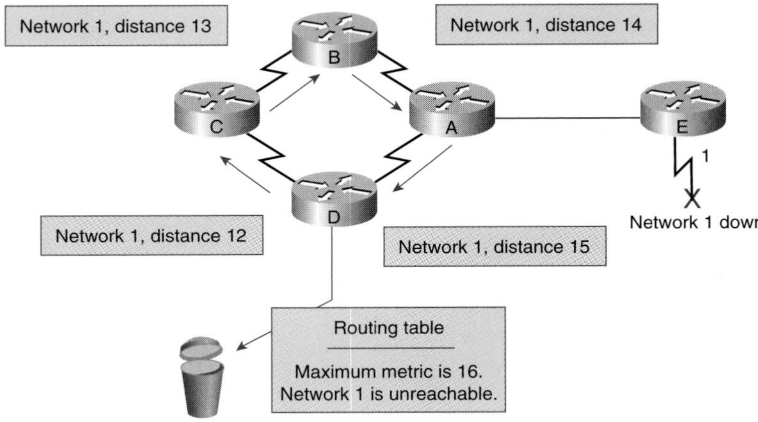

FIGURE 25-19
You can specify a maximum distance vector as infinity.

The Solution of Split Horizon

One way to reduce routing loops and speed up convergence is through the technique called *split horizon*. The logic behind split horizon is that it is never useful to send information about a route back in the direction from which the information originally came.

MOVIE 25.2

Simple Split Horizon

Split horizon explained.

Another possible source for a routing loop occurs when incorrect information that has been sent back to a router contradicts the correct information that it sent. Here is how this problem occurs:

1. Router A passes an update to Router B and Router D, indicating that Network 1 is down. Router C, however, transmits an update to Router B, indicating that Network 1 is available at a distance of 4, by way of Router D.
2. Router B concludes incorrectly that Router C still has a valid path to Network 1, although at a much less favorable metric. Router B sends an update to Router A advising it of the new route to Network 1.
3. Router A now determines that it can send to Network 1 by way of Router B; Router B determines that it can send to Network 1 by way of

Router C; and Router C determines that it can send to Network 1 by way of Router D. Any packet introduced into this environment will loop between routers.

4. Split horizon attempts to avoid this situation. As shown in Figure 25-20, if a routing update about Network 1 arrives from Router A, then Router B or Router D cannot send information about Network 1 back to Router A. Split horizon thus reduces incorrect routing information and reduces routing overhead.

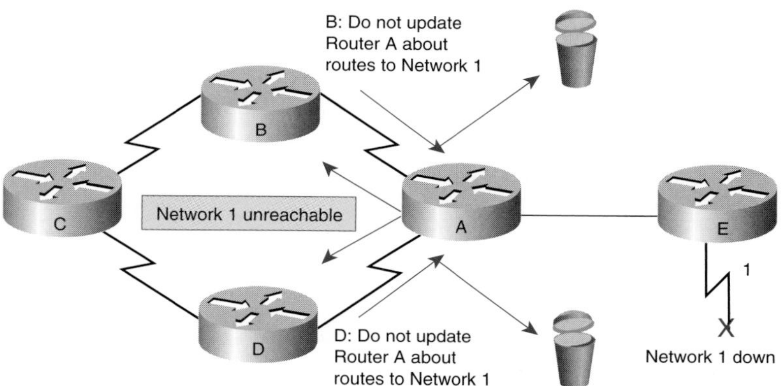

FIGURE 25-20 Split horizon ensures that information about a route is never sent back in the direction from which the original packet came.

The Solution of Hold-Down Timers

Hold-down timers are used to prevent regular update messages from inappropriately reinstating a route that might have gone bad. You can avoid a count to infinity problem by using hold-down timers. When a network connected to a router fails, the router sends a triggered update (poison reverse) to its neighbor routers. In a triggered update, hold-down timers work as follows:

1. A router receives an update from a neighbor indicating that a previously accessible network is now inaccessible. The router marks the route as inaccessible and starts a hold-down timer, as shown in Figure 25-21. If at any time before the hold-down timer expires, an update is received from the same neighbor, indicating that the network is again accessible, the router marks the network as accessible and removes the hold-down timer.

2. If an update arrives from a different neighboring router with an equal or better metric than originally recorded for the network, the router marks the network as accessible and removes the hold-down timer.

3. If at any time before the hold-down timer expires, an update is received from a different neighboring router with a poorer metric, the update is ignored. Ignoring an update with a poorer metric when a hold-down timer in effect allows more time for the knowledge of a disruptive change to propagate through the entire network.

FIGURE 25-21
A router keeps an entry for the network down state, allowing time for other routers to recompute for this topology change.

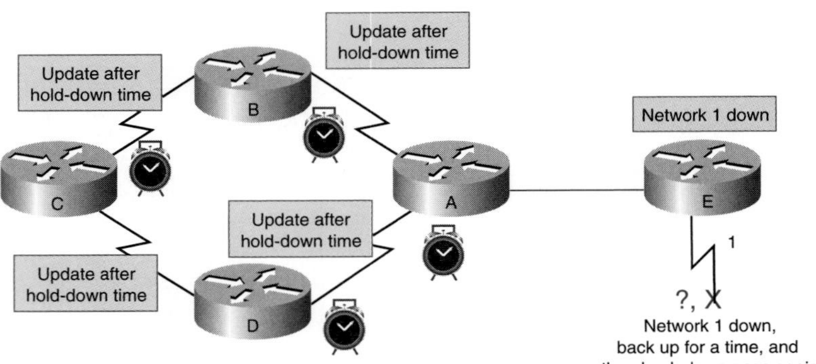

MOVIE 25.3

Hold-Down Timer

When a router goes down and updates.

Link-State Routing Basics

The second basic algorithm used for routing is the link-state algorithm. Link-state–based routing algorithms, also known as shortest path first (SPF) algorithms, maintain a complex database of topology information. Whereas the distance-vector algorithm has nonspecific information about distant networks and no knowledge of distant routers, a link-state routing algorithm maintains full knowledge of distant routers and how they interconnect. Link-state routing uses the following:

- Link-state advertisements (LSAs)
- A topological database
- The SPF algorithm and the resulting SPF tree
- A routing table of paths and ports to each network (see Figure 11-22)

Engineers have implemented this link-state concept in Open Shortest Path First (OSPF) routing. RFC 1583 contains a description of OSPF link-state concepts and operations.

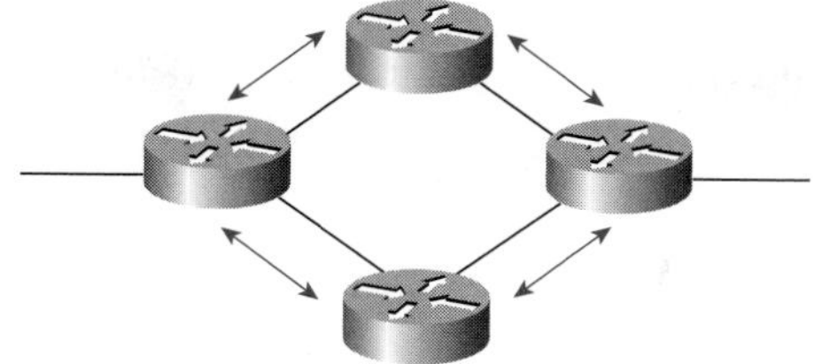

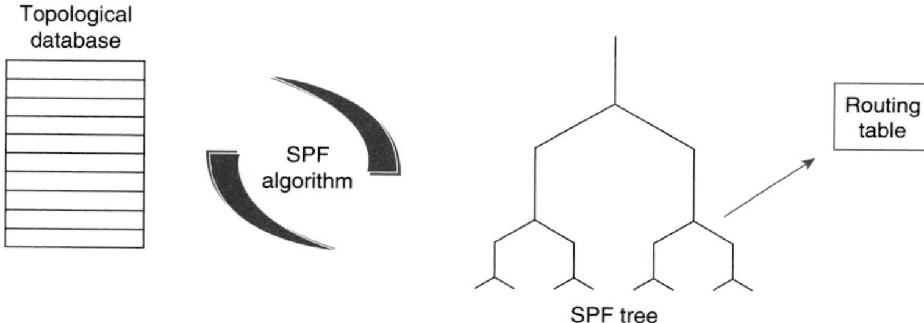

FIGURE 25-22
The link-state algorithm update topology information of all other routers.

MOVIE 25.4

OSPF Routers

Link-state advertisements explained.

How Link-State Protocols Exchange Routing Information

Link-state network discovery mechanisms are used to create a common picture of the entire network. All link-state routers share this view of the network. This is similar to having several identical maps of a town. In Figure 25-23, four networks (W, X, Y, and Z) are connected by three link-state routers. Network discovery for link-state routing uses the following processes:

1. Routers exchange LSAs with each other. Each router begins with directly connected networks for which it has direct, firsthand information.
2. Each router in parallel with the others constructs a topological database consisting of all the LSAs from the internetwork.
3. The SPF algorithm computes network reachability. The router constructs this logical topology as a tree, with itself as root, consisting of all possible

paths to each network in the link-state protocol internetwork. It then sorts these paths shortest path first (SPF).

4. The router lists its best paths and the ports to these destination networks in the routing table. It also maintains other databases of topology elements and status details.

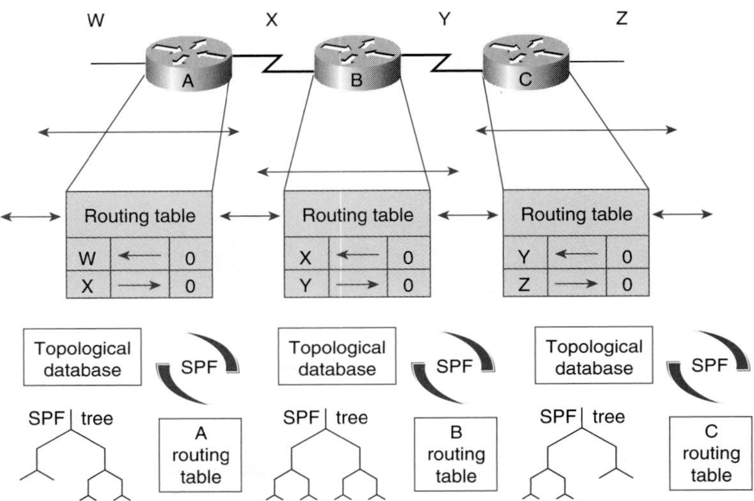

FIGURE 25-23
In link-state routing, routers calculate the shortest path to destinations in parallel.

How Topology Changes Propagate Through the Network of Routers

Link-state algorithms rely on using link-state updates. As shown in Figure 25-24, whenever a link-state topology changes, the routers that first become aware of the change send a new LSA to other routers or to a designated router that all other routers can use for updates. This LSA will be flooded to all routers in the internetwork. To achieve convergence, each router does the following:

- Keeps track of its neighbors, including each neighbor's name, whether the neighbor is up or down, and the cost of the link to the neighbor
- Constructs an LSA packet that lists its neighbor router names and link costs, including new neighbors, changes in link costs, and links to neighbors that have gone down
- Sends out this LSA packet so that all other routers receive it
- When it receives an LSA packet, records the LSA packet in its database so that it uses the most recently generated LSA packet from each router

- Completes a map of the internetwork by using accumulated LSA packet data and then computes routes to all other networks by using the SPF algorithm

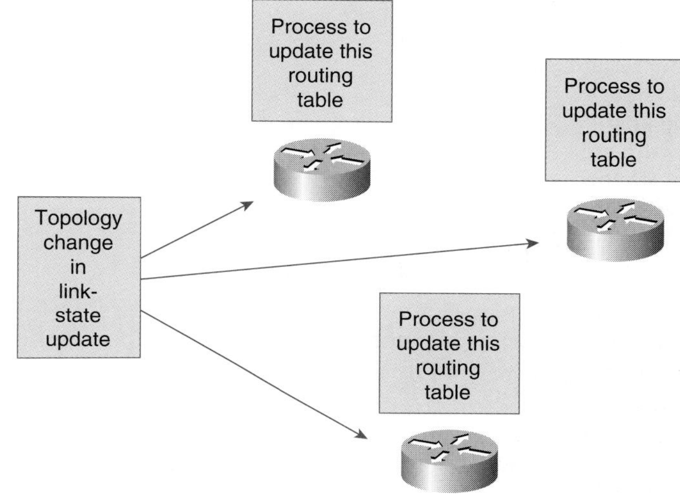

FIGURE 25-24 Update processes proceed using the same link-state update.

Each time an LSA packet causes a change to the link-state database, the link-state algorithm (SPF) recalculates the best paths and updates the routing table. Then every router takes the topology change into account as it determines the shortest path to use for packet routing.

MOVIE 25.5

Link-State Algorithms

Link-state algorithms explained.

Two Link-State Concerns

Two link-state concerns exist: processing and memory requirements, and bandwidth requirements (see Figure 25-25).

Processing and Memory Requirements

Running link-state routing protocols in most situations requires that routers use more memory and perform more processing than distance-vector routing protocols. Network administrators must ensure that the routers they select are capable of providing these necessary resources.

FIGURE 25-25
The two main link-state concerns are processing and memory required for link-state routing and bandwidth consumed for the link-state flood.

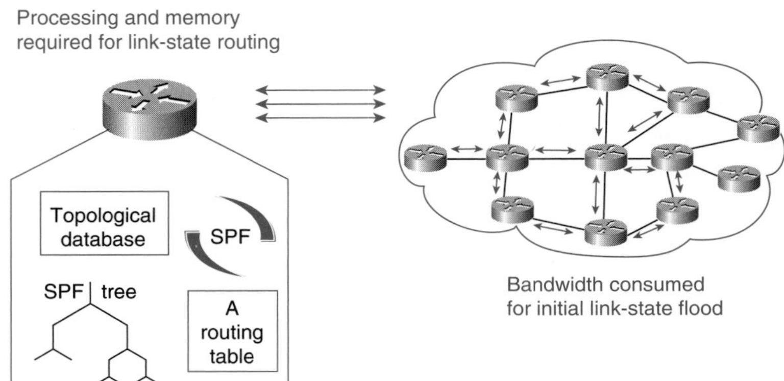

Routers keep track of all other routers in a group and the networks that they can each reach directly. For link-state routing, their memory must be capable of holding information from various databases, the topology tree, and the routing table. Using Dijkstra's algorithm to compute the SPF requires a processing task proportional to the number of links in the internetwork, multiplied by the number of routers in the internetwork.

Bandwidth Requirements

Another cause for concern involves the bandwidth that must be consumed for initial link-state packet flooding. During the initial discovery process, all routers using link-state routing protocols send LSA packets to all other routers. This action floods the internetwork as routers make their *en masse* demand for bandwidth, and temporarily reduces the bandwidth available for routed traffic that carries user data. After this initial flooding, link-state routing protocols generally require only minimal bandwidth to send infrequent or event-triggered LSA packets that reflect topology changes.

Unsynchronized LSAs Lead to Inconsistent Path Decisions among Routers

The most complex and important aspect of link-state routing is making sure that all routers get all necessary LSA packets. Routers with different sets of link-state advertisements (LSAs) calculate routes based on different topological data. Then networks become unreachable as a result of a disagreement among routers about a link (see Figure 25-26). The following is an example of inconsistent path information:

1. Between Routers C and D, Network 1 goes down. Both routers construct an LSA packet to reflect this unreachable status.

2. Soon afterward, Network 1 comes back up; another LSA packet reflecting this next topology change is needed.

3. If the original "Network 1, Unreachable" message from Router C uses a slow path for its update, that update comes later. This LSA packet can arrive at Router A after Router D's "Network 1, Back Up Now" LSA.

4. With unsynchronized LSAs, Router A can face a dilemma about which SPF tree to construct. Should it use paths that include Network 1, or paths without Network 1, which was most recently reported as unreachable?

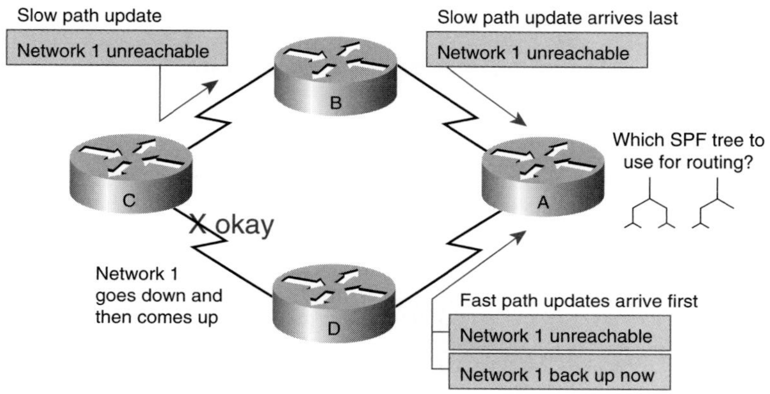

FIGURE 25-26 Unsynchronized updates and inconsistent path decisions make routers unreachable.

If LSA distribution to all routers is not done correctly, link-state routing can result in invalid routes. Scaling up with link-state protocols on very large internetworks can expand the problem of faulty LSA packet distribution. If one part of the network comes up first with other parts coming up later, the order for sending and receiving LSA packets varies. This variation can alter and impair convergence. Routers might learn about different versions of the topology before they construct their SPF trees and routing tables. On a large internetwork, parts that update more quickly can cause problems for parts that update more slowly.

Using Different Routing Protocols in Context

You can compare distance-vector routing to link-state routing in several key areas (see Table 25-1):

- Distance-vector routing gets topological data from the routing table information of its neighbors. Link-state routing obtains a wide view of the entire internetwork topology by accumulating all necessary LSAs.

- Distance-vector routing determines the best path by adding to the metric value that it receives as routing information is passed from neighbor routers. For link-state routing, each router works separately to calculate its own shortest path to destination networks.
- With most distance-vector routing protocols, updates for topology changes come in periodic table updates. The information passes from router to router, usually resulting in slower convergence. With link-state routing protocols, updates are usually triggered by topology changes. Relatively small LSAs passed to all other routers usually result in faster time to converge on any internetwork topology change.

TABLE 25-1 Distance-Vector and Link-State Operational Qualities

Distance-Vector	Link-State
Views network topology from neighbor's perspective	Gets common view of entire network topology
Adds distance vectors from router to router	Calculates the shortest path to other routers
Frequent periodic updates, slow convergence	Event-triggered updates, fast convergence
Passes copies of routing table to neighbor routers	Passes link-state routing updates to other routers

Hybrid Routing Protocols

A third type of routing protocol combines aspects of both distance-vector and link-state routing. This third type is called a *balanced hybrid routing protocol*. Balanced hybrid routing protocols use distance vectors with more accurate metrics to determine the best paths to destination networks. However, they differ from most distance-vector protocols by using topology changes to trigger routing database updates (see Figure 25-27).

The balanced hybrid routing protocol converges rapidly, like the link-state protocols. However, it differs from distance-vector and link-state protocols by using fewer resources such as bandwidth, memory, and processor overhead. An example of a hybrid protocol is Cisco's Enhanced Interior Gateway Routing Protocol (EIGRP).

Basic Routing Processes

Regardless of whether a network uses distance-vector or link-state routing mechanisms, its routers must perform the same basic routing functions. The network layer must relate to and interface with various lower layers. Routers must be capable of seamlessly handling packets encapsulated into different lower-level frames without changing the packets' Layer 3 addressing.

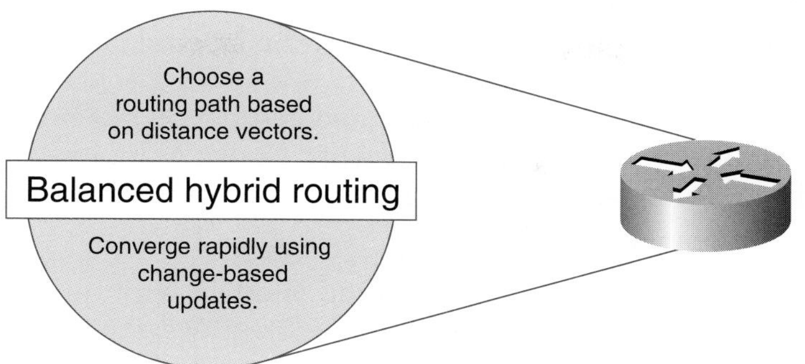

FIGURE 25-27
Hybrid routing shares attributes of distance-vector and link-state routing.

MOVIE 25.6

Router Operation

The responsibilities of the network administrator.

LAN-to-LAN Routing

Figure 25-28 shows an example with LAN-to-LAN routing. In this example, packet traffic from source Host 4 on Ethernet Network 1 needs a path to destination Host 5 on Network 2. The LAN hosts depend on the router and its consistent network addressing to find the best path.

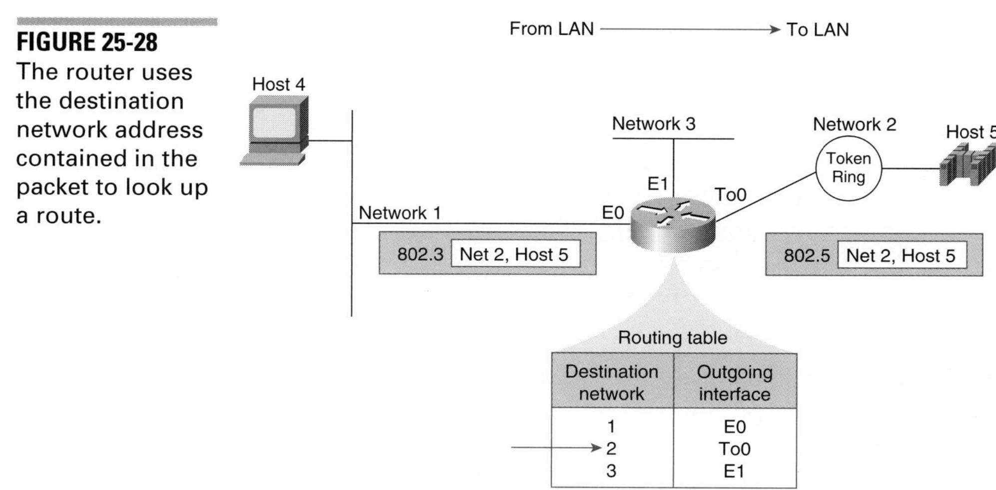

Destination network	Outgoing interface
1	E0
2	To0
3	E1

FIGURE 25-28
The router uses the destination network address contained in the packet to look up a route.

When the router checks its routing table entries, it discovers that the best path to destination Network 2 uses outgoing port To0, the interface to a Token Ring LAN. Although the lower-layer framing must change as the router passes packet traffic from Ethernet on Network 1 to the Token Ring on Network 2, the Layer 3 addressing for source and destination remains the same. In Figure 25-28, the destination address remains Network 2, Host 5, regardless of the different lower-layer encapsulations.

LAN-to-WAN Routing

The network layer must relate to and interface with various lower layers for LAN-to-WAN traffic. As an internetwork grows, the path taken by a packet might encounter several relay points and a variety of data link types beyond the LANs. For example, in Figure 25-29, the following takes place:

1. A packet from the top workstation at address 1.3 must traverse three data links to reach the file server at address 2.4, shown on the bottom.
2. The workstation sends a packet to the file server by first encapsulating it in a Token Ring frame addressed to Router A at the data link layer.
3. When Router A receives the frame, it removes the packet from the Token Ring frame, encapsulates it in a Frame Relay frame, and forwards the frame to Router B.
4. Router B removes the packet from the Frame Relay frame and forwards it to the file server in a newly created Ethernet frame.
5. When the file server at 2.4 receives the Ethernet frame, it extracts and passes the packet to the appropriate upper-layer process.

Routers enable LAN-to-WAN packet flow by keeping the end-to-end source and destination addresses constant while encapsulating the packet in data link frames, as appropriate, for the next hop along the path.

Path Selection and Switching of Multiple Protocols and Media

Routers are devices that implement the network datagram delivery service. They provide interfaces for a wide range of links and subnetworks at a wide range of speeds. Routers are active and intelligent network nodes that can participate in managing a network. Routers manage networks by providing dynamic control over resources and supporting the tasks and goals for internetwork connectivity, reliable performance, management control, and flexibility.

In addition to the basic switching and routing functions, routers have a variety of additional features that help to improve the cost-effectiveness of the internetwork. These features include sequencing traffic based on priority and traffic filtering.

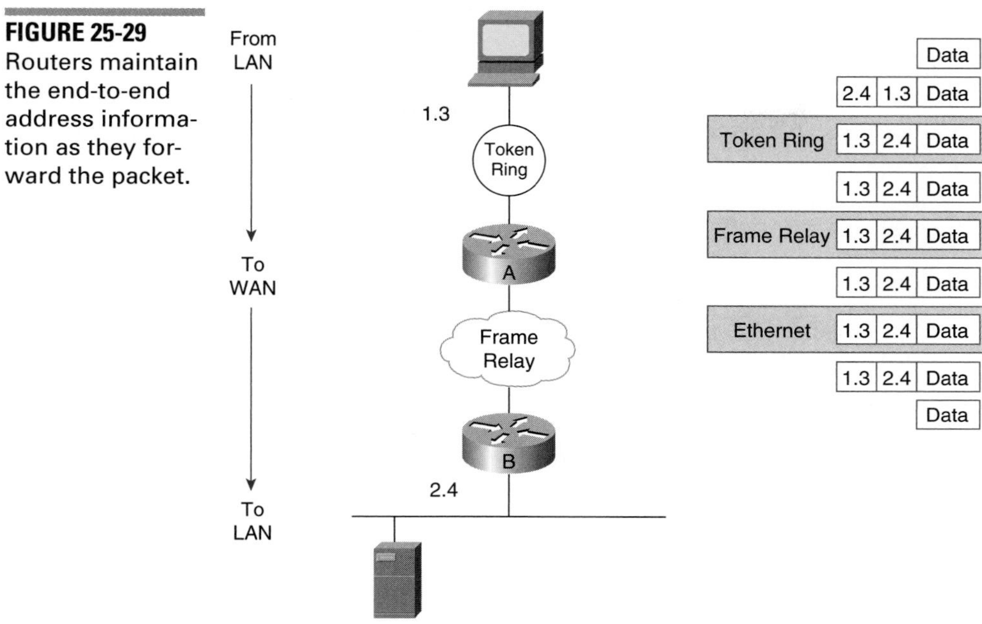

FIGURE 25-29 Routers maintain the end-to-end address information as they forward the packet.

Typically, routers are required to support multiple protocol stacks, each with its own routing protocols, and to allow these different environments to operate in parallel. In practice, routers also incorporate bridging functions and sometimes serve as a limited form of hub (see Figure 25-30). Routers are extremely versatile devices that are responsible for the very existence of the Internet.

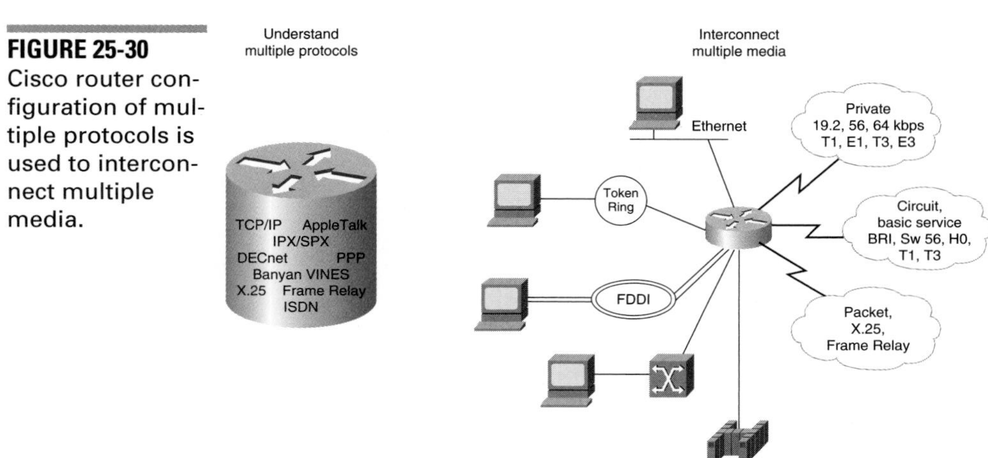

FIGURE 25-30 Cisco router configuration of multiple protocols is used to interconnect multiple media.

Summary

In this chapter, you learned that

- Internetworking functions of the network layer include network addressing and best-path selection for traffic.
- In network addressing, one part of the address is used to identify the path used by the router, and the other is used for ports or devices on the network.
- Routed protocols allow routers to direct user traffic; routing protocols work between routers to maintain routing tables.
- Network discovery for distance-vector routing involves exchange of routing tables; problems can include slow convergence.
- For link-state routing, routers calculate the shortest paths to other routers; problems can include inconsistent updates.
- Balanced hybrid routing uses attributes of both link-state and distance-vector routing.

Check Your Understanding

1. Which of the following best describes one function of Layer 3, the network layer, in the OSI model?

   A. It is responsible for reliable network communication between nodes.

   B. It is concerned with physical addressing and network topology.

   C. It determines which is the best path for traffic to take through the network.

   D. It manages data exchange between presentation layer entities.

2. What function allows routers to evaluate available routes to a destination and to establish the preferred handling of a packet?

   A. Data linkage

   B. Path determination

   C. SDLC interface protocol

   D. Frame Relay

3. How does the network layer forward packets from the source to the destination?

   A. By using an IP routing table

   B. By using ARP responses

   C. By referring to a name server

   D. By referring to the bridge

4. What are the two parts of an network layer address that routers use to forward traffic through a network?

   A. Network address and host address

   B. Network address and MAC address

   C. Host address and MAC address

   D. MAC address and subnet mask

5. Which of the following best describes a routed protocol?
   - **A.** Its address provides enough information to allow a packet to be forwarded from host to host.
   - **B.** It provides information necessary to pass data packets up to the next-highest network layer.
   - **C.** It allows routers to communicate with other routers to maintain and update address tables.
   - **D.** It allows routers to bind MAC and IP addresses together.
6. Which of the following best describes a routing protocol?
   - **A.** A protocol that accomplishes routing through the implementation of an algorithm
   - **B.** A protocol that specifies how and when MAC and IP addresses are bound together
   - **C.** A protocol that defines the format and use of fields within a data packet
   - **D.** A protocol that allows a packet to be forwarded from host to host
7. What is one advantage of distance-vector algorithms?
   - **A.** They are not likely to count to infinity.
   - **B.** You can implement them easily on very large networks.
   - **C.** They are not prone to routing loops.
   - **D.** They are computationally simple.
8. Which of the following best describes a link-state algorithm?
   - **A.** It recreates the exact topology of the entire internetwork.
   - **B.** It requires minimal computations.
   - **C.** It determines distance and direction to any link on the internetwork.
   - **D.** It uses little network overhead and reduces overall traffic.
9. Why do routing loops occur?
   - **A.** Slow convergence occurs after a modification to the internetwork.
   - **B.** Split horizons are artificially created.

C. Network segments fail catastrophically and take other network segments down in a cascade effect.

D. Default routes were never established and initiated by the network administrator.

10. Which of the following best describes balanced hybrid routing?

A. It determines best paths, but topology changes trigger routing table updates.

B. It uses distance-vector routing to determine best paths between topology during high-traffic periods.

C. It uses topology to determine best paths but does frequent routing table updates.

D. It uses topology to determine best paths but uses distance vectors to circumvent inactive network links.

11. What is a network with only one path to a router called?

A. Static network

B. Dynamic network

C. Entity network

D. Stub network

12. Which best describes a default route?

A. Urgent-data route manually entered by network administrator

B. Route used when part of the network fails

C. Route used when the destination network is not explicitly listed in the routing table

D. Preset shortest-distance route that does not need to consider any other metric

13. Which of the following are metrics commonly used by routers to evaluate a path?

A. EMI load, SDLC connections, deterioration rate

B. Bandwidth, load, reliability

C. Distance, hub count, SN ratio

D. Signal count, loss ratio, noise

14. What metric measures the passage of a data packet through a router?
    - A. Exchange
    - B. Hop
    - C. Transmittal
    - D. Signaling
15. Which best describes convergence?
    - A. Messages simultaneously reach a router and a collision occurs.
    - B. Several routers simultaneously route packets along the same path.
    - C. All routers in an internetwork have the same knowledge of the structure and topology of the internetwork.
    - D. Several messages are being sent to the same destination.
16. What do distance-vector algorithms require of routers?
    - A. Default routes for major internetwork nodes in case of corrupted routing tables
    - B. That they periodically send its routing table to its neighbors
    - C. Fast response times and ample memory
    - D. That they maintain a full database of internetwork topology information
17. What is the situation called in which packets never reach their destination but instead cycle repeatedly through the same group of network nodes?
    - A. Split horizon
    - B. End-to-end messaging
    - C. Convergence
    - D. Routing loop
18. How can the count to infinity problem be reduced?
    - A. By using routing loops
    - B. By defining a minimum hop count
    - C. By using hold-down timers
    - D. Both B and C

19. Why are hold-down timers useful?

A. They help prevent a router from immediately using an alternate route that might be the failed route.

B. They force all routers in a segment to synchronize switching operations.

C. They reduce the amount of network traffic during high-traffic periods.

D. They provide a mechanism for bypassing failed sections of the network.

20. What happens if routers have different sets of LSAs?

A. A check sum procedure is initiated, and faulty routing tables are repaired.

B. Routes become unreachable because routers disagree about a link.

C. A comparison is forced and subsequent convergence on a single routing table occurs.

D. A broadcast message is sent with the master copy of the routing table to all routers.

Objectives

After reading this chapter, you will be able to

- Describe initial router configuration
- Describe interior and exterior routing protocols
- Describe RIP
- Describe IGRP

Chapter 26

Routing Protocols

Introduction

Now that you have learned about routing protocols, you are ready to configure IP routing protocols. As you know, routers can be configured to use one or more IP routing protocols. In this chapter, you learn the initial configuration of the router to enable the IP routing protocols of the Routing Information Protocol (RIP) and the Interior Gateway Routing Protocol (IGRP). In addition, you learn how to monitor IP routing protocols.

Initial Router Configuration

After testing the hardware and loading the Cisco IOS system image, the router finds and applies the configuration statements. These entries provide the router with details about router-specific attributes, protocol functions, and interface addresses. Remember that if the router cannot locate a valid startup-config file, it enters an initial router configuration mode called setup mode or system configuration dialog.

With the setup mode command facility, you can answer questions in the system configuration dialog. This facility prompts you for basic configuration information. The answers that you enter allow the router to build a sufficient but minimal router configuration that includes the following:

- An inventory of interfaces
- An opportunity to enter global parameters
- An opportunity to enter interface parameters
- A setup script review
- An opportunity to indicate whether or not you want the router to use this configuration

After you confirm setup mode entries, the router uses the entries as a running configuration. The router also stores the configuration in NVRAM as a new startup-config, and you can start using the router. For additional protocol and interface changes, you can then use the enable mode and enter the command **configure**.

MOVIE 26.1

Router Operation

Determination, transportation, and switching.

Initial IP Routing Table

Initially, as shown in Figure 26-1, a router must refer to entries about networks or subnets that are directly connected to the router. Each interface must be configured with an IP address and a subnet mask. The Cisco IOS software learns about this IP address and mask information from a configuration that has been input from some source. The initial source of addressing is a user who types it into a configuration file.

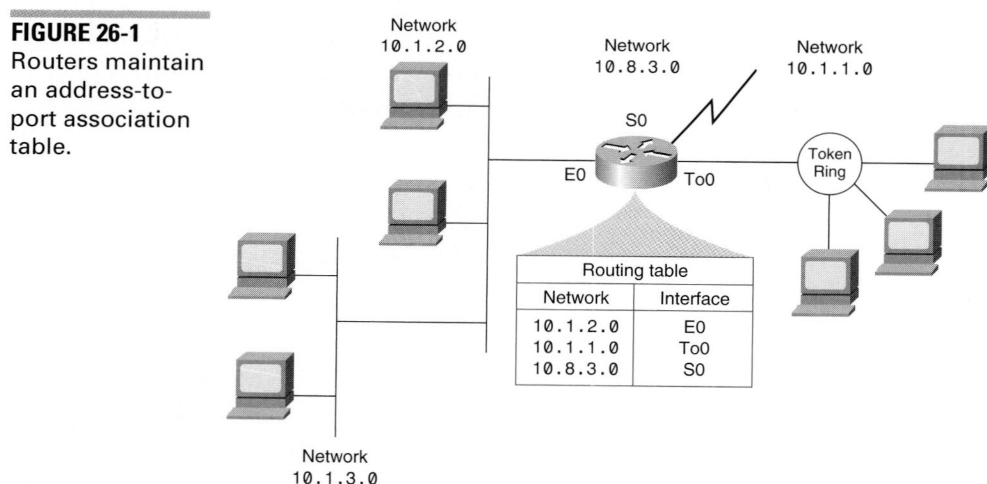

FIGURE 26-1
Routers maintain an address-to-port association table.

MOVIE 26.2

Routing Table

Static routes and dynamic routes are explained.

In this section, you start up your router in a "just-received" condition, a state that lacks another source for the startup configuration. This condition on the router permits you to use the setup-mode command facility and answer prompts for basic configuration information. The answers that you enter include address-to-port information to set up router interfaces for IP.

How a Router Learns About Destinations

Routers learn paths to destinations three different ways:

- **Static routes**—These routes are manually defined by the system administrator as the next hop to a destination. Static routes are useful for security and traffic reduction (see Figure 26-2).
- **Default routes**—These routes are manually defined by the system administrator as the path to take when there is no known route to the destination (see Figure 26-3).
- **Dynamic routing**—The router learns of paths to destinations by receiving periodic updates from other routers.

FIGURE 26-2
A fixed route to address reflects the administrator's knowledge.

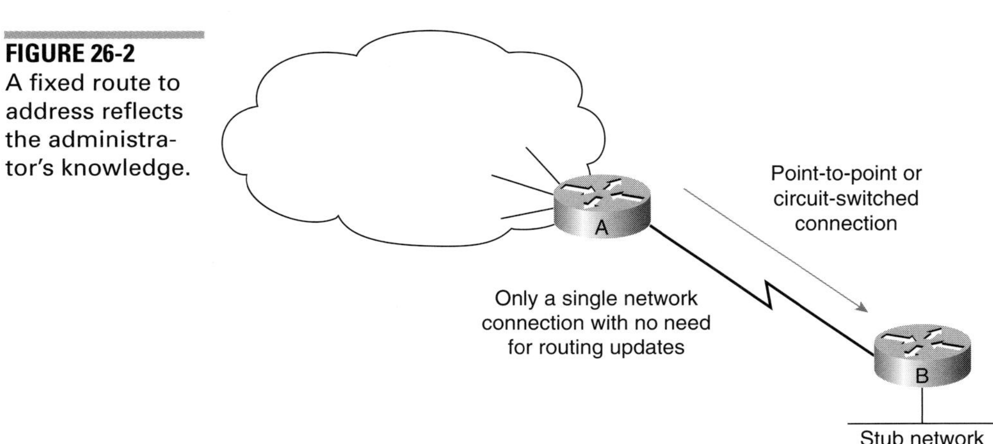

MOVIE 26.3

Static Routes

Static routes are explained.

MOVIE 26.4

Dynamic Routes

Dynamic routes are explained.

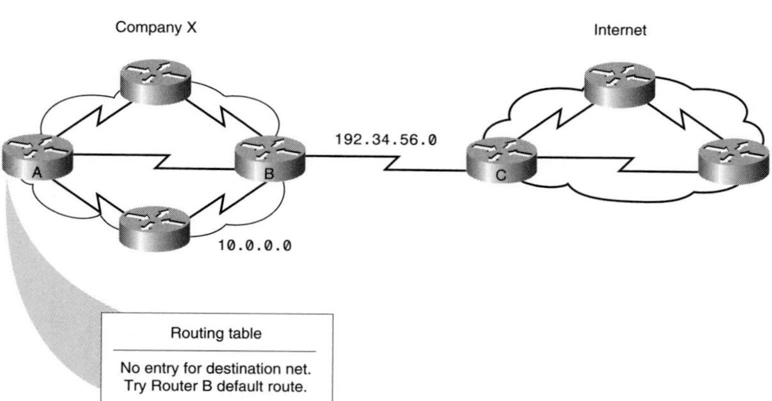

FIGURE 26-3
The default route is used if the next hop is not explicitly stated in the routing tab.

The ip route Command

Static routes are user-defined routes that cause packets moving between a source and a destination to take a specified path. The ip route command sets up a static route and uses the following syntax:

```
ip route network [mask] {address | interface} [distance]
```

The parameters have the following meanings:

network	Destination network or subnet
mask	Subnet mask
address	IP address of next-hop router
interface	Name of interface to use to get to destination network
distance	The administrative distance

The administrative distance is a rating of the trustworthiness of a routing information source, expressed as a numeric value from 0 to 255. The higher the number, the lower the trustworthiness rating.

A static route allows manual configuration of the routing table. No dynamic changes to this table entry will occur. A static route might reflect some special knowledge of the networking situation known to the network administrator.

Manually entered administrative distance values for static routes are usually low numbers (1 is the default). Routing updates are not sent on a link if the link is referenced only by a static route; in this way, static routes conserve bandwidth.

The example shown in Figure 26-4 includes the following values:

ip route 172.16.1.0	Specifies a static route to the destination subnetwork
255.255.255.0	Subnet mask indicates that 8 bits of subnetting are in effect
172.16.2.1	IP address of next-hop router in the path to the destination

FIGURE 26-4
Router A is configured with a static router to 172.16.1.0.

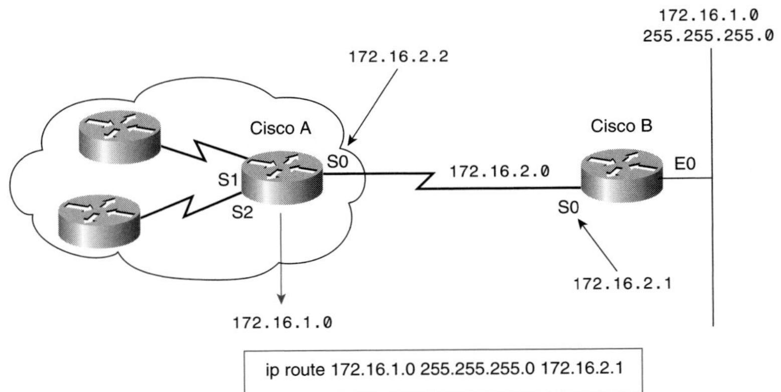

The assignment of a static route to reach the stub network 172.16.1.0 is proper for Cisco A because there is only one way to reach that network. The assignment of a static route from Cisco B to the cloud networks is also possible. However, a static route assignment is required for each destination network, in which case, a default route might be more appropriate.

e-LAB ACTIVITY 26.1

Using the ip route Command

In this activity, you demonstrate how to set up a static route with the administrative distance of 1.

e-LAB ACTIVITY 26.2

IP Static Route Challenge

In this activity, you demonstrate how to configure a static route between neighboring routers.

SKILL BUILDER

Lab Activity: Static Routes

In this lab, you configure a static route between neighboring routers.

The ip default-network Command

A router might not know the routes to all other networks. To provide complete routing capability, the common practice is to use some routers as default routers and give the remaining routers default routes to those routers.

The **ip default-network** command establishes a default route by using the following syntax:

```
ip default-network network-number
```

network-number is equal to the IP network number or subnet number defined as the default.

The **ip default-network** command establishes a default route in networks using dynamic routing protocols. Default routes keep routing tables shorter. When an entry for a destination network does not exist in a routing table, the packet is sent to the default network. Because a router does not have complete knowledge about all destination networks, it can use a default network number to indicate the direction to take for unknown network numbers. Use the default network number when you need to locate a route but have only partial information about the destination network. The **ip default-network** command must be added to all routers in the network or used with the additional command

redistribute static so that all networks have knowledge of the candidate default network.

In the example shown in Figure 26-5, the global command **ip default-network 192.168.17.0** defines the Class C network 192.168.17.0 as the destination path for packets that have no routing table entries.

The Company X administrator does not want updates coming in from the public network. Router A might need a firewall for routing updates. Router A might also need a mechanism to group networks that share Company X's routing strategy. One such mechanism is an autonomous system number.

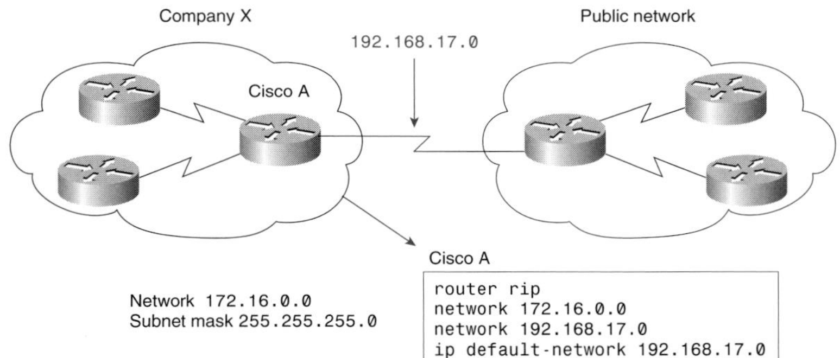

FIGURE 26-5
The **default-network** command indicates where packets are sent when the routes does not know how to get to the destination.

e-LAB ACTIVITY 26.3

Using the ip network default Command

In this activity, you demonstrate how to set up a default network.

Interior and Exterior Routing Protocols

Exterior routing protocols are used for communication between autonomous systems. Interior routing protocols are used within a single autonomous system (see Figure 26-6).

MOVIE 26.5

Routed Versus Router Protocols

Routed and router protocols are explained.

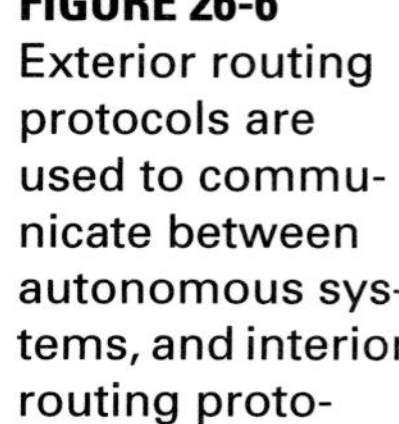

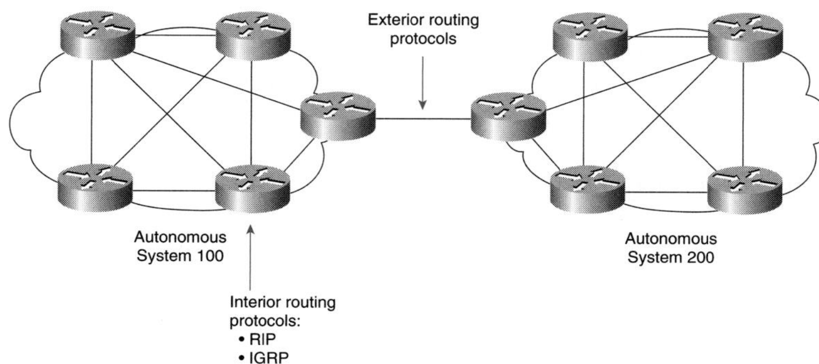

FIGURE 26-6
Exterior routing protocols are used to communicate between autonomous systems, and interior routing protocols are used within a single autonomous system.

Autonomous Systems

An autonomous system consists of routers run by one or more administrators that present a consistent view of routing to the external world. The Network Information Center (NIC) assigns a unique autonomous system (AS) number to enterprises. This autonomous system number is a 16-bit number. A routing protocol such as Cisco's IGRP requires that you specify this unique, assigned autonomous system number in your configuration.

Interior IP Routing Protocols

At the Internet layer of the TCP/IP suite of protocols, a router can use an IP routing protocol to accomplish routing through the implementation of a specific routing algorithm. Examples of IP routing protocols include the following:

- **RIP**—A distance-vector routing protocol
- **IGRP**—Cisco's distance-vector routing protocol
- **OSPF**—A link-state routing protocol
- **EIGRP**—A balanced hybrid routing protocol

The following sections show you how to configure the first two of these protocols.

MOVIE 26.6

Dynamic Routing Protocols

Dynamic protocols, such as RIP, are explained.

IP Routing Configuration Tasks

The selection of an IP routing protocol involves setting both global and interface parameters (see Figure 26-7).

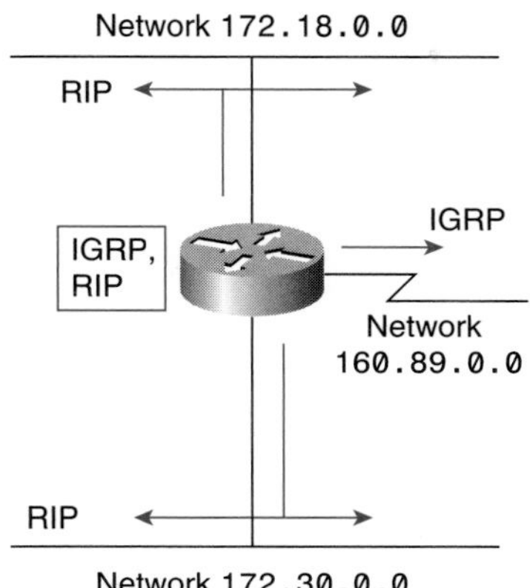

FIGURE 26-7
A router can use more than one routing protocol, if desired.

Global tasks include selecting a routing protocol, either RIP or IGRP, and indicating IP network numbers by way of specific subnet entries. The interface task is to assign network/subnet addresses and the appropriate subnet mask (to each interface). Dynamic routing uses broadcasts and multicasts to communicate with other routers. The routing metric helps routers find the best path to each network or subnet.

Using the router and network Commands

The **router** command starts a routing process. The **network** command is required because it enables the routing process to determine which interfaces will participate in sending and receiving routing updates.

Both of these are used to configure dynamic routing. The **router** command starts a dynamic routing process by first defining an IP routing protocol; its form is as follows:

```
Router(config)# router protocol [keyword]
```

Then the **network** command is needed for each IP routing process:

```
Router(config-router)# network network-number
```

The parameters specify the following:

protocol	This is either RIP, IGRP, or Enhanced IGRP.
network	This could be an autonomous system, which is used with protocols that require an autonomous system, such as IGRP. The **network** command is required because it allows the routing process to determine which interfaces will participate in the sending and receiving of routing updates.
network-number	This is a directly connected network.

The network numbers must be based on the network class addresses, not subnet addresses or individual host addresses. Major network addresses are limited to Class A, B, and C network numbers. You can enter subnets but they'll only appear in the config as "classful" networks.

RIP

RIP was originally specified in RFC 1058. Its key characteristics include the following:

- It is a distance-vector routing protocol.
- Hop count is used as the metric for path selection (see Figure 26-8).
- If the hop count is greater than 15, the packet is discarded.
- By default, routing updates are broadcast every 30 seconds.

MOVIE 26.7

RIP

RIP explained.

MOVIE 26.8

RIP Problems

Hop-count limit is a problem in RIP.

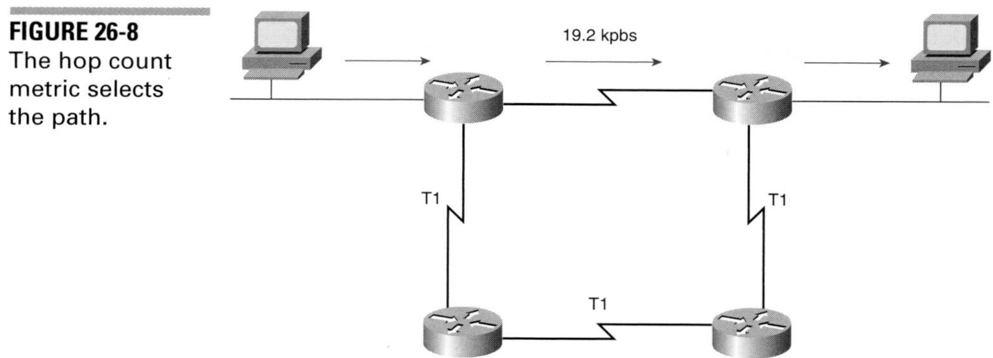

FIGURE 26-8
The hop count metric selects the path.

Using router rip and network Commands to Enable RIP

The **router rip** command selects RIP as the routing protocol and starts the dynamic routing process. The **network** command assigns a network class address to which a router is directly connected. The routing process associates interfaces with the network addresses and begins using RIP on the specified networks.

NOTE

In RIP version 1, all subnet masks must be the same. RIP version 1 does not share subnetting information in routing updates. In this book, we are concerned only with RIP version 1 and will no longer make this distinction when discussing RIP.

Enabling RIP on an IP-Addressed Network

In the example shown in Figure 26-9, the descriptions for the commands are as follows:

- **router rip**—Selects RIP as the routing protocol
- **network 1.0.0.0**—Specifies a directly connected network
- **network 2.0.0.0**—Specifies a directly connected network

The Cisco A router interfaces that are connected to networks 1.0.0.0 and 2.0.0.0 send and receive RIP updates. These routing updates allow the router to learn the network topology.

Monitoring IP Packet Flow Using the show ip protocol Command

The **show ip protocol** command displays values of routing timers and network information pertaining to the router (see Listing 26-1). Use this information to identify a router that you suspect is delivering bad routing information.

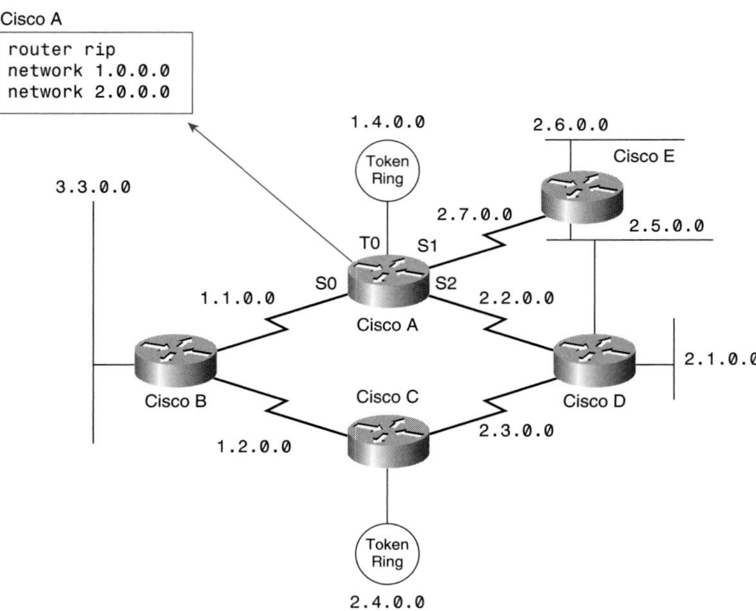

FIGURE 26-9
Cisco A sends information to networks 1.0.0.0 and 2.0.0.0.

e-LAB ACTIVITY 26.4

Setting Up RIP Routing on a Router

In this activity, you demonstrate how to enable RIP on a router.

Listing 26-1 The show ip protocol Command Observing RIP's Behavior

```
Router> show ip protocol
Routing Protocol is rip
  Sending updates every 30 seconds, next due in 13 seconds
  Invalid after 180 seconds, hold down 180, flushed after 240
  Outgoing update filter list for all interface is not set
  Incoming update filter list for all interface is not set
  Redistributing: rip
  Routing for Networks:
    183.8.0.0
    144.253.0.0
  Routing Information Sources:
  Gateway               Distance             Last Update
    183.8.128.12         120                  0:00:14
    183.8.64.130         120                  0:00:19
    183.8.128.130        120                  0:00:03
  Distance: (default is 120)
```

The router in the example sends updated routing table information every 30 seconds (configured interval). Seventeen seconds have elapsed since it sent its last update; it will send the next one in 13 seconds. Following the "Routing for Networks" line, the router specifies routes for the listed networks. The last line shows that the RIP administrative distance is 120.

e-LAB ACTIVITY 26.5

Using the show ip protocol Command

In this activity, you demonstrate how to verify the protocols and network information.

The show ip route Command

The **show ip route** command displays the contents of the IP routing table. The IP routing table contains entries for all known networks and subnetworks, along with a code that indicates how that information was learned (see Listing 26-2).

Listing 26-2 The show ip route Command Displaying the Local Routing Table

```
Router> show ip route
Codes:  C - connected, S - static, R - RIP, M - mobile, B - BGP
        D - EIGRP, EX - EIGRP external, O - OSPF, IA - OSPF inter area
        E1 - OSPF external type 1, E2 - OSPF external type 2, E - EGP
        i - IS-IS, L1 - IS-IS level 1, L2 - IS-IS level 2
        * - candidate default

Gateway of last resort is not set

    144.253.0.0 is subnetted (mask is 255.255.255.0), 1 subnets
C   144.253.100.0 is directly connected. Ethernet1
R   133.3.0.0
R   153.50.0.0 [120/1] via 183.8.128.12, 00:00:09, Ethernet0
    183.8.0.0 is subnetted (mask is 255.255.255.128), 4 subnets
R     183.8.0.128 [120/1] via 183.8.128.130.00, 00:00:17, Serial0
                  [120/1] via 183.8.64.130, 00:00:17, Serial1
C     183.8.128.0 is directly connected, Ethernet0
C     183.8.64.128 is directly connected, Serial1
C     183.8.128.128 is directly connected, Ethernet0
R   192.3.63.0
```

e-LAB ACTIVITY 26.6

Using show ip route Command

In this activity, you demonstrate how to see all the links the router knows by displaying the routing table.

e-LAB ACTIVITY 26.7

RIP Routing

In this activity, you demonstrate how to configure RIP as the routing protocol.

SKILL BUILDER

Lab Activity: RIP Routing

In this lab, you configure RIP as the routing protocol.

IGRP

IGRP is a distance-vector routing protocol developed by Cisco. IGRP sends routing updates at 90-second intervals, advertising networks for a particular autonomous system. Some of the IGRP key design characteristics emphasize the following:

- Versatility that enables it to automatically handle indefinite, complex topologies
- Flexibility for segments that have different bandwidth and delay characteristics
- Scalability for functioning in very large networks

MOVIE 25.9

IGRP

Multipath routing explained.

By default, the IGRP routing protocol uses two metrics: bandwidth and delay. IGRP can be configured to use a combination of variables to determine a composite metric (see Figure 26-10). Those variables include the following:

- Bandwidth
- Delay
- Load
- Reliability

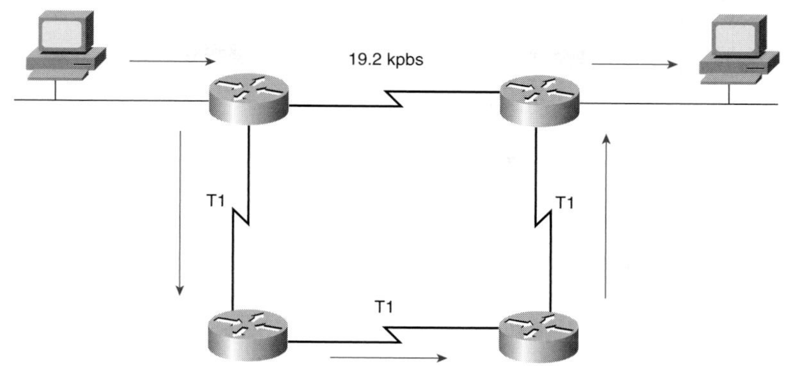

FIGURE 26-10
With IGRP, the composite metric selects the path, and speed is the primary consideration.

The **router igrp** command selects IGRP as a routing protocol and starts the dynamic routing process:

```
Router(config)# router igrp autonomous-system
```

The parameter specifies the following:

autonomous- system	Identifies the IGRP router processes that will share routing information

The **network** command specifies any directly connected networks to be included:

```
Router(config-router)# network network-number
```

The parameter specifies the following:

network-number	Specifies a directly connected network: a classful network number, not a subnet number or individual address

MOVIE 26.10

IGRP

Metrics are explained.

MOVIE 26.11

RIP/IGRP

Metric differences are explained.

Using router igrp and network Commands to Enable IGRP

The **router igrp** command selects IGRP as a routing protocol. The **network** command specifies any directly connected networks that are to be included.

Like RIP, all subnet masks must be the same. IGRP does not share subnetting information in routing updates.

Enabling IGRP on an IP-Addressed Network

In the example shown in Figure 26-11, IGRP is selected as the routing protocol for autonomous system 109. All interfaces connected to networks 1.0.0.0 and 2.0.0.0 will be used to send and receive IGRP routing updates.

- **router igrp 109**—Selects IGRP as the routing protocol for autonomous system 109
- **network 1.0.0.0**—Specifies a directly connected network
- **network 2.0.0.0**—Specifies a directly connected network

e-LAB ACTIVITY 26.8

Setting up IGRP Routing on a Router

In this activity, you demonstrate how to enable IGRP on a router.

Monitoring IP Packet Flow Using the show ip protocol Command

The **show ip protocol** command displays parameters, filters, and network information about all the routing protocol(s) (RIP, IGRP, and so on) that are in use on the router (see Listing 26-3). The algorithm used to calculate the routing metric for IGRP is shown in this display. It defines the value of the K1 to K5 constants and the maximum hop count. The constant K1 affects bandwidth, and the constant K3 represents delay. By default, the values of the constants K1 and K3 are set to 1. K2, K4 and K5 values are defaulted to 0.

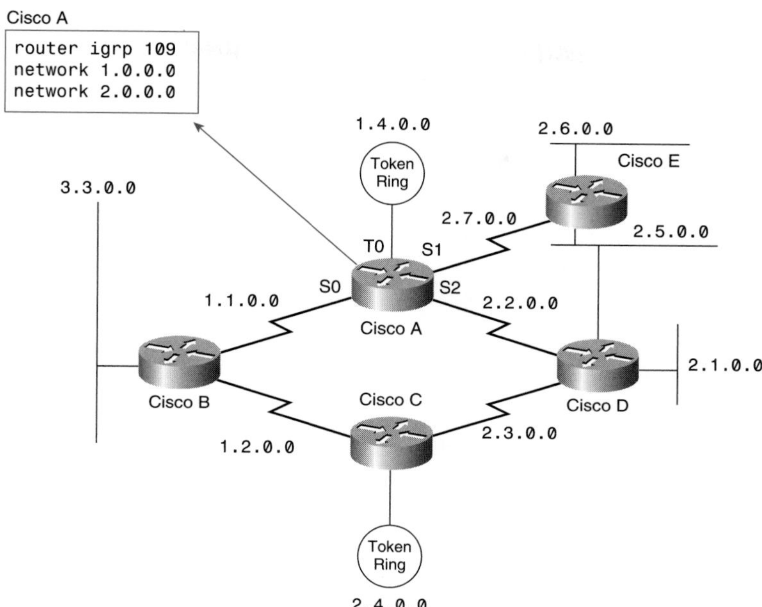

FIGURE 26-11 You use router igrp and network commands to create an IGREP router.

Listing 26-3 The show ip protocols Command

```
Router> show ip protocols
Routing Protocol is igrp 300
  Sending updates every 90 seconds, next due in 55 seconds
  Invalid after 270 seconds, hold down 280, flushed after 360
  Outgoing update filter list for all interfaces is not set
  Incoming update filter list for all interfaces is not set
  Default networks flagged in outgoing updates
  Default networks accepted from incoming updates
  IGRP metric weight K1=1, K2=0, K3=1, K4=0, K5=0
  IGRP maximum hopcount 100
  IGRP maximum metric variance 1
  Redistributing igrp 300
  Routing for Networks:
    183.8.0.0
    144.253.0.0
  Routing Information Sources
    Gateway            Distance            Last Update
    144.253.100.1      100                 0:00:52
    183.8.128.12       100                 0:00:43
    183.8.64.130       100                 0:01:02
  Distance: (default is 100)
 --More--
```

The show ip interfaces Command

The **show ip interfaces** command displays the status and global parameters associated with all IP interfaces (see Listing 26-4). The Cisco IOS software automatically enters a directly connected route in the routing table if the interface is one through which software can send and receive packets; such an interface is marked *up*. If the interface is unusable, it is removed from the routing table. Removing the entry allows the use of backup routes, if they exist.

Listing 26-4 The show ip interfaces Command

```
Router> show ip interfaces
Ethernet0 is up, line protocol is up
  Internet address is 183.8.128.2, subnet mask is 255.255.255.128
  Broadcast address is 255.255.255.255
  Address determined by non-volatile memory
  MTU is 1500 bytes
  Helper address is not set
  Directed broadcast forwarding is enabled
  Outgoing access list is not set
  Inbound access list is not set
  Proxy ARP is enabled
  Security level is default
  Split horizon is enabled
  ICMP redirects are always sent
  ICMP unreachables are always sent
  ICMP mask replies are never sent
  IP fast switching enabled
  IP fast switching on the same interface is disabled
  IP SSE switching is disabled
  Router Discovery is disabled
  IP output packet accounting is disabled
  IP access violation accounting is disabled
  TCP/IP header compression is disabled
  Probe proxy name replies are disabled
--More--
```

e-LAB ACTIVITY 26.9

Overview of the show ip interface Command

In this activity, you demonstrate how to view the status and global parameters associated with IP interfaces.

The show ip route Command

The **show ip route** command displays the contents of the IP routing table (see Listing 26-5). The table contains a list of all known networks and subnets and the metrics associated with each entry. Note that in this example, the information was derived either from IGRP (I) or from direct connections (C).

Listing 26-5 The show ip route Command

```
Router> show ip route
Codes:  C - connected, S - static, R - RIP, M - mobile, B - BGP
        D - EIGRP, EX - EIGRP external, O - OSPF, IA - OSPF inter area
        E1 - OSPF external type 1, E2 - OSPF external type 2, E - EGP
        i - IS-IS, L1 - IS-IS level 1, L2 - IS-IS level 2
        * - candidate default

Gateway of last resort is not set
   144.253.0.0 is subnetted (mask is 255.255.255.0), 1 subnets
C  144.253.100.0 is directly connected, Ethernet1
I  133.3.0.0 [100/1200] via 144.253.100.200, 00:00:57, Ethernet1
I  153.50.0.0 [100/1200] via 183.8.128.12, 00:00:05, Ethernet0
   183.8.0.0 is subnetted (mask is 255.255.255.128), 4 subnets
I  183.8.0.128 [100/180671] via 183.8.64.130, 00:00:27, Serial1
   [100/180671] via 183.8.128.130, 00:00:27, Serial0
C  183.8.128.0 is directly connected, Ethernet0
C  183.8.64.128 is directly connected, Serial1
C  183.8.128.128 is directly connected, Serial0
I  172.16.0.0 [100/1200] via 144.253.100.1, 00:00:55, Ethernet1
I  192.3.63.0 [100/1300] via 144.252.100.200, 00:00:58, Ethernet1
```

e-LAB ACTIVITY 26.10

Using the show ip route Command

In this activity, you demonstrate how to see the IP routing table.

The debug ip rip Command

The **debug ip rip** command displays RIP routing updates as they are sent and received (see Listing 26-6). In this example, the update is sent by 183.8.128.130. It reported on three routers, one of which is inaccessible because its hop count is greater than 15. Updates were then broadcast through 183.8.128.2 and 144.253.100.202.

Listing 26-6 The debug ip rip Command

```
Router# debug ip rip
RIP Protocl debugging is on
Router#
RIP:  received update from 183.8.128.130 on Serial0
      183.8.0.128 in 1 hops
      183.8.64.128 in 1 hops
      0.0.0.0 in 16 hops (inaccessible)
RIP:  received update from 183.8.64.140 on Seria11
      183.8.0.128 in 1 hops
      183.9.128.128 in 1 hops
      0.0.0.0 in 16 hops (inaccessible)
RIP: received update from 183.8.128.130 on Seria10
      183.8.0.128 in 1 hops
      183.8.64.128 in 1 hops
      0.0.0.0 in 16 hops (inaccessible)
```

continues

Listing 26-6 The debug ip rip Command (Continued)

```
RIP:  sending update to 255.255.255.255 via Ethernet0 (183.8.128.2)
      subnet 183.8.0.128, metric 2
      subnet 183.8.64.128, metric 1
      subnet 183.8.128.128, metric 1
      default 0.0.0.0, metrick 16
      network 144.253.0.0, metric 1
RIP:  sending update to 255.255.255.255 via Ethernet1 (144.253.100.202)
      default 0.0.0.0, metric 16
      network 153.50.0.0, metric 2
      network 183.8.0.0, metric 1
```

Use caution when using **debug** commands; they are processor-intensive and can decrease network performance or cause loss of connectivity. Use them only during times of low network usage. Disable the command when finished by using the command **no debug ip rip** or **no debug all.**

e-LAB ACTIVITY 26.11

Checking RIP Routing Updates

In this activity, you demonstrate how to check RIP routing updates as they are sent and received.

SKILL BUILDERS

Lab Activity: RIP Convergence

As a system administrator, sometimes configuring static routes can be very useful. Static routes are useful for stub networks because there is only one way to get to those networks. Security is another reason to use static routes. For example, if you have a network or networks that you don't want the rest of the network to be able to "see," you would not want RIP or other routing protocols sending periodic updates to other routers.

With simple networks (with few routers), it is sometimes more efficient to use static routes because this conserves bandwidth on WAN links. In this lab, you use static routes for troubleshooting purposes and to see their relationship to dynamic routes and routing protocols.

e-LAB ACTIVITY 26.12

Routing Loops Setup Challenge

In this activity, you demonstrate how to create a routing loop for the five-router setup.

SKILL BUILDER

Lab Activity: Routing Loops Challenge

In this lab, you set up a WAN connection between Lab A and Lab E to create alternate paths in the standard router lab setup. Using a set of WAN serial cables, connect Lab A Serial 1 to Lab E Serial 0. Remember to set the clock rate on the DCE side of the cable (Lab E's Serial 0 interface).

SKILL BUILDER

Lab Activity: Routing Loops Prevention Challenge

In the previous challenge lab, you saw how long it took to converge when a link went down. In this lab, your task is to find out how to prevent and control routing loops. Using hold-down timers, defining a maximum hop count, counting to infinity, and using poison reverse and split-horizon are all methods of controlling routing loops. You use the RIP hop count metric to control routing loops in this lab.

Summary

In this chapter, you learned that

- Initially, a router must refer to entries about networks or subnets that are directly connected.
- Routers learn paths to destinations three different ways:
  - Static routes
  - Default routes
  - Dynamic routes
- The **ip route** command sets up a static route.
- The **ip default-network** command establishes a default route.
- Routers can be configured to use one or more IP routing protocols, such as RIP and IGRP.

Check Your Understanding

1. What kind of entries does a router initially refer to?
   - **A.** Entries about networks or subnets that are directly connected
   - **B.** Entries that it has learned about from the Cisco IOS software
   - **C.** Entries whose IP address and mask information are known
   - **D.** Entries that it has learned about from other routers
2. Which of the following best describes a static route?
   - **A.** A routing table entry that is used to direct frames for which a next hop is not explicitly listed in the routing table
   - **B.** A route that is explicitly configured and entered into the routing table and that takes precedence over routes chosen by dynamic routing protocols
   - **C.** A route that adjusts automatically to network topology or traffic changes
   - **D.** A route that adjusts involuntarily to direct frames within a network topology
3. Which of the following best describes a default route?
   - **A.** A routing table entry that is used to direct frames for which a next hop is not explicitly listed in the routing table
   - **B.** A route that is explicitly configured and entered into the routing table
   - **C.** A route that adjusts automatically to network topology or traffic changes
   - **D.** A route that adjusts involuntarily to direct frames within a network topology
4. What are exterior routing protocols used for?
   - **A.** To transmit between nodes on a network
   - **B.** To deliver information within a single autonomous system
   - **C.** To communicate between autonomous systems
   - **D.** To set up a compatibility infrastructure between networks

5. What are interior routing protocols used for?

A. They are used to set up a compatibility infrastructure between networks.

B. They are used to communicate between autonomous systems.

C. They are used to transmit between nodes on a network.

D. They are used within a single autonomous system.

6. Which of the following is a global task?

A. Addressing IP network numbers by specifying subnet values

B. Enabling a routing protocol—RIP or IGRP

C. Assigning network/subnet addresses and the appropriate subnet mask

D. Setting up a routing metric to find the best path to each network

7. What metric does RIP use to determine the best path for a message to travel on?

A. Bandwidth

B. Hop count

C. Varies with each message

D. Administrative distance

8. You suspect that one of the routers connected to your network is sending bad routing information. What command can you use to check?

A. router(config)# **show ip route**

B. router# **show ip route**

C. router> **show ip protocol**

D. router(config-router)# **show ip protocol**

9. Why would you display the IP routing table?

A. To set the router update schedule

B. To identify destination network addresses and next-hop pairs

C. To trace where datagrams are coming from

D. To set the parameters and filters for the router

10. If you want to learn which routing protocol a router was configured with, what command structure should you use?
    - A. router> **show router protocol**
    - B. router(config)> **show ip protocol**
    - C. router(config)# **show router protocol**
    - D. router> **show ip protocol**
11. In the following command, what does the last number stand for? router (config)# **ip route 2.0.0.0 255.0.0.0 1.0.0.2** 5
    - A. The number of hops
    - B. The number of routes to the destination
    - C. The administrative distance
    - D. The destinations reference number in the routing table
12. An administrative distance of 15 indicates which of the following?
    - A. The IP address is static.
    - B. The IP address is dynamic.
    - C. The routing information source is relatively trustworthy.
    - D. The routing information source is relatively untrustworthy.
13. If you just added a new LAN to your internetwork and you want to manually add the network to your routing table, what command structure would you use?
    - A. router (config)> **ip route 2.0.0.0 255.0.0.0 via 1.0.0.2**
    - B. router (config)# **ip route 2.0.0.0 255.0.0.0 1.0.0.2**
    - C. router (config)# **ip route 2.0.0.0 via 1.0.0.2**
    - D. router (config)# **ip route 2.0.0.0 1.0.0.2 using 255.0.0.0**
14. In the IP RIP routing protocol, how often are routing updates sent?
    - A. Every 30 seconds
    - B. Every 60 seconds
    - C. Every 90 seconds
    - D. Only when the admin directs the router to do so

15. If you want to identify destination network addresses and next-hop pairs, what line matches what you would type?

    A. router(config)# **show ip protocol**

    B. router# **show ip table**

    C. router> **show ip route**

    D. router(config-router)# **show ip table**

16. Which of the following is a variable used by IGRP?

    A. Bandwidth

    B. File size

    C. Hop length

    D. Time span

17. IGRP sends routing updates at what interval?

    A. 30 seconds

    B. 60 seconds

    C. 90 seconds

    D. 120 seconds

18. When setting up dynamic IP routing, you must tell the process which interfaces will participate in the sending and receiving of routing updates. Which choice matches the command you would use to do this?

    A. router(config-if)> **network** *<network-number>*

    B. router(config)# **network** *<network-number>*

    C. router(config-router)# **network** *<network-number>*

    D. router(config-router)# **network** *<IP address>* *<subnet mask>*

19. After using the **router igrp** command, why is it necessary to use the **network** subcommand?

    A. It displays the contents of the network routing table.

    B. It allows each router to send its routing table in routing updates to all the networks.

C. It displays the status and global parameters associated with a network.

D. It specifies any directly connected networks to be included.

20. If you wanted to see RIP routing updates as they are sent and received, what command structure would you use?

A. router# **show ip rip**

B. router# **debug ip protocols**

C. router# **debug ip rip**

D. router# **show ip rip update**

Objectives

After reading this chapter, you will be able to

- Describe a general model for troubleshooting
- Describe how to develop a troubleshooting routine

Network Troubleshooting

Introduction

By performing router labs, you become more familiar with the troubleshooting process. In this chapter, you explore troubleshooting in more detail. To some extent, troubleshooting is an individualized process. However, some principles are common to any troubleshooting methodology. In the following pages, we use the language of the OSI model to put troubleshooting in perspective as it relates to Semester 2 router labs. Then we present a general problem-solving approach for networking.

Troubleshooting Semester 2 Labs

You gained quite a bit of skill in troubleshooting during the time you spent configuring routers in Semester 2 (see Figure 27-1). You learned to work upward from Layer 1 of the OSI model, progressing from the physical layer to the data link layer, to the network layer, and beyond. A review of some of the common Layer 1, Layer 2, and Layer 3 issues that you learned to resolve follows.

Layer 1 errors can include these (see Figure 27-2):

- Broken cables
- Disconnected cables
- Cables connected to the wrong ports
- Intermittent cable connections
- Cables incorrectly terminated
- Wrong cables used for the tasks at hand (must use cross-connects, rollovers, and straight-through cables correctly)
- Transceiver problems
- DCE cable problems
- DTE cable problems
- Devices powered off

FIGURE 27-1
Here is the Semester 2 lab configuration with all the usual settings.

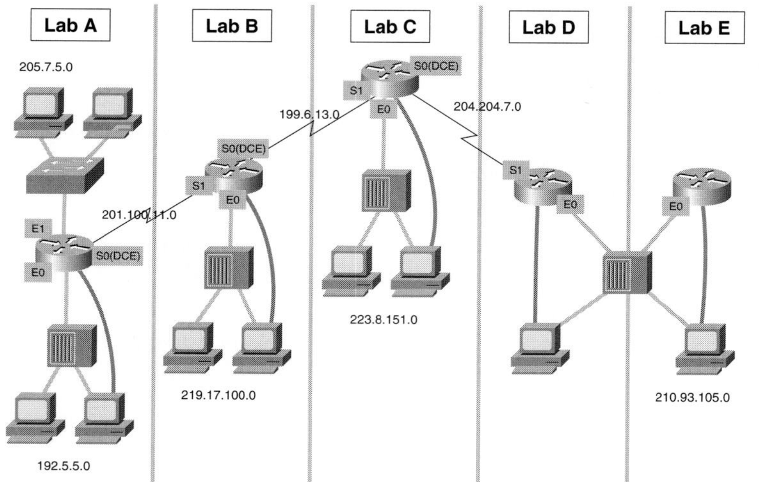

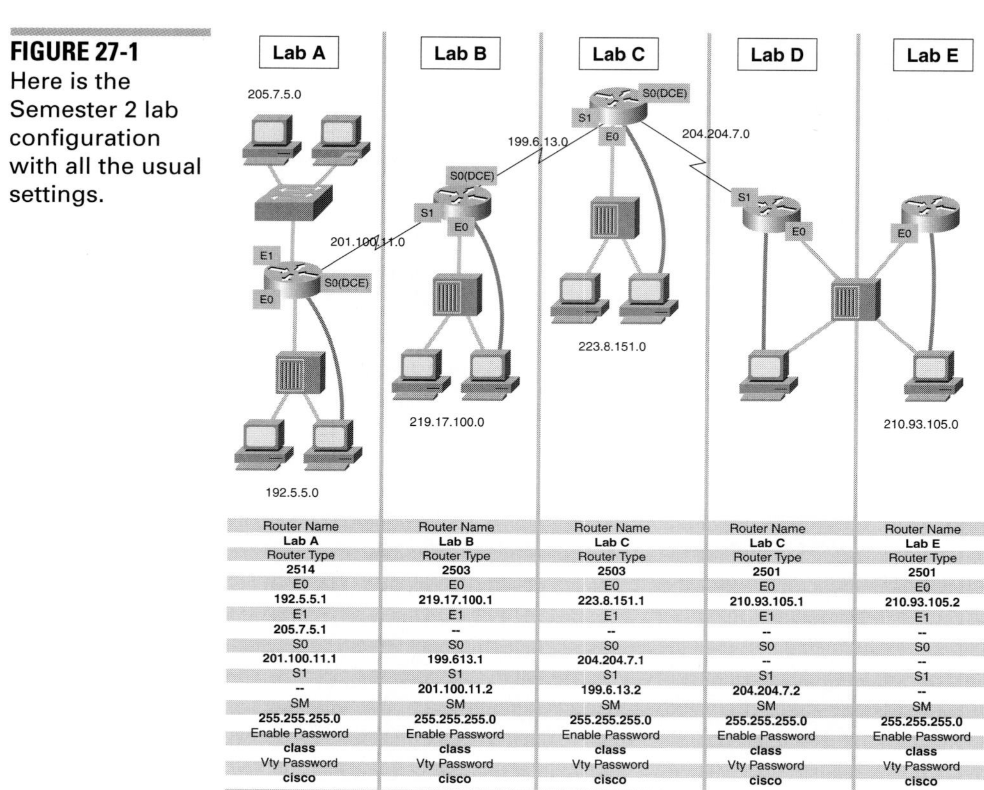

	Lab A	Lab B	Lab C	Lab D	Lab E
Router Name	**Lab A**	**Lab B**	**Lab C**	**Lab C**	**Lab E**
Router Type	**2514**	**2503**	**2503**	**2501**	**2501**
E0	**192.5.5.1**	**219.17.100.1**	**223.8.151.1**	**210.93.105.1**	**210.93.105.2**
E1	**205.7.5.1**	--	--	--	--
S0	**201.100.11.1**	**199.613.1**	**204.204.7.1**	--	--
S1	--	**201.100.11.2**	**199.6.13.2**	**204.204.7.2**	--
SM	**255.255.255.0**	**255.255.255.0**	**255.255.255.0**	**255.255.255.0**	**255.255.255.0**
Enable Password	**class**	**class**	**class**	**class**	**class**
Vty Password	**cisco**	**cisco**	**cisco**	**cisco**	**cisco**

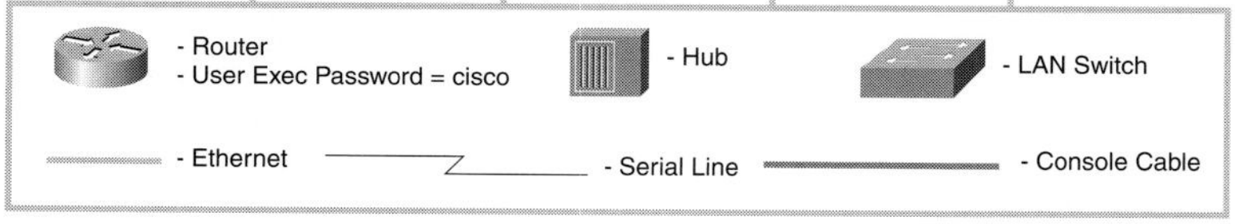

Layer 2 errors can include the following (see Figure 27-3):

- Improperly configured serial interfaces
- Improperly configured Ethernet interfaces
- Incorrect clock rate settings on serial interfaces
- Improper encapsulation set on serial interfaces (HDLC is default)
- Faulty NIC

FIGURE 27-2
Always start troubleshooting by analyzing Layer 1 issues.

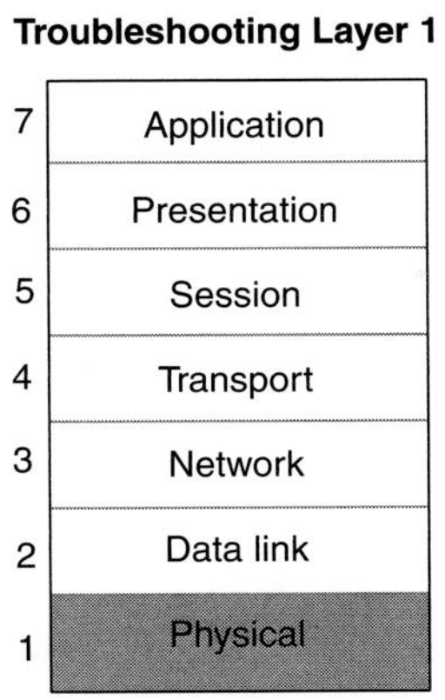

Troubleshooting Layer 1
7 Application
6 Presentation
5 Session
4 Transport
3 Network
2 Data link
1 Physical

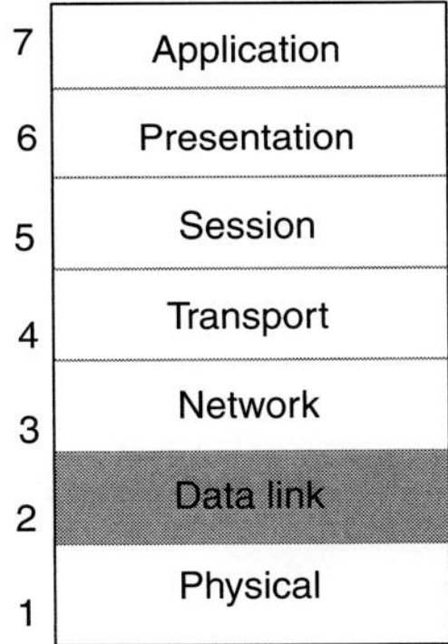

FIGURE 27-3
The second OSI layer that you should troubleshoot is Layer 2.

Troubleshooting Layer 2
7 Application
6 Presentation
5 Session
4 Transport
3 Network
2 Data link
1 Physical

Layer 3 errors can include these (see Figure 27-4):

- Routing protocol not enabled
- Wrong routing protocol enabled
- Incorrect network/IP addresses
- Incorrect subnet masks
- Incorrect interface addresses
- Incorrect DNS-to-IP bindings (host table entries)
- Wrong autonomous system number for IGRP

FIGURE 27-4
Normally, you complete your troubleshooting with Layer 3 of the OSI model.

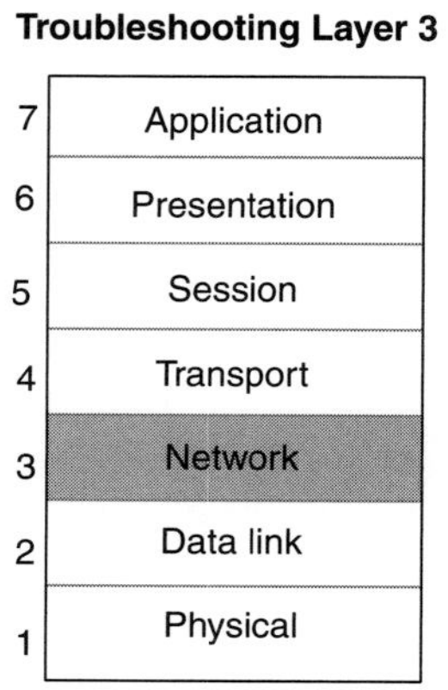

Troubleshooting Layer 3

7	Application
6	Presentation
5	Session
4	Transport
3	Network
2	Data link
1	Physical

It's important to be familiar with troubleshooting the Layer 1, Layer 2, and Layer 3 errors listed. That's not the end of the story, however, because you also need to know where to look for help if you can't immediately determine why a network is not working as desired. Figure 27-5 lists some of these resources. One resource that networking professionals use frequently is the documentation Web site at Cisco Connection Online (CCO), at www.cisco.com.

FIGURE 27-5
Here is a list of troubleshooting resources, in case the usual troubleshooting techniques don't work.

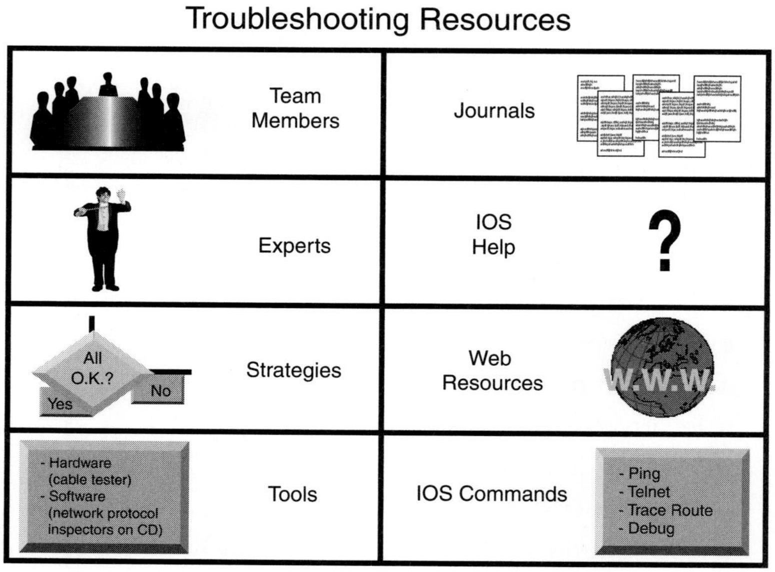

Troubleshooting Resources

Team Members	Journals
Experts	IOS Help
Strategies (All O.K.? Yes / No)	Web Resources (W.W.W.)
Tools: - Hardware (cable tester) - Software (network protocol inspectors on CD)	IOS Commands: - Ping - Telnet - Trace Route - Debug

A General Model for Troubleshooting

It's useful to have a general method to refer to when troubleshooting computer networks. This section outlines one such method used by many networking professionals.

The steps are as follows:

Step 1 Define the problem. What are the symptoms and the potential causes?

Step 2 Gather the facts. Isolate the possible causes.

Step 3 Consider the possibilities. Based on the facts gathered, narrow the focus to areas relevant to the specific problem. This is the step where you set the boundaries for the problem.

Step 4 Create an action plan. Devise a plan in which you manipulate only *one* variable at a time.

Step 5 Implement the action plan. Perform each step carefully while testing to see if the symptom disappears.

Step 6 Observe the results. Determine whether you resolved the problem. If so, the process is complete.

Step 7 Repeat the process. If you did not resolve the problem, move to the next most likely cause on your list. Return to Step 4, and repeat the process until you solve the problem.

Applying the Model for Troubleshooting

Now consider an example of how you can apply the troubleshooting model in a router lab (see Figure 27-6).

When trying to **ping** Lab-E from Lab-A, you receive a series of timeout messages.

```
lab-a#ping lab-e

Type escape sequence to abort.
Sending 5, 100-byte ICMP Echos to 210.93.105.2, timeout is 2 seconds:
.....
Success rate is 0 percent (0/5)
```

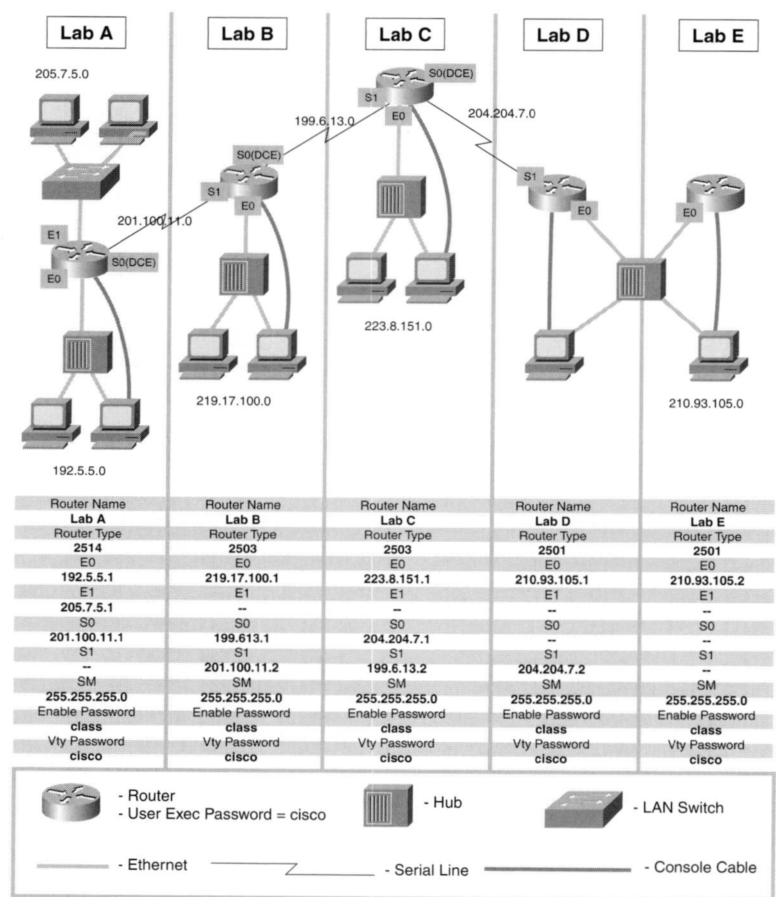

FIGURE 27-6 The familiar Semester 2 router lab diagram.

You now begin Step 1 of the troubleshooting model:

Step 1 Define the problem. What are the symptoms and the potential causes? Begin by listing the symptoms:

Unable to **ping** Lab-E from Lab-A.

Then list the potential causes by layer:

— Layer 1

A. Bad cable

B. Cable not connected

C. Power loss on hub

— Layer 2

A. Interface shut down

B. Improper encapsulation set (HDLC is the default on serial interfaces)

C. Incorrect clock rate settings on serial interfaces

— Layer 3

A. Wrong interface address

B. Wrong subnet mask

C. Wrong routing information

Step 2 Gather the facts. Isolate the possible causes.

You can do this by using the router's **show** commands to isolate the problem. Begin by testing the whole network. Because this network is under the control of one administration, the routing table of each router contains all the networks in the WAN.

Type **show ip route** at the privileged EXEC prompt on Lab-A. This shows the routing table for Lab-A. All eight networks should be displayed. In the following sequence, only seven of the eight networks appear in the routing table:

```
lab-a#show ip route
Codes: C - connected, S -  static, I - IGRP, R - RIP, M - mobile, B - BGP
    D - EIGRP, EX - EIGRP external, O - OSPF, IA - OSPF inter area
    N1 - OSPF NSSA external type 1, N2 - OSPF NSSA external type 2
    E1 - OSPF external type 1, E2 - OSPF external type 2, E - EGP
    i - IS-IS, L1 - IS-IS level-1, L2 - IS-IS level-2, * - candidate default
    U - per-user static route, o - ODR

Gateway of last resort is not set

C  205.7.5.0/24 is directly connected, Ethernet1
R  219.17.100.0/24 [120/1] via 201.100.11.2, 00:00:24, Serial0
R  199.6.13.0/24 [120/1] via 201.100.11.2, 00:00:24, Serial0
R  204.204.7.0/24 [120/2] via 201.100.11.2, 00:00:24, Serial0
C  192.5.5.0/24 is directly connected, Ethernet0
R  223.8.151.0/24 [120/2] via 201.100.11.2, 00:00:24, Serial0
C  201.100.11.0/24 is directly connected, Serial0
```

Step 3 Consider the possibilities. Based on the facts gathered, narrow the focus to those areas relevant to the specific problem. Set the boundaries of the problem. To do this, you must simplify the search area; move from the big picture to a more focused and detailed look of where the problem could be.

The information from the routing table shows that network 204.204.7.0 is two hops away, which is displayed as [120/2] in the line **R 204.204.7.0/24 [120/2] via 201.100.11.2, 00:00:24, Serial0.** Two hops from Lab-A is Lab-C, which is the last router that shared its RIP information. You should begin troubleshooting at the last router from which you received information. Now gather information on a smaller scale. Focus on a single router. Telnet to the router Lab-C. At Lab-C, type **show run** to see the router's running configuration. Be sure to log the configuration file (write the configuration in your journal, or copy and paste the configuration into a Notepad file).

```
lab-a#lab-c
Trying lab-c (199.6.13.2)... Open


User Access Verification

Password:
lab-c>ena
Password:
lab-c#show run
Building configuration...


Current configuration:
!
version 11.3
service timestamps debug uptime
service timestamps log uptime
no service password-encryption
!
hostname lab-c
!
enable password class
<more>
```

```
interface Ethernet0
 ip address 223.8.151.1 255.255.255.0
!
interface Serial0
 ip address 204.204.7.1 255.255.255.0
 no ip mroute-cache
 clockrate 56000
!
interface Serial1
 ip address 199.6.13.2 255.255.255.0
!
interface BRI0
 no ip address
 shutdown
!
router rip
 network 199.6.13.0
 network 204.204.7.0
 network 223.8.151.0
!
ip host lab-a 192.5.5.1 205.7.5.1
ip host lab-b 201.100.11.2.219.17.100.1
<more>
```

Gather information on the interface connected to the last displayed network from the **show ip route** command. At the prompt, type **show int s0**; this displays all the current information about the interface. Log this information.

```
lab-c#sho int s0
Serial0 is up, line protocol is up
 Hardware is HD64570
 Internet address is 204.204.7.1/24
 MTU 1500 bytes, BW 1544 Kbit, DLY 20000 usec,,
  reliability 255/255, txload 1/255, rxload 1/255
 Encapsulation HDLC, loopback not set, keepalive set (10 sec)
 Last input 00:00:01, output 00:00:00, output hang never
 Last clearing of "show interface" counters never
 Input queue: 0/75/0 (size/max/drops); Total output drops: 0
 Queueing strategy: weighted fair
 Output queue: 0/1000/64/0 (size/max total/threshold/drops)
  Conversations 0/1/256 (active/max active/max total)
  Reserved Conversations 0/0 (allocated/max allocated)
```

```
5 minute input rate 0 bits/sec, 0 packets/sec
5 minute output rate 0 bits/sec, 0 packets/sec
  185 packets input, 12570 bytes, 0 no buffer
  Received 185 broadcasts, 0 runts, 0 giants, 0 throttles
  0 input errors, 0 CRC, 0 frame, 0 overrun, 0 ignored, 0 abort
  241 packets output, 20487 bytes, 0 underruns
  0 output errors, 0 collisions, 21 interface resets
  0 output buffer failures, 0 output buffers swapped out
  10 carrier transitions
  DCD=up DSR=up DTR=up RTS=up CTS=up
```

Step 4 Create an action plan. Devise a plan in which you manipulate only one variable at a time.

From the information about Lab-C's running configuration, you see that everything is correctly configured. Looking then at the information from the **show int s0** report, you see that the interface is up and the line protocol is up. This tells you that the cable is connected to a device on the other end and that the data link layer is functional. If the cable is not connected properly, the line protocol will be down. From these two **show** commands, you know that this router is correctly configured and functioning. The problem must be at the next router, Lab-D. This is an example of the process of elimination, or of simplifying the problem. A good action plan would start by attempting to Telnet to router Lab-D and then moving to Lab-D's terminal to check the running configuration for errors. If you do not find errors in the configuration, you might need to examine the S1 interface.

Step 5 Implement the action plan. Perform each step carefully while testing to see if the symptom disappears.

You tried to Telnet to router Lab-D and failed. You must now go to the terminal connected to Lab-D. Enter privileged EXEC mode and type **show run**. From this report, you notice that the routing protocol on Lab-D is IGRP instead of RIP (which router Lab-C uses). To correct this error, you need to enter global configuration mode, type **no router igrp 111**, and enter the command **router rip**. Now enter the network commands **network 210.93.105.0** and **network 204.204.7.0** (these are the networks directly connected to Lab-D). Then type Ctrl-Z and issue the **copy run start** command.

Step 6 Observe the results. Determine whether you resolved the problem. If so, the process is complete.

Now test connectivity by **ping**ing Lab-A and Lab-E.

```
lab-d#ping lab-a

Type escape sequence to abort.
Sending 5, 100-byte ICMP Echos to 192.5.5.1, timeout is 2 seconds:
!!!!
Success rates is 100 percent (5/5), round-trip min/avg/max = 96/100/108 ms

lab-d#ping lab-e

Type escape sequence to abort.
Sending 5, 100-byte ICMP Echos to 210.93.105.2, timeout is 2 seconds:
!!!!
Success rate is 100 percent (5/5), round-trip min/avg/max =  1/3/4 ms
```

Step 7 Repeat the process. If you did not resolve the problem, move to the next most likely cause on your list. Return to Step 4, and repeat the process until you solve the problem.

Although you found an error in the configuration file of the router and corrected it, this might not successfully restore connectivity. Some problems have multiple causes. If this fails to fix the problem, return to Step 4 and develop a new action plan. Just as most network problems are caused by user error, your action plan might also contain errors. Most errors in an action plan are omissions, simply overlooked configuration items. The process of troubleshooting can be frustrating. Remember: Don't panic. If you reach a point at which you need help, don't be afraid to ask.

To put all this in perspective, Figure 27-7 shows a flowchart for the troubleshooting model.

With this guide, you can resolve most network failures that confront you. As a networking professional, troubleshooting plays a vital role in day-to-day work, so it is critical that you get a lot of hands-on experience to improve your troubleshooting skills. For many people, troubleshooting is the most enjoyable and rewarding part of networking. With a little time and patience, the process of troubleshooting becomes second nature.

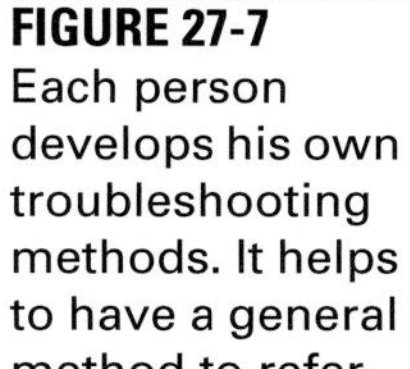

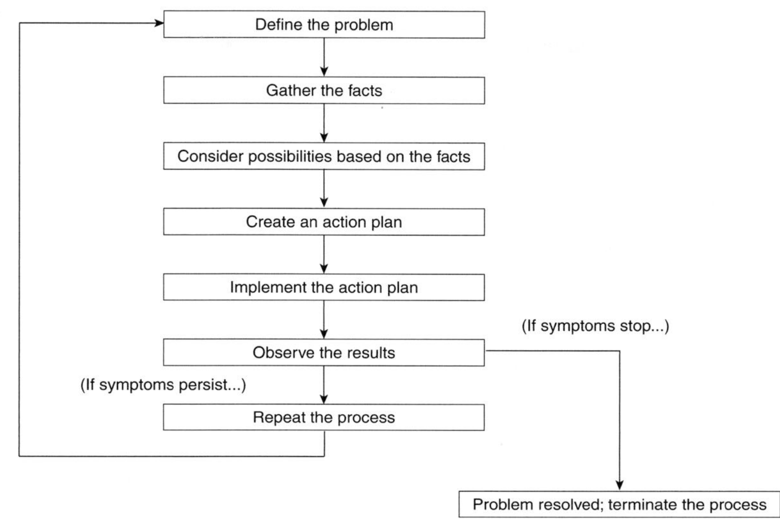

FIGURE 27-7 Each person develops his own troubleshooting methods. It helps to have a general method to refer to if all else fails.

IP Troubleshooting Scenarios

This section covers aspects of troubleshooting IP connectivity problems that have not yet been discussed. This is not intended to be an in-depth analysis of IP network troubleshooting. However, it does cover some of the fundamental skills that anyone supporting an IP network should have. The troubleshooting methodology presented is very structured and uses the process of elimination to isolate the failure to the root symptom. Like many network failures, the root cause of the failure in this scenario may never be known.

Developing a Troubleshooting Routine

Troubleshooting techniques vary significantly from one network engineer to another. They are part science and part artistry. A good network engineer can simultaneously think in a linear fashion (following a logical progression of an event from start to finish) and in a lateral fashion (considering events not directly related to the problem at hand but possibly having an effect).

In general, there is no one correct way to determine the root cause of a problem. However, you can follow a few guidelines:

- Determine as much as possible exactly what problem you are trying to solve, and focus on it. Networks are a lot like cars: You can start out investigating one problem and find 10 other things that may need attention.

Make a note of any unrelated problems, but focus on investigating the primary problem.

- If several users are reporting problems from different areas of the network at the same time, there is a good chance that they are reporting elements of the same problem. Focus on one area at a time. It can be overwhelming to have 1000 or more users down at once, but if the same problem is simply reoccurring in multiple parts of the network, you have to figure it out only once.
- Whenever possible, try to duplicate the problem in a lab and troubleshoot it there. Often, the act of troubleshooting a problem has a greater negative impact on the end-user population than the original problem.
- If any test requires reconfiguring a device, ensure that you can roll back the change after the test, or you might find that you have backed yourself into a corner and cannot proceed.
- Use as few tests as possible to isolate and define the problem.
- Ensure that the results of the tests are unambiguous.
- Validate the test results by repeating each one at least twice. Note that running a command to verify a configuration parameter is not considered a test in this sense and therefore doesn't need to be performed twice.
- Document the tests performed and the results (in case a bug is found).
- Document any changes made to the network during the troubleshooting procedure so that the network can be properly restored to its original condition.
- Document any workarounds that were left in place so that other support personnel will be able to understand how and why the network changed.

Using a Troubleshooting Scenario

The problem in this fictional scenario is that end systems A and B cannot **ping** each other. (Assume that the Frame Relay network is fully functional.) End system A is a Sun Classic running Solaris 2.5, and end system B is a PC running Windows 98, as shown in Figure 27-8.

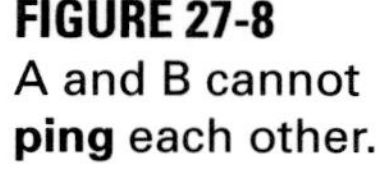

FIGURE 27-8
A and B cannot **ping** each other.

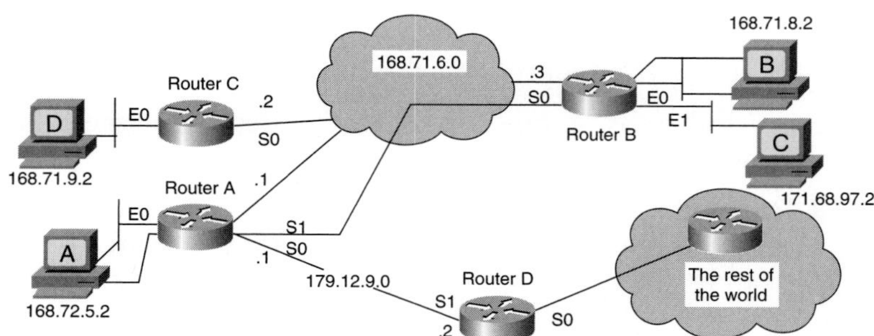

Checking the Available Routes

In the following output of **show ip route 168.71.8.2** from Router A, you can see that Router A has a route to the subnet that PC-B is on:

```
RouterA#show ip route 168.71.8.2
Routing entry for 168.71.8.0 255.255.255.0
  Known via "rip", distance 120, metric 1
  Redistributing via rip
  Last update from 168.71.6.3 on Serial1, 00:00:13 ago
  Routing Descriptor Blocks:
  * 168.71.6.3, from 168.71.6.3, 00:00:13 ago, via Serial1
      Route metric is 1, traffic share count is 1
RouterB#
```

In the following output of **show ip route 168.72.5.2** from Router B, you can see that Router B has a route to this subnet:

```
RouterB#show ip route 168.72.5.2
Routing entry for 168.72.5.0 255.255.255.0
  Known via "rip", distance 120, metric 1
  Redistributing via rip
  Last update from 168.71.6.1 on Serial0, 00:00:23 ago
  Routing Descriptor Blocks:
  * 168.71.6.1, from 168.71.6.1, 00:00:23 ago, via Serial0

      Route metric is 1, traffic share count is 1
RouterB#
```

The previous test has validated that the two routers have knowledge of the subnets that Sun-A and PC-B are on.

Tracing the Route

Another useful tool is the traceroute utility. It is used to trace a route (path) between a device and a host on a remote network or subnetwork address. Most systems with a TCP/IP protocol stack have a version of this utility; in Windows 98, it is called tracert.exe. It is usually found in the Windows directory.

The following output of the **traceroute 168.71.8.2** command from SUN-A shows that the trace dies after reaching Router B. Note that SUN-A resolved the Domain Name System (DNS) entry for PC-B before attempting the trace:

```
SUN-A> traceroute 168.71.8.2
traceroute to pc-b.cisco.com (168.71.8.2), 30 hops max, 40 byte packets
 1  routerb (168.71.6.3)  3 ms  3 ms  3 ms
 2  *    *    *
 3  *    *    *
 4  *    *    *
 5  *    *    *
SUN-A>
```

The following output of the **tracert 168.72.5.2** command from PC-B shows that the trace never really starts. It was necessary to kill the tracert session by pressing Ctrl-C (^C). This typically means that the PC cannot reach its first gateway:

```
c:\windows\ > tracert 168.72.5.2
c:\windows\ >
```

> **NOTE**
>
> Cisco routers also have a **traceroute** utility that can be run from a command prompt. The syntax is **traceroute xxxx.xxxx.xxxx.xxxx**, where every **x** represents a host address. See the Cisco IOS documentation for more information on Cisco's implementation of **traceroute**.

You can test whether the PC is running tracert correctly by tracing the route to itself:

```
c:\windows\ > tracert 168.71.8.2
Tracing route to 168.71.8.2 over a maximum of 30 hops:
  1     2 ms     3 ms     2 ms 168.71.6.3
Trace complete.
c:\windows\ >
```

If the PC fails to run tracert correctly, it appears to freeze after you enter the **tracert** command:

```
c:\windows\ > tracert 168.71.8.2
```

If this happens, you need to terminate the operation by pressing Ctrl-C (^C). You can then use the winipcfg.exe utility to verify that you have an IP address. At a DOS command prompt, type **winipcfg**, which brings up the Windows IP configuration tracking utility.

If your IP address appears as 0.0.0.0, your system doesn't have an IP address configured. Contact your system administrator or refer to the Microsoft documentation on configuring the TCP/IP protocol. If an IP address appears but is not the address you expected, try running **tracert** on this address; it should work.

In this case, PC-B appears to be running tracert.exe correctly. Note that the address was not resolved to a DNS entry, possibly because PC-B could not reach its DNS server.

The problem now appears to be that PC-B cannot reach its local gateway, which prevents PC-B from reaching any hosts on different subnets or networks.

Using Extended pings to Track Connectivity

Another method for quickly determining whether an end system (such as PC-B) has connectivity to its gateway is to use the extended **ping** function available on Cisco routers (see Figure 27-9).

Extended **ping** enables you to select a source address for the **ping**s from any valid IP address in the router. Normally, **ping**s from a router use as a source address the address from the interface attached to the subnet that the **ping**s will exit over.

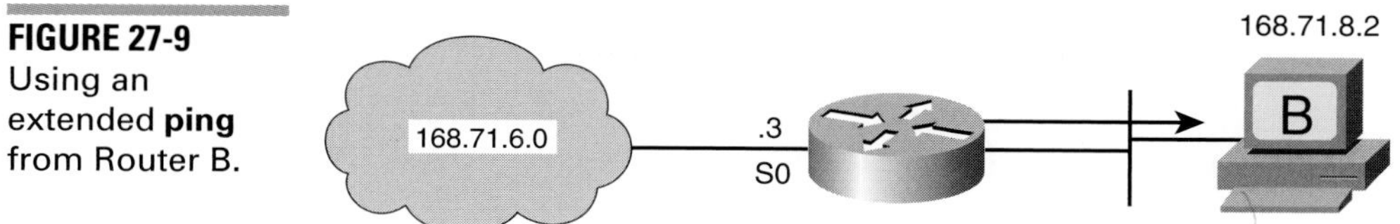

FIGURE 27-9
Using an extended **ping** from Router B.

The following output from Router B **ping**ing PC-B shows that the **ping**s have failed. Note that the source IP address, 168.71.6.3, is not on the same subnet as PC-B, proving that PC-B is having a problem reaching its gateway.

```
RouterB#ping
Protocol [ip]:
Target IP address: 168.71.8.2
Repeat count [5]:
Datagram size [100]:
Timeout in seconds [2]:
Extended commands [n]: y
Source address: 168.71.6.3
Type of service [0]:
Set DF bit in IP header? [no]:
Validate reply data? [no]:
Data pattern [0xABCD]:
Loose, Strict, Record, Timestamp, Verbose[none]:
Sweep range of sizes [n]:
Type escape sequence to abort.
Sending 5, 100-byte ICMP Echos to 168.71.8.2, timeout is 2 seconds:
...
Success rate is 0 percent (0/5)
RouterB#
```

NOTE

See the Cisco IOS documentation for more information on Cisco's implementation of **ping**.

Other Possible Problems

It is too early to assume that the problem lies with PC-B's gateway address. Although it might make sense at this point to skip to checking the gateway address of PC-B, doing so would eliminate the opportunity to show some other useful troubleshooting techniques.

An ARP Problem

It is not unheard of to encounter a problem with the ARP process. An ARP entry can be corrupted. Another example is that the gateway interface MAC address changes when someone installs a new interface. The end system's ARP entry for the old IP/MAC address combination might not have timed out yet, which would cause the end system to send packets to the wrong Layer 2 (MAC) address.

> **NOTE**
>
> Cisco routers do not have the problem of changing the MAC addresses for interfaces when the physical interfaces themselves are changed. This is because Cisco routers download the MAC address for interfaces from a table of addresses held in memory on the system board that holds the CPU. In a 7500-based system, the MAC addresses are held on the RSP.

> **NOTE**
>
> It's possible to manipulate these routing tables temporarily by using the procedures provided in this section. Making the changes permanent requires that the configuration files themselves be modified, which is beyond the scope of this book. Consult the system administrator or the system reference guide for the system in question.

Remember that Layer 2 addresses represent local, point-to-point connectivity on the physical LAN, to which the end system and the gateway are attached. IP addresses, in contrast, permit end-to-end connectivity.

In the following output from the **show arp** command on Router B, you can see the IP/MAC addresses in use. On Cisco routers, the **show interface** command shows the MAC addresses assigned to the interfaces. On a Windows 98 system, the winipcfg.exe utility shows the MAC address in use by the PC.

```
RouterB#show arp
Protocol  Address          Age (min)    Hardware Addr  Type   Interface
Internet  168.71.8.1               -    0000.0c0a.50ca ARPA   Ethernet0
Internet  168.72.8.2               1    0060.9733.e9f5 ARPA   Ethernet0
```

In this scenario, the IP/MAC addresses appear correct. You can compare them to the addresses on PC-B. The **arp -a** command is a fairly universal method for displaying an ARP table on a device running TCP/IP:

```
C:\WINDOWS>arp -a
Interface: 168.71.8.2
  Internet Address  Physical Address      Type
  168.71.8.2        00-60-97-33-e9-f5     dynamic
  168.71.8.1        00-00-0c-0a-50-ca     dynamic
C:\WINDOWS>
```

The following output of **arp -a** from SUN-A is provided for reference only. You already know that SUN-A can reach its local gateway.

```
SUN-A > arp -a
Net to Media Table
Device IP Address                   Mask               Flags     Phys Addr
------ --------------------         ---------------    -----     ---------------
le0    168.72.5.1                   255.255.255.255              00:00:0c:32:93:95
le0    168.72.5.2                   255.255.255.255    SP        00:80:5f:78:79:71
SUN-A>
```

Because all the addresses match, it is probably safe to assume that they are correct. Therefore, the problem lies elsewhere.

Validating End System Routing Tables

The problem now appears to be with PC-B's gateway entry. This section explains how to verify this hypothesis and how to make a temporary change. You previously verified that SUN-A's use of its gateway is correct. (The methods for analyzing its routing table are presented in this section for reference purposes only).

Although neither end system is running a dynamic routing protocol, they both still have routing tables. The information in these tables is derived from configuration files when the systems start.

By displaying the routing table on PC-B, you find the problem. The default route of 0.0.0.0 0.0.0.0 is pointing to the wrong gateway address: 168.71.8.10. The correct gateway is 168.71.8.1:

```
C:\WINDOWS>netstat -rn
Route Table
Active Routes:
  Network Address    Netmask          Gateway Address  Interface     Metric
  0.0.0.0            0.0.0.0          168.71.8.10      168.71.8.2    1
  168.71.8.0         255.255.255.0    168.71.8.1       168.71.8.2    1
  168.71.8.2         255.255.255.255  127.0.0.1        127.0.0.1     1
  168.71.0.0         255.255.0.0      168.71.8.1       168.71.8.2    1
  168.71.255.255     255.255.255.255  168.71.8.2       168.71.8.2    1
  127.0.0.0          255.0.0.0        127.0.0.1        127.0.0.1     1
  224.0.0.0          224.0.0.0        168.71.8.2       168.71.8.2    1
  255.255.255.255    255.255.255.255  168.71.8.2       168.71.8.2    1
Active Connections
  Proto  Local Address          Foreign Address        State
C:\WINDOWS>
```

The following shows how to flush existing gateways and add a new gateway dynamically in Windows 98 at a DOS command prompt:

```
C:\WINDOWS>route -f add 0.0.0.0 mask 0.0.0.0 168.71.8.1
```

The following routing table from PC-B shows the correct gateway address in place:

```
C:\WINDOWS>netstat -rn
Route Table
Active Routes:
  Network Address    Netmask          Gateway Address  Interface    Metric
       0.0.0.0       0.0.0.0          168.71.8.1       168.71.8.2   1
       168.71.8.0    255.255.255.0    168.71.8.1       168.71.8.2   1
       168.71.8.2    255.255.255.255  127.0.0.1        127.0.0.1    1
       168.71.0.0    255.255.0.0      168.71.8.1       168.71.8.2   1
   168.71.255.255    255.255.255.255  168.71.8.2       168.71.8.2   1
        127.0.0.0    255.0.0.0        127.0.0.1        127.0.0.1    1
        224.0.0.0    224.0.0.0        168.71.8.2       168.71.8.2   1
  255.255.255.255    255.255.255.255  168.71.8.2       168.71.8.2   1
Active Connections
  Proto  Local Address          Foreign Address        State
C:\WINDOWS>
```

To make the same kind of a change on a Solaris system (and most other UNIX systems), use the following syntax (as ROOT):

```
SUN-A# route add default 168.71.5.1 1
add net default: gateway 168.71.5.1
```

Again, you use the **netstat -rn** command to display the routing table; the default equals 0.0.0.0:

```
SUN-A# netstat -rn
Routing Table:
```

NOTE

The second line shown in the previous UNIX output (add net default: gateway 168.71.5.1) is SUN-A echoing the command back to the terminal prompt. The word *default* and the address *0.0.0.0* can be used interchangeably.

continues

```
Destination           Gateway            Flags  Ref   Use   Interface
-------------------- ------------------- ----- ----- ------ ---------
127.0.0.1            127.0.0.1            UH       0     80  lo0
224.0.0.0            168.71.5.2           U        3      0  le0
default              168.71.5.1           UG       0   3622
SUN-A>
```

The following output of the **route** command from PC-B shows the various options that this command can accept. The syntax on UNIX systems and NT systems is very similar. You can typically find out the available options by entering the **route** command without any options after it. This is how the information that follows was created.

Remember that these commands are only temporary. Rebooting the PC restores the defaults.

```
C:\WINDOWS\Desktop>route
Manipulates network routing tables.
ROUTE [-f] [command [destination] [MASK netmask] [gateway]]
 -f            Clears the routing tables of all gateway entries. If this is
      used in conjunction with one of the commands, the tables are
      cleared prior to running the command.
 command       Specifies one of four commands:
 PRINT   Prints a route
 ADD     Adds a route
 DELETE  Deletes a route
 CHANGE  Modifies an existing route
 destination Specifies the host to send command.
MASK         If the MASK keyword is present, the next parameter is
             interpreted as the netmask parameter.
netmask      If provided, specifies a subnet mask value to be associated with this
             route entry. If not specified, it defaults to 255.255.255.255.
gateway      Specifies gateway.
```

All symbolic names used for **destination** or **gateway** are looked up in the network and host name database files, NETWORKS and HOSTS, respectively. If the command is **print** or **delete**, wildcards may be used for the **destination** and **gateway**, or the **gateway** argument might be omitted.

The following is an example of adding and then deleting a route on PC-B:

```
C:\WINDOWS>route add 171.68.97.0 mask 255.255.255.0 168.71.8.1
C:\WINDOWS>netstat -rn
Route Table
Active Routes:
  Network Address    Netmask          Gateway Address  Interface     Metric
       0.0.0.0       0.0.0.0          168.71.8.1       168.71.8.2    1
       168.71.8.0    255.255.255.0    168.71.8.1       168.71.8.2    1
       168.71.8.2    255.255.255.255  127.0.0.1        127.0.0.1     1
       168.71.0.0    255.255.0.0      168.71.8.1       168.71.8.2    1
   168.71.255.255    255.255.255.255  168.71.8.2       168.71.8.2    1
   171.68.97.0       255.255.255.0    168.71.8.1       168.71.8.2    1
        127.0.0.0    255.0.0.0        127.0.0.1        127.0.0.11
        224.0.0.0    224.0.0.0        168.71.8.2       168.71.8.2    1
  255.255.255.255    255.255.255.255  168.71.8.2       168.71.8.2    1
Active Connections
```

```
  Proto  Local Address          Foreign Address        State
C:\WINDOWS>
C:\WINDOWS>route delete 171.68.97.0 mask 255.255.255.0 168.71.8.1
C:\WINDOWS>netstat -rn
Route Table
Active Routes:
  Network Address    Netmask          Gateway Address  Interface      Metric
  0.0.0.0            0.0.0.0          168.71.8.1       168.71.8.2     1
  168.71.8.0         255.255.255.0    168.71.8.1       168.71.8.2     1
  168.71.8.2         255.255.255.255  127.0.0.1        127.0.0.1      1
  168.71.0.0         255.255.0.0      168.71.8.1       168.71.8.2     1
  168.71.255.255     255.255.255.255  168.71.8.2       168.71.8.2     1
  127.0.0.0          255.0.0.0        127.0.0.1        127.0.0.1      1
  224.0.0.0          224.0.0.0        168.71.8.2       168.71.8.2     1
  255.255.255.255    255.255.255.255  168.71.8.2       168.71.8.2     1
Active Connections
  Proto  Local Address          Foreign Address        State
C:\WINDOWS>
```

It is safe to practice with these commands because they are reset when the PC is rebooted or power-cycled.

This section has focused on some basic troubleshooting techniques that are useful when the problem appears to be an end system configuration issue.

Summary

This chapter introduced some basic troubleshooting techniques and guidelines. The two main ingredients in all network engineers' troubleshooting techniques are as follows:

- Knowledge of the way things are supposed to behave
- The ability to forget how things are supposed to behave and to have faith that what you are seeing is what is really happening—that is, the ability to step back and look at the situation from a naïve point of view.

Check Your Understanding

1. A loose cable would be classified as a problem with which layer?
   - **A.** Layer 4
   - **B.** Layer 3
   - **C.** Layer 2
   - **D.** Layer 1
2. Using the wrong encapsulation type on a serial interface would be classified as a problem with what layer?
   - **A.** Layer 4
   - **B.** Layer 3
   - **C.** Layer 2
   - **D.** Layer 1
3. Using the wrong subnet mask on an interface would be classified as a problem with what layer?
   - **A.** Layer 4
   - **B.** Layer 3
   - **C.** Layer 2
   - **D.** Layer 1
4. A flow control problem would be classified as a problem with what layer?
   - **A.** Layer 4
   - **B.** Layer 3
   - **C.** Layer 2
   - **D.** Layer 1
5. Incorrect routing protocols would be considered problems with what layer?
   - **A.** Layer 4
   - **B.** Layer 3
   - **C.** Layer 2
   - **D.** Layer 1

After reading this chapter, you will be able to

- Describe why network security is essential
- Describe network security as a continuous process

Chapter 28

Introduction to Network Security

Introduction

Today there is an ever-growing dependency on computer networks for business transactions. As a result, new business practices are driving a multitude of changes in all facets of enterprise networks. Consequently, network security is becoming more prevalent as organizations try to understand and manage the risks associated with the rapidly developing business applications and practices deployed over enterprise network infrastructures.

With the free flow of information and the high availability of many resources, managers of enterprise networks must understand all the possible threats to their networks. These threats take many forms, but all result in loss of privacy to some degree and possibly malicious destruction of information or resources that can lead to large monetary losses.

Restricted use of network infrastructure equipment and critical resources is necessary. Limiting network access to only those who require access is a smart way to deter many threats that breach computer network security. Not all threats are intended to be malicious, but they can exhibit the same behavior and can cause as much harm. It is important to understand what types of attacks and vulnerabilities are common and what you can do at a policy level to guarantee some degree of safe networking.

In this chapter, you learn why network security is essential. Additionally, you learn about the primary threats to network security and the different types of network attacks. Finally, you learn about the steps in the network security as a continuous process.

Why Network Security Is Essential

Network security is essential because the Internet is a network of interconnected networks without a boundary. Because of this fact, the organizational network becomes accessible and vulnerable from computers anywhere in the world. As companies become Internet businesses, new threats arise from persons who no longer require physical access to a company's computer assets to do harm.

In a recent survey conducted by the Computer Security Institute (CSI), 70 percent of the organizations polled stated that their network security defenses had been breached and that 60 percent of the incidents came from within the organizations.

Primary Threats to Network Security

Four primary types of threats to network security exist:

- Unstructured threats
- Structured threats
- External threats
- Internal threats

Unstructured threats consist of mostly inexperienced individuals using easily available hacking tools from the Internet. Some of the people in this category are motivated by malicious intent, but most are motivated by the intellectual challenge and are commonly known as *script kiddies*. These people are not the most talented or experienced hackers, but they have the motivation, which is all that matters.

Structured threats consist of hackers who are more highly motivated and technically competent. They usually understand network system designs and vulnerabilities, and they can understand as well as create hacking scripts to penetrate those network systems.

External threats are individuals or organizations working outside your company who do not have authorized access to your computer systems or network. They work their way into a network mainly from the Internet or dialup access servers.

Internal threats occur when someone has authorized access to the network with either an account on a server or physical access to the wire.

Three Types of Network Attacks

Three types of network attacks exist:

- **Reconnaissance attacks**—An intruder attempts to discover and map systems, services, and vulnerabilities.
- **Access attacks**—An intruder attacks networks or systems to retrieve data, gain access, or escalate their access privilege.
- **Denial of Service (DoS) attacks**—An intruder attacks your network in a way that damages or corrupts your computer system or that denies you and others access to your networks, systems, or services.

Reconnaissance is the unauthorized discovery and mapping of systems, services, or vulnerabilities. This is also known as information gathering and, in most cases, precedes an actual access or denial-of-service attack. The malicious intruder typically **ping**-sweeps the target network first to determine what IP addresses are alive. After this is accomplished, the intruder determines what services or ports are active on the live IP addresses. From this information the intruder queries the ports to determine the application type and version as well as the type and version of operating system running on the target host.

Reconnaissance is somewhat analogous to a thief scoping out a neighborhood for vulnerable homes to break into, such as an unoccupied residence, an easy-to-open door or window, and so on. In many cases the intruders go as far as "rattling the door handle," not to go in immediately if it's open, but to discover vulnerable services that they can exploit at a later time when there is less likelihood that anyone is looking.

Access is an all-encompassing term that refers to unauthorized data manipulation, system access, or privilege escalation. Unauthorized data retrieval is simply reading, writing, copying, or moving files that are not intended to be accessible to the intruder. Sometimes this is as easy as finding share folders in Windows 9x or NT, or NFS exported directories in UNIX systems with read or read and write access to everyone. The intruder will have no problems getting to the files—and, more often than not, the easily accessible information is highly confidential and completely unprotected to prying eyes.

System access is the ability of an intruder to gain access to a machine that the intruder is not allowed access to (for example, the intruder does not have an account or password). Entering or accessing systems that one does not have access to usually involves running a hack, script, or tool that exploits a known vulnerability of the system or application being attacked.

Another form of access attacks involves privilege escalation. This is done by legitimate users with a lower level of access privileges, or intruders who have gained lower privileged access. The intent is to get information or execute procedures that are not authorized at the current level of access. In many cases, this involves gaining root access in a UNIX system to install a sniffer to record network traffic such as usernames and passwords, which can be used to access another target.

In some cases, intruders only want to gain access without wanting to steal information—especially when the motive is intellectual challenge, curiosity, or ignorance. Denial of service occurs when an attacker disables or corrupts networks, systems, or services with the intent to deny the service to intended users. It usually involves either crashing the system or slowing it to the point that it is unusable. But denial of service can also be as simple as wiping out or corrupting information necessary for business. In most cases, performing the attack simply involves running a hack, script, or tool. The attacker does not need prior access to the target because all that is usually required is a way to get to it. For these reasons and because of the great damaging potential, denial-of-service attacks are the most feared—especially by e-commerce Web site operators.

Network Security as a Continuous Process

Network security should be a continuous process built around a security policy. A continuous security policy is most effective because it promotes retesting and reapplying updated security measures on a continuous basis. This continuous security process is represented by the security wheel in Figure 28-1.

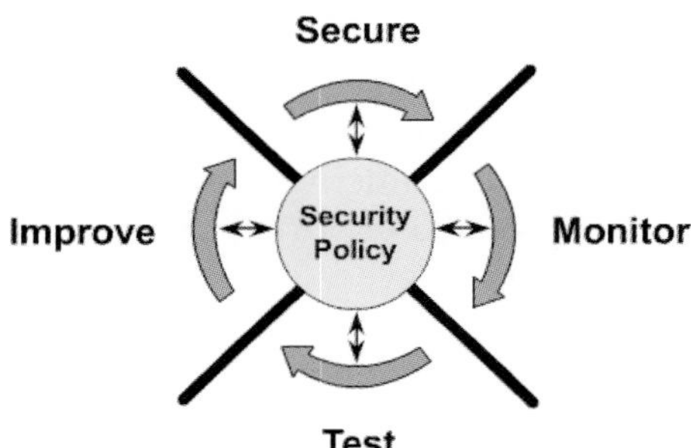

FIGURE 28-1
Network security as a continuous process built around a security policy.

To begin this continuous process known as the security wheel, you need to create a security policy that enables the application of security measures. A security policy needs to accomplish the following tasks:

- Identify the organization's security objectives
- Document the resources to be protected
- Identify the network infrastructure with current maps and inventories

To create or implement an effective security policy, you need to figure out what you want to protect and in what manner you are going to protect it. You should know and understand your network's weak points and how they can be exploited. You should also understand how your system normally functions so that you know what to expect and are familiar with how the devices are normally used. Finally, consider the physical security of your network and how to protect it. Physical access to a computer, router, or firewall can give a user total control over that device.

After the security policy is developed, it becomes the hub upon which the next four steps of the security wheel are based:

Step 1 Secure the system. This involves implementing security devices—firewalls, identification authentication systems, encryption, and so on—with the intent to prevent unauthorized access to network systems. This is where the PIX firewall is effective.

Step 2 Monitor the network for violations and attacks against the corporate security policy. Violations can occur within the secured perimeter of the network from a disgruntled employee or from outside the network by a hacker. Monitoring the network with a real-time intrusion detection system, such as the Cisco Secure Intrusion Detection System, can ensure that the security devices in Step 1 have been configured properly.

Step 3 Test the effectiveness of the security safeguards in place. Use Cisco Secure Scanner to identify the security posture of the network with respect to the security procedures that form the hub of the security wheel.

Step 4 Improve corporate security. Collect and analyze information from the monitoring and testing phases to make security improvements.

All four steps—secure, monitor, test, and improve—should be repeated on a continuous basis and should be incorporated into updated versions of the corporate security policy.

Secure the Network

Secure the network by applying the security policy and implementing the following security solutions (see Figure 28-2):

- **Authentication**—Gives access to authorized users only (for example, using one-time passwords).
- **Encryption**—Hides traffic contents to prevent unwanted disclosure to unauthorized or malicious individuals.
- **Firewalls**—Filter network traffic to allow only valid traffic and services.
- **Vulnerability patching**—Applies fixes or measures to stop the exploitation of known vulnerabilities. This includes turning off services that are not needed on every system; the fewer services that are enabled, the harder it is for hackers to gain access.

NOTE

Remember to implement physical security solutions to prevent unauthorized physical access to the network.

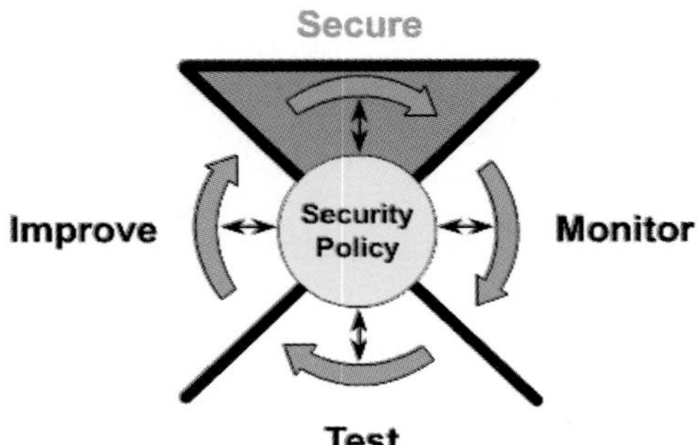

FIGURE 28-2
Implement security solutions to stop or prevent unauthorized access or activities and to protect information.

Monitor the Network

Monitor the network for violations and attacks against the corporate security policy. These attacks can occur within the secured perimeter of the network—from a disgruntled employee or contractor from a source outside your trusted network. Monitoring the network should be done with a real-time intrusion-detection device, such as the Cisco Secure Intrusion Detection System. This assists you in discovering unauthorized entries and also serves as a check-and-balance system for ensuring that devices implemented in Step 1 of the security wheel have been configured and are working properly (see Figure 28-3).

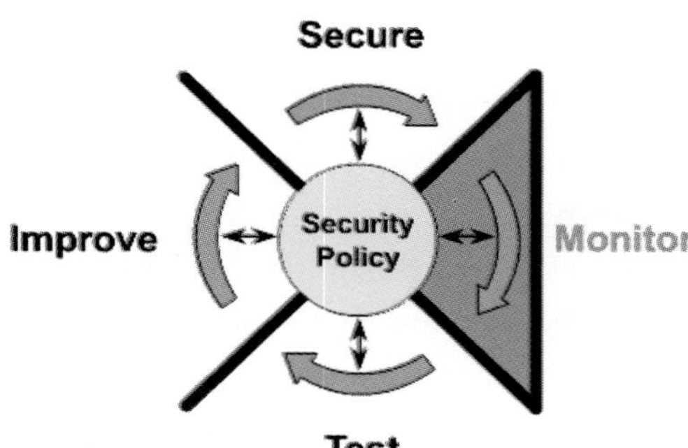

FIGURE 28-3
Monitoring the network involves system auditing and intrusion detection.

Test Security

Validation is a must. You can have the most sophisticated network security system, but if it is not working, your network can be compromised. This is why you need to test the devices you implemented in Steps 1 and 2 to make sure they are functioning properly. The Cisco Secure Scanner is designed to validate your network security (see Figure 28-4).

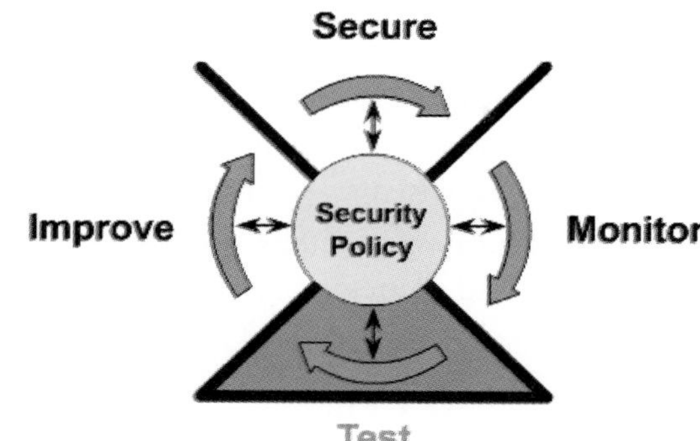

FIGURE 28-4
Testing security validates the effectiveness of the security policy through system auditing and vulnerability scanning.

Improve Security

The improvement phase of the security wheel involves analyzing the data collected during the monitoring and testing phases and then developing and implementing improvement mechanisms that feed into your security policy and the securing phase in Step 1. If you want to keep your network as secure as possible, you must keep repeating the cycle of the security wheel because new network vulnerabilities and risks are created every day (see Figure 28-5).

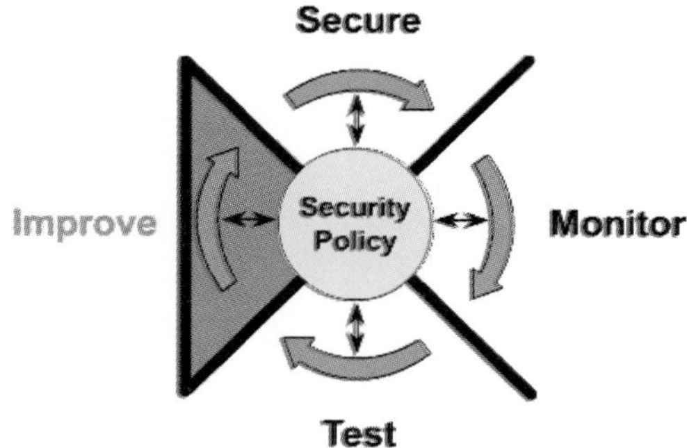

FIGURE 28-5
Use information from the monitor and test phases to make improvements to security implementation.

Summary

Now that you have completed this chapter, you should have a firm understanding of the following:

- Network security is essential because networked computers are accessible and vulnerable from computers anywhere in the world.
- Four types of primary threats to network security exist: unstructured threats, structured threats, external threats, and internal threats.
- Three types of network attacks can take place: reconnaissance attacks, access attacks, and Denial of Service attacks.
- The security wheel is a graphical representation of implementing security as a continuous process.

Check Your Understanding

1. What type of primary threat to network security consists of hackers who are highly motivated and technically competent?

   A. Internal threats

   B. External threats

   C. Structured threats

   D. Unstructured threats

2. What type of attack is similar to a thief scoping out a neighborhood for vulnerabilities?

   A. Access attacks

   B. Intruder attacks

   C. Denial-of-service attacks

   D. Reconnaissance attacks

3. What is the second step in the security wheel?

   A. Test security

   B. Monitor security

   C. Improve security

   D. Secure the network

4. What best describes an access attack?

   A. The unauthorized discovery and mapping of network systems and services

   B. The intrusion into a network to retrieve data or escalate a user's privileges

   C. Disabling or attacking services, rendering them useless for intended users

   D. The corruption or destruction of information that is used to operate a business

5. Which security solution is used to apply fixes or measures to stop the exploitation of know vulnerabilities?
   - **A.** Firewalls
   - **B.** Encryption
   - **C.** Authentication
   - **D.** Vulnerability patching
6. Which Cisco product is specifically designed to validate your network security?
   - **A.** Cisco Secure Scanner
   - **B.** Cisco Secure VPN Client
   - **C.** Cisco QoS Policy Manager
   - **D.** Cisco Secure Intrusion Detection
7. What must be done to keep your network as secure as possible?
   - **A.** Define a new security wheel each week
   - **B.** Keep repeating the cycle of the security wheel
   - **C.** Purchase a firewall for every workstation
   - **D.** Disable NAT on all intranetworking devices
8. Which step of the security wheel is the PIX firewall most effective?
   - **A.** Secure the system
   - **B.** Improve corporate security
   - **C.** Test the effectiveness of the security safeguards in place
   - **D.** Monitor the network for violations and attacks a against security policy
9. How are most people categorized in an unstructured security threat?
   - **A.** Contractors
   - **B.** Script kiddies
   - **C.** Current employees
   - **D.** Former employees

10. Which step of the security wheel is validation a must?

A. Test security

B. Monitor security

C. Improve security

D. Secure the network

Objectives

After reading this chapter, you will be able to

- Identify the functions of various types of audits
- Identify the purpose of a network map
- Identify network software management tools and their functions
- Identify characteristics and functions of SNMP and CMIP
- Identify methods needed to troubleshoot a network
- Identify the purpose of network performance evaluation

Chapter 29

Network Management

Introduction

In this book, you learned how to design and build networks. You learned how to select, install, and test cable, and you have learned to determine where wiring closets will be located. But network design and implementation are only part of what you need to know. You must also know how to maintain the network and keep it functioning at an acceptable level. This means that you must know how to troubleshoot problems when they arise. In addition, you must know when it is necessary to expand or change the network's configuration in order to meet the changing demands placed on it. In this chapter, you begin to learn about managing a network by using techniques such as documenting, auditing, monitoring, and evaluating.

The First Steps in Managing a Network

After a network has been implemented successfully and is in operation, it might seem like the perfect time to relax. A smart network administrator knows that is exactly the wrong approach to take. Instead, what you should be doing is documenting the network. Knowing how the network is supposed to work will make your job easier when problems occur. So instead of relaxing, use the time when the network is operating smoothly to perform an audit of the network. In fact, you need to perform five types of audits on the network: an inventory audit, a facility audit, an operational audit, an efficiency audit, and a security audit. All these types of audits are described in this chapter. You can begin inventory and facility audits almost immediately. Information for the operational, efficiency, and security audits can and should be obtained after the network has begun to function because these audits require data that can only be provided through monitoring and analysis of the network's behavior and performance.

Inventory Audits

An *inventory audit* allows you to take stock of all the network's hardware and software. Ideally, this information should be obtained when the hardware and software is purchased and before it is set up. This will save you time and effort and will reduce the amount of inconvenience experienced by network end users.

An inventory audit of the network's hardware should include the device's serial number, the type of device, and the name of the individual using the device. It should also list the settings on the various workstations and networking devices. Some network administrators find it useful to keep hardware inventory information directly attached to each networking device. Others prefer to store the information in either a written or a computerized database, where it is easily accessible to network support staff.

An inventory audit of the network's software applications should include the types of software used, the number of users for each application, and the operating requirements of each application. During the inventory audit, you should also make sure that the number of users for each software application does not surpass the number of licenses your site possesses.

Facility Audits

A *facility audit* allows you to note where everything is. It should include the cabling, workstations, printers, and internetworking devices (such as hubs, bridges, and routers). In short, it should provide detailed information about the location of all the network's components. Ideally, all this information should have been recorded on a working version of a document called a *cut sheet* at the time the network was installed. When the audit is complete, it is time to transfer the information you recorded on the cut sheets to a set of the building's blueprints.

Network Maps

After you conduct the inventory and facility audits, you should use the information you gathered to generate a network map, which looks similar to a blueprint. The map should include the physical location and layout of all devices attached to the network and the applications that run on them. It should also include the IP and MAC addresses of each device. Finally, the network map should include the distances of each cabling run between nodes on the network. The completed network map should be kept near the location selected for network administration and monitoring.

When monitoring programs and devices report a problem with a network's physical components, they often indicate the location of the problem, such as a break or short, by providing you with its distance from where the monitoring device is located. In other instances, the monitoring program provides you with the address of the device or devices where a problem is occurring. Obviously, locating and solving the problem is greatly facilitated if you have the information you need, which is shown in Figure 29-1, readily available.

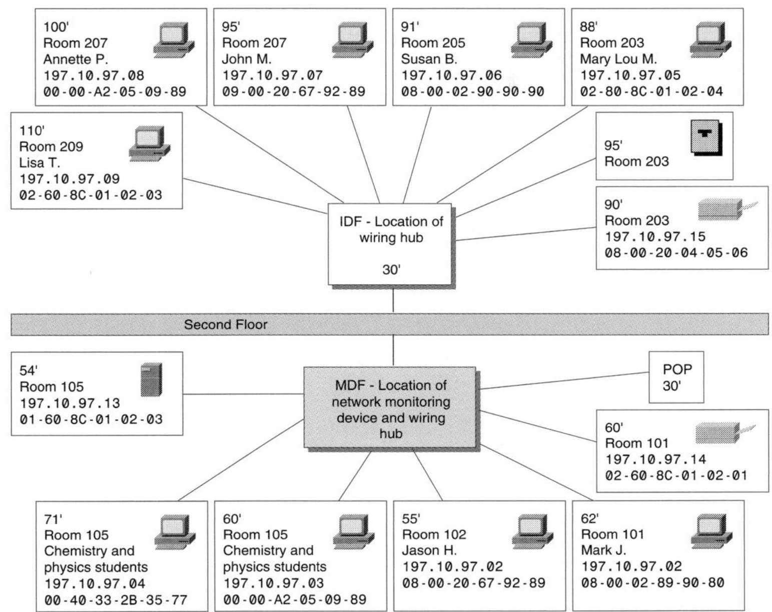

FIGURE 29-1 Information about a network should show the address of the device or devices where a problem might be occurring.

The inventory and facility audits should be done as quickly as possible. These audits should be performed before the network begins providing services to its customers. Having the information provided by these audits at hand will let you troubleshoot problems more rapidly and effectively later, when they do occur.

Operational Audits

An *operational audit* allows you to view the day-to-day activity on the network. It requires the use of specialized software and hardware. In addition to a network monitor, an operational audit can also include the use of such devices as a network analyzer, a time domain reflectometer, breakout boxes, power meters, and an oscillator. Devices such as network monitors and analyzers use specialized software to perform their functions.

Together, all this hardware and software allows the network administrator to keep track of network traffic by counting the number of packets sent, the number of times packets must be retransmitted, packet size, and how the network is being used. Simply stated, these devices and the software they use allow you to detect such events as shorts and breaks in the cable, noise on the networking media, and network bottlenecks.

Of the hardware management tools mentioned here, the ones used most frequently to provide information needed for operational, efficiency, and security audits are network monitors and analyzers. A more detailed discussion of these two devices is provided later in the chapter. For now, it is sufficient that you know these devices are usually centrally located where they can be easily accessed by authorized support personnel.

Network Software Management Tools

Vendors provide a variety of network software management tools. These tools are designed to monitor the nodes on the network, monitor levels of network traffic, watch for network bottlenecks, keep track of software metering, and collect diagnostic information. Most of these applications support vendor-specific types of information and follow one of two network management protocols: Simple Network Management Protocol (SNMP) or Common Management Information Protocol (CMIP). Both of these management protocols use a concept known as the Management Information Base (MIB). Simply put, an MIB contains information, tests, equations, and controls to which all resources on a network conform. Although both SNMP and CMIP share the same mission and use the MIB concept, their methods of retrieving network information differ greatly. In some instances, this may affect which protocol you choose to use in monitoring your network.

SNMP

First released by the U.S. Department of Defense and the developers of TCP/IP in 1988, SNMP is the most used and well known of the network software management tools.

To retrieve network information, SNMP uses a technique called *MIB collection*. This means that it goes from one network device to another, polling them about their status. Then, as shown in Figure 29-2, it copies information regarding each device's status as well as each device's local MIB.

One advantage of SNMP is that devices on the network do not have to be smart enough to report when a problem occurs. SNMP's polling takes care of that task for them. However, in large networks that have many devices and resources attached to them, SNMP's polling technique can be a disadvantage because it contributes significantly to network traffic. This can actually slow the network.

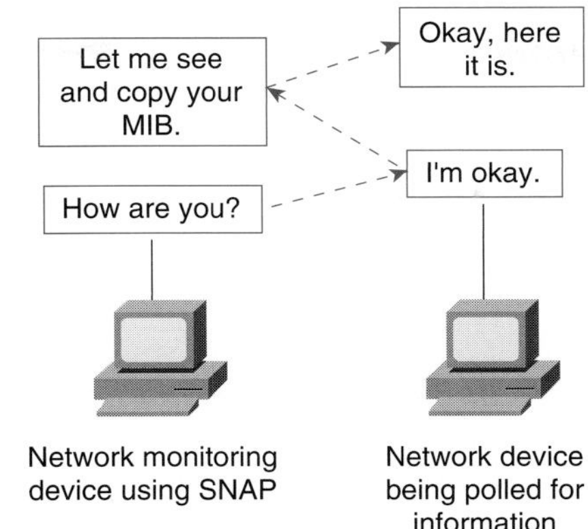
Let me see and copy your MIB.
Okay, here it is.
How are you?
I'm okay.
Network monitoring device using SNAP
Network device being polled for information

FIGURE 29-2 SNMP uses a technique called *MIB collection* to retrieve network information by polling network devices.

CMIP

CMIP was developed by the International Organization for Standardization (ISO). Currently CMIP is not implemented as much as SNMP, particularly in new installations. To obtain information about the network, CMIP uses a technique called *MIB reporting*. Using this technique, as shown in Figure 29-3, the central monitoring station waits for devices to report their current status to it.

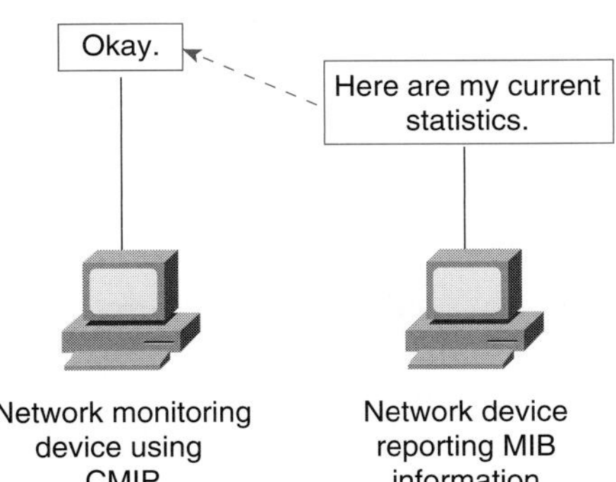
Okay.
Here are my current statistics.
Network monitoring device using CMIP
Network device reporting MIB information

FIGURE 29-3 If concern about the amount of traffic is an issue on your network, CMIP can be a useful network management tool for you.

Networking Monitoring

By monitoring the day-to-day operating of the network, you establish what is "normal" for your network. For instance, by tracking the information over a period of time, you come to learn how busy, on average, the network is. You also discover when the peak traffic times are for the network as measured by the time of day, the time of week, and the time of month. You learn what the network's most and least popular applications are and how they are being used. In some instances, you can identify which network users are most prone to experience difficulties when working on the network. Logs should be kept of all this information. Later, when you notice something that might be a problem, you can compare it against this baseline information showing what normal network operation should be.

Efficiency Audits

An *efficiency audit* allows you to determine that the network is performing to its potential. Like the operational audit, this audit is best performed after the network has begun to provide services to its clients.

For your network's wiring system, a set of baseline measurements meeting Institute of Electrical and Electronic Engineers (IEEE) and/or Electrical Industries Association/Telecommunications Industry Association (EIA/TIA) standards should have been provided by the installer. To ensure that your network's cabling continues to operate efficiently, you should periodically measure its performance for comparison against this baseline.

Other factors that should be included in your network's efficiency audit include a cost analysis of the network, an analysis of the ease with which the network is able to retrieve information, and an analysis of the ability of the network to ensure integrity of its data. Also included should be an evaluation of the workforce in place to support the network. Finally, the efficiency audit should include an assessment of the network's clients and their capabilities in terms of using the network's hardware and software.

Security Audits

A *security audit* reviews the security requirements of the network and what kind of software and hardware security system best meets them. Only observation and experience in how the network and its clients use and access data will provide you with the information needed to complete this audit.

Types of information that should be contained in this type of audit include a list of which segments require limited authorized access or encryption of data; which devices, files, and directories require locks or password protection; which files should be provided with archived backup; how frequently backup procedures should be performed; the type of virus protection being utilized by the network; and, most importantly, information regarding what emergency and disaster procedures will be employed by the network.

If you are uncertain about the types of information that your audits should contain, check with other network administrators to learn how they conduct audits of their networks and what types of network management tools they find most helpful in performing these tasks. Or, you can check with the manufacturers of your network's operating system. They will be able to recommend appropriate network auditing software that can guide you in securing adequate and comprehensive monitoring and analysis of your network.

Network Analyzers

You may want to investigate adding a *network analyzer* to your network. Also called a *protocol analyzer*, this device keeps track of statistical information much like a network monitor does. However, it offers a more sophisticated level of service than does a network monitor. In fact, these devices are so sophisticated and intelligent that they not only detect and identify problems, such as bottlenecks, but they fix them as well.

Troubleshooting Problems on the Network

The key to successfully troubleshooting problems on a network is information. As a general rule, the more information you have, the easier it should be to solve the problem. Information obtained during the audits you conducted will provide a baseline set of measurements with which to compare current data detailing the problem. Additional information must be gathered after the problem has arisen. Just as you did with the information you obtained during the audits, you must record and document this information as well as any solution provided. Such a log or journal is important because it provides a record of your contributions to the system. Later, it can be used to justify requests for additional equipment, personnel, and training. The problems and solutions documented in the log can be useful tools to train additional troubleshooters for your network. The journal also allows you to track trends that help anticipate problems and propose solutions, either with situations or individuals.

Documenting Network Problems

Some network problems will be detected by the network administrator using the network management software and hardware tools. The network support staff will learn of other problems when the network's clients report them. All client requests for help should be documented in a trouble report. The information recorded in each report should be divided into five general categories.

The first category should be an ID number that has been assigned to the call. This will be useful in filing the information or entering it into a database.

The second category should consist of preliminary information. It should include the name of the individual who reported the problem; the time the problem was reported; the method by which the problem was reported; whether the problem was related to previous calls reporting trouble and the ID numbers of those reports; the location of where the problem occurred; whether the problem can be replicated for network support staff; the time when the problem first appeared; whether anything was done differently or changed just before the problem occurred; and whether the problem was periodic or constant in nature.

The third category should consist of information that network support staff gather at the site where the problem occurred. It should include comments by support staff regarding the PC environment, such as power, temperature, humidity, and any others; support staff observations about the problem or difficulty; and a list of what actions were taken to remedy the problem.

The fourth category should provide information that indicates whether the PC had to be taken to a repair area for further servicing, a list of any actions taken, and the result of those actions.

The final category that should appear on the trouble report should be the summary. The summary should list whether the problem was a hardware, software, or user problem: If the problem was a software problem, what software was involved; if the problem was a hardware problem, what hardware was involved.

Analyzing and Solving Network Problems

After you collect all the information available about a problem, start listing possible causes. Based on the performance history you have at your disposal, you should be able to prioritize these causes from most likely to least likely. It will help if you keep in mind how data flows on your network while you do this. Using this list of possibilities, use your network's management tools to further identify the cause of the problem.

Even if you are limited in the types of network management tools at your disposal, you can still successfully troubleshoot problems on your network. Instead of relying heavily on such network management tools as monitors and analyzers, you will need to use the *replacement method*.

To understand how the replacement method works, when a problem occurs, assume you have one healthy entity and one nonfunctioning one. For example, if the information you gather leads you to believe that the problem lies in a particular workstation, get another one that you know works.

Start at the most basic level: the cabling. Switch the patch cords on the PCs. If the malfunctioning machine begins to work properly and the healthy PC becomes sick, you've found the problem on the first try. If nothing changes in the malfunctioning device, replace the patch cords to their original locations and move on to the next most basic level. Continue switching components until the malfunctioning device works and the healthy one quits functioning. Be prepared: Using the replacement method to troubleshoot the problem could take a while.

If you try everything and still cannot solve the problem, don't overlook the obvious. Lack of knowledge, experience, or proper management tools could be part of the problem. After you reach this conclusion, don't hesitate to call in the experts. In the long run, consultants armed with sophisticated diagnostic management tools, more knowledge, and more experience can save you and your organization time, money, and effort. In the process, they can provide you with a valuable learning experience.

The key to successfully troubleshooting problems on the network is to isolate the problem by systematically working your way through a simple hierarchy of troubleshooting procedures.

Troubleshooting Procedures

As you gain experience in working with your network and clients, you will develop a hierarchy of troubleshooting procedures that are best suited for you. In the meantime, the following guidelines may be useful.

In most networks, usually the users—not the hardware or software—are responsible for so-called network problems. Therefore, a logical first step in troubleshooting a user-identified problem is to fix the user.

If you determine that the problem did not originate due to user actions, move to the next most frequent source of network problems: the hardware. Begin by making sure you have the right tools to diagnose the problem. Next, determine whether the problem is local to the device. If necessary, take the PC to a network connection that you know is good and replace it with a portable PC. If you determine that the problem is not local, focus on the network's hardware. SNMP can help you determine whether there is a problem with a particular network segment. Look at the network's wiring system first. See if there were any recent cable changes. Use diagnostic tools, such as a time domain reflectometer. Check all cable connections on the known faulty segment. Begin with connections at the work area first and work back to the wiring closet. If you decide that the cabling and its connections are not at fault, look at the network's file servers. If you have multiple servers, try to determine which is the most likely candidate for causing the problem. If you think the problem lies with a workstation, check the wiring hub, cable, connector, and workstation memory. Don't neglect to use any diagnostic utilities built into the device's network interface card to help diagnose and solve the problem. If you eliminate the network's hardware, follow the appropriate diagnostic procedures to check and fix any software problems.

Network Performance Evaluations

Periodic evaluations of the network are important maintenance and prevention tools that can help ensure that it continues to operate at an acceptable level. The first evaluation should occur after the network has been in operation for a reasonable period of time. It should be based on information provided by the system's network management tools. After they have been compiled, the results of the evaluation should be presented in the form of an *evaluation report*. The evaluation report will allow network management to see whether the network is continuing to work as anticipated and needed by the organization. The purpose of the evaluation report is to reveal the network's strengths and weaknesses so they can be corrected if necessary.

For example, logs maintained by a network analyzer could indicate a trend toward a slower rate of traffic on certain segments of the network. An updated audit of the network's hardware and software could reveal the addition of several new network devices running multimedia applications on those segments. When both sets of data are taken together and presented in an evaluation report, this information can be used by network management as the basis for formulating changes in the system and how it operates.

Procedures for Making Changes to a Network

Network administrators must keep in mind that all organizations change and grow. Consequently, a network that was implemented even a year ago may no longer meet the needs and requirements of that organization. As the organization changes and evolves, so must the network.

When a network administrator believes that changes need to be implemented in a network, particularly those that will alter the way users interface with the network, the services that will be provided by that network, access to information housed in applications that run on the network, or those that will involve additional time, expense, and labor, he or she should draft a request for change. This document should be circulated for review.

The individuals who review the request for change vary from organization to organization. Ideally, the list of reviewers should include individuals in the organization who not only possess a degree of technical knowledge, but are familiar with the types of services, applications, and work the organization must handle.

In some instances, the request for change might trigger responses from reviewers. Usually, such responses range from a brief analysis to extensive investigation and analysis. Occasionally, such investigations might result in a return to an earlier point in the network's life cycle. At others, they could require a complete redesign of the network. If problems identified in the evaluation report are severe and far reaching enough, it could even mean a return to the study phase. In short, a request for change could result in a greatly modified network.

Summary

- The first step in managing a network is to document it.
- To document a network, the following audits must be performed:
  - An inventory audit and a facility audit can be used to help troubleshoot problems on the network.
  - An operational audit allows you to view the day-to-day operations of the network through the use of specialized hardware and software management tools.
  - A security audit reviews the security requirements of the network and what kind of software and hardware security system best meets them.
  - An efficiency audit allows you to determine that the network is performing to its potential.
- Audits are needed to establish a baseline of performance against which a network's continuing performance can be measured.
- Procedures and questions can be helpful in troubleshooting problems, particularly those identified by clients.
- Periodic evaluations of the network are important maintenance and prevention tools that can help ensure that the network continues to operate at an acceptable level.
- Information gathered during a network evaluation is used to prepare an evaluation report that can become the basis for a request for change.

Check Your Understanding

1. What is the purpose of an inventory audit?
   - **A.** To identify the location of every network component
   - **B.** To monitor and analyze the network's performance
   - **C.** To collect vendor specification documents for every network component
   - **D.** To take stock of all hardware and software on the network
2. What is the purpose of a facility audit?
   - **A.** To identify the types of hardware and devices on the network
   - **B.** To identify the location of every network component
   - **C.** To monitor and analyze the network's performance
   - **D.** To transfer the information on a building's blueprints to cut sheets
3. How does a network map aid in locating problems with a network's physical components?
   - **A.** It provides the name of the user of the problem device.
   - **B.** It provides the settings on the problem device.
   - **C.** It provides operating requirements for applications used on the problem device.
   - **D.** It provides addresses for the problem device.
4. Which of the following correctly describes SNMP?
   - **A.** SNMP is rarely used in new installations.
   - **B.** SNMP is a TCP/IP standard.
   - **C.** SNMP uses a concept known as MIB.
   - **D.** SNMP is the best choice for networks with a large amount of traffic.
5. Which of the following correctly describes how CMIP functions?
   - **A.** It uses MIB polling.
   - **B.** It has the central monitoring station wait for devices to report the current status.

C. It copies each device's local MIB.

D. The way it obtains information from devices contributes significantly to network traffic.

6. What is the purpose of an efficiency audit?

A. To monitor and analyze the network's performance

B. To determine whether the network is performing to its potential

C. To identify the types of hardware and devices on the network

D. To provide information regarding emergency and disaster recovery

7. What is the purpose of a security audit?

A. To match security requirements with building and privacy codes

B. To assess the capabilities of clients to use the network hardware and software

C. To identify the network's ability to ensure integrity of data

D. To identify the hardware and software system required for network security

8. After collecting performance data, what are the steps you would use to analyze and solve a network problem?

A. Determine whether the problem is periodic or constant; list possible causes; prioritize causes

B. Prioritize causes; identify cause using network management tools or the replacement method; track trends to anticipate future problems

C. List possible causes; prioritize causes; identify cause using network management tools or the replacement method

D. Determine whether the problem can be replicated; prioritize possible causes; identify cause using network management tools or the replacement method

9. Which of the following is likely to be included in an evaluation report?

A. Identification of network hardware and software that does not conform to industry standards

B. Logs indicating a trend toward a slower rate of traffic on certain sements of the network

C. A description of instances and the location of unauthorized access to files

D. A description of the types of users prone to experience difficulties using the network

10. What should a written request for change to improve network performance and security include?

A. The rationale behind each change requested

B. The type, number, and location of each device on the network

C. A comparison of present performance and anticipated optimal performance

D. A breakdown of costs for equipment and labor

After reading this chapter, you will be able to

- Describe home network integration market drivers
- Describe the home network architecture
- Describe WAN connections
- Describe home network subsystems

Introduction to Residential Networking

Introduction

The concept of home networking is not new. In most cases, multiple home networks, or subsystems, already exist in a home. These might consist of entertainment systems, lighting systems, telephone networks, security systems, heating and air conditioning systems, or other specialty systems such as sprinkler and pool/spa systems. An integrated home network is the connection of independent multiple home network subsystems to a larger control supersystem.

Integration of home networks maximizes efficiency, increases application ease of use, and reduces the cost of running these systems by creating a single point of consumer interaction and simplified infrastructure. Additionally, the infrastructure on the integrated home network allows Internet and Internet-enabled technology to be utilized in home life. This provides for a uniform "look and feel" for interface applications, as well as internal and remote access to the subsystems on a Web browser.

In this chapter, you learn about the emerging home network integration industry. You identify who the participants are in the ecosystem of the industry. You also learn about the emergence of the Internet lifestyle and the behavioral and technological factors that have influenced home network integration. Lastly, you explore the evolution of the subsystems in the home as individual networks into an integrated home network.

Home Network Integration Market Drivers

The desire for communications and multimedia applications in the home is the largest driver of consumer interest in home networking. The Internet is the application that drives the highest demand throughout the home. Consider these statistics:

- Forty-two percent of PC households would use a network to enhance communications with family members.
- Thirty-nine percent want to share the Internet throughout the home.

- Thirty-nine percent want to download video from the Internet and share it throughout the home.
- Thirty-three percent want to do the same with audio.

Additionally, shared entertainment throughout the household is also driving consumer interest in home networking. Market analysts believe that entertainment sharing, both from the Internet and from in-home systems, will soon become the largest driver of the home networking market.

- Thirty-nine percent of PC households want to share audio, such as surround sound, throughout the home.
- Thirty-three percent want to do the same for video.

Consumers have indicated that the need for control of other systems will also contribute to their interest in home networking:

- Thirty-seven percent of PC households would use a network to control and monitor home heating and cooling systems.
- Thirty-six percent would use a network to control home appliances from anywhere in the home.
- Thirty-three percent want additional phone lines as part of the high-speed Internet access package.

High-speed Internet access is the foundation of the home network. Several different technologies provide high-speed Internet access. DSL and cable modem technologies are the most widely used forms of high-speed Internet access, and their deployment into U.S. homes is predicted to grow very rapidly in the coming years. The number of networked homes is expected to triple within the next three years.

The Evolution of Home Networking

The home network integration industry is being fueled by the pursuit of the "Internet lifestyle," the blending of technology with home life to create a connected environment in which one can both communicate with and control the home environment, either from within the home or remotely through Internet access.

Communications Systems Lead the Way

Communications systems have led the way in changing the home environment into an Internet environment with expanded accessibility, control, and functionality. A home computer subsystem typically features applications such as e-mail, online chatting, and online banking. These applications have encouraged a comfort level with computer technology that promotes technology uses throughout the home environment. Additionally, technological advances have promoted high-speed data transmission and "always-on" Internet access to make the Internet an easily accessed and integral part of the home lifestyle.

Connectivity of Other Subsystems

With the computer subsystem in place, other subsystems in the home can now utilize Internet access for simplified onsite access as well as remote access. The integration of other subsystem devices requires that they be "intelligent devices" that possess Internet Protocol technology. With intelligent devices, they can be connected to and controlled by the home network.

- Entertainment networks can be devised to eliminate multiple controls for television, VCR, satellite TV, and cable TV, in favor of a single access and control device for ease and simplicity.
- Security systems are a potential addition to the network, enabling homeowners to monitor the home and property at any time—from any place in the world—via the Internet. Homeowners can access audible and visual security monitoring systems and can control them from within the home, the office, or a vacation destination.
- Other home control networks, such as heating, air conditioning, lighting, and water management can be accessed, controlled, and monitored from any location via the Internet.
- Appliances such as Internet-ready refrigerators can also be connected to the network to be monitored.

In the near future, the home network will become as essential as power, water, and electricity utilities currently in the home. As the overall cost of technology continues to decrease and its availability increases, home network technology will increase in consumer acceptance and accessibility. Standards in connectivity also will increase the simplicity of networking the home subsystems into one supersystem.

Home Network Integration Industry Ecosystem

The home network integration industry is comprised of numerous other industries, all of which converge to supply technology and services to the home environment and connect the technologies within the home.

- **Home integrators**
  - Provide the customer with the right solutions using the right technology.
  - Possess understanding of all subsystems and how to integrate them.

- **Homeowners**
  - — Are central to the decision of what subsystems will be integrated with the home network and what types of services and subscriptions will be used in the home network.
  - — Base their decisions on the available technology, their budget, and their comfort level with technology.
- **Service providers**
  - — Provide a particular service or bundle of services to the home environment.
- **Homebuilders and developers**
  - — Increasingly utilize the home integrator to incorporate structured wiring and some components into the standard or packaged upgrade options in the new home.
  - — The home integrator might initially work with the homebuilder/developer to lay the wiring infrastructure. However, the home integrator might then work with the homeowner at a later stage in construction if customization or additional networking is needed.
- **Architects and Designers**
  - — Work with homebuilders, developers, and home integrators to determine whether any special structural design requirements are necessary to accommodate a fully integrated home network.
  - — Must consider both environmental considerations of network equipment storage (such as heat, cold, and humidity) and general home structure design and room usage (home office, bedroom, entertainment centers, and so on).
- **Manufacturers**
  - — Increasingly are developing components and appliances that use the Internet Protocol (IP) to receive and send data about the device.
  - — Are developing devices that are "plug-and-play." However, certain standards for the integrated network must be followed to truly achieve "plug-and-play" capability.
- **Distributors**
  - — Play a key role for the home integrator by providing local supply of components and equipment necessary for the home network.
- **Retailers**
  - — Constitute the main suppliers of the devices and components that are utilized on the home network.

— Are currently partnering with manufacturers to develop and promote devices and components that are "plug-and-play" to make connection to the home network simple.

- **Media and analysts**
  — Play an important role in disseminating information to consumers and shaping public opinion.
  — The home integrator should be aware of developments in the industry and should be prepared for questions that might arise from homeowners out of publicly shared information.

What Is an Integrated Home Network?

An integrated home network is the federation of subsystems that must be connected to each other and to the Internet. The integrated home network is accessed and controlled by an application that resides on a home network control supersystem.

Home Network Integration Process

Home network integration can be achieved on any scale based on what the homeowner wants to reach and the technology that is currently available. As the home integrator, you will determine the level of integration necessary and, therefore, exactly what activities will be performed within each step of the home network integration process based on the subsystems that a homeowner wants to connect and the method of use. Systems are being installed today that provide scalability for future fully integrated homes.

The home network integration process consists of the following main steps:

Step 1 In the design phase, gather basic network and lifestyle requirements.

Step 2 In the engineering phase, create detailed design requirements and obtain the customer's approval.

Step 3 In the installation phase, complete these steps:

— Rough-in, or pre-wire, the wiring throughout the home.
— Trim the wire by terminating it.
— Finish the installation by connecting components and testing the entire network.

Step 4 Provide ongoing customer service and support.

Safety

Most state and local governmental bodies recommend the establishment, implementation, and maintenance of safety programs for both on- and off-worksite locations. You must check with the regulations to ensure that you are following the required safety practices and documentation standards.

For example, State of California Senate Bill 198 requires that every employer establish, implement, and maintain an effective injury and illness prevention program.

OSHA

The Occupational Safety and Health Administration (OSHA) is a federal and state program. OSHA sets guidelines and practices for safety adherence. If your state has an OSHA program, you are required to follow its guidelines; however, if it does not, you are required to follow the federal guidelines.

Standards and Codes

Standards and codes are guidelines that reflect agreement on products, practices, or operations by nationally or internationally recognized associations or governmental bodies. Because new standards and codes are continually developed, you should regularly monitor governmental legislation and industry association activities.

Some particular standards that you should be aware of are the following:

- **TIA/EIA-570**—This standard defines residential wiring and support devices for telecom applications in the home.
- **TIA 568-A**—This standard governs the use of electrical wire, cable, fixtures, and electrical and optical communications cable installed in commercial buildings. The planning and installation specifications can also be applied to the home environment.
- **FCC Rule Part 68**—The Federal Communications Commission set this standard pertaining to telephone connections.
- **Underwriter's Laboratories** (UL)—UL set many standards for consumer and industrial equipment, and it provides product safety testing information.
- **National Electric Code** (NEC)—This code is a standard that governs the use of electrical wire, cable and fixtures, and electrical and optical communications cable installed in buildings.

Industry Associations and Organizations

The following are some industry associations and organizations:

- **Electrical**
  - — National Electrical Contractors Association (NECA)
  - — National Electric Code (NEC)
- **Electronic**
  - — Custom Electronic Design and Installation Association (CEDIA)
  - — Consumer Electronics Manufacturers Association (CEMA)
  - — Video Electronic Standards Association (VESA)
  - — National Systems Contractors Association (NSCA)
  - — American Electronics Association (AEA)
- **Computer**
  - — International Computer Security Association (ICSA)
  - — National Institute of Standards and Technology (NIST)
- **Telecommunications**
  - — Telecommunications Industry Association (TIA)
  - — Continental Automated Buildings Association (CABA)
  - — Business Industry Consulting Service, International (BISCI)
  - — Canadian Wireless Telecommunications Association (CWTA)
- **Security**
  - — International Association of Home Safety and Security Professionals (IAHSSP)
  - — Security Industry Association (SIA)
  - — National Burglar and Fire Alarm Association (NBFAA)
  - — National Fire Protection Association (NFPA)
  - — National Institute for Certification in Engineering Technologies (NICET)
  - — Canadian Alarm and Security Association (CANASA)
- **HVAC**
  - — Plumbing-Heating-Cooling Contractors Association (PHCC)
  - — American Society of Heating, Refrigerating, and Air-Conditioning Engineers (ASHRAE)

- **Home building**
  - — National Association of Home Builders (NAHB)
  - — National Conference of States on Building Codes and Standards (NCSBCS)
  - — Integration Industry
  - — Home Automation Association (HAA)
  - — Internet Home Alliance

Home Network Architecture

Now that you have an overview of home network integration, you are ready to explore the architecture that supports the home network. You will begin with an overview of some key concepts upon which home network integration is built. You will also review the many different wiring types and terminations that you might encounter in a home network integration project.

In this section, you explore the home network as a local-area network (LAN), the wide-area network (WAN) that resides outside the home, and the LAN/WAN relationship via high-speed Internet access. Finally, you learn about the function of the distribution panel and the different components found in the panel.

Bandwidth

Bandwidth typically indicates the amount of data that can be transmitted in a fixed amount of time. It also means the width of the range of frequencies that an electronic signal occupies on a given medium. Two delivery methods exist for bandwidth: baseband and broadband.

Bandwidth is measured for analog and digital devices, both of which are found in the home environment. Bandwidth is measured in bits per second (bps) for digital devices and in hertz (Hz) for analog devices.

You will be concerned with data transmission rates of the Internet access technology, as well as the media types used in the home, which distribute the Internet service to the devices on the home network. High-speed Internet service is needed for many of the typical application uses on the home network.

Baseband

Baseband is a type of data transmission in which each medium, or wire, carries only one signal, or channel, at a time. Data can be sent or received, but not sent and received at the same time. Because baseband is the primary form of data transmission among devices on the home network, a network management device such as a hub or router is required to manage the data transmission requests.

Broadband

Whereas baseband can carry only one signal at a time, *broadband* is a type of data transmission that can simultaneously carry multiple signals by using a form of frequency multiplexing. (Multiplexing allows the combination of the various signals for transmission and then signal recovery at the receiving end.)

With multiple signal capacity, data transmission can be broken into channels and allocated for simultaneously sending and receiving data. To maximize the total bandwidth available, bandwidth can be allocated at different speeds for the downstream (to the home) and upstream (from the home) directions. For instance, a higher portion of the total bandwidth can be allocated to the downstream channel to deliver multimedia applications to the home. Additionally, multiple devices can communicate simultaneously on a broadband connection without having to compete for bandwidth allocation.

Topologies

At the most basic level, a topology is a network hardware configuration. Several different topologies can be used to configure a network. You should be aware of their application to the various subsystems on the integrated home network.

Daisy Chain

The daisy chain topology flows in a serial manner, beginning at one end, connecting each hardware component in a linear chain, and concluding at the opposite end. The daisy chain is the simplest structure to implement, but it is also the least flexible for home network scalability.

Although daisy chains are easy to implement because they do not require any provisioning of bandwidth, they are inefficient. At any given time, the signal travels through and is available on each device on the network, instead of being addressed to a specific device on the network.

Bus

The bus topology is similar to the daisy chain in that each hardware component is linearly aligned on a backbone that has a beginning and an end. However, the bus topology allows for addressable characteristics when a device on the bus requests signal service for sending and retrieving signals.

Bus topologies are not always appropriate for the home network because the devices on the network compete for available bandwidth. Also, the network is susceptible to a higher rate of failure because any malfunction on the network will adversely affect the entire network.

Star

The star topology individually connects the devices to a central hub that manages data transmission. This configuration is the most flexible and scalable for a home network because it isolates devices and is not affected by problems on any given device. However, the use of a hub introduces a single point of failure. Additionally, the topology is more expensive to implement because it uses a larger amount of wiring than other topologies.

Media Types

This section describes many different media types.

Phone Wire

Phone wire is a type of copper wire that is used to distribute voice service. Although phone wire can also be used to transmit data, it has not been widely accepted as a high-speed data-transmission method because phone lines use filters to suppress frequencies above 3400 Hz for optimal voice service. However, there are technology solutions that utilize high-speed data transmission on phone wire to take advantage of legacy wiring systems in existing residences where a retrofit with Category 5/Category 6 wire is difficult.

Category 5/Category 6 Wire

Category 5 wire is a type of twisted-pair copper wire suitable for high-speed data transmission (up to 100 megabits per second [Mbps]) of voice and data. Category 5 wire is comparable in price to phone wire, so it is an attractive choice in new home building for both voice and data transmissions. Category 6 wire promotes higher-speed data transmission than Category 5 wire, but it is currently in standards development.

Powerline

Powerline refers to the use of existing power cables or electrical circuits for data transmission. The biggest advantage is the use of legacy wiring to accomplish home networking. No remodeling or retrofitting is necessary. However, the disadvantage of powerline is the negative effect that the powerline can exhibit on the data transmission.

Coaxial Cable

Coaxial cable is a type of wire that can transmit voice, audio/video, and data at a speed of up to 10 Mbps, which is much less than Category 5/Category 6 wire. Additionally, the construction of the cable, using layers of wire with insulation in between, makes coaxial cable less susceptible to interference than phone wire or Category 5/Category 6 wire. (Phone wire and Category 5/Category 6 wire consist of pairs of wires twisted around each other, thereby introducing the possibility of interference with each other.)

Coaxial cable is used by the cable industry to distribute cable television, so it is widely used both outside and inside the home. Additionally, coaxial cable exists in many homes already, making it an easy choice for retrofitting home networking solutions.

FireWire (IEEE 1394)

FireWire, originally an Apple development, also called IEEE 1394, supports data transmission rates of up to 400 Mbps. In addition to its high-speed characteristic, FireWire is ideal for applications viewed in real time because it offers a guaranteed data delivery rate, called isochronous data. FireWire is very expensive, and for this reason it is limited to devices that have large throughputs, such as video cameras.

Fiber-Optic Cable

Fiber-optic cable is made of glass or plastic fibers on which data is transmitted as light impulses. Fiber-optic cable possesses very high bandwidth. Also, by transmitting data as light impulses over glass or plastic fibers, it is immune to electromagnetic interference (EMI—refer to the glossary for more information).

There has been a dramatic increase in fiber-optic cable installation for bringing newly developed high-speed Internet access technologies to the home. Fiber-optic cable to the home is also referred to as "fiber to the curb," "fiber to the building," or "fiber to the home" (also called FTTx). The use of fiber-optic cable to the home promises very high-speed security and reliability. Although it is more expensive than other media types, you should consider recommending the installation of fiber-optic cable throughout the home to "future-proof" the home. Fiber-optic cable in the home will allow the same data transmission rates throughout the home network as is promised for the connection to the home.

Wireless

Wireless is a very effective alternative to hardwiring with phone wire, Category 5/Category 6 wire, coaxial cable, or fiber optic cable, especially in retrofit home networking situations or where local mobile access to a network subsystem is desired. Wireless LANs operate using a wireless Ethernet card that is inserted into the computer to transmit signals to a wireless backbone hub or access point. When considering wireless solutions for the home network, you must be aware that signal strength is inversely proportional to distance.

You should also consider the cost of the wireless solution. Although wireless devices are typically more expensive, they might be less costly when used in a retrofit home network project to avoid wiring installation and major wall reconstruction.

You should also be aware that many of the wireless data solutions today operate over the unlicensed 2.4 GHZ frequency spectrum, the same spectrum occupied by many of today's long range 2.4-GHZ phones. Issues of contention between voice and data transmission must be considered in any wireless deployment where wireless phones are also in use.

802.11, 802.11a, and 802.11b

These are standards that provide for different wireless rates of data transmission with different modulation methods:

- **802.11**—1 to 2 Mbps
- **802.11a**—6, 12, and 24 Mbps
- **802.11b**—11 Mbps

Because they offer very high quality, they are also among the most expensive solutions.

Home RF

Home RF (with RF stemming from "radio frequency") is a lower-cost alternative to the 802.11 series, offering 1 to 3 Mbps transmission speed for both voice and data. A new version of Home RF is currently in development to provide up to 10 Mbps. However, the modulation method can slow the data transmission speed because it takes time to settle in on a frequency.

BlueTooth

BlueTooth is another wireless method of data transmission. BlueTooth is positioned as a secure medium for transmission because of its high channel-hopping capacity.

Structured Wiring

Structured wiring is the combination, or bundling, of multiple types of wiring in a group of wires threaded throughout the home. Structured wiring can contain several types of wires and multiple strands of each wire, to provide the fullest complement of wiring for the integrated home network.

The structured wiring used for a home network integration project will vary, depending on the types of wires needed for successful subsystem networking. You must balance cost and performance in your choice of which wire to include in the structured wiring. Although fiber-optic cable is best for performance, it is also the most expensive. And whereas coaxial cable is subject to less interference than Category 5 wire, it also has a slower data transmission speed. Phone line and powerline are the least expensive options and the easiest to implement because of their existing infrastructure in most homes. However, they have the lowest data transmission speed and lower performance than the other wiring types. Finally, wireless is the easiest to implement and provides competitive data transmission speeds to coaxial cable, but it is also a costly option.

Terminations

A wire can be terminated in two ways: Connect it directly to a component or connect it to a jack at a wall outlet location.

Some typical types of wall outlets follow:

- **Phone outlet**—This outlet connects a phone line using an RJ-11 modular connector.
- **Cable outlet**—This outlet connects the coaxial cable using an RG-6–style connection.
- **Data outlet**—This outlet connects Category 5 wiring to Category 5 data jacks (RJ-45).
- **Power outlet**—This outlet connects the powerline to the power connector.
- **Universal outlet**—This outlet is customizable to the types of jacks required at the outlet. Coaxial, phone, Category 5/Category 6 wire, and powerline can connect to a universal outlet.

Distribution Methods

The distribution method that you choose for the home network LAN will depend upon the customer's requirements for speed and access. The following characteristics differentiate LAN distribution methods from one another:

- Topology used to arrange the devices on the LAN
- Protocols used to encode and send data along the LAN
- Media used to connect the devices on the LAN (wiring or wireless)

Ethernet

The most common type of LAN distribution method is Ethernet, which uses a bus or star topology and transmits data up to 10 Mbps. Newer versions of Ethernet are Fast Ethernet, which supports data transmission up to 100 Mbps, and Gigabit Ethernet, with up to 1,000 Mbps of data transmission.

HomePNA

Another distribution method is HomePNA, which uses the phone wire media. The benefit to HomePNA is that it uses the legacy wiring that exists in the home, thereby reducing the complexity and inconvenience of rewiring a home with other media types. However, because the phone wire was not originally designated for high-speed data transmission and it usually exists in a daisy chain topology, the performance is less than optimal when compared to LANs using other media and topology types.

Powerline

Powerline is a third LAN distribution method that uses the existing powerline throughout the home. Powerline is usually laid using a bus topology throughout the home. Powerline is the lowest-performing LAN because of the high tendency for interference between devices that are obtaining AC voltage from the powerline and devices that are transmitting data along the same line.

Wireless

The LAN distribution method of choice for existing homes where rewiring is not possible is wireless, which uses a star topology. Wireless uses radio frequencies (RF) or infrared (IR) waves to transmit data between devices on the LAN. A key component is the wireless hub, or access point, for signal distribution.

Wireless is a costly option, has a range of data transmission speeds (from 1 to 24 Mbps), and has a limited range of transmission. However, wireless might be an appropriate choice for some connections on the LAN where the cost of rewiring the home offsets the cost of the wireless components. Wireless technology is also very convenient for the end user; for example, you can access the Internet from anywhere in your house on your laptop if your laptop has a wireless NIC.

WAN

With a high-speed Internet connection, data, voice, and audio/video can be quickly transmitted to and from the home network. Subsystems in the home that are integrated into the home network can then be remotely accessed, monitored, and controlled from any location in the world.

The connection of the LAN to the WAN via high-speed Internet access is a key element in home network integration. Several high-speed Internet access technologies will connect the WAN to the LAN. (We will explore these technologies in the following sections.) Each technology supports varying data transmission speeds; however, a key characteristic is that they allow the LAN to be always connected to the Internet. The customer does not have to dial up to the Internet and disrupt the traditional telephone service.

High-Speed Internet Access Technology: ISDN

A type of high-speed Internet access from the WAN to the home is Integrated Services Digital Network (ISDN). ISDN in concept is the integration of both analog or voice data together with digital data over the same network. ISDN is provided over the telephone line and differs from other high-speed Internet services in that it is a dialup service rather than a continuous or "always-on" connection.

ISDN requires adapters at both ends of the transmission, so the access provider also needs an ISDN adapter as well as the customer. The ISDN adapter translates the digital signal received from the WAN into a digital signal that can be distributed on the LAN, and vice versa.

Two levels of service exist: the Basic Rate Interface (BRI), intended for the home and small enterprise, and the Primary Rate Interface (PRI), for larger installations. Both rates include a number of B channels and D channels. Each B channel (bearer channel) carries data, voice, and other services. Each D channel (delta channel) carries control and signaling information.

The BRI consists of two 64-Kbps B channels and one 16-kbps D channel. Thus, a BRI user can have up to 128-kbps service. The PRI consists of 23 B channels and one 64-kbps D channel in the United States, or 30 B channels and 1 D channel in Europe and Asia.

ISDN is generally available from the phone company in most urban areas in the United States and Europe. ISDN is at a competitive disadvantage with the following forms of high-speed Internet access because of ISDN's lower transmission rates and higher charges from local telephone carriers.

High-Speed Internet Access Technology: Cable Modem

Cable modem high-speed Internet service is a broadband technology that is provided by cable television service providers and that runs on coaxial cable. Cable modem data transmissions can operate between 320 kbps and 10 Mbps, depending on different factors such as modulation scheme of the signal and type of coaxial cable. The actual speed of the Internet access service coming to the home depends on the service provider. Typically the bandwidth is shared between users in the neighborhood, and an individual cable modem subscriber might experience access speeds from 500 kbps to 1.5 Mbps or more, depending on the network architecture and traffic load.

The advantage of using cable modem high-speed Internet access is that coaxial cable wiring offers greater bandwidth using broadband for more applications to the home network LAN. Additionally, cable lines are already in place in most of the country because of the wide deployment of cable television throughout the last few decades. Therefore, cable modem high-speed Internet access is more readily available in most areas than DSL.

High-Speed Internet Access Technology: Wireless

The wireless high-speed Internet access method, also called fixed wireless, uses radio frequencies (RF) to transmit data signals at various frequencies. Wireless is a broadband method that works on the concept of a footprint, or a large geographical area that is serviced by strategically located towers that provide signal service to all the homes in the designated area.

The benefit of wireless high-speed Internet access is the simplicity in obtaining service. Subscribers within a geographical service area can be added easily without any additional infrastructure to the wireless WAN or physical wiring to the home. The disadvantage of wireless high-speed Internet access is that most wireless service providers operate at a lower frequency that requires a line of sight with the tower. Physical objects, such as trees, can block wireless service.

High-Speed Internet Access Technology: Satellite

Satellite provides another wireless high-speed Internet access method to the home network. In the past, high-speed Internet access via satellite was at a disadvantage because of the lack of interactive data service. The data path used point-to-multipoint transmission, or one-way data-transmission, from the service provider to the home. Therefore, an additional method of data transmission had to be used to send data from the LAN out to the WAN. This made satellite a complicated, expensive, and undesirable choice for Internet access. However, the latest satellite Internet services provide two-way data transmission, thus eliminating the need for a secondary Internet service.

Distribution Panel/Head End

The distribution panel is the physical and logical point of access between the WAN and the home network LAN. The distribution panel consists of a configuration of the basic components that complete the LAN/WAN connection. These components include the following:

- Modem
- Network connection/management devices (switch or hub; router or bridge)
- Home automation control unit
- Audio/video unit
- Telephone unit
- Security control panel
- Home automation controls distribution panels (HVAC, lighting, entertainment)

The concept of the distribution panel is simple. All data, voice, and audio/video signals coming into the home (including broadband access, telephone, cable, satellite, and wireless) are connected through the distribution panel. The signals are then translated and distributed to the various devices attached on the home network LAN. Conversely, the signals sent from the home network LAN to the WAN are also funneled out through the distribution panel. Additionally, signals are sent between the devices on the LAN and are controlled through the distribution panel.

Analog Modem

Several devices that actually connect the home network LAN and WAN are available. The first is the modem. A modem is a device that allows data transmission between a LAN and a WAN over a hard-wired or wireless network. A modem translates signals that are received from the WAN into signals that are distributed throughout the home network LAN. Each method of high-speed Internet access coming into the home must utilize a modem of some type to translate the signal.

A modem can use a variety of different protocols to translate signals; however, protocols are specified at particular rates of data transmission. In addition to the protocol designation, the following characteristics distinguish modem capabilities:

- **Bits per second (bps)**—The speed at which the modem can transmit and receive data
- **Voice and fax capabilities, in addition to data transmission**—Used for expanded home network options
- **Data compression**—For faster data transfer rates

NOTE

The benefits of the modem speed (or bps) depend on the speed at which the signal is received. The signal must be received from the WAN at a speed equal to or greater than the modem speed to transmit at the maximum speed of the modem.

Switch or Hub

A switch is a network management device that filters and forwards data packets between LAN devices. This allows only the recipient device to receive the data packets that are specifically addressed to that device.

A hub differs from a switch in that all devices on the network can see all data packets at any given time. The data packets are not directed to the intended recipient device as with a switch.

One advantage to using a switch over a hub is that devices connected to a LAN using a switch do not compete for bandwidth; instead, devices have dedicated bandwidth that is used only at the time of signal transmission.

Router or Bridge

A bridge is a network management device that connects two similar or dissimilar LANs together. A bridge does not use network layer protocols for addressable data packet forwarding. It does not provide packet analysis or rerouting capabilities.

A router, however, does utilize network layer protocols to forward data to the intended recipient device. A router provides more versatility for the home network by providing a firewall for security on the home network LAN, but it is also more expensive and complex to connect to the LAN. A router must be configured before it can be added to the network.

Residential Gateway

The residential gateway is a preassembled and preconfigured package consisting of a modem, switch or hub, and router or bridge to make the home network installation easy and convenient. Physically, the residential gateway can consist of a full or partial set of these devices to handle signal connection, translation, and direction. The selection and configuration of the devices in the residential gateway depend on the complexity of the network.

Before recommending the configuration for a home network integration project, you should consider how the customer plans to use the network. For instance, if the customer has cable service and cable modem is the chosen high-speed Internet access method, a cable modem should be included in the gateway. You need to review the manufacturer's residential gateway to ensure that it is scalable for future attachments as the customer's home network expands and as technology evolves.

Other Modules

Several additional modules, or units, are present in the distribution panel. The first is the home automation control unit, which connects subsystem modules to the integrated home network. The individual subsystem modules for security, lighting, HVAC, and audio/video connect to the home automation control unit. This allows these modules to function separately from the home network in case the network experiences difficulties. It ensures that there is no single point of failure in the home network.

The entertainment control panel connects to the receiver, which is then connected to the home automation control unit. Another unit of the distribution panel is the telephone unit or private branch exchange (PBX). The PBX unit controls multiple telephone lines and also provides expanded functionality and features to the telephone subsystem. Finally, a power distribution unit is located in the panel to provide multiple power connections and, optionally, surge protection to the subsystems.

Home Network Subsystems

In this section, you learn how the different subsystems can be enhanced when integrated with the home network. You learn about the elements of the subsystem, as well as how the subsystem infrastructure and components connect to each other and to the home network.

Computer Subsystem and the Home Network

The computer subsystem is perhaps the most critical subsystem in the entire home network. The computer subsystem provides the digital data access that enables other subsystems to be accessed and controlled through the home network.

Reasons for networking the computer subsystem include the following:

- **Shared Internet access**—Everyone on the home network can access the Internet simultaneously.
- **Personal e-mail**—Everyone on the network can have personalized email accounts that can be updated on a regular basis.
- **Share efficiently**—Efficiency can be gained in sharing files and peripherals such as printers, backup storage devices, and CD-ROM drives.
- **Provide infrastructure**—Networking provides the basic infrastructure for additional subsystems in the home, such as the entertainment, security, or home automation control subsystems, to communicate over the integrated network.
- **Remote home control**—Home automation controls can be done remotely.
- **Cost savings**—You can realize cost savings by using voice over IP (VoIP) as an alternative to telephone service.

Building Blocks of the Computer Subsystem

High-speed Internet access is the first building block of the computer subsystem, as well as all other subsystems in the home that will be integrated into the home network. The next building block consists of the computer subsystem's distribution devices: hubs or switches that provide physical distribution of the signal between the WAN and the computers on the computer subsystem. It also includes a router or bridge for logical distribution of the data packets. Additionally, if wireless computing will be used, a wireless backbone hub is also installed to distribute the signals to the computers equipped with wireless Ethernet cards.

The next layer is the infrastructure of client computer wiring. This includes Category 5/Category 6 wiring for Fast Ethernet via Digital Subscriber Line

(DSL), ISDN, or cable modem from the demarcation point of the home. It also includes Category 5/Category 6 wiring for each client computer that is connected to the network.

The last building block consists of the devices that are attached to the computer subsystem. These can include components that can be networked, such as desktop and laptop client computers, storage devices, and peripherals such as printers. After the physical components are in place, the computers are assigned an IP address (either by the Internet service provider or the homeowner's router), to enable communication using the TCP/IP protocol.

Elements of the Computer Subsystem

The computer subsystem includes the following elements (see Figure 30-1):

- **High-speed Internet access**—For connection between the LAN and the WAN
- **Switch or hub**—For physical distribution of the signal among multiple devices on the LAN
- **Router or bridge**—For logical distribution of the data packets to IP-addressed devices on the LAN
- **Category 5/Category 6 wiring**—For connection between the modem and client computers
- **Client computers**—Individual computers connected to the LAN
- **Peripherals**—Devices such as printers and scanners

Telephone Subsystem and the Home Network

The telephone subsystem is an analog signal subsystem that delivers telephone services throughout the home. When integrated with the home network, the telephone subsystem can act as a conduit for signal distribution of other subsystems, such as the security and computer subsystems that require telephone lines. Also, by using the structured wiring scheme in an integrated home (instead of the daisy chain wiring topology used in the past), the features and functionality of the telephone subsystem can be augmented with the addition of a private branch exchange (PBX) unit.

Building Blocks of the Telephone Subsystem

With the high-speed Internet access already in place for the computer subsystem, the next building block of the telephone subsystem on the integrated home network is the telephone distributor or PBX unit. These devices are installed in the distribution panel. The wires coming from the demarcation point of the home are fed into the distributor or PBX unit. Then lines are run to each individual room (using the star topology) that is designated for telephone or data use.

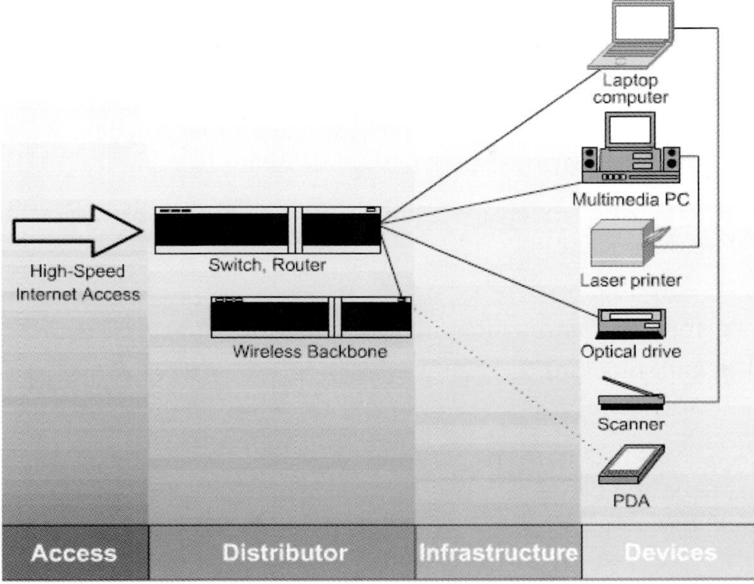

FIGURE 30-1
Elements of the computer subsystem.

The next building block is the wiring. The telephone subsystem begins with wiring the home with phone wire, or preferably Category 5/Category 6 wire because of its scalability and the possibility for VoIP support. The wiring should be laid for every room that will use a phone connection or an Internet connection. At the connection in each room, the telephone handsets are connected to the wiring.

Elements of the Telephone Subsystem

Note that although high-speed Internet access is not necessary for the telephone subsystem itself, it is included here because of the several methods discussed in Chapter 2, "The OSI Model," including DSL and ISDN, which supply high-speed Internet access via the telephone line. Another reason for indicating high-speed Internet access as a building block of the telephone subsystem on the integrated home network is for access to VoIP. VoIP is an Internet solution for telephony services that compliments traditional telephone service. Therefore, high-speed Internet access is included as the first building block of the telephone subsystem that is integrated into the home network.

The next building block of the telephone subsystem consists of the distribution devices that distribute the telephone signals throughout the telephone and computer subsystems in the home. One of the devices might be a splitter. A splitter will be installed by the telephone company for high-speed Internet access to the home via DSL, for example. Another device will be used to distribute the telephone signal. These devices can vary, depending on the system needs. If you are using a standard telephone hub device, you can have up to four telephone lines connected to the hub. You can utilize more than one hub if you have additional phone lines coming into the home. However, you might find that a PBX unit will better suit a customer's needs. A PBX unit adds functionality and features such as the following (see Figure 30-2):

- The use of extensions, which provide multiple interior lines with only one exterior line
- Voicemail
- Intercom and conferencing capabilities
- Call blocking

NOTE

Devices are available that further expand the capabilities of the PBX unit, to include features of the computer subsystem such as Internet service.

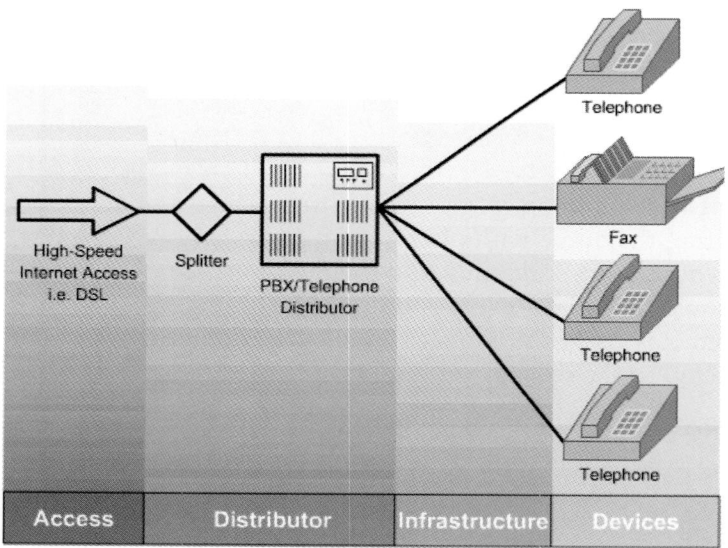

FIGURE 30-2 Elements of the telephone subsystem.

The next building block, the infrastructure, consists of telephone wire or Category 5/Category 6 wire that is distributed using the star topology. This allows multiple lines to be used in designated rooms. Finally, the telephone handset devices are connected to the telephone wire or Category 5/Category 6 wires. Also, client computers are connected to the wires for high-speed Internet service.

Entertainment Subsystem and the Home Network

The entertainment subsystems of today generally consist of some or all of the following: television, home theater, surround sound, CD, DVD, and VCR. The entertainment subsystem functions as its own separate system. However, when connected to the home network via a client computer, entertainment options are exponentially expanded. In addition to regular over-the-air broadcast, cable, or satellite television, it is now possible to have immediate access to on-demand programming, such as music videos, from the Internet. Additionally, the computing subsystem is expanded in that the television becomes merely a monitor and the entertainment subsystem can now function as yet another computing device in the home.

The benefits of networking the entertainment subsystem with the computer subsystem include the following:

- **Richer Internet experience**—A richer and more enjoyable Internet experience is produced because the Internet can now be played or viewed using the home's high-end entertainment equipment instead of on a small computer screen and local computer-based speakers.
- **Better control of entertainment subsystem**—The entertainment subsystem can be controlled from other devices and locations in the home.
- **Download entertainment content**—Users can download, view, and store entertainment programs from the Internet on the computer subsystem.
- **Simultaneous Internet use**—The Internet can be used simultaneously with any broadcast, cable, or satellite programming in use, becoming one more source of entertainment content for the homeowner to choose.

Building Blocks of the Entertainment Subsystem

High-speed Internet access is the first building block of the entertainment subsystem integrated into the home network. The Internet expands the entertainment options that can be accessed throughout the home.

The receiver is the next building block in the entertainment subsystem. It acts as the hub, or distributor of the audio and video signals from the input components (such as cable or satellite television and the CD, DVD, and VCR players) to the other output components (such as the television set and speakers). The next layer is the infrastructure wiring. The wiring consists of the coaxial cable for connection to the cable television or satellite signal, as well as the speaker wires for connecting the speakers to the receiver.

Next, the television set, speakers, and other devices are attached to the network. Also, a client computer (which is networked with the computer subsystem) is attached to the receiver to provide the connection for high-speed Internet access. With the PC attached, the entertainment subsystem components become input and output devices to the entire home network instead of only the entertainment subsystem.

Elements of the Entertainment Subsystem

The entertainment subsystem consists of the following (see Figure 30-3):

- High-speed Internet access
- Entertainment delivery options, such as satellite, broadcast, and cable television
- Receiver, the main distributor for the entertainment subsystem
- Coaxial cable wiring for video distribution
- Category 5/Category 6 or FireWire for data connections
- Speaker wiring for audio distribution
- Input and output devices, such as digital television (or analog television connected to a PC with a video card), satellite dish, speakers, CD player, DVD player, and VCR
- Storage devices such as audio and video storage disks (accessed via the computer network)

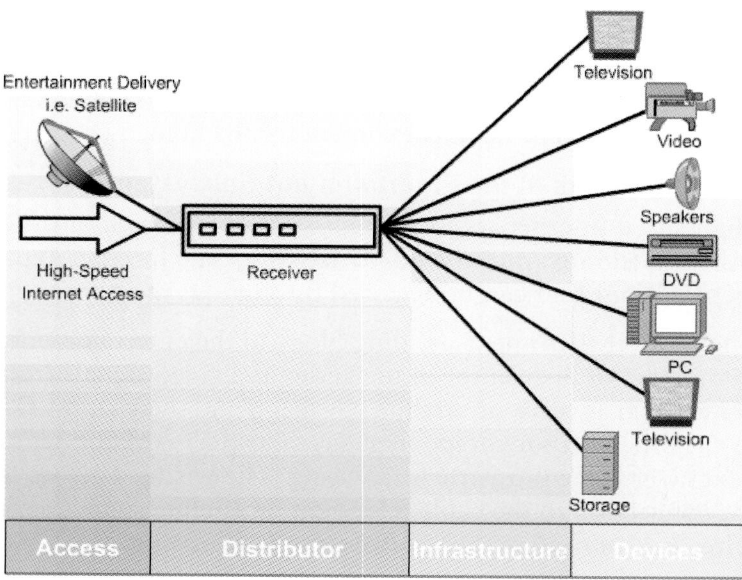

FIGURE 30-3 Elements of the entertainment subsystem.

Security Subsystem and the Home Network

Today's security subsystems are stand-alone systems that report via telephone or cellular to the security monitoring service for fire department and police notification of a security or fire breach. However, the security subsystem that is integrated with the home network can provide the customer with constant monitoring from anywhere in the world. For example, a security camera might be mounted at the front door and in the back yard. The security subsystem could be connected to the computer subsystem, which provides data transmission viewable from a Web browser interface.

The benefits of having a security subsystem networked with the entire home network include the following:

- **Direct alert**—The customer can be directly alerted of a security breach instead of waiting for notification by the monitoring service, the fire department, or the police.
- **Control home access**—With a Web browser interface, the security subsystem can be used to control access to the home for various reasons. Some examples include the following:
    - Allow the housekeeper regular access to the home on Thursdays at 2 P.M., and allow the kids access anytime, using different PIN codes for the system.
    - Allow a delivery person access when the delivery is made and no one is home. When the delivery person rings the doorbell, the customer is notified through his/her personal digital assistant (PDA), cellular phone, or workstation. The customer can deactivate the security system to allow access and monitor the delivery person's actions through a security camera. The customer can reactivate the security subsystem when the delivery person leaves.

Building Blocks of the Security Subsystem

The first building block of the security subsystem integrated with the home network is high-speed Internet access. This allows the security subsystem to be accessed remotely via a Web browser application. The next building block is the security control panel, which is the distribution point of the security subsystem. The security control panel is connected to the home network distribution panel for remote access and notification via the Internet. It is also connected to a second phone line if used as a backup for the subsystem to allow off-network functionality.

> **NOTE**
>
> The operating system in the security control panel is programmed for functionality.

Next, the security wiring is attached from the distribution panel to the contacts on the door and windows as well as to other control devices. Also included is Category 5/Category 6 wiring from the central control panel and the network distribution panel for integration into the entire home network. If a second phone line is used for system backup off the network, then telephone wire or Category 5/Category 6 wiring is also used between the central control panel and the demarcation point of the home.

Next, the components of the security subsystem are added. These components include the security pads or contacts that are usually configured in zones using a combination of star and daisy chain topologies. Keypads for a user interface are connected to the wiring that runs from the central control panel. A client computer is then connected to the subsystem for remote access via a Web browser interface.

Elements of the Security Subsystem

The security subsystem consists of these main components (see Figure 30-4):

- High-speed Internet access
- Security control panel, the hub of the security system
- Operating system programming
- Security wiring, usually laid by zones for a combination of star and daisy chain topologies
- Category 5/Category 6 wiring for connection to security cameras
- Phone wire for connection to the home network distribution panel and the demarcation point of the home (for the backup line)
- Security pads and contacts in each zone
- Keypad or other user interface devices

Home Automation Controls Subsystem and the Home Network

The home automation industry has been slow to progress in networking many of the home automation control subsystems because they have not been data-critical functions in the home. However, with the addition of high-speed Internet access in connection with home automation control subsystems, more people have become interested in controlling and monitoring the subsystems from their home networks.

For example, a customer could turn on the hot tub remotely using a Web browser interface, a cell phone, a wireless PDA, or a similar device one hour before arrival to have it ready for use when he arrives. That customer also could adjust the heat and turn on the landscape lights.

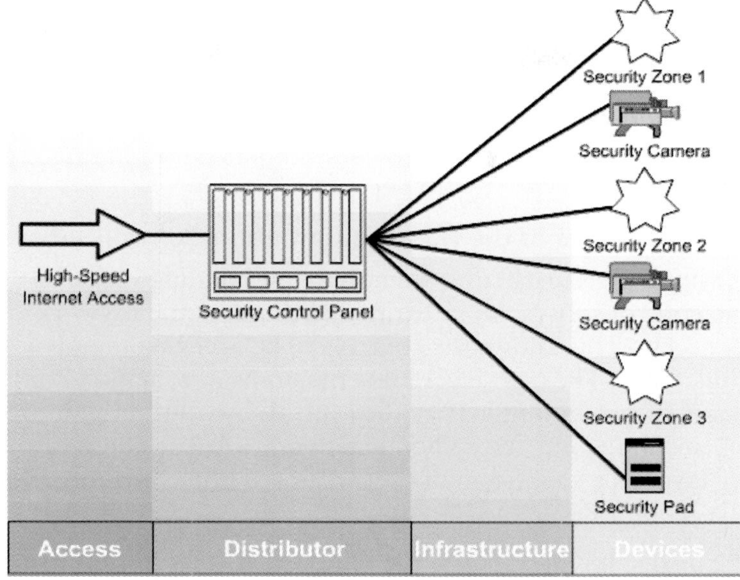

FIGURE 30-4 Elements of the security subsystem.

The home automation controls subsystem could consist of the following:

- Appliances
- HVAC
- Lighting
- Water supply
- Pool/spa
- Sprinkler system
- Shades
- Garage doors
- Lifts

Today, traditional "dumb devices" (those having no IP intelligence) can be controlled on the network if they have a serial port that is connected to a processor. (We will explore this processor, called the home network supersystem control, in a later section). These devices can be controlled for basic or complex functions. However, they each require a separate software "driver" that increases the complexity of the system as you add devices. However, manufacturers are developing "smart devices" that utilize IP intelligence directly within the device to expand control and allow for identification of features and communication with or from the device without the need for specialized individual software drivers.

The benefits of adding home automation control subsystems to the integrated home network include the following:

- **Remote access**—Provides remote access to the subsystems
- **Simplified interface**—Provides simplified user interface with one point of access

Building Blocks of the Home Automation Control Subsystem

As with the security subsystem, the first building block of the home automation control subsystem integrated with the home network is high-speed Internet access. This allows the controls to be accessed remotely via a Web browser application. The next layer adds the home automation control processor from the supersystem that acts as the central distribution point for all the subsystems in the integrated home network. (A discussion of the supersystem control layer as a subsystem in the integrated home network will be covered in the next section.)

The next building block is the wiring that runs from the distribution panel to each component of the control subsystems. That wiring might include power cables, Category 5/Category 6 wiring, and serial and coaxial cables. Additionally, wireless connections might be considered where wiring is restrictive or difficult without major remodeling. Finally, the components and the individual control devices of each control subsystem are added. This can include the HVAC unit, thermostat, lights, pool/spa pump, pool/spa heating unit, sprinkler system timing control, garage door remote and wall switch, and any lift controllers.

Elements of the Home Automation Control Subsystems

The following are elements of home automation control subsystems:

- High-speed Internet access
- Home automation control processor
- Wiring for all media types according to the subsystem requirements
- Components of each subsystem with serial port or IP intelligence within the device
- Control devices for individual subsystem control

Home Network Control Supersystem and the Home Network

The home network control supersystem allows seamless control of all subsystems throughout the house. The home network control supersystem provides access to and monitoring of each subsystem through one device that is equipped with IP technology. Wireless touch-pad devices such as the Crestron, Panga, and Eschelon 1000 are used for the supersystem to allow mobile and convenient interfaces. You might also create a Web browser interface to allow remote access to the entire home network.

Device technology is rapidly advancing. You should check with your distributors or manufacturers to determine which supersystem device best suits your home network infrastructure. A key advancement is the addition of IP intelligence in traditional "dumb devices." IP intelligence allows identification of the device on the network, as well as the transmission of available features and the status of the device's functions without writing a specialized software driver for each device.

Building Blocks of the Home Control Supersystem

As with all other subsystems in the home, high-speed Internet access is supplied to allow the entire integrated home network to be accessed remotely via a Web browser. The next layer is the home automation control processor, which is the main distributor of the supersystem control. The processor is the main distribution point for the subsystems that are connected to the supersystem.

Next, the infrastructure consists of the wiring from each subsystem to the home automation control processor. This could consist of power cables, security wire, phone wire, Category 5/Category 6 wire, coaxial and serial cable. A wireless media solution should be used if a wireless touch pad is used for the user interface device. Finally, the user interface devices are then added to allow wireless control throughout the home with wireless or wall-mounted touch pads. These units provide simplicity with a single point of access for a common interface to the subsystems connected to the supersystem.

NOTE

You should always install the standard individual control devices for each home automation control subsystem for operation off the network. These include devices such as the thermostat or pool pump control. This prevents a single point of failure and allows control of critical control subsystems if the integrated home network becomes inoperable.

Elements of the Home Network Control Supersystem

The elements of the home network control supersystem are listed here:

- High-speed Internet access
- Home automation control processor, operating system, and software application
- Wireless, serial, digital or analog, or power on/off connections to each subsystem
- Security control distributor
- Entertainment control distributor
- HVAC control distributor
- Lighting control distributor
- Wall-mounted or wireless touch pads

Subsystem Subscriptions

Services and subscriptions are necessary to the integrated home network to provide application to the system. The most important subscription for the computer subsystem is high-speed Internet access. High-speed Internet access provides Internet access to the subsystems on the network, greatly expanding their utility.

Several options exist for high-speed Internet access:

- DSL
- ISDN
- Cable modem
- Satellite
- Wireless/fixed wireless

Not all subscriptions are available in all areas. You should check with local service providers to determine what types of high-speed Internet access are available. You should also consider how the customer wants to use the home network with regard to speed and continuous or dedicated Internet connectivity.

NOTE

Many telephone companies bundle their services to offer high-speed Internet access in addition to telephone services.

Telephone Subsystem

The telephone subsystem relies on two telephone services: local and long-distance telephone service.

VoIP also offers another avenue for telephone service. Instead of using the telephone lines to place a call, applications are available that allow voice transmission via high-speed Internet access. Because of lower reliability of the data transmission via high-speed Internet access, many opt to use VoIP capabilities as a secondary communication tool in conjunction with traditional telephone-line access. On the other hand, VoIP is positioned to replace telephony as we have known it.

Entertainment Subsystem

Entertainment subscriptions include several choices:

- Cable television
- Satellite television, such as DirecTV and DSS
- On-demand services, such as TiVo
- High-speed Internet access

Security Subsystem

The security subsystem utilizes a monitoring service that is alerted when there is a security breach. The monitoring service, in turn, alerts the police and fire departments, when necessary. It is important that you check with security monitoring services to be sure that their service agreement allows the security subsystem to be connected to an Internet interface for remote control and access to the system. Currently, many monitoring services will not allow remote access because of the possibility of system hacking.

Summary

In this chapter, you learned about the many industries that constitute the home network integration industry, and you learned how the computer subsystems in the home have driven the growth in home network integration. You learned about the key concepts of bandwidth, baseband, broadband, and IP. You learned about the LAN/WAN connection via high-speed Internet access, which provides the basis for home network integration. Lastly, you learned about the subsystems found in the home and their expanded functionality when they are connected to the integrated home network.

Check Your Understanding

1. Which industry provides a particular service or bundle of services to the home environment?
   - A. Retailers
   - B. Manufacturers
   - C. Service providers
   - D. Home builders
2. Which subsystem is the basis for an integrated home network?
   - A. Entertainment subsystem
   - B. Security subsystem
   - C. Sprinkler subsystem
   - D. Computer subsystem
3. What is an integrated home network?
   - A. A federation of subsystems that must be connected to each other and to the Internet
   - B. The combination of the computer and entertainment subsystems only
   - C. More than one computer with Internet access
   - D. An extension of an office network
4. Which of the following are the four phases of the home network integration process?
   - A. Design, engineering, component installation, and customer service and support
   - B. Sales, service provider research, design, and customer service
   - C. Design, engineering, installation, and customer service and support
   - D. Rough-in, trim, and finish
5. Which of the following is a residential telecommunications cabling standard?
   - A. TIA 568-A
   - B. TIA/EIA 570

C. FCC Rule Part 68

D. CABA

6. What technology is the foundation of home network integration?

A. Baseband technology

B. Coaxial cable

C. High-speed Internet access

D. Modem

7. Bandwidth relates to both broadband and baseband in that it ____________ the amount of data that can be transmitted in a fixed amount of time

A. Defines

B. Allocates

C. Increases

D. Measures

8. Which network configuration is the most flexible and scalable?

A. Bus

B. Daisy chain

C. Star

9. What technology is an addressing scheme used for sending data to a recipient over a network in the form of data packets?

A. Router

B. IP

C. Home RF

D. IR

10. Which media type consists of twisted-pair copper wire and has a data transmission speed of up to 100 Mbps?

A. Coaxial cable

B. Fiber-optic cable

C. FireWire

D. Category 5

11. Which statement about structured wiring is not true?
    - A. Structured wiring is a bundle of multiple types of wiring threaded throughout the home.
    - B. Structured wiring can include coaxial cable.
    - C. Structured wiring consists of BlueTooth, Home RF, or 802.11.
    - D. Structured wiring can be an economical solution for home network integration projects
12. Which LAN distribution method is utilized with existing phone wire?
    - A. Home PNA
    - B. Fast Ethernet
    - C. BlueTooth
    - D. Powerline
13. Which type of high-speed Internet access method operates over a coaxial cable?
    - A. ISDN
    - B. DSL
    - C. Cable modem
    - D. Satellite
14. What is the physical and logical point of access between the WAN and the home network LAN?
    - A. Residential gateway
    - B. Modem
    - C. Distribution panel
    - D. Switch or hub
15. Which component of the entertainment subsystem acts as a distributor of the audio and video signals from the input devices?
    - A. Television set
    - B. Receiver
    - C. Speakers
    - D. Remote control

16. A security system can be remotely accessed and controlled by the homeowner via the use of which of the following?

A. Remote control devices

B. Keypad

C. Web browser application

D. Security monitoring service

17. What component is the distributor of the home automation control subsystem?

A. Home automation control processor

B. Receiver

C. Distribution panel

D. Residential gateway

18. The home network control supersystem provides ____________________ each subsystem through one device that is equipped with IP technology.

A. Instructions on the use of

B. Access to and monitoring of

C. One-way interface with

D. Static data about

19. How do subsystems benefit when they are provided with high-speed Internet access?

A. Subsystem response time is greatly enhanced.

B. Subsystem connectivity is easier.

C. An unlimited number of subsystems can be connected to the home network.

D. Subsystem utility is greatly expanded.

20. VoIP is typically used as a secondary communication tool in conjunction with traditional telephone-line access because of which of the following:

A. High-speed Internet service is not as reliable as telephone service.

B. High-speed Internet service provides poor-quality voice transmission.

C. Some forms of broadband will not support VoIP.

D. The cost of VoIP is prohibitive.

Check Your Understanding Answer Key

This appendix contains the answers to the Check Your Understanding questions at the end of each chapter.

Chapter 1

1. C
2. A
3. B
4. A
5. B
6. A
7. C
8. A
9. B
10. C
11. C
12. B
13. D
14. B
15. C
16. B
17. D
18. B
19. C
20. C

Chapter 2

1. A
2. D
3. C
4. B
5. A
6. B
7. B
8. B
9. A
10. D
11. A
12. C
13. A
14. A
15. B
16. C
17. D
18. B
19. D
20. B

Chapter 3

1. B
2. C
3. D
4. A

5. A
6. B
7. C
8. D
9. A
10. B
11. B
12. C
13. B
14. B
15. C
16. C
17. C
18. A
19. C
20. C

Chapter 4

1. A
2. D
3. B
4. B
5. B
6. B
7. A
8. D
9. A
10. C

11. B
12. A
13. D
14. B
15. C
16. D
17. A
18. A
19. B
20. C

Chapter 5

1. B
2. C
3. B
4. C
5. C
6. A
7. A
8. C
9. B
10. C
11. C
12. A
13. C
14. B
15. A
16. C

17. C
18. B
19. A
20. D

Chapter 6

1. A
2. B
3. C
4. B
5. B
6. C
7. A
8. B
9. B
10. C
11. C
12. A
13. D
14. C
15. C
16. A
17. A
18. B
19. C
20. C

Chapter 7

1. C
2. B
3. A
4. D
5. D
6. D
7. C
8. B
9. A
10. D
11. B
12. C
13. C
14. B
15. D
16. B
17. D
18. A
19. B
20. D

Chapter 8

1. D
2. A
3. A
4. C

5. B
6. B
7. D
8. C
9. A
10. C
11. C
12. C
13. C
14. B
15. A
16. D
17. C
18. C
19. B
20. B

Chapter 9

1. C
2. B
3. C
4. A
5. B
6. A
7. C
8. B
9. C
10. A

11. B
12. B
13. A
14. C
15. C
16. A
17. B
18. B
19. C
20. D

Chapter 10

1. A
2. B
3. B
4. A
5. B
6. C
7. A
8. D
9. B
10. A
11. B
12. B
13. D
14. B
15. C
16. B

17. D
18. C
19. C
20. C

Chapter 11

1. C
2. B
3. C
4. C
5. A
6. A
7. C
8. B
9. D
10. D
11. A
12. A
13. B
14. A
15. A
16. C
17. A
18. D
19. D
20. D

Chapter 12

1. A
2. A
3. B
4. D
5. A
6. A
7. B
8. A
9. D
10. D
11. C
12. C
13. B
14. A
15. A
16. C
17. B
18. A
19. C
20. B

Chapter 13

1. D
2. C
3. C
4. A

5. A
6. D
7. A
8. D
9. D
10. C

Chapter 14

1. A
2. C
3. C
4. C
5. A
6. B
7. C
8. B
9. C
10. A

Chapter 15

1. D
2. A
3. B
4. A
5. D
6. B
7. D
8. A

9. B
10. A

Chapter 16

1. A
2. A
3. B
4. D
5. D
6. C
7. D
8. D
9. A
10. D
11. D
12. D
13. C
14. A
15. D
16. A
17. D
18. D
19. A
20. C

Chapter 17

1. A
2. A

3. B
4. A
5. C
6. A
7. D
8. A
9. D
10. B
11. C
12. D
13. A
14. D
15. C
16. B
17. C
18. A
19. B
20. A

Chapter 18

1. A
2. C
3. A
4. A
5. A
6. D
7. D
8. A
9. A

10. D
11. A
12. C
13. A
14. A
15. D

Chapter 19

1. B
2. C
3. A
4. D
5. A
6. D
7. A
8. D
9. A
10. D
11. D
12. D
13. D
14. D
15. A
16. C
17. D
18. C
19. C
20. B

Chapter 20

1. B
2. C
3. D
4. D
5. B
6. A
7. C
8. A
9. A
10. A
11. A
12. A
13. A
14. A
15. A

Chapter 21

1. A
2. C
3. B
4. C
5. B
6. D
7. B
8. C
9. A

10. D
11. C
12. D
13. A
14. B
15. A
16. B
17. A
18. D
19. A
20. B

Chapter 22

1. A
2. B
3. A
4. B
5. C

Chapter 23

1. A
2. A
3. C
4. D
5. B
6. A
7. D
8. B

9. A
10. C
11. B
12. A
13. D
14. B
15. D
16. C
17. B
18. B
19. D
20. C

Chapter 24

1. A
2. D
3. A
4. D
5. D
6. C
7. D
8. C
9. D
10. A
11. C
12. D
13. C
14. A

15. B
16. D
17. A
18. A
19. C
20. B

Chapter 25

1. C
2. B
3. A
4. A
5. A
6. A
7. D
8. A
9. A
10. A
11. D
12. C
13. B
14. B
15. C
16. B
17. D
18. D
19. A
20. B

Chapter 26

1. A
2. B
3. A
4. C
5. D
6. B
7. B
8. C
9. B
10. D
11. C
12. C
13. B
14. A
15. C
16. A
17. C
18. C
19. D
20. C

Chapter 27

1. D
2. C
3. B
4. A
5. B

Chapter 28

1. C
2. D
3. B
4. B
5. D
6. A
7. B
8. A
9. B
10. A

Chapter 29

1. D
2. B
3. D
4. C
5. B
6. B
7. D
8. C
9. B
10. A

Chapter 30

1. C
2. D

3. A
4. C
5. B
6. C
7. D
8. C
9. B
10. D
11. C
12. A
13. C
14. C
15. B
16. C
17. A
18. B
19. D
20. A

Command Summary

This appendix contains a summary of the commands used in this book and is intended to provide a quick reference. Each command is in alphabetical order with a short description of it. In addition, the table contains cross-references to the chapter in which the command is introduced and explained. This appendix should add to your understanding of the commands used to configure Cisco routers.

Command	Description	Chapter
access-enable	Enables the router to create a temporary access list entry in a dynamic access list.	17
access-template	Manually places a temporary access list entry on a router to which you are connected.	17
appn	Sends a command to the APPN subsystem.	17
atmsig	Executes ATM signaling commands.	17
b	Boots the operating system manually.	21
bandwidth	Sets a bandwidth value for an interface.	20
banner motd	Specifies a message-of-the-day banner.	20
bfe	Sets manual emergency modes.	17
boot system	Specifies the system image that the router loads at startup.	21
calendar	Manages the hardware calendar.	17
cd	Changes the current device.	17
cdp enable	Enables Cisco Discovery Protocol on an interface.	18
clear	Resets functions.	17
clear counters	Clears the interface counters.	18

Command	Description	Chapter
clockrate	Configures the clock rate for the hardware connections on serial interfaces, such as network interface modules and interface processors to an acceptable bit rate.	20
cmt	Starts or stops FDDI connection management functions.	17
config-register	Changes the configuration register settings.	21
configure	Allows you to enter changes to an existing configuration and maintain and store configuration information at a central site.	17, 20, 26
configure memory	Loads configuration information from nonvolatile random-access memory.	20
configure terminal	Configures the terminal manually from the console terminal.	20, 21
connect	Opens a terminal connection.	17
copy	Copies configuration or image data.	17
copy flash tftp	Copies the system image from Flash memory to a TFTP server.	21
copy running-config startup-config	Stores the current configuration in RAM into NVRAM.	20, 21
copy running-config tftp	Stores the current configuration in RAM on a network TFTP server.	20
copy tftp flash	Downloads a new image from the TFTP server to Flash memory.	21
copy tftp running-config	Loads configuration information from a network TFTP server.	20
debug	Uses debugging functions.	17
debug ip rip	Displays RIP routing updates as they are sent and received.	26
delete	Deletes a file.	17
dir	Lists the files on a given device.	17

Command	Description	Chapter
disable	Turns off privileged commands.	17
disconnect	Disconnects an existing network connection.	17
enable	Turns on privileged commands.	17
enable password	Sets a local password to control access to various privilege levels.	20
enable secret	Specifies an additional layer of security over the **enable password** command.	20
erase	Erases Flash or configuration memory.	17
erase startup-config	Erases the contents of NVRAM.	19, 20
exit	Exits any configuration mode, or closes an active terminal session and terminates the EXEC.	17, 20
format	Formats a device.	17
help	Gets a description of the interactive help system.	17
history	Enables the command history function.	17
interface	Configures an interface type and enters interface configuration mode.	20
ip address	Assigns an address and a subnet mask and starts IP processing on an interface.	24
ip default-network	Establishes a default route.	26
ip domain-lookup	Enables name-to-address translation in the router.	24
ip host	Makes a static name-to-address entry in the router's configuration file.	24
ip name-server	Specifies the addresses for up to six name servers to use for name and address resolution.	24
ip route	Establishes static routes.	26
lat	Opens a LAT connection.	17

Command	Description	Chapter
line	Identifies a specific line for configuration and starts the line configuration command collection mode.	20
lock	Locks the terminal.	17
login	Logs in as a particular user. Enables password checking at login.	17, 20
logout	Exits from EXEC mode.	17
media-type	Specifies the physical connection.	20
mbranch	Traces down a branch of a multicast tree for a specific group.	17
mrbranch	Traces up a branch of a multicast tree for a specific group.	17
mrinfo	Requests neighbor and version information from a multicast router.	17
mstat	Shows statistics after multiple multicast traceroutes.	17
mtrace	Traces the path from a source to a destination branch for a multicast distribution tree.	17
name-connection	Names an existing network connection.	17
ncia	Starts/stops the NCIA server.	17
network	Assigns a Network Information Center–based address to which the router is directly connected.	26
no shutdown	Restarts a disabled interface.	20
pad	Opens an X.29 PAD connection.	17
ping	Sends an echo request; diagnoses basic network connectivity.	17, 23, 24
ppp	Starts the IETF Point-to-Point Protocol.	17
pwd	Displays current device.	17
reload	Halts and performs a cold return; reloads the operating system.	17, 19, 21

Command	Description	Chapter
rlogin	Opens an rlogin connection.	17
router	Starts a routing process by first defining an IP routing protocol. For example, **router rip** selects RIP as the routing protocol.	20, 26
rsh	Executes a remote command.	17
sdlc	Sends SDLC test frames.	17
send	Sends a message over tty lines.	17
service password-encryption	Enables the password encryption function.	20
setup	Enters the **setup** command facility.	17, 19, 26
show	Shows running system information.	17
show buffers	Provides statistics for the buffer pools on the network server.	18
show cdp entry	Displays information about a neighbor device listed in the CDP table.	18
show cdp interface	Displays information about the interfaces on which CDP is enabled.	18
show cdp neighbors	Displays the results of the CDP discovery process.	18
show flash	Displays the layout and contents of Flash memory.	18, 21
show hosts	Displays a cached list of hostnames and addresses.	24
show interfaces	Displays statistics for all interfaces configured on the router.	18
show ip interface	Displays the status and global parameters associated with an interface.	26
show ip protocols	Displays the parameters and current state of the active routing protocol process.	26
show ip route	Displays the contents of the IP routing table.	18, 26

Command	Description	Chapter
show memory	Shows statistics about the router's memory, including memory-free pool statistics.	18
show processes	Displays information about the active processes.	18
show protocols	Displays the configured protocols. This command shows the status of any configured Layer 3 protocol.	18
show running-config	Displays the current configuration in RAM.	18, 19, 20, 21
show stacks	Monitors the stack use of processes and interrupt routines and displays the reason for the last system reboot.	18
show startup-config	Displays the saved configuration, which is the contents of NVRAM.	19, 20, 21
show version	Displays the configuration of the system hardware, the software version, the names and sources of configuration files, and the boot images.	18, 21
shutdown	Disables an interface.	20
telnet	Logs in to a host that supports Telnet.	13, 17
term ip	Specifies the format of network masks for the current session.	17
trace	Determines a path that packets will take when traveling to their destination.	18, 24
verify	Verifies the checksum of a Flash file.	17
xremote	Enters XRemote mode.	17
where	Lists active connections.	17
which-route	Does OSI route table lookup and displays results.	17
write	Writes the running configuration to memory, a network, or a terminal.	17

Command	Description	Chapter
write erase	The **erase startup-config** command replaces this command.	20
write memory	The **copy running-config startup-config** command replaces this command.	20
x3	Sets X.3 parameters on PAD.	17
xremote	Enters XRemote mode.	17

e-Lab Activity Index

CD Number	e-Lab Title	Description
16.1	Setting Up Cisco Lab Equipment	In this activity, you demonstrate an understanding of how the Cisco lab routers are set up and connected for the Semester 2 topology.
16.2	Router and Workstation Configuration	In this activity, you demonstrate an understanding of how the Cisco lab routers and workstations are configured for the Semester 2 topology.
17.1	User and Privileged Modes	In this activity, you demonstrate how to use the command that allows you to access the privileged mode of a router.
17.2	User Mode Command List	In this activity, you demonstrate the use of the command that allows you to display the list of commands in user mode.
17.3	Privileged Command List	In this activity, you demonstrate how to use the command that allows you to display the list of commands in privileged mode.
17.4	Setting the Router Clock	In this activity, you demonstrate how to use the command that allows you to set the router clock.
17.5	Using IOS Command History	In this activity, you demonstrate how to use the IOS command history.
17.6	Using the Command-Line User Interface	In this activity, you demonstrate how to use different commands in user mode and privileged mode.
18.1	Examining Router Status	In this activity, you demonstrate how to use the command that allows you to examine router status.
18.2	Show Running and Startup Configurations	In this activity, you demonstrate how to use the command that allows you to see the active configuration file on a router.

CD Number	e-Lab Title	Description
18.3	**show interfaces, show version,** and **show protocols**	In this activity, you demonstrate how to use the **show interfaces, show version,** and **show protocols** commands.
18.4	Router **show** Commands	In this activity, you demonstrate how to use the router **show** commands, which are the most important information-gathering commands available for the router.
18.5	**show CDP neighbors**	In this activity, you demonstrate how to use the **show CDP neighbors** command to display information about neighboring devices.
18.6	CDP Configuration	In this activity, you demonstrate how to enable CDP on a router interface.
18.7	**show cdp**	In this activity, you demonstrate how to use the **show cdp** command to check general CDP settings.
18.8	**cdp neighbors**	In this activity, you demonstrate how to use the **show cdp** command to discover and show information about directly connected Cisco devices (routers and switches).
18.9	Testing Process that Uses the OSI Model	In this activity, you demonstrate how use the **telnet** command to test a connection between two routers.
18.10	Testing the Application Layer by Using **telnet**	In this activity, you demonstrate how to log on to a remote router and gather information about that router.
18.11	Remote Telnet Access	In this activity, you demonstrate how to use the **telnet** command to log on to a remote router and gather information about it by using the **show interfaces, show protocols, show running-config,** and **show startup-config** commands.
18.12	Testing the Network Layer Using the **ping** Command	In this activity, you demonstrate how use the **ping** command to test network connectivity.

CD Number	e-Lab Title	Description
18.13	Testing the Network Layer Using the **traceroute** Command	In this activity, you demonstrate how to use the **traceroute** command to see how data is routed between the two routers each step along the network.
18.14	Testing the Network Layer Using **show ip route**	In this activity, you demonstrate how to use the **show ip route** command to display the router's routing table.
18.15	Testing the Physical and Data Link Layers	In this activity, you demonstrate how to check the status of the physical and data link layers of your network by displaying information about serial interfaces configured.
18.16	Displaying Information about Interfaces	In this activity, you demonstrate how to display information about all interfaces configured on the router.
18.17	Using **show interfaces** and **clear counters**	In this activity, you demonstrate how to use **show interfaces** and **clear counters**.
18.18	Checking Real-Time Traffic with **debug**	In this activity, you demonstrate how to check all possible router traffic as it happens.
19.1	Commands Related to Router Startup	In this activity, you demonstrate how to reconfigure a router from scratch.
19.2	Using the **setup** Command	In this activity, you demonstrate how to enter router setup mode.
20.1	Copying Configuration Files to and From a TFTP Server	In this activity, you demonstrate how to store a current copy of the configuration on a tftp server.
20.2	Router config: TFTP	In this activity, you demonstrate how to use a Trivial File Transfer Protocol (TFTP) server to save a copy of the router's configuration file.
20.3	Using NVRAM Configuration Commands	In this activity, you demonstrate how to load a configuration from NVRAM.

CD Number	e-Lab Title	Description
20.4	Basic Router Configuration	In this activity, you demonstrate how to use the router's global configuration mode and enter one-line commands that change the entire router.
20.5	Entering Terminal Configuration Mode	In this activity, you demonstrate how to enter global configuration mode.
20.6	Router Interface Configuration Challenge	In this activity, you demonstrate how to use the router's interface configuration mode to configure an IP address and subnet mask for each router interface.
20.7	Defining an Interface's Physical Properties	In this activity, you demonstrate how to set the clock rate to 56,000 so that it can be used.
20.8	Router Password Recovery	In this activity, you demonstrate how to use the password recovery procedure on a router.
20.9	Using the **line con 0** command	In this activity, you demonstrate how to go into the console line configuration mode so others can set the password and log in.
20.10	Using the **message of the day** command	In this activity, you demonstrate how to start a message of the day.
21.1	Setting the Configuration Register	In this activity, you demonstrate how to set the router to boot from ROM, and set the configuration register.
21.2	Identifying the IOS Version Number	In this activity, you demonstrate how to verify the IOS version.
21.3	IOS Image Boot	In this activity, you demonstrate how to gather information on the version of IOS software that is currently running on the router.
21.4	Checking an IOS Image in Flash	In this activity, you demonstrate how to check an IOS image in Flash.
21.5	Using **copy flash tftp**	In this activity, you demonstrate how to do a backup to a tftp server.

CD Number	e-Lab Title	Description
21.6	Loading a New Flash Image	In this activity, you demonstrate how to start the process of getting the IOS on the router upgraded.
22.1	Router Configuration	In this activity, you demonstrate how to configure a router from the command line.
22.2	Individual Router Configuration Challenge	In this activity, you demonstrate how to do a step-by-step configuration of a router.
23.1	ARP Challenge	In this activity, you demonstrate how to identify the MAC addresses of each Ethernet interface.
24.1	Assigning an IP Address to a Router Interface	In this activity, you demonstrate how to assign an IP address with the subnet mask to an interface.
24.2	Creating an IP Host Table Entry	In this activity, you demonstrate how to set up a static name-to-address entry on a router.
24.3	Setting Up an IP-Name Server	In this activity, you demonstrate how to set up a router to recognize a new name server.
24.4	Using **no ip domain-lookup**	In this activity, you demonstrate how to turn off **ip domain-lookup**.
24.5	Discovering Host Names	In this activity, you demonstrate how to determine whether there are any host names linked to IP addresses.
24.6	Using the **telnet** Command	In this activity, you demonstrate how to **telnet** to the Serial 0 interface of a remote router.
24.7	Using the **trace** Command	In this activity, you demonstrate how to **trace** to a workstation.
26.1	Using the **ip route** Command	In this activity, you demonstrate how to set up a static route with the administrative distance of 1.
26.2	IP Static Route Challenge	In this activity, you demonstrate how to configure a static route between neighboring routers.

CD Number	e-Lab Title	Description
26.3	Using the **ip network default** Command	In this activity, you demonstrate how to set up a default network.
26.4	Setting Up RIP Routing on a Router	In this activity, you demonstrate how to enable RIP on a router.
26.5	Using the **show ip protocol** Command	In this activity, you demonstrate how to verify the protocols and network information.
26.6	Using **show ip route** Command	In this activity, you demonstrate how to see all the links the router knows by displaying the routing table.
26.7	RIP Routing	In this activity, you demonstrate how to configure RIP as the routing protocol.
26.8	Setting Up IGRP Routing on a Router	In this activity, you demonstrate how to enable IGRP on a router.
26.9	Overview of the **show ip interface** Command	In this activity, you demonstrate how to view the status and global parameters associated with IP interfaces.
26.10	Using the **show ip route** Command	In this activity, you demonstrate how to see the IP routing table.
26.11	Checking RIP Routing Updates	In this activity, you demonstrate how to check RIP routing updates as they are sent and received.
26.12	Routing Loops Setup Challenge	In this activity, you demonstrate how to create a routing loop for the five-router setup.

Movie Index

The following table lists the movies that you can find on this book's CD-ROM.

Movie Name	Title and Description	Chapter
Movie 1.1	**What Is Internetworking?** A collection of networks.	1
Movie 1.2	**The Evolution of Internetworking** The growth of the computer industry.	1
Movie 1.3	**The Evolution of Internetworking** Stand-alone computers with printers attached.	1
Movie 1.4	**The Evolution of Internetworking** Replacing old printers on a LAN with high-speed network printers.	1
Movie 1.5	**The Evolution of Internetworking** New offices—each has a LAN, software, hardware, and network administrator.	1
Movie 2.1	**The Evolution of Internetworking** Three problems—duplication of equipment and resources, inability to communicate efficiently, and lack of LAN network management.	2
Movie 2.2	**The OSI Model** The ISO researched networks, including DECnet, SNA, and TCP/IP.	2
Movie 2.3	**The OSI Model** The OSI model enhances interoperability and comprehension.	2
Movie 2.4	**The OSI Model Conceptual Framework** Protocols allow communication to occur.	2
Movie 2.5	**The Internet** Technology and networking.	2

Movie Name	Title and Description	Chapter
Movie 3.1	**Network Interface Cards** The MAC address is hard coded onto the NIC.	3
Movie 3.2	**Internetworking Devices Connect Networks** Repeaters, bridges, LAN extenders, routers, and WANs are introduced.	3
Movie 3.3	**Repeaters Amplifying Signals** A repeater cleans, amplifies, and resends a signal that is weakened by long cable length.	3
Movie 3.4	**Repeater Disadvantages** Repeaters can't filter traffic.	3
Movie 3.5	**Bridges** Bridges divide a network into segments and filter traffic.	3
Movie 3.6	**Bridge Problems** Bridges always propagate frame.	3
Movie 3.7	**Routers** Problem of excessive broadcast traffic can be solved by a router.	3
Movie 3.8	**Router/Bridge Difference** Bridging occurs at Layer 2 and routing occurs at Layer 3.	3
Movie 7.1	**Ethernet and 802.3 LANs** Ethernet and 802.3 LANs are broadcast networks.	7
Movie 7.2	**CSMA LANs** CSMA LANs use Ethernet and 802.3.	7
Movie 10.1	**IP Addressing Format** An IP address has a network number and a host number, and uses dotted-decimal notation.	10
Movie 10.2	**IP Address Classes** Five classes of addresses explained.	10
Movie 10.3	**Where to Get an IP Address** You can get IP addresses from an ISP and InterNIC.	10

Movie Name	Title and Description	Chapter
Movie 10.4	**IP Class Addresses** Class B addresses explained.	10
Movie 10.5	**IP Class Addresses** Class C addresses explained.	10
Movie 10.6	**IP Reserved Addresses** Extensions explained.	10
Movie 10.7	**Addressing Without Subnets** An explanation of addressing without subnets.	10
Movie 10.8	**Addressing With Subnets** An explanation of addressing with subnets.	10
Movie 10.9	**Subnet Addresses** A subnet address includes the network number, subnet number, and host number.	10
Movie 10.10	**Creating Subnet Addresses** Bits explained.	10
Movie 11.1	**Address Resolution** MAC addresses and ARP explained.	11
Movie 23.1	**Broadcast Transmission** Source node to network transmission.	23
Movie 23.2	**Reachability** The TCP/IP host sends an ICMP echo request.	23
Movie 23.3	**ICMP Time Exceeded Message** Time-To-Live field.	23
Movie 23.4	**TCP Sliding Window** Flow control explained.	23
Movie 23.5	**Router Can't Deliver** ICMP destination unreachable message.	23
Movie 25.1	**Distance-Vector Algorithms** Routing updates explained.	25
Movie 25.2	**Simple Split Horizon** Split horizon explained.	25
Movie 25.3	**Hold-Down Timer** When a router goes down and updates.	25

Movie Name	Title and Description	Chapter
Movie 25.4	**OSPF Routers** Link-state advertisements explained.	25
Movie 25.5	**Link-State Algorithms** Link-state algorithms explained.	25
Movie 25.6	**Routers and Network Administrators** The responsibilities of the network administrator.	25
Movie 26.1	**Router Operation** Determination, transportation, and switching.	26
Movie 26.2	**Routing Table** Static routes and dynamic routes explained.	26
Movie 26.3	**Static Routes** Static routes explained.	26
Movie 26.4	**Dynamic Routes** Dynamic routes explained.	26
Movie 26.5	**Routed Versus Router Protocols** Routed and router protocols explained.	26
Movie 26.6	**Dynamic Routing Protocols** Dynamic protocols, such as RIP, explained.	26
Movie 26.7	**RIP** RIP explained.	26
Movie 26.8	**RIP Problems** Hop-count limit is a problem in RIP.	26
Movie 26.9	**IGRP** Multipath routing explained.	26
Movie 26.10	**IGRP** Metrics explained.	26
Movie 26.11	**RIP/IGRP** Metric differences explained.	26

This glossary gathers and defines the terms and abbreviations related to networking. As with any growing technical field, some terms evolve into several meanings. Where necessary, multiple definitions and abbreviation expansions are presented. Hyphenated terms are alphabetized as if there were no hyphens.

Terms in this glossary are typically defined under their abbreviations. Each abbreviation expansion is listed separately, with a cross-reference to the abbreviation entry. In addition, many definitions contain cross-references to related terms.

We hope that this glossary adds to your understanding of internetworking technologies.

Numerics

4B/5B local fiber 4-byte/5-byte local fiber. Fiber Channel physical medium used for FDDI and ATM. Supports speeds of up to 100 Mbps over multimode fiber.

8B/10B local fiber 8-byte/10-byte local fiber. Fiber Channel physical medium that supports speeds of up to 149.76 Mbps over multimode fiber.

10Base2 A 10-Mbps baseband Ethernet specification using 50-ohm thin coaxial cable. 10Base2, which is part of the IEEE 802.3 specification, has a distance limit of 185 meters per segment. *See also* Ethernet and IEEE 802.3.

10Base5 A 10-Mbps baseband Ethernet specification using standard (thick) 50-ohm baseband coaxial cable. 10Base5, which is part of the IEEE 802.3 baseband physical-layer specification, has a distance limit of 500 meters per segment. *See also* Ethernet and IEEE 802.3.

10BaseF A 10-Mbps baseband Ethernet specification that refers to the 10BaseFB, 10BaseFL, and 10BaseFP standards for Ethernet over fiber-optic cabling. *See also* 10BaseFB, 10BaseFL, 10BaseFP, and Ethernet.

10BaseFB A 10-Mbps baseband Ethernet specification using fiber-optic cabling. 10BaseFB is part of the IEEE 10BaseF specification. It is not used to connect user stations, but provides a synchronous signaling backbone that allows additional segments and repeaters to be connected to the network. 10BaseFB segments can be up to 2000 meters long. *See also* 10BaseF and Ethernet.

10BaseFL A 10-Mbps baseband Ethernet specification using fiber-optic cabling. 10BaseFL is part of the IEEE 10BaseF specification and, although it can interoperate with FOIRL, it's designed to replace the FOIRL specification. 10BaseFL segments can be up to 1000 meters long if used with FOIRL, and up to 2000 meters if 10BaseFL is used exclusively. *See also* 10BaseF and Ethernet.

10BaseFP A 10-Mbps fiber-passive baseband Ethernet specification using fiber-optic cabling. 10BaseFP is part of the IEEE 10BaseF specification. It organizes a number of computers into a star topology without the use of repeaters. 10BaseFP segments can be up to 500 meters long. *See also* 10BaseF and Ethernet.

10BaseT A 10-Mbps baseband Ethernet specification using two pairs of twisted-pair cabling (Category 3, 4, or 5): one pair for transmitting data and the other for receiving data. 10BaseT, which is part of the IEEE 802.3 specification, has a distance limit of approximately 100 meters per segment. *See also* Ethernet and IEEE 802.3.

10Broad36 A 10-Mbps broadband Ethernet specification using broadband coaxial cable. 10Broad36, which is part of the IEEE 802.3 specification, has a distance limit of 3600 meters per segment. *See also* Ethernet and IEEE 802.3.

100BaseFX A 100-Mbps baseband Fast Ethernet specification using two strands of multimode fiber-optic cable per link. To guarantee proper signal timing, a 100BaseFX link cannot exceed 400 meters in length. Based on the IEEE 802.3 standard. *See also* 100BaseX, Fast Ethernet, and IEEE 802.3.

100BaseT A 100-Mbps baseband Fast Ethernet specification using UTP wiring. Like the 10BaseT technology on which it is based, 100BaseT sends link pulses over the network segment when no traffic is present. However, these link pulses contain more information than do those used in 10BaseT. Based on the IEEE 802.3 standard. *See also* 10BaseT, Fast Ethernet, and IEEE 802.3.

100BaseT4 A 100-Mbps baseband Fast Ethernet specification using four pairs of Category 3, 4, or 5 UTP wiring. To guarantee proper signal timing, a 100BaseT4 segment cannot exceed 100 meters in length. Based on the IEEE 802.3 standard. *See also* Fast Ethernet and IEEE 802.3.

100BaseTX A 100-Mbps baseband Fast Ethernet specification using two pairs of either UTP or STP wiring. The first pair of wires is used to receive data; the second is used to transmit. To guarantee proper signal timing, a 100BaseTX segment cannot exceed 100 meters in length. Based on the IEEE 802.3 standard. *See also* 100BaseX, Fast Ethernet, and IEEE 802.3.

100BaseX A 100-Mbps baseband Fast Ethernet specification that refers to the 100BaseFX and 100BaseTX standards for Fast Ethernet over fiber-optic cabling. Based on the IEEE 802.3 standard. *See also* 100BaseFX, 100BaseTX, Fast Ethernet, and IEEE 802.3.

100VG-AnyLAN A 100-Mbps Fast Ethernet and Token Ring media technology using four pairs of Category 3, 4, or 5 UTP cabling. This high-speed transport technology, developed by Hewlett-Packard, can be made to operate on existing 10BaseT Ethernet networks. Based on the IEEE 802.12 standard.

A

A&B bit signaling A procedure used in T1 transmission facilities in which each of the 24 T1 subchannels devotes 1 bit of every sixth frame to the carrying of supervisory signaling information.

ABM Asynchronous Balanced Mode. An HDLC (and derivative protocol) communication mode supporting peer-oriented point-to-point communications between two stations, where either station can initiate transmission.

access list A list kept by routers to control access through or to the router for a number of services (for example, to prevent packets with a certain IP address from leaving a particular interface on the router).

access method 1. Generally, the way in which network devices access the network medium. 2. Software within an SNA processor that controls the flow of information through a network.

ACK *See* acknowledgment.

acknowledgment Notification sent from one network device to another to acknowledge that some event (for example, receipt of a message) occurred. Sometimes abbreviated ACK. *Compare with* NAK.

active monitor A device responsible for performing maintenance functions on a Token Ring network. A network node is selected to be the active monitor if it has the highest MAC address on the ring. The active monitor is responsible for such ring maintenance tasks as ensuring that tokens are not lost and that frames do not circulate indefinitely.

adapter *See* NIC.

address A data structure or logical convention used to identify a unique entity, such as a particular process or network device.

address mapping A technique that allows different protocols to interoperate by translating addresses from one format to another. For example, when routing IP over X.25, the IP addresses must be mapped to the X.25 addresses so that the IP packets can be transmitted by the X.25 network.

address mask A bit combination used to describe which portion of an address refers to the network or subnet and which part refers to the host. Sometimes referred to simply as *mask*.

address resolution Generally, a method for resolving differences between computer addressing schemes. Address resolution usually specifies a method for mapping network layer (Layer 3) addresses to data link layer (Layer 2) addresses.

Address Resolution Protocol *See* ARP.

adjacency A relationship formed between selected neighboring routers and end nodes for the purpose of exchanging routing information. Adjacency is based on the use of a common media segment.

Advanced Research Projects Agency *See* ARPA.

advertising A router process in which routing or service updates are sent so that other routers on the network can maintain lists of usable routes.

AEP AppleTalk Echo Protocol. A protocol used to test connectivity between two AppleTalk nodes. One node sends a packet to another node and receives a duplicate, or echo, of that packet.

AFP AppleTalk Filing Protocol. A presentation-layer protocol that allows users to share data files and application programs that reside on a file server. AFP supports AppleShare and Mac OS file sharing.

agent 1. Generally, software that processes queries and returns replies on behalf of an application. 2. In NMSs, a process that resides in all managed devices and reports the values of specified variables to management stations.

algorithm A well-defined rule or process for arriving at a solution to a problem. In networking, algorithms are commonly used to determine the best route for traffic from a particular source to a particular destination.

ANSI American National Standards Institute. A voluntary organization composed of corporate, government, and other members that coordinates standards-related activities, approves U.S. national standards, and develops positions for the United States in international standards organizations. ANSI helps develop international and U.S. standards relating to, among other things, communications and networking. ANSI is a member of the IEC and the International Organization for Standardization.

API Application Programming Interface. A specification of function-call conventions that defines an interface to a service.

AppleTalk A series of communications protocols designed by Apple Computer consisting of two phases. Phase 1, the earlier version, supports a single physical network that can have only one network number and be in one zone. Phase 2 supports multiple logical networks on a single physical network and allows networks to be in more than one zone. *See also* zone.

application A program that performs a function directly for a user. FTP and Telnet clients are examples of network applications.

application layer Layer 7 of the OSI reference model. This layer provides services to application processes (such as e-mail, file transfer, and terminal emulation) that are outside the OSI reference model. The application layer identifies and establishes the availability of intended communication partners (and the resources required to connect with them), synchronizes cooperating applications, and establishes agreement on procedures for error recovery and control of data integrity. Corresponds roughly with the transaction services layer in the SNA model. *See also* data link layer, network layer, physical layer, presentation layer, session layer, and transport layer.

APPN Advanced Peer-to-Peer Networking. An enhancement to the original IBM SNA architecture. APPN handles session establishment between peer nodes, dynamic transparent route calculation, and traffic prioritization for APPC traffic.

ARA AppleTalk Remote Access. A protocol that provides Macintosh users direct access to information and resources at a remote AppleTalk site.

area A logical set of network segments (CLNS-, DECnet-, or OSPF-based) and their attached devices. Areas are usually connected to other areas via routers, making up a single autonomous system.

ARP Address Resolution Protocol. An Internet protocol used to map an IP address to a MAC address. Defined in RFC 826. *Compare with* RARP.

ARPA Advanced Research Projects Agency. A research and development organization that is part of the U.S. Department of Defense. ARPA is responsible for numerous technological advances in communications and networking. ARPA evolved into DARPA, and then back into ARPA again in 1994.

ARPANET Advanced Research Projects Agency Network. A landmark packet-switching network established in 1969. ARPANET was developed in the 1970s by BBN and funded by ARPA (and later DARPA). It eventually evolved into the Internet. The term *ARPANET* was officially retired in 1990.

ASBR Autonomous System Boundary Router. An ABR located between an OSPF autonomous system and a non-OSPF network. ASBRs run both OSPF and another routing protocol, such as RIP. ASBRs must reside in a nonstub OSPF area.

ASCII American Standard Code for Information Interchange. An 8-bit code (7 bits plus parity) for character representation.

Asynchronous Balanced Mode *See* ABM.

Asynchronous Transfer Mode *See* ATM.

asynchronous transmission Digital signals that are transmitted without precise clocking. Such signals generally have different frequencies and phase relationships. Asynchronous transmissions usually encapsulate individual characters in control bits (called start and stop bits) that designate the beginning and end of each character. *Compare with* synchronous transmission.

ATM Asynchronous Transfer Mode. An international standard for cell relay in which multiple service types (such as voice, video, or data) are conveyed in fixed-length (53-byte) cells. Fixed-length cells allow cell processing to occur in hardware, thereby reducing transit delays. ATM is designed to take advantage of high-speed transmission media such as E3, SONET, and T3.

ATM Forum An international organization jointly founded in 1991 by Cisco Systems, NET/ADAPTIVE, Northern Telecom, and Sprint that develops and promotes standards-based implementation agreements for ATM technology. The ATM Forum expands on official standards developed by ANSI and ITU-T and develops implementation agreements in advance of official standards.

ATP AppleTalk Transaction Protocol. A transport-level protocol that provides a loss-free transaction service between sockets. The service allows exchanges between two socket clients in which one client asks the other to perform a particular task and to report the results. ATP binds the request and response together to ensure the reliable exchange of request/response pairs.

attenuation Loss of communication signal energy.

AURP AppleTalk Update-Based Routing Protocol. A method of encapsulating AppleTalk traffic in the header of a foreign protocol, allowing the connection of two or more discontiguous AppleTalk internetworks through a foreign network (such as TCP/IP) to form an AppleTalk WAN. This connection is called an *AURP tunnel*. In addition to its encapsulation function, AURP maintains routing tables for the entire AppleTalk WAN by exchanging routing information between exterior routers.

authentication In security, the verification of the identity of a person or process.

B

B channel Bearer channel. In ISDN, a full-duplex 64-kbps channel used to send user data. *Compare with* D channel, E channel, and H channel.

backbone Part of a network that acts as the primary path for traffic that is most often sourced from, and destined for, other networks.

backbone cabling Cabling that provides interconnections between wiring closets and the POP, and between buildings that are part of the same LAN.

backoff The retransmission delay enforced when a collision occurs.

bandwidth The difference between the highest and lowest frequencies available for network signals. Also used to describe the rated throughput capacity of a given network medium or protocol.

bandwidth reservation The process of assigning bandwidth to users and applications served by a network. It involves assigning priority to different flows of traffic based on how critical and delay sensitive they are. This makes the best use of available bandwidth, and if the network becomes congested, lower-priority traffic can be dropped. Sometimes called *bandwidth allocation*.

Banyan VINES *See* VINES.

Basic Rate Interface *See* BRI.

binary A numbering system characterized by 1s and 0s (1 = on; 0 = off).

BOOTP Bootstrap Protocol. A protocol used by a network node to determine the IP address of its Ethernet interfaces to affect network booting.

bootstrap A simple, preset operation to load instructions that in turn cause other instructions to be loaded into memory, or cause entry into other configuration modes.

Bootstrap Protocol *See* BOOTP.

BPDU Bridge Protocol Data Unit. A Spanning-Tree Protocol hello packet that is sent out at configurable intervals to exchange information among bridges in the network.

BRI Basic Rate Interface. An ISDN interface composed of two B channels and one D channel for circuit-switched communication of voice, video, and data. *Compare with* PRI.

bridge A device that connects and passes packets between two network segments that use the same communications protocol. Bridges operate at the data link layer (Layer 2) of the OSI reference model. In general, a bridge filters, forwards, or floods an incoming frame based on the MAC address of that frame.

broadcast A data packet that is sent to all nodes on a network. Broadcasts are identified by a broadcast address. *Compare with* multicast and unicast. *See also* broadcast address.

broadcast address A special address reserved for sending a message to all stations. Generally, a broadcast address is a MAC destination address of all 1s. *Compare with* multicast address and unicast address. *See also* broadcast.

broadcast domain A set of all devices that will receive broadcast frames originating from any device within the set. Broadcast domains are typically bounded by routers (or, in a switched network, by VLANs) because routers do not forward broadcast frames.

bus topology A linear LAN architecture in which transmissions from network stations propagate the length of the medium and are received by all other stations. *Compare with* ring topology, star topology, and tree topology.

C

cable range A range of network numbers that is valid for use by nodes on an extended AppleTalk network. The cable range value can be a single network number or a contiguous sequence of several network numbers. Node addresses are assigned based on the cable range value.

caching A form of replication in which information learned during a previous transaction is used to process later transactions.

call setup time The time required to establish a switched call between DTE devices.

carrier An electromagnetic wave or alternating current of a single frequency, suitable for modulation by another data-bearing signal.

Category 1 cabling One of five grades of UTP cabling described in the EIA/TIA 568B standard. Category 1 cabling is used for telephone communications and is not suitable for transmitting data. *Compare with* Category 2 cabling, Category 3 cabling, Category 4 cabling, and Category 5 cabling. *See also* UTP.

Category 2 cabling One of five grades of UTP cabling described in the EIA/TIA 568B standard. Category 2 cabling is capable of transmitting data at speeds of up to 4 Mbps. *Compare with* Category 1 cabling, Category 3 cabling, Category 4 cabling, and Category 5 cabling. *See also* UTP.

Category 3 cabling One of five grades of UTP cabling described in the EIA/TIA 568B standard. Category 3 cabling is used in 10BaseT networks and can transmit data at speeds of up to 10 Mbps. *Compare with* Category 1 cabling, Category 2 cabling, Category 4 cabling, and Category 5 cabling. *See also* UTP.

Category 4 cabling One of five grades of UTP cabling described in the EIA/TIA 568B standard. Category 4 cabling is used in Token Ring networks and can transmit data at speeds of up to 16 Mbps. *Compare with* Category 1 cabling, Category 2 cabling, Category 3 cabling, and Category 5 cabling. *See also* UTP.

Category 5 cabling One of five grades of UTP cabling described in the EIA/TIA 568B standard. Category 5 cabling is used for running CDDI and can transmit data at speeds of up to 100 Mbps. *Compare with* Category 1 cabling, Category 2 cabling, Category 3 cabling, and Category 4 cabling. *See also* UTP.

CCITT Consultative Committee for International Telegraph and Telephone. An international organization responsible for the development of communications standards. Now called the ITU-T. *See* ITU-T.

CDDI Copper Distributed Data Interface. An implementation of FDDI protocols over STP and UTP cabling. CDDI transmits over relatively short distances (about 100 meters), providing data rates of 100 Mbps using a dual-ring architecture to provide redundancy. Based on the ANSI Twisted-Pair Physical Medium Dependent (TPPMD) standard. *Compare with* FDDI.

Challenge Handshake Authentication Protocol *See* CHAP.

CHAP Challenge Handshake Authentication Protocol. A security feature supported on lines using PPP encapsulation that prevents unauthorized access. CHAP does not itself prevent unauthorized access; it merely identifies the remote end. The router or access server then determines whether that user is allowed access. *Compare with* PAP.

CIDR Classless Interdomain Routing. A technique supported by BGP and based on route aggregation. CIDR allows routers to group routes in order to cut down on the quantity of routing information carried by the core routers. With CIDR, several IP networks appear to networks outside the group as a single, larger entity.

circuit A communications path between two or more points.

circuit group A grouping of associated serial lines that link two bridges. If one of the serial links in a circuit group is in the spanning tree for a network, any of the serial links in the circuit group can be used for load balancing. This load-balancing strategy avoids data ordering problems by assigning each destination address to a particular serial link.

Cisco IOS software Cisco Internetwork Operating System software. Cisco system software that provides common functionality, scalability, and security for all products under the CiscoFusion architecture. The Cisco IOS software allows centralized, integrated, and automated installation and management of internetworks while ensuring support for a wide variety of protocols, media, services, and platforms.

client A node or software program (front-end device) that requests services from a server.

client/server computing Distributed computing (processing) network systems in which transaction responsibilities are divided into two parts: client (front end) and server (back end). Both terms (*client* and *server*) can be applied to software programs or actual computing devices. Also called *distributed computing (processing)*. *Compare with* peer-to-peer computing.

client/server model A common way to describe network services and the model user processes (programs) of those services. Examples include the nameserver/nameresolver paradigm of the DNS and fileserver/file-client relationships such as NFS and diskless hosts.

CMIP Common Management Information Protocol. An OSI network management protocol created and standardized by ISO for the monitoring and control of heterogeneous networks. *See also* CMIS.

CMIS Common Management Information Services. An OSI network management service interface created and standardized by ISO for the monitoring and control of heterogeneous networks. *See also* CMIP.

CO central office. A local telephone company office to which all local loops in a given area connect and in which circuit switching of subscriber lines occurs.

coaxial cable A cable consisting of a hollow outer cylindrical conductor that surrounds a single inner wire conductor. Two types of coaxial cable are currently used in LANs: 50-ohm cable, which is used for digital signaling, and 75-ohm cable, which is used for analog signal and high-speed digital signaling.

coding Electrical techniques used to convey binary signals.

collision In Ethernet, the result of two nodes transmitting simultaneously. The frames from each device impact and are damaged when they meet on the physical media. *See also* collision domain.

collision domain In Ethernet, the network area within which frames that have collided are propagated. Repeaters and hubs propagate collisions; LAN switches, bridges, and routers do not. *See also* collision.

common carrier A licensed, private utility company that supplies communication services to the public at regulated prices.

concentrator *See* hub.

congestion Traffic in excess of network capacity.

congestion avoidance A mechanism by which an ATM network controls traffic entering the network to minimize delays. To use resources most efficiently, lower-priority traffic is discarded at the edge of the network if conditions indicate that it cannot be delivered.

connectionless Data transfer without the existence of a virtual circuit. *Compare with* connection-oriented. *See also* virtual circuit.

connection-oriented Data transfer that requires the establishment of a virtual circuit. *See also* connectionless and virtual circuit.

console A DTE through which commands are entered into a host.

contention An access method in which network devices compete for permission to access the physical medium. *Compare with* token passing.

convergence The speed and ability of a group of internetworking devices running a specific routing protocol to agree on the topology of an internetwork after a change in that topology.

count to infinity A problem that can occur in routing algorithms that are slow to converge, in which routers continuously increment the hop count to particular networks. Typically, some arbitrary hop-count limit is imposed to prevent this problem.

CPE Customer Premises Equipment. Terminating equipment, such as terminals, telephones, and modems, supplied by the telephone company, installed at customer sites and connected to the telephone company network.

CSMA/CD Carrier sense multiple access with collision detect. A media-access mechanism wherein devices ready to transmit data first check the channel for a carrier. If no carrier is sensed for a specific period of time, a device can transmit. If two devices transmit at once, a collision occurs and is detected by all colliding devices. This collision subsequently delays retransmissions from those devices for some random length of time. CSMA/CD access is used by Ethernet and IEEE 802.3.

CSU channel service unit. A digital interface device that connects end user equipment to the local digital telephone loop. Often referred to together with DSU as CSU/DSU.

cut sheet A rough diagram indicating where cable runs are located and the numbers of rooms they lead to.

D

D channel Delta channel. 1. Full-duplex 16-kbps (BRI) or 64-kbps (PRI) ISDN channel. *Compare with* B channel, E channel, and H channel. 2. In SNA, a device that connects a processor and main storage with peripherals.

DARPA Defense Advanced Research Projects Agency. The U.S. government agency that funded research for and experimentation with the Internet. Evolved from ARPA, and then, in 1994, back to ARPA. *See also* ARPA.

DAS 1. Dual Attachment Station. A device attached to both the primary and the secondary FDDI rings. Dual attachment provides redundancy for the FDDI ring: If the primary ring fails, the station can wrap the primary ring to the secondary ring, isolating the failure and retaining ring integrity. Also called a Class A station. *Compare with* SAS. 2. Dynamically Assigned Socket. A socket that is dynamically assigned by DDP upon request by a client. In an AppleTalk network, the sockets numbered 128 to 254 are allocated as DASs.

data Upper-layer protocol data.

data flow control layer Layer 5 of the SNA architectural model. This layer determines and manages interactions between session partners, particularly data flow. Corresponds to the session layer of the OSI reference model. *See also* data link control layer, path control layer, physical control layer, presentation services layer, transaction services layer, and transmission control layer.

data link control layer Layer 2 in the SNA architectural model. Responsible for the transmission of data over a particular physical link. Corresponds roughly to the data link layer of the OSI reference model. *See also* data flow control layer, path control layer, physical control layer, presentation services layer, transaction services layer, and transmission control layer.

data link layer Layer 2 of the OSI reference model. Provides transit of data across a physical link. The data link layer is concerned with physical addressing, network topology, line discipline, error notification, ordered delivery of frames, and flow control. The IEEE divided this layer into two sublayers: the MAC sublayer and the LLC sublayer. Sometimes simply called *link layer.* Roughly corresponds to the data link control layer of the SNA model.

datagram A logical grouping of information sent as a network layer unit over a transmission medium without prior establishment of a virtual circuit. IP datagrams are the primary information units in the Internet. The terms *cell, frame*, *message*, *packet*, and *segment* are also used to describe logical information groupings at various layers of the OSI reference model and in various technology circles.

DCE 1. Data Communications Equipment (EIA expansion) or Data Circuit-terminating Equipment (ITU-T expansion). Devices and connections of a communications network that comprise the network end of the user-to-network interface. The DCE provides a physical connection to the network, forwards traffic, and provides a clocking signal used to synchronize data transmission between DCE and DTE devices. Modems and interface cards are examples of DCEs. *Compare with* DTE.

DDN Defense Data Network. A U.S. military network composed of an unclassified network (MILNET) and various secret and top-secret networks. DDN is operated and maintained by DISA.

DDP Datagram Delivery Protocol. An AppleTalk network-layer protocol responsible for the socket-to-socket delivery of datagrams over an AppleTalk internetwork.

DDR Dial-on-Demand Routing. A technique whereby a router can automatically initiate and close a circuit-switched session as transmitting stations demand. The router spoofs keepalives so that end stations treat the session as active. DDR permits routing over ISDN or telephone lines, sometimes using an external ISDN terminal adapter or modem.

DECnet A group of communications products (including a protocol suite) developed and supported by Digital Equipment Corporation. DECnet/OSI (also called *DECnet Phase V*) is the most recent iteration and supports both OSI protocols and proprietary Digital protocols. Phase IV Prime supports inherent MAC addresses that allow DECnet nodes to coexist with systems running other protocols that have MAC address restrictions.

DECnet Routing Protocol *See* DRP.

default route A routing table entry that is used to direct frames for which a next hop is not explicitly listed in the routing table.

demarc A demarcation point between carrier equipment and CPE.

demultiplexing The separating of multiple input streams that have been multiplexed into a common physical signal back into multiple output streams. *See also* multiplexing.

designated router An OSPF router that generates LSAs for a multiaccess network and has other special responsibilities in running OSPF. Each multiaccess OSPF network that has at least two attached routers has a designated router that is elected by the OSPF Hello protocol. The designated router enables a reduction in the number of adjacencies required on a multiaccess network, which in turn reduces the amount of routing protocol traffic and the size of the topological database.

destination address An address of a network device that is receiving data. *See also* source address.

destination service access point *See* DSAP.

DHCP Dynamic Host Configuration Protocol. A protocol that provides a mechanism for allocating IP addresses dynamically so that addresses automatically can be reused when hosts no longer need them.

dial-on-demand routing *See* DDR.

dialup line A communications circuit that is established by a switched-circuit connection using the telephone company network.

distance-vector routing algorithm A class of routing algorithms that iterate on the number of hops in a route to find a shortest-path spanning tree. Distance-vector routing algorithms call for each router to send its entire routing table in each update, but only to its neighbors. Distance-vector routing algorithms can be prone to routing loops but are computationally simpler than link state routing algorithms. Also called Bellman-Ford routing algorithm.

DNS Domain Name System. The system used in the Internet for translating names of network nodes into addresses.

DoD Department of Defense. The U.S. government organization that is responsible for national defense. The DoD has frequently funded communication protocol development.

dotted-decimal notation The common notation for IP addresses in the form *a.b.c.d*, where each number represents, in decimal, 1 byte of the 4-byte IP address. Also called dotted notation or four-part dotted notation.

DRP DECnet Routing Protocol. A proprietary routing scheme introduced by Digital Equipment Corporation in DECnet Phase III. In DECnet Phase V, DECnet completed its transition to OSI routing protocols (ES-IS and IS-IS).

DSAP Destination Service Access Point. The SAP of the network node designated in the Destination field of a packet. *Compare with* SSAP. *See also* SAP (service access point).

DSU Digital Service Unit. A device used in digital transmission that adapts the physical interface on a DTE device to a transmission facility such as T1 or

E1. The DSU is also responsible for such functions as signal timing. Often referred to together with CSU as CSU/DSU. *See also* CSU.

DTE Data Terminal Equipment. A device at the user end of a user-network interface that serves as a data source, destination, or both. DTE connects to a data network through a DCE device (for example, a modem) and typically uses clocking signals generated by the DCE. DTE includes such devices as computers, routers, and multiplexers. *Compare with* DCE.

dual attachment station *See* DAS.

dual counter-rotating rings A network topology in which two signal paths, whose directions are opposite each other, exist in a token-passing network. FDDI and CDDI are based on this concept.

dual-homed station A device attached to multiple FDDI concentrators to provide redundancy.

dual homing A network topology in which a device is connected to the network by way of two independent access points (points of attachment). One access point is the primary connection, and the other is a standby connection that is activated in the event of a failure of the primary connection.

dynamic routing Routing that adjusts automatically to network topology or traffic changes. Also called *adaptive routing*. Requires that a routing protocol be run between routers.

E

E channel Echo channel. A 64-kbps ISDN circuit-switching control channel. The E channel was defined in the 1984 ITU-T ISDN specification but was dropped in the 1988 specification. *Compare with* B channel, D channel, and H channel.

E1 A wide-area digital transmission scheme used predominantly in Europe that carries data at a rate of 2.048 Mbps. E1 lines can be leased for private use from common carriers. *Compare with* T1.

E3 A wide-area digital transmission scheme used predominantly in Europe that carries data at a rate of 34.368 Mbps. E3 lines can be leased for private use from common carriers. *Compare with* T3.

echo channel See E channel.

EEPROM Electrically Erasable Programmable Read-Only Memory. EEPROM can be erased using electrical signals applied to specific pins.

EIA Electronic Industries Association. A group that specifies electrical transmission standards. The EIA and TIA have developed numerous well-known communications standards, including EIA/TIA-232 and EIA/TIA-449.

EIGRP Enhanced Interior Gateway Routing Protocol. An advanced version of IGRP developed by Cisco. Provides superior convergence properties and operating efficiency, and combines the advantages of link state protocols with those of distance vector protocols. *Compare with* IGRP. *See also* IGP, OSPF, and RIP.

encapsulation Wrapping of data in a particular protocol header. For example, upper-layer data is wrapped in a specific Ethernet header before network transit. Also, when bridging dissimilar networks, the entire frame from one network can simply be placed in the header used by the data link layer protocol of the other network. *See also* tunneling.

encoding The process by which bits are represented by voltages.

EPROM Erasable Programmable Read-Only Memory. Nonvolatile memory chips that are programmed after they are manufactured and, if necessary, can be erased by some means and reprogrammed. *Compare with* EEPROM and PROM.

ES-IS End System-to-Intermediate System. An OSI protocol that defines how end systems (hosts) announce themselves to intermediate systems (routers). *See also* IS-IS.

Ethernet A baseband LAN specification invented by Xerox Corporation and developed jointly by Xerox, Intel, and Digital Equipment Corporation. Ethernet networks use CSMA/CD and run over a variety of cable types at 10, 100, and 1000 Mbps. Ethernet is similar to the IEEE 802.3 series of standards.

excess rate Traffic in excess of the insured rate for a given connection. Specifically, the excess rate equals the maximum rate minus the insured rate. Excess traffic is delivered only if network resources are available and can be discarded during periods of congestion. *Compare with* insured rate and maximum rate.

F

Fast Ethernet Any of a number of 100-Mbps Ethernet specifications. Fast Ethernet offers a speed increase 10 times that of the 10BaseT Ethernet specification while preserving such qualities as frame format, MAC mechanisms, and MTU. Such similarities allow the use of existing 10BaseT applications and network management tools on Fast Ethernet networks. Based on an extension to the IEEE 802.3 specification. *Compare with* Ethernet. *See also* 100BaseFX, 100BaseT, 100BaseT4, 100BaseTX, 100BaseX, and IEEE 802.3.

fault management Four categories of network management— accounting management, configuration management, performance management, and security management—are defined by ISO for management of OSI networks. Fault management attempts to ensure that network faults are detected and controlled.

FDDI Fiber Distributed Data Interface. A LAN standard, defined by ANSI X3T9.5, specifying a 100-Mbps token-passing network using fiber-optic cable, with transmission distances of up to 2 km. FDDI uses a dual-ring architecture to provide redundancy. *Compare with* CDDI and FDDI II.

FDDI II An ANSI standard that enhances FDDI. FDDI II provides isochronous transmission for connectionless data circuits and connection-oriented voice and video circuits. *Compare with* FDDI.

Fiber Distributed Data Interface *See* FDDI.

fiber-optic cable A physical medium capable of conducting modulated light transmission. Compared with other transmission media, fiber-optic cable is more expensive but is not susceptible to electromagnetic interference. Sometimes called *optical fiber.*

File Transfer Protocol *See* FTP.

filter Generally, a process or device that screens network traffic for certain characteristics, such as source address, destination address, or protocol, and determines whether to forward or discard that traffic based on the established criteria.

firewall A device that controls who may access a private network and is itself immune to penetration.

firmware Software instructions set permanently or semipermanently in ROM.

Flash memory Nonvolatile storage that can be electrically erased and reprogrammed so that software images can be stored, booted, and rewritten as necessary. Flash memory was developed by Intel and is licensed to other semiconductor companies.

flash update A routing update sent asynchronously in response to a change in the network topology. *Compare with* routing update.

flat addressing A scheme of addressing that does not use a logical hierarchy to determine location.

flow A stream of data traveling between two endpoints across a network (for example, from one LAN station to another). Multiple flows can be transmitted on a single circuit.

flow control A technique for ensuring that a transmitting entity does not overwhelm a receiving entity with data. When the buffers on the receiving device are full, a message is sent to the sending device to suspend the transmission until the data in the buffers has been processed. In IBM networks, this technique is called *pacing*.

forwarding A process of sending a frame toward its ultimate destination by way of an internetworking device.

fragment A piece of a larger packet that has been broken down into smaller units. In Ethernet networks, sometimes also referred to as a frame less than the legal limit of 64 bytes.

fragmentation The process of breaking a packet into smaller units when transmitting over a network medium that cannot support the original size of the packet.

frame A logical grouping of information sent as a data link-layer unit over a transmission medium. Often refers to the header and trailer, used for synchronization and error control, that surround the user data contained in the unit. The terms *cell*, *datagram*, *message*, *packet*, and *segment* are also used to describe logical information groupings at various layers of the OSI reference model and in various technology circles.

frame forwarding A mechanism by which frame-based traffic, such as HDLC and SDLC, traverses an ATM network.

Frame Relay An industry-standard switched data link-layer protocol that handles multiple virtual circuits by using a form of HDLC encapsulation between connected devices. Frame Relay is more efficient than X.25, the protocol for which it is generally considered a replacement. *See also* X.25.

FTP File Transfer Protocol. An application protocol, part of the TCP/IP protocol stack, used for transferring files between network nodes. FTP is defined in RFC 959.

full duplex The capability for simultaneous data transmission between a sending station and a receiving station. *Compare with* half duplex and simplex.

full mesh A network in which devices are organized in a mesh topology, with each network node having either a physical circuit or a virtual circuit connecting it to every other network node. A full mesh provides a great deal of redundancy, but because it can be prohibitively expensive to implement, it is usually reserved for network backbones. *See also* mesh and partial mesh.

G

gateway In the IP community, an older term referring to a routing device. Today, the term *router* is used to describe nodes that perform this function, and *gateway* refers to a special-purpose device that performs an application-layer conversion of information from one protocol stack to another. *Compare with* router.

Gb Gigabit. Approximately 1,000,000,000 bits.

Gbps Gigabytes per second.

Get Nearest Server *See* GNS.

gigabit Abbreviated Gb.

GNS Get Nearest Server. A request packet sent by a client on an IPX network to locate the nearest active server of a particular type. An IPX network client issues a GNS request to solicit either a direct response from a connected server or a response from a router that tells it where on the internetwork the service can be located. GNS is part of the IPX SAP. *See also* IPX and SAP (Service Advertising Protocol).

GUI Graphical User Interface. A user environment that uses pictorial as well as textual representations of the input and output of applications and the hierarchical or other data structure in which information is stored. Conventions such as buttons, icons, and windows are typical, and many actions are performed using a pointing device (such as a mouse). Microsoft Windows and the Apple Macintosh are prominent examples of platforms utilizing GUIs.

H

H channel High-speed channel. A full-duplex ISDN primary rate channel operating at 384 kbps. *Compare with* B channel, D channel, and E channel.

half duplex A capability for data transmission in only one direction at a time between a sending station and a receiving station. *Compare with* full duplex and simplex.

handshake A sequence of messages exchanged between two or more network devices to ensure transmission synchronization before sending user data.

hardware address *See* MAC address.

HDLC High-Level Data Link Control. A bit-oriented synchronous data link-layer protocol developed by ISO. HDLC specifies a data encapsulation method on synchronous serial links by using frame characters and checksums.

header Control information placed before data when encapsulating that data for network transmission. *Compare with* trailer.

hello packet A multicast packet that is used by routers using certain routing protocols for neighbor discovery and recovery. Hello packets also indicate that a client is still operating and network-ready.

holddown A state into which a route is placed so that routers will neither advertise the route nor accept advertisements about the route for a specific length of time (the holddown period). Holddown is used to flush bad information about a route from all routers in the network. A route is typically placed in holddown when a link in that route fails.

hop The passage of a data packet from one network node, typically a router, to another. *See also* hop count.

hop count A routing metric used to measure the distance between a source and a destination. RIP uses hop count as its sole metric. *See also* hop and RIP.

host A computer system on a network. Similar to *node*, except that *host* usually implies a computer system, whereas *node* generally applies to any networked system, including access servers and routers. *See also* node.

host address *See* host number.

host number The part of an IP address that designates which node on the subnetwork is being addressed. Also called a *host address*.

HTML Hypertext Markup Language. A simple hypertext document formatting language that uses tags to indicate how a given part of a document should be interpreted by a viewing application, such as a Web browser.

HTTP Hypertext Transfer Protocol. The protocol used by Web browsers and Web servers to transfer files, such as text and graphics files.

hub 1. Generally, a device that serves as the center of a star-topology network and connects end stations. Operates at Layer 1 of the OSI reference model. 2. In Ethernet and IEEE 802.3, an Ethernet multiport repeater, sometimes called a *concentrator*.

hybrid network An internetwork made up of more than one type of network technology, including LANs and WANs.

Hypertext Markup Language *See* HTML.

Hypertext Transfer Protocol *See* HTTP.

I

IAB Internet Architecture Board. A board of internetwork researchers who discuss issues pertinent to Internet architecture. Responsible for appointing a variety of Internet-related groups such as the IANA, IESG, and IRSG. The IAB is appointed by the trustees of the ISOC. *See also* IANA and ISOC.

IANA Internet Assigned Numbers Authority. An organization operated under the auspices of the ISOC as a part of the IAB. IANA delegates authority for IP address-space allocation and domain-name assignment to the InterNIC and other organizations. IANA also maintains a database of assigned protocol identifiers used in the TCP/IP stack, including autonomous system numbers.

ICMP Internet Control Message Protocol. A network-layer Internet protocol that reports errors and provides other information relevant to IP packet processing. Documented in RFC 792.

IDF intermediate distribution facility. A secondary communications room for a building using a star networking topology. The IDF is dependent on the MDF. *See also* MDF.

IEC International Electrotechnical Commission. An industry group that writes and distributes standards for electrical products and components.

IEEE Institute of Electrical and Electronic Engineers. A professional organization whose activities include the development of communications and network standards. IEEE LAN standards are the predominant LAN standards today.

IEEE 802.2 An IEEE LAN protocol that specifies an implementation of the LLC sublayer of the data link layer. IEEE 802.2 handles errors, framing, flow control, and the network layer (Layer 3) service interface. Used in IEEE 802.3 and IEEE 802.5 LANs. *See also* IEEE 802.3 and IEEE 802.5.

IEEE 802.3 An IEEE LAN protocol that specifies an implementation of the physical layer and the MAC sublayer of the data link layer. IEEE 802.3 uses CSMA/CD access at a variety of speeds over a variety of physical media. Extensions to the IEEE 802.3 standard specify implementations for Fast Ethernet. Physical variations of the original IEEE 802.3 specification include 10Base2, 10Base5, 10BaseF, 10BaseT, and 10Broad36. Physical variations for Fast Ethernet include 100BaseTX and 100BaseFX.

IEEE 802.5 An IEEE LAN protocol that specifies an implementation of the physical layer and MAC sublayer of the data link layer. IEEE 802.5 uses token passing access at 4 or 16 Mbps over STP or UTP cabling and is functionally and operationally equivalent to IBM Token Ring. *See also* Token Ring.

IETF Internet Engineering Task Force. A task force consisting of more than 80 working groups responsible for developing Internet standards. The IETF operates under the auspices of ISOC.

IGP Interior Gateway Protocol. An Internet protocol used to exchange routing information within an autonomous system. Examples of common Internet IGPs are IGRP, OSPF, and RIP.

IGRP Interior Gateway Routing Protocol. An IGP developed by Cisco to address the problems associated with routing in large, heterogeneous networks. *Compare with* EIGRP. *See also* IGP, OSPF, and RIP.

Institute of Electrical and Electronic Engineers *See* IEEE.

insured rate The long-term data throughput, in bits or cells per second, that an ATM network commits to support under normal network conditions. The insured rate is 100 percent allocated; the entire amount is deducted from the total trunk bandwidth along the path of the circuit. *Compare with* excess rate and maximum rate.

Integrated Services Digital Network *See* ISDN.

interface 1. A connection between two systems or devices. 2. In routing terminology, a network connection on the router. 3. In telephony, a shared boundary defined by common physical interconnection characteristics, signal characteristics, and meanings of interchanged signals. 4. A boundary between adjacent layers of the OSI reference model.

International Organization for Standardization *See* ISO.

Internet The largest global internetwork, connecting tens of thousands of networks worldwide and having a culture that focuses on research and standardization based on real-life use. Many leading-edge network technologies come from the Internet community. The Internet evolved in part from ARPANET. At one time called the DARPA Internet. Not to be confused with the general term *internet*.

internet Short for *internetwork*. Not to be confused with the Internet. *See* internetwork.

Internet protocol Any protocol that is part of the TCP/IP protocol stack. *See* IP. *See also* TCP/IP.

internetwork A collection of networks interconnected by routers and other devices that functions (generally) as a single network.

Internetwork Packet Exchange *See* IPX.

internetworking The industry devoted to connecting networks. The term can refer to products, procedures, and technologies.

InterNIC An organization that serves the Internet community by supplying user assistance, documentation, training, registration service for Internet domain names, network addresses, and other services. Formerly called *NIC*.

interoperability The capability of computing equipment manufactured by different vendors to communicate with one another successfully over a network.

IOS Internetwork Operating System. *See* Cisco IOS software.

IP Internet Protocol. A network-layer protocol in the TCP/IP stack offering a connectionless internetwork service. IP provides features for addressing, type-of-service specification, fragmentation and reassembly, and security. Defined in RFC 791. IPv4 (Internet Protocol version 4) is a connectionless, best-effort packet-switching protocol. *See also* IPv6.

IP address A 32-bit address assigned to hosts using TCP/IP. An IP address belongs to one of five classes (A, B, C, D, or E) and is written as four octets separated by periods (that is, dotted-decimal format). Each address consists of a network number, an optional subnetwork number, and a host number. The network and subnetwork numbers together are used for routing, and the host number is used to address an individual host within the network or subnetwork. A subnet mask is used to extract network and subnetwork information from the IP address. CIDR provides a new way of representing IP addresses and subnet masks. Also called an *Internet address*.

IP datagram A fundamental unit of information passed across the Internet. Contains source and destination addresses along with data and a number of fields that define such things as the length of the datagram, the header checksum, and flags to indicate whether the datagram can be (or was) fragmented.

IPv6 IP version 6. A replacement for the current version of IP (version 4). IPv6 includes support for flow ID in the packet header, which can be used to identify flows. Formerly called IPng (IP next generation).

IPX Internetwork Packet Exchange. A NetWare network-layer protocol used for transferring data from servers to workstations. IPX is similar to IP and XNS.

IPXWAN IPX wide-area network. A protocol that negotiates end-to-end options for new links. When a link comes up, the first IPX packets sent across are IPXWAN packets that negotiate the options for the link. When the IPX-WAN options are successfully determined, normal IPX transmission begins. Defined by RFC 1362.

ISDN Integrated Services Digital Network. A communication protocol offered by telephone companies that permits telephone networks to carry data, voice, and other source traffic.

IS-IS Intermediate System-to-Intermediate System. An OSI link-state hierarchical routing protocol based on DECnet Phase V routing whereby ISs (routers) exchange routing information based on a single metric to determine network topology. *See also* ES-IS and OSPF.

ISO International Organization for Standardization. An international organization that is responsible for a wide range of standards, including those relevant to networking. ISO developed the OSI reference model, a popular networking reference model.

ISOC Internet Society. An international nonprofit organization, founded in 1992, that coordinates the evolution and use of the Internet. In addition, ISOC delegates authority to other groups related to the Internet, such as the IAB. ISOC is headquartered in Reston, Virginia, U.S.A. *See also* IAB.

ITU-T International Telecommunication Union Telecommunication Standardization Sector (formerly the Committee for International Telegraph and Telephone [CCITT]). An international organization that develops communication standards.

K

kB Kilobyte. Approximately 1,000 bytes.

kb Kilobit. Approximately 1,000 bits.

kBps Kilobytes per second.

kbps Kilobits per second.

keepalive interval The period of time between each keepalive message sent by a network device.

kilobit Abbreviated kb.

kilobits per second Abbreviated kbps.

kilobyte Abbreviated kB.

kilobytes per second Abbreviated kBps.

L

LAN Local-area network. A high-speed, low-error data network covering a relatively small geographic area (up to a few thousand meters). LANs connect workstations, peripherals, terminals, and other devices in a single building or other geographically limited area. LAN standards specify cabling and signaling at the physical and data link layers of the OSI reference model. Ethernet, FDDI, and Token Ring are widely used LAN technologies. *Compare with* MAN and WAN.

LAPB Link Access Procedure, Balanced. A data link-layer protocol in the X.25 protocol stack. LAPB is a bit-oriented protocol derived from HDLC. *See also* HDLC and X.25.

LAPD Link Access Procedure on the D channel. An ISDN data link-layer protocol for the D channel. LAPD was derived from the LAPB protocol and is designed primarily to satisfy the signaling requirements of ISDN basic access. Defined by ITU-T Recommendations Q.920 and Q.921.

LAT Local-area transport. A network virtual terminal protocol developed by Digital Equipment Corporation.

leased line A transmission line reserved by a communications carrier for the private use of a customer. A leased line is a type of dedicated line.

link A network communications channel consisting of a circuit or transmission path and all related equipment between a sender and a receiver. Most often used to refer to a WAN connection. Sometimes referred to as a line or a transmission link.

Link Access Procedure, Balanced *See* LAPB.

Link Access Procedure on the D channel *See* LAPD.

link layer *See* data link layer.

link-layer address *See* MAC address.

link-state routing algorithm A routing algorithm in which each router broadcasts or multicasts information regarding the cost of reaching each of its neighbors to all nodes in the internetwork. Link-state algorithms create a consistent view of the network and are therefore not prone to routing loops, but they achieve this at the cost of relatively greater computational difficulty and more widespread traffic than do distance-vector routing algorithms. *Compare with* distance-vector routing algorithm.

LLC Logical Link Control. The higher of the two data link-layer sublayers defined by the IEEE. The LLC sublayer handles error control, flow control, framing, and MAC-sublayer addressing. The most prevalent LLC protocol is IEEE 802.2, which includes both connectionless and connection-oriented variants.

load balancing In routing, the capability of a router to distribute traffic over all its network ports that are the same distance from the destination address. Good load-balancing algorithms use both line speed and reliability information. Load balancing increases the use of network segments, thus increasing effective network bandwidth.

local-area network *See* LAN.

local loop A line from the premises of a telephone subscriber to the telephone company CO.

local traffic filtering A process by which a bridge filters out (drops) frames whose source and destination MAC addresses are located on the same interface on the bridge, thus preventing unnecessary traffic from being forwarded across the bridge. Defined in the IEEE 802.1 standard.

loop A route where packets never reach their destination but simply cycle repeatedly through a constant series of network nodes.

loopback test A test in which signals are sent and then directed back toward their source from some point along the communications path. Loopback tests are often used to test network interface usability.

LSA Link-State Advertisement. A broadcast packet used by link-state protocols that contains information about neighbors and path costs. LSAs are used by the receiving routers to maintain their routing tables. Sometimes called a Link-State Packet (LSP).

M

MAC Media Access Control. The lower of the two sublayers of the data link layer defined by the IEEE. The MAC sublayer handles access to shared media, such as whether token passing or contention will be used. *See also* data link layer and LLC.

MAC address A standardized data link layer address that is required for every device that connects to a LAN. Other devices in the network use these addresses to locate specific devices in the network and to create and update routing tables and data structures. MAC addresses are 6 bytes long and are controlled by the IEEE. Also known as a *hardware address*, *MAC-layer address*, or *physical address*. *Compare with* network address.

MAC address learning A service that characterizes a learning switch in which the source MAC address of each received packet is stored so that future packets destined for that address can be forwarded only to the switch interface on which that address is located. Packets destined for unrecognized broadcast or multicast addresses are forwarded out every switch interface except the originating one. This scheme helps minimize traffic on the attached LANs. MAC address learning is defined in the IEEE 802.1 standard.

MAC-layer address *See* MAC address.

MAN Metropolitan-Area Network. A network that spans a metropolitan area. Generally, a MAN spans a larger geographic area than a LAN, but a smaller geographic area than a WAN. *Compare with* LAN and WAN.

Management Information Base *See* MIB.

mask *See* address mask and subnet mask.

MAU Media Attachment Unit. A device used in Ethernet and IEEE 802.3 networks that provides the interface between the AUI port of a station and the common media of the Ethernet. The MAU, which can be built into a station or can be a separate device, performs physical-layer functions, including the conversion of digital data from the Ethernet interface, collision detection, and injection of bits onto the network. Sometimes referred to as a *media access unit*, also abbreviated MAU, or as a *transceiver.* In Token Ring, a MAU is known as a *multistation access unit* and is usually abbreviated *MSAU* to avoid confusion.

maximum rate The maximum total data throughput allowed on a given virtual circuit, equal to the sum of the insured and uninsured traffic from the traffic source. The uninsured data might be dropped if the network becomes congested. The maximum rate, which cannot exceed the media rate, represents the highest data throughput the virtual circuit will ever deliver, measured in bits or cells per second. *Compare with* excess rate and insured rate.

MB Megabyte. Approximately 1,000,000 bytes.

Mb Megabit. Approximately 1,000,000 bits.

Mbps Megabits per second.

MDF Main Distribution Facility. The primary communications room for a building. The central point of a star networking topology where patch panels, hub, and router are located.

media Plural of *medium*. Various physical environments through which transmission signals pass. Common network media include twisted-pair, coaxial, fiber-optic cable, and the atmosphere (through which microwave, laser, and infrared transmission occurs). Sometimes called *physical media*.

Media Access Control *See* MAC.

media attachment unit *See* MAU.

megabit Abbreviated Mb. Approximately 1,000,000 bits.

megabits per second Abbreviated Mbps.

megabyte Abbreviated MB. Approximately 1,000,000 bytes.

mesh A network topology in which devices are organized in a manageable, segmented manner with many, often redundant, interconnections strategically placed between network nodes. *See also* full mesh and partial mesh.

message An application-layer logical grouping of information, often composed of a number of lower-layer logical groupings such as packets. The terms *datagram*, *frame*, *packet*, and *segment* are also used to describe logical information groupings at various layers of the OSI reference model and in various technology circles.

metric *See* routing metric.

MIB Management Information Base. A database of network management information that is used and maintained by a network management protocol such as SNMP. The value of a MIB object can be changed or retrieved by using SNMP commands, usually through a GUI network management system. MIB objects are organized in a tree structure that includes public (standard) and private (proprietary) branches.

modem Modulator-demodulator. A device that converts digital and analog signals. At the source, a modem converts digital signals to a form suitable for transmission over analog communication facilities. At the destination, the analog signals are returned to their digital form. Modems allow data to be transmitted over voice-grade telephone lines.

MSAU Multistation Access Unit. A wiring concentrator to which all end stations in a Token Ring network connect. The MSAU provides an interface between these devices and the Token Ring interface of a router. Sometimes abbreviated MAU.

MTU Maximum Transmission Unit. The maximum packet size, in bytes, that a particular interface can handle.

multicast Single packets copied by the network and sent to a specific subset of network addresses. These addresses are specified in the Destination Address field. *Compare with* broadcast and unicast.

multicast address A single address that refers to multiple network devices. Synonymous with *group address*. *Compare with* broadcast address and unicast address. *See also* multicast.

multimode fiber Optical fiber supporting propagation of multiple frequencies of light.

multiplexing A scheme that allows multiple logical signals to be transmitted simultaneously across a single physical channel. *Compare with* demultiplexing.

multistation access unit *See* MSAU.

multivendor network A network using equipment from more than one vendor. Multivendor networks pose many more compatibility problems than single-vendor networks. *Compare with* single-vendor network.

N

NAK Negative acknowledgment. A response sent from a receiving device to a sending device, indicating that the information received contained errors. *Compare with* acknowledgment.

name resolution Generally, the process of associating a name with a network address.

name server A server connected to a network that resolves network names into network addresses.

NAT Network Address Translation. A mechanism for reducing the need for globally unique IP addresses. NAT allows an organization with addresses that are not globally unique to connect to the Internet by translating those addresses into globally routable address space. Also known as *network address translator*.

NAUN Nearest Active Upstream Neighbor. In Token Ring or IEEE 802.5 networks, the closest upstream network device from any given device that is still active.

NCP Network Control Program. In SNA, a program that routes and controls the flow of data between a communications controller (in which it resides) and other network resources.

neighboring routers In OSPF, two routers that have interfaces to a common network. On multiaccess networks, neighbors are dynamically discovered by the OSPF Hello protocol.

NetBEUI NetBIOS Extended User Interface. An enhanced version of the NetBIOS protocol used by network operating systems, such as LAN Manager, LAN Server, Windows for Workgroups, and Windows NT. NetBEUI formalizes the transport frame and adds additional functions. NetBEUI implements the OSI LLC2 protocol.

NetBIOS Network Basic Input/Output System. An application programming interface used by applications on an IBM LAN to request services from lower-level network processes. These services might include session establishment and termination and information transfer.

NetWare A popular distributed NOS developed by Novell. Provides transparent remote file access and numerous other distributed network services.

NetWare Link Services Protocol *See* NLSP.

NetWare Loadable Module *See* NLM.

network A collection of computers, printers, routers, switches, and other devices that can communicate with each other over some transmission medium.

network address A network-layer address referring to a logical, rather than a physical, network device. Also called a *protocol address*. *Compare with* MAC address.

network address translation *See* NAT.

network administrator A person responsible for the operation, maintenance, and management of a network.

network analyzer A hardware or software device offering various network troubleshooting features, including protocol-specific packet decodes, specific preprogrammed troubleshooting tests, packet filtering, and packet transmission.

Network Basic Input/Output System *See* NetBIOS.

network byte order An Internet-standard ordering of the bytes corresponding to numeric values.

Network File System *See* NFS.

network interface The boundary between a carrier network and a privately owned installation.

network interface card *See* NIC.

network layer Layer 3 of the OSI reference model. This layer provides connectivity and path selection between two end systems. The network layer is the layer at which routing occurs. Corresponds roughly with the path control layer of the SNA model. *See also* application layer, data link layer, physical layer, presentation layer, session layer, and transport layer.

network management Using systems or actions to maintain, characterize, or troubleshoot a network.

network management system *See* NMS.

network number The part of an IP address that specifies the network to which the host belongs.

network operating system *See* NOS.

networking The interconnection of workstations, peripherals such as printers, hard drives, scanners, CD-ROMs, and other devices.

NFS Network File System. As commonly used, a distributed file system protocol suite developed by Sun Microsystems that allows remote file access across a network. In actuality, NFS is simply one protocol in the suite. NFS protocols include RPC and XDR. These protocols are part of a larger architecture that Sun refers to as ONC.

NIC 1. Network interface card. A board that provides network communication capabilities to and from a computer system. Also called an *adapter.* 2. Network Information Center. An organization whose functions have been assumed by InterNIC. *See* InterNIC.

NLM NetWare Loadable Module. An individual program that can be loaded into memory and can function as part of the NetWare NOS.

NLSP NetWare Link Services Protocol. A link-state routing protocol based on IS-IS.

NMS Network Management System. A system responsible for managing at least part of a network. An NMS is generally a reasonably powerful and well-equipped computer such as an engineering workstation. NMSs communicate with agents to help keep track of network statistics and resources.

node 1. An endpoint of a network connection or a junction common to two or more lines in a network. Nodes can be processors, controllers, or workstations. Nodes, which vary in routing and other functional capabilities, can be interconnected by links and serve as control points in the network. *Node* is sometimes used generically to refer to any entity that can access a network and is frequently used interchangeably with *device*. 2. In SNA, the basic component of a network and the point at which one or more functional units connect channels or data circuits.

nonextended network An AppleTalk Phase 2 network that supports addressing of up to 253 nodes and only one zone.

nonseed router In AppleTalk, a router that must first obtain, and then verify, its configuration with a seed router before it can begin operation. *See also* seed router.

non-stub area A resource-intensive OSPF area that carries a default route, static routes, intra-area routes, interarea routes, and external routes. Non-stub areas are the only OSPF areas that can have virtual links configured across them and are the only areas that can contain an ASBR. *Compare with* stub area.

NOS Network Operating System. Distributed file systems. Examples of NOSs include LAN Manager, NetWare, NFS, VINES, and Windows NT.

Novell IPX *See* IPX.

NTP Network Time Protocol. A protocol built on top of TCP that assures accurate local timekeeping with reference to radio and atomic clocks located on the Internet. This protocol can synchronize distributed clocks within milliseconds over long time periods.

NVRAM Nonvolatile RAM. RAM that retains its contents when a unit is powered off.

O

octet 8 bits. In networking, the term *octet* is often used (rather than *byte*) because some machine architectures employ bytes that are not 8 bits long.

ODI Open Data-Link Interface. A Novell specification providing a standardized interface for network interface cards (NICs) that allows multiple protocols to use a single NIC.

Open Shortest Path First *See* OSPF.

Open System Interconnection *See* OSI.

Open System Interconnection reference model *See* OSI reference model.

OSI Open System Interconnection. An international standardization program created by ISO and ITU-T to develop standards for data networking that facilitate multivendor equipment interoperability.

OSI presentation address An address used to locate an OSI application entity. It consists of an OSI network address and up to three selectors, one each for use by the transport, session, and presentation entities.

OSI reference model Open System Interconnection reference model. A network architectural model developed by ISO and ITU-T. The model consists of seven layers, each of which specifies particular network functions such as addressing, flow control, error control, encapsulation, and reliable message transfer. The lowest layer (the physical layer) is closest to the media technology. The lower two layers are implemented in hardware and software, and the upper five layers are implemented only in software. The highest layer (the application layer) is closest to the user. The OSI reference model is used universally as a method for teaching and understanding network functionality. Similar in some respects to SNA. *See also* application layer, data link layer, network layer, physical layer, presentation layer, session layer, and transport layer.

OSPF Open Shortest Path First. A link-state hierarchical IGP routing algorithm proposed as a successor to RIP in the Internet community. OSPF features include least-cost routing, multipath routing, and load balancing. OSPF was derived from an early version of the IS-IS protocol.

OUI Organizational Unique Identifier. Three octets assigned by the IEEE in a block of 48-bit LAN addresses.

P

packet A logical grouping of information that includes a header containing control information and (usually) user data. Packets are most often used to refer to network-layer units of data. The terms *datagram*, *frame*, *message*, and *segment* are also used to describe logical information groupings at various layers of the OSI reference model and in various technology circles.

packet internet groper *See* **ping.**

PAP Password Authentication Protocol. An authentication protocol that allows PPP peers to authenticate one another. The remote router attempting to connect to the local router is required to send an authentication request. Unlike CHAP, PAP passes the password and host name or username in the clear (unencrypted). PAP does not itself prevent unauthorized access, but merely identifies the remote end. The router or access server then determines whether that user is allowed access. PAP is supported only on PPP lines. *Compare with* CHAP.

parallel transmission A method of data transmission in which the bits of a data character are transmitted simultaneously over a number of channels. *Compare with* serial transmission.

partial mesh A network in which devices are organized in a mesh topology, with some network nodes organized in a full mesh, but with others that are connected to only one or two other nodes in the network. A partial mesh does not provide the level of redundancy of a full-mesh topology but is less expensive to implement. Partial-mesh topologies are generally used in the peripheral networks that connect to a fully meshed backbone.

Password Authentication Protocol *See* PAP.

patch panel An assembly of pin locations and ports that can be mounted on a rack or wall bracket in the wiring closet. Patch panels act like switchboards that connect workstations' cables to each other and to the outside.

path control layer Layer 3 in the SNA architectural model. This layer performs sequencing services related to proper data reassembly. The path control layer is also responsible for routing. Corresponds roughly with the network layer of the OSI reference model. *See also* data flow control layer, data link control layer, physical control layer, presentation services layer, transaction services layer, and transmission control layer.

payload A portion of a cell, frame, or packet that contains upper-layer information (data).

PDN Public Data Network. A network operated either by a government (as in Europe) or by a private concern to provide computer communications to the public, usually for a fee. PDNs enable small organizations to create a WAN without all the equipment costs of long-distance circuits.

PDU Protocol Data Unit. The OSI term for a packet.

peer-to-peer computing Calls for each network device to run both client and server portions of an application. Also describes communication between implementations of the same OSI reference model layer in two different network devices. *Compare with* client/server computing.

permanent virtual circuit *See* PVC.

PHY 1. Physical sublayer. One of two sublayers of the FDDI physical layer. 2. Physical layer. In ATM, the physical layer provides for the transmission of cells over a physical medium that connects two ATM devices. The PHY is composed of two sublayers: PMD and TC.

physical address *See* MAC address.

physical control layer Layer 1 in the SNA architectural model. This layer is responsible for the physical specifications for the physical links between end systems. Corresponds to the physical layer of the OSI reference model. *See also* data flow control layer, data link control layer, path control layer, presentation services layer, transaction services layer, and transmission control layer.

physical layer Layer 1 of the OSI reference model. The physical layer defines the electrical, mechanical, procedural, and functional specifications for activating, maintaining, and deactivating the physical link between end systems. Corresponds with the physical control layer in the SNA model. *See also* application layer, data link layer, network layer, presentation layer, session layer, and transport layer.

ping Packet Internet groper. An ICMP echo message and its reply. Often used in IP networks to test the reachability of a network device.

PLP Packet-Level Protocol. A network-layer protocol in the X.25 protocol stack. Sometimes called *X.25 Level 3* and *X.25 Protocol*. *See also* X.25.

point-to-multipoint connection One of two fundamental connection types. In ATM, a point-to-multipoint connection is a unidirectional connection in which a single source end system (known as a *root node*) connects to multiple destination end systems (known as *leaves*). *Compare* with point-to-point connection.

point-to-point connection One of two fundamental connection types. In ATM, a point-to-point connection can be a unidirectional or bidirectional connection between two ATM end systems. *Compare with* point-to-multipoint connection.

Point-to-Point Protocol *See* PPP.

poison reverse update A routing update that explicitly indicates that a network or subnet is unreachable, rather than implying that a network is unreachable by not including it in updates. Poison reverse updates are sent to defeat large routing loops.

port 1. An interface on an internetworking device (such as a router). 2. In IP terminology, an upper-layer process that receives information from lower layers. Ports are numbered, and many are associated with a specific process. For example, SMTP is associated with port 25. A port number of this type is called a *well-known address*. 3. To rewrite software or microcode so that it will run on a different hardware platform or in a different software environment than that for which it was originally designed.

POST Power-on self-test. A set of hardware diagnostics that runs on a hardware device when that device is powered up.

PPP Point-to-Point Protocol. A successor to SLIP that provides router-to-router and host-to-network connections over synchronous and asynchronous circuits. Whereas SLIP was designed to work with IP, PPP was designed to work with several network-layer protocols, such as IP, IPX, and ARA. PPP also has built-in security mechanisms, such as CHAP and PAP. PPP relies on two protocols: LCP and NCP.

presentation layer Layer 6 of the OSI reference model. This layer ensures that information sent by the application layer of one system will be readable by the application layer of another. The presentation layer is also concerned with the data structures used by programs and therefore negotiates data transfer syntax for the application layer. Corresponds roughly with the presentation services layer of the SNA model. *See also* application layer, data link layer, network layer, physical layer, session layer, and transport layer.

presentation services layer Layer 6 of the SNA architectural model. This layer provides network resource management, session presentation services, and some application management. Corresponds roughly with the presentation layer of the OSI reference model.

PRI Primary Rate Interface. An ISDN interface to primary rate access. Primary rate access consists of a single 64-kbps D channel plus 23 (T1) or 30 (E1) B channels for voice or data. *Compare with* BRI.

priority queuing A routing feature in which frames in an interface output queue are prioritized based on various characteristics such as protocol, packet size, and interface type.

PROM Programmable Read-Only Memory. ROM that can be programmed using special equipment. PROM can be programmed only once. *Compare with* EPROM.

protocol A formal description of a set of rules and conventions that govern how devices on a network exchange information.

protocol address *See* network address.

protocol analyzer *See* network analyzer.

protocol stack A set of related communications protocols that operate together and, as a group, address communication at some or all of the seven layers of the OSI reference model. Not every protocol stack covers each layer of the model, and often a single protocol in the stack addresses a number of layers at once. TCP/IP is a typical protocol stack.

proxy An entity that, in the interest of efficiency, essentially stands in for another entity.

proxy Address Resolution Protocol *See* proxy ARP.

proxy ARP Proxy Address Resolution Protocol. A variation of the ARP protocol in which an intermediate device (for example, a router) sends an ARP response on behalf of an end node to the requesting host. Proxy ARP can lessen bandwidth use on slow-speed WAN links.

punch tool A spring-loaded tool used for cutting and connecting wire in a jack or on a patch panel.

PVC Permanent Virtual Circuit. A virtual circuit that is permanently established. PVCs save bandwidth associated with circuit establishment and tear down in situations where certain virtual circuits must exist all the time. In ATM terminology, called a *permanent virtual connection*. *Compare with* SVC.

Q

QoS Quality of service. A measure of performance for a transmission system that reflects its transmission quality and service availability.

queue 1. Generally, an ordered list of elements waiting to be processed. 2. In routing, a backlog of packets waiting to be forwarded over a router interface.

queuing delay The amount of time that data must wait before it can be transmitted onto a statistically multiplexed physical circuit.

R

RAM Random-Access Memory. Volatile memory that can be read and written by a microprocessor.

random-access memory *See* RAM.

RARP Reverse Address Resolution Protocol. A protocol in the TCP/IP stack that provides a method for finding IP addresses based on MAC addresses. *Compare with* ARP.

reassembly The putting back together of an IP datagram at the destination after it has been fragmented either at the source or at an intermediate node.

redirect Part of the ICMP and ES-IS protocols that allows a router to tell a host that using another router would be more effective.

redundancy 1. In internetworking, the duplication of devices, services, or connections so that, in the event of a failure, the redundant devices, services, or connections can perform the work of those that failed. 2. In telephony, the portion of the total information contained in a message that can be eliminated without loss of essential information or meaning.

repeater A device that regenerates and propagates electrical signals between two network segments.

Request for Comments *See* RFC.

RFC Request for Comments. A document series used as the primary means for communicating information about the Internet. Some RFCs are designated by the IAB as Internet standards. Most RFCs document protocol specifications such as Telnet and FTP, but some are humorous or historical. RFCs are available online from numerous sources.

ring A connection of two or more stations in a logically circular topology. Information is passed sequentially between active stations. Token Ring, FDDI, and CDDI are based on this topology.

ring topology A network topology that consists of a series of repeaters connected to one another by unidirectional transmission links to form a single closed loop. Each station on the network connects to the network at a repeater. Although logically they arerings, ring topologies are most often organized in a closed-loop star. *Compare with* bus topology, star topology, and tree topology.

RIP Routing Information Protocol. An IGP supplied with UNIX BSD systems. The most common IGP in the Internet. RIP uses hop count as a routing metric.

RMON Remote monitoring. A MIB agent specification described in RFC 1271 that defines functions for the remote monitoring of networked devices. The RMON specification provides numerous monitoring, problem detection, and reporting capabilities.

ROM Read-Only Memory. Nonvolatile memory that can be read, but not written, by the microprocessor.

route map A method of controlling the redistribution of routes between routing domains.

route summarization The consolidation of advertised network numbers in OSPF and IS-IS. In OSPF, this causes a single summary route to be advertised to other areas by an area border router.

routed protocol A protocol that can be routed by a router. A router must be able to interpret the logical internetwork as specified by that routed protocol. Examples of routed protocols are AppleTalk, DECnet, and IP.

router A network-layer device that uses one or more metrics to determine the optimal path along which network traffic should be forwarded. Routers forward packets from one network to another based on network-layer information contained in routing updates. Occasionally called a *gateway* (although this definition of *gateway* is becoming increasingly outdated).

routing The process of finding a path to a destination host. Routing is very complex in large networks because of the many potential intermediate destinations a packet might traverse before reaching its destination host.

routing metric A method by which a routing algorithm determines that one route is better than another. This information is stored in routing tables and sent in routing updates. Metrics include bandwidth, communication cost, delay, hop count, load, MTU, path cost, and reliability. Sometimes referred to simply as a *metric*.

routing protocol A protocol that accomplishes routing through the implementation of a specific routing algorithm. Examples of routing protocols are IGRP, OSPF, and RIP.

routing table A table stored in a router or some other internetworking device that keeps track of routes to particular network destinations and, in some cases, metrics associated with those routes.

Routing Table Maintenance Protocol *See* RTMP.

routing update A message sent from a router to indicate network reachability and associated cost information. Routing updates are typically sent at regular intervals and after a change in network topology. *Compare with* flash update.

RPC Remote-Procedure Call. The technological foundation of client/server computing. RPCs are procedure calls that are built or specified by clients and executed on servers, with the results returned over the network to the clients.

RPF Reverse Path Forwarding. A multicasting technique in which a multicast datagram is forwarded out of all but the receiving interface if the receiving interface is the one used to forward unicast datagrams to the source of the multicast datagram.

RSVP Resource Reservation Protocol. A protocol that supports the reservation of resources across an IP network. Applications running on IP end systems can use RSVP to indicate to other nodes the nature (bandwidth, jitter, maximum burst, and so forth) of the packet streams they want to receive. RSVP depends on IPv6. Also known as *Resource Reservation Setup Protocol.*

RTMP Routing Table Maintenance Protocol. Apple Computer's proprietary routing protocol. RTMP establishes and maintains the routing information that is required to route datagrams from any source socket to any destination socket in an AppleTalk network. Using RTMP, routers dynamically maintain routing tables to reflect changes in topology. RTMP was derived from RIP.

RTP 1. Routing Table Protocol. A VINES routing protocol based on RIP. Distributes network topology information and aids VINES servers in finding neighboring clients, servers, and routers. Uses delay as a routing metric. 2. Rapid Transport Protocol. A protocol that provides pacing and error recovery for APPN data as it crosses the APPN network. With RTP, error recovery and flow control are done end-to-end rather than at every node. RTP prevents congestion rather than reacts to it. 3. Real-Time Transport Protocol. One of the IPv6 protocols. RTP is designed to provide end-to-end network transport functions for applications transmitting real-time data, such as audio, video, or simulation data, over multicast or unicast network services. RTP provides services such as payload type identification, sequence numbering, timestamping, and delivery monitoring to real-time applications.

S

SAP 1. Service Access Point. A field defined by the IEEE 802.2 specification that identifies the upper-layer process and is part of an address specification. Thus, the destination plus the DSAP define the recipient of a packet. The same applies to the SSAP. 2. Service Advertising Protocol. An IPX protocol that provides a means of informing network clients, via routers and servers, of available network resources and services.

SAS Single Attachment Station. A device attached only to the primary ring of an FDDI ring. Also known as a Class B station. *Compare with* DAS. *See also* FDDI.

SDLC Synchronous Data Link Control. An SNA data link layer communications protocol. SDLC is a bit-oriented, full-duplex serial protocol that has spawned numerous similar protocols, including HDLC and LAPB.

secondary station In bit-synchronous data link-layer protocols such as HDLC, a station that responds to commands from a primary station. Sometimes referred to simply as a *secondary.*

seed router A router in an AppleTalk network that has the network number or cable range built in to its port descriptor. The seed router defines the network number or cable range for other routers in that network segment and responds to configuration queries from nonseed routers on its connected AppleTalk network, allowing those routers to confirm or modify their configurations accordingly. Each AppleTalk network must have at least one seed router.

segment 1. A section of a network that is bounded by bridges, routers, or switches. 2. In a LAN using a bus topology, a continuous electrical circuit that is often connected to other such segments with repeaters. 3. In the TCP specification, a single transport-layer unit of information. The terms *datagram*, *frame*, *message*, and *packet* are also used to describe logical information groupings at various layers of the OSI reference model and in various technology circles.

Sequenced Packet Exchange *See* SPX.

serial transmission A method of data transmission in which the bits of a data character are transmitted sequentially over a single channel. *Compare with* parallel transmission.

server A node or software program that provides services to clients.

service access point *See* SAP.

Service Advertising Protocol *See* SAP.

session 1. A related set of connection-oriented communications transactions between two or more network devices. 2. In SNA, a logical connection enabling two network addressable units to communicate.

session layer Layer 5 of the OSI reference model. This layer establishes, manages, and terminates sessions between applications and manages data exchange between presentation layer entities. Corresponds to the data flow control layer of the SNA model.

shortest-path routing Routing that minimizes distance or path cost through application of an algorithm.

signal reference ground A reference point used by computing devices to measure and compare incoming digital signals.

signaling The process of sending a transmission signal over a physical medium for purposes of communication.

simplex The capability for transmission in only one direction between a sending station and a receiving station. Broadcast television is an example of a simplex technology. *Compare with* full duplex and half duplex.

single-vendor network A network using equipment from only one vendor. Single-vendor networks rarely suffer compatibility problems. *See also* multi-vendor network.

sliding window flow control A method of flow control in which a receiver gives a transmitter permission to transmit data until a window is full. When the window is full, the transmitter must stop transmitting until the receiver advertises a larger window. TCP, other transport protocols, and several data link-layer protocols use this method of flow control.

SLIP Serial Line Internet Protocol. A standard protocol for point-to-point serial connections using a variation of TCP/IP. The predecessor of PPP.

SMI Structure of Management Information. A document (RFC 1155) specifying rules used to define managed objects in the MIB.

SNA Systems Network Architecture. A large, complex, feature-rich network architecture developed in the 1970s by IBM. Similar in some respects to the OSI reference model, but with a number of differences. SNA is essentially composed of seven layers. *See* data flow control layer, data-link control layer, path control layer, physical control layer, presentation services layer, transaction services layer, and transmission control layer.

SNMP Simple Network Management Protocol. A network management protocol used almost exclusively in TCP/IP networks. SNMP provides a means to monitor and control network devices and to manage configurations, statistics collection, performance, and security.

socket 1. A software structure operating as a communications endpoint within a network device (similar to a port). 2. An addressable entity within a node connected to an AppleTalk network; sockets are owned by software processes known as *socket clients*. AppleTalk sockets are divided into two groups: SASs, which are reserved for clients such as AppleTalk core protocols, and DASs, which are assigned dynamically by DDP upon request from clients in the node. An AppleTalk socket is similar in concept to a TCP/IP port.

socket number An 8-bit number that identifies a socket. A maximum of 254 socket numbers can be assigned in an AppleTalk node.

source address An address of a network device that is sending data.

spanning tree A loop-free subset of a Layer 2 (switched) network topology.

spanning-tree algorithm An algorithm used by the Spanning-Tree Protocol to create a spanning tree. Sometimes abbreviated as STA.

Spanning-Tree Protocol A bridge protocol that uses the spanning-tree algorithm, enabling a learning switch to dynamically work around loops in a switched network topology by creating a spanning tree. Switches exchange BPDU messages with other bridges to detect loops and then remove the loops by shutting down selected switch interfaces. If the primary link fails, a standby link is activated. Refers to both the IEEE 802.1 Spanning-Tree Protocol standard and the earlier Digital Equipment Corporation Spanning-Tree Protocol on which it is based. The IEEE version supports switch domains and allows the switch to construct a loop-free topology across an extended LAN. The IEEE version is generally preferred over the Digital version.

SPF Shortest Path First. A routing algorithm that iterates on length of path to determine a shortest-path spanning tree. Commonly used in link-state routing algorithms. Sometimes called *Dijkstra's algorithm*.

split-horizon updates A routing technique in which information about routes is prevented from exiting the router interface through which that information was received. Split-horizon updates are useful in preventing routing loops.

spoofing 1. A scheme used by routers to cause a host to treat an interface as if it were up and supporting a session. The router spoofs replies to keepalive messages from the host in order to convince the host that the session still exists. Spoofing is useful in routing environments such as DDR, in which a circuit-switched link is taken down when there is no traffic to be sent across it in order to save toll charges. 2. The act of a packet illegally claiming to be from an address from which it was not actually sent. Spoofing is designed to foil network security mechanisms such as filters and access lists.

SPP Sequenced Packet Protocol. A protocol that provides reliable, connection-based, flow-controlled packet transmission on behalf of client processes. Part of the XNS protocol suite.

SPX Sequenced Packet Exchange. A reliable, connection-oriented protocol that supplements the datagram service provided by network-layer protocols. Novell derived this commonly used NetWare transport protocol from the SPP of the XNS protocol suite.

SQE Signal Quality Error. In Ethernet, a transmission sent by a transceiver back to the controller to let the controller know whether the collision circuitry is functional. Also called *heartbeat*.

SSAP Source Service Access Point. The SAP of the network node designated in the Source field of a packet. *Compare with* DSAP. *See also* SAP.

standard A set of rules or procedures that are either widely used or officially specified.

star topology A LAN topology in which endpoints on a network are connected to a common central switch by point-to-point links. A ring topology that is organized as a star implements a unidirectional closed-loop star, instead of point-to-point links. *Compare with* bus topology, ring topology, and tree topology.

static route A route that is explicitly configured and entered into the routing table by default. Static routes take precedence over routes chosen by dynamic routing protocols.

STP shielded twisted-pair. A two-pair wiring medium used in a variety of network implementations. STP cabling has a layer of shielded insulation to reduce EMI. *Compare with* UTP.

stub area An OSPF area that carries a default route, intra-area routes, and interarea routes but does not carry external routes. Virtual links cannot be configured across a stub area, and they cannot contain an ASBR. *Compare with* non-stub area.

stub network A network that has only a single connection to a router.

subnet *See* subnetwork.

subnet address A portion of an IP address that is specified as the subnetwork by the subnet mask.

subnet mask A 32-bit address mask used in IP to indicate the bits of an IP address that are being used for the subnet address. Sometimes referred to simply as *mask*.

subnetwork 1. In IP networks, a network sharing a particular subnet address. Subnetworks are networks arbitrarily segmented by a network administrator in order to provide a multilevel, hierarchical routing structure while shielding the subnetwork from the addressing complexity of attached networks. Sometimes called a *subnet*. 2. In OSI networks, a collection of ESs and ISs under the control of a single administrative domain and using a single network access protocol.

surge Any voltage increase above 110% of the normal voltage carried by a power line.

SVC Switched Virtual Circuit. A virtual circuit that is dynamically established on demand and is torn down when transmission is complete. SVCs are used in situations where data transmission is sporadic. Called a *switched virtual connection* in ATM terminology. *Compare with* PVC.

synchronous transmission Digital signals that are transmitted with precise clocking. Such signals have the same frequency, with individual characters encapsulated in control bits (called *start bits* and *stop bits*) that designate the beginning and end of each character. *Compare with* asynchronous transmission.

T

T1 A digital WAN carrier facility that transmits DS-1-formatted data at 1.544 Mbps through the telephone-switching network using AMI or B8ZS coding. *Compare with* E1.

T3 A digital WAN carrier facility that transmits DS-3-formatted data at 44.736 Mbps through the telephone switching network. *Compare with* E3.

TACACS Terminal Access Controller Access Control System. An authentication protocol, developed by the DDN community, that provides remote access authentication and related services, such as event logging. User passwords are administered in a central database rather than in individual routers, providing an easily scalable network security solution.

TCP Transmission Control Protocol. A connection-oriented transport-layer protocol that provides reliable full-duplex data transmission. TCP is part of the TCP/IP protocol stack.

TCP/IP Transmission Control Protocol/Internet Protocol. A common name for the suite of protocols developed by the U.S. DoD in the 1970s to support the construction of worldwide internetworks. TCP and IP are the two best-known protocols in the suite.

Telnet A standard terminal emulation protocol in the TCP/IP protocol stack. Telnet is used for remote terminal connection, enabling users to log in to remote systems and use resources as if they were connected to a local system. Telnet is defined in RFC 854.

TFTP Trivial File Transfer Protocol. A simplified version of FTP that allows files to be transferred from one computer to another over a network.

throughput The rate of information arriving at, and possibly passing through, a particular point in a network system.

Time-To-Live *See* TTL.

timeout An event that occurs when one network device expects to hear from another network device within a specified period of time but does not. The resulting timeout usually results in a retransmission of information or the dissolving of the session between the two devices.

token A frame that contains control information. Possession of the token allows a network device to transmit data onto the network.

token bus A LAN architecture using token passing access over a bus topology. This LAN architecture is the basis for the IEEE 802.4 LAN specification.

token passing An access method by which network devices access the physical medium in an orderly fashion based on possession of a small frame called a token. *Compare with* contention.

Token Ring A token-passing LAN developed and supported by IBM. Token Ring runs at 4 or 16 Mbps over a ring topology. Similar to IEEE 802.5.

TokenTalk Apple Computer's data-link product that allows an AppleTalk network to be connected by Token Ring cables.

topology A physical arrangement of network nodes and media within an enterprise networking structure.

traceroute A program available on many systems that traces the path a packet takes to a destination. It is mostly used to debug routing problems between hosts. There is also a traceroute protocol defined in RFC 1393.

traffic management Techniques for avoiding congestion and shaping and policing traffic. Allows links to operate at high levels of utilization by scaling back lower-priority, delay-tolerant traffic at the edge of the network when congestion begins to occur.

trailer Control information appended to data when encapsulating the data for network transmission. *Compare with* header.

transaction services layer Layer 7 in the SNA architectural model. Represents user application functions, such as spreadsheets, word processing, or electronic mail, by which users interact with the network. Corresponds roughly to the application layer of the OSI reference model. *See also* data flow control layer, data link control layer, path control layer, physical control layer, presentation services layer, and transmission control layer.

transmission control layer Layer 4 in the SNA architectural model. This layer is responsible for establishing, maintaining, and terminating SNA sessions, sequencing data messages, and controlling session level flow. Corresponds to the transport layer of the OSI reference model. *See also* data flow control layer, data link control layer, path control layer, physical control layer, presentation services layer, and transaction services layer.

Transmission Control Protocol *See* TCP.

transport layer Layer 4 of the OSI reference model. This layer is responsible for reliable network communication between end nodes. The transport layer provides mechanisms for the establishment, maintenance, and termination of virtual circuits, transport fault detection and recovery, and information flow control. Corresponds to the transmission control layer of the SNA model. *See also* application layer, data link layer, network layer, physical layer, presentation layer, and session layer.

trap A message sent by an SNMP agent to an NMS, a console, or a terminal to indicate the occurrence of a significant event, such as a specifically defined condition or a threshold that was reached.

tree topology A LAN topology similar to a bus topology, except that tree networks can contain branches with multiple nodes. Transmissions from a station propagate the length of the medium and are received by all other stations. *Compare with* bus topology, ring topology, and star topology.

TTL Time-To-Live. A field in an IP header that indicates how long a packet is considered valid.

tunneling An architecture that is designed to provide the services necessary to implement any standard point-to-point encapsulation scheme.

U

UDP User Datagram Protocol. A connectionless transport-layer protocol in the TCP/IP protocol stack. UDP is a simple protocol that exchanges datagrams without acknowledgments or guaranteed delivery, requiring that error processing and retransmission be handled by other protocols. UDP is defined in RFC 768.

unicast A message sent to a single network destination. *Compare with* broadcast and multicast.

unicast address An address specifying a single network device. *Compare with* broadcast address and multicast address.

universal resource locator *See* URL.

UPS Uninterruptible Power Supply. A backup device designed to provide an uninterrupted power source in the event of a power failure. UPSs are commonly installed on file servers and wiring hubs.

URL Universal Resource Locator. A standardized addressing scheme for accessing hypertext documents and other services using a browser.

User Datagram Protocol *See* UDP.

UTP Unshielded Twisted-Pair. A four-pair wire medium used in a variety of networks. UTP does not require the fixed spacing between connections that is necessary with coaxial-type connections. *Compare with* STP. *See also* twisted pair.

V

VINES Virtual Integrated Network Service. A NOS developed and marketed by Banyan Systems.

virtual circuit A logical circuit created to ensure reliable communication between two network devices. A virtual circuit is defined by a VPI/VCI pair and can be either permanent (PVC) or switched (SVC). Virtual circuits are used in Frame Relay and X.25. In ATM, a virtual circuit is called a virtual channel. Sometimes abbreviated VC.

VLAN Virtual LAN. A group of devices on a LAN that are configured (using management software) so that they can communicate as if they were attached to the same wire, when in fact they are located on a number of different LAN segments. Because VLANs are based on logical instead of physical connections, they are extremely flexible.

W

WAN Wide-area network. A data communications network that serves users across a broad geographic area and often uses transmission devices provided by common carriers. Frame Relay, SMDS, and X.25 are examples of WANs. *Compare with* LAN and MAN.

watchdog packet A method used to ensure that a client is still connected to a NetWare server. If the server has not received a packet from a client for a certain period of time, it sends that client a series of watchdog packets. If the station fails to respond to a predefined number of watchdog packets, the server concludes that the station is no longer connected and clears the connection for that station.

watchdog spoofing A subset of spoofing that refers specifically to a router acting especially for a NetWare client by sending watchdog packets to a NetWare server to keep the session between client and server active. Useful when the client and server are separated by a DDR WAN link.

watchdog timer 1. A hardware or software mechanism that is used to trigger an event or an escape from a process unless the timer is periodically reset. 2. In NetWare, a timer that indicates the maximum period of time that a server will wait for a client to respond to a watchdog packet. If the timer expires, the server sends another watchdog packet (up to a set maximum).

window size The number of messages that can be transmitted while awaiting an acknowledgment.

X

X.25 An ITU-T standard that defines how connections between DTE and DCE are maintained for remote terminal access and computer communications in PDNs. X.25 specifies LAPB, a data link layer protocol, and PLP, a network-layer protocol. Frame Relay has to some degree superseded X.25.

XNS Xerox Network Systems. A protocol suite originally designed by PARC. Many PC networking companies, such as 3Com, Banyan, Novell, and UB Networks used or currently use a variation of XNS as their primary transport protocol.

Z

ZIP Zone Information Protocol. An AppleTalk session-layer protocol that maps network numbers to zone names. ZIP is used by NBP to determine which networks contain nodes that belong to a zone.

zone In AppleTalk, a logical group of network devices.

zone multicast address A data-link-dependent multicast address at which a node receives the NBP broadcasts directed to its zone.

Numerics

Symbols

A

B

C

D

E

F

J-K

L

O

P

Q–R

T

U

V

W

X-Y-Z

Hey, you've got enough worries.

Don't let IT training be one of them.

Get on the fast track to IT training at InformIT, your total Information Technology training network.

www.informit.com

■ Hundreds of timely articles on dozens of topics ■ Discounts on IT books from all our publishing partners, including Cisco Press ■ Free, unabridged books from the InformIT Free Library ■ "Expert Q&A"—our live, online chat with IT experts ■ Faster, easier certification and training from our Web- or classroom-based training programs ■ Current IT news ■ Software downloads ■ Career-enhancing resources

InformIT is a registered trademark of Pearson. Copyright ©2001 by Pearson.